Aboriginal History

Aboriginal History A Reader

Edited by

Kristin Burnett and Geoff Read

OXFORD
UNIVERSITY PRESS

OXFORD
UNIVERSITY PRESS

Oxford University Press is a department of the University of Oxford.
It furthers the University's objective of excellence in research, scholarship,
and education by publishing worldwide. Oxford is a registered trade mark of
Oxford University Press in the UK and in certain other countries.

Published in Canada by
Oxford University Press
8 Sampson Mews, Suite 204,
Don Mills, Ontario M3C 0H5 Canada

www.oupcanada.com

Library and Archives Canada Cataloguing in Publication

Aboriginal history : a reader / edited by Kristin Burnett and Geoff Read.

Includes bibliographical references.
ISBN 978–0–19–543235–0

1. Native peoples—Canada—Historiography.
I. Burnett, Kristin, 1974– II. Read, Geoff, 1975–

E78.C2A1457 2012   971.004'97   C2012-900059-0

This book is printed on permanent (acid-free) paper ∞.

Printed and bound in Canada

1 2 3 4 — 15 14 13 12

Contents

FOUR   War, Conflict, and Society

FIVE   The Fur Trade

SIX   Locating Métis Identity

Contributors

Naomi Adelson
York University

Betty Bastien
University of Calgary

David Bentley

Robin Jarvis Brownlie
University of Manitoba

Alexander V. Campbell

Sarah Carter
University of Alberta

J.W. Daschuk
University of Regina

Laurie Meijer Drees
Vancouver Island University

Dorothy Harley Eber

Lorena Sekwan Fontaine
University of Winnipeg

Paul Hackett
University of Saskatchewan

Celia Haig-Brown
York University

David Henige
University of Wisconsin–Madison

Bonita Lawrence
York University

John Lutz
University of Victoria

Scott MacNeil

Dennis H. McPherson
Lakehead University

Jaime Mishibinijima
University College of the North

Brenda Murphy
Wilfrid Laurier University

Jarich Oosten
University of Leiden

Gabrielle Parent
McGill University

Sherry Pictou
World Forum of Fisher Peoples,
Bear River First Nations

Liza Piper
University of Alberta

J. Douglas Rabb
Lakehead University

Arthur J. Ray
University of British Columbia

Cornelius H.W. Remie
University of Nijmegen

Daniel K. Richter
University of Pennsylvania

Brett Rushforth
College of William & Mary

Paul Rynard

Joan Sangster
Trent University

Hugh Shewell
Carleton University

Susan Sleeper-Smith
Michigan State University

Martha Stiegman
Concordia University

Alan Taylor
University of California, Davis

Cora Voyageur
University of Calgary

Todd Webb
Laurentian University

Acknowledgements

We would like to acknowledge and thank the following people who contributed to the publication of this volume:

Olive Patricia Dickason, whose groundbreaking book, *Canada's First Nations: A History of Founding Peoples from Earliest Times*, redefined the teaching of Aboriginal history in Canada and remains a powerful text and pedagogical tool. Sadly, she passed away in March 2011; we dedicate this volume to her memory.

Lawrence Barkwell, Lynn Berthelette, Sarah Carter, Chris Dooley, Paul Hackett, J. Douglas Leighton, Mary Jane McCallum, Dennis McPherson, Carolyn Podruchny, Colin Read, and Rob Robson, for their advice and guidance.

Naomi Adelson, Betty Bastien, Laurie Meijer Drees, Lorena Sekwan Fontaine, Celia Haig-Brown, Bonita Lawrence, John Lutz, Jaime Mishibinijima, Gabrielle Parent, Sherry Pictou, Liza Piper, Joan Sangster, Hugh Shewell, Martha Stiegman, Cora Voyageur, and Todd Webb, for contributing original essays to this volume, working hard to meet deadlines and make revisions, and, in some cases, helping to identify and secure primary documents. Special thanks to Bonita Lawrence for helping to find an author on short notice when a contributor had to withdraw.

Julie Bennett, Robin Jarvis Brownlie, Lauren Kolodziejczak, Roger Lewis, Leah Otak, and Christina M. Thompson, who helped us acquire the primary documents.

Chris Blow and Steve Gamester, who helped us locate relevant films.

Kathryn Schade and Matthew Sitter, whose invaluable work saved us many hours.

Mark Blagrave, Ursula Boyd, Rebecca Mudge, Huron University College, and Lakehead University, who ensured that Kathryn and Matthew got paid for their work.

The staff at Oxford University Press, particularly Alan Mulder, who suggested we undertake this project in the first place, and our editors: Jodi Lewchuk, Katherine Skene, Caroline Starr, Kathryn West, Janna Green, and, especially, Patti Sayle, whose patience and hard work was and continues to be much appreciated.

Robert Adlam, Mount Allison University; Rick Monture, McMaster University; and Fred Shore, University of Manitoba, who reviewed this reader for the press and whose input greatly strengthened the final product.

Our children, Adrian Burnett and Zachary, Zoe, and Parker Read, who felt the impact of the demands this project placed on our time. Kristin's furry children—Avery, George, Mary, and Sam—who love when Kristin spends so much time at her computer and provides a nice warm lap to sleep in. Dylan Burnett, who passed away suddenly in 2009. And Geoff's partner, Sarah Read, who shouldered more than her fair share of the housework and childcare at times so that work could be done on this volume and yet remained supportive throughout the process, despite working full-time and, for the past eight and a half months, being pregnant.

The final product is very much our own; whatever errors that have been made in the editing process are our responsibility. Nevertheless, the book could not have come to fruition without the contributions—both great and small—of all the people listed above, and for that we are deeply grateful.

Kristin Burnett and Geoff Read
Thunder Bay, ON, and London, ON
15 June 2011

Aboriginal History in a Colonial Context

Kristin Burnett with Geoff Read

The inspiration for this project was a conversation with my Oxford University Press sales representative, during which I lamented the paucity of a suitable reader to complement Olive Patricia Dickason's influential work, *Canada's First Nations: A History of Founding Peoples from Earliest Times*. At the time, I was determining the reading requirements for an Aboriginal history survey course that I was teaching. While a great many outstanding collections addressing specific experiential, theoretical, and disciplinary aspects of Aboriginal history have been published—particularly since the late 1990s—none were broad enough geographically, temporally, or thematically for a survey course. Nor did these collections include a broad range of primary sources, a necessary tool to expose students to how we recover and interpret the past. The challenge thus became to find something that contained all these elements and exposed students to the rich history of Canada's Aboriginal peoples, including the challenges they have encountered and overcome in the face of European and Canadian colonialism.

As one of the first works of its kind in Canada, Dickason's text is significant in that it tries to provide a synthesis of Aboriginal history in the geographical area that came to be known as Canada. Now in its fourth edition, it remains unmatched—this speaks to both the quality of Dickason's work and, sadly, the degree to which Aboriginal history remains marginal within the discipline of history and, by extension, within Canadian history departments.[1] When Dickason wrote her textbook in 1992, she did so as a challenge to non-Aboriginal individuals who believed 'that Canada [was] a country of much geography and little history'.[2] This statement, made by Prime Minister William Lyon Mackenzie King in the House of Commons on 18 June 1936, lays bare the pervasiveness and strength of the perception that North America lacks history. Dickason wrote her text to show that Aboriginal people were, in the truest sense, North America's 'first nations', challenging the Eurocentric notion that North American history began with the arrival of Europeans and that Aboriginal peoples' histories are rightly relegated to pre-history and archaeology. Such thinking reflects the belief that the 'art of writing history' is bound by written documents penned by 'dead white men'.

To combat this perspective, *Aboriginal History* contains a variety of primary sources that reflect the breadth and diversity of available materials. Many were created by Aboriginal people, contradicting the common perception that their history is at risk of being 'lost' because 'Indians', as supposed primitives, did not leave their own records behind. Such assumptions recall King's comment and are patently false. We include photographs, oral history accounts, maps, newspaper articles, government documents, letters, diary excerpts, baptismal records, and more. In this diverse set of documents, Aboriginal people's voices come through loud and clear, ensuring that their stories are told and remembered and demonstrating, in many cases, their past and present struggle to counter the Eurocentric narratives of the colonizing newcomers. Given that, as Gayatri Chakravorty Spivak suggests, silencing Aboriginal voices and erasing Aboriginal history is an integral part of the colonial project,[3] such documents are invaluable for historians who wish to deconstruct the Eurocentrism of traditional Canadian history.

In specific instances, we chose to draw on records created by the Canadian government and non-Aboriginal people. We did so not because we believe that they accurately reflect the experiences of Aboriginal people but because they reveal the context within which Aboriginal people operated and the constraints to which they were subjected. The Indian Act, for instance, remains 'an aggressive colonizing project of assimilation'[4] and continues to govern the day-to-day lives of Aboriginal people. To cite only three of its invasive provisions, the Act determines who is legally considered a Status Indian, controls where Aboriginal people can live, and requires that Aboriginal people obtain permission from their Indian agent to sell agricultural produce. Because the Act clearly (though unfortunately) continues to exercise a powerful influence over the lives of Aboriginal people, it is important for students to consider. In examining it, students can learn about the restrictions placed upon Aboriginal people as well as the racist and discriminatory means by which Canada, as a colonial state, has sought to control, subjugate, assimilate, and (at times) eradicate Aboriginal peoples and cultures. Looking at primary sources of diverse types and authors also forces students to think about the different media we use to learn about the past, how individuals can look at and interpret the same text in very different ways, and how the Eurocentric bias dominates the documentary record relied upon by the history profession.

In addition to querying sources, historians need to break down the disciplinary boundaries they have constructed, which create documentary and disciplinary hierarchies that privilege one kind of source or methodology over another. In order to do so, we must, as Winona Wheeler urges, find

> a place in history for Other Ways of Knowing. . . . It requires us to develop new ways of learning and understanding, and to step outside of our rigorously trained comfort zones. . . . Our task is not only to create a space for other ways of knowing as an object or subject of study, but also to create space to apply the teachings that guide the learning, keeping, and transmission of Indigenous knowledge. If we are not willing to step out of our comfort zones, we are culpable for the obliteration of our world . . . we would be responsible for our 'becoming nothing.'[5]

This reader thus uses an interdisciplinary approach to reflect the richness, diversity, and breadth of the topic.[6] We include articles from a wide variety of disciplines, including anthropology, philosophy, social work, sociology, history, and Indigenous learning. Historians cannot claim sole authority to 'knowing' the history of Aboriginal people. The rigid policing of disciplinary boundaries has served only to isolate Aboriginal history within national narratives and preclude the employment of Aboriginal historians in history departments.[7]

The slow but steady entry of more Aboriginal people into the academy has also changed the landscape of the histories that are being written, the focus of these works, and the discipline's relationship to the sources. In a special issue of *American Indian Quarterly*, Mary Jane McCallum and Susan Hill describe the relationship of Aboriginal historians to archives and archival sources:

> [W]e read them both as academics and as members of families and communities. We also read archives as a minority among those who access them as skilled researchers and as people who have been subjected to multiple forms of state imposed regulation aimed at our elimination. Thus, in our readings of archives we often have to negotiate around the very government documents that define us as their products.[8]

The 'intellectual repatriation' of records and the perspectives of Aboriginal scholars provide valuable lessons for non-Aboriginal people who seek to learn more about the history and experiences of Aboriginal people. It forces us to acknowledge that historians are not infallible, that Aboriginal people are not objects, and that the records we examine to learn about the past have very real implications in the present. In other words, Aboriginal people are not relics frozen in the past but part of a dynamic and diverse present and future.

Terminology

There is no universal term for Aboriginal people in North America. The terminology has evolved to reflect a growing awareness and understanding of Indigenous peoples and cultures both in Canada and around the world. In Canada, the term *Aboriginal* is used to refer to all the 'Aboriginal people in Canada collectively, without regard to their separate origins and identities'.[9] While the term *Indian* is considered outdated and historically inaccurate in contemporary academic circles, it reflects legal categories that have very real meanings for Aboriginal people in Canadian society. The three legal categories of Indians as defined under the Indian Act are Status Indians (individuals who are registered with the federal government according to specific criteria), Non-Status Indians (individuals who are members of a First Nation but whom the federal government does not recognize as Indians), and Treaty Indians (individuals who are Status Indians and recognized as members of a First Nation that signed a treaty with the Crown). In the chapter introductions of this reader, we use *Aboriginal* and *Indigenous* to refer to Status and Non-Status Indians, Métis, and Inuit. *First Nation* is also used to refer to individual bands, for example, the Pelican Lake First Nation. The authors of original articles use the terminology that they believe to be most appropriate, often in direct reference to the legal language. Some of the reprinted articles use terminology that is considered outdated today. The glossary provided at the end of the text includes definitions of these various terms.

The 'simplest' definition of a Métis person is someone who is of mixed Aboriginal and European ancestry.[10] However, recent constitutional and judicial developments have both enhanced and complicated the Métis identity as defined by the state. For instance, in the 2003 Powley decision the Supreme Court of Canada ruled that Métis people possess Aboriginal hunting and fishing rights in a particular area only if they can prove that they have ancestors who lived there before Confederation. The 1982 Constitution Act also recognizes Métis people as one of Canada's founding Aboriginal peoples, but they are considered part of that founding nation only if they self-identify as Métis and can trace their ancestry back to a historical Métis community. These definitions are further complicated by the individual membership criteria of different Métis organizations across Canada. Such processes have constructed narrowly defined categories of identity that often bear little relationship to the realities of people's lives.

We also use terms such as *colonialism, colonial project, newcomer/settler*, and *settler society* throughout the reader. Traditional definitions of colonialism describe it as the 'implanting of settlements on a distant territory'.[11] However, as this reader clearly shows, colonialism is messy and, at times, nebulous. At its root, colonialism can be understood as a relationship of domination by one group over another that is simultaneously a social experience, a political arrangement, and an intellectual process. A settler society is one that is 'intent on making a territory their new home while continuing to enjoy metropolitan living standards and political privileges' and that continues to draw on the technologies of power and control employed earlier to assert their dominance.[12] Finally, in defining the terms *settler* and *newcomer*, we borrow from Adam Barker, who rejects the notion that defining settlers/newcomers as merely non-Indigenous is too simplistic. Settlers/newcomers 'include most peoples who occupy lands previously stolen or in the process of being taken from their Indigenous inhabitants or who are otherwise members of the "Settler society," which is founded on co-opted lands and resources'.[13]

Chapter Descriptions

This volume is divided into 15 chapters. With the exception of Chapter One, each chapter includes two articles supplemented by primary documents and/or photos. While the geographic coverage provided by the articles is by no means comprehensive, it does encompass the histories of First Nations in the West, the North and far North, central Canada, Quebec, and the Maritimes. To a degree, the content is shaped chronologically, which is also how history survey courses are generally taught. Ideally, this reader would follow Aboriginal societies from their birth to the present and include the origin stories of each First Nation, stories that identify the Americas as the place of origin for Aboriginal peoples. Recent archaeological evidence illustrates that human beings were present in the Americas as early as 70,000 years ago.[14] To cover 70,000 years of history of the diverse nations and cultures present within the (artificial) boundaries of present-day Canada in one reader is a vast and impossible undertaking. Instead, we have chosen to draw on the historical knowledge and perspective of Aboriginal people and scholars regarding particular periods within Aboriginal history.

This volume seeks to decentre those historical events and processes of Canadian history that have been highlighted as part of our national narrative—such as the establishment of Quebec City, the Conquest, Confederation, the building of the intercontinental railway, Vimy Ridge, peacekeeping, and the patriation of the Constitution—while alternative histories, particularly those that account for Aboriginal histories and ways of knowing, have been excluded. As Germaine Warkentin and Carolyn Podruchny suggest, in undertaking an examination of Aboriginal history we must subject what we 'know' of history to scrutiny and recognize that it 'is only recently that we have attempted to do so from the point of view of the Native peoples who were living here when the Europeans arrived, inhabiting the same historical epoch but with very different ideas of its history'.[15]

In Chapter One, Dennis H. McPherson, J. Douglas Rabb, and Betty Bastien inform readers that Aboriginal people have their own history and historical traditions (which should be an obvious statement but is sadly necessary). Writing from an Ojibwa perspective, McPherson and Rabb state that 'Native spirituality and identity have, despite all odds, survived colonialism.' Together with Bastien, they show how Western knowledge and perspectives often run contrary to Aboriginal people's ways of knowing and understanding the past and the world around them. Indeed, McPherson and Rabb's article is a rallying cry to Aboriginal people to reclaim their histories and traditions and to resist the erasure or re-telling of the past.

Betty Bastien argues that 'learning is premised on a "knowing" that is generated through a participatory and experiential process.' To illustrate, Chapter Two offers Aboriginal perspectives of contact with Europeans and suggests a range of possibilities in imagining the first encounters that took place along the eastern coast of North America. When different peoples first came into contact with each other, they did not 'discover the unexpected' but 'went into new territories full of expectations, ideas, and stereotypes: what they found was—in large measure—what they expected to find.'[16] In other words, Aboriginals and Europeans alike used pre-existing cultural meanings and categories to interpret what they witnessed, heard, and experienced when they met new people. Both Daniel K. Richter and Dorothy Harley Eber point out that Aboriginals and Europeans understood and experienced their first encounters with each other in radically different ways. Therefore, contact with the European world, while drastically affecting the First Nations that resided in the Americas, needs to be re-imagined and re-examined from different points of historical reference and 'knowing' and incorporate Aboriginal world views and perspectives. 'First contact' can no longer be understood as a single event with a clear beginning and end. Instead, we should perceive contact as both a 'spatial and temporal movement' that sweeps through what Mary Louise Pratt has called the 'contact zone'.[17] Within this contact zone, cultures met, grappled with each other, and arrived at some sort of accommodation, however unequal. Contact initiated a 'dialogue which, once commenced, could not be easily broken off' and, indeed, continues to this day.[18]

Just as contact was not a singular event, it was also not confined to physical encounters between peoples. In Chapter Three, we explore the impact of disease on Aboriginal peoples and societies. David Henige's article outlines more conventional debates regarding the size of the Americas' pre-European contact population and the role that the introduction of European disease played in the depopulation of the continent. His article addresses the following questions: To what extent did the first Europeans to arrive actually see untouched Aboriginal communities? Were the relatively sparsely populated societies and villages they encountered actually remnants of much larger societies devastated by disease? J.W. Daschuk, Paul Hackett, and Scott

MacNeil complicate the etiology of epidemic diseases, situating them within the ecological, economic, and political changes caused by one group imposing its hegemony over another. They also demonstrate that diseases that were a function of poverty and malnutrition continued to have detrimental and at times disastrous consequences for First Nations well into the twentieth century.

More conventional histories of North America have focused on those events that fuelled economic and geographic expansion of European empires and led to the building of modern nation-states, focusing in particular on the wars of empire and conquest. Until recently, Aboriginal people and nations were seen as peripheral to, or at best casualties of, this enterprise. We argue that not only were Aboriginal people and nations not peripheral but that they also had very different understandings of, perspectives on, and agendas during these events. Because Aboriginal people did not conform to contemporary definitions of nations and states, their histories of territorial expansion and political manoeuvrings during the seventeenth and eighteenth centuries have been overlooked, especially in conjunction with the jostling of European empires occurring in North America. However, Aboriginal people were not marginal figures but negotiated political, economic, and social agreements with other First Nations and Europeans. Sometimes the interests of Aboriginals and Europeans were compatible, and at other times they were not. In Chapter Four, Brett Rushforth examines the nature of French–Aboriginal alliances during the eighteenth century and how they were profoundly shaped by the French's Aboriginal partners. These allies reshaped the geopolitical map to their advantage through establishing and perpetuating New France's reliance on slaves, especially those from the Fox Nation. In doing so, they ensured a state of perpetual war with the Fox. Similarly, Alan Taylor's article focuses on the actions and interests of the Haudensaunee (Iroquois, or Six Nations) in the aftermath of the American Revolution and offers a reinterpretation of the meanings of national borders. Taylor reveals how the Haudensaunee used conflicts between European powers to protect their own interests. Aboriginal people were present at, involved in, and affected by European conflicts but perceived and experienced these conflagrations very differently than did their European enemies, neighbours, and allies. For example, as Taylor shows, the American Revolution presented Aboriginal nations with opportunities and stark choices. Among the Haudensaunee, different members of the confederacy took different actions depending on how they perceived their own interests, actions which have had far-reaching consequences. Indeed, for most Aboriginal people involved in the American Revolution, the conflict did not end with the Treaty of Paris in 1783, once again signifying the differing positions and perspectives of Aboriginal peoples from those of European background.

Similarly, older works that outlined the fur trade characterized it as an enterprise performed primarily by Europeans and men. In Chapter Five, Arthur J. Ray's article challenges this narrative. Ray's work places Aboriginal people and societies at the centre of the fur trade. Indeed, without Aboriginal people, their knowledge, and trading networks, trade would not have been possible. The fur trade also produced a socio-cultural complex that drew on Aboriginal and European traditions. Susan Sleeper-Smith shows how important the fur trade was to the emergence of a hybrid culture that operated in what Richard White has referred to as the 'middle ground'.[19] In this interstitial space, Aboriginal women were central actors in the family and economic politics of the Great Lakes region and elsewhere. The fluidity of this familial and economic space produced its own unique cultural and social formations. Sleeper-Smith also demonstrates the varied strategies employed by Aboriginal women as they cemented relationships between their kin networks and French merchants and pursued their own and their families' interests with vigour.

Chapter Six examines the Métis in Canada, focusing on identity formation and articulation. Over the past decade, scholarship on the Métis has exploded in its diversity and depth. This research has moved beyond just looking at the struggles between Métis free-traders and the Hudson's Bay Company and those between Louis Riel and the Canadian state as the only significant moments and places of Métis identity formation. Alexander V. Campbell's work traces the multifarious lineages of the Métis community, suggesting that it was not just the fur trade that produced intimate and 'tender ties' between Indigenous women and European men. Instead, Campbell points to the relationships that formed between military personnel and Aboriginal people, especially women, as a widespread and common component of imperial expansion in the nineteenth century. Accordingly, 'such dynamics produced a distinct subset of Aboriginal families descended from British troops who were determined to marry, trade, and settle' in North America. Picking up on the thread of empire, Geoff Read and Todd Webb show how the identity of the Métis took on national and international importance as journalists, politicians, and social commentators from Australia to France discussed the Métis and their unique identity. Indeed, the Métis were not an unknown people confined to the periphery of empire, but 'the degree to which the broader international community acknowledged Métis claims and nationhood shaped the socio-political terrain upon which the Métis had to operate.'

Chapters Seven to Ten explore the state's assimilationist efforts and the resistance of Aboriginal people. Two years after Confederation, the federal government passed its first Indian Act in accordance with section 91(24) of the British North American Act, which gave Canada exclusive jurisdiction over 'Indians and lands reserved for Indians'.[20] This 1869 Act mapped out Canada's vision of its relationship with Aboriginal people. In 1876, all legislation pertaining to Aboriginal people was consolidated, reflecting the preoccupation of the federal government with land management, First Nations or band membership, and local governance. These years witnessed tremendous shifts in federal Indian policy and signalled the hardening of boundaries between Aboriginal and non-Aboriginal people in Canada. During the 1870s, the numbered treaties were negotiated, Aboriginal people were increasingly confined to reserves, alien systems of governance were imposed, and the pass system was instituted. In 1880, the Department of Indian Affairs (DIA) was created. These events made it extremely difficult for First Nations people to resist the growing intrusion of the colonial Canadian state. Dwindling food resources led to starvation and an increasing incidence of diseases associated with poverty and poor living conditions. The late nineteenth and early twentieth centuries and the operations of the DIA laid the foundations of Canada's Indian policy, which remained remarkably constant over the next century.

In 1920, Duncan Campbell Scott, one of the major architects of Canadian Indian policy, stated before a special parliamentary committee:

I want to get rid of the Indian problem. I do not think as a matter of Fact, that this country ought to continuously protect a class of people who are able to stand alone. That is my whole point. Our objective is to continue until there is not a single Indian in Canada that has not been absorbed into the body politic, and there is no Indian question, and no Indian Department and that is the whole object of this Bill.[21]

Such opinions shaped government policies that sought to transform Aboriginal people into European Canadians through education in residential schools, the transformation of families, and the imposition of individualist capitalist wage labour.

Chapter Seven examines the development and implementation of Indian policy in the late nineteenth and twentieth centuries. Hugh Shewell looks at the rise and entrenchment of the bureaucratic administration and management of First Nations in Canada during the early twentieth century. His article outlines the repressive administration of Scott and its implications for Aboriginal people. Health and health care also became central components of Indian policy. Laurie Meijer Drees's article examines the Nanaimo Indian Hospital, one of the major centres of tuberculosis treatment and containment, as well as a site of cultural resistance and persistence. Drawing on oral history, Meijer Drees shows how Aboriginal people resisted the DIA and understood their experiences at the hospital both as patients and visitors.

Chapters Eight and Nine outline the personal consequences of Indian policy on First Nations people and communities. In Chapter Eight, both Bonita Lawrence and Jaime Mishibinijima unveil the intimate violence that the Indian Act has perpetrated on the lives of Status and Non-Status Indians. This race-based legislation has created inequities not only between Aboriginal and non-Aboriginal people but also among Aboriginal people themselves. Lawrence discusses how federal policies towards Aboriginal people have 'caused profound chaos within communities, including the fracture of family ties; the loss of knowledge of language, ceremonies, songs, and rituals; and the demise of a daily living relationship to the land'. Mishibinijima looks at Bill C-31, an amendment to the Indian Act passed by Parliament in 1985, and how the Indian Act and its attendant legislation have had profound and often destabilitizing effects on Aboriginal families.

Chapter Nine focuses on the ongoing impact of residential schools on Aboriginal people and their communities. Drawing on the voices of residential school survivors Celia Haig-Brown and Lorena Sekwan Fontaine shows how the effects of residential schools are real and present and not just part of Canada's history. From my own experiences as a teacher, I am constantly surprised at how little students know about the history and objectives of Canada's residential school system or how long this system lasted. Similarly, Fontaine describes how, after teaching a history course on residential schools, many students told her that they had not considered the continuing effect that the residential schools have on Aboriginal communities or the ongoing pain that survivors experience. These are important truths to acknowledge about Canadian history and the reality of Canada's Indian policy.

In Chapter Ten, Cornelius H.W. Remie and Jarich Oosten survey a number of phenomena in the northern Inuit community of Pelly Bay (Kugaaruk) in present-day Nunavut. The efforts of Roman Catholic missionaries to convert the Inuit at Pelly Bay had important consequences, but the authors also reveal how the Oblates transcended their religious roles and took on important functions within the community, providing social welfare, food, and other necessities. Mission organizations and their workers often stepped in when the federal government failed to act or refused to do so. Moreover, Remie and Oosten argue that our understanding of conversion needs to be complicated because the Inuit's Catholicism was of a decidedly syncretic bent. In their words, the Inuit 'integrated [their own cultural beliefs and traditions] into Catholicism, thus developing a form of religiosity that was reshaped to suit their own existential and cultural needs'. Conversion was no top-down affair—the Inuit did not receive the benefits of Christianity passively from their European 'betters' but selectively adopted the teachings of the missionaries to suit their own purposes and circumstances. In her study of a seemingly isolated Cree community in northern Quebec, Naomi Adelson likewise focuses on the community's agency in its adoption of modern communications technologies. In particular, she looks at how new technologies helped this seemingly isolated community expand upon its existing network of kinship relations and increase its interconnectedness with the wider world. Adelson argues that the availability of such technology has enabled the Whapmagoostui First Nation to re-imagine and practise culture in new ways.

The works in this reader also seek to make Aboriginal people visible in those areas of political, economic, and social history in which they have been traditionally written out of the narrative. In Chapter Eleven, John Lutz's article highlights the important roles that Aboriginal people played in the development of British Columbia's economy, making them visible in the wage economy of the post-fur trade era. Similarly, Joan Sangster seeks to rescue Aboriginal women workers from obscurity and looks at labour placement programs aimed at Aboriginal women in the post-World War II period. Conventional histories of labour in Canada do not include Aboriginal people, let alone Aboriginal women. Indeed, in a traditional survey of Canadian history, the role of Aboriginal people in the development of the Canadian economy tends to disappear with the decline of the fur and robe trades of the mid-nineteenth century. Indian policy and residential schools wanted to produce a particular type of Aboriginal worker: Aboriginal men would fill positions as the most menial of labourers and Aboriginal women would be domestic servants. The perpetuation of this fallacy and exclusion of Aboriginal people from Canadian economic history is part of the process of making them appear as outsiders, remnants of the past, and objects of tradition. Lutz and Sangster both take important steps towards correcting this misrepresentation.

Chapter Twelve turns to Aboriginal women and their growing marginalization under the Canadian state. In this context, Aboriginal women faced a double bind, disadvantaged both as women and as Indians. During the early settlement period in western Canada, when the region was struggling to establish white settler societies based on agriculture, an Anglo-Saxon identity, and the nuclear family, Aboriginal communities fought to resist this changing social landscape. Under the 1876 Indian Act, Aboriginal women lost many of their social, political, and economic rights. The Acts of 1868 and 1869 gave Aboriginal women fewer rights under the law than Aboriginal men. For example, women could not vote in band elections or inherit property from their husbands. Accordingly, their maintenance upon the death of their spouses became the responsibility of their children. Women also lost their Indian status if they married non-Aboriginal men. These policies recreated European-style patriarchy in First Nations communities and made Aboriginal women dependent on both men and the colonial state. Sarah Carter's article shows how the process of erasing Aboriginal women from the landscape of western Canada was central to the colonial project and facilitated the efforts of newcomers to make the newly formed white society appear natural and neutral and Aboriginal women out of place, particularly in urban areas, through the use of passes and public humiliation. Cora Voyageur offers an examination of Elsie Knott, the first Aboriginal woman to be elected chief of her band under the Indian Act. This event was possible only after the Act was revised in 1951 and allowed women to participate in band politics and to hold office. Both Carter and Voyageur demonstrate that Aboriginal women rejected the passive roles ascribed to them by Canadian authorities and asserted their agency in multiple ways.

The interconnectedness of Aboriginal cultures, Aboriginal peoples' well-being, and the environment is the central theme of Chapter Thirteen. Both Liza Piper and Gabrielle Parent explore how the degradation of the aquatic environment deeply affected the well-being of First Nations people. Piper looks at how the importance of fishing to Aboriginal people in the Canadian northwest was undermined by the desire of non-Aboriginal people to acquire access to the rich fisheries in the region. Indeed, the avarice of non-Aboriginal people in collusion with provincial and federal governments led to extensive environmental damage and growing incidents of ill-health in the region, particularly among Aboriginal people. Exploring similar themes in a different time and place, Gabrielle Parent emphasizes the significance of the aquatic environment to the Northern Ojibwa and Oji-Cree's culture, belief system, and economy and the impact that settlement and industrial development had on their way of life. In so doing, Parent suggests both the degree to which the colonial and industrial projects of the Canadian state were intertwined and the need for scholars, when examining environmental degradation, to consider the special relationship that Aboriginal peoples had with their environments. In picking up on the latter theme, Parent re-emphasizes a point made by both McPherson and Rabb and Bastien in Chapter One.

The final two chapters outline how Aboriginal people have resisted state efforts at assimilation. Although this resistance has gone on for over 500 years, these articles deal primarily with the twentieth century. Conventional histories of Aboriginal activism cite World War II as the watershed moment, looking at the rise of civil rights movements in the 1960s and the growing use of court challenges to force the federal government to keep treaty promises and to strike down legislation that violates human rights. The public and more visible nature of court challenges over the last 30 years has hidden the resistance and activism of Aboriginal people prior to World War II.[22] As Robin Jarvis Brownlie clearly shows in her article in Chapter Fourteen, Aboriginal people have been articulating and defending their rights since the abrogation of treaty and hunting rights began. David Bentley and Brenda Murphy outline how the Métis community of Kelly Lake acted to redefine their marginal and subordinate position within Canada's social, political, and economic system to address the chronic and pressing health care needs of their community. In doing so, the Métis of Kelly Lake took control of how they, as Métis people, were located and identified within Canadian society.

Chapter Fifteen looks at the actions of the state to abrogate treaties and agreements negotiated in good faith with First Nations. These articles show that the illegal and corrupt actions of the state are not a function of the distant past but a very real part of the present. Paul Rynard looks at the negotiations that took place around the James Bay Agreement and the role of the federal and provincial governments. He argues that 'public policy needs to be analyzed in light of the Canadian state's chronic subservience to the needs of powerful social interests and the exigencies of the market economy.' Martha Stiegman and Sherry Pictou discuss how recent court challenges, while seeming to address immediate problems, do not change the fundamental nature of the system—a liberal capitalist economy and a colonial state—that underpins it. Accordingly, Stiegman and Pictou suggest that present-day Aboriginal activists would be well served to build alliances with non-Aboriginal producers, as many have begun to do. Stiegman and Pictou are echoed by Rynard, who ultimately believes that the capitalist economy drives the resource extraction that leads Canada and the provinces to violate their legal obligations to Aboriginal peoples, often with dire consequences for First Nations. These two articles provide an appropriate conclusion to the volume by tying together many of the themes emphasized by the other essays, including the interconnectedness of Aboriginal peoples with their environments, the rapacious nature of the Canadian state, and the need to draw on alternative world views for solutions.

While it should be painfully obvious that Aboriginal history is a vital area of research in and of itself and integral to the history of Canada, the perspective that North America lacks history prior to 1492 continues to hold currency. In an August 2008 interview with Montreal newspaper *La Presse*, Richard Pound, former vice-president of the International Olympic Committee, stated that '400 years ago, Canada was a land of savages, with scarcely 10,000 inhabitants of European origin, while in China, we're talking about a 5,000-year-old civilization.'[23] In a demonstration of just how widespread Pound's fallacious view is, many social commentators rushed to defend it, including the *Globe and Mail*'s Margaret Wente, whose piece surpassed Pound's original comments in terms of offensiveness.[24] In choosing the articles for this reader, we sought to accomplish several objectives, but chief among them was to counter the views of Pound, Wente, and others by showcasing the diverse and dynamic history of Canada's Aboriginal peoples. The topics of the reader seek, as Jacques Derrida eloquently posits, not to 'reduce [Aboriginal people] to our own categories'[25] but to show that the histories of Aboriginal people and non-Aboriginal peoples are deeply interconnected and at times separated by a gulf of misunderstanding. Different moments held greater significance and meaning for Aboriginal peoples than for European Canadians. Their perceptions were frequently vastly different than those of 'white' Canadians but in no way inferior or subservient to them. We want to expose students to the diversity of primary sources that are available to learn about the past, particularly those created by Aboriginal people. In doing so, we show that Aboriginal history is not at risk of being lost and that Aboriginal people are not relics of a, to use Pound's term, 'savage' past. Finally, the reader serves as a challenge to those individuals who would erase the past of Aboriginal peoples by denying their histories and experiences. Indeed, such denials are part of a larger project to 'rid Canada of its Indian problem'. Clearly, this eradication of the 'Indian problem' has not taken place—Aboriginal people have resisted and flourished in spite of the best efforts of the state.

ONE

World Views

Introduction

This chapter is an exploration of **Aboriginal** world views. One of the most damaging aspects of the colonial project lies in its attempt to erase the traditions and bodies of knowledge of Aboriginal people and societies. This epistemological violence has several consequences. It makes the attempts of Europeans and then European Canadians to assimilate Aboriginal people appear benevolent and makes Aboriginal people seem in desperate need of 'salvation and civilization'. By creating the fiction that Aboriginal people are without traditions, knowledge, or history, colonial discourses simultaneously cast them as naive children and as newcomers. Doing so reaffirms the European explorers' descriptions of North America as a *terra nullius*, Latin for 'land belonging to no one'. And if no one owned this land, it was available for the taking.

The two articles in this chapter encourage us to think about how people from different cultures and traditions understand the world around them and their history. Dennis H. McPherson and J. Douglas Rabb believe that, in spite of the state's best efforts, concepts of Indigeneity have survived and that, in order to learn about the past, Aboriginal people must use the beliefs of contemporary Elders and Aboriginal scholars in conjunction 'with early contact accounts in the historical record'. To do so, we would have to 'dig beneath the foreign matter' to repatriate the history of Aboriginal people.

The second article, by Betty Bastien, outlines the world view of the *Siksikaitsitapi* (Blackfoot-speaking people), offering an alternative to the Western lens through which most North Americans see the world. Bastien, a member of the Siksika Nation, urges us to move away from Eurocentric individualism, the typically Western desire to dominate and control the natural world, and the characterization of everything outside the Western tradition as primitive and outmoded. Instead, she encourages people to see themselves as part of a complex system of kinship relations that require respect and reciprocity. In her discussion, Bastien uses several Blackfoot terms, which are defined in an accompanying glossary.

Using these articles as a starting point, we challenge you to examine history from an Aboriginal perspective, to examine the documentary record with a healthy skepticism, and to question the Eurocentrism of traditional Western historical narratives. European explorers and empires that described North America as a *terra nullius* did so deliberately in order to justify their conquest and possession of it. Indeed, Europeans invoked elaborate ceremonies to legitimize their assertions of sovereignty over North America.[1] More insidious still was the characterization of Aboriginal people as 'primitive' and without 'civilization'. Such depictions initiated an ongoing tradition of undervaluing Aboriginal perspectives and ways of knowing.

Chapter Objectives

At the end of this chapter, you should be able to

- identify elements of Aboriginal epistemology and their influence on Aboriginal world views;
- identify some of the major differences between Aboriginal and Western world views;
- consider how Eurocentric world views of Aboriginal people contributed to elements of the colonial project in Canada; and
- examine critically the development of Aboriginal studies programs in Western institutions, such as in universities.

Secondary Source

1.   Indigeneity in Canada: Spirituality, the Sacred, and Survival

Dennis H. McPherson and J. Douglas Rabb

This paper is written from an **Ojibwa** perspective. [Among] the **Anishnabe** people, the Ojibwa are known as the 'faith keepers'.[2] It is therefore most appropriate that a discussion of Native spirituality in Canada be written from an Ojibwa perspective. We will show how it has been and still is possible for a growing number of Indigenous people to maintain traditional spiritual values and Indigenous world views, thereby holding on to a dignified sense of self in spite of Canadian policies of assimilation. This is not meant in any way to minimize the damage done by such policies. In fact, Canadian philosopher J.T. Stevenson has argued that their implementation today would violate the security of person provision in the 1948 United Nations Declaration of Human Rights.[3] As Stevenson has argued:

> If you wanted a recipe for the destruction of personality, one such would be this: destroy the material base of a culture; force the people into an environment which provides little means of economic activity; foster the culture of dependency by means of minimal handouts; make ignorant and racist attacks on the

structure and superstructure of what remains of the culture; as the adults disintegrate from these shocks, experiment blindly with their children.[4]

It is now, finally, widely acknowledged that this was in fact the fate of Native people in Canada.[5] However, we wish to show how, in spite of everything, the concept of Indigeneity has survived this assault.

Pre-Contact Spiritual Values and World Views

[B]y the concept of Indigeneity we mean to encompass traditional pre-contact spiritual values and world views. We may glimpse some of these through the early contact accounts of European explorers, missionaries, traders, and settlers. We are, in a sense, forced to use such accounts in order to see beyond the horizon of 1492, before which it is impossible to obtain any kind of written confirmation acceptable to the academic world. These early contact accounts can be compared with one another and with oral and narrative traditions as well as with more objective ethnological accounts and contemporary Native voices.[6] Of the early contact literature, we have found *The Jesuit Relations* to contain a good deal of useful documentation concerning Native spirituality, values, and world views. Unlike most modern ethnologists, the **Jesuits** at least had a commitment to the religious and were, therefore, perhaps in a better position to understand spiritual concerns than the more objective ethnologists today. Of course *The Jesuit Relations* are written with an obvious ethnocentric and religious bias. However, the Jesuit philosophy is well understood and any trained philosopher should be able to make allowances for it. A good example of this approach is found in the work of Canadian philosopher Michael M. Pomedli, particularly in his *Ethnophilosophical and Ethnolinguistic Perspectives on the Huron Indian Soul.*[7]

A considerable body of evidence from first and early contact accounts supports the recent contention by Native scholars that, contrary to the Hollywood version of the savage, warlike redskin: 'hundreds of indigenous cultures have existed side by side on this continent "forever" without the "violent ethnic conflict now plaguing the world."'[8] This view of the pre-Columbian peoples of the Americas is sometimes dismissed as a naive romanticization of the past. For example, our own 1993 study, *Indian from the Inside: A Study in Ethno-Metaphysics*, was criticized as 'verging on the fanciful'.[9] The only historical evidence offered to support this criticism is the opinion of Francis Parkman, in his adventure narrative *The Oregon Trail*, that for the 'Sioux Indians' in the American West of 1846 'life [was] incessant war.'[10] However, more systematic studies such as Calvin Luther Martin's *In the Spirit of the Earth: Rethinking History and Time* conclude that 'the romantic myth of the "Noble Savage" . . . might not be so mythic and romantic after all.'[11] [Richard] Maundrell is not the only philosopher naive enough to go on record as supporting the myth of the savage redskin. Environmental philosopher J. Baird Callicott has reacted strongly against the contention by contemporary Native scholars cited above that 'It was, in fact, the acceptance (and even *celebration*) of a rich cultural and ethical diversity . . . that made it possible for hundreds of cultures to flourish side by side . . .'.[12] As Callicott puts it: 'No historical evidence whatever for this claim is offered; and the evidence that does exist supports an opposite conclusion.'[13] Callicott seems to dismiss contemporary Native voices as simply irrelevant:

> [Lee] Hester et al. write with complete certainty about indigenous thought. But search their footnotes for the cultural artifacts—or any evidence at all—upon which their pontifications are based. . . .
>
> Why then, when weighed against the cultural artifacts that I have amassed, meticulously studied, synthesized, and summarized . . . should we trust Hester et al.'s account of the beliefs, attitude and values of indigenous peoples and accept their criticism of mine. Apparently, because two of the authors identify themselves as indigenous.[14]

Callicott clearly believes most contemporary Indigenous people have been assimilated. He says explicitly that he suspects that 'such efforts may have been to some extent successful.'[15] To emphasize the point, he goes on to state: 'I also suggest that adopting nonnative technologies (such as the automobile and the television) and the replacement of native languages by European languages (such as Spanish and English) as mother tongues, might have further attenuated the process of cultural transmission and reproduction . . .'.[16] In an earlier article Callicott proclaimed: 'To buy guns, motors, and mackinaw jackets is to buy, however unintentionally, a world view to boot.'[17] Supposedly, for Callicott, contemporary Native people know nothing of traditional values and world views because 'the process of cultural transmission and reproduction' was 'attenuated' by largely successful policies of assimilation. We, on the contrary, are arguing that the beliefs of contemporary Elders and arguments of contemporary Native scholars should be compared with each other and with early contact accounts in the historical record.

Though perhaps not often mentioned in the schools of the dominant society, many early contact accounts in fact 'describe natives who are caring, loving, and sharing among themselves and with others'.[18] Even Christopher Columbus said of the Natives he first encountered:

> They are so . . . free with all they have, that no one would believe it who has not seen it; of anything that they possess, if it be asked of them, they never say no; on the contrary, they invite you to share it and show as much love as if their hearts went with it . . .'.[19]

About 3,000 miles to the north of Columbus's first encounter, in what was to become Canada, we find Father Paul Le Jeune of the Society of Jesus recording his thoughts concerning the Hurons in *The Jesuit Relations*:

> We see shining among them some rather noble moral virtues. . . . Their hospitality towards all sorts of strangers is remarkable; they present to them in their feasts, the best of what they have prepared, and as I have already said, I do not know if anything similar, in this regard, is to be found anywhere. They never close the door upon a Stranger, and once having received him into their houses, they share with him the best they have; they never send him away, and when he goes away of his own accord, he repays them with a simple 'thank you.'[20]

More than 200 years after Father Le Jeune's experiences with the Huron, and about 3,000 miles to the west on what is now the Canadian Prairies, a Ukrainian settler describes his encounter with an elderly Indian stranger:

> . . . He waved to me to come over. I was kind of scared and didn't go at first. Finally I went and as I got nearer I saw that he was eating these berries. Slowly, he picked off a berry and dropped it into his mouth. He was showing me I should do the same. I finally did and tasted the juiciest berry I ever had. I smiled and tried to thank the man. . . .[21]

There are also well-documented accounts of very similar acts of hospitality from the American West of the late 1600s. Frank Waters's *Book of the Hopi* contains a revealing description of the arrival of the Navaho, often regarded as the traditional enemy of the Hopi:

> . . . [L]ittle **bands** of men, women and children came, all dressed the same way, all hungry and homeless. The Hopi were good to these barbarians. They fed and sheltered them. They taught them to work in the fields, to weave baskets, and to spin cotton.[22]

The Hopi respected and welcomed a people so different from themselves that they could be thought of as 'barbarians'. Of course, the Navaho eventually outstayed their welcome, as did, incidentally, the Spanish, and hostilities did break out. But as Waters also reports, even after the Hopi were victorious over the Spanish, in the **Pueblo Revolt of 1680**, and shortly thereafter over the Navaho:

> The Hopi were left with a great sadness. They were a people of Peace who did not believe in war, yet they had been forced into killing both [the Navaho] and the Castillas [Spanish] in order to protect their homes and their religion.[23]

It is important to note here that the Hopi are reported to have gone to war in order to *preserve* their religion and way of life, not to *impose* their religion or their ways on anyone else. This represents a very different value system from that which the Christian missionaries brought to, and tried to impose on, the Native people of the Americas.

Respect, Autonomy, and Non-Interference

The Native values may be summed up in words like *respect* and *non-interference*. As we have documented above, they were at least at first contact widespread among Native people from different regions of the Americas. These values have also been identified by Cree-Métis philosopher Lorraine Brundige in her 1997 thesis, 'Continuity of Native Values: Cree and Ojiibwa'. She explains 'the most prevalent value, that of non-interference' by noting that 'an Aboriginal person does not tell another Aboriginal what to do. The act of directly interfering in someone's life is considered rude.'[24] The ethics of non-interference, which is a function of respect for the autonomy of the other, manifests itself in all aspects of Indigenous culture from social interactions through child-rearing practices to **treaties** between nations. The level of complete autonomy granted by

Indigenous parents to their children was noticed and remarked upon with much astonishment by the early missionaries. Father Le Jeune again in *The Jesuit Relations*:

> There is nothing for which these people have a greater horror than restraint. The very children cannot endure it, and live as they please in the houses of their parents, without fear of reprimand or of chastisement.[25]

Brundige argues that even today the 'use of personal stories and native narratives, rather than direct intrusive instruction, demonstrates the extent to which Native parents value the autonomy of their children'.[26] This is a further manifestation of the ethic of non-interference. It is a common remark that if you ask an Elder for advice you will never get a straight answer. You will often be told a story which seems to have nothing whatever to do with the question asked or the problem raised. You are given the autonomy to discover the relevance of the reply and hence to work out the problem for yourself. This is a sign of respect. It is also a method of instruction which fosters independent thinking and self-reliance. [T]here is compelling evidence for this kind of respect for autonomy in the child-rearing practices of Indigenous people today.[27] To give but one example, the British Columbia Ministry of Education's *Native Literacy and Life Skills Curriculum Guidelines*, in comparing Native and non-Native children, suggests that 'at the age of mobility' the Native Indian child is 'considered a person' and is 'free to explore his own environment' whereas the non-Native 'is watched and controlled by parents throughout childhood'. In this document, which was compiled by a committee made up mostly of Native people, the word *autonomous* is used to describe the Native child whereas his or her non-Native counterpart is said to be 'dependent'. The non-Native child is raised with more rigid routines dominated or controlled by adults. In the extended family of Native society 'rarely is a child punished in a systematic way' whereas the non-Native child can expect 'punishment for failure to comply with adult expectations'.[28]

[T]hese same values of autonomy and non-interference also served as the governing principles in treaties and other agreements between Indigenous Nations. This can be seen, for example, in the famous **Iroquois Confederacy**. In the traditional narrative of the founding of the Confederacy, Deganawidah (Dekanaweda) creates a symbol of the union by taking an arrow from each of the Five Nations 'which', he says 'we shall tie up together in a bundle which, when it is made and completely tied together, no one can bend or break.' Immediately after declaring, 'We shall tie this bundle of arrows together with deer sinew which is strong, durable and lasting and then also this institution shall be strong and unchangeable,' Deganawidah introduces a further symbol—the autonomous members of the Confederacy united as a single person. 'This bundle of arrows signifies that all the lords and all the warriors and all the women of the Confederacy have become united as one person.'[29] This, it is important to remember, does not lessen the importance or uniqueness of the individual member of this ideal, united person without whom it would not be what it is. This ideal person is a unity which includes difference, a unity not a uniformity. The individual members of the Iroquois Confederacy are all one person yet maintain their individual identities.

> Before the real people united their nations, each nation had its council fires. . . . The five Council Fires shall continue to burn as before and they are not quenched.[30]

This confederacy of nations was conceived by the Iroquois as one which accommodates the diversity and autonomy of those nations. The Deganawidah narrative states explicitly that 'Whenever a foreign nation is conquered or has by their own free will accepted the Great Peace, their own system of internal government may continue so far as it is consistent but they must cease all strife with other nations.'[31] This Indigenous ideal of diversity in unity is recommended for the present day by Lumbee tribal member Robert Williams. In his 1997 study *Linking Arms Together*, he argues: '. . . Deganawidah's message envisioned a multicultural community of all peoples on earth, linked together in solidarity under the sheltering branches of the Tree of the Great Peace.'[32]

From the Ethnocentric to the Polycentric

We began this paper with the claim that we were writing from an Ojibwa perspective. It now looks as if we are advocating something closer to a pan-Indian perspective. To resolve this paradox, it should be noted that another common feature in most North American Indigenous cultures is a concept we have called 'the polycentric perspective' as opposed to say Eurocentric, ethnocentric, or anthropocentric perspectives.[33] It is closely connected to or is a manifestation of 'non-interference'. This multi-perspectival approach is illustrated beautifully in the following account of a traditional 'sharing circle' by Cree scholar Michael Hart:

> Symbolically, the topic is placed at the centre of the circle and everyone has a chance to share their views about the topic. Since everyone is in a circle they will each have a different perspective of the topic or part of the picture. Everyone expresses their views so that a full picture of the topic is developed. Individual views are blended until consensus on the topic is reached. A community view is developed and knowledge is shared for the benefit of all members.[34]

We are convinced that this polycentrism is pervasive in Indigenous cultures. The concept has been picked up by Cherokee philosopher Jace Weaver. He explain[s] the significance of the polycentric perspective for what he calls Native theology using a story told by Osage scholar George Tinker:

> . . . Imagine two Indian communities who live in close proximity to each other, separated by a mountain. A non-Native visitor arrives at the first community. In the course of the stay, she is informed that the tribe's council fire is the center of the universe and creation myths are told to demonstrate this concept. The following day, the outlander and representatives of the first tribe travel to the other community. The elders of the new tribe declare that their council fire is the center of the universe, and the members of the first tribe nod their assent. Confused, the visitor asks her host, 'I thought you said that your fire was the center.' The Indian replies, 'When we're there, that is the center of the universe. When we are here, this is the center.'. . .[35]

As **Mi'kmaq** scholar Marie Battiste and her Chichasaw husband, Sa'ke'j Henderson, argue: 'Indigenous communities accept more diversity than most linguistic communities.'[36] It is important not to be misled into thinking that this kind of Indigenous pluralism entails relativism. As Canadian historian Michael Ignatieff argues in defending his 'patchwork-quilt vision' of Canadian identity: 'Pluralism does not mean relativism. It means humility.'[37] We are not surprised that Ignatieff argues in this way since we suspect that this distinctive feature of Canadian culture actually has Indigenous roots.[38] Nor does [Indigenous pluralism] entail the uncritical acceptance of incompatible beliefs, 'reconciling contradictory positions . . . at the cost of giving up the principle of non-contradiction', as Maundrell argued in his dismissal of Indigenous philosophy.[39]

The polycentric perspective does not prevent Indigenous people from taking a critical stance, though they may express it in a non-confrontational way compatible with the value of non-interference. For example, we suggest that most Indigenous people would find themselves in accord with the Mi'kmaq perspective as expressed by Marie Battiste when she says: 'From a Mi'kmaw perspective, the teachings of Moses, Jesus Christ, and Mohammed are part of the teachings of *npuoinaq* or medicine people—nothing more, nothing less.'[40] We simply cannot comprehend how some adherents of these so-called world religions can possibly regard themselves as having the One True Religion. This kind of arrogance is simply incompatible with the humility inherent in polycentrism and non-interference. These three 'world religions' all share a common origin and even share some sacred places, such as the Temple Mount in Jerusalem, but this does not seem to help them celebrate their mutual diversities. Perhaps they should try to see themselves from an Indigenous perspective.

Sacred Sites and Spirituality

Indigenous peoples too have their sacred sites. In order to understand the spiritual significance of sacred places for Indigenous peoples, we shall look briefly at one example of how the Canadian government has dealt with a sacred site. We will then try to portray the event from an Indigenous perspective. The site we have in mind is the sacred rock in the Qu'Appelle Valley, SK, which came to be known as 'Mistaseni'. The story of its fate is gracefully told in Trevor Herriot's *River in a Dry Land: A Prairie Passage*. We choose this story because it represents government insensitivity to Indigenous spirituality, not back in the eighteenth or nineteenth century, but in the mid-twentieth century. On 1 December 1966, Mistaseni was blown up because it was to be inundated in the creation of what is now called Lake Diefenbaker.[41] But Mistaseni was acknowledged to be a sacred rock.

The fate of Mistaseni makes an interesting story. Much thought had been given to moving the rock rather than blowing it up. Herriot describes the efforts to raise funds for the project:

> University of Saskatchewan students went door to door asking for donations to 'save the rock.' Even the provincial government said it would throw a couple of thousand dollars into the hat. In the spring of 66, folksinger Buffy Sainte-Marie, born twenty-three years earlier on Piapot reserve in the central Qu'Appelle Valley, headlined a benefit concert. . . . Meanwhile, Saskatchewan members of Parliament rose in the House of Commons somewhere east of the rock and

said heroic things, demanding the rescue of this 'ancient Indian shrine' and pointing out that Canada had recently sent hundreds of thousands of dollars to help move historic monuments threatened by the Aswan Dam project in Egypt. One of these champions was John Diefenbaker, the man who initiated the dam project while he was prime minister, the man whose name now graces the reservoir.[42]

In the end, however, insufficient funds were raised and the alternative method of 'preservation' using 60 sticks of dynamite was adopted.[43] A monument using some of the rubble from the blast was erected overlooking the lake. Herriot cites an internal memo dated 5 June 1967: 'As you know the Mistaseni Rock is made of black granite which does not shear or split like normal field stone. Consequently the cairn has been constructed mainly of field stone with an occasional piece of Mistaseni inserted when possible.' Even this cairn was moved some 20 years later to make way for a golf course.[44] Herriot describes seeing its final resting place:

> We walked toward the cairn for a closer look. It sat there askew, in high weeds, in the attitude of discarded things. Things that soon gather moisture, grow a shaggy beard, and tilt at the forces that were powerful enough to wash them aside.[45]

But this was a sacred rock. Early contact documents such as Henry Youle Hind's 1858 *Exploring Expedition* narrative describes 'Indians' placing 'offerings to Manitou' of tobacco, beads, and so on upon it.[46] The archaeological evidence from a 1959 dig at the base of the rock intended to recover anything of significance before the area was flooded, uncovered over 1,000 artifacts which Herriot describes as 'the tribute of countless travelers who had come to pay their respects, and yield something of their tools, adornment, and themselves, to the power indwelling in stone'.[47] This was a stone whose sides were worn smooth by buffalo rubbing themselves against it. This was a living rock which Elders say was created through various transformations from lost child to buffalo to stone.[48] The site had long-standing significance for the people. From an Indigenous perspective that is criterion enough for everyone to regard it as a sacred site.

To capture the sheer horror of Canada's treatment of this sacred site, try to imagine this 'Canadian solution' adapted to solve, say, the violence in the Middle East. Imagine a Canadian corps of engineers blowing up the Temple Mount in Jerusalem and distributing pieces of the rubble to representatives of the three 'world religions' offended by this sacrilege. We are suggesting that from an Indigenous perspective, the blowing up of Mistaseni was just as much of a sacrilege and is, most certainly, equally offensive.

The Resilience of Indigenous Values and World Views

A recent article by Regna Darnell explains that pre-contact **Algonquian** peoples including the Ojibwa were semi-nomadic hunting societies. They expand[ed] and contract[ed] like an accordion, depending on the season. According to Darnell, a summer gathering group might involve as many as 1,500 people trading and visiting by a lake or river. In the winter, 35 to 75 people might hunt together. If the game was scarce, this could be reduced to one or two extended families hunting together, as few as 10 people, though they would always remain in contact with other groups who could be of help. As Darnell puts it: 'Algonquian social organization is not one of random movement on land but of an accordion, a process of subsistence motivated expansion and contraction of social groups in relation to resource exploitation.'[49]

It is important to realize that Darnell is using the pre-contact, traditional, accordion-like social organization of peoples like the Ojibwa to understand Native identity in the present day. She argues:

> It is clear that Algonquian band-level societies have been adapting their traditional cultures to rapidly changing conditions since contact. . . . The system [today] looks different in terms of the number of people living together, but the underlying assumptions about repeated subsistence-driven changes in who lives with whom and why have not changed. What has changed is the availability of additional options: in New England, trapping for furs, cash labour, whaling, mercenary soldiering, crafts, and other occupations motivated geographical mobility without loss of perceived ties to home place and home people. In northern Canada, logging and oil rigs provided additional seasonal employment opportunities.[50]

In Darnell we find recognition not only of the continuity of Native values and identity but also of social organization. In many cases, the process is the same; the underlying assumptions have not changed since pre-contact times. We suggest that it may well be, in part, this very form of social organization which makes Native cultures so resistant to assimilation and Indigenous values so resilient. Even if only relatively few families continue to teach and practice Indigenous values, traditional ways can always be re-established. As Darnell points out: 'This accordion-like system has a considerable advantage under stress conditions because it can regenerate complexity from any component part.'[51]

From Colonialism to Neo-colonialism

By way of conclusion we will outline briefly this notion of neo-colonialism and the kind of research which remains to be done if the problem of neo-colonialism is to be overcome. In his book *Tortured People: The Politics of Colonization*, [Métis philosopher and historian Howard] Adams argues that neo-colonialism 'involves giving some benefits of the dominant society to a small privileged minority of Aboriginals in return for their help in pacifying the majority'.[52] His contention is borne out by the historical record. Many government policies were originally put in place to pacify the Indians, to ensure that they did not (or could not) cause trouble. For example, at the end of his 1880 book, *The Treaties of Canada*, negotiator Alexander Morris explains how 'Chiefs' and 'Councillors' have been 'strongly impressed with the belief that they are officers of the Crown, and that it is their duty to see that the Indians of their tribes obey the provisions of the treaties'. He explains that is why they are paid by the Government. They become government employees through 'payment of an annual salary of twenty-five dollars to each Chief, and of fifteen dollars to each

Councillor, or head man, of a Chief (thus making them in a sense officers of the Crown)'.[53]

In explaining to the chiefs why they receive 'suits of official clothing' under the provisions of the treaty, Morris states: 'I wear a uniform because I am an officer of the Queen, the officers of the police wear uniforms as servants of the Queen. So we give to the Chiefs and Councillors good and suitable uniform indicating their office, to wear on these and other great days.'[54] The implication would not be lost. The 'Chiefs and Councillors' as officers of the Queen, like the police officers, are expected 'to keep order amongst their people'.[55] They are working for the Queen, not for their people. This is not to say that chiefs and **band councils** today do not try to work for their people. Of course they do. But the problem is systemic. The system is not set up for chiefs and band councils to work for the people. They work for the Crown. When the system was established, the people were feared. Even their 'wandering mode of life' was seen by the dominant society as 'a difficulty which the assignment of **reserves** was calculated to obviate'.[56] Morris is more than clear about what the reserves were intended to accomplish. He says: 'I regard the Canadian system of allotting reserves to one or more bands together, in the [widely scattered] localities in which they have had the habit of living, as far preferable to the American system of placing whole tribes in large reserves . . . the breaking up of which, has so often led to Indian wars. . .'.[57] The reserve system in Canada was created, at least in part, to diminish the strength of the Indians in the 'remote contingency' of Indian uprisings. Morris states quite explicitly that 'the Canadian system of band reserves has a tendency to diminish the offensive strength of the Indian tribes, should they ever become restless . . .'.[58] The reserves together with their chiefs and band councils were set up to control the Indians. Speaking specifically of the chiefs, Morris describes 'how much advantage it is to the Crown to possess so large a number of Indian officials, duly recognized as such, and who can be inspired with a proper sense of their responsibility to the Government. . . .'[59] This was the beginning of neo-colonialism in Canada. This was the beginning of internalizing oppression within Native communities, just as the Indian residential schools were the beginning of the attempt to internalize the oppressor within the individual.[60]

From Residential Schools to Canadian Universities

[B]y the end of the twentieth century the instruments of neo-colonialism had moved from residential schools to institutes of higher education. [Adams] argues at some length that in Canada 'governments have developed a neo-colonial, conservative ideology among the young Aboriginal Peoples through university education, training programs of administration and management of small business.'[61] Adams shows how 'Neocolonialism involves the use of Métis and Indian elite to control other Aboriginal Peoples.' [D]rawing on close to 25 years of teaching experience at universities in both Canada and the United States, [he] argues in strong and bitter terms:

> Neocolonialism altered the attitude and aspirations of Indian and Métis people. One significant way this was done was through education. In Regina, the government supported **Status Indians** to establish their own college, which grants Bachelor Degrees in several disciplines. Similarly, there are Native Studies

Departments at almost every large university in Canada and many teacher institutes offer special programs to train Natives to be teachers. But their perspectives and ideology are quite consistent with mainstream . . . courses. There are also university programs to train Aboriginals in law, administration and commerce. All of these courses indoctrinate Native students to conservative middle class ideologies. They are orientated toward creating . . . a small privileged minority of Aboriginals in return for their help in pacifying the majority.[62]

Adams represents a growing number of Aboriginal academics who have spent their careers encouraging Native students to pursue post-secondary education, only to find that the system has let them down. We have documented elsewhere the systemic racism inherent in a university system run by members of the dominant society.[63] Such universities inevitably deal with Native issues and education in terms of what we call outside-view predicates. There is always the danger that Native students will apply such predicates to themselves, though some do not. We have seen them fight the system. To apply an outside-view predicate to yourself is much more than seeing yourself as others see you. It is permitting others to tell you who you are, fitting in with the plans and projects of others, making it easy for them to manipulate you for their own ends, for their own purposes. As we have argued in more detail elsewhere, 'It is, in a very real and frightening sense, to lose yourself, to become alienated, to become a stranger, an alien to yourself.'[64] Battiste and Henderson confirm this difficulty in Canadian universities. After years of attempting to develop appropriate Aboriginal programming in universities and educational systems run by the dominant society, [they] find it necessary to admit [that] '. . . Canadian educational systems view Indigenous heritage, identity and thought as inferior to Eurocentric heritage, identity and thought'.[65] They are forced to conclude that 'educators still know very little about how Indigenous students are raised and socialized in their homes and communities, and even less about how Indigenous heritage is traditionally transmitted.'[66] This, sadly, confirms our own findings 'that when a modern university administration attempts to understand what culturally appropriate education means to Native students without realizing that the entire non-Native world view may well be incommensurable with that of the students, the decisions reached may well result, not merely in misunderstanding, but in actual systemic discrimination'.[67]

We submit that the kind of research necessary to confront the problem of neo-colonialism is not going to come out of Canada's mainstream universities as they are currently configured. As we have seen in Adams, and Battiste and Henderson, the studies to date show that the kind of research which still remains to be done requires Indigenous scholars working in and for Indigenous communities.[68]

Community-Based Research and Indigenous Identity

Indigenous values and world views, ceremonies and practices, can still be found if one knows where to look and how to identify them. As we have argued, they can be extrapolated from the cultural interactions within Indigenous society. But this can only be done by people who are so much a part of those cultural intersections that their very being has been shaped by them, by their communities. Fortunately there are today a growing number of Indigenous scholars equipped to engage in critical dialogue with Elders and others in the community. There are also Elders who recognize the necessity of such critical dialogue, who no longer wish to serve simply as 'informants' for strangers trying to earn a doctorate from some foreign university. There have always been such Elders, but until recently, there have not been the right kind of scholars with the experience necessary to listen openly for the voice of the community.

This exciting new research should, of course, be combined with the more usual academic research, involving early contact literature and more modern ethnological analyses etc. Battiste and Henderson note, for example, that 'there is a collection of material in the social sciences literature on Aboriginal traditions and ways of life and on the spiritual relations between traditions and the land, including detailed studies of kinship, religion, and family structures.' They go on to argue: 'Although most of these writings are contaminated by Eurocentric bias, once they are decontaminated they may be helpful in understanding the nature and scope of Indigenous knowledge and heritage.'[69] We are not convinced that decontamination is quite the right concept to use in this context or if it is even necessary. We prefer [using a] conceptual archaeology metaphor [that] is equally applicable to both the writings of the early Christian missionaries and the contemporary social sciences literature. At both levels it is necessary 'to dig beneath the foreign matter'. Community-based research by Indigenous scholars using similar methodologies is necessary to deal with neo-colonialism, for it will provide balance to the Eurocentric bias of contemporary social sciences literature. We have learned in our research, and in our experiences, that balance is certainly not going to happen in universities run by members of the dominant society. Accordingly, Battiste and Henderson argue that '[t]he establishment of community-based institutions for supervising research, promoting education and training, and conserving collections of important objects and documents, is clearly essential.'[70] In a similar vein and for similar reasons, Adams argues:

> Ideally Aboriginals, not Euro-Canadian academics, should research Aboriginal culture. Indigenous institutions should be staffed by Native scientists who grow up in Aboriginal societies and, therefore, identify themselves with the future well-being of Aboriginal nations.[71]

Adams is not suggesting the building of community-based research institutions as simply one more community economic development scheme. He is arguing, we are all arguing, that, given the way in which neo-colonialism developed by the end of the twentieth century, the kind of community-based research we have been discussing is absolutely necessary for the survival of Native spirituality, even for the survival of Native identity. It is up to the Native communities themselves to implement this research. No one else is going to do it for them, simply because no one else can do it for them.

As we have demonstrated in this paper Native spirituality and identity have, despite all odds, survived colonialism. Our concern is that if the Indigenous peoples in Canada continue to sit idly by and do nothing about neo-colonialism, not only will their Native spirituality and their Native identity not survive, they themselves will not survive. For the first time since contact with Europeans more than 500 years ago, the opportunity to survive as distinct peoples rests truly in their own hands.

Secondary Source

2.   Indigenous Pedagogy: A Way Out of Dependence

Betty Bastien

This article explores the pedagogical practices of *Siksikaitsitapi*. Traditional learning is premised on a 'knowing' that is generated through a participatory and experiential process involving kinship relationship networks known as alliances. In the Indigenous paradigm, an understanding of the dynamic and intricate relationships among *Mokaksin*, *Pommaksinni*, and *Aistommatop* knowledge originates and is experienced from the living, fluid, and transforming world of the Blackfoot people. The organic nature of the universe is understood and emulated through the powers of life, which *Siksikaitapi* call *Ihtsipaitapiiyo'pa*. Referring to *Ihtsipaitapiiyo'pa* reminds us of the sacred spirit. In this context, the word *spirit* is understood as universal consciousness.

This sacred power structures all relationships among and between humans, nature, and the universe. The *Siksikaitapi* perspective thus emulates natural patterns of the universe. The universe's patterns constitute a web of interconnectivity, a system that maintains balance and harmony that preserves and strengthens *Ihtsipaitapiiyo'pa*. By echoing these natural relationship and life processes, *Siksikaitapi* harmonize with nature. Harmony is achieved through their relationships, as revealed through their relationship with *Natosi*, the manifestation of the source of life that is at the core of human and planetary survival. Subsequently, *Natosi* is an integral partner in our renewal of responsibilities in maintaining balance and thus is central to the Blackfoot world. The inclusive nature of relationships with the natural and cosmic world and with the sacred is at the heart of the Blackfoot ontological perspective. Self/identity is premised on the integrative spirit of *Ihtsipaitapiiyo'pa*.[72]

Ontological Perspective

Siksikaitapi ontological theory is premised on experience with the sacred *Ihtsipaitapiiyo'pa*. The individual's experience of the sacred guides *Niitsitapi* (real people, as in the Blackfoot-speaking people) in understanding what it means to be human. Therefore, human development is based on experiences, which connect the individual to the transformational powers of the universe. This includes a complex system of kinship relationships through which *Niitsitapi* teach their children the meaning and purpose of life. Children discover the meaning of life through experiences grounded in the sacred relationships of alliances. The understanding of what it means to be a human being is premised on the connections with the sacred and on transformational experiences. In essence, the identity of the people and the theory of human development are based on a framework of moral and ethical relationships.

These spiritual relationships have been referred to generically as the spirituality of Indigenous people. They are the basis of becoming and being *Niitsitapi*. The tribal identity of *Siksikaitsitapi* begins with having good relations. Prayer is not only the path for good relations among one's alliances, but it is also the process of making alliances and acknowledging them. This has been expressed as follows by one

Kaaahsinnooniksi: 'In order to regain our identity and maintain our way of life we need to have good relations. We don't leave out prayer in anything that we do. This is our way.'[73]

The Indigenous and Eurocentred conceptions are diametrically opposite in their approach to relationships and to defining the purposes of human activity. The most striking cultural difference is that in the Eurocentred concept an objectified self represents the universal nature of humanness. This denies the cosmic essence of humanity originating with *Ihtsipaitapiiyo'pi* as the source of the relationships of *Siksikaitsitapi*. The nature of humanity in the *Siksikaitsitapi* world view orginates from spiritual relationships. Human development and governance are shaped through these relationships, and human beings strive to be in balance with all relationships. In summary, the ontological experience of the sacred arises within a complex system of kinship relations.

Niitsitapi's conception of self is intricately linked with an organic universe; alliances with the natural world are the relationships from which life is lived. *Niitsitapi* cosmic self is understood as part of the natural order and is ethically and morally located in all of time. Subsequently, knowing is the knowing of all time. On the other hand, in the Eurocentred view, the objectified self stands alone and powerless. The ideas of self are totally reversed between these two paradigms. Understanding these differences means recognizing and distinguishing the construction and the dynamics of dependency.

Using the European self-image and concept of power automatically victimizes tribal people, since these conceptions continually reconstruct powerlessness, victimization, deficiency, or inferiority as characteristics of Indigenous peoples. A post-colonial paradigm must not only deconstruct the assumption of the Eurocentred ideological process but also begin by reaffirming and reconstructing tribal concepts, the fundamentals of Indigenous theories and ontological assumptions. The validation and use of tribal ontologies begins the process of the reconstruction of self and the identification of one's place in a cosmic universe allowing for Indigenous ways of knowing. For *Siksikaitsitapi*, the beginning point is the awareness of their alliances that are at the heart of the culture. Alliances shape tribal and personal identities. Through these relationships, *Niitsitapi* identity can manifest and express itself outside the colonial paradigm, wholly and self-sufficiently engaged in its own discourse.

By advancing a universal definition of self, the Eurocentred perspective denies other forms of knowledge, other forms of knowing, and thus other forms of humanity. This denial of other views has been central to genocide and colonialism. As a result, for many Indigenous persons, the self has become disassociated from the natural world. In this experience, knowing is understood as a cerebral activity located in the intelligence of humankind, and science is seen as an isolated and objective exercise dependent upon the ability to separate the self from the world. In fact, in the context of the Eurocentred mind, to understand the self as a cosmic being is to be powerless and without much agency. It is politically unwise and undesirable; furthermore, it is considered morally reprehensible, primitive, and outmoded.[74]

The general framework that constructs *Niitsitapi* dependency is the objectified self and subsequent analysis of deficiency and pathology that support the paradigm. 'The North American indigenous self has been seen as deficient. Further, the indigenous self has become contaminated or damaged through the effects of genocide. "Damaged", in this context, refers to the individual's inability to achieve his/her purpose in life as framed within the value system of the dominant society.'[75]

The concept of an objectified self is consistent with and part of the Eurocentred concept of culture. 'Self' is seen as composed of characteristics that are distinguished by intelligence and by the ability to separate and isolate phenomena. Notions of reality are intricately linked with this concept of self (as with any other), a self premised on an absolute autonomy. A clear distinction is made between what is and what is not self. This autonomous conception of self has been forced upon tribal peoples. Subsequently, pathological characteristics have also been imposed and projected on the now isolated Indigenous self. As a result, the objectification of self is one of the fundamental bases for the denial of the existence of other forms and expressions of humanity. This objectification has been imposed via Eurocentred theories of human development and education, which are used to interpret the behaviour of tribal peoples. The abstracting definition of self is a premise fundamental to Eurocentred science and knowledge and determines how reality is perceived and how a society comes to knowledge.[76] Culture and self thus have become abstractions that can be controlled and manipulated in accordance with the values of Eurocentred societies.

Siksikaitsitapi Ways of Knowing: Epistemology

Epistemology concerns itself with theories of knowing and provides frameworks for discussing validity issues. It provides cultures with a philosophical and theoretical structure for seeking knowledge as well as for processes that define truth. Epistemology affects the informal and formal educational process that is dependent upon theoretical interpretations and understandings of the nature of the universe, reality, and truth. The educational foundation of a culture originates from its epistemological assumptions, its pivot of reality interpretation and maintenance.[77]

Most Eurocentred epistemologies are premised on rationality and the objectification of knowing. As a result, nature is understood to be made of identifiable qualities that are potentially knowable. Scientific inquiry is the pursuit of discerning the knowable qualities of an objectified universe. The rational goal of objectified observation is to identify the discrete parts that are assumed to exist and from which understanding and knowledge are derived. By identifying the component parts of the universe, or understanding how these parts are interconnected, the knower garners the power to control, manipulate, and predict the movements of people and objects.[78] Scientific rationality and objectivity are considered possible because of the assumption that humans are fundamentally rational beings. The Eurocentred paradigm distinguishes human beings not only as separate from each other but also as separate from the natural world by virtue of their intellect or ability to reason.

In this model, we must control an object in order to gain knowledge of it. We can do this only if we are emotionally detached from it. And we gain emotional distance from the 'object' by first and foremost gaining control over ourselves, by placing our intellect in control of our emotions. Marimba Ani describes Eurocentred epistemologies as invoking certain ontological foundations that have a cognitive bias.[79] These assumptions are embedded in the structure of the English language. Language in general is the medium through which structures of power are perpetuated, and concepts of 'truth', 'order', and 'reality' established.[80] 'Truth' is what counts as true within a system of rules for a particular discourse; 'power' is that which annexes, determines, and verifies truth. Truth is never outside or deprived of power, and the production of truth is a function of power; we cannot exercise power except with the production of truth.[81] Power lies in the understanding that truth is contextual to the science and methods of a culture.

For *Niitsitapi*, intelligence means participating within the world from which one has acquired the wisdom of nature and the knowledge of experience. The objectification of knowledge through the manipulation and control of observation has negated alternative epistemologies, modes of cognition, and world views, thereby limiting the ability for people to experience the universe as cosmic.[82] *Niitsitapi* epistemologies are premised on a set of assumptions through which knowledge and validity are constituted. Within these assumptions, all knowledge rests within a cosmic union of human beings who are interconnected with the natural order through the spiritual forces coming from *Ihtsipaitapiiyo'pa*. They constitute the collective consciousness of *Niitsitapi*, which is based on the spirituality of a cosmic order. A *Kaaahsinnoon* shares his experience with *Siksikaitsitapi* epistemologies:

> I had moved to the Sundance with my parents. X (an older person who was a member of *Omahkohkanakaaatsiisinni*) approached me to assist him with his dancing [ceremony]. He said, 'Would you assist me when I dance out from *Tatsikiiyakokiiysinni*, the centre tipi?' I did not want to do it. I did not feel good about doing it.' Y (another man, who overheard X asking for my assistance) interjected and said, 'He is asking for your assistance, why don't you want to assist him?' I then agreed to help X with his dancing. X said, 'You watch me, when I come out of *A'mii, Tatsikiiyakokiiysinni*. I will wave to you.' X did as he said and I entered the center and danced with *Omahkohkanakaaatsiisinni*.
>
> In the morning, I was sleeping and was awakened by the sound that people make when they want to enter a lodge. The sound is a way of announcing their arrival. My mother called to them to enter. Three *Omahkohkanakaaatsiisinni* members had come to visit my father.[83]

One of the *Omahkohkanakaaatsiisinni* began with,

> 'Your son created a grave imbalance yesterday [by dancing with the *Mopisstaan* without proper preparation], it is not good. He went to the center and danced with the bundle.' X continued, 'When it is midday, he will go to the center lodge. The person who is going to paint his face will be sitting waiting for him.' X did not say whether I would dance with the Bundle again. After they left, my mother told me, 'Do as you are told, go to the center lodge.' She gave me offerings (gifts) for *Kaaahsinnoon* who was going to paint my face.
>
> At midday I went to the center lodge. X was there. He pointed to *Kaaahsinnoon* who was going to paint my face. Later, I danced with the bundle. This was an imbalance I made. It bothered me.[84]

In the above narrative, *Kaaahsinnoon* addresses how he was guided by the ancestors and the alliances among *Omahkohkanakaaatsiisinni* in becoming a grandfather.

His participation began with an imbalance that could have had severe consequences for him and his family. However, he was protected by the members' advice. Through this experience, *Kaaahsinnoon* began to live in balance and harmony. In particular, he shared the proper movements within the lodge, which maintain an agreeable equilibrium among the occupants.

Pommaksinni, a process of transferring spiritual knowledge through kinship relations, is central to *Siksikaitsitapi* epistemology. 'Kinship' in this context has a wider meaning than a biological/genealogical relationship. *Siksikaitsitapi* ontology and epistemology are inextricably intertwined. The following epistemological assumptions illustrate these relationships:

- The nature of the universe is interconnectedness.
- The universe is interconnected through *Ihtsipaitapiiyo'pa*.
- It is the nature of the universe to work for balance.
- The universe has sacred power and influence; it works in reciprocal ways among its interdependent parts.

Siksikaitsitapi epistemology creates a way of being, a way of relating to the world that embodies the kinship–relationship system. Relationships entail responsibilities that connect to an experiential 'body' of knowledge. In this way, knowing becomes a part of the knower. *Mokaksin*, meaning knowledge itself, has spirit that is 'transferred' in the relationships between the knower and known. Through these methods and rules of knowing, knowledge and self become one.

Additionally, transformation is achieved by changing the relationship between knower and known. In describing an experience of *Siksikaitsitapi* epistemology in action, a *Kaaahsinnoon* said,

> There are certain things in our way of life that I understand are given to us. You have to do certain things. That is your life. These are the real personal things that *Siksikaitsitapi* must do. These things cannot be handed down. I think that in some cases those of you, who are attempting to learn our ways, you are trying to understand this aspect of our way of life.
>
> It comes directly from *Ihtsipaitapiiyo'pa* to you. It will be shown to you in one way, shape, or form. It will be taught to you.
>
> It is given to you, for you to use in a good way.[85]

In this example, *Kaaahsinnoon* refers to one of the most powerful assumptions of Indigenous epistemologies: it is in the nature of the universe to give gifts, blessings, and lessons, which are meant to be used in a positive way.

Our theory of knowledge is found in the sacred stories, which are the living knowledge of the people. These stories, accumulated over millenia, explain the nature of reality, the science, and the economic and social organization of *Siksikaitsitapi*. The knowledge contained in the stories remains alive because it is applicable across generations. Each generation of *Kaaahsinnooniksi* is responsible for retelling the stories to the next, which must adapt the lessons and apply them to the present. The ways of knowing, of acquiring knowledge and truth, are dependent upon observational skills, or *Kakyosin*. Knowledge lives in the process of observing, in reflecting on connections among observations, and in applying the experiences of *Akaitapiwa*, our ancestors.

Knowledge also derives from applying one's personal observations and experiences to the interrelationships of alliances.

Niitsitapi epistemologies represent knowledge as being experienced in an infinite and all-encompassing moment. Following *Niitsitapi* logic means experiencing the whole, the interconnectedness of an indivisible universe. Rationality, on the other hand, denies the spiritual nature of knowledge and sacrifices the wholeness of human beings.[86] One example of the denial and sacrifice that results from Eurocentred logic comes from my friend, colleague, and ceremonialist Duane Mistaken Chief. He shared the following with me regarding the use of plants and herbs: 'Eurocentred scientists dissect the herb and extract the elements of the herb that they have found to have medicinal properties. However, what they don't understand is that the plant functions as a whole—other properties of the plant may be important because of their cleansing functions.'[87]

The nature of the universe to function as an interdependent whole has profound implications for education and the process of learning. The following principles encompass the epistemologies of *Niitsitapi*:

- Knowledge, truth, and meaning are revealed to *Niitsitapi* through their relationship with *Ihtsipaitapiiyo'pa* and through a network of interdependent kinship relations. Knowledge is holistic and every aspect of nature contains knowledge that can be revealed.
- Knowing, learning, and teaching are reciprocal in nature. *Niitsitapi* learn the nature of existence through the guidance of kinship alliances.
- The reciprocal nature of knowing is understood and appreciated through *Pommaksinni*. The reciprocal nature of knowing is premised on creating and generating the knowledge necessary for maintaining balance.

These principles of coming-to-knowing correlate with the manner in which education and human development processes and practices are traditionally organized among *Niitsitapi*. The primary medium for seeking to understand *Niipaitapiiysin* and, for *Mokaksin*, *Ihtsipaitapiiyo'pa* is kinship relations. Knowledge is transferred through these relationships and exists in a process of renewing and generating alliances for knowing.

A common sense of transformation and transcendence is experienced through ceremonies. The meanings associated with *Pommaksinni* are shared by the people.[88] As long as the people retain their transfers, they will retain their connection to the transformational ways of being. The people will continue to renew their responsibilities as instructed in the original *Pommaksinni* described in the old stories. Song, prayer, dance, and other mimetic movements were given that embody the vibrational patterns by which the power of the alliances can be transferred to *Siksikaitsitapi*. For example, in *Pommaksinni* of sacred power and knowledge of *Niinaimsskahkoyinnimaan*, *Ksisstsi'ko'm* said:

> Here is my pipe. It is medicine. Take it and keep it. Now, when I come in the Spring, you shall fill and light my pipe, and you shall pray to me. . . . For I bring the rain which makes the berries large and ripe. I bring the rain which makes all things grow, and for this you shall pray to me, you and all the people.[89]

Furthermore,

> Whenever you transfer the Pipe to anyone, steal quietly upon them just before daybreak, the time I am on the move, and take him by surprise, just as I do, chanting my song, and making the sound of a bear charging. When you catch a man and offer him the Pipe, he will not dare refuse, but must accept it and smoke it. It is sure death to refuse, because no one dares to turn away from the grizzly bear. The owl is also a prominent figure in the Pipe because he is a bird of the night. When the society is after a new member, they chant Owl songs and pray to Owl for sacred power to enable them to catch him in a deep sleep. In this way, a spell is cast over him and he cannot escape.[90]

The *Niinaimsskahkoyinnimaan* story lives in the ceremonies and through the lives of *Aawaatowapsiiks* and *Kaaahsinnooniksi*, who renew these alliances to bring peace and prosperity to the people. Each year after *Ksisstsi'ko'm* is first heard, *Niinaimsskaiks* know it is their responsibility to hold the annual Thunder Pipe dance. The narrative illustrates the reciprocal responsibilities of prosperity and balance between *Ksisstsi'ko'm* (including all the alliances represented in the bundle) and the people. The protocol requires people to show respect, seek good relations, and maintain alliances with *Ksisstsi'ko'm* each year when *Niinaimsskahkoyinnimaan* are opened, the ceremonial dances are performed, and songs are sung to honour and renew the *Siksikaitsitapi–Ksisstsi'ko'm* alliances for another season.

Thunder Pipes are used for curative purposes. In contemporary Indigenous societies, many individuals abuse drugs and alcohol; one-third of Aboriginal people die violent deaths; and incarceration and unemployment are at unprecedented levels that continue to rise. These conditions indicate the need to reconnect with the healing knowledge generated through sacred alliances, such as with the Medicine Pipes (a form of Thunder Pipe). Healing in this sense means reclaiming and regaining the tribal ways of generating knowledge and restoring the responsibilities to life itself. Learning the responsibilities of traditional alliances is the path of coming to know one's purpose in life and of learning the sacred knowledge that can address adversity experienced by contemporary *Niitsitapi*.[91]

The sacred power of the universe is pervasive and reveals itself through all of creation, including thoughts, objects, speech, and actions. It speaks through rocks and animals and may take the form of an animal that transforms into a person or begin with a person who transforms into an animal.[92] As part of the transformational power of the universe, people migrate regularly into 'dream worlds'. These migrations provide the meaning and knowledge sought and acquired by *Siksikaitsitapi*. In fact, all human beings, according to the Plains cultures, transcend the limits of their embodiment through these dream-world migrations. They are considered unexceptional experiences.[93]

Knowledge is Coming-to-Know *Ihtsipaitapiiyo'pa*

In the traditional context, knowledge comes from *Ihtsipaitapiiyo'pa* and knowing means connecting with *Ihtsipaitapiiyo'pa*. Knowledge not only has spirit but also *is* spirit.

Knowledge grows through the ability to hear the whispers of the wind, the teachings of the rock, the seasonal changes of the weather. By connecting with the knowing of the animals and plants, we strengthen our knowledge. As in all relationships, consent must be given and obligations and responsibilities observed.[94] Ceremonies embody the delicate balance of the cosmic order and thus provide connections to knowing. These relationships are also evident in creation stories and cosmology.

The social organization of *Niitsitapi* reflects the influence and teaching role of *Akaitapiwa*. As Ronald Goodman illustrates in his discussion of Lakota star knowledge, the star world and the microcosmic world of the Plains are intricately interconnected.[95] The same connections are considered important among *Siksikaitsitapi*. In partial fulfillment of this relationship, we have four annual major ceremonies that correspond to the seasons: *Niinaimsskahkoyinnimaan*, the Medicine Pipes, which are opened after the first *Ksisstsi'ko'm* in spring; *Aako'ka'tssin*, the Sundance, which is held in July or when the Saskatoon berries ripen; *Ksisskstakyomopisstaan*, the Beaver Bundle, held after the ice breaks in the spring; and *Kano'tsisissin*, the All Smoke, held in the winter when the nights are long. These ceremonies are the collective consciousness of *Siksikaitsitapi*, which places them at the centre of their universe. During these ceremonies, we acknowledge and give thanks to our alliances for another cycle. We ask for continued protection, prosperity, long life, growth, and strength.

This knowledge is a living knowing. It is illustrated through the heart of *Siksikaitsitapi* epistemologies and pedagogy: *Pommaksinni* is the central approach to teaching the traditional knowledge of the tribe. In this way, the initiated take care of the bundles and pipes that are the connections of alliances, the partners of *Siksikaitsitapi* in maintaining the delicate balance of life. This includes an all-encompassing responsibility to teach and pass on the knowledge to the next generation of initiates and to ensure the survival of all. *Pommaksiistsi* are the ceremonies that transfer knowledge and maintain the tribal integrity of *Siksikaitsitapi* ontology and epistemology.

The basic ontological responsibility, *Kiitomohpiipotokoi*, of giving and sharing is embedded in the fundamental philosophical premises of *Siksikaitsitapi* education. Sharing and giving connect to and perpetuate *Ihtsipaitapiiyo'pa*. They are consistent with the natural order of the universe and help to maintain it in balance. According to *Siksikaitsitapi*, a fundamental aspect of the cosmic universe is reciprocity, which is experienced in *Aipommotsspists*, the practice of ceremonial transfers. As a *Siksikaitsitapi* word, *Aipommotsp* means 'We are transferred; it was given, or passed on.' The word depicts reciprocal responsibilities or an exchange of responsibilities among participants. The natural law of reciprocity is not limited to ceremony but is extended by *Siksikaitsitapi* to their daily customs and activities.

The ethical and moral behaviour identified through customs, language, values, and roles is often referred to as protocol or ritual. Protocols and rituals encapsulate the *Kiitomohpiipotokoi* that are the means for returning to a state of balance or ensuring good relations. This was mentioned earlier in regard to joining sacred societies for ceremony and living arrangements of the tipi. A few daily examples are the strictures to give food and drink to visitors, to not walk in front of ceremonial people or *Kaaahsinnooniksi*, to greet and acknowledge everyone with some gesture, and to always move in a sun-wise direction if you are moving in a circle. Tribal protocol acknowledges the sacred state or the good relations of food, the energy of individuals, and the movement of life. One *Kaaahsinnooniksi* shared the following comment on the seeming inexplicability of the rationale behind these protocols:

> These are the things for which we cannot give you an answer. I ask why is it that you cannot enter the lodge (home) of a *Niinaimsskaiks* with a cigarette. Why is it, if I have given you something to eat when you come to visit me, that you have to tell four stories, if you want to take the food out of the home? This is our way of life. These are the things that are taught to us.[96]

Through generations of *Aipommotsspists*, *Kaaahisinnooniksi* have been taught the rigorous and sacred science of participating in ceremonies. The knowledge inherent in their ceremonial protocols transcends the classical Eurocentred conceptions of reality and nature. However, experiments in quantum mechanics have revealed that reality is the manifestation of a 'set of relationships', which, upon interacting with an observing system, change knowledge and physical reality discontinuously.[97] This particular scientific view is consistent with *Siksikaitsitapi* understanding. *Ahkoyinnimaan* can be said to be a web of kinship relationships that, through active participation of *Siksikaitsitapi*, alters and transforms reality. Included in this web of interconnectivity are *Siksikaitsitapi* relationships with animals, who also have roles and responsibilities in the transformation of life. Through participation, *Siksikaitsitapi* become a conscious part of an interactive system and are transformed in the process. Once the transfer has occurred and become part of the living body, the initiated becomes *Aipommotsp*. The alliances collectively strengthen life for the sake of life, for the survival of humankind, and for the universe.

In the sacred story of *Ksisstsi'ko'm*, this knowledge is given to the people as *Aipommotsp*, the transfer of *Ahkoyinnimaan*. The relevant alliances that are active here are illustrated in the following excerpt:

> A long time ago, Thunder struck down a man. While he lay on the ground, the Thunder Chief appeared to him in a vision, showing him a pipe and saying, 'I have chosen you that I might give you this Pipe. Make another just like it. Gather together also a medicine bundle, containing the skins of the animals and birds which go with it. Whenever your people are sick, or dying, a vow must be made and a ceremony given with a feast. The sick will be restored to health.' The Grizzly Bear afterwards appeared to the man and said to him, 'I give you my skin to wrap around the sacred bundle, because it is larger than the skins of other animals.' The owl possesses knowledge of the night. The Medicine Pipe is wrapped with raw hide and decorated with feathers and the winter skins of the weasels. Many animal and bird skins are gathered for the sacred bundle, wrapped in a large grizzly bear skin. In the spring, when the first Thunder is heard, the Pipe is brought out and held up.[98]

Niitsitapi education is distinct from the Eurocentred educational system in that it is governed by the natural law of balance and harmony. *Aipommotsspists* are the means of maintaining the reciprocity and generosity required to preserve balance among *Siksikaitsitapi*. Transfers also sustain the natural order that makes possible the gifts of life; reciprocity is essential for the survival of all life. *Aipommotsspists* are the embodiment of this way of life, forming the fabric of *Siksikaitsitapi* culture and the social organization of a people.

Aipommotsspists: Transfer of Knowledge and Ontological Responsibilities

Aipommotsspists exemplifies the concept that traditional learning is experiential. Transfers bring *Siksikaitsitapi* ontology, epistemology, and pedagogy together by transmitting sacred responsibilities and knowledge from generation to generation. They are the initiations into sacred knowledge and responsibilities that are passed down through each generation to ensure the renewal of cosmic alliances. These medicine bundles have been transferred to *Siksikaitsitapi* with the original instructions for coming-to-knowing, *Akaotsistapi'takyo'p*, so that 'we have come to understand (not merely know) it.'[99]

During the original *Aipommotsp* of the medicine bundles, the initiates were instructed on how to conduct the ceremonies. In essence, the transfer ceremony is working with *Ihtsipaitapiiyo'pa*, from which knowledge is revealed or transferred. As such, the transfers are the processes of renewing the original responsibilities as taught to the *Siksikaitsitapi* in the original transfer.

Kaaahsinnooniksi said:

Tribal identity is learned through experience. Conversely, students and non-Native people who want to learn of our ways often will use the literature; they do not realize that the literature is fraught with inaccuracies and false information. The language and the experience of our relationships has been our way of teaching and learning.

Aipommotsspists are a medium for becoming one with the universe. They are the connections to all time, as well as the ancestors and ancients, and ensure the continuance of *Siksikaitsitapi*. As one ceremonialist said,

It is our responsibility, in the *Siksikaitsitapi* way, to give back what we have been transferred. . . . For example, those who have received an education return and give it back to the people. The *Siksikaitsitapi* way, our way, the *Niitsitapi's* way is to help, to assist, and then *Ihtsipaitapiiyo'pa* will help us.[100]

The ontological theory is a complex kinship system of relationships from which knowing originates. Coming-to-knowing involves a lifetime process of learning, understanding, and knowing. Knowledge is a way of living and being, a way of being in the world, and also a way of learning. Humans' participation in this process creates partnerships in the co-creation of balance in our physical reality. Knowledge is thus relational, acquired through experience and relationships. However, it is also spirit and independent of human beings and a relationship that human beings engage in. Through coming to understand the process of renewal, one understands balance and the process of living that strengthens the balance.

Science currently describes the nature of reality thus: 'Everything is intimately present to everything else in the universe.' In other words, material objects are no longer perceived as independent entities but as concentrations of energy of the quantum field. The universe is portrayed as a quantum field that is present everywhere in space, while its particles have a discontinuous, granular structure.[101] Indigenous people have long understood the universe to be, as physicists now suggest, an indivisible whole.

The ways of knowing and understanding manifest in the interactive exchanges within the context of relationships. These relationships are based on the responsibilities as understood through the reciprocal nature of the universe. *Niisitapi* come-to-know through connection with family, environment, geography, animal world, the universe, and so on. In their relationships, they experience the knowledge and achieve an understanding of their responsibility for maintaining the balance of their world.

In conclusion, protocols and ethics of Indigenous knowledge are embedded in our responsibilities and place in the universe. The academy must begin to respect the reality that, in the generation of knowledge and in respecting Indigenous epistemologies and pedagogy, Indigenous people will regain their independence. From the inner strength of an Indigenous/tribal identity, *Siksikaitsitapi* will remember how to apply the traditional knowledge in the following aspects:

- knowing one's tribal and cosmic responsibilities;
- experiencing the knowing of tribal alliances;
- incorporating knowledge and skills acquired for the well-being of a cosmic universe; and
- passing on one's knowledge and skills to the next generation.

Indigenous ways of knowing live in the experience of being in tune with the source of life; our responsibility is to pass it on, do the transfers, so that others too will live. Indigenous pedagogy teaches *Niisitapi* and others the ways of knowing and being within the Blackfoot world so that all will thrive and survive. The Elders quoted here have lived the *Siksikaitsitapi* ways of knowing, making possible the doctoral research that produced my book *Blackfoot Ways of Knowing*. It is their lived experiences with sacred knowledge that ensures another generation's survival.

Glossary

A'mii, Tatsikiiyakokiiysinni The centre tepee; over the centre tepee.

Aako'ka'tssin Sundance; literally, circle encampment.

Aawaatowapsiiks Ceremonialist; those who have the right to take part in sacred activities and ceremonies; in certain ceremonial contexts, an individual.

Ahkoyinnimaan Pipe.

Aipommotsp (Aipommotsspists) We are transferred; it was given or passed on.

Aistommatop Transformed; literally, embodying the knowledge.

Akaitapiwa (Akaitapiiks) Ancestor; literally, the old [days] people or people of the past.

Akaotsistapi'takyo'p 'We have come to understand (not merely know) it'; to be cognizant of and discern tribal connections; sacred science; knowing as experiential knowing.

Ihtsipaitapiiyo'pa Sacred power, spirit, or force that links concepts; life force; term used when addressing the sacred power and the cosmic universe;

source of life; sun as manifestation of the source of life; great mystery; together with *Niitpaitapiiyssin*, identifies the meaning and purpose of life; that which causes or allows us to live. It is through *Ihtsipaitapiiyo'pa* that all 'natural laws' are governed.

Ihtsipaitapiiyo'pi The reason why we are caused to live through the source of life.

Kaaahsinnoon Grandfather.

Kaaahsinnooniksi 'Our grandparents'; used by *Niitsipoyi* to refer to familial grandparents and by members of the various societies or bundle and pipe holders to refer to previous society members, bunder holders, pipe holders, etc.

Kakyosin Observational skills; 'to align' or 'to balance' referring to the *Siksikaitsitapi* understanding that there is an order of things or pattern that we can discern if we are observant. Through *Kakyosin*, we align ourselves with these patterns and can achieve the same things the observed beings can. For example, one time a man was starving and he came upon a decomposed carcass of a *Makoiyi* (wolf). When he slept, the spirit of the *Makoiyi* spoke to him in song and gave him its pelt as a gift. The spirit told him how to conduct a ceremony around these gifts and instructed him to conduct it every time before using them. With this knowledge, the man was able to transform into a *Makoiyi* and hunt sucessfully.

Kano'tsisissin All Smoke ceremony; a night ceremony attended by past and present members of the various societies, bundle holders, medicine pipe holders, and others, all of whom have had sacred transfers, or Iipommowai, at one time or another.

Kiitomohpiipotokoi Role and responsibilities; 'what you have been put here with.'

Ksisskstakyomopisstaan (Ksisskstakyomopisstaanistsi) Beaver Bundle.

Ksisstsi'ko'm Thunder.

Mokaksin Knowledge; intelligence; wisdom; coming to know.

Mopisstaan Bundle (object).

Natosi 'Sacred power'; the sun.

Niinaimsskaan (Niinaimsskaiks) 'The Medicine Pipe holders'; the Thunder Pipe holders.

Niinaimsskahkoyinnimaan Thunder/Medicine Pipe; reference is to the ceremonial bundle of the Thunder Pipe, which would include the alliances of the pipe.

Niipaitapiiysin Way of life; constant motion of breath; together with *Ihtsipaitapiiyo'pa* identifies the meaning and purpose of life; to teach the way of life.

Niitsitapi Generic term for real people or all Indian, Aboriginal, or Indigenous peoples.

Omahkohkanakaaatsiisinni Big All Comrades Society; the ultimate sacred society, which has the central role in the annual Sundance ceremonies.

Pommaksinni (Pommaksiistsi) The practice of transferring; the method of teaching.

Siksikaitsitapi All Blackfoot-speaking tribes; 'Blackfoot-speaking real people'.

Tatsikiiyakokiiysinni The centre tepee.

Questions for Consideration

1. How do McPherson and Rabb define Indigeneity?
2. Based on the evidence that McPherson and Rabb present, do you agree with them that Indigeneity has survived the colonial experience? Why or why not?
3. What does Bastien say lies at the heart of the 'Eurocentred concept of culture'? How is that different from its *Siksikaitsitapi* counterpart?
4. In Bastien's understanding, how do the *Siksikaitsitapi* view and understand their natural environment? How might that understanding conflict with a Eurocentred conception of the environment?
5. Has a Eurocentric perspective led non-Indigenous Canadians to misunderstand Aboriginal world views? If so, how?

Further Resources

Books and Articles

Bastien, Betty. *Blackfoot Ways of Knowing*. Calgary: University of Calgary Press, 2004.

McClintock, Walter. *The Old North Trail: Life, Legend and Religion of the Blackfeet Indians*. Lincoln: University of Nebraska Press, [1910] 1992.

McPherson, Dennis H., and J. Douglas Rabb. *Indian from the Inside: A Study in Ethno-Metaphysics*. Thunder Bay: Lakehead University Centre for Northern Studies, 1993.

Weaver, Jace. *That the People Might Live: Native American Literature and Native Community*. New York: Oxford University Press, 1997.

Printed Documents and Reports

British Columbia Ministry of Advanced Education. *Native Literacy and Life Skills Curriculum Guidelines*. Victoria: Ministry of Advanced Education and Job Training and Ministry Responsible for Science and Technology, 1989.

Mealing, S.R., ed. *The Jesuit Relations and Allied Documents: A Selection*. Ottawa: Carleton University Press, 1990.

Morris, Alexander. *The Treaties of Canada with the Indians of Manitoba and the North-West Territories: Including the negotiations on which they were based, and other information relating thereto*. Toronto: Prospero Books, originally ublished in [1880] – 2000.

Films

First Nations: The Circle Unbroken. DVD. Directed by Geraldine Bob, Gary Marcuse, Deanna Nyce, and Lorna Williams. NFB, 1993.

The Medicine People: First Nations' Ceremonies. DVD. First Nations Films, 2000.

Totem: The Return of the G'psgolox Pole. DVD. Directed by Gil Cardinal. NFB, 2003.

Waban-aki: People from Where the Sun Rises. DVD. Directed by Alanis Obomsawin. NFB, 2006.

Websites

Canadian Museum of Civilization: Storytelling: The Art of Knowledge
www.civilization.ca/cmc/exhibitions/aborig/storytel/introeng.shtml

First Nations Pedagogy Online
http://firstnationspedagogy.ca/index.html

TWO

Perspectives on Contact

○○○○○○○ ○○○○○ ○○○○○○○○○○○○○○○○ ○○ ○○○○

Introduction

In mid-October 1492, Christopher Columbus and the Tainos people of the Caribbean first encountered each other in present-day Bahamas. Conventional histories of first contact have located this momentous meeting as the 'starting point' from which all other contacts flowed. However, this myopic view lacks complexity. Contact was not a singular moment but occurred for various groups at many different times over the last thousand years. In 1000 CE, Aboriginal people encountered the Vikings at present-day L'Anse aux Meadows, NL, more than 500 years before Jacques Cartier made landfall on the northeastern shores of North America. On the West Coast of present-day Canada, Aboriginal people first met the Spanish aboard their vessel, the *Santiago*, in 1774. This contact was soon followed by the penetration of fur traders into the interior of present-day British Columbia from the east.[1]

Aboriginal peoples who occupied the interior of North America and the far North also encountered Europeans at wildly different times and in incredibly varied ways. Given the extensive Aboriginal trading networks that penetrated the entire contin-ent, the acquisition of European goods and technology often took place long before Aboriginal people met Europeans face to face. Both Daniel K. Richter's and Dorothy Harley Eber's articles capture this point beautifully. Information about Europeans trickled through these networks and 'rumours and objects, not men and arms, were the means of discovery.' Imaginations must have run wild with the 'skimpy evidence that reached them'.[2]

The meanings and understandings that have been applied to contact have fascin-ated historians and have sparked what historian Bruce Trigger refers to as 'a large body of speculative literature'.[3] As both articles reveal, culture was a deciding force in the shaping of contact; the ways in which people understood themselves and their place in the world shaped the contours of these meetings. Until recently, most of this speculation has come from the European perspective. However, drawing on the stories and memories of Inuit Elders, as Eber does, offers extremely dif-ferent and interesting versions of and perspectives on contact. Aboriginal people saw Europeans through their own cultural lenses. Initially, many Aboriginal groups were willing to co-operate to some degree with Europeans. However, this readiness could and usually did change over time. For instance, while initially welcoming, the Stadaconans quickly tired of Jacques Cartier and his crew. Similarly, the arrival and departure of the *Fury* and the *Hecla* at Igloolik under William Edward Parry in 1822–3 was marked by conflict. According to Igloolik Elder Rosie Iqallijuq, the misbehaviour of Parry's men resulted in the prolonged isolation of the region until the curse laid by a local shaman was lifted. Most notably in these encounters, Aboriginal people did not perceive themselves as inferior to Europeans.[4] Indeed, from an Aboriginal rather than European perspective, some of the Europeans' behaviours and misadventures, such as the unpreparedness of Cartier and his followers for the North American winter of 1535–6 and the corporal punishment that Parry carried out over a minor theft, might very well have been taken as evidence of European inferiority, cruelty, and ignorance.

Chapter Objectives

At the end of this chapter, you should be able to

- identify some of the core myths and beliefs about Aboriginal people that resulted from the story of first contact;
- identify ways in which Aboriginal people first reacted to European travellers;
- understand better the different Aboriginal and European perceptions of contact; and
- query the chronology and geography of contact.

Secondary Source

1.   Imagining a Distant New World

Daniel K. Richter

'History', said Carl Becker, is 'an imaginative creation'.[5] Perhaps no historical subject requires more imagination than the effort to reconstruct the period when Indian country first became aware of a new world across the ocean. All we have to go on are oral traditions of Indians who lived generations after the events described, written accounts by European explorers who misunderstood much of what happened in brief face-to-face meetings with Native people, and mute archaeological artifacts that raise more questions than they answer. Yet this very lack of information places us in much the same situation as most eastern North American Indians during the era of discovery. They probably heard mangled tales of strange newcomers long before they ever laid eyes on one in the flesh, and, when rare and novel items reached their villages through long-standing channels of trade and communication, they discovered European *things* long before they confronted European *people*. Rumours and objects, not men and arms, were the means of discovery, and we can only imagine how Native imaginations made sense of the skimpy evidence that reached them.

On the coast of what will one day be called either Newfoundland or Labrador, Native hunters find that several of the traps they had set are missing, along with a needle they need to mend their fishing nets. In the place where these items had been is a smoothly polished upright timber crossed near the top by a second piece of wood, from which hangs the carved effigy of a bleeding man. Flanking this remarkable construction are two other poles from which pieces of some woven substance flap in the breeze: one is white with two strips of red, mimicking the shape of the crossed timbers; the other bears an image of a four-footed, two-winged beast holding something in its paw.

Somewhere near the mid-Atlantic coast, an old woman hides in the woods with her daughter and several grandchildren. Both women scream as some 20 pale, bearded men, sweating in heavy armour and helmets, stumble upon them. The Elder's suspicions abate a little when the men courteously offer her something to eat, but the younger disdainfully flings the food to the ground. As the women try to fathom the strange sounds issuing from what they consider to be incredibly ugly hairy faces, the men suddenly snatch one of the male children away from the grandmother and lunge for the young woman, who flees screaming into the forest, never to see her nephew again.

In an Indian dwelling, a woman tells her granddaughter about the first meeting between Native people and Europeans. One day, she says, a floating island appeared on the horizon. The beings who inhabited it offered the Indians blocks of wood to eat and cups of human blood to drink. The first gift the people found tasteless and useless; the second appallingly vile. Unable to figure out who the visitors were, the Native people called them *ouemichtigouchiou*, or woodworkers.

These three scenes are imagined, but they are rooted in verifiable historical events. The hunters' missing traps were purloined in 1497 by explorer John Cabot and his crew; the mid-Atlantic child was snatched from his kinswomen in 1524 by a detachment of Giovanni de Verrazano's mariners; and the tale of sailors who ate sea biscuits and drank wine was told to a French missionary in 1633 by a Montagnais who in turn had heard it from his grandmother years earlier.[6] This much we know from surviving documents, which also explain the nature of what the Europeans left behind and took with them. Cabot's crucifix and flags were sacred symbols that laid legal claim to the land for, respectively, his God (whose Son was portrayed dying on the wooden cross), his English sponsors (whose patron, Saint George, was evoked on the kingdom's white banner by a red cruciform), and his home republic of Venice (whose patron, Saint Mark, was represented on its flag by a winged lion bearing a book of the Gospel). To convince his sponsor, Henry VII of England, that a land in which 'he did not see any person' was indeed populated, Cabot collected 'certain snares which had been set to catch game', along with a large, red-painted wooden 'needle for making nets'.[7] Similarly, Verrazano justified taking 'a child from the old woman to bring into France' in terms of his need to bring his sponsor, Francis I, living proof of his exploits and a potential interpreter to aid future travellers.[8]

Documentary evidence illuminates the European cast of characters, yet only imagination can put Indians in the foreground of these scenes. [T]here is no record of

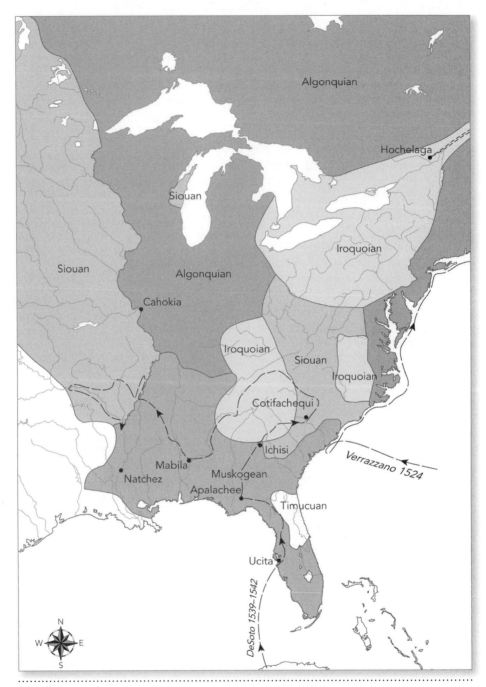

Map 2.1 Eastern North America and the sixteenth-century discovery of Europe: Approximate distribution of major Native American linguistic families and routes of principal European incursions. (Reprinted by permission of the publisher from FACING EAST FROM INDIAN COUNTRY: A NATIVE HISTORY OF EARLY AMERICA by Daniel K. Richter, pp. 16-17, Cambridge, Mass.: Harvard University Press, Copyright © 2001 by the President and Fellows of Harvard College.)

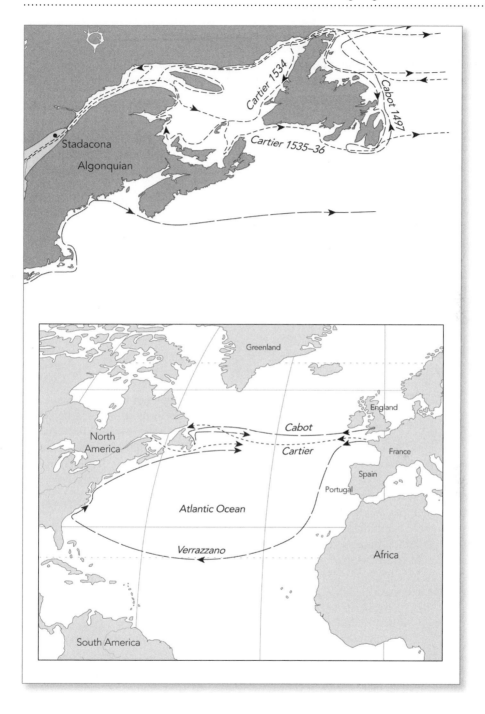

what happened to Cabot's crucifix and flags. Yet we know that if the Indians who owned the missing snares and needle had come upon them, they would not have found the idea of symbolic memorials to important events unfamiliar: northeastern Native people sketched elaborate pictographs in their houses or on the bark of living trees to record the success of war parties, hunting expeditions, and other exploits, and they carved images that they either raised on poles or affixed near the entrances to their houses.[9]

For eastern Indians, the world was a morally neutral universe of potentially hostile or potentially friendly spiritual forces—some human, most other-than-human—with whom one had to deal. All of these relationships depended on reciprocal exchanges of goods and obligations, material or ceremonial. Especially when dealing with beings whose power was greater than one's own, it was important to fulfill ceremonial obligations that demonstrated not only reciprocity but respect.[10]

In light of this emphasis the exchange of goods—gift giving—becomes a dominant motif in each of our three scenes. Yet the gifts are always unanticipated, if not disrespectful. To our conjectured hunters, the unseen Cabot apparently reciprocated for a red needle an incomprehensibly abstract red-and-white symbol, and for an animal trap an image of a strange beast. The crucifix he also left behind was carved with a degree of detail inconceivable to people unfamiliar with iron tools, but it clearly represented a man enduring torture. What kind of gift was this? And what kind of gift givers were Verrazano's men, whose unexpected behaviour lay not in the matter-of-fact arrogance with which they seized a child (Indian war parties routinely took captives of all ages), but in their offering of food, which deceived the grandmother into believing they were allies rather than enemies? And gifts of food also define the unanticipated in the story of the floating island: the wood was worthless, the blood inhumane.

The gifts defined the givers. Montagnais people, the grandmother said, called Europeans 'woodworkers'; elsewhere in eastern North America, Indians commonly described them as 'clothmakers', 'metalworkers', or 'axemakers'.[11] Whoever the bestowers of such things were, they seemed—initially at least—to come from a world quite unlike that in which ordinary human persons lived.

In the early decades of the sixteenth century, European ships regularly converged on the Atlantic coast. Sometimes they stopped to trade with the Natives; when Verrazano in 1524 reached the shore of what later would be known as New England, he found Indian people ready and waiting with the furs they already knew that the newcomers coveted.[12] At other times, particularly on the vast coastline of the territory the Spanish called *la Florida*, which stretched from the peninsula north-ward to Chesapeake Bay, raiders such as Ponce de Leon in 1521, Lucas Vázquez de Ayllón in 1526, and Pánfilo de Narvàez in 1528 came ashore to seek gold or slaves to work in the mines of Cuba and elsewhere. An occasional castaway or newcomer taken in battle learned a Native language and provided the first firm clues about the customs and intentions of the invaders. Welcome or unwelcome, the travellers left behind weapons, tools, jewellry, and clothing that fell into the hands of Indian people.

On two extended occasions during the 1530s, flesh and blood replaced rumours and things in the North American discovery of a new European world. Because the Europeans involved in these contacts wrote about their experiences, we have slender platforms from which to observe the events and—reading against the authors' grain—to imagine how the arrival of Europeans might have looked from a perspective in Indian country.[13] Transporting ourselves to the shores of Tampa Bay on the Gulf coast of Florida on Sunday, 25 May 1539, we barely see the sails of nine Spanish ships anchored three miles or so off the coast to avoid the treacherous shoals closer in. A party of 10 Timucuan-speaking Natives watching with us are familiar enough with Spanish sails to know that these are no floating islands and that although their inhabitants may wield considerable spiritual power, their disembarkation is unlikely to be beneficial. As the first small boats set out for shore, they send word for those women and children not already dispersed to spring fishing or hunting camps to abandon their villages, and they set signal fires to warn others at a greater distance. The wisdom of those preparations becomes clear when the scouts encounter a Spanish advance party and find themselves in a skirmish. The Timucuas kill a pair of Spanish horses before being forced to retreat, but they leave two of their own people dying on the ground.

We are not sure if this is the first time these particular Florida Natives have encountered horses, but we are certain they have never seen so many of the great beasts: more than 200 land in the first boats. During the next week some 600 men follow with a contingent of dogs trained for war and with at least 13 pregnant sows. In command of this assemblage—which far outnumbers the force any village in the area can mount—is Hernando de Soto, the recently appointed governor of Cuba and *adelantado* of *la Florida* [who] bears royal authority to invest his considerable personal fortune in an effort to conquer the people and presumed riches of southeastern North America. Within a week his army takes over an abandoned village named Ucita or Ozita and rechristens it *Spiritu Sancto*, 'Holy Spirit'. As the *adelantado* ensconces himself in the chief's residence, his men dismantle the remaining houses and destroy a temple topped by a carved wooden bird, salvaging the materials to build barracks for themselves. Meantime they brutally seize replacements for four previously captured Timucuan men brought with them to serve as interpreters and guides. When three of these in turn escape, a Native woman who supposedly helped them is thrown to the dogs. The same fate meets the remaining interpreter when he proves a less than cooperative guide.[14]

In a village a couple of days' journey inland are two people who regard the Spaniards' arrival more positively than do the kin of the Ucita victims. One used to call himself Juan Ortiz, although now he uses a Timucuan name and has nearly forgotten the language of his native Seville. A dozen years earlier he was captured on the coast by the people of Ucita. Subsequently he escaped to the rival town of a headman named Mocoço. There he abandoned any real hope of seeing Spaniards again, despite his host's repeated assurances 'that, if at any time, Christians should come to that land, he would release him freely and give him permission to go to them'.[15] The promises were neither empty nor disinterested. Mocoço apparently hopes his guest will broker an alliance with the Spanish that will help him defeat his coastal enemies of Ucita and three other towns and, presumably, open a channel of trade with the newcomers previously blocked by his inland location.

When word of de Soto's landing reaches Mocoço, therefore, he sends Ortiz along with a reception committee that, taking no chances in enemy territory, travels well armed. The Timucuans show themselves to the mounted Spanish, but before any pleasantries can be exchanged, the invaders' horses charge and send the Native people fleeing into the woods. Ortiz barely escapes death by making the sign of the cross and shouting the name of the Virgin and a few other remembered Castilian words.

To the *adelantado*, Ortiz, with his mastery of two Timucuan dialects and his knowledge of Indian culture and diplomacy, is a welcome discovery, yet little else seems promising. The small coastal villages of Tampa Bay hoard no gold or silver and, particularly in the spring well before harvest time, do not even contain enough stored maize to feed his troops. In what seems like a deliberate attempt to protect their immediate neighbourhood, both Ortiz and Mococo deny any knowledge of the wealth the Spanish desire, but they speak vaguely of a much larger town a hundred miles or so to the north, where a chief extracts tribute from all the villages in the region and where the land is 'more fertile and abounding in maize'.[16] So, taking Ortiz along as interpreter, the army vacates Tampa Bay, and a pattern is established: No, one set of Native leaders after another tells the invaders, there is no gold and little food here, but if you travel farther (into what just happens to be the country of my enemies), you might find what you seek. Thus, when de Soto is disappointed at the town of the Paracoxi, his destination becomes Anhaica Apalachee (modern-day Tallahassee). To that southernmost of the surviving Mississippian cities, his army fights its way by late October. There de Soto finds sufficient food to support his men and settles in for the winter, apparently only slightly inconvenienced by Native raiding parties that attack work details or set fires in the town.

By March de Soto is ready to resume his quest. His entourage plods northeastward through present-day Georgia, perfecting tactics first used in the previous year's march through the Florida peninsula. Occasionally the Spaniards capture a hunting party and, if the Indians fail to provide satisfactory information on what lies ahead in words Juan Ortiz can fathom, throw a victim to the dogs or burn him alive to encourage others to talk. More often, de Soto goes through the motions of Mississippian diplomatic ritual; the *adelantado* even carries a chair in which to seat himself during ceremonies with chiefs carried on their retainers' shoulders. Invariably the formalities end when leaders agree to provide several hundred men, who are shackled together to haul the army's equipment. Also likely to be requisitioned are several dozen women, who, after a hasty baptism by one of de Soto's four priests, will satisfy what one Spaniard describes as the soldiers' 'lewdness and lust'.[17] To preclude trouble, the chief and his retinue are held hostage until the army—pillaging corn supplies, burning the occasional refractory village, and planting crosses on temple mounds—reaches the territory of the next chiefdom, when the cycle begins again.

Native leaders repeatedly claim that the riches the Spanish seek lie farther on, in the chiefdom of Cofitachequi. In May 1540, near present-day Camden, SC, de Soto's army finally reaches a spot directly across the Wateree River from its capital. The town's inhabitants are already familiar with Spanish goods, if not with Spanish people; they not only have carefully preserved glass beads and metal items but have also fashioned leather helmets, armour, and footwear in styles that seem strikingly familiar to the Castilians. We watch as a young female leader—the Spanish call her 'The Lady of Cofitachequi'—is carried to the riverbank in a white-cloth-draped litter, from which she enters a canoe graced by a canopy of a similar material. When she reaches de Soto's side of the stream, she removes a string of freshwater pearls from her neck and places it over the *adelantado*'s head. Gifts of blankets and skins, turkeys and other foods, follow.

De Soto rends the ceremonial drama with a blunt inquiry about where more of the pearls might be found. The Lady directs him to one of several nearby towns abandoned two years earlier when 'a plague in that land' forced the inhabitants to seek new homes.[18] There, he and his officers loot a mortuary temple of more than 200 pounds of pearls preserved in the body cavities of the deceased.[19] The corpses also yield European glass beads, rosaries and crucifixes, and 'Biscayan axes of iron'.[20] The pearls are loaded with other booty on the backs of the inevitable requisition of Cofitachequi porters, and the army sets off again holding the Lady hostage.

And so we follow de Soto's trek: across the Appalachian Mountains into the modern states of North Carolina, Tennessee, Georgia again, and Alabama, always chasing reports of wealth in the town over the next hill or down the next river. Armed resistance builds steadily until, in October, the Spaniards' luck runs out in the Tascaloosa city of Mabila, in what will later be called western Alabama. Several thousand warriors hide inside Mabila's houses as a ceremonial welcome for de Soto and his advance party provides cover for Indians waiting in ambush. When the attack comes, several Spaniards die before the remainder flee the town and regroup for a daylong battle that culminates in ruthless slaughter. When it is over, Mabila lies in smoking ruins. Inside are the bodies of perhaps 2,000 Tascaloosas, along with the ruins of all the pearls and other treasure de Soto has collected. Twenty or so Spaniards, including de Soto's nephew, are dead. The wounds of some of the nearly 200 invaders who are seriously injured are treated with the fat of their slaughtered enemies.

For nearly a month de Soto's now ragged army, reduced by cumulative losses to closer to 400 than 600 men, tries to recover strength. It sets off again and huddles for a brutally cold winter in a small abandoned village in what will be known as northeastern Mississippi. In March 1541 the town's former inhabitants burn the Spanish camp, and with it most of the invaders' remaining saddles and padded armour. Still the Spanish plod on, in a journey as increasingly nightmarish for them as for the Indians whose countries they continue to pillage and whose people they continue to enslave when they can. They move across the Mississippi River and into the country of the Caddos in modern-day Arkansas, another winter comes and goes, and in March 1542 Juan Ortiz dies after a brief illness. In May, in the Natchez country, when disease also claims the *adelantado*, his men sink the corpse in the Mississippi River to protect it from the indignities they are sure Indians will perpetrate on it. At last, after the survivors wander through much of what will later be Arkansas and east Texas, they improvise a forge on the banks of the Mississippi and pound the chains of their slaves into nails and hardware for boats. In June 1542 they board the seven vessels they have been building and float out of sight, down the river to the Gulf and the Spanish settlements on the Mexican coast. As they fade from view, a few of the pigs they leave behind—later residents of the area will call their descendants 'razorbacks'—remain with us on the shore, but surviving documents reveal nothing about how, if at all, Native people recovered from the devastation the conquistadores left behind or what stories they told themselves to make sense of invaders from another world.

As de Soto lay dying in the spring of 1542, far to the north, in what is now called St John's Harbor, NL, Frenchman Jacques Cartier prepared to head home, convinced that he had found not only the gold the *adelantado* had been looking for, but diamonds too. This was Cartier's third voyage to a country he called Canada. [W]hen Cartier returned to France, experts confirmed that his ship contained nothing but iron pyrite ('fool's gold') and commonplace quartz crystals.[21]

In search of how Cartier and his entourage may have looked to the people of Canada, we might travel backward in time to July 1534, when the Frenchman arrived on the first of his three voyages.[22] Standing on the southern coast of what is now called the Gaspé Peninsula, we see 40 to 50 canoes full of Micmacs abandoning their fishing as two ships come into view. Hoisting the skins of fur-bearing animals aloft on pieces of wood, they try to lure the newcomers ashore to trade. Inexplicably to the Indians, Cartier's ships turn about and sail for the opposite shore. Micmac canoeists give chase and surround the ships, waving and shouting 'We wish to have your friendship!'[23] but two panicky musket shots drive them off. Shortly, however, they return and get close enough to be struck by a pair of lances wielded from the decks before they have to retreat again. The next day, when the Europeans' nerves have calmed and they have found safe anchor for their ships, they send two men ashore with a load of knives, hatchets, and beads. Soon some 300 Micmac men and women are wading through the shallows dancing and singing and rubbing the arms of Cartier's crew as a sign of welcome. Trading proceeds until the Indians have 'nothing but their naked bodies' left to exchange!ary[24]

That the Natives have clearly come to trade demonstrates that European ships are already familiar sights to the Micmacs. Fifty miles or so to the northeast, on the Bay of Gaspé, however, a group of **St Lawrence Iroquoians** from the interior is far less acquainted with floating islands, although they almost certainly have heard of their existence. Later in the month, as the Iroquoians, fishing for mackerel, look up to see Cartier's vessels approach, they therefore hesitate before surrounding the ships with their canoes. The now more experienced Europeans almost immediately toss them iron knives, glass beads, and other small items, but the Iroquoians are prepared with nothing to exchange for these gifts.

As the French get ready to sail on, they erect a 30-foot wooden cross, in the centre of which they place a shield decorated with fleur-de-lis and letters spelling out *Vive le roi de France*. The Iroquoians' leader boards a canoe with his brother and three sons and follows the Europeans to their ships.[25] Luring the canoe closer with a gesture that promises an iron axe in exchange for the bearskin the headman wears, the Europeans drag the whole party on board. By gestures, Cartier assures the Indians that he means them no harm and offers them food and drink. The cross, he dissimulatingly explains, stakes no claim to their territory; it is merely a marker to allow the French to find the spot again when they return along with two of the headman's sons, who will be taken home to be trained as interpreters.[26] How much of the message gets through clearly is uncertain, but, after an additional bestowal of iron gifts and brass necklaces, the headman, his brother, and one of the young men return to shore reasonably amicably. The others, named Taignoagny and Domagaia, remain on deck wearing ill-fitting French shirts, coats, and caps.

Cartier and—perhaps more astonishingly to their kin—Taignoagny and Domagaia return to Canada within the year, this time with three ships and plans to stay the winter.

We know almost nothing about the intervening experiences of the two Iroquoians in [Europe]. During those months, however, they apparently learned enough French, and their hosts enough St Lawrence Iroquoian, to communicate some important pieces of information about their native land. Their home village (or at least the principal of the five communities that spoke their language) lies far inland along a broad river (the St Lawrence), whose entrance Cartier had missed in his survey of the gulf. From that village of **Stadacona** (the word means 'here is our big village'), on the site of present-day Quebec City, the river continues much farther to a large town called **Hochelaga** ('place at the mountain') at modern Montreal, and thence far onward, perhaps toward a passage to Asia.[27] Taignoagny and Domagaia also speak vaguely about what the French understood to be a fabulously wealthy 'Kingdom of Saguenay', located far to the north and west along a river flowing into the St Lawrence. In part, the tale includes wishful thinking on the part of Cartier, a desire to please (or dupe) their hosts on the parts of Taignoagny and Domagaia, and the same kind of rumour of riches over the next hill that de Soto chased through the southeast.

As the fleet casts anchor near what the French would christen the Île d'Orléans, a few miles down the St Lawrence from Stadacona, Taignoagny and Domagaia struggle to make themselves recognized in their strange clothing and the long hair that has replaced the partially shaved heads with which they left home. When the confusion is cleared up, a group of women dances, sings, and brings all the visitors fish, maize, and melons. The next day Donnaconna, the principal headman of Stadacona, leads a fleet of canoes to conduct a welcoming oration; Cartier reciprocates with the ubiquitous sea biscuits and wine, carried to Donnaconna's canoe. According to the region's diplomatic customs, the visitors should debark from their vessels for additional ceremonies outside the village gates and then enter the town to take up lodging in the houses of its leaders. Days of feasting, speeches in council, and exchanges of gifts should follow to seal the alliance.

None of this happens. Instead, Cartier finds a harbour for his two larger ships at the Île d'Orléans, and, before even visiting the village itself or distributing more than a few token metal items, he demands that Taignoagny and Domagaia guide his third craft on to Hochelaga. Not surprisingly, after an evening of consultations with Donnaconna and other village leaders, the two weary Native travellers lose their enthusiasm for the voyage and offer excuses, warnings, and ruses designed to prevent the French and their precious cargo from going to a rival town. Donnaconna ceremoniously gives three children to the French for adoption; one is his own niece, another Taignoagny's brother. Cartier reciprocates with a gift of swords and brass bowls, but, despite a visit the next day from three shamans bringing warnings from the spirit world of dangers upriver (and a similar call from Taignoagny and Domagaia, who deliver messages allegedly from Jesus and Mary), he persists in his design. Without Native guides, Cartier and some of his men set off for a visit to Hochelaga and several villages and fishing camps along the way.

Donnaconna is less than enthusiastic in welcoming Cartier back [in mid-October]. While their leader was gone, the French had constructed a trench, palisade, and artillery emplacements to protect the ships on which they continued to sleep and eat. Spurning their hosts' hospitality, the Europeans settle in for the winter behind their trench and palisade on the Île d'Orléans. While to all appearances most of the Stadaconans nonetheless interact with the French 'with great familiarity and love', a minority, led by Taignoagny, expresses considerably less pleasure with their ill-mannered guests.[28]

In December Cartier forbids all contact with Stadaconans of both factions, when he learns that disease has killed some 50 villagers. Despite the precautionary quarantine, the French are soon falling desperately ill as well. By March 1536, 25 of the 110-member crew have died, and only a handful can walk. We do not know what is killing the Stadaconans, but the French ailment is an uncontagious nutritional disorder, **scurvy**. Were Cartier not so intent on concealing from his Native hosts the extent of his men's weakness (on one occasion he has them throw stones at Stadaconans who get too near, and on another he orders the few who are able to lift tools to make a furious racket to suggest that the entire crew is busily preparing the ships for departure), he might learn far sooner from Domagaia that a concoction brewed from the vitamin C-rich bark and leaves of the white cedar would restore his men to health.[29]

During the winter the French, shivering in their sickbeds, remain incommunicado for weeks on end, encouraging their hosts to suspect the worst of them. In April Donnacona and Taignoagny bring several hundred newcomers to Stadacona. Perhaps this is a normal seasonal migration of the sort typical among many of the Iroquoians' Algonquian-speaking neighbours, whose small winter communities commonly join much larger agglomerations for the spring and summer. Or the newcomers may be allies whom Taignoagny has convinced Donnacona to recruit for an assault on guests who have long overstayed their welcome. We will never be sure, because, under cover of a friendly council, Cartier takes Donnacona, Taignoagny, Domagaia, and two other leaders prisoner. In a replay of events in 1534, Cartier then assures his prisoners, and the women who bring strings of shell beads to redeem them, that he will restore them safely the next year. Donnacona publicly pledges to return in a few months, and the ships set off downriver.

Five years pass before we see Cartier's ships at Stadacona again. With him in 1541 are several hundred prospective French colonists but none of the Iroquoians who left Canada in 1536. When Donnaconna's successor inquires after their fate, Cartier admits that the chief has long since died in France, but then claims that the others 'stayed there as great lords, and were married, and would not return back into their country'.[30] In fact all but Donnaconna's niece have perished, and she has been prevented from returning to keep the distressing news secret. The Stadaconans, who remember Taignoagny's less-than-enthusiastic tales of Brittany, no doubt suspect as much, but their new headman welcomes Cartier nonetheless, by placing his headdress on the Frenchman's brow and wrapping shell beads around his arms. Cartier reciprocates with 'certain small presents', promises more to come, and partakes of a feast![31] At a place he calls Charlesbourg-Royal, some nine miles above Stadacona, at the mouth of the Cap Rouge River, the French build a fort, plant a crop of turnips, and find their worthless fool's gold and quartz crystals. As the colonists settle into Charlesbourg-Royal for the winter, our ability to imagine the scene suddenly ends. The published narrative left by a participant ends abruptly with the words 'The rest is wanting.'[32]

Yet other sources reveal that Cartier's people—or most of them—survived until spring, as increasingly unwelcome guests. Not only had they settled in the Stadaconans' territory without permission, but they had also done so at an upstream location likely to cut the town off from any trade benefits the Hochelagans and other inland peoples might enjoy. Come spring, Cartier, having lost perhaps 35 men in skirmishes with his hosts, packed up his colonists and sailed for home. In the Newfoundland waters where we first imagined meeting him, he encountered a fleet bearing more colonists under the command of Jean François de la Roque, seigneur de Roberval, who replaced Cartier at Cap Rouge. We know few details of the reception this party encountered except that, after a punishing winter during which untreated scurvy killed at least 50 of their number, in 1543 they too abandoned Canada. As far as we know, no Europeans travelled up the St Lawrence River for another 40 years.[33]

If anything emerges from the shadows of the sixteenth-century Indian discoveries of Europe, it is a persistent theme of conflict and distrust. But the nature of that conflict bears close attention, for its most remarkable aspect is not the violence that erupted between Natives and newcomers. Cartier clearly wore out his welcome, and nothing can be said in defence of the vicious de Soto. Nonetheless, almost everywhere they went, these Europeans found people trying to make some kind of alliance with them, trying to gain access to the goods and power they might possess, trying to make sense of their flags, their crucifixes, and their sea biscuits. These efforts to reach out to people of alien and dangerous ways are more striking than the fact that, in the end, enmity won out over friendship. But most striking of all is the way in which the arrival of the newcomers exacerbated conflicts of one Native group with another: Mococo versus Ucita, Micmacs versus Stadaconans, Stadaconans versus Hochelagans; everyone discouraging advantageous Europeans from travelling to the next town, but encouraging dangerous ones to pay their neighbours a visit. Both within and among Native communities, contact with the new world across the seas inspired bitter conflicts over access to what the aliens had to offer—conflicts that would spiral to unimaginably deadly levels in the decades ahead.

Primary Document

2.

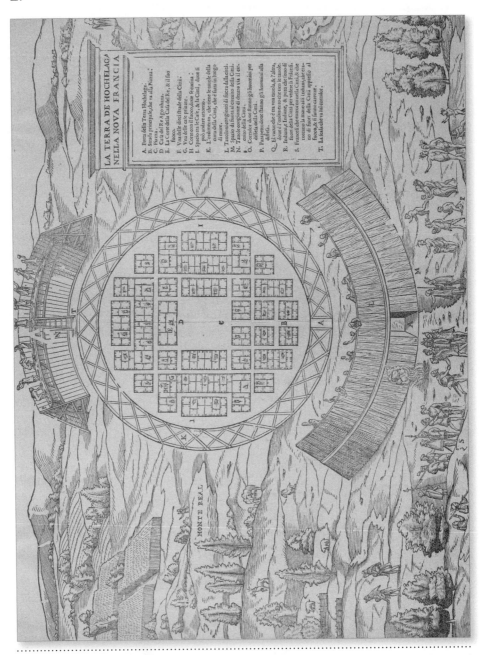

Plan of Hochelaga picturing contact, Cartier, 1556, by Ramusio (Italian chronicler of voyages). (Library and Archives Canada, R9266-3416.)

Primary Document

3.

Jacques Cartier and his first interview with Indians at Hochelaga, 1850, by Andrew Morris. (Library and Archives Canada, R9266-3339.)

Secondary Source

4. Into the Arctic Archipelago: Edward Parry in Igloolik and the Shaman's Curse[34]

Dorothy Harley Eber

The colours of the Arctic today are blue and dove grey, like a Toni Onley watercolour, and on this brilliant clean morning John MacDonald, director of the Igloolik Research Centre, is driving us over the road that leads to the point off which William Edward Parry of the Royal Navy—whom **Inuit** call Paarii—anchored his expedition in the winter of 1822–3.

Vehicles pass us on their way to a summer tent colony at Igloolik Point, where hunters and their families are camped for the walrus hunting, a resource as sustaining today as it was during Parry's visit. Large herds, he wrote on the day he drew within sight of Igloolik, 'were lying with their young on almost every loose piece of ice we saw'.[35] 'We're going to visit Mr Elder,' says MacDonald. In fact, five of us are going to picnic at Mr Elder's grave.

After a while, we stop at a circle of tumbled stones just off the road. They and a tombstone, which juts out of the centre, are encrusted with golden and crimson lichen. The words on the tombstone read:

Mr. Alexander Elder
Greenland Mate
HBM
Ship Hecla
Obit April 15, 1823
Aged 36 years

[Elder] was buried here, near where Parry's observatory stood, having died, wrote Parry, from 'confirmed dropsy which having attacked the region of the heart, rapidly terminated his existence'.[36] But the late Igloolik Elder Mark Ijjangiaq left another version of his end:

That man's death was caused by a **shaman**. It had something to do with a thing that someone wanted from him. One of the higher officials refused the request.

Parry's Farthest, attained on his first voyage into the Arctic archipelago during 1819–20. The sketch shows HMS *Griper* off the west end of Melville Island. (HMS *Hecla* is round the point, a few miles to the west). Watercolour over pencil on wove paper. By Midshipman Andrew Motz Skene (1796-1849), 1820. (Library and Archives Canada, C-132217.)

Of course, they were low on their supplies and had to turn the request down. But that man wanted the thing so badly that with the help of his shaman's powers he killed that white man. That is what I have heard.[37]

The *Fury* and the *Hecla* were the first ships ever to reach Igloolik. No more would come for a hundred years, and this isolation too was the shaman's revenge. I learn the reason why from Rosie Iqallijuq, Igloolik's most senior citizen:

When the two ships were leaving, they were cursed by a shaman never to return. Naturally the crew of the ships had been getting girlfriends—no wonder, they were men! Perhaps the Inuit men were jealous types. One of the wives who got involved with a crew member was the wife of the shaman Qimmungat and he—the shaman—*suvijavininga*—he blew the ship away! From that day on, no ship arrived. The curse of the shaman persisted for a long long time and so no ships were able to make it to this area.[38]

The Start of Nineteenth-Century Arctic Exploration

When Parry anchored off Igloolik, he was 32 and already well on the way to his position as Britain's towering figure in nineteenth-century Arctic exploration. Deeply religious, diligent but daring, his rapid rise to prominence began after he captained the *Alexander* on the British Navy's first attempt to reach the Pacific from the Atlantic via a Northwest Passage.

The British Admiralty had decided to energetically pursue a program of Arctic exploration. In the aftermath of the Napoleonic wars, a window of opportunity had opened up: vessels and men were freed up with the peace and needed employment, and climate conditions were propitious. Whalers reported open water in high latitudes and a remarkable melting of icefields.

It was known that above continental North America a polar sea existed. But the geography of the Arctic Sea and its fractured land masses was unknown. The Northwest Passage was still to be discovered.

Parry's Farthest

[The task to discover the passage went first to John Ross, but] after [his] failure to discover that Lancaster Sound was a Strait, the Admiralty readied a new expedition. They gave the command to William Edward Parry, and, still a lieutenant but in command of his own expedition, Parry made his most revolutionary voyage: he sailed through Lancaster Strait, across the Arctic archipelago, and wintered triumphantly with the *Hecla* and the *Griper* far to the west in Winter Harbour at Melville Island. Ice blocked his further progress—no one would sail further west for 30 years—but Parry knew he had discovered that a sea route existed from Baffin Bay to the Pacific.[39]

He had, in fact, explored one of the several routes by which a Northwest Passage can be accomplished. But the heavy pack ice he encountered had made him believe there was likely to be a more southerly, superior passage.

Portrait of Edward Parry, drawn during Parry's 1821–3 expedition. The word *Captain* at the left was added by the collector George F. Lyon, who brought the drawing back to England. (Scott Polar Institute.)

It was the search for this passage, which he rightly thought would lie close to the coast of continental America, that brought Parry in the years 1821–3 through Hudson Strait and the Bay on a voyage during which he would winter twice in the ice, the second time off Igloolik Island. Igloolik lies at the eastern end of what is now the Fury and Hecla Strait. This ice-choked strait separates the north shore of Melville Peninsula from Baffin Island. It would not provide the route he sought. In fact, the records he and second-in-command, 25-year-old George F. Lyon, kept and published of their close contact with Native people would supply for many years to come the best accounts of Inuit life. These accounts, with their geographic and ethnographic data, endure as classic texts of exploration.

But Igloolik Inuit now have their own well-filed, well-shelved historical record. Since 1986, when the first interviews were recorded, many of the contributors have died, but their stories are alive and readily accessible through the archives of the Inullariit Elders' Society in the Igloolik Research Centre. They grow more valuable year by year.

Paarii in Igloolik, as Inuit Tell It

As soon as possible after I arrive in Igloolik, I go with interpreter Leah Otak to visit Rosie Iqallijuq, the community's foremost authority on Paarii and his times (sadly, Rosie died in 2000). We find her sitting on her bed. 'I know of explorers from what I have heard,' she says. 'It is a long time ago that Igloolik first saw a ship.'

I am anxious to pursue the story of the shaman's curse, its origins and outcome—but, to begin with, from the Inuit point of view, why did Parry come to Igloolik in the first place? From her own Elders, the famous Ataguttaaluk and her husband, Ituksarjuat, whom southerners called the King and Queen of Igloolik, Rosie learned a version of the ancient Inuit creation myth that links Parry's arrival with the coming into existence of the Inuit, white people, and Indians (who traditionally were enemies):

There once was a girl called Uinigumasuittuq who was married to her dog. Because she was married to her dog, her father got bothered in his sleep. So he took his daughter to the island of Qikiqtaarjuk, so she could have her husband with her there. She gave birth to six babies—two were Inuit, two were intimidating half-Indian half-dogs, and two were half-white half-dogs. The father brought the half-Indian half-dogs over to the mainland, and it is said that is why there are unapproachable people there—because of the dogs the father took to the mainland.

The two half-white half-dog babies were put into the sole of a *kamik* [a boot made of caribou hide or sealskin] with two stems of grass and let go into the ocean. Then all of a sudden there was fog; there were bells ringing in the air, and the father could see a mast from the grasses, and sails of a boat like the sails of the boat in which Paarii came. You could see this boot sole, with the two babies in it, leaving the shore. There were only the two babies in the boot sole—a girl and a boy—but that's how the white people multiplied; they had children from one another. Uinigumasuittuq created the white people—these two children who had so many babies. Paarii and his people came around here for the skull of their mother and took it from Qikiqtaarjuk—but we didn't see that![40]

John MacDonald makes the case that to the Inuit of Parry's day this creation story made good sense. 'White men had never appeared around Igloolik before. People must have wondered why they were there; the nature of their mission was difficult to comprehend. Given Parry's interest in the island and obsession with the bones he found lying around, what better interpretation could there be?' For Parry and his crews did take away skulls.

We learn about this in Parry's journal entry for 23 July, when shortly after his arrival in Igloolik he goes to visit an abandoned Inuit winter camp:

In every direction around the huts were lying innumerable bones of walruses and seals, together with the skulls of dogs, bears, and foxes . . . We were not a little surprised to find also a number of human skulls lying about among the rest, within a few yards of the huts; and were somewhat inclined to be out of humour on this account with our new friends, who not only treated the matter with the utmost indifference, but on observing that we were inclined to add some of them to our collections, went eagerly about to look for them, and tumbled, perhaps, the craniums of some of their own relations, into our bag . . . [41]

Inuit today will tell you that before the missionaries came they did not put their dead in boxes—indeed, they had no wood. 'We put rocks around the body and eventually the animals scattered the bones.' And for a long time there were Elders who asked to be buried in the old Inuit way. 'Some people feared the priests' burial—they feared their spirits would be caught by the weight of the rocks on top of them.'[42]

Rosie heard many of her stories from Ulluriaq, a potent personality of the past with whom she once shared the igloo. Ulluriaq lived to a great age and, according to local tradition, was a child herself when Paarii came to Igloolik. Rosie met Ulluriaq when she was about 13, after she had travelled by dog team from Chesterfield Inlet to begin her arranged marriage to an older man:

I first saw Ulluriaq when I got to this area. She was already very old—handicapped by old age—and was sharing the abode with us. I was married to Amaroalik, an old man, very much older than me. Ulluriaq used to tell me stories of the shamans, stories of the explorers. It was basically to put a smile on your face . . .

Ulluriaq told of the time when the ship first arrived—Paarii and his group. Ulluriaq's family were living in Pinngiqalik—Pinger Point—and the ship was travelling towards Igloolik. The hunters got on their kayaks, taking some women with them, and followed the ship, and when it anchored the kayaks went down to the anchored ship.

Describing this same event, on 16 July 1822, Parry wrote:

> At thirty minutes past nine A.M. we observed several tents on the low shore immediately abreast of us, and presently afterwards five canoes made their appearance at the edge of the land-ice intervening between us and the beach. As soon therefore as we had satisfactorily made out the position and state of the ice, I left the *Fury* in a boat, accompanied by some of the officers, and being joined by Captain Lyon went to meet the Esquimaux.[43]

Says Rosie, 'It was then that the community of Igloolik was first established. They wintered at Ungaluujat, past Igloolik Point. You can see the camp grounds today, and you can see that it was a very well established camp.'

There were always Inuit camps—and there still are seasonal Inuit camps—at Igloolik Point, but Parry anchored five miles away in what he called Turton Bay (Inuit call the bay Ikpiarjuq— 'raised beaches') off Ungaluujat. On this point near Parry's anchorage, the expedition set up tents. Quite soon Inuit began to visit and camp out, building their own sod houses, and sometimes using old Thule houses.

Qallunaat [people who are not Inuit] Gifts

When the Inuit first met the white men, Rosie says, their goods initially seemed useless:

> Apparently Inuit received some tobacco from the ship and at that time the tobacco came in the form of squares which had to be cut into small pieces—and apparently Ulluriaq started using these tobaccos as her toys—they were perfectly square. In those days, they were still living in sealskin tents, and one day it started to rain. As a result, the square chunks of tobacco got wet, and when her parents . . . came into the tent, they started to smell something foul. They wondered what it was. So they went over to where Ulluriaq kept her toys and realized it was those square things. The tobacco had gotten wet and was stinking up the tent. Ulluriaq told her parents, 'The smell is coming from my pretend blocks.' Her father collected all the square tobaccos and threw them away. . . .

Foodstuffs were similar puzzles:

> When the ice broke up and the ships were leaving, Ulluriaq's parents received sacks of flour, and at that time flour came in large bags. They also received tea, sugar, and biscuits from the ship. . . . And not realizing that biscuits were made for eating, Ulluriaq and other children started tossing them back and forth. And the sacks of flour were also discarded. When the children realized when you hit the sack it would appear to smoke, they had themselves a time hitting the flour sacks. They hadn't a clue about flour or biscuits—they dare not cook them or eat them, because they didn't know they were food in the first place.

In Parry's account, flour was carried in barrels; but was flour perhaps sometimes distributed in bags? Or is this an instance of blended oral history, a later story now contributing to Rosie's account of Parry's largesse, but which perhaps originally related to supplies received from other sources, possibly the whalers, and heard by Rosie during her childhood?

Certain things were rapidly integrated into the culture. 'At that time,' says Rosie, 'they started drinking tea and using sugar.' And suddenly all the women were resplendent with beads. 'They liked the beads so much they started beading and used them for bracelets. . . . I've heard that those who received beads for the first time—when the first white man wintered here—made bracelets from the beads.'

In fact, at the time of Parry's visit, beads were not unknown. Parry wrote that he found beads already in use among Igloolik women. Like other goods, beads spread through inter-Inuit trade. Trade beads came to Canada with the first explorers. Merchants and explorers took beads with them as objects of trade, and when the first Europeans entered the Gulf of St Lawrence, Venetian beads arrived in their vessels. The **Hudson's Bay Company (HBC)** established its first

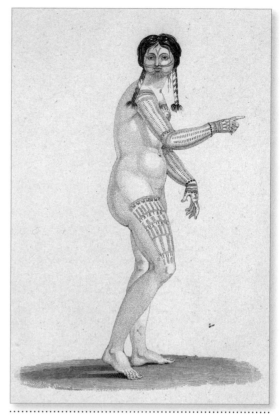

The Manner in Which the Esquimaux Women Are Tattooed. Drawn by George Lyon, 1822-3. (Library and Archives Canada, C-099264.)

post at Churchill on the west coast of the Bay in 1685 and intermittently sent sloops up the coast to trade for oil, whalebone, and ivory. In all probability, on board were glass seed trade beads. Igloolik Inuit may also have begun to receive beads from the whalers, who in 1817 had begun operating high off the east Baffin coast. But the expedition's presence made beads abundant. 'Many of the [women], in the course of the second winter, covered the whole front of their jackets with the beads they received from us.'[44]

The Inuit women also made themselves beautiful with tattoos. [Lyon] had himself tattooed:

She took a piece of caribou sinew, which she blackened with soot. She began the work by sewing a rather deep but short stitch in my skin. When the thread was drawn beneath the skin, she pressed her thumb on the spot so as to press in the pigment . . . The work went slowly . . . When she had sewed forty stitches and the strip was about two inches long, I felt it was enough.[45]

Lyon's skin was then rubbed with whale oil.

Beaded Amautik. The artist, Germaine Arnaktauyok, is the niece of Igloolik storyteller Rosie Iqallijuq. Private collection of the artist. (Arnaktauyok, 2005.)

Why the Curse Was Laid

Despite some squeamishness about Inuit burial practices, relations between the visitors and the Inuit during their winter of residence were harmonious. By the time the expedition left, it had altered the Inuit material culture. The expedition had been peacefully received—its presence useful to the Inuit, and the Inuit helpful to the expedition. The Inuit wanted to trade and were eager to barter, though the white men often gave freely without expecting return. The Inuit had drawn maps, repaired and sewn clothes, and on occasion hospitably hosted officers and crews in their sod houses and tents. Parry had tended the Inuit sick, had set up a makeshift hospital, and shortly before the *Fury* and the *Hecla* began their journey home, he left sledges, wood for bows and arrows, and many useful items for Inuit use, spreading them out around Igloolik so that as many as possible would benefit. Before departure, as per Admiralty instructions, he set up a flag-staff at a site on the Melville Peninsula, which almost certainly did not stand long. 'The wealth of materials invested in the site—wood, metal, canvas, and rope—must have been too valuable an asset for reasonable Inuit to leave intact,' says MacDonald. 'They may well have considered the mast a final, though curious, parting gift from Parry.'[46]

But unfortunately, towards the end of the expedition's stay, harmonious relations were disrupted—a missing shovel brought forth the *qallunaat*'s wrath.

'On the 3d of March [1823],' wrote Parry,

the Esquimaux were excluded from the *Fury* for some hours, on account of a shovel having been stolen from alongside the preceding day. Soon after this, Oo-oo-took, a middle-aged man, who had seldom visited the ships, was in Mr. Skeoch's cabin, when that gentleman explained to him the reason of his countrymen being refused admittance; upon this he became much agitated, trembled exceedingly, and complained of being cold. There could be no doubt he thought Mr. Skeoch had dived into his thoughts; for hastening upon deck, he was a minute or two afterwards detected in bringing back the lost shovel from the place where he had buried it behind our wall. A day or two before this occurrence, Captain Lyon had in a manner somewhat similar recovered a knife that had been stolen from him, for which, by way of punishment, the offender was consigned to solitary confinement for some hours in the Hecla's coal-hole.

As, however, the Esquimaux only laughed at this as a very good joke, and as the time was shortly coming when numerous loose stores must be exposed upon the ice near the ships, I determined to make use of the present well-authenticated instance of theft, in trying the effect of some more serious penalty.

Parry administered naval discipline:

The delinquent was therefore put down into the Fury's store-room passage, and closely confined there for several hours; when having collected several of the natives on board the *Fury*, I ordered him to be stripped and seized up in their presence, and to receive a dozen lashes on the back with a cat-o'-nine tails. The instant this was over, his countrymen called out very earnestly, '*Timun, timunna,*' (That's right, that's right,) and seemed much relieved from the fright they had before been in while the fate of the thief seemed doubtful. . . . This example proved just what we desired; in less than eight-and-forty hours, men, women, and children came to the ships with the same confidence as before, always abusing Oo-oo-took, pronouncing themselves and us uncommonly good people, but evidently more cautious than before of really incurring our displeasure.[47]

But according to the stories told today, the Inuit were not as pleased about this retribution as Parry appears to have thought. '*Taima, taima*' can be interpreted as 'the end, the end,' or 'enough, enough.' When the story was told more than 40 years later, the thief had become a heroic victim.

[Charles Francis] Hall heard his version from a woman called Erktua, who had visited Parry and Lyon's ships:

Oo-oo-took, a superior *an-nat-ko* [shaman] was charged by Parry when at Ig-loo-lik with the crime of theft for taking a shovel . . . Then Parry caused him to be whipped with something that was made of ropes with knots in them—cat-o'-nine-tails. The Innuits standing around and witnessing all this wanted to help Oo-oo-took defend himself, but he said: 'Let the *Kob-lu-nas* to kill me; they cannot, for I am an *an-nat-ko.*' Then Oo-oo-took's hands were untied, after which the *kob-lu-nas* tried to cut his head and hands off with long knives—probably swords. Every time a blow was struck, the extreme end of the knife came close to Oo-oo-took's throat; occasionally the blade came just above the crown of his head, and when the attempt was made to cut off his hands the long knife came down very near his wrists; but, after all he was uninjured because he was a very good *An-nat-ko.*

After the flogging, the shaman was confined below decks:

After Oo-oo-took had been one day and one night in the dark hole, he thought he would use his power as an *an-nat-ko,* and destroy the vessel by splitting it through the middle from stem to stern. So he commenced calling to his aid the Good Spirit, when a great cracking noise was made, now and then, under the ship, and at the end of the two days and two nights' confinement, the *kob-lu-nas*, fearing from such great and terrific noises that the ship would be destroyed, let Oo-oo-took go.[48]

For generations this story has circulated not only in Igloolik but all along the Arctic Ocean coast, sometimes melded with stories of other expeditions, and certainly with additional colourful elements. In the versions people tell today, sometimes the theft of the shovel is mentioned; sometimes it is not.

Lena Kingmiatook of Taloyoak, tells a particularly full and dramatic version:

These white people took an **Inuk** prisoner whose name was Eqilaglu. This little man was also a shaman and the reason he became a prisoner was because he didn't want his wife to be abused by these white people. He was probably trying to protect his wife. These authorities took him and tied him upside down to a mast so he would agree that these white people could do whatever they wanted to do to his wife. That's why they captured him and treated him very roughly. They had a big axe and they tried to kill him, but since he was such a powerful shaman the axe would go right through him and just cut the wooden pole. No marks on him!

The little man had a tent made of sealskin probably—not cotton as we have today, for sure. Every time they tried to kill him, every time they swung the axe, other Inuit watching could see him walking into his tent, his spirit going to his tent. . . . At that time we didn't have the rifles or guns or weapons that the white people had. All we had were harpoons, spears, and knives made of bones. So although there were some Inuit there watching, they were not helping him. The white men tortured him, tried to kill him with an axe, and hung him upside down so the blood would go up to his head and he would go crazy and be unable to use his power.

The little shaman was very helpless. He didn't want to give up his wife and also his steel snow knife, but he didn't have enough power. The other Inuit people know he is asking for help. All the shamans get together and they mumble and mumble in a low, low voice and it sounds like thunder roaring in the tent. It was a prayer to bring help to the little man. He began getting more power from the other shamans; that way he got harder and harder to kill.

Even though he was tied up, as soon as people looked away from him, he'd completely disappear and walk right into his tent. Each time, someone would bring him back, and tie him up, and try to kill him again. The ice was breaking up and they tried to get him to agree they should take his wife along. But he wouldn't agree and the ship stayed there even though they could travel now. Then the captain told them: 'Now it's up to me. We leave this man alone now and give him back his wife. We cannot do anything more because we do not have his power.'

They brought Eqilaglu back to his tent and gave him back his wife. And they began to rush, rush, getting ready to leave at a certain time of day. But the little man said to himself, 'That ship, those white people, have treated me so badly.' Then the little man said a certain word 'Pamiuluq!' That's old language. Pamiuluq is a spirit with a bad tail. The little man said, 'Pamiuluq will chew up their ship.' That's what he said, looking at the ship. 'The white people treated me so badly so Pamiuluq will chew up their ship.'

Hervé Paniaq of Igloolik gives a horrific account of the shaman's sufferings and subsequent action:

> He had stolen a shovel so he was taken. He was made to lie on his back on deck with his hands tied. The white people wanted to axe off his arms . . . He was made to lie on his back, but his arm could not be axed. When they tried to axe his arm, it looked as if his arm was severed, so much so that the blade would stick fast to the deck, but each time his arm was untouched. After numerous attempts had been made, they gave it up. When they were done with him, he blew them away and told them never to return again. As the ship had spent a good deal of time in the region, they kept wanting to return but it was no longer possible.[49]

Pauli Kunnuk also recorded his version of how the shaman took revenge:

> . . . An Inuk had stolen a shovel. It is said that the white person really got mad over the incident, which is understandable because of the theft. Because of the way the man got mad over it the Inuk made it not possible for ships ever to return on account of the ice. That's what I heard, whether there is any truth in it or not I cannot say. But it is said that through shamanism it was no longer possible for ships to make it here. Certainly without a doubt, shamanism was practiced in those times.[50]

After Paarii wintered, for more than a hundred years, no vessel came to Igloolik. This was the shaman's curse.

The Lifting of the Curse

As a small boy in the early 1900s, Mark Ijjangiaq believed white men were rare. 'I thought there were only a few worldwide. . . . I thought Inuit were numerous in comparison—because I knew there were a lot of them.'[51]

In fact, by the early 1900s, Inuit in certain areas of the Canadian Arctic had had contact—often close—with *qallunaat* for three-quarters of a century. The whalers *Elizabeth* and *Larkins*, which appeared high off Baffin Island's northeast coast five years before Parry wintered at Igloolik, were harbingers of many more. In pursuit of the bowhead, Scottish and English vessels whaled in numbers down the east Baffin coast and eventually into the whale-rich waters of Cumberland Sound. Here, Americans joined the chase; they introduced wintering and set up shore stations, and then in the 1860s their vessels sailed into Hudson Bay and Roes Welcome Sound. The Inuit soon became necessary partners in the North's first industry. When the whalers took their leave, for the most part before the First World War, the traders, in pursuit of white fox furs, were there to take their place. They set up permanent trading posts, and the missions and sometimes the Royal Canadian Mounted Police (originally the Royal North West Mounted Police) set up shop next door.

But because of ice conditions—and the shaman's curse—Igloolik Inuit remained profoundly isolated.

Igloolik has a vigorous tradition about how the curse of the shaman was vanquished.

Aya, I think I have heard—
(He has heard from the wind)
I think I have heard—
(He thinks he has heard)
The sound of wood out in the wild
Aya, Aya, Aya.

[The late] Noah Piugaattuk recalls that around the turn of the twentieth century (some consider the song is of earlier origin, even pre-dating Parry) an Igloolik Inuk made up this song for use in a drum dance. The composer, whose name was Imaruittuq, danced with the drum, while his wife and another woman sang his song. In many verses, the song tells that after years without contact the white man will soon come again to Igloolik. But will he come by water or by land? The verses of Imaruittuq's song allow for either possibility.

I think I have heard
He thinks he has heard from the sea
I believe that I hear
He believes that he hears
The sound of wood from the sea.

The song that asked the question was sung in the giant igloo when Piugaattuk was a child. 'The song was made long ago, knowing the inevitability of white settlement.'[52]

Igloolik people say the first white man came by land—in 1913, by dog team. They say he was the French-Canadian explorer Alfred Tremblay—whom Inuit call 'Tamali'. (In fact, Charles Francis Hall had visited Igloolik just 44 years after Parry. Inuit received him hospitably and told him their stories. They called him 'Mistahoh', and Rosie made a brief reference to him after Leah and I asked if she had ever heard of him: 'He was here for a while; then he went on towards Hall Beach and on from there.' Rosie expressed the opinion that he was related to a member of the lost Franklin crews. 'That's why he was anxious to find them. . . .')

According to Igloolik Elders, it was Tremblay who broke the shaman's spell. He had shipped in 1912 with Captain Joseph Bernier on the *Minnie Maud*, an old fishing schooner hastily fitted out to pursue a rumour of 'a new Eldorado' in North Baffin Island. Gold nuggets were said to have been found in the bed of the Salmon River flowing into Eclipse Sound. Tremblay set off overland with Inuit guides to look for minerals, game, and anything else of interest.

He reached Igloolik on 20 March 1913. 'When morning broke I saw the low lying land of Igloolik Island ahead of me . . . we struggled into the native village, at the south-eastern extremity of the island, about noon, and standing on the shore I saw four Eskimos. . . .' Tremblay had no knowledge that Hall had preceded him. 'These natives were very astonished when they saw me as I was the first white man to visit Igloolik since Sir W.E. Parry . . . Some of these natives had never seen a white man before and held them in fear. They had heard of Parry and his men only through tradition.' Tremblay and his guides were too exhausted to explain their presence. They slept for 24 hours in their host Eetootajoo's igloo. But on 23 March, Tremblay set out to explore Igloolik Island.[53]

Noah Piugaattuk was a little boy when Tremblay arrived. '. . . He walked to Igloolik Point and looked at [remains of] the old sod houses there. On his return from his walking journey, he said his exploration had been like capturing an animal—which then becomes available for food. Now people would easily come here and do whatever they needed to do.'[54]

Rosie says Tamali shot up the island. 'It is said that he had a pistol and with it he shot up the island of Igloolik as he walked around the shoreline. Afterwards, he said Igloolik was dead—ships would now be able to get to the island.'

Though Tamali had lifted the curse, it would still be two decades before Igloolik saw a ship. The pace of change quickened after the HBC and the Catholic **Oblate** Mission arrived at Chesterfield Inlet in 1913. But, say Igloolik people, 'Igloolik was the last to have white people.' Only in 1931 did the first ship since the *Fury* and the *Hecla* appear offshore.[55]

Rosie, who had spent her childhood around Chesterfield Inlet when there were already white people, was there to watch when the ship bringing the wood to Igloolik for the first mission came into view:

> I recognized that boat when it was arriving. It was the *Tiriisikuluk* [the *Theresa*], only a small one. The women who were living in the same camp as me began yelling out '*Umiaqjuaraaluuk*!!—A huge big ship!' They seemed to have lost their minds. I became scared of these ladies who went crazy over the ship . . . but they were only happy because the boat was arriving. I said it was really not such a very big ship. They were amazed!
>
> Ever since that time, ships have come regularly again. It seems in the past they had been blown away by the shaman.'[56]

Primary Document

5. Excerpt from an Interview with Rosie Iqallijuq

Interview and translation by Louis Tapardjuk
Edited by Leah Otak

Q: Have you ever heard of Ulluriaq?
A: Ulluriaq was from originally a Kivammiut [people of Kivalliq] but she got married to someone that lived in this area so she was taken here where she made it her home from that time on, this also happened to me.

She lived at Uqquat (pn) until her husband died who was known as Pittiulaaq, not the Pittiulaaq that we know but his namesake. She was brought over by her half son who actually was the son of [her] former husband. She remarried but I cannot remember the name of the person whom she got married to.

She had spent her formative years in this area, it was in her childhood that she remembered the time when white people arrived by boat. She remembered the time when white people came, as a matter of fact she was the first Inuk to have seen white people before anyone else as the rest of the people that saw those white people died but she lived on so she was the only one that ever saw white people for a long time in this area. She said that the ship wintered in this place.

According to her recollection of that particular time they were given things that were really good to play with. One item that made a good toy was black hard cubes which turned out to be tobacco plug. They would use them in their play house as utility boxes; they smelled but nevertheless they were good toys. Another was the biscuits used as *sakkattangit*. They were not considered to be food as a matter of fact they would play with them. They would be given some food from the ship but they did not know what they were so they would just play with them for they did not know what they were.

That is all I have heard about her, she did not bear too many children. I knew one of her children but I have forgotten what she was called. Her grandchild is still alive and that is the wife of Kunuruluk.

Q: Have you ever heard of anything more about the white people that wintered here, I believe they were referred to as Paarii?
A: Yes, that is right they were Paarii and the rest. I believe they wintered here for two winters where their ships were frozen in just in front of us where they sometimes made camp at the point Ungaluujat. The reason why it is called Ungaluujat is connected to the tent rings where there would be a tent and a wall of stones for wind break. They use to have stones surrounding the tent for wind break because it would be a long time before they got enough snow in the autumn for them to make snow dwellings. There are a few of them around so these were used for the winter camp. Some were staying at Igloolik in *qarmaq* [sod house] using whale bones for rafters and the walls made with stones and sod at the time when Paarii wintered here. At Ungaluujat (pn) there is a grave of a white man who is said to have died at the time when Paarii wintered.

I heard at the time when Paarii wintered there was a shaman who was jealous over his wife when she started to go around with some white people. When the ships departed it is said that with the help of his helping spirit he blew the ship away so that no other ship can ever make it back to Igloolik.

From that time on no ship ever came this far. Then there were some others that went to Igluligaarjuk (pn) [Chesterfield Inlet] and Aivilik (pn) [Repulse Bay area]. When they met with some people at Mittuq they made it known to them that they wanted to go to Igloolik. But most of the people refused to go with them except for one individual who was not very smart. When he was asked to go with them he readily agreed to go as he barely ever refused anyone as he was the type of a yes man. It was at that time he came to Igloolik, this was after Paarii voyage. I have not heard if they ever wintered here or not.

After this a white man by the name of Taamali was brought over by dog team from Mittimatalik (pn) [Pond Inlet]. It was said that he was clerk of the trading post. This story is what I have heard from Ittuksaarjuat. They had arrived here from Mittimatalik by dog team which happened before Ittuksaarjuat was born.

It is said that he had a pistol so with it he shot the island of Igloolik as he walked around the shoreline. After he had shot the island he said that Igloolik was dead and that a ship will now be able to get to the island.

It was until very recently when I had started to live in this area that we were able to get a ship into Igloolik. This was a small ship called *Tiriisikuluk*; they brought over the materials for the mission to be built. From that time on we finally started to get ships once in a while.

Before I came to this area I use to see ships so when the people in this area saw this small ship they said that it was big ship, but it was a small one slightly larger than a scow.

. . .

Q: Do you recall the time when they started to get converted to Christianity?
A: Yes, as a matter of fact I had arrived to this place when they were just getting converted to Christianity. Before that time I witnessed an experience where people started to get converted to Christianity. This was the parents of Ujarak, which are Ava and Urulu along with Qaunnaq and his wife. I saw them at the time when they were just getting converted to Christianity. This day walruses and seals were caught. Liver was cut into small pieces and placed to the edge of a small plate; in addition there was the heart, piece of the intestine and part of the head. These were all cut into small pieces; they were too small for one to get a good bite of. They were about the same size as a pill placed on top of the plate.

At this gathering there was a general confession to all the people that were gathered in the central location. As they confess their wrong doings they would be filled with remorse and would cry in their confession. This process of *siqqitiqtut* [converting to Christianity] was called *siqqitiqtut*. After everything that needed to be said had concluded a prayer followed. All the adults in the gathering were offered a piece of meat from the plate where they swallowed the meat which was a voluntary breach of taboo. From this time on they no longer would have taboos to follow. This all happened while we were at Pituqqiq (pn).

I just realize that I never did go through the process of *siqqitiqtut*. I knew about Christianity at that time but I still had not been baptized.

That spring I was taken to this area by Amarualik where we first went to Iqaluit (pn), on our return trip we had to walk home as the ice almost left before we got back. When we arrived I went over to our tent just to discover that there was no one in it. Then I went to Uuliniq's tent but it too was vacant. At that moment I could hear some voices from the dwelling of my in-laws that is Iqipiriaq since they had the largest tent. I told Amarualik that all the people might be in there, he replied that was true. He added that they might be *aaniaqtut* [sick], that his confessing their wrong doings to the gathering. I immediately told him that we should go there, but he found no point in going as it was pointless to go. So I went there alone leaving him behind as he had things to do.

I went in and discovered that there were two plates with meat in them, I immediately got a flash back to the time when I saw people going through the process of *siqqitiqtut*. As it turned out with each of the animals caught this process would continue with each different animals. It was comparable to that of receiving a Communion. When I resided at Igluligaarjuk (pn) before this I use to go to church when the priest were saying Mass and saw when they were giving Communion, so this process of *siqqitiqtut* reminded me of that particular time. This was the time when they started to convert to Christianity and the time when they started to let go [of] the taboos that they were restricted.

Certainly there were those that did not know what to do and how to go about being a Christian. My real mother-in-law Ukkanngut thought it was useless to go through the process of *siqqitiqtut*.

Q: Who was instrumental in getting the people to convert to Christianity?

A: It was Umik, who is said to have been started off by a minister called Uqammak. He had shown the people how to go about converting the people to Christianity, so since Umik was from this region the minister sent him over to convert the people to Christianity.

He was the grandfather of Louis Alianakuluk, Piujukuluk and the rest of the kinship from their mother's side.

Umik soon experienced mental imbalance for he was trying hard to convert the people to Christianity, at the same time his son committed a murder who was taken away to a penitentiary. It was so pitiful to see him in his state. He would hurt himself and he just kept on talking and talking, he was trying to keep his physical abuse to himself and very careful that he did not hurt other people.

He talked so much when he was in that state. I remembered the time he shook my in-law's hand, which is Ukkanngut and Itturiligaq, when he arrived at Ugliarjuk (pn) [Chesterfield Inlet] when we were the only people in that place at that time. They had passed through on the way back from their journey to Mittimatalik (pn) [Pond Inlet], it was at that time his son was arrested and taken away. He said as he shook hands with my father-in-law: '*Gutip irninga qallunaat nunaannut angirraujaungmat, paliisillu kana-itallu piungittumik piqujijunniiqtualuungmata.*' ['The son of God had been taken home to the land of the white people, the police and the Canadians have discouraged anyone from doing wrongful acts'].

This was the first time I ever heard of Canadians mentioned, as I was young at that time I would not forget what I just heard.

Qattuuraannuk and Ittuksaarjuat were living at Akunniq that year; my brother-in-law had gone to Akunniq so that Qattuuraannuk could be advised. So I found that their dwelling did not have anyone so I made up the sleeping platform for them. I was tired but all along Umik just talked and talked, so I went to sleep. After I woke I discovered that he was still talking. The following day they took him to Akunniq where he did the same thing, just talked and talked so that no one could get to sleep on account of it.

The following spring he passed way from exhaustion.

. . .

Questions for Consideration

1. What did Aboriginal peoples and Europeans think of each other when establishing contact and why? What did they want from each other?

2. Do you find Richter's 'imaginings' to be an effective method to capture Indigenous perspectives on contact with Europeans? Why or why not?

3. Discuss whether Ramusio's plan of Hochelaga (see the photo on page 40) should be understood as his 'imagining' of the Huron settlement and whether it is comparable to Richter's imaginings of contact.

4. What evidence of cultural misunderstanding between Parry's expedition and the people of Igloolik exists in both the Inuit Elders' testimonies and the writings of Parry and George Lyon?

5. How do you assess oral histories such as those of the Igloolik Elders? Do you see them as more, less, or equally as valid as written historical documents such as Parry and Lyon's observations? Why or why not? How might considering this question from an Inuit perspective produce a different answer than considering it from a Western or Eurocentric one?

6. Based on the interview with Rosie Iqallijuq, how would you say the Inuit perceived Parry and his men? According to her testimony, what effect did 'contact' with Europeans and Canadians have on her community?

7. Considering the evidence provided in this chapter, would you say that contact should be understood as a single momentary event or as an ongoing process? Give reasons to support your answer.

Further Resources

Books and Articles

Eber, Dorothy. *Encounters on the Passage: Inuit Meet Explorers*. Toronto: University of Toronto Press, 2008.

Richter, Daniel K. *The Ordeal of the Longhouse: The Peoples of the Iroquois League in the Era of European Colonization*. Chapel Hill: University of North Carolina Press, 1992.

Trigger, Bruce. *Natives and Newcomers: Canada's 'Heroic Age' Reconsidered*. Montreal: McGill-Queen's University Press, 1986.

Printed Documents and Reports

Burrage, Henry S. *Early English and French Voyages, Chiefly from Hakluyt, 1534–1604*. New York: C. Scribner's Sons, 1906.

Clayton, Lawrence A., Vernon James Knight Jr., and Edward C. Moore, eds. *The De Soto Chronicles: The Expeditions of Hernando De Soto to North America in 1539–1543*, 2 vols. Tuscaloosa: University of Alabama Press, 1993.

Parry, W.E. *Journal of a Second Voyage for the Discovery of a North-West Passage . . . in the Years 1821–22–23*. London: John Murray, 1824.

Snow, Dean R., Charles T. Gehring, and William A. Starna, eds. *In Mohawk Country: Early Narratives about a Native People*. Syracuse: Syracuse University Press, 1996.

Films

Canada: A People's History, Episode 1. DVD. Executive produced by Mark Starowicz. CBC, 2000.

Websites

Library and Archives Canada, Aboriginal Peoples Collection
www.collectionscanada.gc.ca/aboriginal-peoples/index-e.html

THREE

Population Debates

Introduction

In 1973, Alfred Crosby observed that the contact and interchange between continents during the Columbian Exchange involved not only people but also germs, diseases, plants, and animals. Ten years later, Henry Dobyns set out to delineate the human cost of that exchange by looking at the enormous toll of European diseases on the **Indigenous peoples** of the Americas. Dobyns first examined the loss of life and then considered the consequent destruction of cultural, economic, social, and political structures. He argues that the earliest epidemics were not confined to the regions of direct contact but spread across the Americas in three wavelike pandemics. So destructive were these diseases that, in Dobyns's view, the Indigenous peoples that Europeans encountered in the succeeding centuries were but the remnants of much larger populations and more complex cultures.[1]

Dobyns's work joined an academic debate regarding the nature of the impact of European diseases on the Americas that persists to this day. Much of this discussion is shaped by perceptions of pre-contact Indigenous groups. These perceptions, in turn, are often informed by Eurocentric concepts of civilizations, evolution, appropriate land and resource use, and the ability of people to adapt to new and difficult situations. For instance, a small pre-contact population has been used to suggest that Aboriginal people had not evolved to the point where the exploitation of local resources (according to European standards) and the subsequent development of fixed settlements, agriculture, and extensive trade contracts allowed for the growth of a large population. We now recognize that such claims are false and that these value-laden assumptions are used to imply a lower stage of social, political, and economic organization among Indigenous cultures. Conversely, much doubt has been cast on the pre-contact population estimates that Dobyns and others have put forward. David Henige's work is part of this debate. He takes what he refers to as 'High Counters' to task for their poor methodology and their use of historical demography to explain away what he describes as the 'celerity of the initial conquest'.

J.W. Daschuk, Paul Hackett, and Scott MacNeil's article complicates the discussion further. They argue that individual **First Nations** had vastly different experiences with European diseases and that there were wide variations in terms of the timing and severity of outbreaks. The manner in which Aboriginal groups experienced diseases was a result of the intersection of a complex range of factors, including the epidemiology of a particular disease, the environment in which a particular community or people resided, and the social, political, and economic contexts within which both diseases and Indigenous peoples operated.[2] In other words, Aboriginal people contracted diseases and died in extremely high numbers not just because they lacked previous exposure—a trait they shared with many Europeans—but also because they faced other environmental stresses, such as declining food resources and poor living conditions, that made them particularly vulnerable to contagion. Daschuk, Hackett, and MacNeil's work reminds us, moreover, that disease continued to ravage Aboriginal peoples long after contact. It is in this context that we see the real, continuous, and long-term impact of disease.

Chapter Objectives

At the end of this chapter, you should be able to

- understand the role of disease in European colonization of the Americas;
- understand what motivated the Canadian government's response to the health crisis amongst the Aboriginal peoples of the Plains in the late nineteenth and early twentieth centuries;
- develop a better understanding of pre-contact medicinal practices;
- understand some of the methodology regarding the collection and analysis of data from societies without written records; and
- appreciate how quickly individual communities changed in some cases, including the rapid destruction of long-standing political, economic, and cultural institutions in the face of new settlers, new cultures, new animals, and new diseases.

Secondary Source

1. Recent Work and Prospects in American Indian Contact Population

David Henige

I

In the February 2006 issue of *Discover* readers found an article on epidemics in sixteenth-century Mexico. The article was introduced with the statement that 'in 1519, the native population [of Mexico] numbered about 22 million. By the end of the century . . . only 2 million people remained.'[3] We can reasonably assume that at least

2 million people were exposed to this categorical statement, and most of them will take it to be another of those facts of history. In this article I discuss recent work on the subject of the contact population of the Americas and ask whether such claims are indeed facts of history after all.

II

No one seriously argues any longer that there was not a sharp decline in American Indian population levels, apparently beginning shortly after the arrival of Europeans and continuing for several centuries. The evidence we have—largely from archaeology and eyewitness accounts—converges persuasively on this conclusion. What neither of these can tell us is the magnitude of the decline, because neither source can tell us what population levels around the hemisphere actually were at the moment the decline began.

Not content with this, many observers have used arithmetic to supply the missing information. In turn this has led others—myself included—to question the premise that modern arithmetical procedures can be *evidence* of/for anything. Despite studious efforts to make this distinction, this criticism of method has routinely been taken to be criticism of the idea of decline itself.

III

Views about and estimates of American Indian population and depopulation began forming with Columbus's first landfall, and progressed through a series of zeitgeists, the most recent of which features attempts to calculate population levels as part of a larger reaction against the cycle of indifference and denigration that ran from the mid-nineteenth century well into the twentieth. Previously, although there had been a few high estimates, scholarly opinion favoured lowish estimates based on (pre)conceptions regarding environmental carrying capacities, levels of socio-political organization, and the like. In the process, depopulation was attributed in large part to poor gene pools and ill-treatment by Europeans that resulted in high morbidity, low birth rates, and starvation both before and after 1492. Most either saw no reason to assign numbers or, for that matter, any possibility of doing so.

Beginning in the 1930s, culminating in the 1970s and 1980s, and continuing today, sweeping efforts were undertaken to determine the population levels of the Americas immediately prior to contact with Europe. The catalyst for this enterprise was a series of publications by Carl O. Sauer, Woodrow W. Borah, and Sherburne F. Cook, largely in the 1930s and 1940s, at first on **Mesoamerica** and the Caribbean.[4] Borah and Cook eventually concluded that the population of central Mexico around 1500 might well have been as great as 25 million. They arrived at this figure by a series of extrapolations based on the central assumption that colonial counts were only partial efforts to estimate remnant populations; at best they were parts of parts, and needed to be analyzed, evaluated, and projected accordingly, and in ways markedly different from existing orthodoxy.

Although Borah and Cook considered European diseases to be one factor in what was effectively a 90 plus per cent depopulation, others soon made disease the undisputed centrepiece of their argumentation, which came to be termed 'the disease model'. Most notable of these was Henry Dobyns, who, from the 1960s into the 1990s, pursued both disease and depopulation in the historical record, and when he found what he took to be such an instance, he too hypothesized depopulations of 90 per cent or more. Since he described early epidemics spreading from one pole to the other, he thought it likely that hemispheric population at contact exceeded 100 million, or approximately 13 times most scholarly estimates before the 1930s. Dobyns, and others who followed his line of reasoning, adopted the premise that epidemics usually preceded any European presence, and therefore that whatever numbers could be counted were only scattered remnants of much larger pre-contact populations.[5]

The enterprise of the High Counters flourished and metastasized rapidly. Eventually there was hardly an area from Alaska to Tierra del Fuego that had not been addressed and quantified—and always with numbers that were much greater than had previously been broached. Not all agreed with this change of course, but misgivings met largely with indifference. The enterprise coalesced into a cadre whose members adopted virtually identical hypotheses and methods of building on them. It is not too soon to look back and discuss the most recent approaches and effects of this enterprise. This canvass focuses largely on publications in the last 10 years, although earlier work is occasionally mentioned to provide background and perspective. It is an opportunity to concentrate on the real issues in the debate, which are less about how many people lived in the Americas in 1492 than about how we moderns think that we can find this out.

IV

From the beginning, the High Counters' modus operandi has always been remarkably uniform. The historical record is scoured for references to disease or illness; all instances of these are treated as examples of communicable diseases; unprecedentedly high mortality rates are assigned to these occasions; counts carried out by the colonizers are treated as incorporating remnants of remnants and are used to posit figures many times larger; generic figures in the chronicles are treated as accurate, or even as underestimates; diseases, especially smallpox, are assumed to have spread hemispherically even before the arrival of Europeans in most areas; carrying capacity is uniformly judged to have been adequate to support the numbers advanced; and population growth in the Americas before 1492 is held to have been relatively unconstrained by disease, war, or drought.[6]

A covering premise is that quantitative measures, particularly extrapolation, could be applied on a heroic scale. Some High Counters distinguish among times and places (e.g., dry highlands and wet lowlands, sparsely populated and densely populated areas), but the depopulation ratios adopted consistently exceed 80 per cent. A further assumption is that the newly introduced diseases *by themselves* account [for] these depopulation rates.

The figures at which the High Counters eventually arrive are never countenanced by congruent figures in the historical record, but are constructions springing from a series of working assumptions that are untestable. [B]ut, as we will see, resistance has actually been slight. We now can look at some of the work that has been carried out in the past 10 years or so by historians and historical demographers, medical doctors, historians of epidemics, and catastrophists.

V

In a recent canvass of hemispheric depopulation the historical demographer Massimo Livi-Bacci is cautious in his numbers. For example, he thinks that **Hispaniola**'s contact population was 'several hundred thousands' rather than the 2 million to 8 million estimates proffered by various High Counters.[7] Beyond Hispaniola, Livi-Bacci is wary even of providing ranges of estimates, and does not do so for either Mesoamerica or the Andes.

Livi-Bacci concentrates on the disease scenario required by the High Counters as the only mechanism that could account for the catastrophic declines they postulate. In one instance after another he argues how unlikely the High Counters' arguments are— unrealistic at best, impossible at worst. For instance, in commenting on the notion that smallpox ravaged the Incan empire in the mid-1520s, he notes that '[e]pidemiologists would characterize this hypothesis as improbable if not impossible.'[8] Livi-Bacci thus attacks the root assertion of the High Counters, seeking to destroy the basis of their arguments regarding the sufficiency and early spread of European diseases. In effect he argues that no plausible disease model can come close to explaining the deaths of as many American Indians as the High Counters have reprised.[9]

The High Counters have not been idle, however. The most important recent restatement of their views regarding contact population consists of a set of papers appearing in the *Revista de Indias* in 2003. Several long-standing combatants in the debate contributed, including N.D. Cook, William M. Denevan, and Linda Newson. Dealing with Amazonia, Denevan renounces both the 'habitat-density method' and 'tribe-by-tribe counts plus estimates based on various criteria' that he and others had previously employed. Nevertheless, he now believes that the population of 'Greater Amazonia' was '*at least* 5 to 6 million', or as great or greater than his earlier conclusion that it had ranged between 5.1 million and 6.8 million.[10] Newson continues to maintain that the contact population of what today is Ecuador was about 1.5 million at contact and declined by 85 per cent by 1600.[11]

In general these essays sustain the model that diseases were almost solely responsible for such catastrophic losses. Cook advocates the likelihood that smallpox arrived in Hispaniola as early as 1493, although he can cite no mention of the disease in the relatively copious documentation for the time and place.[12] In contrast, in his contribution Livi-Bacci agrees with most observers that smallpox first reached the Americas only in 1518.[13] Juan and Judith Villamarín favourably rehearse recent estimates for the territory of modern-day Colombia, some as high as 9 million. The Villamaríns do not, however, offer an aggregate figure of their own.[14] Finally, W. George Lovell and Christopher H. Lutz treat the *Audiencia* of Guatemala, which encompassed most of Central America, and to which they attribute a contact population of slightly more than 5 million, which declined precipitately immediately thereafter.[15]

Other work on American Indian depopulation has been carried on as well, although of a different character. Cook and Suzanne A. Alchon have recently produced overviews of the arrival and impact of new diseases in the Americas. Both frame these in the disease model, but neither is disposed to use modern projections, even those they previously advanced themselves, to help make their case. Cook eschews the issue entirely, even for the Incan area, on which he has written extensively.[16] Alchon relegates her discussion to an appendix that frames the issue as an unresolved debate.[17] She completes her analysis by conceding that 'it is clear that it will never be possible to know for sure how many humans lived in the Americas in 1492,' adding significantly that 'perhaps that [is] not what is most important anyway.'[18] It is too soon to say whether this is a harbinger or not, but the success of her work and that of Cook in making the case for depopulation without belabouring population level issues underscores that numbers are less important than defensible explanations of the overall phenomenon.

VI

Scholarly disputations and hypotheses often percolate into the public domain, usually in watered-down fashion, allowing the more extreme aspects of a case to leave the greatest impression. The contact population debate is no exception, and has featured frequently in discussions of the Columbian Exchange; the development of disease models; attempts at catastrophic explanations of the human past, including epidemics; and studies of American Indians in general.[19]

The High Counters have found an enthusiastic following in the small corpus of writing by medical doctors for other medical doctors. These efforts show little interest in considering the problematic aspects of the case, or in consulting primary or even recent secondary sources. Rodolfo Acuña-Soto et al. accept a figure of 'between 15 and 30 million' for Mexico in 1519, with proportionately heavy losses during the next several decades, culminating in the great epidemic of 1576/81.[20] The propensity of medical authors to rely on secondary and tertiary sources sometimes leads to contradictory statements by the same authors. R. Sessa et al. accept that the population of Mexico and Peru combined 'fell from 60 to 10 million' yet 'in Mexico . . . the population fell from an initial 10 million to only 2 million.'[21]

In 2000 Acuña-Soto and two colleagues wrote that 80 per cent of 6.4 million Indians died in Mexico between 1545 and 1549.[22] Four years later Acuña-Soto and a different set of colleagues stated that 'in three years' this epidemic 'killed an estimated 5–15 million people, or up to 80% of the native population at the time'.[23] Just a year later Acuña-Soto and yet a different ensemble of co-authors wrote that there were 11 million deaths from a population of 14 million, citing the 2000 article as their source![24] These three estimates offer a range from 5 million deaths to 12 million, with no attempt at clarification and perhaps not even an awareness of the need.

VII

More important is the work of those scholars who work on the influence of epidemics in world history more generally, and write with a far wider audience in mind. The increasingly abundant literature on epidemiological history has taken notice of the unequal effects of the Columbian Encounter in this respect. A major impetus for recent work was William McNeill's popular and popularizing *Plagues and Peoples*, which sought to establish disease transmission as a basic explanatory model for much of human history.[25]

In its turn, Sheldon Watts's *Epidemics and History: Disease, Power, and Imperialism* attempts to explain the success of European colonialism as a function of varying disease vulnerabilities. Watts describes himself as taking 'a moderate position', which he defines as '[a]ccepting that 80–90 percent of any virgin soil (non-immune) *local* population might have died when smallpox first appeared'.[26]

Alfred J. Bollet has relatively little to say about the effects of epidemics on the post-contact Americas other than to assert that 'the combined ravages of smallpox and measles killed more than 18 million of the original population of 25 million' in Mexico.[27] Most recently, John Aberth discussed the effects of smallpox in the Americas. He admitted that the range of mortality estimates varied widely depending on the presumptions brought to the calculations, and had the disease spreading throughout the **Inca** empire in the mid-1520s and throughout eastern North America 'after being introduced' by members of Hernando de Soto's expedition.[28] Finally, Ano Karlen tells his readers that 'perhaps [a hemispheric population of] 100 million was reduced by about 90 per cent.'[29]

In contrast, another textbook-like presentation is quite circumspect in its arguments. Including no numbers at all in its main text, its author quarantines discussion to an excursus aptly entitled 'unresolved historical issues' and presents a fair summary of differing opinions there ('Did ninety million die or nine?').[30] A rarity, J.N. Hays's discussion illustrates how effectively the epic magnitude of the tragic depopulation in the Americas after 1492 can be evoked without number-mongering. Hays's treating the numbers controversy separately yet explicitly allows his readers to appreciate issues and viewpoints without necessarily predetermining their interpretation of the overall process and its effects, and might be the best introductory treatment of the issue now available.

VIII

Almost by definition authors who want their works to be reviewed in the popular media must appeal to popular taste, including making choices about such things as whether to emphasize caution or sensation. Two prominent examples in our case are works by Charles C. Mann and Jared Diamond, both representing the catastrophist school of thought. A science writer by profession, Mann published his take on what the Americas looked like just before everything changed forever. Mann's *1491* is a gallant attempt to synthesize carefully selected aspects of recent thought regarding American Indian societies on the eve of contact. Mann's work represents the default effort to represent American Indian societies in the brightest possible light, and of course he discusses population levels.

Mann takes the High Counters at their word and adopts their depopulation ratios exceeding 90 per cent.[31] He is unabashedly sympathetic to the notion of dense populations scattered throughout the hemisphere, which were virtually obliterated by the onset of European diseases spreading unchecked. Although Mann neither advances nor supports any particular range of numbers, he cites only the highest figures proposed by the High Counters, depriving readers of the chance to decide for themselves from the range of opinion. He accepts the premise that imputing lower population figures to American Indian societies—or even citing none at all—is *necessarily* a reflection on socio-political accomplishments in the Americas. More people can only mean more sophistication and complexity and vice versa.

With similar goals in mind, Jared Diamond also comments on American Indian population levels at contact. He is free of any uncertainty: '[t]he Indian population of Hispaniola declined from around eight million, when Columbus arrived in A.D. 1492, to zero by 1535.'[32] As for Mesoamerica, '[by] 1618, Mexico's initial population of about 20 million had plummeted to about 1.6 million.'[33] According to Diamond, examples of such depopulation 'could be multiplied indefinitely'.[34] He attributes these staggering losses entirely to widespread pandemics of introduced diseases.

As might be expected, textbooks are particularly apt to cite population figures without compunction. Using Mexico as an example of the larger phenomenon, we find repeated instances of this. The authors of one popular textbook tell students that Mexico might have had 'a population approaching 30 million' as well as providing a chart using only Borah and Cook's estimate of 25.2 million.[35] In another case we are told that the Aztec empire alone 'included between 11 and 20 million people'.[36] A third textbook advises users that an 'estimated 20 million Indians liv[ed] in Mesoamerica' in 1519, while a similar work by a well-known Mexicanist speaks of a 'total estimated population of 25 million' for the area roughly comprising present-day Mexico.[37] The impression left behind can only be that all or parts of Mexico had a population of more than 20 million in 1519.

IX

In search of themes that could unite the experiences of the past by showing the effects of interaction and common patterns, practitioners of the up-and-coming field of world history or 'big history' tend to be sympathetic to the conclusions, as well as to the arguments, of the High Counters, as two recent big books about big history testify. David Christian has several things to say about contact population levels. For instance, he asserts that '[u]p to 2 million people lived in and around Tenochtitlán in 1500,' 200,000 to 300,000 in the city itself. More generally, 'populations in the Americas as a whole may have fallen anywhere from 50 to 70 percent.'[38] In context, these figures are moderate, but there is a buy-in into the premises of the High Counters that contact populations can be calculated.[39] John Richards's *Unending Frontier* is another attempt to tie the past together. A specialist in south Asian history, Richards relies for his information on the effects of the Columbian Exchange on Denevan's 'systematic, region-by-region scholarly synthesis . . . of 54 million (or a range of between 43 and 65 million, with a 20 percent margin of error) in 1492'. Between them, central Mexico and the central Andes comprised about 26 million people.[40]

There are also examples of big-picture authors rejecting the conclusions of the High Counters. Livi-Bacci repeats his view that population levels were much lower than proposed by the High Counters.[41] Fernand Braudel addressed the question of contact population very briefly in his enormously influential work. He regarded the early High Counters' figures as 'very inflated' and hoped that 'no one would believe them blindly'.[42]

In *The World Economy*, Angus Maddison estimates the population levels of many parts of the world at fixed intervals beginning in 1 CE. For the Americas in 1500, Maddison opts for Rudolph Zambardino's estimates of between 5 and 10 million.[43] For Peru [he] accepts Cook's '"minimal" estimate of 4 million'.[44] For North America Maddison suggests 2.25 million but does not explain his preference.[45] He makes no apparent effort to search out the most justifiable figures before the nineteenth century, and this could constrain some from accepting his choices, which are based on intuition or crude averaging rather than on textual exegesis or methodological rigour.

X

One ubiquitous practice among the High Counters' modus operandi is the use of percentages or fractions, but problems abound. Thus Bartolomé de las Casas wrote that the population of Hispaniola had been reduced by more than two-thirds 'from the year of 1494 to that of [149?]6'.[46] Such ratios, however, imply knowledge of the size of the whole as well as the part, yet at that very time, the spring of 1494, Columbus was writing that the Indians on the island were 'innumerable'; in fact he 'believe[d]' that they might even number 'a million millions', that is, nothing less than a trillion.[47]

Las Casas and Columbus were bandying numbers and depopulation ratios that meant only that they neither knew the numbers nor cared that they did not. Neither was exceptional in this, but it is clear that in such cases no depopulation ratio can be legitimized. The lesson is clear—if the ratios meant nothing to those propounding them at the time, they can mean nothing to us.

From the very beginning the High Counters recognized the need to use agricultural carrying capacity to justify their claims, and a large number of hypothetical scenarios regarding production and consumption patterns characterize their work. Calculations of carrying capacity involve a number of variables whose values are inevitably at the mercy of whoever applies them. On the other hand, the High Counters have not [been] interested much in other logistical issues. Thus they accept European estimates of urban and battlefield numbers without considering the constraints that logistics must have placed on these. Nor do they consider the facts that in the Americas the wheel was not used for transportation, ironworking was unknown, and there were no large pack animals. Such logistical facts of life act as constraints on efforts to accept or project large numbers, whether of humans, animals, or raw materials.

XI

A signature component of the High Counters' overall argument is that the population of the pre-contact Americas grew continuously [and] virtually untrammelled by poor health, poor nutrition, and strife. In this tableau American Indians husbanded their resources carefully, maintained peaceable relations with each other and the environment, and died of old age.

There was never much evidence in favour of this belief and the evidence against it continues to accumulate.[48] The Aztec and Inca histories collected after the conquest speak of little but warfare. Even worse, for a long time the **Mayan** civilizations were held up as perfect exemplars of transcendently peaceful societies, but as soon as the Maya hieroglyphs began to be understood, this portrayal radically changed, as it became clear that the numerous Maya polities engaged unceasingly in internecine strife, blood sacrifice, and campaigning.[49] Archaeological and documentary analysis of other areas in the Americas is likewise making it increasingly clear that organized violence was a routine feature of the landscape, if on a less apocalyptic scale.[50]

As for pre-contact patterns of health and nutrition, recent research conclusions have not been kind to the Eden idea either. For instance, in a survey of recent developments Richard H. Steckel observ[ed] that '[t]he natives encountered by Christopher Columbus either acquired or evolved with pathogens, which interacted with their subsistence patterns and other life ways, to cause substantial morbidity and shorten life' and restrict the reproductive cycle.[51] In other words, conditions existed that did not reduce existing populations so much as they kept these from expanding very rapidly in the first place. It does not require large-scale epidemics to reduce populations if these populations had never been allowed to grow large because of long-standing and chronic morbidity and mortality.

Local and regional studies elsewhere contribute toward a picture of widespread endemic health and disease problems that make it unambiguously clear that the pre-contact world proposed by the High Counters is proving more and more a will o' the wisp. The result all but removes the possibility of justifying high numbers on grounds that population growth was not inhibited by the usual suspects—the Four Horsemen rode in the New World just as they did in the Old.[52]

It must be unambiguously emphasized that using epidemic diseases and their effects in the Americas to conjure high population levels is moot. The trouble with the disease model is less with the model itself—that diseases played the most important role in reducing hemispheric populations is undeniable—than the uses to which it has been put. Even the worst-case scenario—that all the illnesses mentioned in the historical record were high-casualty epidemic diseases that spread from one end of the hemisphere to the other—does not imply that as a result the populations they struck were ipso facto larger. Yet the implicit notion undergirding the disease model is that concentrating on disease as a depopulation mechanism gives licence to project indiscriminately. This is as if to argue that the development of the atomic bomb meant that the populations of Hiroshima and Nagasaki were larger than they were when conventional ordnance was dropped on them.

XII

Archaeology has been an inconstant friend of efforts to count American Indians. Archaeological evidence is notoriously elusive, but the preponderance for the Americas does suggest a marked decline in population from the early sixteenth century on, but this can tell us little about precise timing and nothing about magnitude, as a recent study of a site in northern Florida illustrates.[53]

Florida was the focus of an entire book by Henry Dobyns, in which he projected a contact population of over 700,000, which was reduced within a few decades by the usual 90 plus per cent, as diseases promptly spread throughout the area.[54] A look at the evidence from Tatham Mound, an extensive site in west-central Florida, suggests quite a different scenario. As the excavator puts it:

> The evidence from Tatham Mound suggests that shortly after de Soto's march [in 1539] . . . infectious diseases may have played some role in accelerated mortality, but the mass graves that are often associated with mass death (epidemics, warfare, mass disaster) are not present. . . . The evidence supports the silence in the historical records regarding illness as an immediate and universal factor in depopulation.[55]

This is an argument from silence, but in this case the silence is especially impressive—after all, the Tatham Mound was directly in the path of de Soto's expedition, which passed through not long after debarkation, when infectivity of any introduced disease among the Spaniards would have been at its zenith.

XIII

Back in 1991 Suzanne Alchon seemed surprised that '[t]he debate over the size of the pre-Columbian population of the Americas *still* rages.'[56] Apparently she felt that the new approaches should have resolved the issue. But since the debate is based on argument rather than evidence, it is hard to see just what could bring it to an end. There is little likelihood that there can ever be a Kuhnian resolution to the issue since this depends on new evidence—or new interpretations of existing evidence—that cannot take place here.

As it happens, one sentence by William Denevan encapsulates the issue remarkably well:

> [g]iven inadequate data, this is a topic that will never be resolved, but a variety of forms of physical, archaeological, and documentary evidence indicates much higher populations (at least fifty million) than generally thought prior to 1950.[57]

Even the most hopeful diehards must agree with the first clause and all but a few calloused skeptics would accept the major premise in the second, while the last clause is beyond dispute. But for those interested in ontological questions, introducing the parenthetical expression raises entirely different concerns about evidence and its use. About all that it is possible is something along the lines of 'more rather than less', but not 'at least fifty million' or, for that matter, not 'no more than twelve million'.

This said, it nevertheless appears that the disease model complete with high population estimates is set to flourish in the foreseeable future, both inside and outside the academy. Its advantages are manifold: it purports to explain extraordinary events straightforwardly; [it] uses impressive arithmetical means to reach and validate specific population levels high enough to satisfy the need to be shocked; and it has been able to acquire the advantages of incumbency. That it cannot defend itself well against criticism is not likely to matter in the short term.

XIV

In conclusion let me raise the perplexing question: what accounts for the ready accept-ance of these high numbers and the methodology underlying them? Most beliefs, even in academia, have a social/socializing context; clearly the zeitgeist-effect I mentioned earlier has played a role. In this case the rise and growth of area and ethnic studies provided more than enough impetus to give rise to differing perspectives on the past. While some of these were long overdue, others piggy-backed on the spirit of the times, which they used to make their cases cheaply.

The notion that a very small portion of humanity was able to explore and exploit an area far greater than itself merely on fortuitous epidemiology grounds is a comfort-able one in today's world. In this view of things, the disease model goes a long way to-ward exonerating the American Indians from being in any way inferior to Europeans, whether it be in technological levels, socio-political sophistication, or basic well-being. If the defeat of the Aztecs and the Incas by vastly inferior numbers of Europeans can be laid to disease, then all is well. Thus the disease model serves as a convenient *deus ex machina* for those who object to the interpretations once in place. For the Aztecs there is certainly some evidence for this, for the Incas none to speak of, but what evidence there is falls well short of explaining the ease and celerity of the initial conquest.

Primary Document

2.   Natural [Herbal] Medicine

Joseph-François Lafitau

Joseph-François Lafitau was a French Jesuit missionary who, in the 1710s, recorded his observations of Aboriginal medicines among the peoples of present-day Quebec, Ontario, Michigan, and New York.

The subject of the natural medicine of the Indians would be a novel and quite inter-esting one to treat. Both continents of America, in their vast extent, are filled with admirable plants from which there come many remedies for certain ailments and with which their doctors make surprising cures. But it would be difficult to make the study because, apart from the fact that a missionary has scarcely the time to apply himself to this research and is even afraid to do so for fear of appearing to approve of the superstitions and the foolish imaginings of the Indians on [the subject of] their sim-plest remedies, they guard very jealously all information about them and each one of them makes a mystery of those which he has discovered or the knowledge of which is hereditary in his family. If I had stayed at my mission, however, I should not have despaired of making more useful discoveries than I did, but my duties during the time when I was there did not give me free time.

The curing of wounds is the masterpiece of their medical science. In this branch [of medicine] they accomplish things so extraordinary as to be almost unbelievable. I could cite a number of examples of this, but I shall content myself with reporting only two of them which have had many witnesses. The first is that of an Abenaki who, after being wounded when he was drunk, having his entrails cut open and pierced, was cured by the people of his tribe who treated him in Montreal and saved him, in spite of an unfavourable prognosis of doctors and surgeons. The second is that of one of our warriors who went to war against the Outagami or Fox tribe. In the attack on a village of Kikapoos, he was wounded by a bullet and had his shoulder crushed. Since the person who was taking care of him was killed a little later when he imprudently went off the path looking for plants, the patient was then badly cared for, and had a great deal to suffer from hunger and the other discomforts of a journey of more than seven hundred leagues. After that, he gave up with a wound which, since he had it for more than six months, might easily have passed as incurable. The Indians undertook to cure it, however. And, although he was so ill that I had to administer the last sacraments and it seemed that no cure was possible for so old a wound, he improved and recovered his health where a European would, perhaps, have lost a thousand lives [died a thousand deaths].

The Iroquois make a therapeutic liquid[58] for wounds which produces marvellous results. This composition is of different sorts. One kind is made of healing plants which are divided into different classes according to the different degrees of their [remedial] virtues. The second is of vulnerary trees from whose trunk or root they take some chips of which they make their remedy. The third, finally, is derived from the body of different animals, and especially from the heart which they cause to be dried and of which they make a powder or a kind of paste.

This therapeutic liquid of one of these compositions is very thin because they put little solid matter in it. It appears very little different from ordinary water except that it is a little more yellowish. Its effect is to drive out not only the poisonous humours which are usually formed in the wound, but even the splinters of broken bones and the iron of arrowheads which can be seen falling out by virtue of this dittany.

The sick person begins by drinking this water which takes the place of all nourishment while he is in danger. The doctor, after inspecting the wound, drinks some of it also so that his saliva may be impregnated with it before he sucks or syringes [the wound] with his mouth.[59]

After the wound has been well syringed, the doctor covers it in such a way that nothing touches the flesh which has been cut open. At most, he puts around it a circle of medicinal herbs of which he has made a decoction. They [the Indians] are persuaded that any foreign body which touches a wound would only irritate it and change the humours into pus which, remaining around the poultice, would corrode, rot and poison the flesh, and could only retard the cure instead of advancing it.

They lift the poultice at regular intervals and repeat the same treatment which is so efficacious that no discharge or infected flesh which has to be burned away by caustics remains in the wound. The edges of the wound are always red, the flesh always clear. Provided that the ill person follows a sensible regimen and commits no indiscretion, he is soon cured.

Some people believe that, since the Indians use no salt, they have a sweeter and better flesh than ours. That may contribute to their cure, I confess, but I am persuaded that it comes principally from the efficacy of their poultices and, perhaps, still more from their manner of applying them and from the care they take to cut off air from the wound.

They succeed no less well with ruptures, hernias, dislocation, sprains and fractures. People have seen broken bones knitted together again and consolidated in such a way that a week from the time of the fracture the patient had the entire use of them again.

In general, their local remedies are very good. It is not the same with their emetics and purgatives. Patients have to be dosed very strongly with them for them to produce an effect. They are like decoctions of very disgusting enemas. They knot up the stomach. Besides, the Indians do not think themselves sufficiently purged if they do not take very strong medicines which clear them out to excess and might well kill a horse.

They have endless secrets for maladies for which formerly almost no remedy existed. An Indian at Michilimackinac cured, in a week, one of our missionaries of a general paralysis which made all his members useless and forced him to have himself taken to Quebec for treatment. The secret of the cure was known but has been lost. All that I have been able to learn of it is that he went to the marshes to look for some root which he then mixed with water hemlock.[60] I saw an Indian woman in my mission who, people assured me, had been cured of a well developed [case of] dropsy. I neglected to learn from her how and by what remedy. The Indians protect themselves from and cure themselves of the venereal diseases[61] which the Europeans have brought back from America to Europe by shavings of gayac or sassafras wood. A singular thing is that they have the custom of making a cabin in the woods for people attacked by these infamous diseases, separating them from others as the Jews used to do to those who were victims of leprosy. In pleurisies and all maladies where there is some focal point of pain, they try to break up the focus of infection by reflected heat and by applying treatments to the opposite side. In fevers, they bring down the temperature and prevent delirium by cold lotions of medicinal herbs which make a contrast with the heat.

Secondary Source

3. Treaties and Tuberculosis: First Nations People in Late-Nineteenth-Century Western Canada, A Political and Economic Transformation

J.W. Daschuk, Paul Hackett, and Scott MacNeil

The 1870s were years of unprecedented transformation on the Canadian Plains. Politically, the region shifted from the nominal control of the Hudson's Bay Company [HBC] and became a satellite territory of the fledgling Dominion of Canada. At the beginning of the decade, the First Nations of the west were self-governing peoples relying almost exclusively on the bison hunt as the basis for their economy. As the new Dominion sought to consolidate its control over the region through the treaty process, it passed the **Indian Act** in 1876 thereby making all 'Indian' inhabitants of the Plains legal wards of the Canadian state. By the 1880s a second stage of the transformation signalling a catastrophic ecological collapse accompanied these political changes. The bison were all but extinct. Although the conversion to agriculture was the economic cornerstone of most of the numbered treaties, the adoption of agriculture was still in its infancy when the bison disappeared. Traditional Plains societies could no longer sustain themselves. Their economy devastated, the First Nations people were compelled to seek assistance from their new treaty partners. They needed assistance not only to re-orient their hunting economy to farming, but in many cases to simply secure enough food for short-term survival. As a result of the transformations of the 1870s, these people emerged in the early 1880s as a 'subjugated' people.[62]

A third aspect of the transformation was also at work during the 1870s. Weakened by their loss of political autonomy and of their most important food resource, the First Nations of the west were left open to the ravages of a 'new' disease. Prior to Canada's acquisition of the territory, acute infectious diseases such as smallpox, influenza, and measles periodically appeared to sweep the west in epidemic form. Within years of the initiation of treaties on the Plains, tuberculosis, a chronic infectious disease that thrives on disruption and human privation, had established itself as the dominant threat to the health of the First Nations population of the region.[63] The impact among the vast majority of reserve communities was nothing short of devastating. And yet, critically, its effect was not felt evenly throughout the region; some groups escaped the brunt of the disease, while others were ravaged. As a result, tuberculosis left a mottled pattern upon the human geography of the west.

Generally speaking, tuberculosis is a reluctant disease. It is not easily contracted in the absence of underlying health challenges, for the tuberculosis bacillus is only weakly communicable. Unlike measles or smallpox, very few of those exposed to an active tuberculosis carrier will themselves become infected with the bacillus. Most healthy individuals who may become infected have sufficient resistance to prevent the emergence of active tuberculosis indefinitely.[64] Tuberculosis also differs from most other communicable diseases in that the infection can lie dormant until a later period when stress lowers the individual's immune system.[65] When social conditions break down, when poverty, constant stress, and malnutrition become part of everyday life, and when the tuberculosis bacillus is present, the disease may emerge in active form in the individual, and in epidemic form in the community. On the Plains, amidst the new political and environmental reality stemming from the transformation of the late 1870s and early 1880s, many of the negative social and economic factors associated with the early reserve experience contributed directly to the explosion of tuberculosis among reserve communities in the west.

When Canada acquired **Rupert's Land** in 1870, there were no professional physicians on the Plains west of the **Red River Settlement**. The Canadian government and its nascent western administration were often slow in responding to the medical needs of the Plains Indian population. In fact, local administrators were without accurate information regarding even the location of the Indian communities across the region. In 1870, Lieutenant-Governor Archibald of the Northwest Territories sought to rectify this situation by ordering Lieutenant William Butler to the Plains to ascertain both the extent of the recent smallpox epidemic and the general state of affairs in the region. He made no mention of consumption.[66]

The first direct reference to tuberculosis, or more specifically to scrofula,[67] among the Plains people during this period was made by George Munro Grant, a member of Sandford Fleming's Pacific Railway expedition in 1872. In his memoir of the journey,

Grant [stated], '. . . Almost all of the Indians of the Northwest are scrofulous.'[68] Grant then described the situation among the Blackfoot, who had come under the influence of American traders, 'supplied with a poisonous stuff, rum in name . . . This is completing the work that scrofula and epidemics and the causes that bring about scrofula and epidemics were already doing too surely . . .'.[69]

The situation changed for the Blackfoot with the arrival of the **North-West Mounted Police** [NWMP] in the late summer of 1874. Within a year of their establishment in southern Alberta, police reports indicated that the Pikanis (Peigan) had regained their affluence. They had between 5 and 8,000 horses at their camp in the Cypress Hills.[70] In addition to quickly stamping out the whiskey trade, the force brought the first medical doctors (outside the fur trade) and systematic recording of health conditions within the Blackfoot Confederacy. Police physicians were instructed to 'attend any Indians who came for medical or surgical assistance to the post'.[71] According to Commissioner French, 'this course . . . would impress the Indians with the belief that the Government really mean to deal fairly with them.'[72]

Mounted Police physicians began their work among First Nations groups even before their arrival in southern Alberta in the fall of 1874. Surgeon John Kittson, attached to the southern Column of the force, recorded his first encounter with Plains people, near Old Wives Lake, southwest of the present city of Moose Jaw. The band, identified by the surgeon only as Teton Sioux,[73] was composed of nine men, seven women, and several children. After negotiating with their 'herb man', Kittson conducted a 'sick parade'[74] for the group. The physician recorded: one case of pannus (blooded eye), one of sciatica, two cases of dyspepsia, and three of phthisis (pulmonary tuberculosis). Dr Nevitt accounted for the presence of the latter two conditions, '[t]hat such disease as consumption and dyspepsia, should be common, among the Indian women did not surprise me, two diseases, which PAR EXCELLENCE [sic], follow in the wake of want, hardship and exposure.'[75]

Hunger became an increasingly common fixture within Aboriginal Plains communities during the early 1870s. By that time, the disappearance of the bison herds from western Manitoba was fact, an ominous portent of things to come. Periodic but severe famines were reported at various localities. Joseph Christie of the HBC reported that adverse weather conditions in January 1873 had led to widespread famine across the Plains.[76] Even communities that had supplemented their hunt with agrarian production experienced hardship resulting from environmental factors. Consecutive grasshopper infestations through the early years of the decade were reported across the Plains.

As the decade progressed, hardship and periodic starvation became increasingly common on the Plains. Widespread famine and deaths from starvation were reported among the Cree along the North Saskatchewan between Fort Carlton and Edmonton during the spring of 1874. Charles Napier Bell, who spent 1872–3 hunting and trading along the Saskatchewan River, reported that many of the Cree along the North Saskatchewan had been forced to eat their horses prior to succumbing to hunger as 'there were no buffalo on the plains all winter.'[77] Communities in the parklands to the east were also experiencing increasing hardship. At the Touchwood Hills Mission, the Anglican Minister Joseph Reader reported to his superior that the Saulteaux had also eaten their horses and even the missionary's pet dog because of the scarcity of food.[78]

Early in 1875, Reader's reports indicated that the members of George Gordon's Band who were at the mission were not eating regularly and were receiving donations of clothing from England. Reader lamented, '. . . It is no wonder that . . . many of them are weak and sickly in the chest.'[79]

Some Native leaders recognized early that the bison hunt was no longer sustainable and that their economies would have to be re-oriented towards agriculture in order to survive. As early as 1871, the North Saskatchewan Cree Chief, Sweet Grass, requested a treaty with the Dominion government. Along with a formalizing of relations and medical care, Sweet Grass requested cattle, agricultural implements, and assistance to the conversion to agriculture as 'our country is no longer able to support us.'[80] The pledge of government assistance in the shift to agriculture was a key feature in both Treaties 4 and 6. The latter, concluded after days of intense negotiation at Fort Carlton in the late summer of 1876, included clauses dealing with farming assistance [and] famine and pestilence relief. Government officials saw the treaties as a means to settle the question of ownership of the land, opening the country for the expected flood of immigrants who would transform the Plains into what some promoters called an agrarian 'Eden'.[81]

Within months of the completion of the Carlton Treaty, an example of the health risks inherent in large-scale immigration was in evidence in the region surrounding Gimli, MB, when Icelandic immigrants inadvertently brought smallpox with them to Lake Winnipeg. Large numbers of both Icelanders and Aboriginal people died.

In 1877, Daniel Hagarty was hired to serve as medical superintendent of the **Department of Indian Affairs (DIA)**.[82] His appointment signalled an acknowledgement on the part of Dominion authorities that [the department] needed to improve its monitoring of First Nations health conditions. During Hagarty's three-year tenure he and the NWMP physicians vaccinated a substantial part of the Indigenous population of the west. In effect, from the late 1870s onwards smallpox ceased to be a large-scale health threat to Aboriginal people in the west, replaced instead by tuberculosis.

Reports by Hagarty and the Mounted Police physicians during their vaccination campaign in the late 1870s provide a record of changing health conditions across the Prairies. In his January report in 1877, Surgeon Nevitt reported that among the Niitsitapi at Fort Macleod,[83] he had treated nearly 300 Natives, 'including of course women and children' during the previous year. He reported on the general well-being of the population under his care: '[t]he presence of phthitic disease[84] is not marked to the extent I had anticipated. . . .' Although the surgeon was kept busy with his medical work for Indian Affairs, his report indicates that the medical situation in southern Alberta, at least, was under control at the beginning of 1877.

Through 1877, tension mounted throughout the Prairies over the increasingly precarious food situation. The arrival of several thousand refugee Sioux from the United States exacerbated the food shortage as dwindling bison herds were incapable of providing adequate sustenance for all groups on the Plains.[85] The bison population in American territory was further undermined by increased hunting, augmented by the arrival of a railway in Dakota Territory, and an outright extermination program undertaken by the US Army as a means of 'pacifying' the Aboriginal population.[86] In addition to pressure on the herds from the south, 3,600 people who had taken treaty and had moved to reserves abandoned their new homes to follow the dwindling herds to the Cypress Hills, temporarily abandoning agriculture for the hunt.[87] To check the increasingly chaotic situation in the southwestern Plains the Dominion government hastily completed Treaty 7 during the summer of 1877.

The authors of a book on the Blackfoot Treaty have noted that the document was first and foremost a peace treaty.[88] Land issues and agriculture do not appear to have been discussed. Hunger does not appear to have been a factor in the completion of the treaty. At the negotiations, the Blackfoot Chief, Crowfoot, refused to accept government food until his concerns were addressed, a sign that his people were not in immediate need of food.[89] The Blackfoot were more concerned with achieving an agreement that protected their communities from the coming waves of white migration.

Through 1877, police physicians recorded no significant changes in health conditions among their Aboriginal patients. Dr Nevitt at Fort Macleod reported a large case load of Aboriginal patients. He recorded 286 patients between the treaty in September and the end of the year. Even Chief Crowfoot himself had been under Nevitt's care for sciatica.[90] Nevitt's reports for this period made no mention of any specific or serious outbreaks.

Surgeon George Kittson, Nevitt's colleague at Fort Walsh, provided a more detailed account of health conditions in the Cypress Hills.[91] [He] referred to his tuberculosis patients: '[c]onsumption prevails more among women than among the men.[92] . . . Although scrofula in all its forms are very common, still very few cripples are seen among them, as victims succumb to the disease in a very short time.' Clearly, tuberculosis was present among the First Nations in the Cypress Hills but eye disease [remained] the bulk of [Nevitt's] caseload up until 1877. The precarious food situation developed into a full-blown crisis during the winter of 1877–8, known as the 'Black Winter'.[93]

Accounts of hardship and starvation resulting from exceedingly warm temperatures and the dearth of snow were reported as far north as the Athabasca and the Mackenzie, and as far to the northeast as Cumberland House.[94] Police Commissioner James Macleod's report in the spring of 1878 stressed that the situation on the southern Plains was 'entirely different from any we have experienced since the arrival of the force in the country'.[95] The hunt among the Blackfoot was a complete failure and many groups were forced to travel as far as 100 miles from their usual winter locations to find remnant herds. With the exception of a few camps, Macleod wrote, most 'were in a starving condition'.

On the southern Plains, where the population had been almost exclusively dependent on the bison, the conditions deteriorated through 1879. Official correspondence of the Indian Department acknowledged deaths from 'actual starvation' at Blackfoot Crossing and 'young men who a few months before had been stout and hearty were reduced to perfect skeletons.'[96] At Macleod, Dr George Kennedy noted the prevalence of venereal disease, phthisis, and other chest infections.[97] Acute diseases such as typhoid, measles, and scarlet fever also spread through the weakened population.

By the summer of 1880, an estimated 2,500 destitute people were drawing rations from the police post at Fort Walsh. Scarlet fever was killing as many as 30 people each month.[98] In keeping with his assigned role as a front-line physician for First Nations people, Surgeon Kittson wrote a long letter to the Indian Department outlining the inadequacy of government rations being supplied to the hungry and sick population gathered at Walsh.[99] He stated that with the extinction of the bison, hunting could no longer be considered a realistic mode of subsistence. Rations were the only short-term means of keeping the population alive. The approved allotment of government food, 1/2 pound of flour and 1/2 pound of meat per person per day was, according to Kittson, 'totally insufficient'. To underscore the point, the physician noted that even state prisoners in Siberia were given a daily ration of a pound of meat, four pounds of bread, and a quarter pound of buckwheat flour. His report was forwarded eventually to John A. Macdonald, who acted both as prime minister and the superintendent general of Indian Affairs for almost a decade after his return to power in 1878. The report had little immediate effect on Macdonald's policy and, although some increase in the ration amounts was eventually granted, it was not enough.[100] In light of what can only be termed the buffalo famine, it is not surprising that after 1880, tuberculosis became the primary cause of death on the Blackfoot Reserve, the disease striking especially hard among children.[101]

The precipitous decline of health conditions among the Blackfoot between 1877 and 1879 can be attributed to their absolute dependence on bison for sustenance and an inadequate supply of food from government officials. The area covered by Treaty 7 in southern Alberta was unsuitable for agriculture, and such a conversion does not appear to even have been discussed during the negotiations at Blackfoot Crossing in 1877. In contrast, the Aboriginal communities which signed Treaties 4 and 6 had prepared for the end of the bison as a viable staple food. At the onset of the famine in 1878, the vast majority of treaty signatories were still unable to adequately feed themselves through agriculture. Many were forced to revert to hunting as a means to survive.[102] In 1878, more than half of the reserve populations in the areas covered by Treaties 4 and 6 abandoned their homes for the Cypress Hills in a desperate search [for] food.[103]

In April 1878, M.G. Dickieson, the **Indian agent** for Treaty 6, began regular trips to Montana to purchase cattle for the hungry population.[104] By the summer, a stockade was built around the government's Battleford storehouse to protect supplies from those same Aboriginal people.[105] Between 1878 and 1880, officials in the new territorial capital at Battleford were under almost constant pressure from hungry people requesting relief.

Although famine was becoming prevalent on the Plains, it was not universal in the summer of 1878. Fishing was still a reliable subsistence strategy along the lakes to the north, providing some bison hunting communities with a fall-back strategy to meet their immediate needs. Dr Andrew Everett Porter, who had recently arrived in the northwest, noted that acute infections, particularly scarlet fever and influenza, were on the increase among the Aboriginal population owing to more frequent contact with whites, but he made no mention of tuberculosis.[106]

On the northern Plains, fishing proved but a temporary reprieve. In his report from Edmonton for 1879, Indian Agent James Stewart lamented the inadequate supply of food for the hungry, '. . . It was not only the want of buffalo, but everything else seemed to have deserted the country; even fish were scarce.' Stewart reported that many spent the intensely cold winter naked, and had eaten their horses and dogs.[107]

For the increasingly malnourished Indigenous population of the west, the food crisis worsened with the election of the Conservative government under John A.

Macdonald in the fall of 1878. Indian policy shifted from a position of ignorance under the Liberals[108] to one which used 'food rations' as a tool of 'coercion' under the Tories.[109] Macdonald's agenda of mass immigration for the west was contingent on the subjugation of Plains people to facilitate both the building of the railway and the settlement of the Prairies.[110] Prior to the arrival of the railhead at Maple Creek in 1883, rations were withheld from thousands of starving people until they complied with orders for their relocation away from areas of imminent development. With this, First Nations communities were, with very few exceptions, permanently expelled from the South Saskatchewan River Basin in what would later become the province of Saskatchewan.

Edgar Dewdney, the new Conservative administration's appointee as Indian commissioner for the territories, came into conflict with the police who had been attempting to mitigate the effects of the famine. Dewdney refused, in his words to give 'carte blanche' [emphasis in original] to ration all of the hungry gathering at police detachments.[111] Although official accounts noted that the hardship on the eastern Plains was not as severe as that in the Treaty 7 area, starvation and deaths from 'exposure and want' were recorded at Qu'Appelle, Touchwood, and Moose Mountain in the summer of 1879.[112] By August, the Prime Minister was informed that 14,000 people west of Fort Ellice were 'on the point of starvation'.[113] Yet government food ration policy continued to be used to control the Indigenous population.

Dr Hagarty's report of his vaccination efforts in eastern Saskatchewan in the summer of 1879 detailed the precipitous decline in health conditions that were a consequence of the famine. Reporting on White Bear's band at Fort Ellice on 5 August, the physician remarked: '[t]he Indians at this place are very much emaciated. Hunger has shown its terrible effects upon them and scrofula and other kindred diseases are becoming deeply rooted. . . .'[114]

Constrained by the inability of physicians to secure food [for] their hungry and increasingly sick patients, the delivery of health care to the Aboriginal population of the west was further undermined by the dismissal of Hagarty, a Liberal appointee, by the Conservative government, because his services 'were no longer necessary' in the spring of 1880.[115] Medical care for the First Nations people was to be entrusted to the police and local physicians in Manitoba and the Northwest Territories. This was, according to the Prime Minister, the best course 'for the Indians and the most economical for the Government'.[116]

Hagarty's inability to improve the food situation among the hungry population was not confined to the Qu'Appelle area. Near Battleford, Robert Jefferson, a teacher at Red Pheasant's reserve noted that medical care delivered by the Indian Department was hamstrung by physicians being unable to supply food, except to the very sick. Jefferson observed the connection between malnutrition and infection as a key factor in the increasingly serious tuberculosis situation in the Eagle Hills, stating 'sick people need more than pills.'[117]

By 1879, Dr Hagarty's report revealed that as a result of food privation Saskatchewan's Indigenous population was well on its way to showing signs of a full-blown tuberculosis epidemic. Those whose traditional subsistence base was collapsing and whose shift to agriculture had yet to reap any benefits fell victim to tuberculosis; those whose resources remained intact, at least for the time being, were spared. As such, the pattern of disease in western Canada was growing increasingly complex, reflective of the changing circumstances brought about by the ongoing political and economic transformation.

The physician's report from western Manitoba indicates that the Dakota bands who were working both on and off their reserves [along the Assiniboine River] were healthy in relation to the reserve populations to the west in the Qu'Appelle Valley who were undergoing severe privation and sickness. Rather than presenting a threat of tuberculosis infection to the Dakota people, the presence of settlers in western Manitoba provided these people with opportunities to maintain their economic and physical well-being. Along the Assiniboine River, their proximity to settlers was a benefit to the Dakota, who were already skilled farmers willing and able to adapt their means of production to meet the demands of the local market.[118] By the end of the 1880s, many of the men of Standing Buffalo were working off their reserve, including on the construction of the Qu'Appelle, Long Lake, and Saskatchewan Railway. Those who remained on the land had shifted their cultivation away from grain and were selling root crops to settlers.

Because the Dakota were accepted as refugees from the United States, they were not participants in the treaty-making process, sparing them from direct intervention in their daily lives by Indian Affairs. Because they did not receive, and did not require, much assistance from the authorities, 'they were allowed to design their own economic strategies with a freedom not enjoyed by other Indians of the Prairies, or even by the Dakota themselves since the 1840s in Minnesota.'[119]

This flexibility was critical for the Dakota, as it enabled them to escape the devastation of tuberculosis experienced by their neighbours, despite being infected as a group prior to their arrival north of the border. In contrast, the Cree and Saulteaux located on [nearby] reserves in the Qu'Appelle Valley were reported to be suffering from serious nutritional stress and sickness. To the north, even communities such as the Cree on the James Smith reserve at the forks of the Saskatchewan River who had established an agricultural community in the 1850s under the tutelage of missionaries suffered a significant decline of both their economy and their health in the years after signing Treaty No. 6 in 1876. With their entry into a formal treaty with the Dominion government the James Smith people were subjected to the interference of the Indian Department in their daily lives. By 1881, the breakdown of their agrarian practices was having a severe effect on their health; departmental records show two band members were suffering from consumption and were 'at death's door'.[120]

The continued economic success of the Standing Buffalo people and their relatively good health through the late nineteenth century stand as an example of positive deviance[121] in contrast to the experience of the vast majority of other First Nations on the Plains. The reason for this good health may have been their economic adaptability, at least compared to those neighbours who were hindered by the political control of the federal government.

Elsewhere in western Canada, communities further removed from imminent economic hardship and government intervention continued, like the Dakota, to enjoy comparatively good health, at least in the short term. The Red Earth Cree, who were immune from the effects of large-scale European immigration on their reserve at the Pas Mountain in the Manitoba parklands, did not undergo a serious decline in their health until the 1920s. [In 1898], their good diet, which included 'the free use of vegetables and the abundance of salt', was noted as a factor in 'the remarkably good' health of the people in the community, and only one case of scrofula was reported.[122]

Others fell somewhere in the middle in terms of their health. Further west, in the parklands northwest of Prince Albert, the Sandy Lake Mission, which became the Ahtahkakoop Reserve, underwent a period of hardship through the 1880s. In March 1884, Reverend John Hines, who established the agricultural Mission at Sandy Lake, reported to his superior, 'I am certain our Indians would have been better off to-day if the government would not have taken them under their charge.'[123] At the Pas Mission, the connection between malnutrition and mortality was observed by the beginning of the 1880s. In 1882, Joseph Reader reported to his superior: 'I think I am right in saying that nearly every death that has occurred since we have been here has been premature through starvation.'[124]

By the early twentieth century most First Nations communities on the Canadian Plains had been exposed to epidemic tuberculosis. However, what is notable about the outbreaks of tuberculosis on the Plains is the chronology of the appearance of the disease among its victims and the differences in the severity of their experiences. Clearly, the impact of the disease varied according to specific, local, conditions, even within small geographical areas. The overall pattern of outbreaks of tuberculosis in western communities, then, corresponds to the statement by [George W.] Comstock and [Richard J.] O'Brien on the 'sharply localized' nature of the disease.[125] The apparent well-being of the Standing Buffalo Dakota, though they were surrounded by hungry and increasingly sick Cree and Saulteaux communities, is an example of differential experiences with disease among First Nations, and of positive deviance in relation to the overwhelming trend of economic dislocation, malnutrition, and decline from tuberculosis that marked the post-treaty period in the west. This diverse pattern continued well into the twentieth century, with an even more pronounced differential between First Nations and non-Aboriginal communities. In the 1920s, Dr R.G. Ferguson, perhaps the pre-eminent authority on tuberculosis in western Canada in the early twentieth century, reported that tuberculosis deaths were 20 times more frequent among the First Nations of the Qu'Appelle than among their white neighbours.[126] In general, this varied spatial–temporal pattern of tuberculosis was due to marked differences in the local timing of the paired fundamental transformation, the political and the economic, that virtually all First Nations communities underwent at some time following the transfer of the west from the HBC to Canada. In turn, this reinforces the view that the general decline of health among the Aboriginal population was not simply the case of infection from an introduced disease, and that the decline resulting from tuberculosis was not an inevitable or simply organic process. Rather, the process was a direct consequence of an ecological catastrophe coupled with a subjugation policy emanating from the colonial process that began with the transfer of sovereignty to the Canadian government in 1870.

Primary Document

4.   Report of Acting Superintendent M.G. Dickieson, July 1879

Office of the North-West Indian Superintendent, Battleford, N.W.T., 21st July, 1879.

The Right Honorable
The Minister of the Interior,
Ottawa.

SIR, - I have the honor to submit the following report of the transactions in this super-intendency for the half year ending 30th June, during the last three months of which I have been acting as Superintendent. I have kept the head office informed by every mail of the turn events were taking, and of my actions; but think it advisable at the close of the financial year to send a short general summary of proceedings.

1. During the winter a very hidden number of Indians visited this office for assist-ance. A general impression existed in their minds that they had been promised, when the treaty was concluded, that they should be fed whenever they were in want. This erroneous idea has been to a great extent done away with, and they are now beginning to understand that, while the Government will not allow them to starve, they must exert themselves to earn the food given them.

It was hoped that with the advent of spring the demands for assistance would have lessened, but such, unfortunately, has not been the case. At one time nearly all the Indians had gone away from Battleford, but as they found few buffalo they soon came back; and though every exertion was made to induce them to leave, and try to make their living by hunting and fishing, the number who remained in the vicinity of the agency remained nearly the same—from 500 to 900 persons; no sooner had one party gone away than another arrived to take its place.

I have been visited by Crees, Salteux, Stonys, Chipewyans, Bloods, Blackfeet, Sarcees, Piegans and Sioux. The necessity of attending to so many different parties has taken up a great part of my time, and left me sometimes for days no leisure to attend to correspondence and other official work, much less to visit outposts of the agency, where my attendance was almost indispensable, and several matters requiring attention have consequently been al-lowed to stand, very much against my wish, and with detriment to the Department.

I at first employed those able to work in cutting and piling cordwood, and had a number engaged in improving the road and river crossing. Though this was not dir-ectly remunerative, as there was no demand for the greater quantity of the wood cut, yet indirectly it was valuable. Some of those thus engaged had never done [a] stroke of manual labor, and then for the first time handled a hoe or an axe. The prejudice in their minds against working was broken down, and the oft-repeated assertion that the Plain Indian would never work has been shown to be incorrect. One band of Sarcees under 'The Drum' have worked well, and Mosquitoe's band of Stonys have shown that when pressed by hunger they can and will work.

Finding I could not keep them in employment, I determined to commence a farm working on which would teach them how to break up land, and at the same time not be entirely unremunerative to the Government. I selected a location about eight miles from Battleford, where there is a hidden section of excellent land, and hired a man to help and direct them. A good many have gone to work, and the experiment has been as successful as I anticipated. Though the actual amount of work done has not been commensurate with the outlay, the result has been satisfactory. I have been able to say to the Indians 'there is no necessity for your begging from the Government or settlers; you can earn your food, and if you do not wish to work, I will supply you with ammunition, and you can hunt.' A great many preferred hunting to working, and went away. I am convinced, if no work had been provided, and they had been supplied with food on their asking for it, that before this time at least 2,000 Indians would have been collected here, and it would have been very difficult to provide food for such a number of Indians or to prevent them from committing some depredation. I have followed one principle of action, viz., to get the Indians to do as much as possible for themselves, and with this end in view, I have not stinted the supplies to those who were working, or ammunition to those who preferred hunting, while I have not been more liberal than I was actually forced to be to those who would neither work or hunt.

On the 24th May, a deputation of Blackfeet from Old Tom's band came in, who stated that they had left about 60 lodges behind, and that the Indians were very badly off; that several had died, as they were unable to live on the roots, & c., which were their only means of subsistence. I sent out some carts loaded with provisions and ammunition, and advised them to go south, knowing that they would thus sooner meet with buffalo if any were coming north, and if compelled to fall back on the Government for assistance, it would be cheaper to help them there than here.

To prevent the Indians from leaving their usual places of residences, and coming to Battleford, a quantity of provisions has been issued at Carleton, Prince Albert, Fort Pitt, Victoria, and Edmonton, by the Hudson's Bay Company, and at Fort Saskatchewan by Inspector Jarvis. Statements showing the quantity so distributed, as well as what I have given at Battleford, have been forwarded from time to time to Ottawa.

Very little provisions have been given out in Treaty No. 4. This led to a demand accompanied by a show of force, being made on the Hudson's Bay Company at Qu'Appelle, which ended in the delivery of the Government supplies stored there. The full details of this occurrence have been sent to the head office in previous letters. At Moose Mountains the Indians were in a most deplorable condition, and it is reported that several died from exposure and want of food.

I have forwarded suggestions as to what steps ought, in my opinion, to be taken to meet the starvation which threatens the Indians next winter, and need not say anything on the subject here.

I enclose statements of the quantities of provisions supplied to the different bands in Treaty No. 6, at planting time, and also of the seed distributed to them. Nearly all the seed given out was put in the ground, and so far as I have heard, there is every prospect of a fair crop. From the enclosed statement you will find that in Treaty No. 6 there were purchased and given to the Indians, 677 bushels of wheat, 1,759 bushels of potatoes, and 565 bushels of barley, besides turnips, and other small seeds, an increase over last year of 390 bushels of wheat, 595 of potatoes, and a decrease of 93 of barley.

In Treaty No. 4 there were distributed 703 bushels of potatoes, 4 of wheat, and 51 of barley, being an increase of 861 of potatoes, 19 of barley, and 4 of wheat. It must be remembered that some of the Indians had seed from last year, besides that given by the Government. Great difficulty was experienced in procuring a sufficient quantity of barley and potatoes, and more would have been planted could seed have been procured. You will notice that the quantity of provisions distributed overran the appropriation for that purpose, supplemented though it was by an extra grant of $1,000. A part of the provisions given out was remaining from what had been provided for the annuity payments, and I deemed it better to use these supplies then, thus enabling the Indians to put in more seed. Even with the hiddenly increased quantity provided, there was considerable regret expressed when it came to be divided that more could not be given to each band. This arose from the fact that the Indians understood (or at least now said they did) when the treaty was concluded that $1,000 worth of provisions was to be given to each band. They consequently were disappointed when they received their share. The following bands on Treaty No. 6 have broken up the greatest acreage: James Smith, John Smith, Seemmis, Ahtahacoop, Mistawasis, Little Hunter, and Red Pheasants. The first three bands have been farming more or less for some years. The two bands under James and John Smith are hiddenly composed of **half-breeds** and Swampy Indians who have removed from Manitoba, where they have been accustomed to work. Seemmis is the White Fish Lake band who have had a Wesleyan Mission established among them for many years. The other bands named have been entirely dependent on the chase up to the last few years, and the progress they have made is encouraging, and in another year they ought to raise enough to prevent actual starvation. None of the other bands have done much, some of them having made their first attempt at farming this spring. The assistance given by the instructors was of great service, and the expenditure has been a judicious one.

In my letter of the 26th February last, I gave you the position of every band in the Territories, and as the change from that time has not been marked, I need not repeat what I then said.

A quantity of seed was given to the Stonies at Morleyville by sub-Inspector Deuroy under instructions from His Honor Lieutenant-Governor Laird.

Regarding the schools in the Superintendency I need say little, as regular quarterly returns are sent in from those which receive Government aid. I have not been able to visit any except at planting time or when making the payments on which occasions the scholars were not in attendance in consequence of these events.

Schools should be established on several reserves, but the Government cannot expect to get capable teachers for $300 or less per annum.

I wish to call your attention to the school at White Fish Lake which does not receive Government aid, though attended by a hidden number of scholars. Rev. Mr. McDougall made a verbal application to me in May last, but as he was then on his way to Canada, and I understood, intended to bring the matter before you personally, I have not written heretofore on the subject.

In addition to the Indians included in the treaties, there are two bands of Sioux under 'White Cap' and 'Standing Buffalo,' who have begun farming, the former on the South Saskatchewan, the latter near Qu'Appelle. They, as you are aware, have been in the country since 1862, and are well disposed, peaceable, and good workers.

I have had no intercourse with or communication from any of the hostile Sioux who crossed lately from the United States.

I have the honor to be,
Sir,
Your obedient servant,
M.G. Dickieson,
Acting Superintendent.
Swan River Barracks,
North-West Territories, 21st July, 1879.

Questions for Consideration

1. What does Henige think is wrong with the methodologies of the 'High Counters'? Do you agree with his view that these problems discredit their conclusions? Why or why not?
2. What factors does Henige suggest kept pre-contact population levels lower than High Counters argue? How does his view of pre-contact North America compare to McPherson and Rabb's in Chapter One? Whose portrayal do you find more convincing and why?
3. What do Joseph-François Lafitau's observations reveal about the Indigenous medical practices he encountered? Did they challenge his own Eurocentric prejudices? What might his observations suggest about pre-contact death rates in North America?
4. Why did tuberculosis epidemics ravage many Aboriginal communities of the Canadian west in the late nineteenth and early twentieth centuries?
5. How would you characterize and explain the Canadian government's response to the health crisis amongst the Aboriginal peoples of the Plains during the late nineteenth and early twentieth centuries?
6. What light does Dickieson's report shed on the health crisis and the government's response?
7. What role did disease play—and continue to play—in European colonization of the Americas?

Further Resources

Books and Articles

Crosby, Alfred W., Jr. *The Columbian Exchange: Biological and Ecological Consequences of 1492*. Westport: Greenwood Press, 1973.

Dobyns, Henry. *Their Number Become Thinned: Native American Population Dynamics in Eastern North America*. Knoxville: University of Tennessee Press, 1983.

Henige, David. *Numbers from Nowhere: The American Indian Contact Population Debate*. Norman, OK: University of Oklahoma Press, 1998.

Owram, Douglas. *Promise of Eden: The Canadian Expansionist Movement and the Idea of the West, 1856-1900*. Toronto: University of Toronto Press, 1980.

Printed Documents and Reports

Ferguson, R.G. *Tuberculosis among the Indians of the Great Canadian Plains: Preliminary Report of an Investigation Being Carried Out by the National Research Council of Canada.* London: Adlard & Son, 1929.

Morris, Alexander, ed. *The Treaties of Canada with the Indians of Manitoba and the North-West Territories.* Saskatoon: Fifth House, 1991.

Films

The Gift of Diabetes. DVD. Directed by John Paskievich and O. Brion Whitford. NFB, 2005.

The Last Days of Okak. DVD. Directed by Anne Budgell. NFB, 1985.

Websites

CBC, 'Davis Inlet: Innu Community in Crisis', 1992–2005
http://archives.cbc.ca/society/poverty/topics/1671/

CBC, 'TB Plagues Northern Natives', 4 Nov. 1991
http://archives.cbc.ca/health/disease/clips/5326/

CBC, 'Tuberculosis: Old Disease, Continuing Threat', 1943–2001
http://archives.cbc.ca/health/disease/topics/883/

FOUR

War, Conflict, and Society

Introduction

The relationship between history, Aboriginal peoples, war, and conflict is complicated. Until recently, stories of white women being held captive, scalping, and 'blood thirsty savages' held a great deal of currency in colonial narratives of Aboriginal warfare. While inaccurate, the salacious stories of Aboriginal captivity and the potential for Aboriginal violence have fascinated Euro-Canadian audiences and driven the formulation of colonial and, later, Canadian Indian policy.[1]

Recently, historians seeking to reclaim and make respectable the military traditions of Aboriginal peoples have cast them as 'long-standing allies of the Crown from the colonial era through to the twentieth century'.[2] Historian J.R. Miller argues that, during the eighteenth century, relations between Aboriginal and European people were defined by military alliances—a function of the protracted conflicts in which Europeans found themselves embroiled in North America and abroad.[3] While Aboriginal people were undeniably involved in what are perceived as 'European conflicts', they entered these struggles for their own geopolitical reasons, switching alliances between European powers and various Aboriginal Nations in order to secure and pursue their own interests. Brett Rushforth's article outlines how those First Nations allied with the French used the Europeans' conflict with the Fox Nation to ensure that they controlled access to European goods and weapons. In doing so, First Nations retained their dominant position as middlemen in the lucrative trading networks between Aboriginal nations further west and the French.

Alan Taylor's piece examines the period from 1783 to 1815, which encompasses the end of the **American Revolution** and the War of 1812. Although these wars have a clear beginning and end for Europeans (i.e. declarations of war and formal peace treaties), the same cannot be said for First Nations whose territories were bisected during this period of solidifying national boundaries and border-making. Typically, this era is seen as the beginning of the end for Aboriginal peoples' ability to manoeuvre effectively between the two European powers in these 'borderlands'. Taylor complicates this narrative and asserts that the solidification of borders, 'the limitation of Native peoples within the boundaries of nation', and the settlement of Aboriginal people on reserves was a central feature of nation-building. In other words, the creation and solidification of the modern nation-state was dependent on restraining Aboriginal people and appropriating their land.

Chapter Objectives

At the end of this chapter, you should be able to

- explain why New France and its Aboriginal allies went to war with the Fox;
- discuss why the Six Nations moved from present-day New York State to the southwest of present-day Ontario and why tensions regarding this land still run high in places such as present-day Caledonia;
- understand how the drawing of the international boundary between the United States and British North America affected Aboriginal peoples; and
- identify how Aboriginal people shaped events as the French, British, and Americans expanded their territories and influence.

Secondary Source

1.   Slavery, the Fox Wars, and the Limits of Alliance

Brett Rushforth

On the bitterly cold evening of 13 December 1723, Jean Becquet, master of the house at the governor's residence, called for Father Étienne Boullard. When Boullard arrived, he found an ailing Indian woman called Marguerite-Geneviève, whom he promptly baptized. Returning to his small residence at the seminary, the priest recorded what he had learned about the woman during his visit. She was 35 years old. She had a 14-year-old daughter called Marie Louise, whom he also baptized. She was a Fox Indian. And she was a slave: 'captured in Fox territory by the Marquis de Vaudreuil', the governor of **New France**, 'with whom she presently resides'.[4]

Only two months earlier, Vaudreuil had written a letter to France congratulating himself on successful peace negotiations with Marguerite-Geneviève's people in an ongoing conflict historians call the Fox Wars. Pitting New France's Indian allies against a coalition of Fox, Sauk, Kickapoo, and Winnebago, this series of clashes claimed thousands of lives and destabilized the Upper Country for the better part of 30 years. Charged with maintaining the region's Indian alliances, Vaudreuil proudly announced that he had thwarted recent plans by his Native allies to attack Fox villages by sending a well-respected French officer to the region 'to Persuade them to be Reconciled and to Live in peace'.[5] As he had done many times before, Vaudreuil pressured Upper Country Indians to embrace the Fox as allies rather than enemies, seeking greater regional stability to facilitate French commercial and territorial expansion.

Governor Vaudreuil never mentioned to his French superiors that his household, like scores of others in New France, was served by Fox slaves who had been captured in the very attacks he claimed to oppose. For the previous 10 years, these slaves had trickled into Canada as allied Indians attacked Fox villages, making Fox men, women, and children the primary source of enslaved labour in the St Lawrence River Valley during the 1710s and 1720s. Because these slaves do not appear in the official reports that have informed earlier studies, their lives have been noted, if acknowledged at all, as interesting but insignificant side notes to the story of French–Indian diplomacy.[6] Yet the records discussing these slaves, produced by parish priests, notaries, and court reporters, offer a valuable new perspective on the Fox Wars.

This reassessment of the Fox Wars suggests that it was neither inherent Fox aggression nor domineering French leadership that fuelled the violence. Instead the Fox Wars grew out of a much more mundane disagreement over the limits of the emerging French–Indian alliance. Whereas French imperial officials sought to enlarge their influence in the west, connecting with an ever-growing number of commercial and military partners, those Natives already attached to the French wished to limit this expansion, blocking their enemies' access to French goods and support. As the French embraced the Fox, allied Indians violently asserted their prerogative to define the parameters of alliance, demanding that the French honour their friendship by shunning their historical enemies.

By raiding Fox villages for captives, and then giving or selling these captives to the French as slaves, [New France's Native allies] drove a deep and eventually fatal wedge between the French and their erstwhile Fox allies. French colonists' demand for Fox slaves supported this strategy, ultimately ensuring its success by alienating the Fox from French interest and finally compelling them to war. In addition to illuminating the role of Indian slavery in structuring the western alliance system, the wars also powerfully illustrate the ways in which Indians shaped the contours of the alliance to their advantage against French wishes.

Throughout the latter part of the seventeenth century, the French and the Fox shared a mutual desire for friendship. With the Iroquois threat looming, each side profited from the other's assurances of protection, and both could benefit from the trade that accompanied such relationships. But it was clear from the beginning that the French had a problem. New France's allies, including the Illinois, Ottawas, Ojibwa, Miami, and Hurons, detested the Fox. Even as these peoples needed Fox co-operation during the Iroquois Wars, they expressed deep enmity toward their Fox neighbours, seeking their exclusion from French protection and trade.

During the 1670s and 1680s, Fox villages came under attack from all these groups, sparking rounds of reprisals. These conflicts ebbed and flowed with the currents of the Iroquois threat, but animosity remained the norm. The cramped proximity forced by Iroquois attacks often sparked new violence among these historical enemies, creating a tense atmosphere in western refugee villages. Illinois, Ottawa, Ojibwa, and Huron war parties clashed with the Fox throughout the 1680s and 1690s, even as they faced a common Iroquois enemy.[7]

By the time of the general peace conference in Montreal in 1701, the Fox delegate to the peace negotiations expressed his desire to have a French presence in their territory. If the Fox 'had a black robe, a blacksmith, and several Frenchmen among us,' he pleaded with the French governor, 'the Chippewa [Ojibwa] would not be bold enough to attack us.' Although each of these peoples agreed to French alliance, the Ojibwa were not the only ones who wanted to drive the Fox out. The Illinois described the Fox as 'devils on earth, they have nothing human but the shape. . . .' Still the French wanted the Fox within the alliance, so they invited the Fox to the 1701 peace as full partners.[8]

The French decision to establish a new settlement at Detroit the same year only deepened these divisions. Although never exclusive middlemen in the Great Lakes fur trade, the Ottawas, Ojibwa, and Illinois lived much closer to the French and thus could command a larger proportion of their commerce. As the French moved westward, these peoples were faced with the dual threat of having the Fox become better armed and of losing their position of strength within the region's fur trade networks.[9]

Meanwhile the absence of the Iroquois threat removed what little incentive Ottawas, Ojibwa, and Illinois felt to remain at peace with the Fox. In 1703 and 1708, Fox warriors attacked the Ojibwa near the southeastern corner of Lake Superior, killing several warriors and seizing a large number of Ojibwa captives. Counter-raids began later that year. Despite these conflicts French officers persisted in their efforts to join these peoples 'together in feelings of peace and union', hoping to avoid taking sides in a dispute among peoples they considered allies.[10]

In this tense environment, the French naively invited the Fox to live among the allied peoples whose villages surrounded Detroit. Articulating his vision of an expansive western alliance, Governor Vaudreuil ordered Jacques-Charles Renaud Dubuisson, Detroit's new post commander, to 'give all his attention to preventing the Indian allies from making war on one another'.[11]

Instead violence erupted almost immediately. During one attack the Fox struck two Huron and Ottawa villages, capturing the wife of a powerful Ottawa chief who vowed revenge. Needing little encouragement a group of Ottawas, Hurons, Ojibwa, Illinois, Potawatomi, and some Miami surrounded the fortified Fox town near Detroit, threatening to kill all of them unless they released their prisoners and returned to their lands west of Green Bay.[12] Rather than embracing the Fox as kin like Vaudreuil had hoped, the Native alliance violently articulated their intention to define the Fox as enemies.

Besieged and badly outnumbered, the Fox desperately appealed for French mediation. At a hastily arranged meeting in late 1712, Fox War Chief Pemoussa begged French military officers for mercy. Following protocol for cementing alliances, Pemoussa offered several slaves to signify his friendly intentions, defining himself as a kinsman to the French and their allies. 'Remember that we are your brothers,' he said to the assembly of Native leaders.[13] In this dangerous world of symbolic diplomacy, no gift carried greater weight than a human body, and Pemoussa wisely offered slaves as his best hope to save his people.

Still, speaking for the French-allied nations, an Illinois warrior rejected Pemoussa's claim to kinship. Defined as enemies the best [the Fox] could hope for was to be kept alive as slaves. Making one final appeal to kinship, this time depicting the Fox as the most beloved Elder in a young man's life, Pemoussa begged again: 'Remember . . . that you are our grand-nephews; it is your own blood you seem so eagerly to thirst for; would it not be more honorable to spare it, and more profitable to hold us as slaves[?]'[14]

Map 4.1 Location of major participants in the Fox Wars, c. 1701. Adapted from Helen Hornbeck Tanner, ed., *Atlas of Great Lakes Indian History* (Norman, OK: University of Oklahoma Press, 1987), 32–3, 40–1; R. David Edmunds and Joseph L. Peyser, *The Fox Wars: The Mesquakie Challenge to New France* (Norman, OK: University of Oklahoma Press, 1993), 12–13; and Gilles Havard, *Empire et métissages: Indiens et Français dans le Pays d'en Haut, 1660–1715* (Paris: Les Éditions du Septentrion, 2003), 227. Drawn by Rebecca L. Wrenn. (Helen Hornbeck Tanner, ed., 2003.)

Rejecting Pemoussa's offer of peace, the Fox's enemies surrounded and attacked them. One French observer reported that, after allowing Pemoussa a safe retreat, 'all the [Fox] were cut in pieces before they could regain their weapons. The women and children were made slaves, and most of them were sold to the French.'[15]

These events fit rather uneasily into the prevailing model of French–Indian relations, first developed in [Richard White's] *The Middle Ground*, which presumes a fundamental 'tension between the Algonquian ideal of alliance and mediation and the French dream of force and obedience'.[16] At Detroit in 1712, this formulation was turned on its head. French officials pursued a policy of mediation with the Fox, while their Algonquian-speaking allies manoeuvred for dominion over them. Rather than a cultural compromise initiated by Native diplomats, orders to mediate came from the highest levels of French imperial authority.

Indeed, Dubuisson's most notable concession to Native demands came when he agreed to participate in the bloodshed. This represented French acknowledgement of their allies' expectations. From the perspective of many allied nations, the French did not breach the terms of alliance through violence but rather when they sought mediation and peace with enemy nations.

But as violence around Detroit dragged on, French officials wearied of the fighting. From 1713 to 1716, French policy wavered between grudging support for the war against the Fox and efforts to secure a peaceful resolution. After three years of intermittent warfare, in 1716 French and Native forces defeated a large group of Fox, grinding the violence to a bloody halt.[17]

That fall, under heavy pressure from the French, the Fox and their enemies gathered in the St Lawrence River Valley to negotiate peace. Once again led by Pemoussa, the Fox arrived at Quebec hoping to restore their standing as French allies. Pemoussa performed several public displays of friendship. He gave gifts to French officers, returned prisoners to allied nations, and allowed himself to be baptized. The Fox would return prisoners and give symbolic gifts, including slaves captured in distant regions, to their fictive kin, both Native and French. Through this process they would replace the dead who had fallen, restoring the bonds of kinship severed by the war.[18]

Obviously pleased by this turn of events, Governor Vaudreuil praised the agreement.[19] To the Ottawas and other Indian peoples, however, it must have seemed the height of arrogance for the French governor to dictate how they should feel about their enemies. After all, the military commander who first proposed the armistice claimed to have the support of New France's Native allies, yet one Frenchman admitted that 'he deceived himself, if he really thought so.'[20] Asserting their prerogative to define the limits of the French–Indian alliance, these groups rejected French efforts to force mediation. During the following decade, they would slowly draw the French into renewed, and far more destructive, war with the Fox, limiting the expansive reach of French imperialism through strategic violence.

The 1716 treaty acknowledged the symbolic power of slaves to end French–Fox bloodshed. But if slaves offered the greatest hope for peace, they could also spark renewed warfare. The French had received scores of Fox slaves during the previous four years. By accepting these slaves, French colonists had symbolically acknowledged their enmity against the Fox, implicitly committing military support to their allies in future disputes.

Visiting Montreal two years later, a Fox delegation begged the French to 'dissipate the fear which still Possessed them, by restoring to them some of their Children—that is, some of their people who were Slaves among the French'.[21] Beginning in 1718 every recorded complaint made by the Fox against the French and their Native allies centred on the return of Fox captives, the most significant issue perpetuating the Fox Wars into subsequent decades.

Despite clear instructions to the contrary—issued repeatedly from Versailles and Quebec—French colonists retained and continued to acquire new Fox slaves following the 1716 peace accords. Emanating from every level of Canadian society, the French demand for slaves offered ample opportunity for Ottawa, Ojibwa, and Illinois warriors to capture Fox villagers and offer them to the French, thereby driving a wedge between these erstwhile allies. Over time the French enslavement of Fox would erode whatever hope for peace existed in 1716, sparking the second, and far more destructive, phase of the Fox Wars.

New France's appetite for Fox slaves originated in the bloody battles of 1712, when the French and their allies captured large numbers of Fox women and children. Many French officers and merchants returned from the Fox campaigns with young captives. From 1713 to 1716, about 80 Fox slaves appear in the colony's parish and court records, belonging to as many as 60 different French families. The actual number of slaves and slaveholders was certainly much higher, given the improbability that every slave and every master appear in surviving records.[22]

These Fox slaves served families in Montreal and Quebec, as well as in smaller seigneurial villages. In 1714, for example, a Sulpician priest baptized a young Fox slave, named François-Michel, who belonged to Jean Baptiste Bissot de Vincennes. Vincennes had been second-in-command in Detroit during the 1712 siege of the Fox. During the final stages of the standoff, a Fox emissary addressed him: 'I will surrender myself; answer me at once, my Father, and tell me if there is quarter for our families. . . .' Vincennes responded with a promise that he knew he could not keep. According to the French report, 'Sieur de Vincennes called out to them that he granted their lives and safety.' When the Fox surrendered, and slaughter ensued, Vincennes gave his own sort of quarter to this young boy, who became his slave in Montreal.[23]

In another example Pierre Legardeur de Repentigny baptized his Fox slave, Mathurine, in 1713. Repentigny, a captain in the colonial troops, participated actively in several western campaigns. The potential to return home with slaves gave French military officers a personal stake in supporting violence against the Fox, but lower-ranking soldiers also benefited by obtaining Fox slaves. In Batiscan, for example, Marie Catherine Rivard-Loranger appears either as owner or godmother to several slaves from 1713 to 1716. Her son, a **voyageur** among the Illinois who fought in the early battles of the Fox Wars, returned with the Fox slaves in 1714.[24]

Occasionally, voyageurs and merchants connected to the war also obtained Fox slaves. Michel Bisaillon exemplifies this type of trader. He used his long-standing trade relationships with Illinois Indians to mobilize their support for French attacks during the first phase of the war. As a result he acquired several Fox captives that he subsequently sold as slaves to Montreal merchants. In 1717, for example, he sold a young female slave to René Bourassa, dit La Ronde for 400 livres.[25]

Many other merchants active in Detroit also acquired slaves during the early Fox campaigns, including the well-positioned Pierre Lestage, who garnered at least two young Fox slaves, Ignace and Marie-Madeleine. The children's godfather, Ignace Gamelin, also traded Indian slaves in Montreal and Detroit, acquiring one for his own household by early 1714. Pierre Biron, who supplied goods to the military during the Fox Wars, obtained a young Fox girl as his slave the same year. Called Marie-Joachim, she would serve as a house slave for nearly 20 years until her death in 1733.[26]

Many well-placed French officials also received their share of Fox slaves during the first four years of the conflict. François-Marie Bouat, a powerful Montreal judge, baptized his Fox slave, Marguerite, in 1713. In 1713 François, a Fox boy, was baptized as the slave of Augustin Lemoyne, with highly visible and powerful godparents: Charles Lemoyne de Longueuil and Catherine de Ramezay, daughter of Montreal's governor and future interim governor of the colony. Even more visible was Guillaume Gaillard, a member of New France's Superior Council and Governor Vaudreuil's close associate, who had purchased at least three Fox slaves by 1716 to serve in his home as domestics.[27]

[The] growing rift between the French and the Fox weakened French claims of the Fox as allies, subtly but steadily edging them out of the alliance just as the other Native allies had hoped. To deepen the divide, allied Indians continued to attack Fox villages in violation of the 1716 peace agreement, trading or giving slaves to French officers as tokens of alliance. The Illinois, especially, raided the Fox for captives and sold them as slaves to their French allies.[28]

Fox men, women, and children captured in these raids continued to stream into Montreal even after the French-brokered peace. Many colonists buying these slaves either hid their purchases or identified their slaves as *panis*, rather than Fox, Indians. For instance, when Joseph-Laurent Lefebvre bought a Fox slave in 1722, the notary initially recorded that she was a Fox Indian. In an apparent attempt to conceal the slave's origins, the notary then boldly struck out *Renard* and replaced it with *panise* (feminine of *panis*). With diplomats clamouring for the return of Fox prisoners, a notarized acknowledgment of a Fox slave's origins could undermine the slave owner's claim to legal possession. Despite obvious French efforts to obscure the identity of Fox slaves, nearly 100 more appear in New France's colonial records following the 1716 treaty. The distribution of these slaves, like those captured before the peace negotiations, suggests a pervasive acceptance of and demand for the enslavement of Fox Indians.[29]

These slaves performed many tasks, including domestic service, urban skilled labour, and even fieldwork. During the 1710s, for example, the tiny village of Batiscan acquired a disproportionate number of Fox slaves, who were employed in a hemp-growing scheme supported by the colony's intendant, Michel Bégon. Other Fox slaves worked on Montreal's riverfront, loading and unloading canoes for western trade. Most were house servants, many of them selling for as much as 400 livres—a third of a French officer's annual salary.[30]

During the early 1720s, the Fox four times requested French intervention to prevent the Illinois and other allied Indians from attacking their villages for captives. Finally, their patience grew thin and they retaliated with great force. Vaudreuil conceded that 'the [Fox] were less in the wrong than the Ilinois for the war they have had together. . . .' The Fox, he explained to the commandant of Illinois country, 'claim to have Grievances against the Illinois, because the latter detain their prisoners. I am convinced that, if they were to give satisfaction to the [Fox] on this point, it would not be difficult to induce The latter to make peace.' Although Vaudreuil owned at least two Fox slaves from these very attacks, and saw many others serving his neighbours, he blamed the Illinois rather than the French colonists who made slave raiding so advantageous.[31]

By 1724 the Fox made it clear to the French that they would resume intense warfare with the Illinois and their French defenders unless Fox captives were returned. 'They Are indignant,' wrote Constant Le Marchand de Lignery, 'because, when peace was made in 1716, they sent the illinois back Their prisoners while The illinois did not return Theirs, As had been Agreed upon in The treaty.'[32]

To placate the Fox and their allies, Vaudreuil proposed an inspection of Illinois villages to determine if they held any Fox prisoners. Reporting the results of the inspection conducted in 1725, a French officer flatly declared, 'Our Illinois have no Slaves belonging to the Foxes.' An Illinois chief, Anakipita, offered a similarly calculated denial: '[The Fox chief] says that his Slaves have not been given back to him. Where are they? Is there a single one in our villages?' Anakipita and his French counterpart spoke a literal truth to conceal Illinois guilt in the Fox attacks. As Vaudreuil knew the disputed Fox slaves were already in French hands, far from the Illinois communities that had initially seized them.[33]

Even at this late date, the Fox still seemed willing to return to the French alliance if they could secure the return of their captives. In 1726 the Fox again approached the French, this time at Green Bay, begging for the governor to mediate these disputes. French authorities, wishing to expand trade in the area, were only too happy to oblige.[34]

Yet by this time hundreds of French colonists had given a decade of support to anti-Fox slave raids, rewarding their allies' violence with valuable goods and often with military support for the expeditions themselves. Many French post commanders had private interests in the slave trade, placing them in a poor position to negotiate a peace. And both of New France's governors who dealt with the Fox problem—Philippe de Rigaud de Vaudreuil and Charles de Beauharnois—owned a host of Indian slaves, including several Fox. Despite their need to avoid warfare among potential allies, French officials supported the Illinois, Ottawas, Ojibwa, and Hurons against the Fox.

Faced with continuing raids in violation of French assurances, and never receiving the promised return of their captives, Fox warriors finally abandoned their efforts to secure a French alliance, declaring open war on New France and all its Indian allies. In the spring of 1727 they murdered a party of seven French soldiers, launching a series of attacks. These new raids bred deep and mutual resentment among the French, their allies, and the Fox, finally putting an end to French–Fox efforts to expand the Upper Country alliance.[35]

The warfare that followed brutalized the Fox. Convinced by western post commanders to pursue the war wholeheartedly, French authorities invested soldiers and money to crush a people they had once called children. From 1728 to 1731, French–Indian war parties scored a series of victories over Fox warriors, but each triumph proved ephemeral, followed shortly by a Fox resurgence. Frustrated and facing pressure from his superiors, Beauharnois issued an order for his soldiers and his allies to 'kill [the Fox] without thinking of making a single Prisoner, so as not to leave one of the race alive in the upper Country'. In the process, Beauharnois hoped to maintain the supply of slaves that had been one of the Fox Wars' greatest benefits to his colony (and to his own household: he owned at least eight Fox slaves). 'If [the Sieur de Villiers] is obliged to exterminate the Men,' he added, 'the women and Children who remain will be brought here, Especially the Children.'[36]

This bloody contest exacted a costly toll from the Fox, who dwindled from a population of several thousand in the 1710s to only a few hundred by the mid-1730s. Yet, this victory came at a high price for the French. Not only did thousands of men, women, and children die in the conflict, but the Fox's retaliation limited French commercial and imperial expansion, blocking New France's westward reach just as its allies had hoped to do.[37]

During the height of the fighting, New France's intendant, Gilles Hocquart, sent a letter and a gift to his friend, a Monsieur de Belamy, in La Rochelle, France. The letter contained 'news of the defeat of the Foxes' by the French and their Native allies, detailing the heroics of the French officer who had led the charge. Sent on the same ship, Hocquart's gift supplied tangible evidence of the news. He instructed the captain of the ship to 'remit to M. de Belamy a Fox slave' who was on board.[38]

In a similar move, Beauharnois, the colony's governor, apparently sent a Fox slave to his brother, François, who served as the intendant of Rochefort, France. As he had done with at least one African slave from Saint Domingue, Beauharnois likely

Slave of Fox Indians or Népissingué slave, ca. 1732, anonymous. (Estampes et photographie, OF-4(A)-FOL, Bibliothèque nationale de France.

registered his slave with French authorities, claiming that he brought the slave to France 'to have him instructed in the Catholic religion and to have him learn a trade'. Rather than returning to the Americas with improved skills, however, Beauharnois's Fox slave remained in France until his death, eventually encountering an artist who rendered his dubious likeness.[39]

Like these unfortunate survivors of the Fox Wars, hundreds of slaves entered New France as tokens of alliance between that colony and its Native allies. These slaves permeated, and powerfully influenced, the history of the Fox Wars. When the Fox wanted to forge an alliance with their attackers in 1712 [and when they made peace in 1716], they offered slaves. When Fox diplomats pressured the French for greater support, it was invariably to recover those of their nation captured by enemies. Perhaps most significantly, when Indian allies perceived that the French wanted them to embrace the hated Fox, they used slave raids to register their dissatisfaction with the French, defining the limits of alliance through strategic violence.

This violence allowed New France's Indian allies to exert their control over the alliance system, blocking French expansion whenever it threatened to strengthen their enemies. When French officials sought to bring the Fox into the alliance, their allies fought what they perceived to be a betrayal of their friendship. By raiding the Fox for slaves, and then placing these slaves into French hands, Illinois, Ottawa, Ojibwa, and Huron warriors alienated their Fox enemies from their French allies, drawing the two sides into war.

By shifting the angle of vision from French imperial aims to the local objectives of their Indian allies, it becomes difficult to view intercultural relations in binary terms, with Euro-Americans on one side, Indians on the other, and a world of mutual invention in between on a middle ground. This was a much more complicated world where fault lines formed between peoples with competing interests but not necessarily between those with incomprehensible cultures. Through a process of negotiation that White describes so elegantly, Vaudreuil and Pemoussa found a common ground on which to work out their differences. Yet the relatively similar cultures of the Fox and the Ottawas could not.

The Fox Wars also highlight important divisions within the French and Algonquian societies that generally constitute the units of analysis in the history of the Upper Country. Personal interest, overlapping spheres of authority, and local demands combined to make French imperial policy highly complex and difficult to predict. In the

1710s and 1720s, for example, the closer one got to Versailles the more likely one would be to support generous mediation with the Fox. Driven by their own set of interests, post commanders in the Upper Country clamoured for war, whereas governors and crown officials ordered peace.

'Algonquian' offers an even more problematic western bracket for the middle ground. The very fact of war between the Fox and their neighbours calls into question the presumed unity of the region's Algonquian-speaking peoples. Despite French insistence that Algonquian peoples shared the bonds of kinship as children of a French father, the Natives themselves had other ideas. When Pemoussa expressed his concurrence with the French vision of inclusive Algonquian kinship, his would-be brothers denied his claims and violently enforced the divisions they wished to maintain.

By doing so these Indians ensured that they, rather than the French, would determine the limits of the Upper Country alliance. They also defined its character. But if this alliance was 'largely Algonquian in form and spirit', that is not because it reflected an Algonquian culture of mediation rather than a French culture of 'force and obedience'.[40] Such false dichotomies obscure the intimate connections between warfare and alliance that placed the slave trade at the heart of the Fox Wars. Like Marguerite-Geneviève—a Fox slave serving a French governor who wanted peace with her people—all Fox captives embodied the tensions between mediation and violence that riddled both Algonquian and French societies. During the Fox Wars and beyond, Upper Country Indians used these tensions to their advantage, compelling their French father to accept their enemies as his own.

Primary Document

2.   Baptisms, 21 September 1713[41]

B Marg Marguerite Guichard	On the twentieth of September of the year seventeen hundred and thirteen was baptized marie marguerite nee [. . .] daughter of jean guichard, master surgeon, and marguerite gerbau, his wife. the godfather was mr. françois poulain and the godmother miss marguerite la morille daughter of [. . .] la morille [. . .].
	[signatures] Guichard [. . .] Poulin marguerite la morille Belmont priest
B Ignace Lamage	On the twenty-first of september of the year seventeen hundred and thirteen was baptized ignace lamage, roughly seven years old, from the fox nation living in the service of mr. Lestage a town merchant. The godfather was ignace gamelin, the godmother miss françoise le maître wife of mr. guillemin. [signatures] gamelin
	[. . .] guillimin Belmont pr.

B Marie Medelene Lamagelle	On the twenty-first of september of the year seventeen hundred and thirteen was baptized marie madelene lamagelle, roughly seven years old, of the fox nation also living in the service of the aforementioned mr. Lestage. The godfather was mr. Ignace gamelan. The godmother Marie Trudeau, wife of mr. Arnault. [signatures] Guillimin Marie [. . .] Belmont pr.
B Mathurine Lamagelle	On the twenty-first of september of the year seventeen hundred and thirteen was baptized Mathurine Lamagelle, roughly seven years old of the fox nation, living in the service of mr. Serapentigny. The godfather was mr. charles guillimin town merchant. The godmother mrs. agathe de [. . .] Wife of mr. serapentigny. [signatures] Agathe [. . .] Guillimin Belmont pr.
B Marg Lamagelle	On the twenty-first of september of the year seventeen hundred and thirteen was baptized Marguerite Lamagelle, roughly seven years old, of the fox nation, living in the service of mr. charles de [. . .] The god father was mr. charles guillimin, the godmother mrs. Agathe de [. . .]. [signatures] Agathe de [. . .] Guillimin Belmont pr.
B Marg Lamagelle	On the twenty-first of september of the year seventeen hundred and thirteen was baptized Marguerite Lamagelle, roughly six years old, of the fox nation, living in the service of mr. Boriat. The godfather was françois le pallieur, son of Mr. Michel Le pallieur. The godmother Catherine Le pallieur also daughter of the aforementioned Mr. Le pallieur. [signatures] Lepallieur [. . .] le pallieur Belmont priest

Secondary Source

3. The Divided Ground: Upper Canada, New York, and the Iroquois Six Nations, 1783–1815

Alan Taylor

In recent years, historians have paid increasing attention to borders and borderlands as fluid sites of both national formation and local contestation. At their peripheries, nations and empires assert their power and define their identity with no certainty of success. Nation-making and border-making are inseparably intertwined. Nations and empires, however, often reap defiance from peoples uneasily bisected by the imposed boundaries. This process has been especially tangled in the Americas where empires and republics projected their ambitions onto a geography occupied and defined by Indians. Imperial or national visions ran up against the tangled complexities of interdependent peoples, both Native and invader. Indeed, the contest of rival Euro-American regimes presented risky opportunities for Native peoples to play off the rivals to preserve Native autonomy and enhance their circumstances.[42]

At Paris in 1783, British and American negotiators concluded the War of the American Revolution, recognizing the independence of the United States while reserving the Canadian provinces to the British Empire. American independence and Canadian dependence required a new boundary between the young republic and the lingering empire. The negotiators ran that boundary through the Great Lakes and the rivers between them, including, most significantly, the 36-mile-long Niagara River.[43]

Along the Niagara River, the Iroquois **Six Nations** clung to their position as autonomous keepers of a perpetual and open-ended borderland, a place of exchange and interdependence. Recognizing their own weakness in numbers and technology, the Natives sought renewed strength in their geographic and political position between the Americans and the British. By exploiting the lingering rivalry between the republic and the empire, the Iroquois Six Nations hoped to remain intermediate and autonomous rather than divided and absorbed by the rivals. In 1790 the Six Nations spokesman Red Jacket explained to the Americans, 'that we may pass from one to the other unmolested . . . we wish to be under the protection of the thirteen States as well as of the British.' A year later, he reminded the Americans, '[we] do not give ourselves entirely up to them [the British], nor lean altogether upon you. We mean to stand upright as we live between both.'[44]

Before the American Revolution, the six Iroquoian nations sustained a loose confederation of villages located south of Lake Ontario and east of Lake Erie, within the territory claimed by the colony of New York. From east to west, the Six Nations were the Mohawk (in the Mohawk Valley), the Oneida and the Tuscarora (both south of Lake Oneida), the Cayuga and Onondaga (in the Finger Lakes region), and the especially numerous Seneca (in the Genesee, Allegheny, and Niagara valleys). Culturally similar, they spoke kindred languages of the Iroquoian family and their population aggregated to about 9,000 on the eve of the war. Occupying and cultivating the most fertile pockets of alluvial soil, they reserved most of their broad hinterland as a forest for hunting and gathering. Of course, American settlers coveted that vast hinterland, which they regarded as wasted upon Indians and properly rededicated to their own farm-making.[45]

The War of the American Revolution proved catastrophic for the Six Nations. Under severe pressure from both sides, the Iroquois divided. Most of the Oneida and some of the Tuscarora assisted the American rebels, but the great majority of the Iroquois allied with the British as their best bet for resisting expansionist settlers. Whatever their alliance, the Six Nations all suffered devastating raids that destroyed almost all their villages, especially in 1779. The Oneida fled eastward, taking refuge at Schenectady within the American frontier, while the other Iroquois shifted northward into British-held Canada or westward to the vicinity of the British fort at Niagara. The raids and flights depopulated a broad and bloody no man's land between Niagara and Schenectady. The violent dislocations also promoted malnutrition and disease, combining to reduce Iroquois numbers by a third, from a pre-war 9,000 to a post-war 6,000.[46]

In 1783, the war-weary British government offered remarkably generous terms and boundaries to the United States. The British retained Canada, but conceded everything south of the Great Lakes to the Americans—although most of that vast region actually belonged to Indians, including the Six Nations. The border even sacrificed the most important British forts along the Great Lakes, including Fort Niagara, at the mouth of the Niagara River, on the southwestern shore of Lake Ontario. For the United States, a nation verging on financial collapse and unable to defend its long frontier against Indian raids, the peace treaty was a stunning victory. But the British-allied Indians suffered a shocking betrayal, for the treaty did not even mention them, treating the Natives as mere pawns passed into American control.[47]

Outraged by the treaty and the new border, the Indians pressured and menaced the British officials, officers, and traders throughout the Great Lakes, threatening violence if they tried to evacuate the border posts. By alarming the post commandants, the Indians compelled a dramatic decision by Major General Frederick Haldimand, the overall British commander in Canada. 'To prevent such a disastrous event as an Indian War', he delayed turning over the forts during the summer of 1783. He also appealed to his superiors in London to render that retention permanent, by obliging the Americans to accept a broad buffer zone, possessed by the Indians.[48]

In early 1784 the home government recognized that the peace treaty line compromised both the security and the economy of Canada. Moreover, with growing signs that the American union of republican state governments was faltering, the British wanted to be in a strong position for the anticipated collapse. Finally, the British government found principled grounds for retaining the posts in two American violations of the peace treaty: the states withheld payment of pre-war debts owed to British merchants and obstructed Loyalist efforts to reclaim their properties confiscated by the state governments.[49]

By catalyzing Britain's policy shift, the Indians demonstrated that they were more than mere pawns in an imperial game. Far from intimidating the Indians, the British troops and their posts functioned as hostages, enabling the Indians to compel concessions. Those concessions exposed the fallacy that an artificial boundary suddenly could separate Native peoples from their British allies.

American leaders, however, continued to nurture a fantasy of division and separation. In October 1784 at Fort Stanwix, American commissioners, backed by armed troops, dictated a one-sided treaty to literally captive Iroquois chiefs. The treaty extorted a four-mile-wide strip along the Niagara River and all Six Nation lands *west* of the mouth of Buffalo Creek, at the southwestern edge of the Niagara corridor. From a federal perspective, the critical matter in 1784 was to affirm that the 1783 peace treaty with the British had established a firm international boundary at Niagara without any intervening Indian borderland. A strip of federal territory prevented the Six Nations from interposing between British Canada and America New York and, instead, separated the Iroquois from their allies, British and Native, to the west. The Niagara strip affirmed that the **Treaty of Paris** made the United States 'the sole sovereign within the limits . . . and therefore the sole power to whom the [Indian] nations living within those limits are hereafter to look up for protection'. Like the 1783 peace treaty boundary, the 1784 Fort Stanwix line was a political concept bluntly imposed on space in defiance of the social geography. Indeed, the line ran through the pre-eminent cluster of Six Nations villages at Buffalo Creek, and (if enforced) dispossessed the Iroquois of their villages at Cattaraugus. Of course, the Six Nations chiefs, in council at Buffalo Creek, promptly disavowed the treaty as dictated by force on their captive delegates.[50]

By keeping the border posts, the British reassured the Indians but angered the Americans: an exchange the British were willing to make during the 1780s. The British shift initiated a state of cold war along the frontier, as their officers annually supplied presents of guns and ammunition to the Indians. The British meant for the well-armed Indians to give the Americans pause in their drive to settle the borderland. To the west, the Indians of the Ohio country employed their British munitions to resist American intrusions and to raid American settlements. In New York, the Iroquois hoped to preserve their lands without entering the war by preserving an armed neutrality instead.

To increase their diplomatic leverage, the Americans worked to defeat the Ohio Indians and to woo the Iroquois Six Nations during the late 1780s and early 1790s. Both efforts became more significant after 1788, when the American states ratified a new constitution endowing their federal government with enhanced revenues and increased power. After 1789, the new federal leaders—principally President George Washington, Secretary at War Henry Knox, and Indian Commissioner Timothy Pickering—hoped to enlist [the Six Nations'] aid in pressuring and inducing the western Indians to make a peace. Embarking on a charm offensive, the federal government treated the Six Nations with diplomatic respect and generous presents. On the New York frontier, at Tioga in November 1790 and Newtown Point in July 1791, Pickering held two conciliatory councils with Six Nations chiefs. In early 1792, federal leaders also hosted a successful visit to Philadelphia by a large delegation of Six Nations chiefs, primarily Seneca, including Red Jacket and Farmer's Brother. That spring, the Washington administration appointed Israel Chapin as the new superintendent for Iroquois affairs. The chiefs regarded Chapin as their asset: as a conduit for information and patronage conveniently placed in their country.[51]

For a few heady years during the early 1790s, Six Nations chiefs found themselves courted by two ardent and generous suitors. To compete with the British Indian agents, Chapin matched their hospitality to chiefs and their annual delivery of presents (mostly cloth, jewellry, gunpowder, and shot). In June 1792 Chapin reported to Pickering: 'be persuaded, Sir, that as long as [the British] are able to make [the Indians] more presents than they receive from us, they will have the most with them.' Recognizing the centrality of property to Euro-Americans, Indians regarded generosity as the measure of their sincerity. In 1794 Chapin explained to his superiors that a recent shipment of clothing 'Confirmed them in opinion of your Friendly Disposition towards them & that your friendship did not appear by words only but by actions also'. The new American attention and presents upped the ante, obliging the British officials to respond in kind. In turn, enhanced British generosity inspired the chiefs to expect even more from the Americans. In April 1794 Chapin sighed, 'The Expences of the Indians increase very fast. Their demands increase with the importance [that] they suppose their friendship to be of to us.'[52]

The presents flowed unevenly to reflect the political geography of Iroquoia. During the mid-1780s, the Six Nations peoples had shifted around in search of the best locations for their post-war villages. About a third (2,000) abandoned their crowded refugee villages near Niagara or Schenectady to rebuild in their former homelands, in the broad intervening territory depopulated by the war. A second group of Iroquois, led by the Mohawk, preferred to withdraw behind the British line to resettle within Canada. Numbering about 1,350, they clustered at Tyendinegea (150) to the north or Grand River (1,200) to the west of the Niagara Valley. The third, and largest, group of Iroquois clung to villages in the Niagara corridor, especially at Buffalo Creek (present Buffalo, New York, at the outlet of Lake Erie into the Niagara River).[53]

The three Iroquois groupings reflected varying degrees of British and American influence. Those within Canada accepted British presents and advice (but never command). Those deep within New York felt the lure of American presents and the pressure of westward-migrating American settlers. By 1790 this Iroquois group was already outnumbered by 14 to 1 by the 29,000 inhabitants of New York's two western-most counties, Ontario and Montgomery. Growing settler numbers gave them an empowering sense of security. On the other hand, as settler fears waned, the local Indian anxiety grew. In April, a federal emissary reported that the Genesee Seneca anticipated a frontier war and 'wished to join the U[nited] States because if they took the other side, they knew that ultimately they must be driven from the[ir] lands'.[54]

If Grand River was too close to the British and Genesee (and points south and east) too nigh the Americans, then Buffalo Creek was just right, equidistant between the two powers, and the special beneficiary of their competing presents. At Buffalo Creek in 1791 Thomas Proctor found the inhabitants 'far better clothed than those Indians were in the towns at a greater distance, owing entirely to the immediate intercourse they have with the British'. The Buffalo Creek chiefs, who included Red Jacket and Farmer's Brother, recognized the benefits of their middle position in both diplomacy and geography.[55]

That middling position eroded after September 1794, when an American army defeated the hostile western Indians at Fallen Timbers in the Ohio country. The British lost credibility and influence when their troops failed to help the retreating Indians. That November, in London the British government also concluded a treaty with American emissary John Jay, resolving the lingering differences of the post-war era. In the **Jay Treaty**, the British accepted the 1783 peace treaty boundary through the Great Lakes and promised to surrender the border posts during the summer of 1796—which promise they kept. In an important concession to Native interests, the treaty's third article guaranteed the right of 'the Indians dwelling on either side of the said boundary line' freely to cross and recross with their own possessions.[56]

The defeat of the western Indians and the Jay Treaty cost the Six Nations much of their leverage with the Americans. News of the battle at Fallen Timbers reached Canandaigua in western New York in October 1794, where and when Timothy Pickering and Israel Chapin were holding another council with the chiefs of the Six Nations. The news undercut the most defiant chiefs, and strengthened the proponents of compromise, leading in early November to a comprehensive treaty that confirmed the ascendancy of American influence over the Indians within New York State. Preferring comity to confrontation, Pickering made important concessions. He rescinded the most controversial part of the cession extorted at Fort Stanwix in 1784; the United States relinquished its claims to the lands in the vicinity of Buffalo Creek and Cattaraugus: the southern half of the strip along the Niagara River and the Lake Erie Shore as far as the Pennsylvania border. He made that concession to secure a tract more immediately important to the United States: the northwestern 'triangle' of Pennsylvania on the shores of Lake Erie. The 'Erie Triangle' gave Americans access to that lake as it potentially cut off the Six Nations from direct communication with the Indians of the Ohio country. The Treaty of Canandaigua enabled Pennsylvanians to develop settlements in the triangle and permitted the federal government to erect a fort to guard the harbour at Presque Isle.[57]

In rapid succession, the Battle of Fallen Timbers (September 1794), the Canandaigua Treaty (November 1794), the Jay Treaty (November 1794), and the American occupation of the Erie Triangle (summer 1795), set new bounds to the Six Nations. In August of 1796, American troops garrisoned Fort Niagara after the British withdrew across the river to the eastern shore. In early September, Israel Chapin Jr (his late father's successor as federal agent for the Iroquois) noted a new and demoralizing sense of confinement among the Six Nations. He anticipated the Native's growing sense of weakness, as the American advent at Niagara initiated two decades of tension over the proper meaning of the border. The Indians never went meekly, but the terms of the debate kept shifting against their autonomy, as each new confrontation exacted more concessions.[58]

On 21 September, the new American commandant at Niagara, Captain James Bruff, held a council with the Six Nations to explain their new situation within an American boundary: 'Lines are fixed, and so strongly marked between us [the British and the Americans], that they cannot be mistaken . . .'. Citing the boundary, Bruff announced new restrictions on the Six Nations. He demanded that the Iroquois cease their profitable practice of tracking British deserters for British rewards within the new American line. Ignoring the Jay Treaty, Bruff also insisted that the chiefs could no longer send delegations of chiefs and copies of American speeches across the border to British agents without first obtaining his permission. And the captain discouraged their expectations that the Americans would continue the British practice of freely feeding Indian visitors to Fort Niagara. Bruff's speech alarmed the Six Nations as an assault on three long-standing rights—rewards for deserters, open communication with both empires, and official hospitality to visiting chiefs.[59]

The Six Nations did not acquiesce quietly. In his pointed reply, Red Jacket argued that the Six Nations remained an autonomous people situated *between* the British and the Americans:

> You are a cunning People without Sincerity, and not to be trusted, for after making Professions of your Regard, and saying every thing favorable to us, you . . . tell us that our Country is within the lines of the States. This surprises us, for we had thought our Lands were our own, not within your Boundaries, but joining the British, and between you and them. . . .

Red Jacket understood that the Six Nations lost their sovereignty if the American boundary line coincided with the limits of Upper Canada. Bending, but not capitulating, the Six Nations dwelling in the Niagara corridor stopped tracking British deserters, but persisted in communicating with, and taking presents from, British officials at Fort George.[60]

Long the keepers of a broad and porous borderland, the Iroquois of the Niagara corridor now confronted a double set of restricting boundaries: first, the international border along the Niagara River and, second, the private property lines demarcating Indian reservations as enclaves within a settlers' world. The two sets of lines were interdependent, as the assertion of the first facilitated the American pressure that established the second—which, then, reinforced the meaning of the nearby international boundary. Emboldened by Fort Niagara in American hands, settlers pressed across the Genesee River into westernmost New York by the hundreds after 1796.[61]

Unable to keep the intruders out, the Seneca chiefs felt obliged to negotiate with land speculators. Making the best of a bad situation, the leading chiefs (including Red Jacket) secured private payments and future pensions in return for facilitating the 1797 Treaty of Big Tree with the Holland Land Company. The Seneca surrendered almost all of their remaining lands, holding back 11 reservations, totalling about 200,000 acres, and including Buffalo Creek, Cattaraugus, and Allegheny. They received a principal of $100,000 vested in American bank stock, which yielded an annual payment of $6,000. This initially seemed impressive until divided among 1,500 Seneca to provide a modest $4 apiece per year. The Cayuga and Onondago dwelling in western New York got no payments and no secure reservation, which led many to move across the border to resettle at Grand River.[62]

The new boundary also curtailed the power of the Six Nations freely to trade to the British side of the border. In May 1802 at Buffalo Creek an American customs collector seized the goods of a petty trader, Mrs Elisabeth Thompson, of Fort Erie village on the western shore of the Niagara. Israel Chapin Jr characterized Thompson as a 'lame Widow woman, who . . . has been fiddling among the Six Nations for a livelihood'. She appealed to both Indian sympathy and self-interest. Critical of the cold competitiveness of the invading society, Natives liked the opportunity to patronize a poor white woman—especially because she charged lower prices than did the American traders. Those traders complained that Thompson violated American customs regulations in crossing the new border to conduct her old trade at Buffalo Creek. Their complaint induced the customs collector to act—and the Indians to react. They broke open the government warehouse, liberated her goods, and spirited them to safety across the river in Upper Canada.[63]

The Seneca insisted that their sovereignty gave them control over trade into their reservation, but the new American secretary of war, Henry Dearborn, trumped that sovereignty with his nation's control over the boundary. Denouncing the 'glaring outrage on the laws of the United States', Dearborn demanded the Seneca pledge never again to interfere with American customs officers. He threatened to withhold the value of the liberated goods from their annuity payment. Given the Indian dependence on that annuity for their clothing, the chiefs formally apologized for their action, grudgingly conceding that the boundary gave federal control over their trade with Canada.[64]

While constraining the Indians, the boundary empowered unscrupulous white settlers to prey on Native property. Between 1805 and 1810 the Tuscarora dwelling near Fort Niagara counted 17 cattle and 2 horses stolen by settlers. The thieves exploited the nearby border to convey the rustled animals into Upper Canada for ready sale beyond the jurisdiction of American magistrates. Worse still, American authorities and missionaries gradually and reluctantly concluded that it would be easier to move the Indians west than to protect their reservations from their most ruthless neighbours. Indian removal seemed a humanitarian measure to New York's leaders—if not to the Indians, who preferred the enforcement of their **treaty rights**.[65]

In 1802 some of those aggressive whites also endowed the state of New York with a murder case to assert its legal jurisdiction over the Seneca. On 25 July 1802, a Seneca known to settlers as 'Seneca George' got into a drunken fracas outside a tavern in the frontier village of New Amsterdam (now Buffalo) adjacent to the Buffalo

Creek reservation. Pursued and beaten, George pulled a knife to stab two white men, one fatally. The Seneca chiefs reluctantly surrendered George for incarceration in the Ontario County jail at Canandaigua, pending trial. In general, Natives dreaded prolonged imprisonment as worse than a violent death. They also distinguished, in Red Jacket's words, murders 'committed in cool blood' from killings while intoxicated, which they blamed on the alcohol rather than the drinker.[66]

The Seneca chiefs' spokesman, Red Jacket, protested George's arrest and trial as incompatible with the Seneca standing as a sovereign people:

> Did we ever make a treaty with the state of New-York, and agree to conform to its laws? No. We are independent of the state of New-York. It was the will of the Great Spirit to create us different in color; we have different laws, habits, and customs from the white people. We shall never consent that the government of this state shall try our brother.

Citing the several murders of Seneca by whites that had been resolved by giving presents, rather than by demanding executions, Red Jacket insisted, 'We now crave the same privilege in making restitution to you, that you adopted toward us in a similar situation.'[67]

Governor George Clinton replied that settling a murder with presents was 'repugnant' to the laws of New York, which he meant to enforce throughout its bounds. The national government also disappointed the Seneca by declining to intervene.[68]

At Canandaigua on 22 February 1803, a trial jury convicted Seneca George of murder, establishing New York's criminal jurisdiction over the Iroquois. But neither the jurors nor the governor and legislators of New York thought it wise to complete the process with an execution. The county grand jurors petitioned the governor to suspend the execution and call on the legislature for a pardon. Declaring that George acted in self-defence the grand jurors suggested that both 'policy' and 'justice' called for a pardon. The secretary of war, Henry Dearborn, agreed. On 5 March, Governor Clinton suspended the execution and recommended a pardon because of 'extenuating circumstances . . .' and 'considerations of a political nature . . .'. A week later the legislators pardoned Seneca George, with the proviso that he leave the state permanently. Having established their legal precedent, the New Yorkers could afford to be magnanimous. Once again, the Iroquois compelled a compromise from the new keepers of the border—but every compromise marked a further shift in the balance of power in the Americans' favour.[69]

During the August 1802 meeting with the Seneca chiefs in Albany, the governor pressed for another land cession: a one-mile-wide strip of shoreline beside the Niagara River, as well as the islands in the middle. The New Yorkers wanted to promote commerce along the river [and] facilitate a new federal fort at Black Rock, at the mouth of Buffalo Creek, as a counter to Fort Erie on the British shore.[70]

The New York state Indian commissioners secured half of their prize—the shoreline but not the islands. The Seneca, [Governor Clinton] insisted, accepted that the Black Rock fort would serve 'for our mutual protection and defense'. By intruding a fort between Buffalo Creek and the British line, the Americans meant to divide and isolate the two great centres of the Six Nations—Grand River and Buffalo Creek—in anticipation of a future war with the British.[71]

That conflict came in June 1812, when the United States declared war on Great Britain and prepared to invade Canada. The federal Indian agent, Erastus Granger, bluntly warned the Buffalo Creek Indians that they risked extermination if they helped the British, but he promised security if they kept out of the war. Granger observed, 'The United States are strong and powerful; you are few in numbers and weak, but as our friends we consider you and your women and children under our protection.'[72]

The Buffalo Creek chiefs agreed to send a delegation to Grand River to preach a Six Nations unity in neutrality. The delegated chiefs sadly conceded that they spoke from a position of weakness:

> The gloomy Day, foretold by our ancients, has at last arrived; —the Independence and Glory of the Five Nations has departed from us; —We find ourselves in the hands of two powerful Nations, who can crush us when they please. . . .

In reply, the Grand River spokesman, John Norton, recognized the plight of the Buffalo Creek Indians: 'The Americans have gained possession of all your Country, excepting the small part which you have reserved. They have enveloped you:—it is out of your power to assist us,— because in doing so,—you would hazard the Destruction of your families.' To defend their autonomy, the Grand River Indians would uphold their alliance with the British: 'If the King is attacked, we must support him, we are sure that such conduct is honourable.'[73]

Division and war proved disastrous for the Six Nations. In 1812 and early 1813 the Grand River warriors helped repel the American invasions of the Niagara Peninsula. Frustrated American officers broke their former promises and cajoled the Buffalo Creek warriors into joining the war. Despite their best efforts, the Six Nation warriors could not always avoid combat with one another, in a war that served none of them. After the Americans and the British made peace in late 1814, both empires viewed the Indians as obstacles to economic development. Once keen to keep the Iroquois securely within their boundaries, after 1815 New York's leaders pressed for their removal west.[74]

From the end of the American Revolution in 1783 through the War of 1812, the Americans contended to realize and master the boundary imagined by the peace treaty that concluded the first conflict. For the Americans, securing that boundary required subordinating the Iroquois Six Nations and discouraging their ties with the British side. The process was reciprocal, for once the Americans gained a secure perch on the Niagara River, they could consolidate their ascendancy over the Indians by restricting movement, regulating trade, demanding land cessions, and enforcing criminal jurisdiction. Formerly, in Richard White's phrase, 'a middle ground', Iroquoia became a divided ground—with harsh consequences for the Native people who had so long and so ably resisted that development against overwhelming odds. The diminution of Iroquoia served to consolidate the United States as a nation-state with pretensions to a secure northern border. In Iroquoia, as throughout North America, the limitation of Native peoples within the boundaries of nation and the subordinate lines of reservations helped constitute the United States.[75]

That said, Six Nations people never accepted their division by boundary or the denial of Native sovereignty implicit in that boundary. To this day, Indian activists defend

Article III of the Jay Treaty, which guarantees their rights freely to pass and repass over the international boundary. During the 1920s, restrictive American immigration and naturalization laws led Six Nations people, under the leadership of Chief Clinton Rickard (Tuscarora), to organize the Indian Defense League of America. Winning a test case in 1927 (*McCandless v. Diabi*) the Indian Defense League instituted a celebratory march across the border at the Niagara Falls Bridge, a march that has become an annual tradition. In 1995 Chief Rickard's granddaughter, Jolene Rickard, wrote that the march gave her 'a sense of freedom, [of] my inherent right to move freely in Iroquoian territories and that is what the fight is all about for Indian people . . .'. The Native challenge to boundary restrictions suggests that the Canadian–American border will remain a contested ground—with new possibilities of fluidity, as well as renewed pressures from officials for greater closure.[76]

Primary Document

4.   Speech by Red Jacket, 21 November 1790

On 21 November 1790, Seneca Chief Red Jacket met with Timothy Pickering, the US government's commissioner to the Iroquois (Six Nations), to discuss alleged fraudulent behaviour on the part of land speculators and mistreatment of the Seneca at the hands of the US government.[77]

Br. [Brother] Now you begin to hear the situation of our lands. Mr. Phelps and D. Barton[78] came up to make one the fire again at Canadasago. After they were come then Mr. Phelps sped [?] on to Niagara and sent to our old friend Col. [Colonel] Butler[79] whom he met at a tavern home of Col. B. [. . .] at Canadasago [. . .]. He said that he came to kindle a fire at Canadasago at which then [*sic*] Col B. told him that Canadasago was not a fit place at which to kindle a fire and that our custom was to kindle a fire at our castle. Col B. told him that he thought he might build a fire at Buf. [Buffalo] Creek[80] and if he did that he believed he would attend the treaty. Mr. Phelps expressed his fear that if he held the treaty there he wld. [would] meet with some difficulty. Then L. [Little] Billy[81] and the Heap of Dogs[82] went to Canadasago, took Mr. Phelps by the hand and led him to our Council Fire at Buffaloe [*sic*] Creek. All these people here know what speech Mr. Phelps put on – (he points to F. [Farmer's] Brother[83] and Billy) these went to Canadasago to see what the Council was. These all know and Mr. Street[84] knows that Mr. Phelps held up a long paper with a seal as big as my hand.

When he opened his mind to us we took it hard. We wanted to keep a large piece of land but it was not in our power. Mr. Street (pointing to him on the Bench) you know very well a treaty was held all night to fix on the boundary and the price of the land. These men (Mr. Smith, J. Obeil,[85] Little Billy, Heap of Dogs, [. . .] and I were there) know very well that the proposal was that Mr. Ph. wd. give 10,000 dollars for the purchase and 500 dollars annual rent. That was the agreement made that night. The bargain was not finished till morning, and just as we went out of the house the first of morn. we sought for persons to draw it in writing. The persons chosen were Mr. Kirkland,[86] Col B., and Capt. [Captain] Chandler [?]. Mr. Street was not then present. After this the

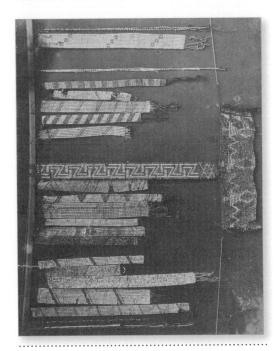

Wampum belts of the Fire Keepers of the Six Nations Indians, 1872. (Library and Archives Canada, PA-124105.)

Red Jacket, Seneca war chief. (Library of Congress Prints and Photographs Division Washington, D.C.)

bargain being completed Mr. Street took our papers with him to Niagara and last summer a year ago we came to Canadaraga expecting to receive 10,000 dollars but then we found we had but 5,000 to receive. When we discovered the fraud we had in mind to apply to see if the matter cd. [could] not be rectified. For when we took the money and shared it every one here knows we had but about a dollar a piece for all the country. Mr. Street you know very well that all our lands come to [. . .] but the price of a few [. . .] of tobacco. Gentlemen who stand by do not think hard of what has been said. At the time of the treaty twenty branches wd. not buy half a loaf of bread. Further, when the [. . .] home there was not a [. . .] about us [?]. The last spring again Genrl. [General] St. Claire[87] stretched out his hand to us to give a little fire at Big Flats[88] and then I had a little talk with him and finding we had but a shilling a piece to use we did find him to [. . .] his hand again. This is all we have to have to say at this time. Mr. Street knows how hard it was for us to part with our land. And this we have said because we wish the President to know how we have been treated.

Now B. the 13 States you must open yr. [your] ears. You heard what has happened respecting our lands. You told us from this time the Ch. of Fr. [Chain of Friendship] wld. Be brightened. Now B. we have begun to brighten the Ch. of Fr. and we will follow the path of our for fas [forefathers]. We will take this paper then we may sit easy and choose where and how large our seats shd. [should] be. The reason we find this necessary is that the president over all the 13 colonies may make our seats easy. We do it that the chain of friendship may be brightened with the 13 states as well as with the British; that we may pass from one to the other unmolested. B. this is what your [. . .] chiefs and warriors have to say to you, relative to brightening the ch. of frshp. We wish to be under the protection of the 13 states as well as of the British.

Questions for Consideration

1. What role did France's Aboriginal allies—the Illinois, Ottawas, Ojibwa, Miami, and Hurons—play in the enslavement of the Fox in New France?
2. Why did the Fox become the implacable enemy of the Aboriginal allies, with whom they shared a language and (to some degree) a culture? Why were the French allies of the Illinois, Ottawa, Ojibwa, Miami, and Huron allied with the French against the Fox Nation?
3. How many of the people listed in the baptismal register are identified as being from the Fox Nation? What roles did these individuals occupy in society? Why did they have these positions?
4. Why did the Six Nations resist the imposition of the British North America–United States border in the Niagara region?
5. How successful was Six Nations' resistance to the imposition of the border in the short and long terms? Give reasons to support your answer.
6. Discuss whether Red Jacket's speech portrays him as a supplicant to representatives of the US government or as a spokesperson for an independent nation.
7. To what degree did Indigenous people influence events as the French, British, and Americans expanded their territories? How did the creation of European nation-states in North America alter relationships between Aboriginal people?

Further Resources

Books and Articles

Edmunds, R. David, and Joseph L. Peyser. *The Fox Wars: The Mesquakie Challenge to New France*. Norman, OK: Oklahoma University Press, 1993.

Taylor, Alan. *The Divided Ground: Indians, Settlers, and the Northern Borderland of the American Revolution*. New York: Alfred A. Knopf, 2006.

———. *The Civil War of 1812: American Citizens, British Subjects, Irish Rebels, & Indian Allies*. New York: Alfred A. Knopf, 2010.

White, Richard. *The Middle Ground: Indians, Empires, and Republics in the Great Lakes Region, 1650–1815*. New York: Cambridge University Press, 1991.

Printed Documents and Reports

Snyder, Charles M., ed. *Red and White on the New York Frontier: A Struggle for Survival: Insights from the Papers of Erastus Granger, Indian Agent, 1807–1819*. Harrison, NY: Harbor Hill Books, 1978.

Thwaites, Reuben Gold, ed. *Collections of the State Historical Society of Wisconsin* vol. 16. Madison: State Historical Society of Wisconsin, 1902.

Films

Six Miles Deep. DVD. Directed by Sara Roque. NFB, 2010.
You are on Indian Land. DVD. Directed by Mort Ransen. NFB, 1969.

Websites

Archiving Early America: Full Text of the Jay Treaty
www.earlyamerica.com/earlyamerica/milestones/jaytreaty/text.html

The Mohawk Council of Akwesasne, 'Aboriginal Border Crossing Rights and the Jay Treaty of 1794'
www.akwesasne.ca/jaytreaty.html

Six Nations of the Grand River
www.sixnations.ca

FIVE

The Fur Trade

Introduction

Early histories of the fur trade in North America, such as Harold Innis's 400-page tome, *The Fur Trade in Canada*, focused on the trade as integral to the economic development of the area that came to be known as Canada.[1] European men figured prominently within this narrative of progress. Aboriginal people, on the other hand, remained in the background, portrayed as pre-modern obstacles to the growth of the trade and eventually rendered obsolete and dependent on industrious Europeans for survival. Arthur J. Ray's seminal work, *Indians in the Fur Trade*, refocused the lens of fur trade history onto Aboriginal people as central actors in the trade.[2] Published in 1974, the book draws on the records of the Hudson's Bay Company—made available to the general public only one year earlier—to trace the roles that Aboriginal people played in the establishment, success, and eventual decline of the fur trade. Ray's article in this chapter reflects this revision of fur trade history, a revision that its author argues is necessary to rectify the old stereotypes and misunderstandings that continue to inform Aboriginal and non-Aboriginal relations.

This picture has been further complicated by scholars such as Sylvia Van Kirk and Jennifer Brown, who both include women in their examinations of fur-trade history.[3] Van Kirk, in particular, highlights the centrality of women's cultural knowledge and labour. The significance of these two works is that they initiated a new perspective on the fur trade: the beginning of a socio-cultural complex that drew on the traditions of both parents and produced its own unique culture and lifeways. Susan Sleeper-Smith's article in this chapter builds on the foundations laid by Van Kirk, Brown, and others by looking at how Aboriginal women became 'negotiators of change' both at the personal level through their marriages to fur traders and more broadly by mediating their community's relations with traders and the European economy. Through a careful reading of the record, Sleeper-Smith investigates how four Aboriginal women identified themselves and were paramount in creating new Catholic kin networks that ran parallel to, and often intersected with, Aboriginal society. Moreover, these networks were extremely important in the pursuit of familial, social, and economic success and remained a necessary component of the fur trade. Thus, a complete examination of fur-trade history in North America cannot be undertaken from an economic perspective alone but must include the social, cultural, and personal enterprise that was forged in this period.

Chapter Objectives

At the end of this chapter, you should be able to

- understand the role that Aboriginal people played in the fur trade;
- discuss the implications of a history that downplays or even eliminates the role of Aboriginal people in the fur trade;
- see the history of the fur trade from an Aboriginal perspective; and
- explain how Aboriginal women were, from an economic and socio-cultural perspective, important figures in the fur trade.

Secondary Source

1.   Fur-Trade History as an Aspect of Native History

Arthur J. Ray

Howard Adams, among others, has made the point that the dominant white Euro-Canadian culture has projected racist images of the Indians that 'are so distorted that they portray natives as little more than savages without intelligence or beauty'.[4] He argued further that the Indians 'must endure a history that shames them, destroys their confidence, and causes them to reject their heritage'.[5] There is a great deal of truth in Adams's statements, and clearly a considerable amount of historical research needs to be done to correct these distorted images. One important aspect of any new meaningful Indian history necessarily will be concerned with the involvement of the Indian peoples in the fur trade and with the impact of that participation upon their traditional cultures as well as those of the European intruders. Work in this area will be important not only because it holds a potential for giving us new insights into Indian history, but also because it should serve to help establish Indian history in its rightful place in the mainstream of Canadian historiography. As some of Canada's most prominent historians have emphasized, the fur trade was a moulding force in the economic, political, and social development of Canada,[6] and the Indian peoples played a central role in this enterprise. For these reasons Indian history should not simply be devoted to recounting the manner in which the Aboriginal peoples of Canada were subjugated and exploited, but it must also consider the positive contribution that the Indian peoples made to the fur trade and, hence, to the development of Canada. If this positive contribution is recognized, it should help destroy some of the distorted images that many Canadians have of Indians and their history.

Until relatively recently the Indian peoples have not figured prominently in works dealing with the fur trade.[7] Rather, they generally appear only as shadowy figures who are always present, but never central characters, in the unfolding events.[8] In part, this neglect appears related to the fact that historians have been primarily concerned with studying the fur trade as an aspect of European imperial history or of Canadian business and economic history.[9]

Although the tendency to consider the fur trade primarily as an aspect of Euro-Canadian history has been partly responsible for the failure of scholars to focus on the Indians' role in the enterprise, other factors have been influential as well. One of the basic problems with most studies of Indian–white relations has been that ethnohistorians and historians have taken a retrospective view. They see the subjugation of the Indian peoples and the destruction of their lifestyles as inevitable consequences of the technological gap that existed between European and Indian cultures at the time of contact.[10] From this technological-determinist perspective, the Indian has been rendered as an essentially powerless figure who was swept along by the tide of European expansion without any real hope of channelling its direction or of influencing the character of the contact situation. The dominance of this outlook has meant that in most fur trade studies the Indian has been cast in a reflexive role. Reflecting this perspective, until recently most ethnohistorical research has been approached from an acculturation-assimilation point of view. The questions asked are generally concerned with determining how Indian groups incorporated European technology as well as social, political, economic, and religious customs into their traditional cultures.

While also interested in these issues, historians have devoted a considerable amount of attention toward outlining the manner and extent to which Euro-Canadian groups, particularly missionaries and government officials, helped the Indians to adjust to the new socio-economic conditions that resulted from the expansion of Western cultures into the new world.[11] Often historical research has taken a certain moralistic tone, assuming that members of the dominant white society had an obligation to help the Indians adopt agriculture and European socio-economic practices and moral codes, so that the Indian peoples could fit into the newly emerging social order.[12] Thus, historians who undertake these types of studies are frequently seeking to determine whether or not the traders, missionaries, and government officials had fulfilled their obligations to help 'civilize' the Indian.

Granting that much good work has been done in the above areas, it is my opinion that many new insights into Indian history can be obtained if we abandon the retrospective, technological-determinist outlook and devote more attention to an examination of Indian involvement in the fur trade in the context of contemporary conditions. Such an approach would necessarily recognize that the nature of the trading partnerships that existed between Indian groups and various European interests changed substantially over time and place, making it difficult, frequently misleading, and certainly premature, given the amount of research that still needs to be done, to make any sweeping statements at this time about the nature of Indian–white relations in the context of the Canadian fur trade.

In order to pursue this work effectively, two courses of action need to be followed—one is not currently popular, and the other is extremely tedious. First, students of Indian history need to abandon the assumption that the Indians were ruthlessly exploited and cheated in all areas and periods by white traders. At present this is a very popular theme for both Indian and liberal white historians. All of us have heard the story many times of how the Indians sold Manhattan Island for a few pounds of beads, and we have been informed of the many instances when Indians parted with valuable furs for trinkets and a drink. But, why are we never informed of what the Indians' perceptions of trade were? It may well be that they too thought they were taking advantage of the Europeans. For example, in 1634, when commenting on Montagnais beaver trapping in eastern Canada, Father Le Jeune wrote:

> The Castor or Beaver is taken in several ways. The Savages say it is the animal well-beloved by the French, English and Basques,—in a word, by the Europeans. I heard my [Indian] host say one day, jokingly, *Missi picoutau amiscou*, 'The Beaver does everything perfectly well, it makes kettles, hatchets, swords, knives, bread; and in short, it makes everything.' He was making sport of us Europeans, who have such a fondness for the skin of this animal and who fight to see who will get it; they carry this to such an extent that my host said to me one day, showing me a beautiful knife, 'The English have no sense; they give us twenty knives like this for one Beaver skin.'[13]

While there is no denying that European abuses of Indians were all too common, there are several things wrong with continually stressing this aspect of the fur trade and Indian history. As the previous quote suggests, it gives us only half the story. Of greater importance, by continually focusing only on this dimension of the trade, we run the serious risk of simply perpetuating one of the images in Indian historiography that Adams, among others, most strongly objects to, namely, the view that the Indians were little more than 'savages without intelligence'. It also glosses over a fundamental point that must be recognized if the Indian is to be cast in an active and creative role. We must not forget that the Indians became involved in the fur trade by their own choice. Bearing that in mind, an objective and thorough examination of the archival records of the leading trading companies, admittedly a wearisome task, gives considerable evidence that the Indians were sophisticated traders, who had their own clearly defined sets of objectives and conventions for carrying on exchange with the Europeans.

This can be demonstrated by following several lines of inquiry. One of these involves attempting to determine the kind of consumers the Indians were at the time of initial contact and how their buying habits changed over time. Probably one of the most striking pictures that emerges from an examination of the early correspondence books of the Hudson's Bay Company is that, contrary to the popular image, the Indians had a sharp eye for quality merchandise and a well-defined shopping list. In short, they were astute consumers and not people who were easily hoodwinked.

If this is doubted, the early letters that the traders on Hudson Bay sent to the governor and committee of the Hudson's Bay Company in London should be read carefully. A substantial portion of almost every letter deals with the subject of the quality of the company's trade goods and with the Indians' reactions to it. Not only do these letters reveal that the Indians could readily recognize superior merchandise, but they also indicate that the Indians knew how to take advantage of the prevailing economic situation to improve the quality of the goods being offered to them. The following quote, typical of those that were written in the period before 1763, demonstrates the point and at the same time indicates one of the problems that is associated with carrying on research of this type. On 8 August 1728, Thomas McCliesh sent a letter from York **Factory** to the governor and committee in London informing them:

> I have sent home two bath rings as samples, for of late most of the rings [which] are sent are too small, having now upon remains 216 that none of the Indians will Trade. I have likewise sent home 59 ivory combs that will not be traded, they having no great teeth, and 3900 large musket flints and small pistol flints, likewise one hatchet, finding at least 150 such in three casks that we opened this summer which causes great grumbling amongst the natives. We have likewise Sent home 18 barrels of powder that came over in 1727, for badness I never saw the like, for it will not kill fowl nor beast at thirty yards distance: and as for kettles in general they are not fit to put into a Indian's hand being all of them thin, and eared with tender old brass that will not bear their weight when full of liquid, and soldered in several places. Never was any man so upbraided with our powder, kettles and hatchets, than we have been this summer by all the natives, especially by those that borders near the French. Our cloth likewise is so stretched with the tenter-hooks, so as the selvedge is almost tore from one end of the pieces to the other. I hope that such care will be taken so as will prevent the like for the future, for the natives are grown so politic in their way of trade, so as they are not to be dealt by as formerly . . . and I affirm that man is not fit to be entrusted with the Company's interest here or in any of their factories that does not make more profit to the Company in dealing in a good commodity than in a bad. For now is the time to oblidge [sic] the natives before the French draws them to their settlement.[14]

From McCliesh's letter one gets the impression that few of the goods on hand were satisfactory as far as the Indians were concerned. Taken out of context, comments of this type, which are common in the correspondence from the posts, could be construed to indicate that the governor and committee of the Hudson's Bay Company hoped to enhance their profits by dealing in cheap, poor quality merchandise whenever possible. However, such a conclusion would distort the reality of the situation and overlook important developments that were underway in the eighteenth century. If one examines the letters that the governor and committee sent to the Bay during the same period, as well as the minutes of their meetings in London and correspondence with British manufacturers and purchasing agents, other important facts emerge.

These other documents reveal that from the outset the governor and committee were concerned with having an array of the types and quality of goods that would appeal to the Indians. From the minute books of the company we learn that in the earliest years of operations the London directors relied heavily upon the experience and judgment of Pierre-Esprit Radisson to provide them with guidance in developing an inventory of merchandise that would be suitable for their posts in Canada. Radisson helped choose the patterns for knives, hatchets, guns, and so forth that manufacturers were to use, and he was expected to evaluate the quality of items that were produced for the company.[15] The governor and committee also sought the expertise of others in their efforts to maintain some quality control. For instance, in 1674 they attempted to enlist the services of the gunsmith who inspected and approved the trade guns of the East India Company.[16] They wanted him to evaluate the firearms that the Hudson's Bay Company was purchasing.

In their annual letters to the posts on the Bay, the governor and committee generally asked the traders to comment on the goods that they received and to indicate which, if any, manufacturer's merchandise was substandard. When new items were introduced, the directors wanted to know what the Indians' reactions to them were.

The question that no doubt arises is, if the governor and committee were as concerned with the quality of the products they sold, as suggested above, then why was there a steady stream of complaints back to London about their goods? Before a completely satisfactory answer to this question can be given, a great deal more research needs to be done in these records. However, several working hypotheses may be put forth at this time for the sake of discussion and research orientation. In developing its inventory of trade goods, the Hudson's Bay Company, as well as other European groups, had to deal with several problems. One of these was environmental in character. Goods that may have been satisfactory for trade in Europe, Africa, or Asia often proved to be unsuitable in the harsh, subarctic environment. This was especially true of any items that were manufactured of iron. For example, one of the problems with the early flintlocks was that the locks froze in the winter.[17]

The extremely cold temperatures of the winter also meant that metal became brittle. Hence, if there were any flaws or cracks in the metal used to make mainsprings for guns, gun barrels, knives, hatchets, or kettles, these goods would break during the winter. In this way the severe environment of the subarctic necessitated very rigid standards of quality if the goods that were offered to the Indians were going to be satisfactory. These standards surely tested the skills of the company's suppliers and forced the company to monitor closely how the various manufacturers' goods held up under use.

Besides having to respond to environmental conditions, the traders also had to contend with a group of consumers who were becoming increasingly sophisticated and demanding. As the Indians substituted more and more European manufactures for traditional items, their livelihood and well-being became more dependent upon the quality of the articles that they were acquiring at the trading posts. This growing reliance meant that the Indians could no longer afford to accept goods that experience taught them would fail under the stress of hard usage and the environment, since such failures could threaten their survival. It was partly for these reasons that the Indians developed a critical eye for quality and could readily perceive the most minute defects in trade merchandise.

Indian groups were also quick to take advantage of competitive conditions. They became good comparison shoppers and until 1821 used European trading rivalries to force the improvement of quality and range of goods that were made available to them. For example, during the first century of trade on Hudson Bay, the Indians frequently brought to Hudson's Bay Company posts French goods that they judged to be superior to those of English manufacture. The Indians then demanded that the Hudson's Bay Company traders match or exceed the quality of these items or risk the loss of their trade to the French. Similar tactics were used by the Indians in later years whenever competition was strong between Euro-Canadian groups. Clearly such actions were not those of 'dumb savages', but rather were those of astute traders and consumers, who knew how to respond to changing economic conditions to further their own best interests. The impact that these actions had on the overall profitability of the trade for Euro-Canadian traders has yet to be determined.

The issue of profits raises another whole area of concern that is poorly understood and should be studied in depth. To date we know little about how the economic motivations of the Europeans and the Indians influenced the rates of exchange that were used at the posts. In fact, there is still a great deal of confusion about the complicated system of pricing goods and fur that was used in Canada. We know that the Hudson's Bay Company trader used two sets of standards. There was an official rate of exchange that was set by the governor and committee in London which differed from the actual rate that was used at the posts. Of importance, the traders advanced the prices of their merchandise above the stated tariff by resorting to the use of short measures. Contemporary critics of the Hudson's Bay Company and modern Native historians have attacked the company for using such business practices, charging that the Indians were thereby being systematically cheated, or to use the modern expression, 'ripped off'.[18] But was this the case? Could the company traders have duped the Indians over long periods of time without the latter having caught on? Again, common sense and the record suggest that this was not the case.

The traders have left accounts of what they claimed were typical speeches of Indian trading leaders. One central element of all of these addresses was the request by these leaders that the traders give the Indians 'full measure and a little over'.[19] Also, the Indians usually asked to see the old measure or standards. Significantly, the Indians do not appear to have ever challenged the official standards, while at the same time they knew that they never received 'full measure'. What can we conclude from these facts?

In reality, the official standards of trade of the Hudson's Bay Company, and perhaps those of other companies as well, served only as a language of trade, or point of reference, that enabled the Indians and the traders to come to terms relatively quickly. The traders would not sell goods at price below those set in the official standard. The Indian goal, on the other hand, was to try to obtain terms that approximated the official rate of exchange. An analysis of the Hudson's Bay Company post account books for the period before 1770 reveals that the company traders always managed to advance prices above the standard, but the margin of the advance diminished as the intensity of French opposition increased.[20] And even under monopoly conditions such as existed in western Canada before the 1730s, the Hudson's Bay Company traders were not able to achieve an across-the-board increase that exceeded 50 per cent for any length of time.[21] This suggests strongly that the Indians successfully used competitive situations to improve the terms of trade and that they had their limits. If prices were advanced beyond a certain level, the Indians must have perceived that their economic reward was no longer worth the effort expended, and they broke off trade even if there was no alternative European group to turn to.

These remarks about the *overplus* system apply to the period before 1770. What we need to know is the extent to which the Indians were able to influence the rates of exchange during the time of bitter Hudson's Bay Company and **North West Company** rivalry. A preliminary sample of data from that period suggests their impact was much greater and that range of price variation was much more extreme than in the earlier years. Similarly, it would be helpful to have some idea what effect the re-establishment of the Hudson's Bay Company's monopoly after 1821 had on trade good prices and fur values in western Canada. Being able to monitor prices under these contrasting conditions would enable us to obtain some idea of how the Indians were coping with the changing economic situation and how their responses influenced the material well-being of the different tribal groups.

Although this sample of the early accounting records shows that the Indians were economic men in the sense that they sought to maximize the return they obtained for their efforts, the same documents also indicate that, unlike their European counterparts, the Indians did not trade to accumulate wealth for status purposes. Rather, the Indians seem to have engaged in trade primarily to satisfy their own immediate requirement for goods. On a short-term basis their consumer demand was inelastic. In the early years this type of response was important in two respects. It was disconcerting to the European traders in that when they were offered better prices for their furs, the Indians typically responded by offering fewer pelts on a per capita basis. This type of a supply response was reinforced by gift-giving practices. Following the Indian custom, prior to trade tribal groups and the Europeans exchanged gifts. As rivalries for the allegiance of the Indians intensified, the lavishness of the gifts that the traders offered increased.

The ramifications that Indian supply responses to rising fur prices and to European gift-giving practices had for the overall conduct of the fur trade have yet to be fully explored. Clearly the costs that the Europeans would have had to absorb would have risen substantially during the periods when competition was strong, but to date no one has attempted to obtain even a rough idea of the magnitude by which these costs rose during the time of English–French or Hudson's Bay Company–North West Company rivalry. Nor has serious consideration been given to the manner in which such economic pressures may have favoured the use and abuse of certain trade articles such as alcohol and tobacco.

Concerning the use of alcohol, the excessive consumption of this drug was an inevitable consequence of the manner in which the economies of the Indian and European were linked together in the fur trade and of the contrasting economic motives of the two groups. As rivalries intensified, the European traders sought some means of retaining their contacts with the Indians, while at the same time keeping the per capita supply of furs that were obtained at as high a level as was possible. However, in attempting to accomplish the latter objective, the Europeans faced a number of problems. The mobile life of the Indians meant that their ability to accumulate material wealth was limited, especially in the early years when the trading posts were distant from the Indians' homelands. And, there were social sanctions against the accumulation of wealth by individual Indians.[22] To combat these problems, the traders needed to find commodities that could be transported easily or, even better, consumed at the trading post.

Unfortunately, alcohol was ideal when viewed from this coldly economic perspective. It offered one of the best means of absorbing the excess purchasing power of the Indians during periods of intensive competition. Furthermore, alcohol could be obtained relatively cheaply and diluted with water prior to trade.[23] Hence, it was a high profit trade item, an article that helped the traders hold down their gift-giving expenses, and it could be consumed at the forts. Given these characteristics, the only way that the abusive use of alcohol in trade could have been prevented in the absence of a strong European or Native system of government was through monopoly control.

The traditional Indian consumer habits and responses to rising fur prices were important in another way. They were basically conservationist in nature although not intentionally so. By trapping only enough furs to buy the goods they needed in the early years, the pressures that the Indians exerted on the environment by their trapping activities were far less than they would have been had the objective been one of accumulating wealth for status purposes. If the latter had been the primary goal, then the Indians would have been tempted to increase their per capita supply of **peltry** as fur prices rose, since their purchasing power was greater.

In light of the above, the period between 1763 and 1821 is particularly interesting and warrants close study. During that period Euro-Canadian trading rivalries reached a peak, and one of the consequences of the cutthroat competition that characterized the time was that large territories were overhunted and trapped by the Indians to the point that the economies of the latter were threatened.[24] The question is, had the basic economic behaviour of the Indians changed to such an extent that it facilitated their overkilling fur and game animals? Or, was the heavy use of addictive consumables such as alcohol and tobacco a major factor in the destruction of the environment?

Yet another aspect of the fur trade that has received too little attention is the connection that existed between the European and eastern North American markets and the western Canadian operations of the trading companies. It needs to be determined how prices for trade goods and furs in these markets, as well as transportation costs, influenced rates of exchange at the posts. For instance, it has become popular to cite cases where European traders advanced the prices of certain articles by as much as 1,000 per cent over what it cost the companies to buy them in Europe. Similarly, accounts of occasions when the Indians received a mere pittance for valuable furs[25] are common. But it is rarely reported, and indeed it is generally not known, what percentage of the total gross revenues of a company were made by buying and selling such items. Nor is it known if losses were sustained on the sales of other commodities. Equally important, there is not even a rough idea of what the total overhead costs of the companies were at various times. Hence, their net profit margins remain a mystery, and what was considered to be a reasonable profit margin by European standards in the seventeenth, eighteenth, and early nineteenth centuries is not known. Answers to all of these questions must be found before any conclusions can be reached about whether or not the Indian or the European trader was being 'ripped off'.

And indeed, the Indian side must be considered when dealing with this question and when attempting to understand how the trading system responded to changing economic conditions. Even though Harold Innis pointed out that Indian trading specialists played a crucial role in the development and expansion of the fur trade, a common view of the Indians in the enterprise is still one that portrays them basically as simple trappers who hunted their own furs and accepted whatever prices for these commodities that the traders were willing to give them. The fact of the matter is that the records show that, in the period before 1770, probably 80 per cent of all of the furs the Europeans received in central Canada came from Indian middlemen who acquired their peltry through their own trading networks.

Furthermore, these middlemen charged the Europeans substantially more for these furs than they had paid to obtain them from the trapping bands with whom they dealt. In turn, the middlemen advanced the prices for their trade goods well above the levels they had been charged by the Europeans, sometimes by margins of almost 1,000 per cent.

These practices of the Indian middlemen raise a difficult question. If the Indians were not engaged in the trade to accumulate wealth, as suggested earlier, then why did the middlemen advance their prices to the extent that they did? Did their price levels simply enable them to maintain a material standard that they had become accustomed to? Before this question can be answered, a great deal more needs to be known about the problems that the Indian middlemen had to cope with in their efforts to acquire and transport goods and furs. A clearer understanding of their motives for engaging in the trade is also required. For example, why did some Indian groups quickly assume the middleman role while others were apparently content to continue as trappers? How did middlemen groups fare, economically, in comparison with trapping groups?

The Indians played a variety of other roles in the fur trade. They served as provision suppliers, canoe builders, canoe and boat men, and farm labourers around the posts, to name only a few. The Indians quickly assumed these roles as economic conditions changed, rendering old positions obsolete and opening up new opportunities.

This brings to mind another broad research area that should be explored more fully than it has been to date. It deals with determining how the various Indian groups perceived and responded to changing economic situations. Work in this area would serve to destroy another distorted image that many Euro-Canadians have of Indian societies, namely, the view that these societies are rigid and incapable of responding to change. Historically there is little evidence to support such a notion for the period before 1870. While the fur trade was a going concern and the Indians were not tied to the reserves and shackled with bureaucratic red tape, they made many successful adaptations to new circumstances. More needs to be written about this aspect of Indian history. If this work is done, perhaps a picture will emerge that shows the Indians to be innovative, dynamic, and responsive people, whose creativity and initiative have been thwarted in the post-treaty period.

In conclusion, this paper has focused upon the early phases of the western Canadian fur trade, and the discussion has been restricted primarily to the economic dimension of trade. However, this restriction is justified because many of the problems of Indian–white relations are rooted in the past. Also, many of the distorted images that Euro-Canadians currently hold regarding Indians, thereby causing problems in the relationships between the two groups, have been generated and perpetuated by the manner in which the fur-trade history has been written. Correcting these images requires starting at the beginning, and it is not simply a matter of rewriting what has already been done. New research has to be conducted in the various archival collections across the country and records that have received little attention to date, such as accounting records, need to be exhaustively explored. In conducting this research and presenting our results, the urge to overcompensate for past wrongs and inaccuracies by placing the Indian on a pedestal must be resisted. If the latter course of action is taken, a new mythology that will not stand the test of time will be created. Even more serious, it would probably serve only to perpetuate the warped images that such research set out to destroy, because it would fail to treat the Indians as equals with their own cultures and sets of values. Finally, if one of the objectives of studying the fur trade is to attempt to obtain a better understanding of Indian–white relations, it must be based on solid objective historical research.

Primary Document

2.   Minutes from the Excise Committee of the Hudson's Bay Company, 24 March 1673

a Comittee at the Excise office the 24th march 1673
Presente
Earle of Shaftsbury
Sr. James Hayes
Mr. Hawkins
Ordered That a letter bee written to Mr Pierce of Plimouth in answer to one from him with order to him for Sendeing all the beaver there p. the first good conveyance by Sea hither to bee consigned to Mr. Hawkins, the Custome to bee payd there, & to bee charged by bill of exchange together with all other charges thereon upon Mr. Hawkins here for his reimbursement, which is accordeingly written & Signed by this Comittee & recommended to Mr. Rastells care to bee Sent away & to gett Mr. Millington's hande to it.

That Mr. Holmes forthwith gett patternes of brasse kettles & the Lowest prices, as well ready made up, as unmade up, for better Sattisfaction of the Comittee.

That the *Messinger* Dogger bee forthwith turned into a pinke[26] & to bee fitted with 3 mastes & Sayles to them proportionably by Mr. Yeames the Shipwright, & that Mr. Holmes the husbande with the advise of Captain Shephard & mate Thompson take care & agree about it, & alsoe take Speedy care for fitteing up the *Prince Rupert*, & reporte to the Comittee upon thursday next what the charge may bee thereof.

That 200 hatchetts more bee provided wth. Square heades for tryall.

That Mr. Thompson who Surveys & examines the gunns for the East india Company bee desired to attende the Comittee next thursday.

That Mr. Rastell or Mr. Heatley give noates to the gunsmithes that are agreed with for the quantities of gunns they are to make, that is 50 Mr. West, 50 Mr. Palmer, 50 Mr. Boulton, 50 Mr. Ireland, & 100 Mr. Shaw & his partner.

Secondary Source

3.   Women, Kin, and Catholicism:
New Perspectives on the Fur Trade

Susan Sleeper-Smith

Scholars who have studied the fur trade of the western Great Lakes offer conflicting interpretations of its impact on Native American societies. Those who view the trade as synonymous with the intrusion of market forces, particularly the pursuit of profit, generally link both Indigenous decline and the depletion of animal populations with the trade. Other scholars contend that the fur trade had overarching political and diplomatic ramifications and that profit-making was often subordinated to maintain the Algonquian–French alliance.[27] Most recently, Richard White has envisioned the fur trade as integral to an ever-evolving arena of cultural negotiation, which he labelled the 'middle ground'. For White 'the creation of the middle ground involved a process of mutual invention' created by 'people who shared neither their values nor their assumptions about the appropriate way of accomplishing tasks' and 'which grew according to the need of people to find a means, other than force, to gain the co-operation or consent of foreigners'.[28]

This article focuses on four Native women, married to French fur traders, whose lives offer insight into the process of sociological and cultural adaptation that occurred as Indian villages of the western Great Lakes became increasingly involved in the trade. This essay suggests that the conception of White's *Middle Ground* is a viable way in which to describe interaction between Indian and Euro-Americans and that it should be expanded to emphasize the prominent role that Native women played as cultural mediators. The Indian women who married fur traders were 'negotiators of change'.[29] They lived in a region where the exchange process occurred primarily at wintering grounds or in villages, and, because trade had social as well as economic ramifications, intermarriage played an integral role in the trade's evolution. Traders who married these women thus had an advantage over their rivals. Marriage, either in the 'manner of the country' or performed by missionary priests, assured traders' inclusion as members of Indigenous communities and facilitated access to furs.[30]

A fur trader's presence enhanced the importance of the community where he lived and simultaneously enhanced his wife's authority and prestige among her people. Native women did not marry out; rather, they incorporated their French husbands into a society structured by Native custom and tradition.[31] Although access to trade goods enhanced the power and influence of these Native women, they did not simply re-invent themselves as French.

The Native women who are the focus of this article can be identified in Jesuit records by both their Indian and Christian names. Because we are aware of their Native ancestry, we can consequently see how they were involved in the creation of Catholic kin networks. Baptism and marriage provided the means through which this diverse and real fictive kin network could be continually expanded. Marital and baptismal records suggest that these networks, created by Catholicism, facilitated access to peltry while simultaneously allowing these women to negotiate for themselves positions of prominence and power. By the mid-eighteenth century an identifiable Catholic kin network had evolved that was compatible with and often parallel to that of Indigenous society.

The contention that Catholicism had important social ramifications that enhanced female autonomy contradicts the view that Catholicism instituted a male patriarchal order, which increasingly subordinated Native women to men. These conclusions do not appear uniformly applicable to all Native communities in the western Great Lakes. Instead, this article suggests that Catholicism could also serve as a pathway to social prominence.[32] The Jesuits generally recruited catechizers or instructors among Native women. These female converts were often the most visible proof of Jesuit success. It would have been foolhardy for these priests to foster female subjection to the authority of men whom the Jesuits frequently despised. Indeed, most missionary priests viewed the fur-trade husbands of these converts as licentious drunkards who undermined Christian ideals; the Jesuits even vigorously supported a seventeenth-century royal policy that banished traders from the western Great Lakes. The Jesuits also frequently dismissed the Elders of Native communities, many of whom scorned Christianity. Therefore, it would have been problematic for the Jesuits to support the establishment of a male patriarchal order that subjected their pious female converts to the authority of male fur traders and unconverted headmen.

Just as the profit-making dimensions of the fur trade were mediated by the Algonquian–French political alliance, the repressive patriarchal order was mediated by the Jesuit's reliance on Native women. During the eighteenth century these women were also the beneficiaries of the dramatic decline in the number of Jesuit priests. Not only did missionary fervour wane, but in the last quarter of the century the Jesuits were temporarily disbanded. In the absence of priests, many female converts fashioned a type of 'frontier Catholicism' in which they assumed the role of lay practitioners.

Amid the dynamics of this changing social landscape, Indian women who married fur traders relied on the interface between two worlds to position themselves as mediators between cultural groups, to assume leadership roles in religious training, to influence commodity production, and eventually, at least in a few cases, to establish themselves as independent traders. Through it all these women retained their Indian identity, as evidenced by their language, names, and tribal affiliations. More important, they relied on their Catholicism to maintain relative autonomy in relation to their husbands. The complicated dynamics of such behaviours are evidenced by four women, whose lives spanned the seventeenth and eighteenth centuries. Two of the women were Illini: Marie Rouensa-8cate8a[33] and Marie Madeleine Réaume L'archevêque Chevalier.[34] Each used Catholicism to resist and reshape Indigenous societal constraints. Over time, the syncretic nature of Catholicism facilitated the creation of an ever-expanding kin network that extended the parameters of women's worlds from those of their immediate family and community to fur-trade posts throughout the Great Lakes and Mississippi River Valley.

These women used the fictive ties created by godparenting to create an ever-expanding kinship network, and by the end of the eighteenth century these networks had evolved as strategic alliances that enabled some Native women to establish themselves as independent fur traders. This was the case for Magdelaine Marcot La Framboise and Thérèse Marcot Lasaliere Schindler, who were raised in Odawa communities and were incorporated from birth into the Catholic kin networks of fur-trade society.[35] They negotiated the hazardous world of the late-eighteenth- and early-nineteenth-century fur trade when Frenchmen were displaced, first by the English and later by American traders. Both La Framboise and Schindler prospered [and retained their independence] because their centrality in Indigenous kin networks gave them access to a stable supply of furs.

These women, who have appeared tangentially in the fur-trade literature, have been depicted either as historical outliers or as women who did not challenge traditional spheres of male authority.[36] White used Rouensa to exemplify the cultural inventions of an evolving middle ground, when compromise, rather than force, convinced Rouensa to marry the fur trader Michel Accault. After her marriage, Rouensa disappeared from the 'middle ground'.[37] Marriage was not her gateway to invisibility, however. Marriage, coupled with her Catholicism, afforded access to power and prestige, which is apparent when examining the whole of Rouensa's life.[38]

Her centrality as a historical actor resulted from the economic and social adaptations that Indian communities experienced as they became increasingly involved in the western Great Lakes fur trade. Rouensa's village, located just south of Lake Michigan, became involved in the fur trade in the late 1670s, when Robert La Salle established a French presence in Illinois Country. Her father was an important headman among the Kaskaskia, one of the seven nations of the Iliniwek Confederacy.[39] In 1790 he arranged for Rouensa to marry a fur trader who had ventured west with La Salle in 1679.

Among the Kaskaskia, women were free to reject such arranged marriages. But in the 1690s, when the Fur Trade Wars engulfed the Great Lakes, access to trade goods and alliances with the French were considered important strategies that countered Iroquois hostilities. Rouensa would have experienced tremendous community pressure to accede to her father's request and to the wishes of her village. Had she acquiesced to such pressure, her behaviour would have escaped historical attention. But Rouensa refused to marry, and she turned to the Jesuit Father Jacques Gravier for support.

Christian conversion enabled Rouensa to position herself as a teacher among her people. She expanded the culturally innovative dimensions of the middle ground when she translated Gravier's Christian message into her Kaskaskia language.

Gravier further reinforced such behaviours of young female proselytes when he shared with them stories of female saints. Virtue and mystical experiences produced European celibates, and strong similarities in Indigenous behaviour encouraged the Kaskaskia converts to dedicate their lives to the church. Illini women who traditionally elected to remain single usually entered warrior society. Christian conversion created an alternative option, and, facing the threat of an undesirable marriage, Rouensa 'resolved to consecrate her virginity to God'. Catholic conversion encouraged her to resist a proposed marriage, even though it was arranged by her parents. Her professed devotion to virginity, to the love of Christ, intensified when her parents chose for her husband Michel Accault, a 50-year-old grizzled veteran of the fur trade. Rouensa called on Gravier to defend her decision to remain a celibate Catholic woman.[40]

Gravier supported his young convert's decision. To have abandoned her would have resulted in the inevitable loss of his female congregation. Although Gravier proposed prayer as the solution for the impasse, Rouensa proposed a more practical solution. She consented to marry the disreputable French trader if her parents agreed to become Christian converts. They readily assented to her demands.

In this manner Rouensa used Catholicism to reshape an otherwise potentially dismal outcome.[41] A marriage 'in the manner of the country' would have given her minimal control over a husband who was 'famous in this Illinois Country for all his debaucheries'.[42] Now she could demand Christian reformation of Accault's character. As the priest's able assistant, Rouensa helped define what was expected of a Christian husband, and she relied on both her parents and her community to apply the necessary social pressures.

French fur traders were eager to marry Native women with extensive kin networks, particularly socially prominent women like Rouensa. The exchange of trade goods for peltry occurred on a face-to-face basis, along a kinship continuum. Kin networks controlled access to furs and marriage ensured Euro-American men inclusion as kin. When French traders married Illini women, they joined their wives' households. This gave women, who controlled productive resources, increased access to trade goods. Trade goods reinforced ritual gift-giving and enhanced both the power and prestige of matrifocal households and individual women.

Households, like that of Rouensa, remained rooted within Indigenous society and proved highly resistant to any efforts to impose patriarchal authority. Gravier was justifiably reluctant to accord Accault authority over his wife, for she was both an effective Catholic proselytizer and a more rigorous and faithful Christian than her husband. In this instance Catholicism proved to be a socially innovative mechanism that enhanced female authority. For Rouensa, her household, and her community, Accault was a desirable spouse, but only because this amorous adventurer was transformed into a reliable presence.

Such households not only frustrated attempts to impose hierarchical notions of European authority on Native women, but they also fostered the expansion of the Western fur trade. Native women became active participants in the trade because they controlled access to resources, particularly agricultural produce. European fur traders in the western Great Lakes were dependent on the Indigenous food supply. Trade permits allowed each recipient only two canoes for the upper country, and men who married into these Indigenous households were able to devote the limited cargo space of transport canoes almost entirely to trade goods. That was because the matrifocal households to which they were connected produced an agricultural surplus sufficient to feed not only their immediate family but also the more transient fur trade population.

Rouensa was left a widow after seven years of marriage to Accault, after which she married another Frenchman, Michel Philippe.[43] For the next 20 years the Kaskaskia baptismal records detail the evolution of their increasingly large family. Rouensa gave birth to six more children, and by her death in 1725 she had amassed an estate that was sufficient to probate and inventory.

Over time, communities like Kaskaskia evolved as a blending of Indigenous and French cultures, but for the first generation they were more Illini than French.[44]

Agriculture, for instance, remained the province of women. The continuity of these matrifocal households encouraged French husbands to become traders rather than farmers. But fields mounded in Indian fashion or cultivated by the small French *en bardeau* plows led travellers to condemn French men as lazy, simply because Native women's agricultural work was invisible to these Euro-American outsiders. These women also resisted the women's work associated with French households. Among the probated wills and inventories of the river community residents, there were none of the traditional tools associated with French home industry—spinning wheels, looms, or even knitting needles.[45] In these communities it appears that Indigenous gender roles gave women the management and allocation of resources.

Illini Catholicism was a shared female experience that was initially facilitated by Jesuit missionaries who consciously shaped Catholicism to be compatible with Indian beliefs and practices. Catholicism was then taught to Indian women by other female converts and was probably transformed further by the verbal transmission process. By the mid-eighteenth century, when Jesuit priests declined in number and when the order was suppressed in 1773, these Catholic women thus emerged as Catholicism's primary proselytizers. It was therefore not surprising that Catholicism then appealed to larger numbers of Native people.[46]

Catholicism acquired increased centrality in the fur trade because of its social ramifications. During the eighteenth century, female converts used their 'frontier' Catholicism to construct kin networks, both real as well as fictive. Native women married to fur traders served as godmothers to each other's children, and during the eighteenth century these women constructed kinship ties with distant and dispersed communities throughout the western Great Lakes region. In the interface of two disparate worlds, these women relied on long-established kinship behaviours to recreate the familiar within a Christian context. Catholicism did not entail the dissolution of Indigenous culture.

Distinctive Métis communities eventually evolved from these Catholic kin networks as mixed-ancestry women married Frenchmen or mixed-ancestry fur traders. Métis communities existed at important fur-trade posts, like Michilimackinac and Green Bay, but at smaller fur-trade communities the lives of these women continued to be shaped by the Indigenous communities in which they lived. The power of habit structured their lives, just as it organized Indian society and enabled traditional economies to meet the demands of an emerging transatlantic market economy.[47]

Catholic kin networks were indispensable to the fur trade because they linked the larger fur-trade posts (the centres of exchange) with the smaller posts (the sources of supply). How that kinship system operated is apparent in the life of another Illini woman, Marie Madeleine Réaume.[48] She was born early in the eighteenth century, shortly before Rouensa's death. Réaume's life was illustrative of the prominent role women played in the evolution of fur-trade communities. Her life bridged two disparate worlds and illustrated how kin networks linked Indigenous and French societies. Exchange remained embedded in social relationships, kinship mediated that process, and Catholic kin networks linked the distant fur-trade outposts of an expanding fur-trade society. For Native people, however, trade remained a process of collective exchange, while for Europeans exchange was an increasingly individualistic transaction within an emerging transatlantic market economy.[49]

Réaume, like the other women discussed in this article, was married 'in the eyes of the church'. Her husband was Augustin L'archevêque, a licensed trader in the Illinois Country.[50] During the course of their 16-year marriage, Réaume gave birth to six children and remained relatively anonymous until her husband's death.[51] Her name then started to appear in the fort's reimbursement records. Réaume's household produced both a marketable agricultural surplus as well as specific goods for the trade.[52] Her agricultural holdings paralleled those of Rouensa, although they were far less significant.[53] Such women, and the agriculturally oriented communities in which they lived, were common throughout the Great Lakes.

Réaume's first attempt to expand her familial and fictive kin network to other prominent fur-trade families took place after her husband's death.[54] She had kin connections in the Illinois Country, but it was Michilimackinac that was emerging as the most important entrepôt of the eighteenth-century fur trade. In the summer of 1748, the 38-year-old widow travelled north to Michilimackinac. Réaume relied on baptism and marriage to incorporate her family into the more prominent Catholic kin network of Michilimackinac. Members of the Bourassa and the Langlade families served as godparents to Réaume's son and as witnesses at the weddings of her daughters.[55] Both daughters and their fur-trader husbands returned to St Joseph and became part of Réaume's household.

After the marriage of Réaume's daughters, increasingly complex behavioural strategies enveloped this entire household and included not just the children but also Réaume herself. Three years after the 1848 trip to Michilimackinac, Réaume, then 41 years old, gave birth to a son. The child's father was a prominent Michilimackinac trader, Louis Thérèse Chevalier, whom Réaume later married at the St Joseph mission.[56]

The apparent marital strategy of Réaume was to join her prosperous agricultural household to Michilimackinac, which was the most important trading outpost in the western Great Lakes. For Chevalier marriage extended his already extensive kin network and provided him with an entrée into the prosperous St Joseph trade. Following Chevalier's marriage to Réaume, the Chevaliers garnered a substantial portion of the St Joseph trade.

Marriage integrated these two distant families, and in time the offspring migrated to other fur-trade communities. Mobility strengthened kinship ties not only with Michilimackinac but also to the south, creating a network that became increasingly important to the entire St Joseph River Valley when the British took control of the western Great Lakes.

Kinship facilitated fur-trade exchange and had political, as well as social and economic, dimensions. French authority over the North American interior rested on the hegemony of these kin networks. The French traders living among Native people were central to New France's highly effective communications network that linked distant western outposts. French traders relayed messages, solicited warriors, and mediated potentially disruptive disputes. Following the French and Indian War, when the British displaced the French, these kin networks frustrated the transfer of power. The garrisoning of former French forts proved an explosive event, when fur traders failed to assume their traditional role as mediators. Instead, in the uprising of 1763, they remained passive observers as the forts at Le Boeuf, Michilimackinac, Miami, Ouiatenon, Presqu'Isle, St Joseph, Sandusky, and Verango fell to Native American forces.[57]

England lacked a sufficient presence to govern through force, and when the English ignored or attempted to displace French traders and their Native wives, this threatened to destabilize a highly complex, kin-related world of the upper Great Lakes region. Although Chevalier was described by the British as 'so connected with the Potawatomis that he can do anything with them',[58] this influence was actually attributable to his wife.[59] Communities like St Joseph were the locus of Catholic kin networks, and women like Réaume were the demographic links in a world defined by kinship. Her behaviour followed the pattern of godparenting common in the western Great Lakes. She was the godmother to the children of her children, her slaves and their offspring, fellow Native American converts, and even to the children of unconverted Native women. Eventually, Réaume's kinship network extended south to Saint Louis, Cahokia, and Kaskaskia; north to Michilimackinac; and west to Green Bay.

Kinship facilitated the exchange process and had important social ramifications as well. Jesuit baptismal registers reveal a great deal about the nature of kinship and describe a complex social system wherein one was less an individual and more a member of a larger kinship group.[60] The kin networks that evolved from intermarriage between fur traders and Native American women were rooted in and paralleled, extended, and further complicated those of Native American society. The more visible dimensions of these interrelationships were personified by the Catholic kin networks of women like Réaume.

English commandants who ignored women such as Réaume and their French fur-trader husbands thwarted effective governance in the western Great Lakes. Those francophobic English commandants who advocated removal of French fur traders failed to appreciate that many mixed ancestry offspring were now indistinguishable from the Indian people among whom they lived. In 1780, when Patrick Sinclair, the Michilimackinac commandant responsible for the St Joseph post, ordered the forcible removal of the 48 French people resident at St Joseph, including Réaume and Chevalier, he learned a bitter lesson about the folly of ignoring these kinship ties.[61] Shortly after their arrival, the English fur traders sent to Fort St Joseph were attacked by Réaume's Illinois kin network. This force was composed of her immediate family, her son-in-law, and 30 of his friends.

The St Joseph invasion is often described as a minor skirmish of the Revolutionary War, but such descriptions fail to appreciate the extent to which such events reflected fur trade rather than military rivalries. This 1781 incident prevented the establishment of British traders in the St Joseph River Valley and secured the economic interests of the L'archevêque–Chevalier kin network.

Kinship facilitated the exchange process, and by the beginning of the nineteenth century, access to the best peltry in the western Great Lakes was increasingly controlled by these complex kin networks. When the **American Fur Company** entered the Great Lakes trade, company managers relied on this established kinship network and chose to supply two Odawa women, rather than their male competitors. They were Thérèse and Magdelaine Marcot, who were born into the St Joseph kin network. They were part of an intermediate link that joined that river valley to the Odawa community 50 miles farther north, in the Grand River Valley. Direct access to trade goods encouraged their emergence as independent traders.

Thérèse and Magdelaine were the children of an Odawa woman known as Thimotée and a French trader named Jean Baptiste Marcot. Marcot was a St Joseph trader and, along with the Chevaliers, his family had been forcibly removed in 1781.[62] Thimotée returned with the children to her Odawa community in the Grand River Valley, while her husband relocated to present-day Wisconsin.[63] Both children were baptized at Michilimackinac, and their godparents were members of generationally prominent fur-trade families, part of the Chevalier, Barthe, and La Framboise kin networks. Thérèse and Magdelaine, despite being Catholic and the daughters of a French father, were identified as Odawa by the missionary priest.

Thérèse and Magdelaine were raised in Indigenous society and married French fur traders. Magdelaine remained in the Grand River Valley with her husband, Joseph La Framboise, and he traded among her people; Thérèse moved with her fur-trader husband, Pierre Lasaliere, to the St Joseph River Valley.[64] After several years Lasaliere and Thérèse separated, and he moved to the west side of Lake Michigan to join the Wisconsin trade.[65] Like her mother, Thérèse returned to raise her daughter in her Odawa village in the Grand River Valley. Her second husband was an Anglo fur trader, George Schindler, who started trading among the Odawa in 1800.[66]

Early in the nineteenth century the lives of the two sisters changed dramatically. In 1804 their country marriages were consecrated by a missionary priest at Michilimackinac. Joseph La Framboise had lived with Magdelaine for 10 years and they had two children.[67] In 1806, several years after the Michilimackinac celebration of his marriage, Joseph was killed by an irate Indian.[68] Magdelaine buried her husband and continued on her journey to the Odawa wintering ground with her infant son Joseph, two African-American slaves, Angelique and Louison, and 12 voyageurs.[69]

After her husband's death, Magdelaine emerged as an independent trader. She chose not to remarry. Magdelaine's centrality in the Catholic kin networks of fur-trade society, her social prominence as a young Odawa woman, and her experience in the fur trade coincided with trader John Jacob Astor's eager search for an entrée into the Great Lakes trade. Kinship worked to Magdelaine's advantage and encouraged her independence. For the next 15 years, until she retired from the trade in 1822, she travelled annually between the Grand River Valley and Michilimackinac to exchange peltry for trade goods. She lived among her Odawa kin in the Grand River Valley, and each year wintered with them. Magdelaine established herself as Madame La Framboise, obtained trading licences, first from the British and then, after the War of 1812, from the Americans. She hired voyageurs to accompany her, secured trade goods on credit, and returned each June to Michilimackinac to sell her furs and re-supply her outfit.

Several years after Joseph La Framboise's death, a stroke left George Schindler an invalid.[70] Thérèse, like Magdelaine, became an independent fur trader, but traded at L'Arbe Croche, the Odawa community closest to Michilimackinac. Thérèse's operations rapidly expanded. She often served as Magdelaine's supply source for the Grand River Valley trade, but she also supplied a large number of French fur traders, men drawn from her kin network.[71] She sold goods to traders from the Barthe, Chevalier, and La Framboise families, all members of her fictive kin network. Thérèse increasingly acquired prominence as a supplier, while her sister Magdelaine remained an active, independent trader.[72]

In 1816, when the American Fur Trade Company acquired greater control of the Great Lakes trade, it incorporated both women. These women negotiated for themselves positions of prominence in an era when the fur trade proved to be a precarious male venture. Many independent male traders were eliminated when John Jacob Astor and the American Fur Company gained control of the Great Lakes trade. The furs Thérèse Schindler and Madame La Framboise had first sold to Ramsay Crooks, Astor's representative in the Great Lakes, established their standing with Astor's newly formed American Fur Company.[73]

Marie Rouensa, Marie Madeleine Réaume L'archevêque Chevalier, Magdelaine Marcot La Framboise, and Thérèse Marcot Lasaliere Schindler were part of a world where identity was defined not by nationality but by kinship. Kin networks, like those of the St Joseph community, characterized every fur-trade community in the western Great Lakes. The fictive and familial relationships created by the umbrella of frontier Catholicism further strengthened and expanded an already complex Indigenous kinship system.

In 1680 and 1711, Rouensa and Réaume were born into a demographically chaotic and socially unstable world. Indian women emerged as the cultural mediators of this eighteenth-century landscape. The Jesuit presence offered Native women an opportunity to interface between two disparate worlds, and as Catholic converts these women constructed an ever-expanding world of real and fictive kin under the umbrella of Western religion. They raised children conversant with European and Indigenous cultures, drew a livelihood for themselves and their households from the emerging market economy, and facilitated the evolution of the fur trade in the western Great Lakes. Fur-trade exchange was clearly much more than the simple economic transaction of a marketplace economy; instead, it was defined by kinship. The fur trade remained collective on one side and individualistic on the other, and this world of individual and collective exchange was bridged by Native women.

Great Lakes people defined themselves by their relatives, while Anglo outsiders identified them as French or Native American. During the nineteenth century a distinctive Métis society developed from the intermarriages within kin networks, especially those involving the more prominent fur-trade families.[74] At Fort St Joseph, the forcible removal of the French traders and their families abruptly terminated a society evolving in that direction. Social boundaries remained ill-defined and children of Native American mothers and fur-trade fathers identified themselves as French or Canadian, but many preferred their Indigenous identity. Réaume's son Louison, for example, was referred to by the British as Indian. Chevalier's son, Amable, by his first wife, became an important Odawa headman.[75] The Great Lakes kin network, with its diversity and multiplicity of names and identities, can never be fully untangled. It led to anonymity but simultaneously determined one's social position.

Change for these women was always defined by the extensive kin networks that controlled and mediated the exchange process of the fur trade. Three of these women were the daughters of fur traders, and many of their daughters married fur traders. Marriage served as a planned extension of familial kin networks, further extended through the fictive kinship of Catholic ritual. Therefore, as offspring moved to other fur-trade communities, mobility became the warp on which the fabric of the fur trade was woven.

Native women married to fur traders played a pivotal role in the spread of Christianity among Great Lakes people, just as they mediated the face-to-face exchange of goods for peltry. These women suggest alternative perspectives from which we might revise prevailing views about the fur trade and Catholicism. Native women were 'negotiators of change', were active participants, and emerged as central actors in the colonial era of the western Great Lakes.

Primary Document

4. Reminiscences of Early Days on Mackinac Island

Elizabeth Thérèse Baird

As a child, Elizabeth Thérèse Baird visited and then lived on Mackinac Island from 1812 to 1824. Here she recalls female Aboriginal fur trader Magdelaine La Framboise, whom she encountered there.

In 1809, Laframboise left Mackinac with this wife and baby-boy (daughter being at Montreal at school) for his usual wintering place on the upper part of the Grand river, in Michigan. They traveled in Mackinac boats, or *bateaux*. There were two boats, with a crew of six men to each. There were also accompanied by their servants,—old Angelique, a slave and her son, Louizon,—all of whom made a large party. At the last encampment, before reaching Grand river, Laframboise, while kneeling in his tent one night saying his prayers, was shot dead by an Indian, who had previously asked for liquor and had been refused. The widowed wife, knowing that she was nearer Grand river than her own house, journeyed on, taking the remains of her husband with her, and had them buried at the only town in that vicinity, which was near the entrance of the river—the present Grand Haven, Mich. Now was developed the unselfish devotion of her servant, Angelique, whose faithfulness was displayed in many ways through the deep affliction which had fallen upon her mistress. She greatly endeared herself to Madame Laframboise, and was ever after her constant companion in all journeyings, Madame becoming in time dependent upon her; the tie that bound them together remained unbroken until the death of the mistress.

After Madame Laframboise had laid away her husband, she proceeded to her place of business. Here she remained until spring, trading with the Indians. Then she returned to Mackinac and procured a license as a trader, and added much to her already large fortune. In the course of that winter the Indians captured the murderer of Laframboise, and, bringing him to her, desired that she should decide his fate,—whether he should be shot or burned. Madame addressed them eloquently, referring, in words profoundly touching, to her dead husband, his piety, and his good deeds. Then, displaying in her forgiving spirit a most Christ-like quality, she continued: 'I will do as I know he would do, could he now speak to you; I will forgive him, and leave him to the Great Spirit. He will do what is right.' She never again saw that man.

Madame Laframboise would in June return with her furs to Mackinac. The servants whom she left in care of her home there, would have it in readiness upon her arrival, and here she would keep house for about three months and then go back to her work. Among these servants was one notably faithful, Genevieve Maranda, who remained with her until her death.

Madame Laframboise was a remarkable woman in many ways. As long as her father, Jean Baptiste Marcotte, lived, his children, when old enough, were sent to Montreal to be educated. But she and her sister, Grandmother Schindler did not share these advantages, they being the youngest of the family, and the father dying when Madame Laframboise was but three months old. Her mother was of chiefly blood, being the daughter of Ke-wi-na-quot (Returning Cloud), one of the most powerful chiefs of the Ottawa tribe. She had not book-lore, but many might be proud of her attainments. She spoke French easily, having learned it from her husband. All conversation in that day was as a rule held in French. Robert Stuart, a Scotchman, who was educated in Paris, used to say that her diction was as pure as that of a Parisian. She was a graceful and refined person, and remarkably entertaining. She always wore the full Indian costume, and there was at that time no better fur trader than she. She had both the love and respect of the Indians that her husband had had before her. She, indeed, had no fear of the Indians, no matter what their condition; she was always able to control them.

Questions for Consideration

1. How does looking at the history of the fur trade from an Aboriginal perspective change the traditional interpretation of it?
2. What roles did Aboriginal people play in the fur trade and why? According to Ray, what are the broader implications of these roles in terms of the functioning of the industry?
3. If the minutes of the Hudson's Bay Company's Excise Committee were the only source you had available, what might you conclude about the nature of the trade between Aboriginal traders and the company? Why, in Ray's view, might your conclusions be erroneous? What does this imply about the traditional Euro-Canadian narrative of the fur trade?
4. What role did Indigenous women play in the fur trade, according to Sleeper-Smith?
5. Based on the information provided in this chapter, why did European men marry Aboriginal women and vice versa?
6. How does the picture that Elizabeth Thérèse Baird paints of Magdelaine La Framboise conform to the picture of Aboriginal women traders painted by Sleeper-Smith? How does it differ?
7. Was the fur trade shaped by the dictates of the European companies and traders; by the Aboriginal hunters, trappers, fishers, guides, and traders; or by some combination of both? Give reasons to support your answer.

Further Resources

Books and Articles

Podruchny, Carolyn. *Making the Voyageur World: Travelers and Traders in the North American Fur Trade*. Lincoln & Toronto: University of Nebraska Press & University of Toronto Press, 2006.

Ray, Arthur J. *Indians in the Fur Trade*, 2nd edn. Toronto: University of Toronto Press, [1974] 1998.

Sleeper-Smith, Susan. *Indian Women and French Men: Rethinking Cultural Encounter in the Western Great Lakes*. Amherst, MA: University of Massachusetts Press, 2001.

Van Kirk, Sylvia. *Many Tender Ties: Women in Fur Trade Society, 1670–1870*. Winnipeg: Watson & Dwyer, 1980.

Printed Documents and Reports

Rich, E.E., ed. *Minutes of the Hudson's Bay Company, 1671–74*. Toronto: Champlain Society, 1942.

Thwaites, R.G. *The Jesuit Relations and Allied Documents*, 71 vols. New York: Pagent Book Company, 1959. Available at http://puffin.creighton.edu/jesuit/relations/.

Films

Canada: A People's History. Episode 6. DVD. Executive produced by Mark Starowicz. CBC, 2000.

The Other Side of the Ledger: An Indian View of the Hudson's Bay Company. DVD. Directed by Martin DeFalco and Willie Dunn. NFB, 1972.

Websites

Canadiana.ca, 'Exploration, the Fur Trade, and Hudson's Bay Company'
www.canadiana.ca/hbc/stories/aboriginals1_e.html

CBC, 'Happy Birthday Hudson's Bay—From Canada's Indians', 12 Dec. 1970
http://archives.cbc.ca/society/native_issues/clips/15985/

CBC, 'Hudson's Bay Company Ends its Fur Trade', 30 Jan. 1991
http://archives.cbc.ca/economy_business/consumer_goods/clips/2740/

Hudson's Bay Company Heritage
www2.hbc.com/hbcheritage

SIX

Locating Métis Identity

Introduction

The **Métis** past is contentious and no issue is more significant than the question of Métis identity. As Métis scholar Paul Chartrand recently noted, while the Canadian Métis share many cultural attributes, they are a diverse group with varied historical trajectories and senses of identity. Moreover, just who is legally defined as 'Métis' in the Canadian **Charter of Rights and Freedoms**, which recognizes the Métis as one of Canada's Aboriginal peoples, is arguable, and the definition reflects neither the heterogeneity of the community nor the historical elasticity of its boundaries.[1]

Historians have also grappled with this problem. In 1985, for example, Jacqueline Peterson and Jennifer S.H. Brown cautiously suggested using the term *Métis* to describe those descended from the 'Red River Métis' and therefore belonging to the 'Métis Nation' as defined by the Métis National Council, while designating others as lowercase-m métis. This practice, they argued, created a second 'inclusive category' to describe all those of 'mixed ancestry'. Peterson and Brown's own book, however, made the difficulties of this distinction apparent, as the authors chose to stick to the latter spelling rather than 'take it upon [themselves] to decide who belongs to socio-political categories that are still subject to redefinition and evolution'.[2] A survey of the most recent literature shows that most scholars are similarly reluctant but prefer to use *Métis*'.[3] This is the spelling we have chosen to use in this textbook.

As Peterson and Brown's conundrum suggests, one of the many distinctions among the Métis derives from the prominence of Red River in Métis history. This focus led Trudy Nicks and Kenneth Morgan to complain, in 1985, that historians were suffering from 'Red River myopia', concentrating on the Red River Colony at the expense of Canada's many other Métis communities.[4] Answering Nicks and Morgan's call to correct this problem, many scholars (particularly Métis historians) have been busily unearthing the histories of the Métis beyond Red River. Ute Lischke and David McNab's recent edited collection, for example, includes articles focusing on the Métis in present-day Ontario, Alberta, and the United States.[5] Chapter 14 of *Aboriginal History* includes an article on a Métis community in northern British Columbia.[6]

In this chapter, Alexander Campbell contributes greatly to our understanding of Métis identity formation. Complicating the predominant narrative of the Métis as emerging from Indigenous and European unions resulting from the fur trade, he traces the evolution of Métis families descending instead from British military personnel and Aboriginal women. In so doing, Campbell illustrates the different paths Métis families could take, the myriad Métis identities that could develop, and the wide geographical distribution of Métis people. The second article, by Geoff Read and Todd Webb, looks at the degree to which the wider Western world recognized the Métis as a unique community and as a nation during the latter half of the nineteenth century. In the process, Read and Webb discover that, from 1869 to 1885, the Métis were widely discussed by commentators outside Canada's borders. Their research also serves as a stark reminder of the colonial and racist confines within which the new nation had to act and sheds light on why the Canadian government treated Louis Riel and his followers so pitilessly. These two articles suggest that locating Métis identity requires searching far beyond the Red River Colony.

Chapter Objectives

At the end of this chapter, you should be able to

- identify when, where, and how the Métis emerged and address the complexity of determining who 'belongs' to the Métis community;
- discuss how the existence, history, and influence of Métis people descended from British military officers and Aboriginal women complicates our understanding of the Métis in Canada; and
- understand how and why Aboriginal peoples are often silenced in Western discussions of their own identities and fates.

Secondary Source

1.   'I Shall Settle, Marry, and Trade Here': British Military Personnel and Their Mixed-Blood Descendants

Alexander V. Campbell

King George's armies had campaigned across large parts of eastern North America during the course of the Seven Years War (1756–63). Official correspondence, personal journals, and published accounts reveal that redcoats were enthusiastic about the economic promise of the lands through which they traversed. Keen observation about the diversity of native flora and fauna, soil fertility for future country seats, and the abundance of natural resources excited comment among all ranks.[7] Troops assigned to duty in the advanced posts were especially bullish about the empire's newly acquired territories. Soon after surveying captured Fort Niagara's environs, one officer, Captain Charles Lee, apprised family members that he would not be returning to the

United Kingdom because more favourable opportunities awaited in the Great Lakes watershed where, he wrote, 'I shall settle, marry, and trade here.'[8]

Lee's dreams to prosper from hinterland commerce with Native communities were not illusory, despite modern scholarly accounts that decried interaction between redcoats and the First Nations. Historians, preoccupied with events surrounding Pontiac's resistance movement (1763–4), have vilified the King's men as vectors for European exploitation, expansion, and disease. Their complicity in the spread of pox-infected blankets among villagers and their removal of white captives from adoptive Amerindian homes have all become *causes célèbres*.[9] Emphasis upon events from the Seven Years War era, however, distorts the *true* nature of this dynamic association. In truth, British regulars were eventually grafted into an extant socio-political system already evolving between Europeans and various tribal groups, primarily the Nations of the Three Fires and Iroquoian Confederacies. Diplomacy, military aid, philanthropy, and even intermarriage were essential parts of the matrix, ultimately linking army and Indigenous communities together for almost a century.[10]

Three patterns of military involvement with Amerindian peoples contributed to an increase in the overall mixed European-Indian ancestry population as well as the establishment of a distinct community, which asserted title to the soil and declared itself a 'New Nation' under the leadership of Cuthbert Grant. Garrison commanders, who supervised frontier posts throughout the Great Lakes basin and the Ohio Valley, are noteworthy because they dealt with First Nations during their forward deployments and cohabited with Native women as had French officers before them. A second stream of mixed families owes their existence to the influence of regulars recalled to the United Kingdom immediately after the conflict. Although precluded from establishing consequential ties with Aboriginal women themselves, protégé kinsmen sponsored in the fur trade did sire offspring with country wives. Finally, another cadre of half-pay officers and retirees did exactly what Captain Charles Lee espoused: they settled in the New World and became active participants in the Atlantic economy. Military patronage relationships gave them considerable advantages over rivals because former regimental colleagues now supervised the posts where licensed markets operated. From such commercial networks flowed another stream of Métis children whose families resisted the foreign occupation of Red River and, in so doing, became progenitors of the Métis nation. Modern Aboriginal pedigrees are thus dotted with the names of commissioned gentlemen who had spent at least a portion of their careers in North America.

Garrison Commanders

The adaptation of Georgian land forces to New World realities was a slow process of trial and error. Amerindian diplomacy was just one responsibility of frontier duty that took regular personnel time to master. Notable success in this arena was first achieved during the early phases of the Seven Years War among southern villagers. Successful alliances with Catawba and Cherokee warriors acclimated officers to the intricacies of treaty negotiations as well as other local protocols, such as present distribution and adoption.[11] Knowledge of backwoods diplomacy was subsequently put to good use when dealing with tribal communities where reciprocal obligations required the army to protect ancestral lands, safeguard local enterprise in the fur trade, and shield villagers from the murderous rage of frontiersmen like the Paxton Boys.[12]

Humanitarian relief efforts were less dramatic yet equally important instances of military support for the Native population at times when they were under great stress. Medical aid was furnished gratis by regimental surgeons or other qualified soldiers with the costs borne by the imperial government.[13] Similarly, post commanders fed the hungry and clothed the threadbare when needy supplicants appeared before British gates. As with the case of presents, senior officers were allowed to render aid as transient hunting, trading, or war parties needed, despite the fact that supplies only reached army magazines after a great deal of intensive labour by the troops.[14] Such support continued even after the Peace of Paris when traditional harvesting methods should have provided for the First Nations' corporeal needs. As late as 1772, however, detachment heads informed headquarters that they were still 'under the necessity of humoring' tribesmen with provisions shipped for the sole use of the king's men. While government fare was not always of the highest quality, it was repeatedly given to villagers free of charge and in greater amounts than the soldiers themselves received for rations.[15]

Pure altruism alone cannot explain benevolent attitudes displayed towards the Natives by many officers. Conceivably kinship obligations were also a strong motivator because interracial liaisons formed a vital part of the local political dynamic, which astute commandants could not avoid.[16] Since these unions were arranged by local matriarchs for advantageous alliances, detachment heads, like other European predecessors who had profited from the Indigenous knowledge, social connections, and companionship of Amerindian brides, also cohabited with chieftains' daughters.[17] Certainly, the practice of marrying according to the manner of the country became so common among garrison principals that one British officer could jestingly write, 'Now to Mitchilimackinack, We soldiers bid adieu, And leave each squa a child on back, Nay some are left with two.'[18]

Kinsmen and Country Wives

Withdrawal from the Upper Posts did not end the birth of Aboriginal children with important British military antecedents. A noteworthy circle of Métis families trace their origins to European immigrants apprenticed to fur-trade concerns by prominent redcoat sponsors. For instance, the Small/McDonald clan from Ile-à-la-Crosse, SK, owes their existence to Major-General John Small who secured employment in the North West Company for younger kinsmen. The general was a scion of the Perthshire gentry granted an initial commission with the Scots/Dutch Brigade during the War of Austrian Succession (1744–8). Subsequently transferred into the Forty-second (Royal Highland) Regiment of Foot, he came to North America in 1756 as a subaltern and served on Colonel Henry Bouquet's staff throughout the masterful 1764 expedition against insurgent Ohioans. Small, thereafter, commanded a battalion of the Eighty-fourth (Royal Highland Emigrant) Regiment of Foot during the American Revolution, ensuring that family members received companies at his side. Those not disposed to a life at arms were provided for by other means since their benefactor's extensive patronage network reached into the highest royal circles.[19] The first Small involved with the fur trade was the field officer's nephew, Patrick, who spent the majority of his career associated with the North West Company's English River Department. His marriage to a Cree woman helped establish a family fiefdom strengthened locally through the birth of a son, Patrick, and two girls, Nancy and Charlotte. The daughters would later go on to marry John McDonald of Garth and David Thompson, respectively.[20]

The Nor'Wester mantle next fell to another clansman after Patrick's return to Scotland in 1791. That same year, John McDonald of Garth—whose mother was Magdeline Small—set sail from Greenock to Canada with letters of introduction from the general who had secured an appointment in the same merchant concern for his grandnephew. McDonald, too, spent key years in the Churchill River watershed, becoming a formidable presence there by 1804. During this time he met and married his mixed Scottish-Cree ancestry cousin, Nancy Small, 'according to the rites & ceremonies of that country', when she was only 16 years old. Their union produced four Métis offspring in the *pays d'en haut*: William (born along the Saskatchewan River in 1801); Eliza (born at Fort William in 1804); Agnes (born along the Saskatchewan River in 1806); and Rolland (born at Fort Qu'Appelle during 1810). Magdalen (1816), the fifth child, was born shortly after McDonald's retirement to Upper Canada after an adventurous career reckoned even against those of flamboyant peers.[21]

Never a modest man, McDonald expended a disproportionate share of his wealth upon a spacious Regency-style home located on a large estate, overlooking the St Lawrence River astride the Stormont–Glengarry boundary at Gray's Creek. Title to Inverarden House, as the Parks Canada historical site is officially known, remained in the female line even after the fur trader deserted his Native wife for a white woman in 1823. Eliza, the eldest daughter, retained possession of the manor home and 150 choice acres with the tacit understanding that she and her new husband, John Duncan Campbell, maintain any dependent kin from the first marriage.[22] Nancy McDonald, the spurned country wife, lived out her days at Inverarden. By twist of fate, she survived her younger rival by more than a quarter century, witnessing her own children prosper while the issue of the later union slowly bankrupted themselves in a series of rash business ventures.[23]

The Aboriginal household living in the North West Company's premier retirement community in Eastern Ontario flourished despite their father's abandonment. The eldest children had received superb educations while lodged at Park House under the aegis of their guardian, Chief Justice James Reid of Montreal. William McDonald, described by one contemporary as an 'uncommonly clever' young gentleman, attended Alexander Skakel's Classical and Mathematical School, becoming a successful provincial surveyor before his premature demise at New Carlisle, QC, in 1867.[24] Rolland, the younger brother, exhibited more humanistic proclivities, which ultimately led to a distinguished legal career. He also represented his home town of Cornwall three times in the Canadian legislature through the mid-nineteenth century. His successful law practice was rewarded with a Queen's Counsel appointment in 1856, capped by elevation to the Ontario bench some years later.[25] Eliza's instruction followed that obligatory for women of higher colonial station 'under the most competent teachers obtainable at Montreal', including the celebrated poetess Mrs Ann Cuthbert Knight.

Inverarden House. (© Parks Canada Agency.)

There she earned a wide reputation as a 'pianist of no mean order, and the old Scotch melodies and Scotch reels, which charmed the gallants of three quarters of a century ago, she used to play up to her last years'. It was at this formative stage of life that Eliza met and married John Duncan Campbell, who had just retired from the North West Company after its 1821 amalgamation with metropolitan competitors. His career paralleled that of Eliza's father and was the result of birth into another extended British military family.[26]

Commercial Networks

The genesis of a final stream of Métis children with close ties to the Crown's land forces arose from commercial networks established by redcoat veterans who settled in the New World after the Seven Years War. Their decision to remain in North America was predicated upon extant military patronage links that aided their adjustment to civilian life and furthered business pursuits, such as the fur trade. The most ambitious consortium was established by Major Walter Rutherfurd and Lieutenant John Duncan who received permission to establish a settlement on the Niagara portage less than two months after resigning their commissions in 1761. This entrepôt was built to support the garrison, expedite transportation along this difficult overland route, and, more importantly, provide a permanent base from whence agents could draw merchandise and cache peltry bundles obtained in the Upper Country.[27]

Much of the consortium's early success was due to the partners' influence over senior officials at headquarters plus friendship with active duty comrades who supervised scattered posts throughout the Great Lakes basin. Battalion officers abetted the company's activities by winking at the occasional use of their men to labour on private building projects, guard valuable company wares, or transport merchandise between posts in *bateaux* and sleighs.[28] This last concession was especially important when a season's furs had to be moved down the Great Lakes waterways for disposal at Albany. While other traders were required to absorb high freight charges, veterans' cargo travelled all the way from the head of Lake Huron at no cost. Further advantages also accrued to the partnership whenever army colleagues took it upon themselves to warehouse expensive company property in their own quarters while managing business affairs in the absence of accredited representatives. Even officers at the furthermost blockhouses abetted the Rutherfurd initiative by collecting arrears from traders who had acquired items on account but absconded into the wilderness to avoid repayment. Since this practice was a constant annoyance for merchants, the New York partners had one of the most effectual recovery systems in the lawless interior. Assets belonging to debtors or their associates were seized by soldiers when required and marked with the company blazon as a means of repayment.[29]

The Second Generation

While there is no evidence to suggest that either Rutherfurd or Duncan ever fraternized with women 'of the Copper hue', this particular fur-trade/military settler matrix produced a second generation of Britons willing to marry Native women. Typical was John Duncan Campbell, baptized in honour of the veteran campaigner with expectations that his distinguished namesake would serve as an influential patron in later life.[30] Campbell's father, Alexander, had come to North America in 1756 with the British army, establishing a post-war residence in the Mohawk River Valley where he operated a number of commercial ventures besides serving as a magistrate for Albany County. His tavern proved a favourite watering hole for the Schenectady, NY, fur-trade elite.[31] Betrothal to Magdalena Van Sice brought the Scottish immigrant into the influential Johnson orbit through his father-in-law, Johannes Van Sice, who served as an Indian Department gunsmith at Onondaga and was well known throughout the Iroquois Confederacy. Such consequential family ties to both sides of frontier society presaged John Duncan Campbell's apprenticeship to the North West Company begun in 1793.[32]

Campbell spent almost 30 years in the fur trade. Like so many of his fellow Highland Scots, he began as a clerk and was promoted to a wintering partnership within a decade. His family tradition of army service prepared him well for success in a business concern whose social and operational structure reflected a palpable military ethos. Indeed, contemporaries described North West Company principals as soldier-merchants who united 'the gallantry of the one with the shrewdness of the other'.[33] Such qualities were needed in the struggle against Hudson's Bay Company rivals during the whole of John Duncan Campbell's long career, which lasted until the 1821 amalgamation of both interests. There was no room in the new concern, however, for a man who had spent most of his career contesting English expansion into the hinterland and had been arrested for his support of the Red River insurgents led by Cuthbert Grant during the years 1814–17.[34]

The association between the North West Company and its mixed European-Indian ancestry progeny was a complex relationship shaped by personal, social, and economic considerations. The connection between father and child was present at the most basic level, since Nor'Westers of all ranks had been encouraged to marry *à la façon du pays* and many had their own mixed European-Indian children for whom to care. Complementing this parental responsibility was a wider societal sense of clan obligation rooted in the Scottish character of the North West Company partnership, members of which perceived themselves as Highland chieftains bound by the dictates of *noblesse oblige* to protect the welfare of their retainers. Finally, there existed joint economic interests, linking employer and employee in a common commercial pursuit, because mixed European-Indian ancestry males were an important managerial and labour source for the North West Company. All of these interrelated currents played a role in the Red River cauldron, where the mixed European-Indian ancestry population asserted title to the soil and declared themselves a 'New Nation' under the leadership of Cuthbert Grant.[35]

Descendants of the New Nation

The insurrection at Red River was a defining moment in the history of the mixed European-Indian ancestry population associated with the northwestern fur trade. Two groups of mixed European-Indian ancestry people were involved: 'the Canadian Half Breeds', whose loyalties were with the North West Company, and those born around Hudson's Bay Company outposts after the English concern began to tolerate country marriages in the late eighteenth century.[36] Historians have noted, however, that it was only among the former group that notions about distinct identity and nationhood first appeared.[37] In fact, Hudson's Bay dependents in the conflict zone echoed their superiors' disdain for the biracial offspring of the Montreal-based traders, requesting arms and training so that they could crush 'those lawless Rascals which the North West Company have with so little regard to every feeling of humanity brought in to Notice & rendered of Consequence'. Cuthbert Grant and his mixed European-Indian confreres, on the other hand, began to refer to each other as 'countrymen', an appellation which included those mixed European-Indian ancestry dependents of the North West Company then receiving an education in distant Upper Canada. As one partner explained to his sister, the **Battle of Seven Oaks** had recently been won by the 'countrymen' of her mixed Scots-Ojibwa nephew John McIntosh, who was attending school in Cornwall.[38]

Aside from these few allusions to 'countrymen' in contemporary correspondence, other early self-ascriptive labels have not yet come to light. Outsiders, however, had a great deal to say about the composition of this 'New Nation' that had dramatically appeared in British North America. Remarkably, early definitions had little to do with actual residence at the Red River flashpoint, because most of that area's mixed European-Indian ancestry males were employed in Fort William canoe brigades during the summer and could not participate in the active resistance. Rather than association with a particular geographic locale, connection to the North West Company seemed to be the defining mark of membership in this distinctive mixed-ancestry community. As the Earl of Selkirk succinctly expressed:

These half-breeds (or *Bois Brulés* as they were now to be called) have been described as a Nation of independent Indians: but they are in fact with very few
exceptions in the regular employment and pay of the North West Company,
mostly as canoemen, some as interpreters and guides, and a few of better education as clerks. The latter are the progeny of partners of the Company, at
whose expence most of them have been brought up, and through whose influence they may look to be themselves partners. These are the chiefs of this 'New
Nation.'[39]

Other eyewitnesses echoed this sentiment that '*Bois Brulés*' and 'metifs' were mere
synonyms for the 'children of the partners and servants of that Company, by Indian
women, from their different posts'.[40] North West Company support for their mixed
European-Indian ancestry dependents came in various guises. Political backing was
an important form of assistance since they were the first to acknowledge publicly that
their Métis kinsmen were the rightful 'owners of the Country and Lords of the Soil' at
Assiniboia, not the Earl of Selkirk and his colonists. This resolve was disseminated to
a wide audience through the press and by way of pamphlets published on both sides
of the Atlantic.[41] A petition addressed to the Governor of Canada from 'the Free half
breeds of Red River', expressing concern about the loss of their lands, was also ghost-
written by Nor'Westers for circulation in the capital.[42] Finally, the mixed European-
Indian ancestry insurgents were presented with a distinctive flag at Fort William by
the partners at the 1815 annual meeting. This emblem of nationhood—a white infinity
sign, first on a red, and later a blue field—was repeatedly displayed throughout the
conflict with the Selkirk interest and was flown in triumph over captured Hudson's
Bay Company standards.[43]

Political advocacy was complemented by military aid and logistical support.
This is evident from the actions of John Duncan Campbell, the partner in charge of
Cumberland House in 1816, who dispatched an armed party of nine men from his
post to strengthen the largely Métis force concentrated at Fort Qu'Appelle under the
command of Alexander McDonell (Greenfield) and Cuthbert Grant. Before leaving, he
instructed his men to neutralize enemy leaders should an engagement occur.[44] This
order was taken to heart by the detachment head, Thomas McKay, who brought down
one of Selkirk's principals in early exchanges at the Battle of Seven Oaks fought on
19 June 1816. McKay by the way, described as 'one of the best Shots in the Country
and very cool and resolute among the Indians', was one of the numerous Métis children sent east to be baptized at his father's church near the family home in Glengarry
County, Upper Canada.[45]

John Duncan Campbell's support of the Métis nation did not go unnoticed by
Hudson's Bay Company adversaries who sought to prosecute him for his role in destroying the Red River Colony, 'in furtherance of which said conspiracy an attack was
meditated and made on the said Colony wherein Robert Semple Esqr. and 20 other
persons were killed.' He was finally seized by the 'Honourable Company's' thugs in
1819 on his way to Fort William with the English River canoe brigade and impris-
oned at York Factory for several months.[46] He was eventually released from custody
and made his way to Montreal where he met and married Eliza McDonald, the Métis
daughter of John McDonald of Garth, in 1822. Within a year, the ex-winterer had

established a permanent residence in Upper Canada's Cornwall Township with his new wife. They raised four children, Elizabeth Reid (1823), Magdalen Ann (1824), James Reid (1826), and John Duncan (1828), at Inverarden House.[47]

Aboriginal lineage did not present an immediate social impediment to the Campbell minors who were nurtured in a Highland settlement where their father enjoyed a great deal of local standing during his latter years. Next to northwestern Canada itself, the counties of Stormont and Glengarry provided a tolerable home for numerous country-born sons and daughters because, as Heather Devine has so presciently observed, these Loyalist settlers perceived 'the Northwest fur trade as an economic extension of their own community'.[48] Prior to a premature 1835 demise, 'his strong constitution having been affected by his sufferings while prisoner of Lord Selkirk', John Duncan's prestige was confirmed by a company command in the First Regiment of Stormont Militia followed by appointment to an Eastern District magistracy. The Campbell/McDonald family union thus merged different elements of fur-trade society that had originally been predicated upon beneficial alliances between British soldiers and Canada's First Nations.[49]

***

Scholarly deprecation of relations between military personnel and Amerindians ignores the fact that intermarriage between these two peoples became less exceptional as the British Empire expanded through the nineteenth century. Indeed, after Canada's 1763 surrender to George III, contemporary **wampum belts** characterized this new partnership as an age of endless sunshine with 'the red coat (by its bounty) warm[ing] the 24 Tribes or nations'.[50] Matrimony was a vital part of this relationship of which three patterns are evident. First, garrison commanders acquired Native spouses according to the custom of the country but generally left their Métis children to be raised by tribal in-laws. Another group of military personnel, unable to participate directly in the Atlantic economy, sponsored kinsmen in the fur trade who appropriately took winter wives. Finally, a third cadre of veterans became New World residents engaged in hinterland commerce themselves or apprenticed their children to fur-trade concerns. Such dynamics produced a distinct subset of Aboriginal families descended from British troops who were determined to marry, trade, and settle here.

Primary Document

2.   Métis Nationalism: Then and Now

Yvon Dumont

In October 1991, Lieutenant Governor of Manitoba[51] and former president of the Manitoba Métis Federation Yvon Dumont addressed a symposium on 'The Battle of Seven Oaks' at the University of Manitoba. His speech made the case for Métis Nationhood in the past and present and discussed the many obstacles that Métis face within Canada. In so doing, he also offered a critique of Canadian historians.

I am honoured to have been asked to address a conference of scholars on the topic of Métis nationalism. As you know I am not a scholar and my presentation will have to be put in a different category. That is nothing new for us Métis, of course, as we have always been put in different categories. I am here to talk to you about Métis nationalism and I am glad to be able to do that and I am quite comfortable in doing that as I talk about that all the time. It's not often though that Métis, and especially a non-scholar Métis, get a chance to make some points to an audience of learned people.

Learned people, such as yourselves, are in such an advantaged position because you can pass on your views to so many other people in the course of your careers. Not only that, but you are privileged to be able to have as your audience the best and brightest minds of the community. And so you are able to influence the thinking of many of those who will come to be the important decision-makers in the public life of Manitoba and of Canada. Given the rare opportunity that I have today to influence the thinking of such a privileged audience, I hope you will be kind enough to forgive me for taking advantage of my presentation to throw in a few incidental points that some of you scholars may decide are not entirely germane to my topic.

I'll start right now by saying that I must qualify my statement about your audiences usually including the best and brightest minds of the community. My point is that Canadian society has not provided the Métis people with equal access to the benefits of an advanced education so it is that many of our best and brightest minds have never seen the inside of a university. I can assure you that some of the best storytellers, some of the best literary minds, some of the best philosophers that I have ever met are Métis people who happen to have very little formal education.

Let me turn now to my discussion on Métis nationalism, and I suppose it is appropriate that my initial focus should be on the event that took place in North End Winnipeg a long time ago. I am confident that scholars will be digesting the events of La Grenouillère, or Seven Oaks, in some detail today. All I want to do is take an extract of a contemporary statement to show that the stresses and strains with colonial, and then Canadian, society have always been a factor that has worked to cement our collective identity as a people.

When we are attacked and often vilified by strangers the effect is of course to draw us together in order to better assert our own identity. I take the following statement from a small book published in London in 1817 which was republished in 1970 as part of the Coles Canadiana Collection. There is stated, on page 87 in French, 'Mr. Robertson said that we [the Métis] were blacks, and he shall see that our hearts will not belie the colour of our bodies.' So Robertson is saying that for them our hearts can be as black as our bodies. That is a rare reference in the literature to the term *black* that has continued to be used to refer to us, as well as the odious term *half-breed*. But we have been called worse things, as I shall come to show.

I want to remind you that invective is invective, even if it falls from the mouth of an historian. Regardless of the fact that the Métis created a structure of Métis nationalism in the early days, it has never been doubted, even by the mainstream traditional historians, that by the time Manitoba joined the Canadian Federation, the Métis were a distinct nation in the West. Permit me to quote just briefly from the work of W.L. Morton, a University of Manitoba historian, whose works are better known to you than to me.

Métis cart brigade camped on the Prairies, 1874. (Library and Archives Canada, C-81787.)

'The new nation was a unique ethnic and political reality,' he wrote, 'brought from the continental fur trade and it was not aware both of its uniqueness and of its dependence on the old way of life and also its need to adapt itself to the changes which had been foreseen for at least a decade before 1869.' The same author said that the Canadian government had no idea that it was dealing with a corporate entity, a new nation. That point was of course driven home to the Canadian officials, by L'abbé Ritchot, the special negotiator for the Métis, and as a consequence provision was made in Section 31, of the Manitoba Act, for a community land settlement scheme. I will return later to discuss the significance of that provision.

It is in the great events surrounding the creation of Manitoba that historians have traced the role of Louis Riel, one of the great figures of Métis history and Métis nationalism. Riel is one of the great figures of Canadian and Manitoba history because of his role as the founder of the province and so one of Canada's Fathers of Confederation.

Historians have also traced the role of Riel in the events surrounding the patriotic Battle of Batoche in 1885. And out of these roles they have asked themselves the simplistic question, was Riel a hero or a traitor? It isn't as if history could resolve itself by giving simple answers to simple questions that might force a yes or no answer. Unfortunately, this is the stuff that is fed to our children and to yours in the schools of today. No wonder there is a need to re-examine the Canadian identity today. Identity is, of course, very much defined by one's conception of the past and so one should not be at all surprised if Louis Riel means for the Métis something that is not shared by others. The fact is that to the Métis, Louis Riel is very important. He is very important because he is a significant part of our sense of nationalism and a sense of nationalism is derived and developed, not upon a pedantic examination of historical minutia, but rather upon the crystallization of an idealized antiquity. That is so for the Métis people, as it is for all peoples.

A national movement develops as an expression of the political will of the people. The expressions of nationalism and the political will that we are seeing in Eastern Europe today[52] are certainly not movements that have resulted directly from the tidy conclusions of national historians. They are the untidy expressions of peoples' political will. This is not to say that an examination of history has no role to play in the maintenance of a national identity. It has. When we consider the history, as it has been written by your historians however, we see many reasons to be concerned. First of all there is a pattern of undiluted racism that comes across in much of the writing. It is very hard to come to see ourselves as part of one Canadian nation when Canadian history either ignores us in defining the soul of the nation, or else vilifies us in praising the glory of their own national accomplishments.

Let me just give you just one small example of what I regard as a racist historical view of Métis people. It is taken from the work of Marcel Giraud, the French social scientist who is widely regarded, I am told, as the one who has written the best accounts of the story of the Métis. The extent to which he is revered can be gauged, I suppose, by the fact that one of the most recent books published locally on the Métis has a full-page photograph of Giraud at the front of it. The example I want to use is taken from an article written in 1937. It dealt with the Métis who lived away from the Red River

Louis Riel, 1868. (National Archives of Canada, C-007625.)

at the time in two small villages, one of which was St Laurent on the southeast shore of Lake Manitoba. It so happens that St Laurent is my hometown, and the place which I still call home. 'Tiny villages like these,' stated Giraud, 'are now occupied by very backward groups.' Here he stated that 'the mental traits of the Métis appear as incompletely developed as their biological composition. As soon as severe intellectual discipline is required the mixed bloods give up every exertion.' Giraud, of course, tried to throw in a few qualities, probably realizing that no one would believe that an entire people can be all bad. 'They have an acute sense of observation,' [he wrote], 'which allied with their artistic mind explains their curious gift for drawing.'

Now, having had such drivel driven home to them from their school days, how are our children expected to stand tall and to insist on taking their place in the sun, along with the children of immigrants, in order to forge one national vision? The fact is that we have been poorly served by historians. Not only us but all of Canada. The spirit of Canada is poorer today, partly because of the drivel that has been used to forge a national identity. How can you forge a proud and true national identity based on denigrating other people? Where historians have not vilified us they have ignored us. Everyone has heard of the Aboriginal Justice Inquiry of 1991. How many of you, however, have heard of the Aboriginal Justice Inquiry of 1881 in Manitoba? That one dealt with the dispossession of Métis infant land and it only came to light in recent years as a result of a land claims research project conducted by the Manitoba Métis Federation.

I am glad to be able to say that in recent years some historians have started, through their investigations, to give the country a truer version of the history of Canada and of the Métis. The work of Professor Doug Sprague, in leading the research of the Manitoba Métis Federation, is notable, along with subsequent publications derived from that work, and his more recent endeavours. Professor Nicole St-Onge at the College St Boniface, has also done a lot of work researching the history of the Métis. Some of what she has uncovered in the archives has corroborated some of our own oral history. That is pretty exciting stuff.

I want to make one point clear. I am not for one moment suggesting that historians should go out and try to create a version of history that better suits contemporary outlooks. What I have tried to demonstrate is that racist attitudes have infested historical writing. I am aware of the dangers of attempting to rewrite history which would inevitably be described by the media as an attempt, for example, to upgrade Riel and to downgrade John A. Macdonald. Let the system redress the social and economic imbalance that has kept our children out of university. Let us develop Métis historians and other scholars. The writing of history is crafted by human beings and must never be regarded as a truly scientific or objective craft. I am sure that the telling of our story by Métis historians is bound to create a better vision of Canada for all of us.

So we are not looking to rewrite history. But we may be looking at writing some unwritten chapters of history. Then we could insert those chapters into the history books of our school system so that our children can learn Métis history from the Métis perspective. And not just our children, but everybody's children; your children, your grandchildren, my grandchildren, so that we can all have a better understanding of where we all come from, where we all are, and why we are where we are. I think it would help to build a greater understanding of each other and it would be a better ingredient for building a better and more understanding Canadian society in general.

After that tangent I would like to return to the consideration of Métis nationalism. I have left that consideration at the point where it had been agreed, by everyone, that in the second half of the nineteenth century Métis nationalism existed as a fact in western Canada. The conventional wisdom is that, after 1885, when many of our people escaped to the United States in search of a better place in society, and the rest of us were marginalized and abused, that Métis nationalism effectively ended. Well it may have been muted somewhat, but it certainly did not die. Strong feelings of Métis identity have always remained amongst our people wherever they may be found. We should not be confused with the Aboriginal peoples who have been referred to as 'Indians', and we certainly are not Europeans. In the entire history of Canada, Métis nationalism

Pascal Breland, a Métis magistrate in the White Horse Plains district, member of the Council of Assiniboia and the first Legislature Assembly of Manitoba, and between 1872 and 1887 a member of the Council of the Northwest Territories. (Archives of Manitoba, MacLeod, Margaret Arnett collection 23-1, N9337.)

may have been strongly manifested only now and then. But the expression of Métis nationalism never died. I will only give two examples from my own experience.

The first is an extract from an original document, a draft petition written by the people of St Laurent, MB, in 1908 and addressed to the federal government. This is the community where I come from, and people ask me today when we take our case to court: 'Well how come you waited a hundred years?' There were petitions sent to the government all along. One was in 1908 and it comes from my own community. It reads in part

> Since 1870, the government has flooded both Manitoba and the Northwest with immigrants from all parts of the world. The government has given large tracks of land to railway companies, who are making millions of dollars on them. All those millions are the proceeds of the land which is our inheritance. Our forefathers have fought and shed their blood to defend and preserve that inheritance. Now today we are robbed of it and our children are driven out like buffalo, which has now disappeared from the prairies. That inheritance was deeded to us by our forefathers and sealed with their blood. It is our inalienable right which no civilized nation can deny. Misery, discontent, sorrow and war are the results of injustice. In evidence of the above we make mention of the Northwestern Rebellion and the Boer War.

This is the Métis of my community writing to the Government of Canada. We waited all these years and now people wonder why it is that we want to take the government to court on this very issue. It is because we haven't been listened to and we have never had the resources before to be able to take it to court. The government now is using all of the Canadian resources against the Métis of western Canada, who are still of limited means. They are trying to break us in a sense that they think if they keep us fighting over technicalities long enough that we are going to run out of money. Well what they don't know is that we didn't have any money to start with. But we've got a heck of a good lawyer.[53]

How about that for an expression of Métis nationalism? How about that for a version of history that our children could take pride in and use as a basis for the kind of security that would permit them to stand shoulder to shoulder with the children of immigrants to craft together a better version of Canadian society?

My second example comes from a short trip that I took a few years ago to a small place in North Dakota called Belcourt. It was named after a missionary and an Indian reservation is located there. However, all the residents of that American Indian

Métis hunter at Red River, photographed by H.L. Hime, 1858. (Library and Archives Canada, C016447.)

reservation are not Chippewa, as they are called in the United States. Many of them are Mitchif. They are our relatives from the Red River. They are the descendants of Métis people who have been travelling back and forth across the international boundary, ever since the boundary was erected, and who were moving back and forth in that area long before the boundary was established. Those Mitchif people have a very strong sense of national identity. They know they are one with us. But they strongly dislike this Canadian anglicized version of 'Métis'. They told me personally, 'You keep that word Métis up there north of the border, because down here we are Mitchif.' Those Mitchif people in Belcourt have done a lot to advance their identity. They have courses in Mitchif history in their colleges, as well as courses in the Mitchif language. What do we have here on the north side of the line?

The resurgence of public manifestations of Métis nationalism in recent times in Canada has occurred along with a general resurgence of nationalism amongst Aboriginal peoples, not only in the rest of the country, but around the world. Witness the formation of various Aboriginal political organizations in the late 1960s and early 1970s. The Métis organizations were born here in western Canada, some of them in the 1930s, 1940s, 1950s, and 1960s, and they got together and formed the Native Council of Canada in the early 1970s. I was a founding vice-president of the Native Council of Canada in 1972. But as we invited other provincial organizations of Non-Status Indians to join the Native Council of Canada, we soon began to lose our identity. The whole drive of the Native Council of Canada seems to be on Indian Rights and the Métis were beginning to be lost. So in 1983 we withdrew from the Native Council of Canada, not because we didn't support their initiative, because we did. They were right in what they were trying to do, but the issues of the Métis were being left out and were put on the back burner, so to speak. So the Métis National Council was born. Today I am also the spokesman for the Métis National Council.

The Métis were instrumental in setting up the World Council of Indigenous People. That was another fellow, one of those backwards people from St Laurent, MB, who was biologically not developed, I suppose. His name was Guy LaVallee, Father Guy LaVallee, and one who had been its president, the president of the World Council of Indigenous People, and that's Clem Chartier.

Métis nationalism, like the nationalism of other Aboriginal peoples, continues to face serious obstacles. Although the United Nations has recognized that social harmony is best promoted by the recognition of the rights of all distinct people to self-determination, the practice has not favoured the equal application of the principle to the Aboriginal peoples who are caught as enclave populations within national boundaries.

We are not in a position to rent the country apart, as is being done in the former Yugoslavia. Look at how quickly the tanks were brought out against the **Mohawks** last summer.[54] Look at how quickly we were shot and plundered in 1885. We can only try to appeal to Canada's sense of justice. We can only appeal to you to apply to us the same principles that you apply to all peoples and that you apply to yourselves. You recognize the right of self-determination for people in far-off lands and you recognize the right of self-determination for the Quebecois, because there is a political boundary drawn around them. I notice in Manitoba we are so quick to say that if Quebec was to separate from Canada that they could not take all that land because all of northern Quebec belongs to the Aboriginal peoples. But we are not so quick to recognize that fact in northern Manitoba. I don't see much difference. But because we have no boundary you deny us the right that you claim for yourselves and your children. It is shameful to note that we had a boundary but that you took it away.

The **Manitoba Act** of 1870, in Section 31, provided for the establishment of a community land base to permit us to survive as a people. But the governments of Manitoba and Canada took that boundary away from us by unlawful action. We are fighting that battle in Canada's own courts today, which again underscores the weak position that we are in. At the same time we have chosen the gentle and persuasive approach. We are not expressing our nationalism out of the barrels of rifles. We are expressing our nationalism by trying to show you that justice demands that your sense of nationalism will always be tainted if it does not do justice to us. Our general approach is not being quickly rewarded. While world attention is being focused on the situation of the Mohawks, the federal and provincial governments are using all of their resources to attack our case in the courts, delaying and stalling with every conceivable legal technicality. These actions help us to build our sense of national identity and I do not like the picture that is portrayed. Neither do I like the picture of Canadian society that is portrayed by those academic writers who are making a career of attacking our endeavours by using tactics that should shame any nation.

One day I hope we will have the respect of the children of immigrants. That day will come after you have learned to show respect by using capital letters to write words like Aboriginal and Métis. This, our scholars have pointed out to us.

In advancing the cause of Métis nationalism, we aim to advance the cause of Canadian nationalism. A local scholar who worked for a while with the Manitoba Métis Federation has written a small book about the reformulation of the Métis identity. What we the Métis aim to do now, in the context of the national unity debate, is to urge a new vision of Canadian nationalism. We want to urge the reformulation of the Canadian identity. It is not going to be easy. It will not be easy to cast off the effects of the vilification of the Métis by generations of Canadian scholars. The reformulation of the Canadian identity is caught up in a process of constitutional reform and is complicated by the new factor of significant symbolic value that the Constitution of Canada has now taken. The symbolism that is required by the Quebecois and other groups is going to have to make room for the symbolic expression of the nationalism of the Métis and other Aboriginal peoples.

What of Métis nationalism then and now? Métis nationalism then was a part of a great continental movement. When new peoples were advancing across the North American continent they looked to establish for themselves a proper place in the emerging national political institutions. Métis nationalism now is part of a larger movement. It is part of a worldwide movement where people are asking anew the basic question: What is a country for? The shrinking physical and economic world is forcing the design of new political institutions to provide collective security that flows from a distinct culture and a unique historical inheritance. Now that the world has become smaller the stage on which Métis nationalism is being played out has become larger than it was then.

So many people have lost their identity. But we continue to push that dream that our ancestors had, even the dream from my home community where they were sending petitions to the federal government to try and enforce their rights to land. A couple of years ago I was speaking in a community not far from Winnipeg and one young

Unidentified Métis settlers from St François-Xavier, MB, c. 1880. (Archives of Manitoba, Letourneau, H. collection 25, N13674.)

Métis man came to see me afterwards, and he said, 'You know I always wondered what I was and where I fit in.' He said, 'My father spoke French but I wasn't French. My mother spoke Cree but we weren't Indians, and we all spoke English but we weren't English and today,' he said, 'I found myself.' It was very important to that young man; he found out and he began to identify with the Métis. Today he is on the board of directors of the Manitoba Métis Federation.

Last weekend I attended a conference [in] Parksville, BC. Parksville is just a few miles north of Nanaimo on Vancouver Island and it was there that about 100 Métis had gathered. We were told, of course, that there were no Métis there, but we found out that there are quite a few of them. And one young man came to see me and said, 'I have my ancestors from Winnipeg, or from Manitoba.' He was adopted out when he was young, just a few weeks old. He was raised by a family that wasn't Métis and he was raised to be racist against Indians and especially the Métis because the Indians knew their place, but the Métis, they were kind of wild, he was told. He didn't know he was a Métis and as he grew up he suddenly realized that he was a different colour than the people that he had grown up with. Finally they told him that he was adopted. Earlier on this year, he began looking for his roots and he found out that he was a Métis and he then joined the

Métis Association and they found his mother. They sent his mother a letter saying that they'd found her son and if she wanted to contact him they could give them the phone number. The mother was 71 years old and she was afraid to call her own son because she didn't know what the reaction would be. She had been ill when she was young and she had lost all her children and then three years later when she was able to look after them again, she went looking for them and she found every one of them except the young man. They had told her that he had been adopted out already; there was nothing they could do. But he said that he found out later that he wasn't adopted until 1957 and so they lied to her in 1951 when they said he was already adopted out. But he said, 'Finally my mother phoned me and she said, "Do you know who this is speaking?"' And he replied, 'Yes, you're my mother.' So he chatted with his mother and she said, 'I feel like I just had a baby. They sent me a picture of you and you look like your brothers. You look like your family.' He said, 'I sat there on the phone and I had tears in my eyes. It never happened to me before. Suddenly I belonged. I was a Métis and I found that out and now I found my family.' That sense of belonging, of knowing where you come from, where your roots are is very, very important. As we travel throughout Canada we find that Métis nationalism is still there, and still very strong.

Secondary Source

3. Only Pemmican Eaters? The International Press and Métis Identity, 1869–85

Geoff Read and Todd Webb

Few episodes in Canadian history have received more attention than the 'Riel rebellions' of 1869–70 and 1885.[55] Pitting the Métis peoples of the Prairies against the Canadian state, the Métis resistance to the colonization of the West has fascinated historian and citizen alike. This is, in part, because the resistance evokes fundamental divisions between Aboriginal and settler, French and English, Protestant and Catholic, and Liberal and Conservative.

The questions of Métis identity and nationhood are particularly contentious. Some historians, such as D.N. Sprague, have argued that, by the early nineteenth century, the Métis in the vicinity of Red River possessed a distinct identity and constituted a nation that was repeatedly wronged by the Canadian state.[56] The Métis themselves, particularly those tracing their ancestry to the Red River Métis, strongly support this perspective and forcefully assert their distinctiveness and nationhood in both the past and the present. For example, the Manitoba Métis Federation proclaims in boldface on its website that 'Manitoba is the birthplace of the Métis nation.'[57] Conversely, some anglophone historians have sought to undermine such assertions. Gerhard J. Ens has stated that when the fur-trade economy collapsed at Red River on the eve of the resistance of 1869–70, so too did any chance of creating a genuine Métis nation in what was to become Manitoba. Similarly, Tom Flanagan has asserted that the Métis currently have no claim to redress because they were fairly compensated in the Manitoba Act of 1870.[58]

While this article does not attempt to settle this dispute, it does seek to shed light on the debate from a new angle. A number of scholars have examined how the Métis resistance was depicted in the English- and French-Canadian press in order to explore the position of the Métis in the expanding dominion.[59] Likewise, many historians have examined Métis identity formation and ethnogenesis across present-day Canada and the northern United States. Their studies reveal an undeniably distinct community—within Red River and well beyond—manifesting a group consciousness roughly within the timeframe outlined by Sprague and others.[60] The focus of research has, quite properly, been on the Métis themselves: Did they or did they not see themselves as a nation? However, this essay asks a different question: Did the transatlantic community recognize either a distinct Métis identity or Métis nationhood? As John E. Foster has pointed out, when determining 'who is and who is not a member of a particular people' or nation, it is vital to consider the 'views of the historical actors, both "insiders" and "outsiders"'. In other words, we need to determine not only 'when a particular population saw itself' as Métis but also when, or even if, 'outsiders shared this view'.[61] The degree to which the broader international community acknowledged Métis claims and nationhood shaped the socio-political terrain upon which the Métis had to operate. A survey of the press coverage of the Métis resistance—particularly in newspapers in Canada, the United States, France, Great Britain, Ireland, and Australia—suggests that those 'outsiders' had mixed views about what it meant to be Métis and the existence of a Métis nation in the West.

Underlying much of the discussion of Métis nationhood is the group's hybridity. As a people with both European and Indigenous heritage, the Métis occupied what Homi K. Bhabha would call 'liminal space' between Indigenous and Euro-Canadian cultures.[62] While their cultural and ethnic duality marked the Métis as unique and as a people of interest among commentators in the transatlantic media, it also exposed them to the assertions that, on the one hand, they were 'racially' and culturally inferior as an Indigenous people and, on the other, indistinct from French Canadians. Certainly, the Métis appear to fit theorist Gayatri Chakravorty Spivak's definition of the term *subaltern* as 'the oppressed' whose 'identity is its difference'. Spivak also suggests that 'there is no unrepresentable subaltern subject that can know and speak itself,' and that the 'subaltern cannot speak.'[63] As a racialized minority standing in the way of Canadian expansion, the Métis, despite their constant efforts to make themselves heard and recognized, increasingly found their voices drowned out in the domestic and international press. This situation suggests that while Julie F. Codell and Alan Lester, both historians of British imperialism, are right to say that colonized peoples could, as Codell puts it, 'write back', they did so under constrained circumstances and were often ignored.[64] The subaltern might have been able to speak, but that did not mean anyone was listening. In the Canadian context, this attitude translated into a federal government that wantonly trampled the Métis' rights and claims to nationhood while also stealing their land and attempting to obliterate their culture.

The Métis Nation

By the time Louis Riel was executed for treason in November 1885, the Métis had little doubt about their status as a distinct people or nation. Whether viewed in terms of race, culture, or language, the Métis were different from the Europeans and constituted an Aboriginal people in their own right. As their name suggests, the Métis were a 'mixed-blood' community, the product of unions between Aboriginal women and European men. Some of the Métis were English-speaking and Protestant, but the majority were French-speaking and Catholic. For the most part, the latter group defined what it meant to be Métis. The Métis were neither exclusively European farmers nor Aboriginal hunters. While most had farms that they worked for part of the year, they

| | MAJOR SETTLEMENTS |
| | MINOR POSTS OR TRADING STATIONS |

1	Cadotte's Post	28	St. Croix Falls
2	LaPointe	29	Fort Snelling
3	L'Ance	30	Prairie du Rocher
4	St. Joseph's I.	31	Grand River
5	Drummond's I.	32	Ste. Genevieve
6	St. Ignace	33	Kaskaskia
7	Fort Wayne	34	Cahokia
8	Godfrey's Town	35	Peoria
9	Bertrand's	36	Prairie du Chien
10	Parc aux Vaches	37	Shanty Town
11	Terre Coupee	38	Green Bay
12	Bailleytown	39	Bay Settlement
13	Bourbonnais	40	Grand Rapids
14	Grosse Pointe	41	Fort Gratiot
15	Petit Fort	42	Grosse Pointe
16	Rockton	43	Amherstburg
17	Milwaukee	44	River Rouge
18	Sheboygan	45	Oviatanon
19	Two Rivers	46	Vincennes
20	Marinette	47	Chicago
21	Kaukauna	48	Mackinac I.
22	Butte des Morts	49	Gros Cap
23	Portage	50	Michili-Mackinac
24	Wisconsin Rapids	51	Sault Ste. Marie
25	Lac Vieux Desert	52	Fond du Lac
26	Lac du Flambeau	53	River Raisin
27	Lac Court Oreilles		

Map 6.1 Great Lakes Metis Settlements, 1763–1830. (Map by Connie Peterson. Métis Culture & Heritage Resource Centre.)

also played a major role in the buffalo hunt. Another indication of the Métis' status as a unique community was their dress. Métis women were masters of needlework, producing clothing for their families that combined European and Aboriginal elements. By the mid-nineteenth century, these Métis artisans were selling their handiwork to European travellers and settlers, and the clothes they produced were valuable precisely because there was nothing else like them. Even more significantly, some Métis developed their own language. Like almost everything else in Métis life, **Michif** was an Indigenous and European hybrid, mixing Cree verbs and French nouns.[65]

Between 1816 and 1885, the Métis articulated their nationhood in conflicts with European and Canadian groups. At the Battle of Seven Oaks in 1816 and at the trial of Métis fur trader Guillaume Sayer in 1849, the Métis of Red River defined and defended what they saw as their territory and rights against European interlopers and the trade monopoly of the Hudson's Bay Company (HBC). In both instances, the Métis' struggle created a sense of shared purpose in pursuit of their collective interests. That self-identification as a nation was articulated most clearly, however, when they resisted the expansion of the recently created Dominion of Canada in 1869–70 and 1885. In 1869–70, the HBC's sale of Rupert's Land to Canada threatened the Métis, who felt that their rights had been ignored in the transaction. In response, they seized control of Red River, formed their own provisional government, and commenced negotiations with the Tory government of Sir John A. Macdonald. The resulting Manitoba Act of 1870 brought Red River into Confederation as a province but failed to secure the Métis' future. As Riel stated in a letter to US President Ulysses S. Grant, the Métis entered 'the Canadian Confederation, on the faith of a treaty which, Canada, as one of the two contracting parties, does not fulfil'. Instead, the fate of the Métis in the Dominion was to suffer 'prosecutions', 'unwarranted arrests', 'confinement in irons', 'condemnation to death', 'outlawry', and 'the banishment of the Métis Leaders and representative men'.[66]

Indeed, after the Canadian government sent an army to pacify the new province, many Métis fled further west, while Riel went into exile in the United States. Riel returned in 1884 to help the Métis press their ongoing grievances with the federal government. Thanks to the government's unresponsiveness, both the Indigenous people of the West and the Métis took part in related but separate armed uprisings in March 1885. The Métis went into battle declaring that '[i]f we are to die for our country, we will die together.' Many of them did die during and after the Canadian army's suppression of this final episode of armed resistance. Riel was hanged at Regina on 16 November 1885. Even in defeat, however, the Métis saw themselves as a nation defending their territory,[67] and their leaders—including Riel's former lieutenants, such as Gabriel Dumont—continued to press their case with politicians both north and south of the border. In a letter, Dumont even assured his Métis brethren in Canada that he had enlisted the help of 'an exalted person' in France, who 'sympathizes with our cause'.[68]

During the resistance, the Métis, with Riel as their spokesperson, attempted to make their voice heard in the press, both in Canada and abroad. In 1869–70, however, the Métis message was a mixed one—a reflection of Red River's unique political position as a former HBC settlement within the British Empire but not yet legally a part of Canada. In proclamations that were reprinted in the English-Canadian, French-Canadian, and American press, Riel declared that, in resisting the Canadian government, the Métis were defending both 'the rights of nations and our rights as British

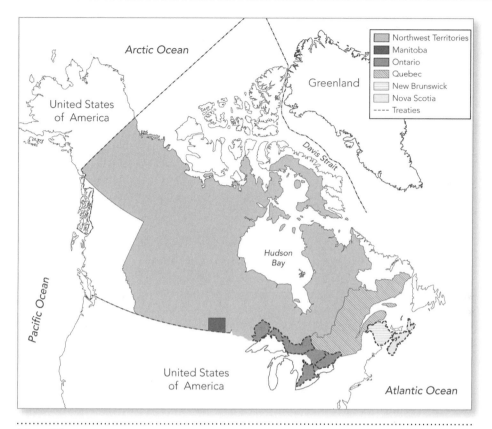

Map 6.2 Canada 1870, Territorial Evolution Map. (Indian and Northern Affairs Canada.)

and American press, Riel declared that, in resisting the Canadian government, the Métis were defending both 'the rights of nations and our rights as British subjects'. He also described the West as 'our country', though, given the fact that the **Red River Resistance** relied on the support of groups besides the Métis, his language was necessarily vague. That was no longer the case in 1885. During the **1885 Resistance** and in the months after his capture, Riel outlined the character and grievances of his followers in the clearest terms. In interviews first printed in the newspapers of western Canada and then reprinted in Ontario and Quebec, Riel portrayed the Métis as an independent people who 'never sold their rights, or agreed . . . to recognize the Dominion Government'. 'We did not rebel,' he argued, 'we defended and maintained rights which we enjoyed and had neither forfeited nor sold.' On several occasions at his widely reported trial, Riel referred to the Métis as a 'nation' with all the rights that such a description entailed.[69] In effect, he repeatedly made the case for a Métis nation in the most public forum available to him. But Riel could not control how either the Canadian or international press framed the Métis story.

The Anglophone World and the Métis

From the beginning, the English-Canadian and English press seemed determined to brush aside the idea that the Métis were a distinct nation. In this approach, Toronto's *The Globe*, the most influential English-Canadian newspaper of its time, set a pattern that others followed. Like the majority of English journalists on both sides of the Atlantic, *The Globe*'s editor, George Brown, firmly believed that Canada was destined to colonize the West and did not look kindly on anything that stood in the way. He consistently denied the Métis resisters' autonomy, stating that they were 'a few desperadoes, reckless of bloodshed' driven on by Riel's despotic will or that of 'some other evil genius behind him'.[70] Reflecting the racist and colonialist mentality of their age, the rest of the English and English-Canadian press agreed that, even if the Métis were a separate people, they were dupes of Riel with no significant will of their own. They were 'irresponsible demi-savages' and 'ignorant half breeds' who were racially incapable of independent action and had been delivered into Riel's hands by the HBC, the Catholic clergy, various American wire-pullers, or an incompetent Conservative government in Ottawa.[71] 'Riel feeds them on **pemmican**,' *The Globe* reported in April 1870, 'and as long as they can get nothing better they will stick to him till they eat what he has.'[72] The Métis might be linguistically and ethnically distinct and have some legitimate grievances, as the London *Times* and *The Anglo-American Times* noted, but they were considered a primitive people, somewhere 'between French and Indians' who could not possibly 'resist the British Empire'.[73]

In 1885, the English-Canadian press appeared to be more willing to support the Métis argument that the Canadian government had treated them badly. Papers friendly to the Liberal Party, eager to strike a blow against Macdonald's Conservative government, stated regularly that the Métis were 'neglected, despised, wronged'.[74] Even the staunchly Conservative *Toronto Daily Mail* accepted this image of the Métis. They could 'complain, and justly, that the Dominion has not treated them fairly', it noted. If the federal government had disrupted the Métis way of life, the *Mail* concluded, they certainly deserved 'compensation'.[75] And when Riel's Métis supporters adopted a revolutionary Bill of Rights in March, a correspondent from the *Mail* was present to record their actual thoughts that 'the Government had for fifteen years neglected to settle the half-breed claims, though it had repeatedly . . . confessed their justice' and so a provisional government had become a necessity.[76] It had taken a decade and a half, but the English-Canadian press seemed ready to deal with the Métis with a measure of cultural sensitivity.

That possibility proved illusory as both Tory and Liberal papers resurrected the racist image of the Métis as simple savages in efforts to gain advantage over their political opponents, undercutting the Métis claim to nationhood in the process. The newspapers of English Canada stressed that the Métis were 'a people who knew little of the world'. They were a 'peaceable' and 'loyal people' who were 'naturally easy-going'.[77] It made political sense for editors, on both sides of the partisan divide, to describe the Métis as naive innocents. Doing so allowed Tory papers to depict them as fooled by Riel, thus exonerating the federal government. The Liberal papers, in contrast, portrayed the Métis as being taken advantage of by both Riel and the Conservatives, whose incompetence had delivered the resisters into Riel's hands.[78] According to the

English-Canadian press, the Métis of 1885 were a unique but dependent group in the West whose ability to influence events was limited. They were the victims of Louis Riel, the federal government, or both. The Métis were not and could never be an autonomous force and, by implication, did not constitute a nation.

In 1885, the British imperial press was far more interested in the events unfolding in the Canadian West than it had been in 1869–70, though newspapers in England, Ireland, and Australia continued to follow the English-Canadian editorial lead. Editors across British world suggested that the Métis were a unique group in western Canada, distinct from the Native people and white settlers and divided into 'Métis-Francais' and the 'Métis-Anglais'.[79] The imperial press also concurred that the 'grievances of the half-breeds are undoubted' and sometimes blamed Canada's federal government for the uprising.[80] From there, however, editors in England and Australia attempted to fit the Métis into the wider context of British imperial affairs, the better to help their readers make sense of events in the Saskatchewan country. According to the London *Times*, the Métis were the Canadian equivalent of 'the Boer adventurers of Bechuanaland', a reference to the Dutch settlers of Southern Africa who stubbornly resisted British rule in the 1870s and 1880s.[81] In Australia, the *Brisbane Courier* likened the Métis to the Maori of New Zealand, similarly determined opponents of British 'land-grabbing'. From this point of view, the Métis could not be dismissed as 'only pemmican eaters': '[M]en fighting for their old free, open-air life of trapping will fight for what they hold to be their own, pemmican eaters, or not. They are just as fond of their rights as if they had been nourished on the most delicate fare.'[82]

In other words, both the English and Australian press characterized the Métis as one of the subject peoples of the British Empire, a rhetorical device that Riel himself employed.[83] However, this portrayal did not necessarily earn the Métis any respect. The *Brisbane Courier* denounced them as 'little better than a pest', while papers in England and Ireland argued that they were under Riel's spell.[84] This confusion—the Métis were a proud and distinct people but also the simple-minded victims of Riel's plotting—reflected the reliance of the Empire's newspapers on their English-Canadian counterparts.[85] With little direct knowledge of Canadian affairs, the editors had to make sense of the partisan wrangling of the Canadian coverage. Under such circumstances, the resulting image of the Métis was bound to be contradictory.

Readers seeking more clarity would have found it in the American press, particularly the two leading newspapers of New York, *The New York Times* and the *New York Tribune*. In 1869–70, the New York newspapers provided their readers with a somewhat nuanced view of Red River and its people. According to the *Times* and the *Tribune*, the Métis were separate not only from various groups of Anglo-American settlers but also from '[t]he Scotch and English half-breeds'.[86] Nor were the French and Catholic Métis to be confused with the Aboriginal peoples of the West.[87]

The American newspapers also had no time for the notion that the Métis were the puppets of some other more powerful group. In 1874, the *Times* published an account of the resistance from the Métis point of view to counteract English-Canadian and English claims that Louis Riel was 'the leader of a mob of French half-breeds, whose chief purpose was plunder' and terror. It strongly suggested that the Métis constituted a nation, arguing that they were a people with genuine grievances, stemming from their deep roots in the region.[88]

But, influenced perhaps by a general hardening of American attitudes towards any obstacle to western expansion in the 15 years after the Red River Resistance, the New York newspapers were less uniformly supportive of the Métis cause in 1885 than they had been in 1869–70. Like editors in English Canada and the British Empire, New York journalists told their readers that the Métis had 'suffered at the hands' of the Macdonald government 'and inch by inch their land is slipping from them.'[89] At the same time, however, the New York press drew on English-Canadian papers that argued that Louis Riel was 'the cause of all the troubles'.[90] At one extreme, the *Times* depicted the Métis as Riel's enraptured followers: 'Of 30,000 half breeds he is the idol,' it stated, 'he has chained them to him by his gift of fiery eloquence and by his undaunted courage.'[91] The *Tribune*, in contrast, was less sure. Taking up the role played by the *Times* in 1869–70, the *Tribune* stressed Métis agency. The aims of Riel and the Métis were not necessarily synonymous, it pointed out, and it might be possible to convince the latter that their leader 'is standing between them and their interests'. If that happened the Métis 'would almost certainly abandon' Riel and 'make terms for

Louis Riel, a prisoner in the camp of Major F.D. Middleton, c. 16 May 1885, Batoche. (Library and Archives Canada, C-003450.)

themselves'. They would behave, in other words, as rational actors, even though they remained fundamentally a 'half-savage people'.[92]

This picture of Métis distinctiveness became muddied after the resistance collapsed and the Canadian army captured Riel. Observing the drama of Riel's trial, conviction, and execution from a distance, the *Tribune* noted that any idea of the Métis as a unique people in Canada was fading fast. As Riel's execution approached, the Métis became subsumed within a larger French-Canadian nation: Riel's fate became the fate of the Métis, and the fate of the Métis became that of French Canada as a whole.[93] At the moment of their greatest international notoriety, US commentators transformed the Métis' story into nothing more than another episode in the long battle between English and French Canada. Certainly, there was no evidence of a widespread understanding of or sympathy for Métis claims to nationhood.

The Francophone North Atlantic and the Métis

In French Canada and France, the story of the Métis nation followed a different trajectory. In the initial stages of the Red River Resistance, commentators shared George Brown's ignorance of the Métis. Although there was more sympathy for the Métis in francophone ranks, confusion reigned over what exactly bound the Métis together.[94] Montreal's Liberal paper *Le Nouveau Monde* listed traits that it thought typified the Métis, but these in no way distinguished them from French Canadians.[95] This uncertainty prevailed despite attempts by some Métis to outline their culture and lifestyle to Quebec newspapers and, through them, to French Canadians. For example, in response to a patronizing piece that appeared in *Le Nouveau Monde*, a Métis letter-writer underlined that the Métis enjoyed many of the accoutrements of European culture. Even 'on the Mackenzie River, at Great Slave Lake,' he remarked, 'one can find pianos and musicians to play them. So don't be surprised if there's a piano at Fort Garry.'[96]

Perhaps the most interesting coverage appeared in *Le Courrier de St. Hyacinthe*, an influential conservative paper published outside Montreal, which printed regular reports from a man in the field who identified with the resisters and was likely Métis. As he wrote on 1 March 1870, 'Mr. Riel . . . is the leader of the nation, which recognizes him as such.'[97]

In French Canada, and to a lesser degree in France, serious discussion of the issues behind the Red River Resistance transpired. This was particularly true of *Le Nouveau Monde*, in which editorials explained the Métis' assertion that, as they had not been consulted by either the HBC or the government over the sale of Rupert's Land, Canadian sovereignty in the region was null and void. The newspaper went so far as to suggest a referendum in Red River on joining Confederation.[98] Even Conservative Member of Parliament Joseph Édouard Cauchon allowed that government agents had run roughshod over the Métis' claims to the land and had been insensitive to their concerns; he urged an even-handed resolution to the conflict.[99] Thus, in French Canada, the commentariat understood Métis disquiet and conceded its legitimacy.

Eventually, what emerged in the francophone discussion of Red River was a construction of Métis identity that emphasized the purported rebels' French heritage and frontier lifestyle. Absent was any meaningful discussion of the Métis' Indigenous heritage: it was their European ancestry that allowed them to be seen as civilized and so worthy of recognition. In this instance, the Métis' hybridity worked to their advantage. The respected Parisian daily *Le Temps*, for instance, carried a lengthy discussion of the disturbance at Red River. 'Most of the insurgents,' noted *Le Temps*' Washington correspondent, 'have French blood in their veins.' They were 'pioneers of civilization, simple and honest men'. The author counted the Métis among the 20,000 'white' inhabitants of the Red River Valley and at one point even referred to them as '[French] Canadian peasant[s]'.[100] Thus, the erasure of the Indigeneity of the Métis fostered sympathy for their cause.

In 1885, by contrast, French-language coverage of the resistance was much more extensive than in 1869–70 and was driven initially by an interest in the 'red peril'. Newspapers ran lurid accounts of 'redskin' violence and alarmist reports of a mass uprising among western Aboriginal peoples. Even Paris's Marxist *Le Cri du Peuple*, later sympathetic to the Métis' plight, initially stoked the racist fears of its readers by predicting 'a war between [the Indians] and the whites, which will be long and bloody'.[101] This sensationalism reached a fever pitch following the kidnapping of two white women by Cree warriors in early April 1885. The spectre of white women under the control of Aboriginal men was, in the minds of French-Canadian and French

Mistahi Maskwa (Big Bear). (Library and Archives Canada, C-001873.)

journalists, beyond horrifying, and newspapers fuelled their readers' outrage with speculation that the leader of the Cree resisters, Big Bear, planned to take the captive Theresa Delaney as a wife.[102]

To the extent that such reporting reveals anything about the authors' perceptions of Métis identity or nationalism, it indicates incomprehension and a conflation of the Métis with their Cree allies, a pattern that persists to this day. Thus, whereas the Métis' French heritage had won them sympathy in 1869–70, in 1885 their Indigenous ancestry initially alienated potential supporters. However, understanding of the Métis did improve and the francophone press on both sides of the Atlantic made a substantial effort to inform their readers of Métis culture and grievances. For example, Montreal's papers attempted to distinguish the Métis from 'the savages', insisting that only the former were 'civilized'.[103] Racist though this discourse was, it represented a step towards recognition of the Métis as a unique group by francophone journalists.

A further move in this direction came with the elucidation of the Métis' lifestyle. Many publications, for instance, underlined that the Métis were hunters and trappers; others emphasized their religiosity; and still others examined Métis appearance, dress, and history.[104] Oftentimes, these investigations were, to borrow Edward Said's term, Orientalist.[105] A peculiarly persistent tendency was to liken the Métis to Bedouins. Both groups, journalists informed their readers, possessed remarkable horseback riding and sharpshooting skills. Several publications, in both Canada and France, likewise compared Riel to another 'rebel' of 1885: Muhammad Ahmad al-Mahdi, who led a Sudanese rebellion against Egyptian (and by extension British) authority.[106] Thus, the Métis became an exotic 'other'.

Others made more concrete attempts to educate the public about the Métis and their grievances. In France, *Paris-Canada* explained to its readers that the dispute was over the dispossession of the Métis' land, adding that the Métis were a culture apart, descended from Indigenous and French unions. The pro-Canadian bent of the publication, however, led the author to ascribe the Métis' plight to their supposed indolence. They had, he explained, 'abandoned Manitoba for the North-West, meaning hard work and industry for hunting and fishing'.[107] *Paris-Canada* thus constructed the Métis as separated from the Indigenous peoples by their French heritage and Catholic religion but, due to their Indigenous origins, unsuited to the 'hard work' of modern life. In so doing, of course, the paper drew on the racist trope of Indigenous peoples as inherently lazy. As *Paris-Canada* stated condescendingly: 'The population is nomadic, anxious, easily offended, [and] childlike.'[108]

Commentators also made the Métis' racial hybridity a centrepiece of their coverage. A common theme was that the Métis played a role as intermediaries between 'Indians' and whites in the Northwest.[109] Crude though this obsession with the duality of Métis identity was, it was often accompanied by serious consideration of the Métis' grievances. Paris's *Le Figaro*, for example, explained that the Métis' main sources of discontent were their being pushed off their land and 'persecutions' at the hands of white settlers.[110] Perhaps the most comprehensive analysis came courtesy of Alexandre Taché, the Catholic archbishop of St Boniface, MB. Taché had a personal relationship with Riel and had been accused by the anglophone press of fomenting Métis unrest. Nevertheless, the archbishop bravely outlined the many ways in which the Métis' concerns had been ignored and concluded that the responsibility for the violence was widely shared among the government, the settlers, and the resisters themselves.[111] In short, sympathy for the Métis' plight, if not their violent actions, was nearly universal in the francophone North Atlantic. As left-wing firebrand Henri Rochefort wrote in Paris, the Métis were one of many 'peoples enslaved, stripped [of their rights], and decimated by English oppression'.[112]

Thus, within the French-language transatlantic conversation about the Métis in 1885, it is clear that commentators recognized the Métis' unique hybrid identity and conceded the legitimacy of their complaints. Did this constitute an international recognition of Métis nationhood? One searches in vain for any commentator not connected to the Métis who used the language of nation to describe them. Yet, particularly during the rigorous discussion of the justice of Riel's conviction and hanging, observers plainly viewed him as a defender of his 'people'. This was especially evident on the political left in both French Canada and France. The organ of the French Workers' Party described Riel as 'the heroic leader of the rebellious Canadian Métis'; French liberal theorist Gustave de Molinari portrayed him as motivated by 'patriotism'; and French-Canadian journalist P.-Ernest Tremblay dubbed Riel a 'champion of the rights of an oppressed people'.[113] Moreover, commentators of all political stripes cast the Métis leader as a martyr. For example, Charles Longuet, Karl Marx's son-in-law and a fervent Marxist, stated that Riel was a 'prisoner of war' who was treated as a 'criminal' and rendered a 'martyr' by his executioners.[114] While there was no widespread recognition of Métis nationhood, at least some commentators on both sides of the Atlantic certainly recognized the Métis as an independent people.

The passionate defence of Louis Riel that arose in both French Canada and France also saw a repetition of the pattern of 1869–70. As authors came to identify with the Métis, they underscored their French heritage and conflated the Métis with French Canadians. Suddenly, just as the story of the resistance of 1885 reached its international climax with Riel's execution, the key theme became 'the conquered [French] race against the conquering [English] one'.[115] In an extreme case, the Parisian paper *Le Figaro* explained: 'Riel . . . is a Métis, a half-Frenchman; but in Canada, where the love of the mother country, of France, is so deeply rooted in people's hearts, a half-Frenchman could pass for a Frenchman and a half. Thus, there, on the banks of the St. Lawrence, a Frenchman is in distress for having defended his home!'[116]

This metamorphosis resulted principally from the political purposes of francophone authors, always eager in both French Canada and France to rouse their readers against 'the Ontarian devourers of priests' or 'cowardly England'.[117] Unfortunately, clarity over Métis identity fell victim to expediency. Once again, therefore, the Métis' hybridity shaped the recognition of their singular identity but paved the way for their effacement within a larger French-Canadian whole. That their effacement transpired despite the continued political activity of the Métis and their claims to be recognized as a distinct nation[118] illustrates all too clearly the hegemony of the predominant view of Indigenous peoples in the Western world.

Conclusion

If the test of nationhood is domestic and international recognition, the Métis of 1869–70 and 1885 did not qualify, as transatlantic francophone and anglophone commentators did not extend such acknowledgement. On the whole, this indifference was unsurprising given that even the most radical commentators assumed the inevitability of the extension of Canadian colonialism in the West. That the grievances of a few thousand 'mixed-race' farmers and hunters might prevent the forward march of 'civilization' was unimaginable to the vast majority of Western observers in the context of the day.

In their discussion of Riel's trial and execution, both francophones and anglophones increasingly referred to the Métis in terms synonymous with French Canadians. Thus, the hybridity of the Métis proved doubly disadvantageous. Their Indigeneity enabled their representation as 'uncivilized', while their French heritage led to their distinctiveness being erased or overlooked.

Did this Western inability to perceive the nationhood and political maturity of the Métis matter? Certainly, the Canadian government was sensitive to the criticisms of its conduct in the international community, as shown by its defence of its actions to the Committee of the Privy Council in Great Britain.[119] Had that community made the case for a Métis nation it might well have given Canada pause. More importantly, the pervasiveness of this mentality on both sides of the Atlantic offers a window into the Western mindset of the late nineteenth century, a mindset that shaped Canadian policy and was hostile to the rights of Aboriginal peoples. Alas, the climate of the times was such that John A. Macdonald confessed publicly without hesitation or shame that the Canadian government's chief aims in dealing with the Red River Métis were 'to obtain possession of the country' and 'the extinguishment of the Indian title'.[120]

That does not mean, however, that the Métis did not possess a national identity or that the international press ignored them entirely. By the time Riel was hanged in November 1885, the Métis self-identified as a unique community in the Canadian West, and many Métis asserted their rights and nationhood in the strongest possible terms. As Riel proclaimed during his trial, the Métis were a 'nation' possessing land— their 'inheritance from God'.[121] Moreover, despite the repression they suffered post-1885 at the hands of Canada, the Métis endured and their culture thrived. For their part, in 1869–70 and 1885 the transatlantic French community and the majority of the anglophones of the British Empire and United States portrayed the Métis as a distinct group, acknowledging, to varying degrees, the legitimacy of their grievances.

Primary Document

4.   The Insurrection in Manitoba

Brisbane Courier, 16 May 1885

A telegram which we publish this morning from our correspondent at Montreal shows that the half-breed insurrection in the North-west of Canada has become very serious. On Thursday the insurgents gained a victory over the Government troops and police. A Canadian Cabinet Council has, our correspondent says, determined to send 2000 men against the rebel force. The question now agitating the Dominion is whether the Indians, some 16,000 in number, will join the rebels. If not, the rebellion will be easily crushed. If they do, the resources of Canada will be heavily taxed. Louis Riel, the half-breed leader, appears to have been making inflammatory speeches about the disabling effect of the dispute between England and Russia, while the Fenians along the American border are threatening to join in the fray. But we are certain that the crisis will be met with courage and coolness by our gallant fellow-subjects, and that Lord Lansdowne will not be wanting to the occasion. The origin of the insurrection is the same as it was in 1869. Everybody has heard of the Red River expedition and many people have a confused idea that some one up a river had to be "smashed," and that Colonel, now General Lord Wolseley smashed him. This conception of what occurred is wanted in exactitude. M. Louis Riel, who led the Red River insurgents, withdrew when Colonel Wolseley's men appeared on the horizon. But though he withdrew, M. Riel was not quite disposed of. He lived to fight another day; the other day has arrived, and his followers are formidable. "What they fought each other for?" is a question that has puzzled more mature historical inquirers than Southoy's little Peterkin. In ancient days men did battle for a woman, or a well, and things were intelligible. Now they grow too confusing, from the intricacy of tribal and national interests, and from the enormous distances of space still covered by our Empire. The causes of quarrel between M. Louis Riel and the British Government in 1870 may be gathered from Colonel Butler's very interesting book, "The Great Lone Land." The Red River Settlement was in insurrection under Riel, because of certain arrangements between the Governor of Canada and the Hudson's Bay Company. The dwellers on the Red River Settlement, the half-French, half-Indian people, wish themselves to be regarded as protesting against land-grabbing. That is really what their case comes to. Ever since English history begins we have been acquiring land, and the natives have protested. Sometimes they protested with polished, neolithic, stone-headed weapons. Sometimes, as when we took the isle of Albion, they protested with laments, which may be read in Gildas. When we occupied New Zealand, they appealed to green-jade axes and *patu patus*.

What was it which really occurred on the Red River? "The native," says Colonel Butler, "knew this land was his, and that strong men were coming to square it into rectangular farms, and to push him further west by the mere pressure of civilisation . . . What were these new people coming to do to him?" Manifestly to "eat him up," as the Zulus say. The plan to which the "rebels" under Riel objected transferred land in the North-west from the Hudson's Bay Company to the Crown. It would have been a most commendable transfer, but there were 15,000 people living in the territory, and "they objected to have themselves and their possessions signed away without one word of consent or one note of approval." So the resisting natives got out their powder horns, put new flints in their old guns, and attacked the surveying parties. Louis Riel, who led freedom's battle, is occasionally described as a half-breed, but there seems to be a divergence of opinion about his lineage. French, or half French half Indian, his energy of character is highly spoken of by some of his biographers. He had rather an excellent opportunity, for no pains were taken by the Hudson Bay Company, or the Imperial Government, or the Dominion Government, to settle the rights and wrongs of the question on the basis of justice and honesty. The Metis the discontented half-breeds, were called "only pemmican eaters," and that was supposed to be a sufficient refutation of their claims. Now, men fighting for their old free, open-air life of trapping, will fight for what they hold to be their own, pemmican eaters, or not. They are just as fond of their rights as if they had been nourished on the most delicate fare. The Red River natives drove the Governor of the country appointed by Canada out of the frontier station at Pembina. They fortified the road between Pembina and Fort Garry. Lastly, they seized Fort Garry, which was their Khartoum, for there they found a battery of nine pounders, with musketry and ammunition. All this was done in a style admired by Colonel Butler. "One hates so much to see a thing bungled," says this distinguished officer, "that even resistance, though it borders upon rebellion, becomes respectable when it is carried out with courage, energy, and decision." All these qualities had, so far, marked the performances of M. Louis Riel.

Although Riel's conduct was at first bold and energetic, he had to be "smashed," or at the very least "disintegrated." Colonel Wolseley, with men in boats, was sent to smash, but only succeeded in disintegrating. The expedition drew near to Fort Garry; it was not fired upon, like that unhappy relief of Khartoum, but was welcomed by all the Scotch and English of the settlement. They were tired of Dictator Riel. Still Riel held out in Fort Garry, just when France was being driven back from her frontiers by the overwhelming weight of the German armies. Fort Garry was reached by our expedition, but there was no sign of hostile occupation. The banner of the insurgents did not flaunt the breezes; in fact there was no banner at all. The gate was open—anyone could go in. An officer of the Hudson's Bay Company was on the threshold to welcome Colonel Wolseley. M. Riel had made war-like preparations. His gallant force had loaded their rifles, and afterwards thrown them away, because they interfered with a speedy strategic movement to the American frontier. "Twenty hands, with an aggregate of perhaps two and a-half hearts among them, were all Riel had to depend on at the last moment." The Dictator, M. Riel, escaped with his life. But he has not forgotten, nor have his kindred forgotten, how they were disposed of, quite without a plebiscite, as Imperial France would have arranged their transfer. The Catholic clergy, no doubt, dislike the increase of Protestant or perhaps agnostic sheep in their fold. The Indians are restless. Then, across the frontier, are our old enemies, the American Irish, who are not likely to keep out of any fighting in which the United States permit them to take part. There is a blood feud between Louis Riel and civilisation. In 1870 he more or less judicially murdered one Thomas Scott, and Scott's slaying is unavenged. The state of things, as we have said, is grave. But we have the satisfaction of knowing that it is being faced with a thorough determination to protect Canadian territory from turbulent risings and lawless raids.

Questions for Consideration

1. How does the existence and history of a considerable and influential population of Métis people with British and Aboriginal ancestry alter our understanding of a) Aboriginal/British relations; b) the fur trade; and c) the Métis?
2. What cultural practices and norms do the Métis descendants of British military officers and Aboriginal women appear to have maintained from each side of their

heritage? Do these individuals appear to have developed a new, unique identity and culture? Give reasons to support your answer.

3. What critique does Yvon Dumont make of Canadian historians' and scholars' interpretations of the Métis? Discuss whether such interpretations should be considered part of the colonial project of subjugating and dominating Aboriginal peoples.

4. Did the international press recognize the Métis as possessing a distinct identity or nationhood? How could this treatment have affected the Métis resistance?

5. Does the perception of the Métis resistances of 1869–70 and 1885 support the view that colonial subjects are silenced by the colonizing society? Why or why not?

6. In what ways does the article from the *Brisbane Courier* afford the Métis any recognition of their distinct identity or nationhood?

7. When, where, and how did a Métis identity emerge? Who contributed to the construction of this emergent identity and who comprised the Métis community?

Further Resources

Books and Articles

Barkwell, Lawrence J., Leah Dorion, and Darren R. Préfontaine, eds. *Métis Legacy.* Winnipeg: Pemmican Publications, 2001.

Lischke, Ute, and David T. McNab, eds. *The Long Journey of a Forgotten People: Métis Identities and Family Histories.* Waterloo: Wilfrid Laurier University Press, 2007.

MacDougall, Brenda. *One of the Family: Métis Culture in Nineteenth Century Saskatchewan.* Vancouver: UBC Press, 2009.

Sprague, D.N. *Canada and the Métis, 1869–1885.* Waterloo: Wilfrid Laurier University Press, 1988.

Printed Documents and Reports

Sprague, D.N., and R.P. Frye. *The Genealogy of the First Métis Nation: The Development and Dispersal of the Red River Settlement, 1820–1900.* Winnipeg: Pemmican Publications, 1983.

Stanley, George F.G., Raymond J.A. Huel, Gilles Martel, Thomas Flanagan, and Glen Campbell, eds. *The Collected Writings of Louis Riel*, 5 vols. Edmonton: The University of Alberta Press, 1985.

Films

Canada: A People's History, Episode 10. DVD. Executive produced by Mark Starowicz. CBC, 2000.

Richard Cardinal: Cry from the Diary of a Métis Child. DVD. Directed by Alanis Obomsawin. NFB, 1986.

Riel Country. DVD. Directed by Richard Duckworth. NFB, 1996.

We Are Métis. Web video. Directed by Stephen St Laurent. 2008. Available at http://vimeo.com/6216205.

Websites

Manitoba Métis Federation
www.mmf.mb.ca

Métis Bill of Rights, 1869
www.canadahistory.com/sections/documents/thewest/metisbillrights.htm

Métis National Council
www.metisnation.ca/

The Virtual Museum of Métis History and Culture heritage exhibit
www.metismuseum.ca/exhibits/heritage

SEVEN

Federal Indian Policy

Introduction

The British laid the foundations of Canada's Indian policy with the **Royal Proclamation of 1763**. In part, the Proclamation was an attempt to ensure peaceful coexistence between Aboriginal and non-Aboriginal peoples by creating guidelines to regulate trade, settlement, and land purchases. Over the next century, the focus of this policy changed drastically. In 1830, the Indian Department was transferred to civilian control in Canada and partnerships were formed with various Christian churches to pursue a policy of 'civilization and assimilation'. The government and missionaries sought to isolate Aboriginal peoples on reserves, encourage their adoption of European-style agriculture, and gradually assimilate them through the inculcation of the social and cultural values and practices of European-Canadians. The federal government expected that, in the process of Aboriginal peoples assimilating, the state would acquire their land and resources.

In the 1850s, fur trader and politician William B. Robinson negotiated what came to be known as the Robinson Treaties, which involved territories along the northern shores of Lake Huron and Lake Superior. These treaties signalled the beginning of a more formalized system of land surrender that continued to develop through the negotiation of the western numbered treaties during the 1870s. The 1850s also witnessed the passage of increasingly restrictive legislation that controlled all aspects of Aboriginal peoples' lives, determining such things as where they could live; whom they could marry; what types of social, cultural, and religious beliefs were acceptable; and how their children would be educated. Although the foundations were laid in the nineteenth century, the bureaucrats who came to work in the Department of Indian Affairs during the twentieth century pursued these policies with renewed vigour and enthusiasm, and, for the most part, a complete lack of awareness of and disregard for Aboriginal cultures and peoples.

In light of the coercive and draconian nature of much of Indian policy, it has been a long time since it has been described as benevolent by historians. There is general acknowledgement that such policy was not only a failure but also cultural genocide. In the 1960s and 1970s, the work of Aboriginal scholars, academics, and activists such as Howard Adams, Harold Cardinal, Maria Campbell, and Vine Deloria Jr forced both the academy and North American society to open their eyes to the injustices of Indian policy. That said, global decolonization and civil rights movements in the post-war period, in conjunction with the efforts of Aboriginal peoples to challenge the policies and actions of the federal government, have created a popular perception that Indian policy after 1945 improved dramatically and abandoned its most coercive practices. Hugh Shewell's article presents a welcome corrective to this assumption and provides a broad overview of Indian policy in the twentieth century. Shewell argues that the goal of Canada's Indian policy—to, in the infamous words of Duncan Campbell Scott, 'rid Canada of its Indian problem'—remains the same as it was at the turn of the century.[1]

Health care as part of Indian policy had been overlooked until recently. The state used ill-health in Aboriginal communities to assume the guise of protector of Aboriginal peoples' well-being. In turn, the persistent ill-health of Aboriginal peoples was blamed on their failure to become more like European Canadians—their failure to assimilate, in other words. Historians, however, have shown that the actual culprits for the pervasive health problems in Canada's Aboriginal communities include substandard rations, hunger, ragged clothing, cultural dislocation, and pervasive poverty.[2] Laurie Meijer Drees, while acknowledging this situation and its damaging effects on the bodies and minds of individuals, seeks to understand how Aboriginal peoples experienced the system and resisted it. Refocusing historians' attention, Drees shows how Aboriginal peoples, despite being forced to remain in Indian hospitals for long periods, continued to practise their culture and pursue their own understandings of health and well-being—often while doctors and nurses remained dismissive or unaware of these efforts.

Chapter Objectives

At the end of this chapter, you should be able to

- understand and explain the goals of Indian policy;
- recognize the ideological framework underpinning this policy and identify the tactics used to carry it out;
- recognize how the Canadian government used health care services as part of the wider colonial project;
- understand how Aboriginal peoples used and continue to use the health system without abandoning their traditional health practices; and
- recognize how Aboriginal peoples resisted federal Indian policy.

Secondary Source

1.   Dreaming in Liberal White: Canadian Indian Policy, 1913–83

Hugh Shewell

The period from 1913 to 1983 represents the rise and entrenchment of the bureaucratic administration and management of First Nations in Canada, beginning with the repressive administration of Duncan Campbell Scott and ending with the release of the **Penner Report**, which 'unexpectedly' endorsed First Nations **self-government**.[3] While some at the time thought that the report's recommendations meant the end of the federal Indian administration,[4] it was not to be. In this article, I trace the historical path of Indian policy during this time frame and argue that the policy and its implementation, while appearing to be more benevolent in the post-World War II era, remained assimilationist, seeking to dissolve First Nations into white, liberal Canadian society. In this context, the term *liberal* refers to a political philosophy that espouses progress and the amelioration of society.

The roots of Canada's Indian policy can be found in the Royal Proclamation of 1763, the subsequent approach to Indigenous peoples adopted by the British Colonial Office up to the mid-nineteenth century, and the eventual ascendancy of responsible government in the colonies of British North America.[5] The Proclamation was designed to maintain good relations with First Nations peoples and to manage interactions between them and the rising numbers of settlers.[6] Thus, it sought first to recognize First Nations peoples as the legitimate occupants of the land and, second, to guarantee their continued use of it. Contrapuntally, it provided a procedure by which lands could be ceded for settlement, a procedure that necessitated First Nations agreement.

The Royal Proclamation thus provided the original constitutional framework by which British colonial authorities, well before Confederation, struggled with what was to become of First Nations in British North America (sometimes termed the 'Native question'). While the plans of British officials differed to some degree from colony to colony, the ultimate solutions were roughly the same: Indians were to be assimilated into the broader Euro-Canadian society.[7] At first, assimilation was generally understood to mean that First Nations peoples would participate collectively in the developing market society but would, broadly speaking, retain their autonomy.[8] By 1841, however, military administration had given way to civil authority. The new civil administrations that represented and promoted the interests of settlers saw First Nations as a nuisance and barrier to settlement. The outright extermination of First Nations was considered, but the permanent undersecretary of the Colonial Office, Herman Merivale, never thought this a viable idea and decided instead on insulation and amalgamation. The latter was to take the form of 'Euthanasia of savage communities'; through miscegenation and acculturation, Indigenous societies and their cultures would eventually cease to exist.[9]

Historian John S. Milloy argues that, by the late 1840s, the colonial legislatures began to see the solution to the Native question not in amalgamation but individual **enfranchisement**, meaning that the Native peoples' 'full civilization . . . could be achieved only when Indians were brought into contact with individualized property.'[10] This approach required a revised constitutional relationship permitting a reconstruction of the Indian as an individual requiring development and acculturation to liberal values and behaviour. Central to liberalism is the belief that people are autonomous, self-contained, sovereign beings endowed with the right to own and exploit property.[11] This concept of the sovereign individual was contrary to nearly all First Nations' cultures and belief systems, which place far greater emphasis on the collective society, communal needs, and an interconnectivity with the land.

In the mid-nineteenth century, Western imperialists viewed their expansionism in terms of a moral mission to spread the grace of their 'superior' civilization. Thus, not only were First Nations peoples to be contained to allow unfettered economic expansion, but they were also to be educated, 'elevated', and 'civilized'. In 1857, the legislature of the United Canadas passed the Gradual Civilization Act, which formed the basis of the Indian Act of Canada and the policies that flowed from it. The Gradual Civilization Act created an enduring paradox: while its stated purpose was to civilize and integrate Indians into Canadian society, making them legally indistinct from other Canadians, it also separated them from Canadian society by defining who was an Indian and denying them the majority of legal rights accorded to Euro-Canadians.[12] In an attempt to eliminate resistance to these policies, the federal government introduced the Gradual Enfranchisement of Indians Act in 1869, in which traditional forms of band governance were abolished and replaced by municipal government-like forms whose actions were constantly supervised by the Department of Indian Affairs. In 1876, government policy was further rationalized under a new Indian Act, the net effects of which were to deny the original peoples of Canada any partnership in Confederation, to subjugate and strip them of their autonomy, and to devalue their cultures. They became dependent wards of the state, children in need of development.[13]

Subjugation, Repression, and Tutelage, 1913–45

How did the federal government propose to integrate these 'uncivilized' peoples? The methods proposed were to confine them to reserves; morally elevate and educate their children; teach them to be agriculturalists, gardeners, mechanics, or domestic servants; and suppress or ban their cultural practices.[14] Accompanying these techniques was a policy of chipping away at Indian lands by stealth or negotiated surrender so that settlement and commerce could proceed unimpeded.[15]

These policies were institutionalized by the time Duncan Campbell Scott became the deputy superintendent general of Indian Affairs in 1913. One of his first actions was to issue a lengthy policy statement to all Indian agents, instructing them on 70 specific points covering nearly every aspect of the Indians' lives, including their agriculture, education, occupations, relief (welfare assistance), and subjection to 'the ordinary law, both civil and criminal, except in so far as the Indian Act makes special provision for their exemption'. Scott determined to fashion a tightly run, parsimonious department that emphasized Indian self-reliance. As he wrote, 'In whatever occupations the Indians are engaged they should be encouraged in habits of industry and thrift.'[16] In addition, the Indian agents were to pursue vigorously the education of Indian children so as to turn them away from their own cultures that 'tend to destroy the civilizing influences of the education imparted' to them.[17] For Scott, the 'civilizing' of Indians meant only one thing: their complete absorption and disappearance into the general population. In his view, the 'great forces of intermarriage and education will finally overcome the lingering traces of native custom and tradition.'[18]

When Scott became deputy superintendent, Indian Affairs employed 651 Indian agents across the country.[19] He demanded absolute loyalty from them and suffered little criticism—like Indians, 'good' agents were obedient agents. The agents developed a clear, paternalistic relationship with the people for whom they were responsible. Thomas Deasy, Indian agent for the Queen Charlotte Islands, was a typical example. In 1920, he prepared a pamphlet for Scott that he thought might serve as an introduction to the role of the agent. He wrote, 'Since the introduction of . . . "Responsible Government," the authorities considered it advisable to appoint men . . . to educate, christianize [sic] and protect the tens of thousands of people emerging from the darkness of superstition, idolatry and self-constituted authority, through which all nations passed, in earlier stages of history.'[20]

With respect to the 'economic progress' of Indians, little was done to develop the economies of Indian communities apart from agriculture.[21] Even so, Scott's administration continuously attempted to press Indians (mainly adult males) into employment and other forms of self-sufficiency by discouraging dependence on relief, which at that time was issued only in the form of rations or clothing. Hence, if relief was given, it was so minimal as to deter the desire for its further provision.[22]

In addition to the three fundamentals of Indian policy—education, agriculture, cultural repression—Scott's administration focused on land surrenders and transfers to commercial and settler interests, compulsory enfranchisement, and the suppression of Indian resistance and political organizing. Scott had been directly involved in the negotiation of Treaty No. 9 over the summers of 1905 and 1906 and was influential in its final extension to other bands in 1929 and 1930. He also helped to frame Treaty No. 10 in northern Saskatchewan and Treaty No. 11 (the Mackenzie River Valley) in 1921–2.[23] In all cases, he was determined to make the terms as advantageous to the federal and provincial governments as possible by limiting the payments to First Nations and by minimizing the ongoing obligations of the state. Certainly, the enormous profits subsequently realized by mining and forestry interests, as well as the Canadian Pacific Railway and the government-owned Canadian National Railway, far outstripped any benefits that accrued to the signatory bands. As historian E. Brian Titley notes, the profit immediately gained by mining companies 'makes it impossible to dispute that fraud of a high order was involved' in these land surrenders.[24]

This type of treatment can also be seen during and following World War I. At the outset of the war, Indian Affairs did not think that Indians could make a useful contribution to the war effort. By its mid-point, however, there was active recruitment of Indian men. Even before the administration's encouragement, Indian men enlisted in far greater proportion to their numbers than did non-Indians, a phenomenon that was repeated in World War II.[25] When the war ended, Scott's administration failed to understand that returning veterans, who had stood side by side with other Canadians in the trenches, were not prepared to suffer discrimination or the denial of their rights. The formation of the **League of Indians of Canada** under the leadership of F.O. Loft, a Mohawk and war veteran, represented the first movement organized to unite Indians

Duncan Campbell Scott, 16 November 1933. (Library and Archives Canada, PA-165842.)

across Canada in resistance against federal Indian policies. The league strongly objected to federal policies that too readily permitted the surrender and sale of reserve lands
and the discriminatory treatment of Indian veterans who were denied benefits under
the Soldier Settlement Act. These and other grievances fuelled general Indian discontent, to the chagrin of Scott. His response was to find ways to discredit the leadership
of the league, to threaten leaders and followers alike with forced enfranchisement (and
thus revocation of official Indian status), and, in 1927, to engineer an amendment to
the Indian Act that 'forbade bands to pay lawyers or organizers to make claims against
the government'.[26] This last action had the temporary effect of rendering widespread
Indian political resistance extremely difficult.

The most enduring legacy of Indian policy during Scott's tenure, however, was the
expansion of the **residential school system**, especially in western Canada.[27] Despite
increasing evidence of the severe maltreatment of Indian children—including sexual
abuse—and a scathing report by P.H. Bryce in 1909 on the poor health of the children
at these institutions, Scott pressed on because he saw the schools as the most effective means of divorcing Indian children and youth from their societies and cultures.
Unquestionably, Scott's administration viewed residential and day schooling as the
main weapon in the state's arsenal to crush First Nations peoples' collective identities and to transform them into a readily available supply of cheap labour. Between
1912 and 1932 (the year of Scott's retirement), the number of Indian students in
these schools rose by 51 per cent, from 11,303 to 17,163—an increase aided by an

amendment to the Indian Act in 1920 compelling Indian children to attend school. Yet, when the dust had settled on Scott's career, there was no tangible evidence that these children had assimilated in any great numbers. Nevertheless, great damage had been done to First Nations cultures and societies, as well as to the individual students, the effects of which are still felt today.[28]

Dr Harold W. McGill, a crony of Prime Minister R.B. Bennett, succeeded Scott in 1932, when the country was in the depths of the Great Depression. McGill's 12-year tenure was both the apex of the department's repressive measures and the beginning of their undoing. McGill had not been in office long before he issued a directive to his Indian agents informing them that Indians would no longer be entertained by the central office.[29] In effect, he attempted to shut Ottawa's door and further isolate the administration from those it ostensibly served. McGill continued Scott's frugal ways and greatly aggravated the effects of the Depression on First Nations peoples. For example, average per capita relief expenditure on First Nations remained substantially below that provided to other Canadians and actually declined as McGill sought to reduce Indian welfare roles and save the Crown money.[30]

World War II heralded a shift in the government's approach to First Nations. For one thing, the active participation of First Nations militarily and on the home front raised public awareness of their presence and discriminatory treatment. More importantly, Indian political resistance began to reassert itself in the face of an obdurate and repressive administration. The suggestions by the Liberal government of William Lyon Mackenzie King that First Nations might be subject to income tax and conscription propelled them into nation-wide resistance, culminating in the formation of the Committee for the Protection of Indian Rights led by chiefs John Tootoosis and Andrew Paull from western Canada and Jules Sioui from Quebec. The committee staged two national conventions in Ottawa, in 1943 and 1944; the latter attracted some 200 delegates despite McGill's efforts to subvert it.[31] Thomas Crerar, the minister of Mines and Resources (the federal department then responsible for Indian Affairs), agreed to meet with the convention organizers to listen to their complaints. In addition, he spoke at length to the convention delegates and assured them that 'there is an obligation resting upon the people of Canada to see that the Indians are fairly treated and do everything possible to assist them to become useful citizens.' In the same breath, however, he reminded Indians of their responsibility to become self-supporting and to be 'useful citizens in our common country'.[32] Crerar's speech foreshadowed post-war Indian policy, while the convention itself gave rise to the formation of the North American Indian Brotherhood (NAIB) and served notice of a new Indian political consciousness.

Citizenship and Integration, 1946–68

Throughout the Great Depression and World War II, Canadians had begun to demand greater rights and entitlements by virtue of citizenship. This demand was reflected most strongly in the rise and electoral success of the Co-operative Commonwealth Federation (CCF), the forerunner of today's New Democratic Party (NDP). The federal Liberal government responded by taking a more interventionist role in the economy, introducing modest welfare measures, and passing a new citizenship act in 1946 that created Canadian, as opposed to British, citizenship. It also struck a joint parliamentary committee to investigate the Indian Act and its consequent policies and practices. The committee sat for two years and proposed that a new Indian Act replace the Act of 1876 to 'facilitate the gradual transition of Indians from "wardship to citizenship" and . . . help Indians to advance themselves'.[33] Overall, the thrust of the committee's recommendations was to promote the fuller participation of Indian communities in the social, political, and economic life of Canada while permitting them to retain some political and cultural autonomy. In 1949, as if to affirm this new direction, the Indian Affairs branch was transferred into the new Department of Citizenship and Immigration.

Even as the committee met, changes were happening in the administration of Indian Affairs. R.A. Hoey, a progressive man and former minister of Education in Manitoba, had replaced McGill.[34] Expenditures for Indian Affairs were rising: a new housing program was introduced, better-qualified teachers were hired, and new classrooms were built. With the rise of the NAIB, Indian Affairs instituted occasional consultation with Indian leaders to seek general advice on policy and on the proposed new Indian Act.[35]

Although the Indian Act of 1951 rid Indian Affairs of many of the compulsory aspects of the Act of 1876, it remained assimilationist. Like the original, the new Act provided for, in John Tobias's words, 'a co-operative approach between government and Indians towards the goal of assimilation'. It 'returned to the philosophy of [the Gradual Civilization Act of 1857]: civilization was to be encouraged but not directed or forced on the Indian people'.[36] Moreover, the removal of the mandatory portions of the old acts of 1876 and 1880 was illusory. Programs and strategies that fostered assimilation while ignoring legitimate concerns such as land claims showed that the state remained determined to absorb First Nations peoples into Canadian society. To this end, the treatment of Indians was to be normalized, and they were dealt with as though they were in transition to citizenship.

During the 1950s and early 1960s, this approach fell flat. Federal welfare benefits were extended to Indians on reserves, while limited attempts were made to promote economic self-sufficiency. However, as their traditional economies continued to be undermined, Indians were encouraged to seek employment off reserves, and special employment placement offices and Indian Friendship Centres were established in major cities to foster integration into the Euro-Canadian mainstream.[37] Despite the branch's claims that progress was being made, the socio-economic conditions of First Nations peoples relative to other Canadians scarcely improved. Many issues continued to fester. A land claims commission recommended by the 1946 joint committee was never established, and this omission was a source of discontent among Indian leaders. The question of unconditional Indian enfranchisement—that is, the granting of full rights of citizenship without surrender of Indian status—also spurred criticism of the federal government both nationally and internationally.[38] Even other federal government departments were critical of the branch, and many public servants referred to it as 'Colonel Jones's lost battalion'.[39]

A new Progressive Conservative government under John Diefenbaker reacted to these criticisms, first by establishing a joint parliamentary committee on Indian Affairs in 1959 and, second, by granting registered adult Indians the federal franchise in 1960. Like its predecessor, the committee sat for two years and entertained testimony from diverse constituencies. Although the committee heard many 'expressions of

Indian nationalist sentiment, as well as their demand for greater autonomy and self-government', its final report essentially endorsed the integrationist principles of post-war Indian policy.[40] The upshot of the committee's recommendations was business as usual with one important exception: it again recommended the establishment of a land claims commission. The Diefenbaker government accordingly prepared legislation to do so. At the same time, the government also approved a three-year, independent study of the Indians in Canada to provide the information needed to raise their socio-economic status to the same level as other Canadians. The study was headed by Dr Harry B. Hawthorn, a professor of anthropology at the University of British Columbia. Shortly thereafter, however, the government fell and, while the Hawthorn study continued, the land claims commission legislation died.[41]

After coming to power in 1963, Lester B. Pearson's Liberal government began an immediate reorganization of Indian Affairs. Pearson's approach was to position Indian matters in the general 'War Against Poverty', a mantra taken up from the Kennedy and Johnson administrations in the United States.[42] Pearson sought the participation of the provinces in Indian issues as part of co-operative federalism. R.F. Battle, the new (and open-minded) director of Indian Affairs, and his deputy minister, Claude Isbister, introduced a community development program on the reserves to promote Indian responsibility for the management of their own affairs by providing 'a framework for coordinating existing health, education, welfare, and economic development services on the reserves and . . . "reduc[ing] costs in such palliative areas as welfare assistance payments"'.[43] In addition, it was argued that this approach would lead to the full integration of Indian communities into their provincial and municipal jurisdictions.[44]

By 1966, when Hawthorn issued the report of his study, the Community Development Program (CDP) had been implemented and was generating considerable controversy because of its perceived radicalism. Thus, Hawthorn's study was published in a contentious environment. It explored nearly every facet of civil, political, and economic life in Indian communities. In their recommendations, Hawthorn and his researchers grappled with two fundamental issues: the rights of First Nations peoples as distinct from those of other Canadians; and First Nations' marginalization and 'structured poverty'. Hawthorn's team recommended considerable direct economic investment in Indian communities and greater integration of them into provincial jurisdictions. It also wanted, however, to preserve Aboriginal cultures and protect their distinct rights. In other words, Indians were to be 'citizens plus'. The progressive thrust of the report, however, was offset by its assimilative and integrative approach to economic progress.[45]

The **Hawthorn Report** was well received by First Nations leadership, especially its recommendations concerning special status and increased autonomy. As for its reception in official circles, the Liberal government was not ready to entertain the idea of 'citizens plus', especially in the context of the already controversial CDP. However, many of Hawthorn's recommendations influenced subsequent initiatives in welfare, education, skills training, and economic development. Finally, despite its liberality, the report provided a cover for the branch—now part of the Department of Indian Affairs and Northern Development (DIAND)—to maintain control over the management of Indian lives.[46] Eventually, the influence of the Hawthorn Report led to the devolution of Indian program administration and to the replication of Indian Affairs' bureaucratic structure at the band level.

From Near Termination to Near Autonomy, 1969–83

The CDP officially ended in 1968. In that same year, Pearson retired from politics and Pierre Elliott Trudeau became prime minister. Trudeau was a champion of individual civil rights and promised a 'just', participatory, and transparent government. He was anxious to end First Nations' marginalization as quickly as possible. Almost immediately upon taking power, the new government, with a view to developing an entirely new Indian policy, engaged in a year-long process of consultation with Indian leadership. This process, however, turned out to be 'a dialogue of the deaf'.[47] In 1969, Jean Chrétien, the minister of Indian Affairs and Northern Development, announced the *Statement of the Government of Canada on Indian Policy* (the **White Paper**) in the House of Commons. Chrétien outlined the government's intention to end the special legal status that Indians enjoyed because it had 'kept the Indian people apart from and behind other Canadians'.[48] The government argued that equal opportunity for First Nations could be achieved only through terminating their special status and giving them control over their land as though it were private property. DIAND would be shut down and Indians would access services like all other Canadians. After a year of consultation—in which they had expressed their aspirations for 'economic and social recovery without losing their identity'—First Nations peoples felt completely betrayed. By 1970, they had rejected the proposal, and Trudeau had stated, 'We won't force any solution on you.' In 1971, the White Paper was officially withdrawn, and the government announced an end to assimilation policy.[49]

The fallout from the White Paper was twofold: Indian leadership became more assertive in demanding self-government and advancing their peoples' rights; and the government transferred the administration of programs designed to foster integration to the bands while permitting First Nations to maintain their separate identities. Throughout the 1970s and early 1980s, the DIAND began to offer a greater range of programs and services to Indian communities. These were increasingly implemented by the bands themselves, although Ottawa carefully controlled their design, objectives, and funding. In effect, band administrations became agents of the state.[50] Most prominent among these programs were social assistance and related services, economic development, and community infrastructure. Bands were funded to hire social workers to administer social assistance, adult care, and homemaker programs. The new Indian Economic Development Fund targeted investment in First Nations communities where success was deemed likely. Innovative programs began to create jobs on reserves and to stimulate on-the-job training. Other economic development initiatives led to community improvement projects such as the building of new schools, recreation centres, band offices, and roads.[51] The idea behind devolution was to give the appearance that the government supported increased autonomy; at the same time, the policy 'shifted critical attention away from [Indian Affairs] to the local chief, council, and manager'.[52] Devolution, rather than being a step towards self-government, can be understood as preparation for termination of the special relationship between First Nations and the Crown.[53]

Nevertheless, the **National Indian Brotherhood (NIB)**—later to become the **Assembly of First Nations (AFN)**—continued to press its case for greater autonomy and self-government. The NIB did so on two fronts during the 1970s: the establishment of a land claims process; and the control of Indian education. Progress on land claims came with a landmark decision of the Supreme Court of Canada in 1973. Although the court ruled against the Nisga'a's claim to the Nass River Valley, it 'recognized that Aboriginal title existed in Canadian law'.[54] In the wake of this decision, the federal government finally established a land claims process that same year. Also in 1973, the government accepted an NIB position paper, 'Indian Control of Education'. First Nations rightly understood that their survival as autonomous peoples depended on schooling their own children. They began to take control of their own education, including the design and implementation of curricula and the training and hiring of committed and qualified teachers.[55]

Trudeau's return to power in 1980 (after a brief hiatus) provided further impetus to First Nations' demands for self-government. Trudeau immediately focused his energies on repatriating the Constitution from Great Britain to Canada. The AFN recognized this move as an opportunity to have Aboriginal rights formally recognized and their claim to be a third order of government accepted. Reneging on a previous commitment, Trudeau did not include First Nations in the negotiations, but the AFN lobbied strenuously and successfully to have Aboriginal rights entrenched in the new constitution. The details were, however, left to a series of three conferences following repatriation in 1982 and involving the provincial and federal governments, as well as Aboriginal leaders, to work out. In the final conference, Trudeau urged the provincial premiers to recognize the principle of Native self-government, but the western premiers refused.[56] In the meantime, a parallel process had been underway.

During the 1970s, DIAND officials had secretly been developing a new band government policy. First Nations however, rejected the proposal because it failed to recognize their inherent right to self-government and instead made it appear as if the Canadian government was granting them permission to govern themselves.[57] The rejection of DIAND's proposal led to the creation of a House of Commons committee 'charged with reviewing all legal and related institutional factors affecting the status, development, and responsibilities of band government on Indian reserves'. The committee submitted its report in 1983. Informally known as the Penner Report (after the committee's chairperson, Keith Penner), the *Report of the Special Committee on Indian Self-Government in Canada* recommended that Indian self-government be recognized as an inherent right and be entrenched in the Constitution. It also suggested new legislation requiring the federal and provincial governments to recognize Indian governments, develop federal–Indian agreements, and 'allow Indians to govern themselves'.[58] Further, the report recommended that the DIAND be dissolved and its functions taken over by Indian governments. To replace DIAND, the report urged the creation of a new Ministry of State for First Nations Relations that would deal with First Nations on a government-to-government basis. Finally, it also recommended that First Nations' land claims be accelerated and/or that territories be sufficiently large to be economically and jurisdictionally viable.[59] Most importantly, the report reflected the First Nations' point of view—it heard and endorsed their voice.

Although the Trudeau government did not accept the report in its entirety, it began to prepare legislation to enable a new form of Indian self-government. Sadly, the final incarnation of Bill C-52, An Act Relating to Self-Government for Indian Nations, was little better than the original DIAND proposal and died with the dissolution of Parliament in June 1984. Attempts to revive it ensued, but a new Progressive Conservative government led by Brian Mulroney failed to define Aboriginal rights at two constitutional conferences, in 1985 and 1987.[60] Another attempt in 1992 to constitutionalize Aboriginal self-government in the Charlottetown Accord failed in a national referendum. Similarly, the recommendations for self-government made by the 1996 report of the **Royal Commission on Aboriginal Peoples (RCAP)** fell on deaf ears.

Since 1984, the DIAND bureaucracy has continued to flourish, and devolution continues apace. DIAND is no longer personality driven, as it was in the days of Scott. It is systemically driven, guided by a liberal ideology that is firmly embedded in an organizational culture honed over time and capable of absorbing progressive ideas such as self-government and crafting them to its own assimilative purpose. Tightly defined forms of self-government that approximate municipal forms of government exist, but Aboriginal bands must apply to 'qualify' for them, and their funding remains controlled by Ottawa.[61] Overall, despite the brief interlude in the 1980s when real autonomy and self-government seemed possible, the policy of integration and amalgamation—assimilation—with the rest of Canada remains in place. While some bands have materially benefited through economic programs and agreements with resource-based corporations, a great many First Nations remain deeply entrenched at the margins of Canadian society. The dilemma remains: if meaningful self-government is not an option, is the gradual absorption of First Nations into Canada's liberal society a just solution to their marginality? Or is it the death knell of their unique societies and cultures?

Primary Document

2.   Civilizing Influences

A proposed pamphlet by Thomas Deasy, Indian Agent, 1920.

The Indian Agent is much misunderstood, by both Whites and Indians. His duties call for more than those of any other class of officials. Usually, his home is on a main reserve, among the people under his care. He is not there as a 'mentor,' or to interfere with the rights and privileges of the individual. The Indians, as 'Wards,' should look upon their Agent more in the light of a 'father.' It is true that the Indian Agent is clothed with the powers of a Magistrate, in certain cases, and requires compliance with the rules of law and order. He is governed, in his public acts, by the 'Indian Act,' which is carried out for the betterment of all concerned. It is not his privilege, or his duty, to enter into the private life, of a well-meaning member of the Bands, or to interfere with the conduct and management of those who comply with the law and engage in lawful occupations. His advice should be sought, on any question, public or private, which can be elucidated through channels that are not open to the residents of outside localities, sometimes far removed from the course of their advice, legal or otherwise.

It is a mistaken idea, of many of the Indians, that an Indian Agent represents only the powers that control him. His duty should be to forward the work of civilization, in a straightforward, honest, manner. The 'Wards of Government' are approaching the day when they will be thrown on their resources. The majority of them are no longer in a condition where they will need direct guidance in all of their affairs. They must take their places, as men and women, capable of adjusting their own lives, free from direct supervision. Over fifty years of education, and the aid of self-sacrificing missionaries, should be sufficient, to lead a people from 'wardship,' to an understanding of what is required of them, not only for the good of themselves; but also for the public good.

The only law, differing from that controlling the other residents of the localities is one for the good of the Indian, in the prohibition of spirituous and intoxicating liquor and ingredients. Prohibition has been found of benefit to the Indian, to prevent degradation and crime. In no other way are the Indians restricted more than their other neighbours. Indulgence in intoxicants, without restraint, has been the curse of every country. If the individual cannot restrain himself, the government introduces laws, on many other matters, which govern the individual. It is safe to assert that the restriction of the sale and use of intoxicants has been the salvation of the Indians, in this country.

Long experience, with the Indians of a particular Province, shows that the natives have not, as a general rule, advanced as they should. The fault may be theirs, or it may be with those associating with them. No race of people will advance until they comply with the laws of God, and with the laws promulgated for health and sanitation. Education of the mind should mean observance of the law of God, and natural laws of health. It is of little use to store the mind with grammatical phrases, and overlook the betterment, by practice, of the interests of soul and body. 'Cleanliness is next to Godliness' is an old adage. Outward appearance, in the way of gaudy clothing, may cover a body contaminated by lack of bathing and need of underclothing free from dirt. The body, like the soul, must not be contaminated, if health is desired.

Secondary Source

3. Our Medicines: First Nations' Medical Practices and the Nanaimo Indian Hospital, 1945–75[62]

Laurie Meijer Drees

Introduction

In the mid-twentieth century, Canada's federal Indian Health Services (IHS) operated a network of hospitals, clinics, nursing stations, and travelling health units in an attempt to address health issues in Aboriginal communities, especially those of registered Indian people. Before 1945, the Department of Indian Affairs operated various hospitals in conjunction with missionary and other non-denominational organizations. After 1945, the ravages of tuberculosis (TB) epidemics in northern and western Aboriginal communities spurred the federal government's sense of moral duty and public safety enough to drive the creation of a separate bureaucracy and machinery to deal with Aboriginal health: the IHS division, which was later housed within Canada's Department of Health and Welfare.

In creating this new system, Canada's federal government circumvented the previously central role of various Christian churches delivering Western medical care to Aboriginal peoples. The history of the IHS and its predecessors has been dealt with, in broad strokes, by several important histories.[63] At the same time, little research sheds direct light on the actions and perspectives of Aboriginal peoples within—and on—the IHS.[64] How did Aboriginal peoples experience IHS? What impact did the IHS have on Indigenous medical practices?

The Indian hospital system run by the IHS was especially significant because it pushed the Canadian government's influence into Aboriginal lives further than ever before. As historian Mary-Ellen Kelm points out, the IHS—even prior to 1950—aimed to legitimize colonial relations and encourage the assimilation of Aboriginal peoples, in this instance, at the level of Aboriginal bodies.[65] The federal government devised laws and policies designed to enforce the treatment of Aboriginal patients with formal Western medicines. Drawing on the governing structures of Indian Affairs, including the residential school system, Ottawa ensured that Canada's formal Western medical system had access to Aboriginal patients, with or without the patient's consent. Similarly, Kathryn McPherson identifies how the IHS and its staff of doctors and nurses, from 1945 to 1970, continued to operate as a colonizing force in Aboriginal communities. In her view, IHS undermined traditional Aboriginal medical traditions, offered contradictory services in Aboriginal communities, underfunded its system, and as a form of coercive 'charity', maintained relatively strict authoritarian control over its clients and their bodies.[66] As both writers point out, the IHS did little to recognize or work with Aboriginal knowledges associated with health care or healing.[67] Yet McPherson suggests that, in the field and in practice, IHS nurses and health practitioners worked around the coercive colonizing structures of the IHS to provide Aboriginal peoples chances to assert their own definitions of health and care.[68]

On the one hand, it is clear that local Indigenous medical practices continued to coexist alongside formal Western medicine despite the countervailing forces of federal Indian policy, law, and the biomedical treatments offered to Aboriginal peoples through the IHS. On the other hand, it is less clear *how* First Nations' medicines and healing practices fared and *how* they operated in a context where IHS administrators and health care providers officially dismissed their value. My interviews with First Nations community members in the central Vancouver Island region between 2005 and 2009 reveal that these remedies continued to be administered and shared in the same time and space as the formal Western medical treatments offered by the IHS from 1945 to the 1970s. As such, 'Indian medicine' is part of the rich and culturally diverse Canadian medical history. This small case study of the use of local First Nations medicine within the IHS Nanaimo Indian Hospital in Nanaimo, BC, during the post-war period provides a glimpse into the nature of coexisting medical practices, using Aboriginal perspectives.

A central theme conveyed in the oral histories is that 'Indian medicines' moved fluidly in and out of the Indian hospital setting. These treatments were sometimes highly visible; at other times, they were practically invisible to everyone but their provider and recipient. Sometimes IHS doctors encouraged the use of 'Indian medicines', while at other times they were unaware of their presence. As a result, there was more than one form of medicine in the Nanaimo Indian Hospital. The Indian hospital offered a space where medicine moved in and out, depending on availability of practitioners and the needs of patients. As Kelm points out, 'Aboriginal people did not relinquish their belief in their own medicine and its role in preserving their health.'[69] Kelm's thesis is supported here but needs to be refined. In fact, based on oral history evidence, local First Nations' medicines made their way into—and operated within—the government facilities created to subvert them.

Indian Health Services and Hospitals

The Canadian government did not always tolerate Aboriginal self-determination in health care, especially when it concerned infectious and communicable diseases such as TB. In fact, as early as 1914, sections of the Indian Act allowed the government to apprehend patients by force if they did not seek medical treatment.[70] Not only could a person be arrested for avoiding treatment, but any person subject to the Indian Act was also personally responsible for seeking treatment from a 'properly qualified physician'.[71] Such regulations did not recognize treatments given by family or community members. In this way, both federal and provincial law applied its weight to Aboriginal communities, forcing the acceptance of Western medicine and its attendant institutions for the sake of public health.

After 1945, IHS became the new instrument through which the federal government would take care of Indian peoples and their health issues. Underlying the IHS was the attitude that Indian and Inuit peoples would not have autonomy in health care. The IHS would take care of Indian and Inuit health; it would provide 'a complete health service for these [Status Indian and Inuit] peoples' based on a moral, not a legal, imperative. In the words of the IHS, 'Canada's Indian Health Service . . . has arisen, not from legislative obligation, but rather as a moral undertaking to succor the less fortunate and to raise the standard of health generally.'[72]

The IHS also sought to 'improve assimilation' of Indian peoples into mainstream non-Native society. Healthy Indian people were deemed to be more economically independent, less dependent on government, and thus better able to join Canada as workers rather than wards.[73] Finally, within this new health care system there was no support or understanding for traditional Aboriginal health practices. Until at least the 1960s, traditional medicines and practices were viewed as backward and as based on superstition and ignorance. The aim of the IHS was to 'correct' the traditional medical and health practices of Aboriginal peoples.

As part of the new health care system, the number of IHS hospitals operated directly by the Department of National Health and Welfare grew from 17 to 21 between 1945 and 1950.[74] Funding also grew: in 1937, Parliament approved $750,000 for the medical branch of Indian Affairs; by 1948, that amount had increased to $7.5 million.[75] Although some mission and public hospitals remained available to First Nations, the IHS institutions were specifically for registered Indian and Inuit patients. Of all Indian hospitals within the IHS, the largest were located in British Columbia and Alberta. Important questions remain, however: How did Aboriginal people experience IHS policies and facilities, and what was the impact of IHS on Indigenous medical traditions?

Coast Salish Medicine

Hul'qumi'num-speaking peoples, from the central Vancouver Island region, possess a deep and complex philosophy pertaining to the human body and how to best maintain an individual person's health and wellness. As part of this philosophy, a myriad of individual and communal cultural practices serve to enhance a person's well-being, build his or her strength, and support his or her ongoing health. These activities might include bathing, performing specific training exercises, eating particular foods, and engaging in prayer, singing, and specific rituals. Herbal preparations and their application often form another element in treating illness and supporting healthiness in people.

Although many of the practices and preparations are commonly known and communally shared among members of the mid-island First Nations communities, some practices and treatments are kept within specific families, to be used only by those families or by special request. Some practices and preparations are deeply private and never shared, except in special circumstances. Taken together, these elements form the medicine upon which many First Nations peoples draw during challenging times and illnesses. Generalizations about the nature and implementation of this medicine are difficult to make, given the sometimes confidential and often private way in which it is shared and used. What is clear is that there exists a body of thought and of practice that support one another in offering humans a way to be a good person and to stay physically, mentally, and spiritually well.

Perhaps one of the more public aspects of this philosophy of maintaining good health is the body of wisdom known in the Hul'qumi'num language as *snuwuyulth*.[76] *Snuwuyulth* is the teachings, offered by Elders to those individuals who are willing and open to listening, that present guidelines or lessons that convey the life skills necessary to be well and a good person. *Snuwuyulth* is usually offered through storytelling, from which listeners can draw the information they need to help themselves. Shared both publicly and privately, the teachings are all-encompassing, addressing the mental, physical, and spiritual aspects of a person. If an individual is not feeling well, mentally or physically, these teachings assist in rebalancing him or her, including his or her energies, body, and mind. For example, some teachings deal with anger management or offer techniques on how to cope with negative emotions. Other teachings emphasize how people should relate to one another in order to maintain healthy communities, such as including children in daily chores and knowing who one's family is. Still others deal with food or with care of the body. If a person follows the teachings, he or she is sure to have a strong mind, heart, and body and will benefit by being 'well'. Sometimes, if a person is feeling unwell, family or community members offer him or her *snuwuyulth* as a balm or a healing. In this way, *snuwuyulth* forms a type of medicine and is understood and practised as such.

Coast Salish communities also have a long history of understanding the biomedical properties of plants. In various families, traditional knowledge about what plants can be harvested, combined, and prepared to offer remedies for a range of illnesses remains. Some of these remedies have been documented by ethnobotanists, including Nancy Turner, as part of ethnobotanical and traditional ecological knowledge studies. Thus, in the Coast Salish communities of central Vancouver Island, well-established sets of practices dealing with all types of illness and sickness continue to exist and flourish. In contemporary times, these practices can and are frequently used in conjunction with formal Western medical treatments.

Nanaimo Indian Hospital

The Nanaimo Indian Hospital (NIH) was opened in 1945 as part of the IHS hospital network. Located on an old military property in Nanaimo, BC, this particular hospital served First Nations patients from central and north Vancouver Island, as well as the central northwest coast of British Columbia. The NIH was one of the larger hospitals in the IHS system, consisting of over 200 beds in its first decade of operations. It offered surgeries and drug treatments for TB as well as other illnesses, although the vast majority of its patients were admitted for TB treatment and convalescence. As new antibiotic drug treatments emerged to address TB, the Indian hospitals adopted and administered them to their patients. Standard medicines offered to tubercular patients between 1945 and the 1970s included the drugs streptomycin, para-aminosalicylic (PAS), and isoniazid (INH). Another important component of the TB treatment regime was mandatory rest, and patients often found themselves on enforced bed rest for months—even years—at a time. In the early years of the NIH's operation, patients were rarely allowed to venture outdoors; however, by the 1950s, fresh air and light outdoor activity for patients became a regular part of the routine implemented by the staff.

Tuberculosis patients on the hospital steps, Blackfoot (Siksika) reserve, Alberta, 1938; Back row: Howard McMaster and Emil Medicine Traveller. Front row: Herbert Eagle Ribs and Marie Many Bears (Chief's daughter). Photographed by Jane and Lucien Hanks. (Glenbow Archives, PA-3385-147.)

Patients of the NIH during the 1950s and 1960s and their family members have rarely spoken publicly about their experiences within this federal facility. In 2005, I began to actively canvass for oral histories related to the institution from both former patients and former employees. The resulting interviews were far-ranging in subject and tone, yet a common theme that emerged was that First Nations peoples continued to practise their own remedies, both inside and outside the hospital, despite the availability of Western medicine through the hospital and its staff. Although Kelm's examination of the IHS in British Columbia discusses at some length how First Nations' healing traditions persisted in spite of the presence of the IHS and its treatments, just *how* local medicines were employed remains vague. Based on the interviews collected, it appears that First Nations people brought their own treatments to the hospital in Nanaimo, whether or not they were invited to do so by physicians or nurses. In many instances, these medicines may have been entirely invisible to hospital staff, who may not have even realized that local medicines were being offered to patients by their visiting family members. Indeed, it is quite likely that staff members did not recognize the activities of family as constituting the administration of medicine. In this way, the bringing of food, the sharing of time and attention, and the administration of herbal remedies and special rituals went on in the NIH without much notice.

The first person to speak to me about Coast Salish medical practices was Ellen White, a beloved Elder, author, and teacher of the Snuneymuxw First Nation. White was trained as a young child in the preparation and use of certain herbal medicines, as well as in midwifery, by her grandmother. Today, her community recognizes her as a powerful spiritual person and as someone who has specific knowledge related to health and healing. White took the time to speak with me about her interaction with the NIH and the staff who worked there in the 1950s. A small excerpt of our conversation is as follows:

> My granny trained us in all the medical things by telling us story after story. Some stories are about childbirth. Or about behaving properly. Another story would be the power of words and how to cause problems for yourself. She also talked to us about the dangers of using certain words when it's not right to do so, not proper. Words go with certain things and you are supposed to do it right.
>
> The stories train us how to do things—we always say, 'Remember that story?' when we are trying to do something. It's a lot like when you are being trained in the hospital to be a nurse. The stories taught us. We learned about kinds of medicines, how to stop bleeding with things like plantain, and a lot of other things.
>
> I went up to the Nanaimo Indian Hospital now and then. I was called up there and did deliver a couple of babies. Some patients were sent out of the hospital. The hospital, I heard later, didn't want to have some of the women that were really badly affected with TB and refused them. It also didn't want some of those women to give birth. The Doctor, Dr Drysdale, would come in and later on, Doctor Schmidt. Dr Schmidt used me a lot. He was always encouraging me, and came down to the reserve. He encouraged some of us from the reserve to train as health aides. I remember that hospital. I recall how one time Doug carried a ladder up the hill, and how he used it to climb in one of the windows to visit a friend there. That's how he got inside! I was pregnant at the time and wanted to stay away. I didn't really like that place much and I got into trouble

with one of the nurses so I had an excuse. I think she wanted me to stay away. She said, 'It's filthy stuff you're putting on the patients.'[77]

In a separate conversation, White mentioned how she was invited to the hospital at times to help with 'cleansings', a local First Nations ritual of sweeping out negative forces or energies from places, thereby purifying a space or person. The hospital staff allowed her to come in and work through the ceremony for the benefit of the patients in the hospital. Undoubtedly, White also brought stories and teachings to those she treated in the hospital.

In these ways, White brought her traditions of healing into a Western medical facility that otherwise appeared separate from, and in many ways ran counter to, local First Nations' healing practices. As she mentions, one particular doctor—Dr Schmidt—supported her activities. However, some nurses were less than appreciative of what she brought to the hospital in the form of knowledge or herbal remedies, and it was these individuals who eventually encouraged White to stay away from the facility.

Much like Ellen White, Delores Louie (Chemainus First Nation) was a visitor to the NIH in the 1960s. Unlike White, she was not invited by the staff to offer any specific treatments but instead came to the hospital every weekend to visit her family: her father, her brother, her sister, and a niece were all patients within the institution. Along with her mother and sisters, Louie visited the hospital every weekend during the extremely limited visiting hours. In this way, she was able to spend valuable time with her family despite the considerable distance of the hospital from her home on the reserve in Cowichan (Duncan, BC). In her words:

> Back in '59 or '60, when my Dad, Basil Alphonse, ended up in the TB hospital . . . what I can't remember is who was first, my brother Leo Alphonse or Dad . . . anyway, Dad was in there for a number of years. I used to go see him. We were only allowed on the weekends. A certain day we had to be there. We had an old vehicle. I used to drive for Mom. Seems like we were there all afternoon, for visiting!

The importance of family, and sharing time together, is part of the Hul'qumi'num understanding of how to live well. Louie spent many hours visiting her relatives on weekends in the hospital and brought them materials so that they could work on crafts as they rested, crafts that they subsequently sold for pocket money. Through visiting and bringing them work to do, Louie offered her relations a chance to remain active and connected to the outside world. Indeed, she was helping her family in a manner that was consistent with her cultural values and teachings. Her family also assisted its sick members with herbal treatments, although those were not bought into the hospital:

> My brother Leo was only in there for eight months. He didn't have TB, so it's strange that he ended up in there. He mentions that one nurse, Mrs Langlois, just brought him in there to be checked and they kept him. He just had pleurisy. He walked out. He got tired of it and just left one day. Walked out. He said he'd never return. But he went on herb medicine [traditional medicine]. He got better in no time. His mom, our mom, made the medicine! And his wife. Those

herbs are really interesting. It was pine tree bark, and gosh, a few other ingredients. Three ingredients in it. He mentions that when he had three gallons, he drank that completely. They checked him months after and there was nothing. He went back to logging! He was a logger . . .

Louie's family used herbal medicines when the hospital treatment failed to meet their needs, taking care of the health problems themselves. The hospital was not criticized overtly, but the perception in her family was that the hospital was a place where people were not treated in a manner that might always help them:

That hospital, it seems like it just existed and that we just accepted it. We accepted what was happening to our people. It wasn't good or bad. My sister never ever complained about it. But when she did come out she just said she just never ever wanted to go back. Same with Dad. He never ever wanted to go back in there! Even my brother, today I tried questioning him, and he just never wanted to be there. I guess because they weren't allowed to walk and they couldn't visit who they wanted, or needed. It was most likely that stressful regime in there. They were kept busy in there, but it was not good.[78]

It is important to note that Louie emphasizes the significance of visiting and staying busy but that the hospital interfered with those important activities that, according to Coast Salish tradition, are considered good and healthy for a person.

A third way in which local First Nations' ways of maintaining and supporting health were brought into the hospital was by bringing patients gifts of food. Officially, the NIH provided meals for all its patients; however, many family members brought their ailing relatives local and preferred foods to help them get better. Violet Charlie, well-respected Elder of the Cowichan Tribes in Duncan, BC, spent four years at the NIH while she was treated for TB. In conversation with me in May 2008, she mentioned how families brought food to their relations in hospital, especially the much prized 'superfood' commonly consumed in the north central coast First Nations communities of British Columbia: oolichan and oolichan oil called 'grease':

LMD: Someone would bring it in, a family member would bring it in?
VC: Uh-huh. A family member would bring it—this grease.
LMD: And did they bring in fish and things like that, for people?
VC: Ya, they got dried fish, abalone—I never tried that—and they called it candlefish, tiny. I tried it and it's really rich. The nurses didn't object. Mind you, that was the four years I spent in there.[79]

Grease is rich in Vitamin A and is a traditional food that many coastal First Nations community members consider vital to their well-being.[80] In addition to being consumed as a food, the grease can be used to treat skin conditions such as psoriasis or inflammation and even stomach ailments.[81] In this case, the NIH allowed family members to bring food in, although this was done at the discretion of the nursing staff and doctors of the facility.[82]

Conclusion

In these three seemingly small ways, First Nations people, who were either patients or family associated with patients in the NIH, found ways to bring their cultural knowledge and understandings of health and well-being into an institution that otherwise did little to recognize Indigenous cultural practices. The perception by First Nations people that these activities had a positive impact on the health and well-being of First Nations patients is evident in the stories shared here.

From 1945 to the 1970s, Indian hospitals in Canada were authoritarian institutions where the health workers and hospitals possessed the legal power to admit and treat individuals suspected of illness, with or without patient consent. The medical system operating within the hospitals was hierarchical, with clear lines of command and obedience: doctors were at the top, followed by nurses, and then the various support staff. Patients stood outside this hierarchy yet were viewed as subject to the power and authority of the hospital staff. In addition, biophysical diagnoses and treatments held supremacy in this system, and the social or spiritual causes of illness were considered either unimportant or irrelevant, as were cultural perspectives on health and healing. In fact, 'Indian medicine' was deemed to be virtually non-existent in the post-World War II period. In 1974, a visiting anthropologist studying Coast Salish communities commented, 'with the near extinction of other forms of native healing, the winter spirit ceremonial has become the only major non-Western therapy at the disposal of the Coast Salish Indians.'[83] As discussed, First Nations brought some of their own healing techniques into this system, generally with the consent of the medical staff. From a contemporary perspective, it seems contradictory that medical staff who sought to isolate and treat Aboriginal peoples within an institutional setting rather than their home communities (which were viewed as being unhygienic and unhealthy) allowed significant elements of that community to 'leak' into the tightly controlled hospital setting. Perhaps hospital staff allowed family visits for compassionate reasons or simply lacked interest in, or insight into, what visitors actually brought into the facility. The fluidity of 'Indian medicine', its rootedness in relationships and in practices or foods not readily recognizable by doctors and nurses, made for its portability and facilitated its implementation in an otherwise generally hostile environment. 'Indian medicine' quietly flowed from person to person, healing as it moved.

Another irony also emerges from the stories about the health care offered by the First Nations Elders interviewed on this subject. Although their collective experiences with the NIH were generally negative, they all shared their memories with a great deal of humour. The humorous retelling of experiences that very likely took place under trying circumstances reflects First Nations' sense of self-determination and resilience in recalling situations where their dignity and self-reliance were being tested. The success of local medicines in a person's life seems to add to that person's sense of power and self-esteem and to their ability to overcome difficult situations. Such retelling also underscores the significant power of the medicines themselves.

In the end, the treatments and activities related to health care operations within the Indian hospitals were far more diverse than the official record or even anecdotal accounts provided by doctors and nurses suggest. For this reason, it is important to investigate the perceptions and personal experiences of those people whose bodies were subject to the care of institutions. Canadian medical history is a rich field with many different perspectives and experiences, all of which deserve exploration and consideration. Historian Kathryn McPherson argues that it is important to research and theorize the diverse, and often oppositional, ways women relate to their health care systems;[84] by extension, it is important to research and theorize how cultural minorities relate to those same standard systems in society. In this case, Coast Salish perspectives on health care reveal that, contrary to the perceptions of 'outsiders', Indigenous medical practices took on many different forms, were highly portable, and continued to be implemented even when members of that community were perceived by medical 'experts' to be lacking in the ability to deal adequately with illness. As academics, we might presume that specific cultural practices related to health care survive and operate, but we rarely seek to describe or explain *how* they operate within our universal and formal Canadian health care system. Sometimes we have much to learn before we can see.

Primary Document

4. Excerpt from an Interview with Violet Charlie

Interview by Laurie Meijer Drees (LMD), 14 May 2008, Duncan, BC. Others present at the interview were Delores Louie (DL) and Violet Charlie (VC)'s daughter, also named Violet Charlie.

LMD: Someone would bring it [oolichan oil] in [to the hospital], a family member would bring it in?

VC: Uh-huh. A family member would bring it—this grease.

LMD: And did they bring in fish and things like that, for people?

VC: Ya, they got dried fish, abalone—I never tried that—and they called it candlefish, tiny. I tried it and it's really rich. The nurses didn't object. Mind you, that was the four years I spent in there.

LMD: What years were those?

VC: [laughing] I don't remember!

LMD: We can figure it out from the photos maybe.

DL: She was born in 1925, so . . .

LMD: So the photo must have been in the late 1940s. That makes sense.

VC: There were quite a few of us.

LMD: Were you in there with friends?

VC: Not all of them. We became friends . . .

LMD: You were on a ward then, with all young women?

VC: Yes. The ward was barracks, divided. There was a wall and glass . . . there were four or six beds to one cubicle, would you say?

DL: Yes.

VC: I had a corner. You would be so happy if you got the window side! So you could look outside! [laughing] It was very boring. Yes.

LMD: Did they do any activities with you?

VC: Well, not until you're getting better. Then you can do craftworks. I never beaded before I went in for TB. I did do knitting before I went in. When I was knitting the nurse brought me some wool.

LMD: After a while you were allowed up, to walk around?

VC: I don't know, after maybe two years I was allowed to get up. To go to the washroom. Otherwise I couldn't get up.

LMD: Did they allow you to go out on little day trips?

VC: When I was in Coqualeetza I was out for a couple of hours. Out with the bus. I was in Nanaimo first, and then for surgery I went to Coqualeetza, I had a lobectomy.

DL: They didn't take any ribs off, eh?

VC: I wouldn't let them! [laughing] They were going to take five, and I said, 'No way!' Ya, you really get lopsided.

DL: I think Dad's was three ribs.

VC: Did they take them out too?

DL: Ya. His turned to cancer after.

LMD: Did they explain to you, what they were doing?

VC: Oh yes, they explained. I didn't want to come home after seeing the X-ray, and seeing the spots. I decided they should take it off. They explained that it might just come back.

LMD: So you stayed longer?

VC: I had two lobes taken off. And which made it difficult to have surgeries after.

LMD: Was your family able to come and visit you?

VC: Yes, they were. Those that were able to come.

LMD: I heard of some people trying to escape from the hospital.

VC: Ya, I wanted to. Because my mother was very very sick . . . and I couldn't even walk. I couldn't even walk to the end of my bed. I wanted to, but I couldn't.

DL: How did you find out you had TB?

VC: My mother kept giving me Indian medicine. She knew there was something wrong with me. She kept changing it. Try it for one month and then change it again. But I started throwing up blood . . . and the doctor was watching me . . . it was terrible . . . I was afraid I would spread it on the children. . . . I had to get away then.

DL: Was that Goodbrand?

VC: Ya, that's right.

LMD: Was he at the hospital? Or here?

VC: He was the Indian doctor here.

LMD: So who looked after your children?

VC: My husband took care of them, and my late niece took care of them, and my mother took care of my baby.

LMD: That was a big worry for you, I'm sure.

VC: I don't know how many days I cried. It is a lot of stress, all the way around. Having someone gone.

LMD: When you returned did you feel healthy again?

VC: It's kind of difficult, after being . . . I don't know what the English word is . . . being told what to do every day. And all of a sudden I had to decide for myself, and it's different again.

LMD: There must have been a lot of rules?

VC: No, not really. The rule was that we shouldn't exert ourselves if we wanted to get better.

VC: It was not much different than going to Residential Schools. Start listening to the staff.

LMD: The staff that were in the hospital, were they mostly white people?

VC: The patients or the staff?

LMD: The staff.

VC: The workers were Natives, the nurses were non-Native. I know one was German. I couldn't understand her. There were quite a few of them. Campbell was our head doctor. And Dr Gamble. . . . Dr Greer . . . and Dr Schmidt, he was there too! [laughing]

LMD: [talks about Auntie Ellen and how she was allowed to do some of her work in that hospital, on the invitation of Dr Schmidt, until she got into a fight with one of the nurses there.]

VC: [laughing] You had to get into a fight! They weren't very nice! Because we were lying flat, they could see anything they wish! You'll answer them one way or the other. It was something we had to put up with. It wasn't so bad. . . .

LMD: I tried to imagine what it was like.

VC: I don't know, it was . . . I was already doing bad because I had TB, which was likely my own fault because I didn't rest enough.

LMD: Was there anyone in there that didn't have TB?

VC: That's what it is, a TB hospital. My daughter didn't have TB—she had a bone problem—she did the Solarium first, and after I asked her to be brought into Nanaimo.

LMD: Where is the Solarium? What facility was that?

VC: It's somewhere near Sidney. It was a San or something.

DL: Ah, that's right!

LMD: A little hospital over there?

VC: Ya . . . it wasn't an Indian Affairs facility.

LMD: I don't know when Nanaimo closed, as a hospital.

VC: I don't know. I guess I just shut my mind away from it all. Tried to forget about it. I went to see it after, though.

DL: It was 1961, it was still there. Cause that's when Percy and I got married and Dad was still there. In 1962, he walked out. [laughing]

LMD: For your wedding?

DL: Ya.

VC: Quite a few of them walked out. Some came back again.

• • •

LMD: Were people sneaking in Indian medicine too? Or no?

VC: They could have been. Uh-huh.

VC: When people walked away from Coqualeetza, they locked the doors and they weren't allowed back in. Even if it's raining!

LMD: Was Coqualeetza bigger than Nanaimo?

VC: I would imagine that it would be about the same size, except that it was high. A different kind of building. Four or five stories. The Nanaimo was just one story.

• • •

VC: When you look back on all of this. Do you ever find out why it was that the Natives got TB?
LMD: What causes them to have it more? It's a good question. . . .
DL: [listing people who had TB and who may have passed it on to others, unknowingly]

• • •

VC: It depends on your immune system.

• • •

LMD: Do you remember what drugs they gave you?
VC: Streptomycin. After two years of that we switched to something else . . . then I went colour blind from that. Then it was pills. The streptomycin was with needles.
LMD: When you went home, after your four years, did you have to keep taking medication?
VC: No, no.
DL: You didn't go on herb, eh?
VC: No.

• • •

LMD: Was there a problem there with language? Maybe some of the patients didn't speak English? Was that a problem there?
VC: No, not really. There was one granny there that didn't speak English, but she understood. She used to sing in her own language sometimes [laughter]. I don't know where she was from. But she understood very good what to do.
DL: There was quite a few different wings, eh?
VC: There were quite a few wings.
DL: I remember because I'd go see Adeline, and then I'd take off and get lost and end up in another wing.
VC: There were three or four from the front. I think the front was 'G'—Ward G. They were all attached by hallways. The kitchen was around the middle.

• • •

DL: Did they have men, what do you call them, orderlies?
VC: Yes, that would be. There was quite a few orderlies. Native. Not many, but a few of them.
DL: So all the nurses, they were pretty well friendly, eh?

VC: Very few were not. Most of them were very friendly. We argued with some of them. Then they would go to the doctor, and the doctor would come and talk to us!

LMD: Tell you to smarten up?

VC: Yeh, tell us to smarten up!

LMD: Do you remember specific nurses? Would you stay friends with some of those nurses? If you'd been there for so long?

VC: Well . . . we would tolerate them, I guess would be the word. They couldn't become friendly with us . . . not really. Some of the staff we could really be friends with. Very few. I couldn't anyways, because of myself, really.

LMD: But they didn't come and visit you at home, years later, or anything.

VC: No.

DL: I just remember that nurse that raised Leona, eh? She had a real strong English accent.

VC: Violet [daughter] had an English nurse. She was speakin' like an English person when she got home! [laughing]

DL: That's the way my little niece was too. A strong accent!

VC: They would bring her over to see me, but I wasn't allowed to touch her. She had to stand way back.

LMD: That would be hard. That would make me cry!

VC: Ya. [laughter]

Questions for Consideration

1. What was the goal of Canadian Indian policy between 1913 and 1983? What sorts of measures did the Canadian government utilize in pursuit of this objective?

2. In Shewell's view, what ideological framework underpinned Canada's Indian policy? Do you agree with his assessment? Why or why not?

3. How is Thomas Deasy's vision of the ideal Indian agent consistent with Shewell's interpretation of the goals of Indian policy? How is it inconsistent?

4. Why did the Canadian government extend health care services to Aboriginal peoples?

5. How does Meijer-Drees's research regarding the Nanaimo Indian Hospital challenge the traditional view of such institutions and federal Indian Health Services? How were the patients able to practise their own medical treatments while at the NIH?

6. Does Meijer-Drees's interview with Violet Charlie and Delores Louie support her view about the coexistence of Western and Aboriginal medical practices? Does Charlie appear to use humour because of a 'sense of self-determination and resilience'? Give reasons to support your answers.

7. How would you characterize federal Indian policy? How did Aboriginal peoples resist and/or react to federal Indian policy?

Further Resources

Books and articles

Burnett, Kristin. *Taking Medicine: Women's Healing Work and Colonial Contact in Southern Alberta, 1880–1930*. Vancouver: UBC Press, 2010.

Kelm, Mary-Ellen. *Colonizing Bodies: Aboriginal Health and Healing in British Columbia, 1900–50*. Vancouver: University of British Columbia Press, 1998.

Lux, Maureen. *Medicine that Walks: Disease, Medicine, and the Canadian Plains People, 1880–1940*. Toronto: University of Toronto Press, 2001.

Shewell, Hugh. *'Enough to Keep Them Alive': Indian Welfare in Canada, 1873–1965*. Toronto: University of Toronto Press, 2004.

Titley, E. Brian. *The Indian Commissioners: Agents of the State and Indian Policy in Canada's Prairie West, 1873–1932*. Edmonton: University of Alberta Press, 2009.

Waldram, James D., Ann Herring, and T. Kue Young. *Aboriginal Health in Canada: Historical, Cultural, and Epidemiological Perspectives*, 2nd edn. Toronto: University Toronto Press, 2006.

Printed Documents and Reports

The Indian Act and Amendments, 1970–1993: An Indexed Collection. Saskatoon: University of Saskatchewan Press, 1993.

Films

Duncan Campbell Scott: The Poet and the Indians. VHS. Directed by James Cullingham. NFB, 1995.

Websites

Health Canada Aboriginal health policy
www.hc-sc.gc.ca/ahc-asc/branch-dirgen/fnihb-dgspni/index-eng.php

Text of the 1985 Indian Act
http://laws.justice.gc.ca/eng/acts/I-5/

Peoples' Experiences of Colonization: Indian Hospitals
http://web2.uvcs.uvic.ca/courses/csafety/mod1/notes4.htm

EIGHT

Survivance, Identity, and the Indian Act

Introduction

The previous chapter dealt generally with Indian policy in Canada and its goal of transforming Aboriginal people into European Canadians. As we discussed, the contradictory nature of this policy and the resilience of Aboriginal people ensured the failure of this objective. Nevertheless, government policy has had far-reaching and unexpected consequences on the lives of Aboriginal people. This chapter examines some of its more insidious costs.

Two of the most significant pieces of legislation affecting the identity of Aboriginal people were passed in Upper and Lower Canada in 1850. These statutes set a precedent—for the first time, non-Aboriginal people determined who was and was not considered an 'Indian' in Canada and enshrined that definition in law. The matter of categorizing Aboriginal people continued. In 1876, all legislation pertaining to Aboriginal people in Canada was consolidated into the Indian Act, a document that still plays a significant role in the daily lives of First Nations. As Bonita Lawrence addresses in her article, this legislation—in combination with traditional and stereotypical ideas of what constitutes an authentic Aboriginal identity—shapes how Aboriginal people interact with each other and European-Canadian society. According to Lawrence, the need to claim an identity based on legal and cultural stereotypes has led to a feeling of superficiality for some Aboriginal people who do not feel 'Indian enough' and has caused many to jostle one another for access to rights. Moreover, the artificial permanency of these legal categories ignores the fluidity of identity evident within Aboriginal society before contact with Europeans.

Jaime Mishibinijima's article addresses similar themes by using the tools of gender analysis. While roles in Aboriginal communities were organized along gender lines, the nature of these divisions was not the same as in European-Canadian society. In an effort to ensure patriarchy in Aboriginal communities, the government passed statutes in 1868 and 1869 that gave Aboriginal women fewer rights under the law than Aboriginal men. Furthermore, the Indian Act meant different things for women than it did for men. The most damaging discrepancy was found in section 12(1) (b) (often referred to as the 'marrying out clause'), which stipulated that any Aboriginal woman who married a non-Aboriginal man or Non-Status Indian lost her Indian status. Notably, Aboriginal men retained their status no matter whom they married, and their non-Aboriginal wives acquired Indian status. Mishibinijima explores this piece of legislation, the struggles of Aboriginal women to address its unfairness, and the damage it caused them, their families, and their communities. She also queries the impact of **Bill C-31**, an amendment passed in 1985 that allowed for the reinstatement of Indian status, and outlines the intimate consequences of the bill within Aboriginal homes.

Chapter Objectives

At the end of this chapter, you should be able to

- discuss the logistical and ethical complexity of the federal government's attempts to define who is and who is not an Indian;
- discuss the impact of this strategy on different communities and individuals, both in the past and in the present-day;
- identify the ways that the 1876 Indian Act created artificial but harmful divisions between communities;
- consider whether pursuing recognition under the Indian Act is a positive and fruitful strategy for Aboriginal people, nations, and activists; and
- identify how federal Indian policy has discriminated against Aboriginal women as *women* and discuss how they have resisted this discrimination.

Secondary Source

1.   Identity, Non-Status Indians, and Federally Unrecognized Peoples

Bonita Lawrence

The foundation of any Indigenous nation is its cultural identity, which is maintained through language, spirituality, connection to land, and kinship networks. When too many external forces attack cultural identity, it can be so radically and unevenly transformed that the bonds holding the nation together can be broken. A crucial step in this disintegrative process for many communities has been their legal transformation from sovereign nations to 'Indian bands'. This subordination, brought about by the very treaty process that Indigenous nations usually entered into in order to protect their lands and assure their futures, introduced controls over kinship patterns, marriage, and access to land; the suppression of ceremonies; and the imposition of residential schooling and the child welfare system. These policies caused profound chaos within communities, including the fracture of family ties; the loss of knowledge of language, ceremonies, songs, and rituals; and the demise of a daily living relationship to the land.

The result has been individuals who know they are 'Indian' but no longer have clear knowledge of what it means to be Indigenous. Yet the imposition of a hegemonic understanding of the Indigenous self as Indian has sparked significant resistance. This is not, in a sense, surprising when we take into consideration how hegemony works:

> I propose that we use the concept [of hegemony] not to understand consent but to understand struggle, the ways in which the words, images, symbols, forms, organizations, institutions and movements used by subordinate populations to talk about, understand, confront, accommodate themselves to, or resist their domination are shaped by the process of domination itself. What hegemony constructs, then, is not a shared ideology but a common material and meaningful framework for living through, talking about, and acting upon social orders characterized by domination.[1]

For many communities, being Indian and confined to a reserve has become a primary site of resistance to the colonial process, insofar as the relative isolation of reserve life can enable communities to recoup traditional identity and cultural knowledge. In many communities, then, pride in 'being an Indian' has become central to resistance.

In such a context, losing or being denied Indian status has severe repercussions. The colonial state first reduced the citizens of Indigenous nations to being Indians and removed much of the epistemological framework of being Indigenous from them. Next, it instituted multiple processes to eradicate 'Indianness' itself from individuals and communities, thereby eliminating the category through which resistance to these processes had been organized. When Indianness becomes the framework through which cultural resistance and the reclaiming of an Indigenous self are organized, the colonial refusal to acknowledge individuals or whole communities as Indian negates any possibility of Indigenous counter-hegemonic struggle. Yet those citizens denied recognition as Indians experienced much of the same cultural dissolution as those who were recognized, having been forced off their land by settlers or resource development. Being rendered landless, many non-recognized communities have become fragmented because their members are forced to scatter in order to survive. With the loss of connection to community comes the loss of Indigenous languages, as well as knowledge of cultural and spiritual practices related to living on the land. Although both citizens who are recognized as Indian and those who are not have suffered a common loss of traditional cultural knowledge, the latter group has also been deprived of the means to participate in the resistance and cultural reclamation that is organized through an Indian identity.

This article focuses on the ways that Indian status was denied or removed from communities and individuals, as well as the various efforts of both to challenge this lack of federal recognition. Of necessity, this discussion will involve engaging in a basic overview of the issues rather than an in-depth exploration of specific kinds of non-status experience. The essay examines how Canada asserted control over Indigenous identity by replacing 'the nation' with 'the Indian'. It also explores the ways in which Canada subverts efforts to address denial of Indian status and suggests that pursuit of federal recognition may not always be the most useful path to follow for Indigenous peoples. Indeed, efforts at cultural revival can be sidetracked by the quest for recognition.

Becoming a Status Indian: Regulation by Gender and Blood

While Indigenous identities are traditionally constructed through kinship practices and networks, being subordinated under the Indian Act forced powerful constraints on Indigenous communities that gradually transformed Indigeneity into Indianness. Moreover, the treaty process—particularly the numbered treaties—played a key and sometimes decisive role in shaping whether individuals could either acquire or maintain their Indianness.

The 1876 Indian Act consolidated previous legislation regarding Indigenous peoples and regulated matters such as land and money. Most significantly, the Act also determined who could and who could not be recognized as Indian. In this article, the Indian Act is understood as a colonial mechanism of control that not only subverted and transformed how communities lived in relation to the land but was also created with the goal of forcing an entirely new understanding of identity onto Indigenous nations. The primary means by which the Act pursued this objective was by reducing Indigenous peoples to a singular racial category: Indian. Indeed, whether this category is replaced with other generic categories in the hopes of appearing less openly colonial—whether it is called 'Native', 'Aboriginal', or even 'First Nation citizen'—the fact that any such label refers to a singular category discounts and denies the diversity of Indigenous nationhood.[2]

This process of denying Indigenous nationhood transpired at both the local and national levels. While most of the pre-Confederation treaties did not actively deny nationhood, they were signed with communities that had already been fragmented by over a century of the fur trade, missionary pressure, waves of disease, and colonial warfare.[3] Post-Confederation, the nascent Canadian state negotiated treaties that specifically categorized individuals as Indians in ways that denied their Indigenous nationhood discursively and limited it practically.

Legislation passed in Upper and Lower Canada in the 1850s attempted to define the term *Indian* as someone of Indian descent or as a woman who was married to a male Indian. While responsibility for Aboriginal people was officially assigned to the federal government in the British North America Act of 1867, it was another two years before the Gradual Enfranchisement Act was passed, giving the superintendent of Indian Affairs (or his agent) extremely wide powers over almost every aspect of Indigenous life. In terms of regulating identity, section 6 of this Act began a process of defining Indianness based on gender that would not be definitively changed until 1985. Under this section, Indian women were declared 'no longer Indian' if they married anybody who lacked Indian status. On marrying an Indian from another 'tribe, band or body', an Indian woman and her children belonged to her husband's tribe only.[4] As Kathleen Jamieson notes, the Act was initially created to control those Indigenous communities in eastern Canada that had already been induced into farming in settled communities by a combination of missionary programs and settler competition for resources.[5] As Canada pushed north and west into Ojibway and Cree territory, however, the legislation imposed controls on Indigenous patterns of land use, residential practices, and kinship relations. Moreover, with the numbered treaties, Canada began defining individuals as 'non-Indian' not only on the basis of gender but also of 'blood'.

Externalizing the 'Half-Breed'

In 1870, Canada acquired Rupert's Land, the massive territories previously claimed by the Hudson's Bay Company and encompassing the lands west of Lake Superior to the Rocky Mountains and north to the Arctic. From this point on, the definition of Indianness by blood took on increased importance, given that the legacy of the fur trade had produced unprecedented levels of migration and hybridity among the Indigenous peoples of the territory. This resulted in myriad forms of Indigenous communities that included not only 'full-blood' and 'mixed-blood' peoples but also detribalized and transient individuals whose ties to their communities had gradually attenuated through a lifetime engaged in the fur trade. In this complex world of what would soon be designated the Northwest Territories, the status of so-called half-breeds (subsequently known as 'Métis') became a central concern of the Canadian government.

It is important to emphasize that 'Métisness' was never simply a matter of blood, as Canadian authorities asserted. Theda Perdue and Eva Marie Garroutte demonstrate that, in most Native communities, kinship ties were the definitive factor in a person's belonging. Thus, the mixed-blood children of Indigenous women remained part of their tribal communities; moreover, many people who self-segregated as Métis were acknowledged as relatives by their tribal communities.[6]

With Canada's acquisition of Rupert's Land, however, surveyors began encroaching on lands around the Red River that were farmed by mixed-bloods who referred to themselves as Métis. Through their resistance, the Red River Métis were successful in forcing Canada to create a new province, Manitoba, that included recognition of their Indian title, which was to be established not through treaty but through setting aside 1.4 million acres for Métis families to settle on.[7] Subsequently, with the signing of treaties 1 and 2 in the area, the mixed-blood members of Ojibway and Cree bands who regarded themselves and were regarded as Indians were included in the Indian treaties, with the proviso that they were relinquishing any rights as half-breeds.[8] However, the signing of Treaty 3 with the Saulteaux in northern Ontario in 1873 brought the issue of half-breed exclusion from treaties to the forefront. It was clear that the Saulteaux viewed Canada's desire to segregate mixed-bloods from full-bloods as a strategy to divide Indigenous resistance. Treaty 3 was anomalous in that the Saulteaux were negotiating from a position of relative strength—Canada's ability to access the Red River Settlement depended on passageway through their lands. Negotiations for the treaty took an unprecedented three years, and the Canadian government was forced to concede the inclusion of the Métis in its provisions in 1875.[9]

The rigidity with which the government insisted upon a strict racial classification based on blood in the framing of the subsequent numbered treaties revealed the colonial belief that 'race' was crucial in both defining and maintaining control of colonial subjects. Even so, Canadian views of half-breeds and Indians varied over time. On the one hand, Indigenous people were often viewed as 'noble savages' existing in a 'pure' primitive state that racial mixing would destroy. On the other, they were frequently seen as brutish savages needing civilizing, which intermarriage could facilitate. But whether half-breeds were seen as inferior or superior to their full-blooded relatives, treaty negotiators were firm in their conviction that they were immutably different from Indians and that blood was the true measure of Indigeneity. Accordingly, when the Indian Act was created in 1876, it contained a provision that excluded anybody who was not considered to be 'pure Indian' from Indianness. The Act stated, 'No half-breed head of a family (except the widow of an Indian, or a half-breed who has already been admitted into a treaty) shall be accounted an Indian, or entitled to be admitted into any Indian treaty.'[10]

It is clear that, despite the Canadian insistence that half-breeds were distinct from Indians, both groups were ultimately viewed as pre-modern and impediments to the development of modern Canada. Furthermore, the nearly absolute dispossession of Métis people from their lands demonstrates that classifying Indigenous people as non-Indian was a powerful tool deployed by the Canadian state in suppressing anti-colonial resistance.

Externalizing Federally Unrecognized Communities

If the treaty process enabled thousands of individuals to be classified as half-breeds and therefore non-Indian, other communities were denied federal recognition simply by oversight, by lack of a treaty, or by having traditional territories that were bisected by Canadian and provincial borders. The Indian Act not only determined that half-breeds would not be registered as Indian in western Canada, but it also limited what communities would be acknowledged as Indian in Canada. This legislation narrowed federal recognition of Indianness to those Indigenous people living in areas under Canadian control who already lived on recognized reserves or belonged to recognized Indian bands.[11]

This denial of recognition has come about in a variety of ways. For example, some small nations that occupied land spanning the Canadian–American border (such as the Passamaquoddy Nation of New Brunswick or the Sinixt Nation in British Columbia) have been dispossessed in Canada by policies that effectively prevent individuals enumerated as Indians in the United States from 'counting' as Indians in Canada. As a result, these nations are federally recognized in the United States but not in Canada. Other bands are federally unrecognized because Canada has refused to honour historic relationships or has disregarded the traditional boundaries of Indigenous nations.[12]

However, most federally unrecognized bands or nations were created by the treaty process itself. After the 1850s, most treaties were generally not negotiated on a nation-to-nation basis but with multiple Indigenous bands of different nations for large areas of land. Other bands were excluded from the treaty process because they were overlooked by treaty commissioners or were absent when the commissioners arrived to negotiate.[13]

The experiences of federally unrecognized nations have varied depending on the extent to which they faced mining, hydro development, clear-cutting, or direct settler incursion on their lands. In places where resource development has occurred, Indigenous peoples faced the combined efforts of police and natural resource personnel forcing them away from their settlements, in some cases through violent coercion. For many, ongoing risk of settler violence has meant that speaking Indigenous languages was dangerous and therefore discouraged. Some individuals have adopted the identity of the dominant culture and severed their ties to Indigenous communities altogether, while many others have simply made efforts to hide their Indigeneity to protect themselves and their families.[14] Elders from these federally unrecognized communities may retain a strong sense of cultural identity; however, as the suppressed culture becomes increasingly inaccessible to subsequent generations and phenotypic markers of Indianness are lost, many Indigenous people feel that they are 'not really Indian' or 'not Indian enough'.[15] While some communities are focusing on cultural revival to address this phenomenon, it is typical for Indigenous identities in federally unrecognized communities to be in flux.

Making Status Indians into Non-Indians

The final means through which people become federally unrecognized is by having their Indian status rescinded because of the identity section within the Indian Act. As the treaties and the Indian Act whipsawed their way across 'Indian country', gendered racial categories that were tremendously destructive to Indigenous communities, as well as legislation forcing enfranchisement upon individuals and their families, made it difficult for any individual who engaged too successfully in the world outside the reserve to remain an Indian. The 1876 Indian Act dictated, for example, that any Indian who became a professional—a lawyer, doctor, or minister of religion—or who gained a university degree was automatically enfranchised and so lost their status.[16]

The effects of these regulations enforcing loss of status were devastating. On the one hand were the men who were enfranchised—frequently war veterans who returned from serving their country only to find themselves classified as 'no longer Indian'. But of far greater impact in terms of sheer numbers were the women who married non-Indians, for the Indian Act, like the Gradual Enfranchisement Act before it, dictated that Indigenous women who married non-status men forsook their Indian status and could not pass their status on to their descendents.[17] If their marriages broke up, such women frequently found themselves excluded from both white society and their own communities. In many cases, unable to find work or to access welfare, these women squatted at the edges of their former reserves, living in shacks and eking out their livings through fishing, cutting wood to sell, or other marginal activities.

Jamieson has documented the extensive economic and cultural losses, as well as the profound isolation and psychological burden suffered by these women, who were sometimes considered 'traitors to their race' for marrying non-Indians.[18] The children of those who returned home and squatted on-reserve were excluded from the most basic rights: they could not attend cultural events in the community, attend reserve schools, or be bussed to off-reserve schools (so non-status children walked for miles daily just to attend school). They were also frequently taunted by Indian children as being non-Indian because they lacked Indian status. Conversely, those who grew up in primarily white urban environments faced discrimination for being Indian. Understandably, many of these children experienced a profound confusion relating to Native identity, which persisted long after their status was reinstated in 1985 under the provisions of Bill C-31.[19]

The intense struggle waged by a number of individuals, organizations, and communities to reverse over a century of gender discrimination in the Indian Act has been well documented.[20] However, the passing of Bill C-31 did not end this form of bias. This amendment actually makes it easier for Indian people to lose their status by creating what is known as 'partial status'. Individuals registered under section 6(2) of the Indian Act have only one recognized Indian parent; if these individuals marry non-Indians, their children lose status. With this legislation, intermarriage now represents a 'ticking time bomb' in that anybody who has only partial or 'half' status cannot pass status on to his or her children unless the other parent is a Status Indian. Indeed, so many reserve communities currently have large numbers of members with only half status that it is highly likely that increasing numbers of band members will be born without Indian status.[21]

Struggles for Federal Recognition as Indian

Struggles to gain or regain federal recognition have been fraught with different pitfalls. Even successful outcomes have had unexpected negative implications that serve the very government agendas that people sought to challenge by winning recognition. One example of this situation is the Métis' efforts to gain status in the 1970s. While it is unclear whether those who thought of themselves as historic Métis sought Indian status, it is evident that, during this time in Ontario, anyone who lacked Indian status was commonly referred to, by Canadians and by other Indigenous peoples, as Métis. Indeed, in western Canada today, individuals of Métis heritage represent a broad mixture of those who see themselves as essentially 'Indians without status cards', those who are Métis because their Cree grandmothers lost Indian status and married Métis men, and those who see their lineage as pure Red River Métis. Furthermore, many who first expressed themselves as Métis in the late 1970s have begun to refocus their cultural identity on their Indigenous heritage.[22]

The 1982 **Constitution Act** changed the official understanding of Métis identity. After a century of designating Métis people as non-Indian, the government formally recognized them as Aboriginal. However, the Act did not challenge the legal distinction between Indian and half-breed. Instead, disregarding how Métis land rights had been conceptualized as the settling of their Indian title, it defined Métis as irrefutably and perpetually distinct from Indian. As a result, the mutable nature of Métis as a category, which intersected with Indianness and was often indistinct from the category of **Non-Status Indian**, was replaced by a hard-and-fast Métisness entirely discrete from Indianness. The Indian Act created the legal fiction of Indianness to reduce citizenship in multiple Indigenous nations to a singular racial category, and subsequent legislation divided those whose experience of colonization had differed into the categories of Indian and not Indian. Rather than destroying the colonial categories dividing these individuals, the Constitution Act established a new legal fiction, namely that there are and always have been rigid and clear distinctions between Indians and Métis.

The recognition of the Métis as an Indigenous people has allowed them to claim certain rights. Most recently, the 2003 Powley decision extended hunting rights to Métis people that Indians have generally enjoyed as part of their Aboriginal and Treaty rights.[23] However, recognition has also resulted in a drive within Métis organizations to determine who can be considered Métis and an insistence that Métisness is categorically different and distinct from Indianness. One particularly extreme example occurred in September 2002, when the Métis National Council adopted a new definition of Métisness, restricting membership in the Métis Nation to individuals who could claim descent from the historic Red River community.[24] Another sign of this policing of boundaries has been an explosion of scholarship that defines Métisness as 'distinct' from Indians. Unfortunately, much of this scholarship focuses only on defining relations between Métis and Canada, not between Métis and Indians. The cost of recognition for Métis, then, has been permanent segregation from Indianness and a hardening of what was once a mutable and shifting identity.

There are very limited ways in which non-status communities can hope to gain federal recognition. Some can attempt recognition as an Indian band on the basis of distinct historical circumstances (such as the Mi'kmaq of Newfoundland, the Passamaquoddies of New Brunswick, and the Beaverhouse Algonquins in northern Ontario). Others, in areas where no treaties have been signed, can participate in a **comprehensive land claims** process, as the Algonquins in Ontario did. Both methods are fraught with difficulties, and the costs are high. It is precisely through the process of seeking federal recognition that the informal boundaries maintaining 'insider' (Indian) and 'outsider' (non-Indian) status in federally unrecognized communities become formalized. For this reason, it is important to take into consideration the very real problem that anthropologist Bruce Miller highlights: How is membership within federally unrecognized communities to be understood, given the intensity of colonial contact that assaults and fragments Indigenous identities?[25] Because of the massive cultural disarray created in many Indigenous communities, particularly by residential schooling, there is no consensus about what makes a person Indigenous.

Colonial policies have therefore created profound confusion in many communities about the boundaries between who is Indigenous and who is not. As a result, disputes about identity claims frequently arise and divide families and communities.[26] In this respect, Métisness may be more acceptable to Status Indians than the identity claims of their non-status relatives, insofar as the term now represents a different kind of Indigeneity than Indianness and, as such, does not create the potential threat to the identities of Status Indians that claims to Indianness of Non-Status Indians represent. For example, Kirby Whiteduck, chief of Pikawakanagan First Nation, warned the Assembly of First Nations that, while definitions of Métisness were now definite and sufficiently distinct from Indianness not to threaten Status Indian rights, Non-Status Indian identity was too nebulous and ill-defined and so jeopardized the 'distinctness' of Status Indian identity.[27]

Finally, for individuals with reinstated Indian status, a significant problem is that, even as attempts are made to address gender biases, the federal government appears determined to maintain racial categories. With the McIvor decision, for example, the gender discrimination inherent in the 'second-generation cut-off' is deferred by at least a generation; however, nothing prevents future losses of status due to intermarriage. Sharon McIvor attempted to broaden the question to address this racial context, but her appeal was denied.[28] Indianness now inexorably stops at the 'one grandparent' cut-off; gendered categories may be rendered more flexible but racial categories are firmly fixed.

Cultural Identity Rather Than Federal Recognition

Glen Coulthard suggests that there are inherent dangers in casting self-determination efforts in the language of recognition, as has been the practice for the past 30 years. His concern is the manner in which Indigenous peoples seeking federal recognition are forced to accommodate the colonialist state so that their collective rights and identities are recognized only if they do not obstruct the imperatives of the state or capital. The other crucial problem is that struggles for recognition do not allow for revisiting traditional teachings and Indigenous paradigms but frequently demand that individuals institute further changes to accommodate state categories.[29] For example, to be defined as Métis according to the Constitution Act requires the descendents of diverse populations of mixed-blood, detribalized, half-breed, and Métis peoples, who traditionally existed in some form of relationship to their Indigenous nations of origin, to actively prove their difference from Indianness in order to assert Métis distinctiveness. Métis cultural regeneration must involve reclaiming the heritage of the Indigenous nations that constitute part of their Métisness; however, current definitions of the term militate against doing so.

Furthermore, when recognition is negotiated without accommodating the need of the nation involved to pursue cultural regeneration, the terms of recognition often reflect Canada's colonialist agenda.[30] Given that recognition projects in the form of land claims involve the surrender of Aboriginal rights, it is highly dangerous to undertake them without first re-envisioning Indigeneous nationhood. The fundamental question that must be addressed relates to the reason for pursuing federal recognition of Indianness. Many pursue recognition solely for the services and benefits that accrue from it. While poverty is a constant reality in Indigenous communities, Taiaiake Alfred warns against allowing Indigenous vulnerability to facilitate the colonialist project. He suggests that, given the reality of these communities' utter economic dependence on the state for their survival, their resulting susceptibility to paternalistic economic development schemes, and the very limited forms of self-government 'allowed' to communities by the federal government, Indigenous peoples need to think hard about what problems their communities face and whether the status quo can actually address them. He writes:

> The problems faced by Onkwehonwe have very little to do with the jurisdiction and financing of band councils or even with high unemployment rates. The real problems are the disunity of our people, the alienation of our youth, our men disrespecting our women, the deculturing of our societies, epidemic mental and physical sicknesses, the lack of employment in meaningful and self-determining Indigenous ways of working, the widespread corruption of our governments and the exploitation of our lands and peoples—all of which most of our current leaders participate in, rather than resist.[31]

Indeed, both Coulthard and Alfred believe that true empowerment for Indigenous peoples involves working to diminish their dependence on the colonial state, moving towards transformative self-empowerment, and turning away from the assimilative lure of settler state recognition, which comes at such a cost. While the temptation to pursue the acquisition or recuperation of Indianness (or, equally, Métisness) for those who are not federally recognized is undeniably powerful, energies are better spent pursuing the Indigenous identities that classification as Indian attempted to foreclose generations ago.

Primary Document

2.   Indian Act, 1876, Sections 3(3)–3(6)

3. The term "Indian" means –

First. Any male person of Indian blood reputed to belong to a particular band;

Secondly. Any child of such person;

Thirdly. Any woman who is or was lawfully married to such person:

(a) Provided that any illegitimate child, unless having shared with the consent of the band in the distribution moneys of such band for a period exceeding two years, may, at any time, be excluded from the membership thereof by the band, if such proceeding be sanctioned by the Superintendent-General:

(b) Provided that any Indian having for five years continuously resided in a foreign country shall, with the sanction of the Superintendent-General, cease to be a member thereof and shall not be permitted to become again a member thereof, or of any other band, unless the consent of the band with the approval of the Superintendent-General or his agent to be first had and obtained; but this provision shall not apply to any professional man, mechanic, missionary, teacher or interpreter, while discharging his or her duty as such:

(c) Provided that any Indian woman marrying any other than an Indian or a non-treaty Indian shall cease to be an Indian in any respect within the meaning of this Act, except that she shall be entitled to share equally with the members of the band to which she formerly belonged, in the annual or semi-annual distribution of their annuities, interest moneys and rents; this income may be commuted to her at any time at ten years' purchase with the consent of the band:

(d) Provided that any Indian woman marrying an Indian of any other band, or a non-treaty Indian shall cease to be a member of the band to which she formerly belonged and become a member of the band or irregular band of which her husband is a member:

(e) Provided also that no half-breed in Manitoba who has shared in the distribution of half breed lands shall be accounted an Indian; and that no half-breed head of a family (except the widow of an Indian, or a half-breed who has already been admitted into a treaty), shall, unless under very special circumstances, to be determined by the Superintendent-General or his agent, be accounted an Indian, or entitled to be admitted into any Indian treaty.

4. The term 'non-treaty Indian' means any person of Indian blood who is reputed to belong to an irregular band, or who follows the Indian mode of life, even though such person be only a temporary resident of Canada.

5. The term 'enfranchised Indian' means any Indian, his wife or minor unmarried child, who has received letter patent granting him in fee simple any portion of the reserve which may have been allotted to him, his wife and minor children, by the band to which he belongs, or any unmarried Indian who may have received letters patent for an allotment of the reserve.

6. The term 'reserve' means any tract or tracts of land set apart by treaty or otherwise for the use or benefit of or granted to a particular band of Indians, of which the legal title is in the Crown, but which is unsurrendered, and includes all the trees, wood timber, soil, stone, minerals, metals, or other valuables thereon or therein.

Secondary Source

3.   Stuck at the Border of the Reserve: Bill C-31 and the Impact on First Nations Women

Jaime Mishibinijima

In the 27 years since the passing of Bill C-31, An Act to Amend the Indian Act, the impacts of this legislation on the daily experiences of First Nations women, as well as the implications on the sustainability of First Nations communities and memberships, have become clear. The amended Indian Act elucidates some of the persistent identity issues facing First Nations women, which are set to change the face of First Nations communities in Canada dramatically. Many judicial scholars, politicians, and academics are wading through the contemporary interpretations of the Indian Act and trying to systematically reconcile its utility in a modern context.

The Indian Act is a foundational piece of Canada's legislation that provides the framework for the colonial establishment and expansion of Europeans across the country. Although many sections within the Act are no longer relevant, it continues to determine the relationship between the Canadian government and First Nations people. This legislation has been the long-standing centre of controversy with Canada and First Nations people. As First Nations scholar Bonita Lawrence describes:

> to treat the Indian Act merely as a set of policies to be repealed, or even as a genocidal scheme that we can simply choose not to believe in, belies how a classificatory system produces a way of thinking—a grammar—which embeds itself in every attempt to change it.[32]

For First Nations women, the implications of the Indian Act and Bill C-31 have been profound. The dislocation of women from their home communities because of whom they married has resulted in identity trauma that has trickled down to First Nations children. Although the amendment ended the most blatant gender discrimination against First Nations women, gender bias in the Indian Act remains. This article discusses the history of the Indian Act and Bill C-31, the impacts of the latter on First Nations women's identity, the anticipated future of Indian status, and contemporary court challenges to the Indian Act.

The History of the Indian Act and Bill C-31

The Indian Act of 1876 consolidated all legislation pertaining to First Nations people in Canada and created the legislative framework for Indian policy that was applied more or less uniformly across the country. It granted considerable power to the superintendent general and his representatives and ensured that Indians were increasingly subjected to bureaucratic regulation.[33] This Act also determined who was legally able to register as Indian. It decided who was eligible to live on reserves; how those lands were managed, protected from encroachment, disposed, or leased; and how land revenues were invested. The Indian Act also controlled what cultural/social practices could be carried out and how people would be educated.[34] Significantly, this legislation was designed to replicate the gender relations of the white society and nuclear family, where the male was the head of the household. As a result, many components of the Indian Act focus on creating distinctions in rights based on gender. For example, when the federal government passed legislation that divided reserves into residential lots in 1869, widows were unable to inherit their husband's lot.[35]

At the end of the 1940s, a joint committee of the Senate and House of Commons was established to examine policy related to Indian people. The committee recommended broad changes to the Indian Act; however, civilization and assimilation philosophy continued to inform those changes. In 1951, major amendments were made to the Indian Act, including the removal of bans on customs such as **potlatches**, pow-wows, and other ceremonies. Other changes granted women the right to hold office and vote in band council elections.

While the 1951 amendments were an important step in dismantling some of the worst transgressions of the Indian Act, little changed for women. Arguably, these amendments further entrenched the more problematic gender inequities of the Act. For example, before 1951, Indian women who lost status due to the death or desertion of their husbands were given 'red tickets'. These identity cards provided women access to treaty moneys and, in some cases, the right to continue living on reserves, despite having lost their Indian status. After 1951, these women were compulsorily enfranchised, and access to band assets, treaty monies, and the right to live on reserves was terminated.[36]

The next major amendment to the Indian Act did not occur until 1985, with the passage of Bill C-31. This bill ended the process of enfranchisement,[37] or the removal of Indian status through marriage under section 12(1) (b) of the Act. The fight to repeal this section, which ultimately led to the passage of Bill C-31, began in 1971 with Jeanette Corbière-Lavell of the Wikwemikong Unceded Indian Reserve. After her name was removed from the band list for marrying a non-Indian man, Corbière-Lavell brought a court action against the federal government under the Canadian Bill of Rights.[38] During the same period, Yvonne Bédard challenged her band's (Six Nations of the Grand River) refusal to allow her to live in a house on-reserve following her separation from her non-Aboriginal husband, despite the fact that her mother had bequeathed the house to her.[39] Both Corbière-Lavell and Bédard lost their cases. The Supreme Court ruled that the Indian Act did not discriminate against Indian women because, in losing status, they gained rights as white women.[40] Corbière-Lavell's case served as the catalyst for the formation of the Native Women's Association of Canada

(NWAC) in 1974. Its mandate was to achieve equality for all Aboriginal women in Canada.

In 1977, a Maliseet woman named Sandra Lovelace filed a complaint with the United Nations Commission on Human Rights under the Optional Protocol to the International Covenant on Civil and Political Rights because she lost her status when she married a non-Indian man in 1970. After her divorce, she attempted to return to her reserve, the Tobique in New Brunswick, but was forbidden. Lovelace contended that section 12(1) (b) represented a major loss of identity, emotional ties to friends and relatives, and the cultural benefits of living in an Indian community. Lovelace's only recourse was to take her case to the international level. Her lack of options was partly caused by the National Indian Brotherhood (NIB)—later the Assembly of First Nations (AFN)—being opposed to any revision of section 12(1) (b) and its seat on the Joint Committee for Indian Act Policy Changes. In 1978, the committee dissolved over conflict around education rights, and the NIB withdrew. First Nations women's rights, however, remained unresolved. As a result, Lovelace's complaint stayed with the UN because the Canadian government was unable to address her complaint at the national level.

While Lovelace's case was being considered, First Nations women became more organized and the NWAC grew stronger. In 1976, the organization recommended to the federal government that sections 12(1) (a) (iv) and 12(1) (b) be temporarily suspended at the request of individual First Nations. In 1980, the Ministry of Indian Affairs agreed. By 1982, 285 bands had suspended section 12(1) (a) (iv) (the double mother clause, which removed status from children once they reached the age of 21 if their mother and paternal grandmother were Non-Status Indians) and 63 had suspended section 12(1) (b).[41] Because any amendment to the Indian Act would require going through the Joint Committee for Indian Act Policy Changes (which was defunct), the federal government also exempted the Indian Act from the application of the Canadian Human Rights Act (CHRA), closing the door for any challenges based on the CHRA. While this was supposed to be a temporary suspension, it persists to this day.

In 1978, the Canadian Advisory Council on the Status of Women published the first major study of discrimination against First Nations women. Written by Kathleen Jamieson, *Indian Women and the Law in Canada: Citizen's Minus* outlined how 'the deleterious effects of this oppressive legislation on the Indian woman and her children materially, culturally and psychologically could be very grave indeed.'[42] Following the release of this report, a march from the Tobique Reserve to Ottawa took place to protest housing conditions for women on the reserve. This march culminated in a historic rally on Parliament Hill on 21 July 1979. Two years later, the UN reached its decision regarding the Lovelace case: it found Canada to be in violation of Article 27 of the Covenant because it denied Lovelace the right to live in her community and, thus, access to her culture, religion, and language. The federal government stated its intention to amend these sections, and a standing committee of the House of Commons was struck to review all 'legal and related institutional factors affecting the Status, development and responsibilities of band governments on Indian reserves and a study on Aboriginal self-government'.[43]

The 1982 enactment of the Charter of Rights and Freedoms left little time to postpone an examination of gender discrimination under the Indian Act. In 1984, the Liberal government put forth Bill C-47 in an attempt to address the issue. The amendment did not pass Parliament, partially because of the different interpretations of the Charter by groups such as the AFN. The AFN argued that the Charter did not apply to the Indian Act because it focused on individual rights rather than collective rights, which was inconsistent with the right to self-government provided in the 1982 Constitution Act. Bill C-31 passed in 1985, under Brian Mulroney's Conservative government. Along with ending the process of enfranchisement, Bill C-31 provided Aboriginal people who had lost their status with options to regain it (called reinstatement). From 1986 to 2002, 113,254 Aboriginal people registered based on the amendment.[44] The influx of reinstated First Nations women and children stretched the resources of many First Nations communities without corresponding increases in federal funding. There has been a general reluctance to accept new band members because most bands were already unable to meet basic needs with their current resources.[45] Although this general reluctance exists, the reality is that few reinstated band members have returned to their communities.[46]

Bill C-31 also allowed individual bands to control their own membership lists through the development of membership codes specific to the demands of the community. This change meant that people could acquire Indian status under the Indian Act (be put on the general roll) but be denied band membership by their communities. There are also variations in the criteria of individual bands' membership codes, ranging from a degree of legal descent of 50 per cent (previously, Indian and Northern Affairs Canada [INAC] required only 25 per cent), to parental residency requirements and moratoriums on services and rights to reinstated persons.[47] However, the federal government cannot remedy any exclusionary criteria of bands because First Nations are not subject to the CHRA. Section 67 of the CHRA provides that nothing in the Act 'affects any provision of the Indian Act or any provision made under or pursuant to that Act'.[48] For people who are denied reinstatement, remedy must be sought through the courts because there is no process for review or appeal under INAC.

With the passing of Bill C-31, disclosing paternity has also become a crucial issue. For many First Nations women, revealing paternity 'can place them in social jeopardy, perhaps endanger them, and at the very least cause social conflicts where a man either denies paternity or refuses to acknowledge it to state authorities'.[49] Another problem is that, since 1985, unknown or unacknowledged paternity affects the status of future generations. Statistics indicate that this issue is significant: from 1985 to 1999, there were 37,300 births to women with 6(1) Indian status with unstated paternity.[50] These children have 6(2) Indian status, which means they will be unable to extend Indian status to their descendants. The intricacies of Bill C-31 also dictate an even more fundamental change to the Indian Act: the slow removal of status from First Nations people in subsequent generations through mixed parenting or 'exogamous parenting'[51] (marriage or parenting with Non-Status Indians) and the eventual extinction of Status Indians.

Bill C-31 sparked debate amongst many First Nation and Métis organizations and governments across Canada. The AFN, in particular, declared that membership/citizenship were matters of First Nations and could not be dictated by the federal government.[52] This argument was similar to the position that the organization put to the Standing Committee on Aboriginal Affairs in 1982: 'As Indian people we cannot afford to have individual rights override collective rights . . . if you isolate the individual rights from the collective rights, then you are heading down another path that is ever more discriminatory . . . The Canadian Charter is in conflict with our philosophy and culture.'[53] The conflicts between individual rights, as guaranteed by sections 15(1) and 28 of the Charter, and collective rights, those sought through the process of self-government, became the mask that the AFN used to oppose the amendment of section 12(1) (b). The result was to separate the issues of Indian status, band membership, and who can and cannot pass status onto children. This new policy created four types of Indians in Canada: status with band membership, status with no band membership, no status with band membership, and no status with no band membership.[54]

The Impact of Bill C-31 on First Nations Women

Policies are the product of negotiation and compromise, and Bill C-31 is no exception. This amendment was never considered a panacea for the flaws of the Indian Act but a temporary solution to deal with the glaring inequities facing First Nations women who had lost their status and the outdated provisions of the Act. However, these biases were inadequately dealt with in the bill and have persisted.[55] Women continue to face prejudice and inequities in their communities due to the process of reinstatement and the gender discrimination embedded in the Indian Act. Specifically, this treatment consists of community-based lateral violence for Bill C-31 reinstatees, statistical extermination, and family and community fragmentation.

Community-Based Lateral Violence

The experiences of many Bill C-31 reinstatees and their descendents in First Nation communities can be characterized by the term *lateral violence*. Psychiatrist Wolfgang Jilek describes lateral violence as a perceived behaviour in reaction to alienation from history and culture; feelings of frustration, defeat, and discouragement, and low self-esteem associated with aggressive behaviour against oneself and/or others or moral disorientation; and alcohol abuse.[56] For First Nations women, the experiences of lateral violence are closely connected to identity because of the reliance on external validating sources (i.e. family, community members, and political leaders).

The historical use of degree of descent can also foster intra-group conflict, discrimination, or hostility when it is internalized by First Nations people.[57] Criminologist Wenona Victor notes that 'internal colonialism and internal racism is crippling many Indigenous communities. Lateral violence is endemic.'[58] The effect of lateral violence on communities and individuals cannot be underestimated. Victor states: 'Aboriginal communities that have been traumatized (due to colonial processes) display fairly predictable patterns of collective dysfunction', which are expressed through gossip, perpetual social and political infighting, political corruption and lack of accountability and transparency in governance, suspicion and mistrust of others, and an inability to work together to solve community-based problems. These factors result in a lack of progress and capacity building.[59]

The outcomes associated with feeling 'inauthentic' as a First Nations person are far-reaching. The loss of power that a First Nations person can experience might result in multiple and overlapping issues such as depression, anxiety, suicide, and feelings of rejection. For First Nations communities, promoting the notion of 'inauthenticity' through the poor treatment of returning community members can also result in a diminished human resource capacity by forcing members to live and work outside the community. The struggle with not feeling 'Indian enough' serves only to obfuscate 'the real sources of oppression—colonialism and global capitalism'.[60] A 'shared peoplehood' should be the goal as communities work towards sovereignty and self-determination rather than dividing people into self-imposed categories that perpetuate lateral violence.

Statistical Extermination of Status Indians

The number of First Nations people currently seems to be growing. According to INAC's *Registered Indian Population Projections for Canada and Regions from 2000–2021*, the Registered or Status Indian population is expected to rise from 690,000 (in 2001) to 940,000 (in 2021).[61] However, upon closer examination, the rate of growth including and excluding Bill C-31 registrants has declined and will continue to do so. According to projections, 'sometime around the end of the fifth generation (of descendents of Bill C-31 reinstated members) no further children would be born with entitlement to Indian registration.'[62] This conclusion is based on scenarios that assume consistent out-marriage or exogamous parenting and includes factors such as 'higher attendance at post-secondary institutions and increasing employment off reserve', resulting in more social interaction between Status Indians and non-Indian populations and subsequently growing out-marriage.

Figure 8.1 shows that the number of individuals who trace their ancestry entirely through the pre-Bill C-31 population are expected to increase from the current level of 540,800 to 864,800 over the next two generations. Over the course of the following two generations, this segment of the Registered Indian population is expected to decline to approximately 550,000 people. The Bill C-31 population (and those who trace their ancestry through Bill C-31) is anticipated to increase slightly for about a decade before, after years of slow decline, reducing to only 7,900 people in the fourth generation.[63] Projections also show that the registered Indian population will begin to decrease in 50 years.[64]

An even closer look reveals that Bill C-31 registration has steadily and consistently decreased since 1993. Predictions show that the total population of survivors and descendants is likely to increase to slightly more than 2 million within four generations. What is most ironic about the struggles presented by Bill C-31 and the tensions that arise between Status, Non-Status, and Reinstated Status Indians is that, if population forecasts are accurate, 'there may be few Status Indians left and the entire landscape of federal government/First Nations relations that has been built on the basis of Status and non-Status distinctions so carefully maintained through Bill C-31 will have changed beyond recognition.'[65]

The implications of statistically exterminating Status Indians are tremendous for sustaining rural reserve communities. In order to live on-reserve, a person must be a band member or married to a band member. While many communities now face huge housing shortages because of an exploding population, such demands will decrease as

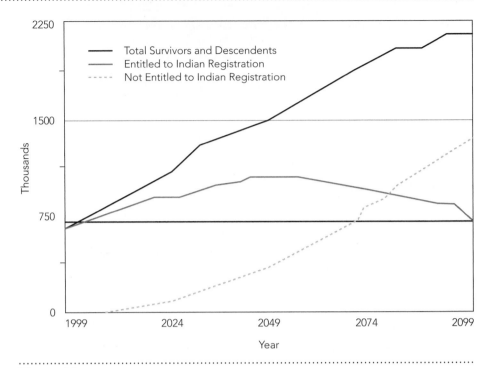

Figure 8.1 Population of Survivors and Descendents by Entitlement to Indian Registration, Canada, 1999–2099
Source: Clatworthy, Stewart. Indian and Northern Affairs Canada. Policy and Strategic Direction. Research and Analysis Directorate. *Re-assessing the population impacts of Bill C-31.* Ottawa: Indian and Northern Affairs Canada, 2004. Figure 17, p.39. Reproduced with the permission of the Minister of Public Works and Government Services Canada, 2011.

the number of people eligible to live on reserves declines. These consequences have further implications for land claims suits, access to treaty rights, and the provision of benefits such as the Post-Secondary Student Support Program and the Non-Insured Health Benefits Program. The inability of communities to sustain themselves in terms of population has clear implications: First Nations people are part of a system that will statistically and legally eliminate them. The socio-economic situation of many First Nation people in Canada has placed them in an untenable position where long-term strategic planning is problematic.

Fragmentation of Families and Communities

Statistics aside, the impacts of Bill C-31 are very real within the family homes and the borders of First Nation communities. The fragmentation that exists politically at the community level and even more so at the national level reduces the sustainability of First Nation communities in Canada. The family and community tension towards Bill C-31 reinstatees can impact personal identity because of the initial rejection of one family member by another. A study by the Aboriginal Women's Action Network (AWAN) found that internalized racism and lateral violence absorbed at the reserve level from the larger society result in attitudes against reinstated band members as not being 'real Indians' or 'pure Indians' and perceptions that women left the reserve 'voluntarily' and want 'something for nothing'.[66]

When the ability of a woman to pass on rights and band membership to her children is lost, her ability to give her children an identity will be destroyed. Being rejected by an entire band is especially difficult for adolescents to endure.[67] Subsequently, these youth may feel alienated and turn to high-risk behaviours (such as solvent and drug abuse), attempt or commit suicide, and abandon education. The internal conflict of legally belonging to an ethnic group with a distinctive culture but not being accepted by those group members has a negative effect on these individuals.

Community members who are raised in off-reserve and urban communities can often feel a sense of being inauthentic, and these negative feelings are often validated by their family members who grew up in the First Nation community. A high proportion of Bill C-31 reinstatees live in urban centres, where they are further disconnected and alienated from their families and First Nation communities. In 2001, 72 per cent of Aboriginal women lived off-reserve.[68] This disconnection, isolation, and alienation can be mitigated when people become involved in their own urban Aboriginal community because there are many people who have a diminished sense of connection to their First Nation.

Eva Marie Garroutte, a Cherokee scholar, discusses the tie to socially constructed determinants of identity through one of her research respondents (Billy S).[69] This respondent felt that knowing your language, songs, and culture is what makes a person an Indian:

> Because it [identity] is not just a legal document; it's a way of life, it's a way of thinking, a way of living, a way of worship that you can't instill on someone with a notarized legal documentation. And I feel that too many times we get into looking at things from a legalistic standpoint and really lose the idea of what it is to be Native.[70]

The resistance and tension that surrounds Bill C-31 reinstatees within families and communities are mainly based on the availability of scarce resources. Fighting for the limited resources offered by the federal government impacts the ability of people to grapple with the bigger picture. The political tension and conflicts between 'automatic' band members and incoming reinstated band members is a very real situation. The impact on some First Nations, especially those with little resources, could be severe and lead to serious conflicts if their need to preserve their social and cultural integrity are disregarded.[71] These tensions exist even within the same family units because brothers and sisters have unequal abilities to pass on status to their descendents. All of these inequalities contribute to strife and division within families and communities. The results will be devastating to adults and children alike.[72]

Bill C-31 remains a colonialist act, 'not even as an event based project with a beginning and an end, but as a contemporary process that is still energized by the particular history and experience of racialized and gendered exclusions in Canada'.[73] Whether or not one can still belong to the group without being a Status Indian remains a difficult question:

living, feeling citizenships, may not be institutionally recognized, but are so-cially and politically recognized in everyday life of the community and that people get called out on them. The challenge to the community is to harden the possibilities into membership policy that may accommodate the simultaneity of these experiences, these different transhistoric discourses (and people), so that these 'feeling citizenships' may then become lived citizenships.[74]

Urban and off-reserve people also struggle with their identity as they attempt to as-similate into communities that have many different cultures that may not reflect their own heritage, history, and value systems. Urban and rural communities are demon-strating the new ways in which Aboriginal communities are developing outside reserve boundaries: 'some Aboriginal people experience marginalization in urban centres, others experience success. Many Aboriginal people maintain strong connections with their rural communities of origin, but many do not.'[75] This is especially true for First Nations women, where discrimination and marginalization associated with Indian status persists. As 'cultural carriers', it is important for First Nations women to have a positive sense of identity so that it can be passed on to subsequent generations.

Contemporary Dialogue on Bill C-31

Today we look to Sharon McIvor as the new champion for First Nations women's rights in Canada. A Nlaka'pamax woman from the lower Salish community in the Lower Nicola Valley First Nation in British Columbia, McIvor has fought the federal govern-ment in courts for decades, challenging the sexual discrimination of the Indian Act. In 1985, McIvor and her children applied for membership with the Lower Nicola Valley First Nation. While McIvor was reinstated as a Status Indian according to Bill C-31, her grandchildren would not have status because their paternal grandfather and their mother were not Status Indians (the 'second generation cut-off'). McIvor, a lawyer, launched a Charter challenge, alleging that the status provisions of the Indian Act dif-ferentially preferred descendents who traced their status through their paternal side.

After 20 years, the government reversed their decision and granted McIvor's chil-dren Indian status on the grounds that McIvor was considered to be an illegitimate child. (The pre-1985 rules indicate that illegitimate children were presupposed to be Indian.) However, the issue of status was not resolved. Due to the fact that McIvor had married and had children with a non-status man, her children would be unable to pass their status onto their children. Despite the concessions of the government, McIvor continued her court challenge for her grandchildren and all other descendents of Aboriginal women who have also lost status. In 2007, the BC Supreme Court judge agreed with McIvor, finding that the Indian Act provisions contravened the Charter by directly discriminating based on sex. The judge called for the immediate registra-tion of all descendents of women who married non-Indians prior to 1985. The fed-eral government believed that it was impossible to implement this broad remedy and sought an appeal based on the argument that, in fact, the Charter was not applicable retrospectively.

In April 2009, the BC Court of Appeal found that section 6 of the Indian Act was indeed discriminatory but in a more limited way than the Supreme Court of British

Table 8.1 Situation under Old Legislation and Situation under 1985 Statute

Situation Under Old Legislation	Situation Under 1985 Statute
Hypothetical Brother Status Indian (s. 11 (e) of pre-1985 Act) Marries non-Indian Maintains Status	Hypothetical Brother Status Indian (s. 11 (e) of pre-1985 Act) Marries non-Indian Maintains Status
Child born—Child entitled to Status	Child born—Child entitled to Status
	1985 Act Comes Into Force
Grandchild of hypothetical brother loses Indian status at age 21 (s 12(1)(a)(iv) of pre-1985 Act) (Double mother rule)	Grandchild of hypothetical brother entitled to Indian status (s. 6(2))
Assume child marries a non-Indian and has children	Assume child marries a non-Indian and has children

Source: Indian and Northern Affairs Canada, 'Changes to the Indian Act Affecting Indian Registration and Band Membership: McIvor v. Canada' (Discussion paper) (Ottawa: Ministry of Indian and Northern Affairs, 2009). Available at http://www.ainc-inac.gc.ca/br/is/bll/exp/dpnc-eng.pdf.

Columbia did. It concluded that the source of the discrimination was the way in which the amended Indian Act dealt with the transition from past registration rules to the future non-discriminatory system. Specifically, the Court was referring to the double mother clause. Bill C-31 eliminated the clause; however, the Court found that, by doing this, a new inequity that disfavoured Sharon McIvor and her descendents followed. The Court of Appeal decision provided a diagram depicting a hypothetical brother and his ability to transmit status as being enhanced by the 1985 amendment (see Table 8.1).

The diagram shows how, prior to 1985, the grandchild of the hypothetical brother would have lost his or her Indian status at the age of 21. With the 1985 amendment to the Indian Act, the grandchild would be entitled to registration. What the Court of Appeal explained is that Sharon McIvor's grandchild cannot be registered and that 'this distinction was not justified by the objective of preserving existing rights because Bill C-31 enhanced the existing "age-limited" right to transmit status to the ability to transmit it for life.'[76]

While the Court of Appeal declared that the amendment to the Indian Act was contrary to the Charter, they chose to leave it to Parliament to determine a resolution, setting a time limit of one year. The deadline ended in April 2010, but the Court allowed for an extension until January 2011. After seeking advice from various stakeholders, the federal government tabled Bill C-3, the Gender Equity in Indian Registration Act, which came into force on 31 January 2011. However, this Act does not address the long-standing issue of First Nations sovereignty over citizenship.

Conclusion

Although Aboriginal identity is inextricably tied to the Indian Act, this archaic legislation has clearly become irrelevant to the needs of First Nations people and is hindering the ability of First Nations communities to plan strategically for long-term sustainability. Bill C-31 has also done little to ameliorate the lives of the First Nations women it sought to help. Despite years of negotiation and lobbying by Aboriginal women's groups and individual claimants, the Indian Act continues to be a blemish on Canada's reputation.

Reinstated members continue to experience lateral violence in their communities as they attempt to access benefits and are often characterized as 'half Indian' or a 'new Indian'. They often feel ostracized because of the reluctance of already economically marginalized communities to accept new members. Alarming trends indicate that, because of the rules of the Indian Act, Indian status will become statistically extinct, which means that the fate of First Nations communities is uncertain. As Sharon McIvor has shown us, Bill C-31 not only failed to stop the loss of Indian status based on gender discrimination, but it also provided new ways for First Nations women to experience differential treatment under the Indian Act. In many cases, a family in which both grandparents hold Indian status may have some grandchildren with Indian status and others without. The result is that some family members can access benefits and rights of Status Indians, including living in the First Nations community, and some cannot. Because Indian status is so closely linked to identity, the ways in which people consider themselves to be 'authentic' are often intimately connected to government-imposed definitions of self.

There are some possibilities for opening up the rigid requirements of the Indian Act through Bill C-3; however, the long-standing issues of who determines membership and citizenship will remain, and the ability of First Nations communities to be self-determining will continue to be limited. McIvor disagrees with the adoption of Bill C-3, claiming that it 'will have the effect of perpetuating discrimination in the status registration provisions. This fact makes the government's proposal unacceptable.'[77] We can continue to look to First Nations women such as McIvor and the women who came before her to ensure the sustainability and perpetuation of First Nations families and communities in Canada, and we can embrace new ways of feeling authentic that have nothing to do with a plastic card issued by the federal government.

Primary Document

4. Excerpt from an Interview with Life History Respondent 12

Interview by Jaime Mishibinijima, 28 July 2008.

I think that there was one thing that kept me in these relationships; I wanted my kids to have status. Once I learned about what all of that meant, I wanted them to get status. It's extremely hard to find a Native man who does not have alcohol problems. With the current guy I'm with, he's Bill C-31 too, so our kids have status. It's been really hard to find a good guy.

When I [. . .] tried to change things, I always heard, 'You didn't grow up here, you're not from here, and you don't know what it's like to grow up on the rez.' That was something I'd heard for so many years, but we had been coming there for many years. That was part of the thing I had a problem with, the inequality.

Primary Document

5.   Indian Act, 1985, Section 6

6. (1) Subject to section 7, a person is entitled to be registered if
   (a) that person was registered or entitled to be registered immediately prior to April 17, 1985;
   (b) that person is a member of a body of persons that has been declared by the Governor in Council on or after April 17, 1985 to be a band for the purposes of this Act;
   (c) the name of that person was omitted or deleted from the Indian Register, or from a band list prior to September 4, 1951, under subparagraph 12(1) (a)(iv), paragraph 12(1)(b) or subsection 12(2) or under subparagraph 12(1)(a)(iii) pursuant to an order made under subsection 109(2), as each provision read immediately prior to April 17, 1985, or under any former provision of this Act relating to the same subject-matter as any of those provisions;
       . . .
   (d) the name of that person was omitted or deleted from the Indian Register, or from a band list prior to September 4, 1951, under subparagraph 12(1)(a) (iii) pursuant to an order made under subsection 109(1), as each provision read immediately prior to April 17, 1985, or under any former provision of this Act relating to the same subject-matter as any of those provisions;
   (e) the name of that person was omitted or deleted from the Indian Register, or from a band list prior to September 4, 1951,
       (i) under section 13, as it read immediately prior to September 4, 1951, or under any former provision of this Act relating to the same subject-matter as that section, or
       (ii) under section 111, as it read immediately prior to July 1, 1920, or under any former provision of this Act relating to the same subject-matter as that section; or
   (f) that person is a person both of whose parents are or, if no longer living, were at the time of death entitled to be registered under this section.
   (2) Subject to section 7, a person is entitled to be registered if that person is a person one of whose parents is or, if no longer living, was at the time of death entitled to be registered under subsection (1).

Questions for Consideration

1. What were the consequences of the federal government's attempts to define who is and who is not an Indian?
2. Why does Lawrence disagree with the strategy often pursued by Aboriginal groups to obtain recognition of their Indian status? What do you think of this tactic?
3. In what ways does the 1876 Indian Act create artificial but harmful divisions between Aboriginal peoples?
4. How have the Indian Act and Bill C-31 shaped Aboriginal women's lives and identities?
5. How have Aboriginal women resisted the discriminatory or injurious provisions of the Indian Act and Bill C-31?
6. Based on the life history respondent's testimony, how have the provisions of Bill C-31 influenced Aboriginal women's decisions regarding their personal relationships?
7. What has been the long-term impact of the Indian Act? What, if anything, should be done with the Act in the present?

Further Resources

Books and articles

Chartrand, Paul, ed. *Who Are Canada's Aboriginal Peoples? Recognition, Definition and Jurisdiction*. Saskatoon: Purich Publishing, 2002.

Garroutte, Eva Marie. *Real Indians: Identity and the Survival of Native America*. Berkeley: University of California Press, 2003.

Jamieson, Kathleen. *Indian Women and the Law in Canada: Citizens Minus*. Ottawa: Native Women's Council of Canada, 1978.

Razack, Sherene, ed. *Race, Space and the Law: Unmapping a White Settler Society*. Toronto: Between the Lines, 2002.

Printed Documents and Reports

Cornet, Wendy. *Executive Summary: First Nation Identities and Individual Equality Rights: A Discussion of Citizenship, Band Membership, and Indian Status*. Prepared for the National Aboriginal Women's Organization, 26 Jan. 2003.

Dead Dog Café Comedy Hour, Vols 1–4 (CD).

Jamieson, Kathleen. *Indian Women and the Law in Canada: Citizens Minus*. Ottawa: Advisory Council on the Status of Women, 1978.

Simpson, Leanne, ed. *Lighting the Eighth Fire: The Liberation, Resurgence, and Protection of Indigenous Nations*. Winnipeg: Arbeiter Ring Publishing, 2008.

Windspeaker (newspaper).

Films

As I Am. DVD. Directed by Nadia Myre. NFB, 2010.
Between: Living in the Hyphen. DVD. Directed by Anne Marie Nakagawa. NFB, 2005.
Club Native. DVD. Directed by Tracey Deer. NFB, 2006.

Websites

Aboriginal Affairs and Northern Development Canada (AANDC)
www.ainc-inac.gc.ca/ai/index-eng.asp

Aboriginal Affairs and Northern Development Canada, 'Basic Departmental Data'
www.ainc-inac.gc.ca/ai/rs/pubs/sts/bdd/bdd-eng.asp

Assembly of First Nations, 'Gathering Voices: A First Nations Dialogue on Citizenship'
www.afn.ca/index.php/en/policy-areas/citizenship

Canadian Human Rights Commission's 'Aboriginal Initiative'
www.chrc-ccdp.ca/nai_ina/default-eng.aspx

NINE

Residential Schools

Introduction

Residential schools embody some of the most brutal, dehumanizing, and destructive elements of Canada's colonial project. The school system, in accordance with the general direction of Indian policy outlined in Chapter Seven, was designed to assimilate Aboriginal children by removing them from the care of their families and communities at a very young age and placing them in boarding schools to receive a European-Canadian education. These schools were funded and run by the state and various church organizations, with very little sympathy for the children in their custody or consideration of their welfare. In fact, given the high death rates of students and graduates of the schools, the degree of sexual, physical, and emotional abuse that occurred within the schools, and the failure of the state or churches to resolve problems even after they became aware of them, it is very clear that the federal government was at best indifferent to the suffering of residential school students. Dr Peter H. Bryce, in his position as chief medical officer of the Department of Indian Affairs (DIA), revealed in a 1906 report that the government's annual expenditure of $2 million on education was largely a waste because almost 75 per cent of residential school graduates died before they reached the age of 18.[1] Bryce's report was neither the first nor the last document that detailed the horrible conditions rampant in the schools. Even more disturbing is that, after the horrendous conditions of these schools were brought to the DIA's attention, they continued to run for almost another century. This system was inherently violent, for at its very core lay the 'intention to "kill the Indian" in the child for the sake of Christian civilization'.[2]

Both articles in this chapter seek to re-centre the history of residential schools by positioning it at the heart of Canada's national history rather than as an unfortunate aberration in an otherwise admirable past. They also emphasize that, given its centrality to Canadian history, the residential school system should be of concern to all Canadians and not just to the victims and their families. Finally, these articles assert that the history of residential schools remains a contemporary concern. According to Celia Haig-Brown, residential schools are part of *our* heritage—'Aboriginal, newcomer, and long-time settler alike'—and they must be remembered and acknowledged by everyone. Lorena Sekwan Fontaine writes from a very personal perspective to address the silence that continues to haunt communities and mask not only the experience of residential schools but also their legacy. Fontaine argues that the violence played out on the bodies and minds of Aboriginal children did not end when they left the schools: 'I realized that the violence that my family had experienced in the schools had been brought into our home.' She further states that 'shame is arguably the most enduring intergenerational impact left by residential schools.' This shame, coupled with the sense of not feeling 'Indian enough' as outlined by Bonita Lawrence in Chapter Eight, can produce a profound sense of cultural dislocation and alienation. Acknowledging this reality is an important part of addressing the shameful legacy of the residential school system. Fontaine traces the slow journey to healing and reconciliation that Aboriginal people, residential school survivors, and European Canadians have begun.

Chapter Objectives

At the end of this chapter, you should be able to

- trace the history of the residential school system, including its goals and the methods used to accomplish them;
- recognize the long-term consequences of the residential school system;
- recognize the complexity of students' responses—including forms of resistance—to the schools' assimilationist project;
- understand the implications of student-on-student violence; and
- consider and debate the place of the residential school system in Canadian history.

Secondary Source

1. Always Remembering[3]: Indian[4] Residential Schools in Canada

Celia Haig-Brown

Introduction

Three things stand out in my mind from my years at school: hunger; speaking English; and being called a heathen because of my grandfather.

George Manuel, 1974[5]

The word or the name 'Spanish' might seem to be no more filled with menace than any other word; but it inspired dread from the first time we Indian boys heard it . . . we knew that 'Spanish' was a place of woe for miscreants, just as hell and purgatory were for sinners. . . . 'Spanish' for us came to mean only one thing: 'the school', known as St. Peter Clavier's Indian Residential School and then later, from 1945, as the Garnier Residential School.

Basil Johnston, 1988[6]

I am holding the Talking Stick. I have been talking about the Indian Residential School in Shubenacadie for many years, and I still don't understand why the hurt and shame of seeing and hearing the cries of the abused Mi'kmaw children, many of them orphans, does not go away or heal. I hope the act of writing it down will help me and others to come up with some answers.

Isabelle Knockwood, 1992[7]

From the early seventeenth century to the late twentieth, missionaries and governments sought to 'Christianize and civilize' the Indigenous peoples of what we now call Canada by establishing various forms of industrial, boarding, and residential schools and hostels. Amazingly, however, we have entered the second decade of the twenty-first century with many Canadians not remembering—or even knowing about—the role that Indian residential schools played in the colonization of this country. Year after year, university students are shocked to hear the extent of the schools' reach. Considering the continuing publicity regarding the schools, the 1996 Royal Commission on Aboriginal Peoples, and the creation of the Aboriginal Healing Foundation in 1998 and the **Truth and Reconciliation Commission (TRC)** in 2009, one is tempted to attribute this oversight to a form of studied amnesia. Those who do know about the residential schools but believe that they belong to a very distant past may be shocked to learn that the last one closed in 1997.

Some people refer to the legacy of residential schools as a dark chapter in Canadian history. Historian John Milloy disagrees:

The system is not someone else's history, nor is it just a footnote or a paragraph, a preface or a chapter, in Canadian history. It is *our* history, *our* shaping of the 'new world'; it is *our* swallowing of the land and its First Nations peoples and spitting them out as cities and farms and hydroelectric projects and as strangers in their own land and communities.[8]

This article makes visible the history of residential schools and their impacts through its re-presentation of fragments of a story that stretches from ocean-to-ocean-to-ocean within this country. It insists on the importance of remembering this heritage for all Canadians: Aboriginal, newcomer, and long-time settler alike.

Origins

The origins of residential schools lie in the philosophies of missionaries who came from Europe seeking to 'Christianize and civilize' the peoples they encountered. The **Récollets**, an order of Franciscan monks, were among the first missionaries to come to the land now called Canada. As the Récollets ministered to the **Innu** on the northern shores of the St Lawrence River in the early 1600s, they were '[d]isturbed by the ability of Native adults to accept Christianity whilst retaining their own cultural and religious framework'.[9] Thus, the missionaries turned their attention to establishing boarding schools offering religious training and French education to children, believing that they would more easily accept a substitute and, in European eyes, superior civilization. These missionaries were the first to separate children from their families and communities. While their schools ultimately failed, a precedent had been set for removing children from community influences in order to hasten assimilation and Christianization. Schooling became a fundamental tool of colonization of the minds, souls, and the territories of the Indigenous peoples in North America.

Extending the Reach

Traditional Indigenous education focuses on life-long learning with no separation of children from adults. Learning takes place in everyday contexts through watching, listening, and then doing. While some Indians initially saw benefits in sending their children to school, such as learning to read, write, and do mathematics in order to prosper within colonial society, many withdrew their support as they recognized government and missionary rejection of all Indian ways.[10] Historian Robin Fisher comments: 'Because missionaries did not separate Western Christianity and Western civilization, they approached Indian culture as a whole and demanded a total transformation of the Indian proselyte. Their aim was the complete destruction of the traditional integrated Indian way of life.'[11]

Sporadic and geographically focused efforts to use schools to influence Aboriginal children were developed from the 1600s, but it was not until the mid-1800s that British North America undertook a systematic investigation into the use of residential schools to serve the goal of assimilation. In 1847, the Province of Canada published a report based on the ideas of Egerton Ryerson, setting future directions in Indian education policy.[12] Clearly expressed is Ryerson's belief in the superiority of Western European cultures and the need 'to raise [Indians] to the level of the whites', as well as the goal of seizing control of Indigenous peoples' land. This aim was implicit in the recommendation that efforts be continued to resettle Indigenous peoples in easily accessible communities to facilitate 'Christianization'. In addition, missionaries were to establish schools focused on teaching menial skills and furthering the assimilationist project. Specifically, 'their education must consist not merely of the training of the mind, but of a weaning from the habits and feelings of their ancestors, and the acquirements of the language, arts, and customs of civilized life.'[13]

Following Confederation in 1867 and the consolidation of existing legislation into the Indian Act in 1876, Regina MP Nicholas Davin was commissioned by the federal government to report on schools for Indians in the United States. In his introduction, Davin references President Ulysses Grant's policy on the so-called Indian question, 'The Industrial school is the principal feature of the policy known as "aggressive civilization".'[14] Reiterating early missionaries' sentiments, Davin wrote:

> the experience of the United States is the same as our own as far as the Indian adult is concerned. Little can be done with him [sic]. . . . The child, again, who goes to a day school learns little, and what he learns is soon forgotten, while

his tastes are fashioned at home and his inherited aversion to toil is in no way combated.[15]

Recommending the establishment of residential schools in Canada, Davin concluded: 'if anything is to be done with the Indian, we must catch him very young.' Clearly, the lessons of the Récollets' failures were long forgotten. Davin's recommendations were widely and quickly implemented. Financed by the federal government, the schools were managed by the churches. This mutually beneficial relationship created a source of funding and a captive audience for the churches and, for the government, facilitated the assimilation of Indigenous peoples and the takeover of their lands.[16] This initiative proved long-lasting and affected thousands of First Nation, Métis,[17] and Inuit children across the developing nation.

By 1920, amendments to the Indian Act included compulsory school attendance for children and boarding schools as the best option. That same year, in a parliamentary discussion concerning revisions to the Indian Act, Deputy Superintendent General Duncan Campbell Scott made his now infamous comment: 'Our object is to continue until there is not a single Indian in Canada that has not been absorbed into the body politic and there is no Indian question, and no Indian department.'[18] Between 1838 and 1985, from British Columbia to Nova Scotia and north to the Yukon and Northwest Territories, over 150,000 students attended 134 schools for Indian, Inuit, and Métis children.[19]

Residential School Life

No matter which schools one considers,[20] the accounts of former students resonate with each other. Memories begin with journeys away from home and family and arrivals at alien institutions. Daily routines were highly structured: early mornings, prayers, morning 'mush', chores, a few hours of school, more chores, more prayers, unappetizing suppers, homework, prayers, and bed. Scattered throughout these endless days are some good memories: learning to read and write; success at sports, dancing, and other competitions; kindnesses of certain staff; and friendships with other children. Many more speak of bad memories arising from the imposition of a foreign culture: general confusion about how things work; dehumanization of institutional life; punishments; loneliness; illnesses; all imaginable forms of abuse; and fundamental disrespect. The Government of Canada acknowledges that 'while some former students have spoken positively about their experiences at residential schools, these stories are far overshadowed by tragic accounts of the emotional, physical and sexual abuse and neglect of helpless children, and their separation from powerless families and communities.'[21] Let us hear what those who attended the schools have to say in their own words.

Arriving

Leaving home and coming to a huge foreign institution stand out in the minds of many residential school students:

> I was five years old and my sister, Mavis, was nine years old when we were sent from home to Edmonton Residential School. Dad took us to Prince

Work and Play, Residential School in Fort Resolution, NT. (Library and Archives Canada, PA-048021.)

Rupert on the freight boat. . . . [There] we were put on a train to Edmonton. At first I found this exciting. . . . But as the train took us farther and farther away I began to feel afraid. At each stop more and more Native children were put on the train. . . . All around there were other children like us, looking and feeling afraid. . . . Finally we stopped in Edmonton; a place far away from home, a place I had never heard of, a place I had never seen. We were crowded into buses which took us into the country. . . . We stopped in front of a huge red brick building full of windows.

Rosa Bell[22]

All of a sudden, here we come in front of this building [Kamloops Indian Residential School]. And after being told to be afraid of white people, you can imagine the feeling we had. . . . We were all standing there, my sister and I hanging on to each other. We were already so scared. . . . Why did my mother and father send us away? Then all of a sudden, we seen somebody coming down the hallway all in black and just this white face and that's when I started just shaking and we all started crying and backing up.

Sophie (pseudonym)[23]

Then one day a 'flyable' took me away from our world through the sky to a dark and desolate place. I do not remember having time to say goodbye to Cyril, my soul mate. I do not remember having time to say goodbye to the puppies or the bright environment before we boarded the RCMP Single Otter to go to Chesterfield Inlet Residential School. . . . Entering 'the hostel', it was impossible to ignore all your senses. Strange voices and languages could be heard in the distance, strange new smells permeated the air at the doorway, and everything was painted in white, in contrast to the people in black.

Jose Amaujak Kusugak[24]

Haircuts and uniforms were standard welcomes:

In keeping with the promise to civilize the little pagan, they went to work and cut off my braids, which, incidentally, according to Assiniboine traditional custom, was a token of mourning—the closer the relative, the closer the cut. After my haircut, I wondered in silence if my mother had died.

Dan Kennedy[25]

Then they brought me to this one room and I had long hair, my hair was really long. And that lady, it was a nun, she said we all have to take a shower. While they were filling the tub up for me, they told me how much I stank. Then they grabbed my hair and told me to sit on a stool. So I sat on it and then they started cutting my hair and I didn't know what was going on. . . . They took me in where the bathroom was. That lady bathed me, and they told me my number was thirteen. That's when they gave me my number and my clothes. It was their clothes and we all had numbers.

Anonymous[26]

Residential School Curriculum

Educationalist Elliot Eisner[27] writes of the three curricula that all schools teach: the implicit, the explicit, and the null. The implicit includes the transmission of attitudes and beliefs, as well as the use of discipline and surveillance to produce what French philosopher Michel Foucault might call normalized behaviours. The explicit refers to the official curriculum, subjects such as reading, writing, and arithmetic. The null curriculum is everything that schools do not teach.

In the residential schools, one day was much like another: the implicit curriculum consumed much of the students' lives. Although students who could afford it and whose homes were close by went home for the summer and winter holidays, others (especially those without families) spent their childhoods in the institution. For them, the days proceeded for years on end with no breaks. Former students speak eloquently of the dehumanizing monotony of their daily routines:

6:15 A.M. Clang! Clang! Clang! I was nearly clanged out of my wits and out of bed at the same time. Never had anything—not wind, not thunder—awakened me with quite the same shock and fright. . . . Clank! Clank! Clank! went the washbasins as they were flipped right side up on the bottom of a long shallow sink that resembled a cattle feeding trough. . . . Clank! Hiss! Gargle!

Inuit children who lived too far away and had to stay at school during the summer. Anglican Mission School, Aklavik, NT, c. 1941. (Library and Archives Canada, PA-101771.)

Scrub-a-dub! Scrape! Choo-choo-choo! were the only sounds from the washing area. . . . Clang! Clang! Clang! *Line up!* Two serpentine columns of listless boys formed.

Basil Johnston[28]

First thing in the morning, we were awakened by the nun's clapping. Then we'd hit the cold floor and say our morning prayers. Then we'd get ready for Mass which lasted for an hour. This was 365 days a year with no let-up.

Betsey Paul[29]

We spent over an hour in the chapel every morning, every blessed morning. And they interrogated us on what it was all about being an Indian. . . . [The priest] would get so carried away: he was punching away at that old altar rail . . . to hammer it into our heads that we were not to think or act or speak like an Indian. And that we would go to hell and burn for eternity if we did not listen to their way of teaching.

Sophie[30]

As for the explicit curriculum, the emphasis in the early years was on learning English: 'The study of the first importance in these schools, for the Indian child, is the acquisition of the English vernacular,' wrote Inspector Martin Benson in 1897. 'Then should follow Reading, Writing, Arithmetic and Hygiene for the needs of the skilled Indian life, some Geography and History, so that he may know something of the world in which he lives and especially the empire of which he forms a part.'[31] By 1910, there was a shift in emphasis. As Deputy Superintendent General Scott explained, religious instruction was the key priority. A clearly gendered division of labour within the school came next.[32] Finally, the teaching of 'the ordinary branches of an English education' was addressed. Jack Funk speaks of 1930s L'École St Henri (Delmas Boarding School) in similar terms, 'The school curriculum had three parts to it. Religious instruction was the first priority, work training was a second while academic studies was a distant third.'[33] Until the 1950s, despite paying lip service to having Aboriginal people become part of 'white stream' Canada, most schools emphasized skills that equipped students for menial jobs at best.

This explicit curriculum influenced the implicit. Students learned quickly that all things related to their own civilization were not tolerated. Not being allowed to speak their language, especially the lasting impact that this loss of language had on family relationships, is a dark memory many shared:

> Neither me nor Teresa could speak a word of English because at home we had spoken all Indian—our native tongue. So they started off with an interpreter who was one of the older kids who told me if I was caught talking Indian again I was to be beaten and that sort of put a fright into me. . . . So inside of four or five years, I forgot all my Indian. . . . Well, just think, it was pounded out of me with a few strappings from the nuns.
>
> Peter Julian[34]

Agnes Grant says that 'the most frequent punishments were for speaking a Native language.'[35] Isabelle Knockwood comments:

> Not only were little children brutally punished for speaking their mother tongue, reducing them to years of speechlessness, but the Mi'kmaw language was constantly referred to as 'mumbo-jumbo' as if it were some form of gibberish. . . . The punishment for speaking Mi'kmaw began on our first day at school, but the punishment has continued all our lives as we try to piece together who we are and what the world means to us with a language many of us have had to re-learn as adults.[36]

Marlene Starr recalls her exposure to the implicit and explicit curricula in this way:

> My formal schooling began in Sandy Bay Residential School in 1963. I did my time for seven years, and there were four significant lessons I learned in that institution. I learned how to be silent and how to be obedient to authority. I learned that being 'Indian' is to be inferior. I also learned to read and write.[37]

In terms of the null curriculum, most students were rarely exposed to traditional knowledge, language, or Indigenous thought within the school.[38] Even now, Indigenous thought is given short shrift in most schools and many post-secondary institutions.

Balancing 'Act'

Emotions run high in contemporary accounts of residential schools, with good reason. For some, the schools hold nothing but negative memories; others seek to redeem some dimensions of their experiences. The accounts vary widely, which is understandable given that there were so many institutions, so many children, so many years, and so many teachers and administrators. In working with former students of St Mary's Indian Residential School near Mission, BC, non-Aboriginal author Terry Glavin seeks a balance.[39] Bill Williams, a former student, says:

> I don't think any of the histories that have been written about the residential schools so far tell the whole story. There is no balance. But in Glavin's work, it is there . . . Chiefs, councillors, band managers, and professional staff, we all learned skills important for our people. . . . I've come out of there with more than I had. I learned how to retain my language and culture in my own way.[40]

Glavin expresses the turmoil even he felt about the school: 'It was an evil place. It was a beautiful place.'[41] In contrast, Bev Sellars, who attended St Joseph's Mission in Williams Lake, BC, stated unequivocally in her speech to the First National Conference on Residential Schools that

> Another comment I have heard is that . . . the schools produced the Native artists, Native leaders, and other Native people who are successful in today's world. Today's successful Native people are proof of the power of Native spirit, and are not as a result of the residential schools. They exist in spite of the residential schools.[42]

Former chief of the Assembly of First Nations (AFN) Phil Fontaine reiterates the tensions characterized above:

> My experiences at residential school taught me to be insecure, to be unsure of myself, to be uncertain of me. I would never send my children to residential school. Further, some people think that residential school was the best thing they could have had because it taught them to work, it taught them discipline, and it helped establish friendships. For those people, I think residential school represented an important part of their lives and one shouldn't take that away from them. . . . But for many others that remember residential schools for the hell-holes they were, they should be given an opportunity to re-examine those negative experiences so they can put them to rest. When you put something to rest it doesn't mean you forget about it. You remember it in different ways, in ways that give you strength.[43]

These 'hell-holes' were places of extreme punishment and, in many cases, sexual abuse. Students talk of the liberal administration of the strap for a variety of offences. 'Pulling ears, slapping heads, and hitting knuckles'[44] were par for the course. Others recount stories of bedwetters being forced to stand with their wet sheets over their heads as a form of public ridicule. One former student speaks of an adolescent girl who was forced to put her bloody underwear on her head.[45] Another recalls hospitalization after being strapped 128 times.[46] Every history of residential schools includes descriptions of harsh physical abuse.

Sexual abuse is also clearly documented. Fontaine is one public figure who speaks openly about the abuse he suffered. Randy Fred writes of his abuse first by an older student and then by a supervisor.[47] In the last few decades, numerous prosecutions have been documented in the media. In 1989 and 1991, an Oblate priest and an Oblate brother who had worked at St Joseph's Residential School in Williams Lake pleaded guilty to sexual assault of 13 boys and sexual abuse of 4 more.[48] In 1995, a former supervisor from the Port Alberni, BC, school was sentenced to 11 years for sexually assaulting boys attending the school between 1948 and 1968. The sentencing judge referred to him as a 'sexual terrorist'.[49] The current TRC will undoubtedly hear many more such stories.

There was also death in the schools. Children died from physical illnesses, such as tuberculosis and blood poisoning. Some people say that children died of heartbreak. Others died while trying desperately to run away from the schools and go home, sometimes in the freezing temperatures of mid-winter.[50]

Despite their environment, students found creative ways to survive and flourish. Almost every text on the schools includes a description of students' resistance to authority.[51] They found places to speak their languages and sources of food and fun,

Boys standing in front of buildings, Tsuu T'ina (Sarcee) Reserve, Alberta, c. 1920. Back row (L–R): Fred Sarcee (Tsuu T'ina) Woman, Reggie Starlight, George Big Plume, Tom Many Horses. Front row (L–R): Stanley Big Plume, Paul Crowchild, Jimmy Big Woman, Alec Big Plume, Edward One Spot, Joe Tony, Pat Dodging Horse, Dick Big Plume. Note that some boys are wearing bandages for tuberculosis. (Glenbow Archives, NA-192-13.)

built lasting friendships, and cared for one another. Some runaways made it home, where their relatives hid them. Families also intervened, hiding their children when the agents came to collect them, appearing at schools to insist that conditions ranging from bad food to harsh punishments be improved, and even having staff dismissed. Rather than simply existing as passive victims of a huge bureaucracy, students and parents found ways to push back as active agents.

The Teachers

Who were the teachers and administrators of the schools? Grant states that they fall into one of two categories: 'those who are remembered because they were kind or were particularly effective teachers and those who inspired fear and anger'.[52] As early as 1891, a former residential school principal wrote of his doubts about the schools:

> How would we white people like it if . . . we were obliged to give up our little children . . . KNOWING that they were taken away from us for the *very purpose* of weaning them away from the old loves and old associations—if we found they were most unwillingly allowed to come back to us for the short summer holidays, and when they came were dressed in the peculiar costumes of our conquerors, and were talking their language instead of the dear old tongue.[53]

While critical of teachers' cruelty, former students also acknowledged the difficulties faced. Mary John of Lejac School says, 'I'm sure they never expected to end up as teachers in the wilds of British Columbia.' Chief John Tootoosis's biographers write:

> His initial impressions of the nuns soon developed into an adversary relationship. Pious and dedicated they were, but also human, and they were almost continually irritated and impatient with their doggedly silent and unresponsive pupils. More and more frequently this continued passive resistance to their efforts exploded into open resentment and anger.[54]

Fontaine acknowledges, 'In spite of all my bad memories, I still end up going to visit the nuns who once taught us at residential school. . . . I need to show them I turned out pretty good in spite of what they thought.'[55]

A recent article tells the story of one teacher and the process of healing with her student. Florence Kaefer, now 75 and never an abuser, found herself increasingly reluctant to speak of her residential school teaching, especially as revelations of sexual abuse were publicized. Recently, she reconnected with a student who had been abused. Kaefer participated with him in a healing circle as they worked together to reconcile their relationship. Former student and country singer Edward Gamblin describes this process as 'reconciliation on a one-to-one basis. That's the only way healing can work.'[56]

Residential Schools in the Twenty-First Century

The fate of residential school buildings exemplifies the current relationship between the school system and its former students, their relatives, their offspring, and their memories. Some buildings are now controlled by local First Nations and are hives of activity. For example, the Woodland Cultural Centre in Brantford, ON—which features a museum, research library, and language department—sits on the site of the former Mohawk Institute. Museum Director Tom Hill comments:

> We are probably the only Cultural Centre in Canada that has had to establish a support counseling program for past students of the Mohawk Institute returning to our site to convince them that they are welcome to come in to see an exhibit, share a public program, visit our library or just browse our Gift Shop.[57]

Certain parts of the school remain untouched, including the carved names and messages of former students that are still visible on the bricks at the back of the building.

The last residential school in existence, the Prince Albert Indian Student Education Centre, operated for a time under the direction of the Chiefs' Council. In 1985, the council took control of the school as others across Canada were either closing or undergoing a radical transformation of purpose. In the face of increasing public criticism of residential schools generally and the withdrawal of federal funding, the centre finally closed its doors in 1997, despite the protests of First Nation parents.

In another show of the power of community action, administration of the Blue Quills Residential School in eastern Alberta was transferred to the First Nation people of the surrounding territories. When the federal government decided to close the school in 1971 without their input, community members and supporters occupied the school and its grounds: 'the old buildings were ringed with tents, hunting parties were sent out for deer, Saskatoon berries and rhubarb, and children went fishing. Elders moved into the gym.'[58] As a result of the occupation, not only did Minister of Indian Affairs Jean Chrétien capitulate, but 23 other schools were turned over to the management of 'properly constituted Indian groups' in 1973.[59] Blue Quills became an adult education centre and eventually an accredited college.

Other buildings remain empty or were burned. The empty Shubenacadie Residential School, like others over the years, burned to the ground in 1968. Rumours circulated that 'Indians' had started the destructive blaze. Former students gathered to cheer the building's demolition. 'There was no sadness, no tears at seeing the building finally being punished and beaten for having robbed so many Indian children of the natural wonders and simple joys of being alive and being Native.'[60] L'École St Henri had burned in 1948 while active. As they watched the fire, 'the nuns cried but the children did not.'[61] The Port Alberni building was torn down by former students, and the rubble remained for several years as a reminder of its horrors. Nothing marks the locations of some schools, though curious visitors comment that strange feelings emanate from the sites.

Always Remembering

Reconciliation, healing, always remembering. Residential schools in Canada are a controversial and complex part of all those who dwell in this land. Grant writes: 'As the twenty-first century begins, it is possible to examine the era, talk about it freely, and seek redress and healing. Though public understanding, formal apologies, and

compensation payments are helpful, it is only from within the cultures that real healing will come.'[62]

Greg Younging makes clear that Canadians need 'to undergo a micro-reconciliation
within themselves':

> The present generation of Canadians need to face up to what has been done in
> their name, and they must own it as being part of who they are. . . . Canadian
> reconciliation must begin with: 1) throwing out all the historical disassociations
> and denials, and 2) getting out of prevailing generation-centric headspace.[63]

Mi'kmaw Sister Dorothy Moore comments, 'It is not where we are that counts; it is
where we are going that matters.'[64]

First Nation, Métis, and Inuit people have more than survived the colonial assault
that the residential schools of Canada exemplify. They have resisted all efforts to assimilate them into the 'white' majority. As Chief Shane Gottfriedson said to the crowds
at the 2010 Kamloopa Powwow, 'They didn't succeed: we are still here.' Indigenous
peoples across the nation are recreating their traditional civilizations in the contemporary context of Canada on their own terms. They are strong leaders, doctors, lawyers, artists, and educators *in spite* of efforts to annihilate them. Certainly, many former
students and their families are still reeling from the intergenerational effects of residential schools; others have found ways to cope. The lessons of the schools and all
that they represent remain for those who consider themselves Canadian. The previous
and (especially) current work of our government and our churches is the collective
responsibility of all Canadians. We will always remember, and now we must find the
best ways to move into honourable relations with one another—First Nation, Métis,
Inuit, long-time settler, and recent immigrant alike.

Primary Document

2.   Program of Studies for Indian Schools, 1897

The Programme of studies herein prescribed shall be followed by the teacher as far as
the circumstances of his school permit. Any modifications deemed necessary shall be
made only with the concurrence of the department.

Subject	Standard I	Standard II	Standard III	Standard IV	Standard V	Standard VI
English	Word recognition and sentence making. Simple sounds of letters of alphabet. Copying words	Sounds continued. Sentence making continued. Orthography, oral and written. Dictation of words learnt and of simple sentences.	Sounds completed. Simple homonyms explained. Orthography, oral and written. Sentences dictated. Composite sentences about objects and actions.	Sounds reviewed. Sentence enlargement. Orthography, oral and written. Letter-writing. Simple composition, oral and written, reviewing work on general knowledge course.	Enlargement and correction of sentences continued. Orthography, oral and written. Letter-writing continued. Easy oral and written, composition, reviewing general knowledge course.	Analysis of simple sentences. Parts of speech. Orthography, oral and written. Letter-writing continued. Oral
General Knowledge	Facts concerning things in school. Develop what is already known. Days of week, month.	The seasons. Measures of length and weight in common use. Colours. Commence animal and vegetable kingdoms, their parts and uses, cultivation, growth, &c. Things in about the school and their parts.	Animal and vegetable kingdoms continued. Money. The useful metals.	Animal, vegetable and mineral kingdoms continued. Uses of railways and ships. Explain manufacture of articles in common uses. The races of man.	Same enlarged. Laws regarding fires, game, &c. of daily use	Social relations. Seats of Government in Canada. System of representation and justice. Commerce and exchange of products.
Writing	Elementary strokes and words on slates. Large round hand.	Words, &c., on slates. Large round hand.	Slates and copy-book No. 1. Medium round hand	Copy-books Nos. 2 and 3. Medium round hand.	Copy-books Nos. 4 and 5. Small round hand	Copy-books Nos. 6 and 7. Small round hand.

Subject	Standard I	Standard II	Standard III	Standard IV	Standard V	Standard VI
Arithmetic	Numbers 1 to 10: their combinations and separations, oral and written. The signs +, -, ×, ÷. Count to 10 by ones, twos, threes, &c. Use and meaning one-half, one-third, one-tenth. Making and showing one-half, one-third, one-fourth, one-eights, one-sixth, one-ninth, one-fifth, one-tenth, one-seventh (no figures). Simple problems, oral.	Numbers 10 to 25: their combinations and separations (oral and written). Count to 25 by ones, twos, threes, &c. Use and meaning of one-half, one-third, one-fourth, &c., to twenty-fifth (no figures). Relation of halves, fourths, eighths, thirds, sixths, twelfths, ninths (no figures). Simple problems, introducing gallons in peck, pecks in bushels, months in year, inches in foot, pound, current coins up to 25c. Addition in columns, no total to exceed 25.	Numbers 25 to 100: their combinations and separations, oral and written. Count to 100 by ones, twos, threes, &c., to tens. Use and meaning of one-twenty-sixth, one-twenty-seventh, &c., to one-one-hundredth (no figures). Addition, subtraction, division, and partition of fractions of Standard II. Roman numerals I to C. Simple problems, introducing seconds in minutes, minutes in hours, hours in day, pounds in bushel, sheets in quire, quires in ream.	Numeration and rotation to 10,000. Simple rules to 10,000. Addition, subtraction, division and partition of fractions already known (figures). Introduce terms numerator, denominator, &c. Roman notation to 2,000. Graded problems, introducing remaining reduction tables. Daily7 practice in simple rules to secure accuracy and rapidity.	Notation and numeration completed. Formal reduction. Vulgar fraction to thirtieths. Denominate fractions. Daily practice to secure accuracy and rapidity in simple rules. Graded problems. Reading and writing decimals to thousandths inclusive.	Factors, measures and multiples. Vulgar fractions completed. Easy application of decimals to ten-thousandths. Easy application of square and cubic measures. Daily practice to secure accuracy and rapidity in simple rules. Easy application of percentage. Graded problems.

Subject	Standard I	Standard II	Standard III	Standard IV	Standard V	Standard VI
Geography			Development of geographical notions by reference to geographical features of neighbourhood. Elementary lessons on direction, distance, extent.	(a) Review of Standard III. Lesson to lead to simple conception of the earth as great round ball, with surface of land and water, surrounded by the air, lighted by the sun, and with two motions. (b) Lessons on natural features, first from observation, afterwards by aid of moulding-board, pictures and blackboard illustrations (c) Preparation for and introductions of maps. (Review of lessons in position, distance, direction with representation drawn to scale). Study of map of vicinity drawn on blackboard. Maps of natural features drawn from moulded forms. Practice in reading	Simple study of the important countries in each continent. Province in which school is situated and Canada to be studied first. The position of the country in the continent; its natural features; climate, productions, its people, their occupations, manners, customs, noted localities, cities, &c. Moulding-boards and map-drawing to be aids in the study. Simple study of the important countries in each continent, &c., &c.	(a) The earth as a globe. Simple illustrations and statements with reference to form, size, meridians and parallels, with their use; motions and their effects, as day and night, season, zones, with their characteristics, as winds and ocean currents, climate as affecting the life of man. (b) Physical features and conditions of North America, South America and Europe, studied and compared. Position on the globe; position, relative to other grand divisions, size, form, surface, drainage, animal, vegetable life, resources, &c. Natural advantages of the cities.

				onventional map symbols on outline maps. (d) General study from globe and maps. The hemisphere, continent, oceans and large islands, their relative positions and size. The continents: position, climate, form, outline, surroundings, principal mountains, rivers, lakes; the most important countries, productions, peoples, interesting facts and associations.	(c) Observation to accompany the study of geography-apparent movements of the sun, moon and stars, and varying times of their rising and setting; difference in heat of the sun's rays at different hours of the day; change in the direction of the sun's rays coming through the school-room window at the same hour during the year; varying length of noon-day shadows; changes of the weather, wind and seasons.
Ethics	The practice of cleanliness, obedience, respect, order, neatness.	Right and wrong. Truth. Continuance of proper appearance and behaviour.	Independence. Self-respect. Develop the reasons for proper appearance and behaviour.	Industry, Honesty. Thrift.	Citizenship of Indians, Patriotism. Industry. Thrift, Self-maintenance. Charity. Pauperism.	Indian and white life. Patriotism. Evils of Indian isolation. Enfranchisement. Labour the law of life. Relations of the sexes as to labour. Home and public duties.

Subject	Standard I	Standard II	Standard III	Standard IV	Standard V	Standard VI
Reading	First Primer	Second Primer	Second Reader	Third Reader	Fourth Reader	Fifth Reader
Recitation		To begin in Standard II, are to be in line with what is taught in English, and developed into pieces of verse and prose which contain the highest moral and patriotic maxims and thoughts.				
History			Stories of Indians of Canada and their civilization.	History of province in which school is situated.	Canadian History (commenced).	Canadian History (continued).
Vocal Music			Simple songs and Hymns. The subjects of the formers to be interesting and patriotic. The tunes bright and cheerful.			
Calisthenics				Exercises, frequently accompanied by singing, to afford variation during work and to improve physique.		
Religious Instruction				Scripture Reading. The Ten Commandments. Lord's Prayer. Life of Christ, &c., &c.		

Note; English. – Every effort must be made to induce pupils to speak English and to teach them to understand it; unless they do, the whole work of the teacher is likely to be wasted.
Reading. – Pupils must be taught to read loudly and distinctly. Every word and sentence must be fully explained to them, and from time to time they should be required to state the sense of a lesson or sentence, in their own words, in English, and also in their own language if the teacher understands it.
General. – Instruction is to be direct, the voice and blackboard being the principal agents. The unnecessary use of text books is to be avoided.
N.B. – It will be considered proof of the incompetency of a teacher, if pupils are found to read in "parrot fashion" only, i.e., without in the least understanding of what they read. And the following remark applied to all teaching, viz.: – Everything must be thoroughly understood, before a pupil is advanced to further studies.

Secondary Source

3.   Reflections on the Indian Residential School Settlement Agreement: From Court Cases to Truth and Reconciliation

Lorena Sekwan Fontaine

On 15 October 2009, Justice Murray Sinclair, chair of the Indian Residential School Truth and Reconciliation Commission (TRC), reminded the Canadian public of the critical nature of the commission's work while cautioning those who view residential schools as something that happened in the past:

> To those of you who would say, 'It's in the past. Why don't they just get over it?' I would say this: 'we—and you—are not out of the past yet. Our families were broken apart, and must be rebuilt. Our relationships have been damaged and must be restored. Our spirits have been stolen and must be returned. Our love for life was turned into fear and we must work together now to learn to trust once again.' We have so much left to learn about the lasting legacy of the schools. Every story told is another opportunity for one individual to be freed from the burden of carrying that story, alone. Today, the Truth and Reconciliation Commission, we hope, will present that opportunity to all who wish to speak up. The Whole Truth can only come from You . . . the Witnesses to this part of our history. . . .[65]

I have heard Elders echo Justice Sinclair's wisdom indicating that, in order for us to move forward as a country, we need to know what has happened in the past. In other words, Aboriginal communities and Canadians need to take the time to look back on what transpired in the schools so that we are able to understand the present. Only when this is done will the country be able to start contemplating how to proceed.

I was faced with a smaller version of this challenge in 2009–10 when I was preparing to teach a seminar on Aboriginal politics in Canada at the University of Winnipeg. My goal was to provide the students with information about the legacy of the Indian residential schools and then work with them on developing ideas about how Canada and Aboriginal peoples can reconcile in the aftermath of this experience. I also wanted the students to be able to articulate some root causes of the hardships that Aboriginal peoples are encountering today. After contemplating how to structure the course for many days, I eventually settled on reading material I located on the Aboriginal Healing Foundation website. The research series was extremely insightful, although some of the vivid descriptions of residential school experiences were hard to read. One article greatly affected me because the author acknowledged the current generation, suggesting that 'Our generation inherited this family history by just being who we are— part of the continuum of our ancestors' legacy right through to the few generations that proceeded us.'[66] As I read this sentence, I realized that I had removed a critical part in preparing for the course—my personal experiences. Perhaps my reaction was natural. For the most part, my experiences are traumatic. After some time, I concluded that it was important for me to include my personal relationship in the topic. I recognized that my experience is relevant because it demonstrates that the legacy of residential schools is not only part of Aboriginal peoples' history but that it also continues to have an impact on lives today. I began the course determined to make the students aware that residential schools are a contemporary issue. By the middle of the semester, many students commented that they had not considered the current repercussions of the schools. Some of them wrote in their reflection papers that they had gained a better understanding of why there was so much violence in Aboriginal communities. Others indicated that they were surprised to find out that residential school survivors continue to suffer so much pain. When the seminar was completed, I was relieved to find out that many of the students felt that the personal human experiences had had the biggest impact on their learning.

As a result of what I learned from teaching my course, I decided to include personal reflection and experience in this article. I will begin, as I did in the seminar, by sharing my family's experience with the residential school system. Then, I will briefly provide an overview of some key events that have occurred over the past 20 years leading up to the first national event of the TRC. Finally, I will provide concluding thoughts on the historic **residential school apology** made by Prime Minister Stephen Harper on 11 June 2008 and on former Assembly of First Nations (AFN) national chief Phil Fontaine's comments on reconciliation to demonstrate that, in spite of the hard work ahead, there is hope for a brighter future.

Until 2001, I knew very little about residential schools. I had casually heard my aunts and uncles mention that they had attended the schools, but their experiences were never revealed to me. My educational experience was even less informative. Residential schools were briefly mentioned in a few sentences of a textbook. As far as I was concerned (at the age of 23), residential schools were an ordinary part of Canada's education system. I received a rude awakening when I attended a keynote address my mother gave during an education conference. Her talk revealed that she had contemplated suicide while dealing with the abuse that she had experienced in the residential school system. That day, I learned that she was forced to live in the schools for 13 years. Although it was mandatory for all Indian children to attend a residential school from the age of five,[67] my mother and her twin sister, for some reason, were forcibly removed from our community when they were merely three years old. My mother also revealed that she was denied the ability to speak Cree, beaten constantly, and subjected to sexual, physical, and spiritual abuse while in the residential school. One of the strongest memories she has is repeatedly being made to feel ashamed of her Cree identity. Her experiences were brutal and devastating, yet I knew very little about them.

Listening to my mother that day was a life-changing experience. Learning about the gross injustices Aboriginal peoples endured while in residential schools provided me with the impetus to research the legislation and policy decisions made during this era. I particularly wanted to know why no one was publicly talking about what had happened. When I searched for answers, I was shocked to find very little material on the topic. I decided to discuss the issue with some of my cousins. Most of us were in shock to find out about the abuse our parents had experienced, but we were unable to enter into long discussions because we did not have enough information. I think that most of us figured that our parents had already been through enough and felt equally awkward about approaching them for answers. There was a lot of silence, a lot of guessing about the reasons why they never informed us. However, by piecing together family comments and speaking to Aboriginal organizations that were conducting research on the topic, I began to discover more about the schools. I also came to startling realizations about the reasons for the silence and the impact on my own life.

The first connection I made was related to the impact of the residential schools on my home life. I realized that the violence that my family had experienced in the schools had been brought into our home. I came to this conclusion after I reflected on my parents, aunts, and uncles growing up in a violent environment without any love or nurturing from their parents and extended families. It finally made sense to me why they had a hard time parenting. I also recognized that none of them had ever gone through counselling or healing from their experiences, so I understood why so many of them turned to alcohol in order to cope.

When I look back on my childhood, I recall that my family's drinking led to erratic behaviour and, ultimately, physical and sexual abuse. All of my cousins, siblings, and I have been affected. Although not all of us directly experienced the physical and sexual violence, we were all witnesses. Witnessing abuse can be (and, in our case, proved to be) as damaging as being its direct victim because of the resulting sense of powerlessness. Evidence of my cousins and I internalizing the violence we experienced is found in the many instances of suicide, eating disorders, and constant drug and alcohol abuse that occurred amongst us. Another damaging impact is the repeated violent behaviour that some of my cousins have brought into their children's lives. We are in the process of dealing with many issues, most of which are associated with feelings of shame.

Shame is arguably the most enduring intergenerational impact left by residential schools. Shame leads to so many issues, so many struggles. Our parents' inability to teach us about our Aboriginal identity was largely due to the shame they were made to feel in the schools. We were never taught to speak our language, and we were never taught about our history at home. No one ever talked about our leaders, our politics, our stories, our songs, or our ceremonies. It was as if our cultural identity did not exist in Canada. This experience affected me in countless ways, including leaving me with paralyzingly low self-esteem, an intense discomfort with my Cree and Ojibway ancestry, and a complete denial of my Aboriginal identity until my early twenties. On a number of occasions, I simply told people that I was French because I had the last name Fontaine.

Court Cases

Shortly after I started to make personal realizations about the legacy of the residential schools, I began to hear about court cases being launched against the federal government and the churches. One case that received national attention was *Barney v. Canada* (originally known as *Blackwater v. Plint*) because it was heard by the Supreme Court of Canada. The case involved a claim against Canada, the United Church of Canada, and Arthur Plint for the sexual and physical abuse that occurred at the Alberni Indian Residential School in British Columbia. Although it must have been very difficult for these brave complainants to bring their case forward in 1998, their case sparked many more. By 2004, there were approximately 14,000 cases involving Aboriginal peoples' allegations of sexual and physical abuse at residential schools before the courts. While I was working as a legal consultant on residential schools, I encountered hundreds of former students across Canada who were also seeking compensation for the physical punishment they experienced for speaking their language, which ultimately constrained their ability to pass the language on to their children and grandchildren. They expressed a great deal of fear over the possibility of their communities losing their traditional languages and cultures within the coming generations.

When the residential school survivors I spoke to were informed that there was nothing expressly stated in Canada's Constitution regarding the right to Aboriginal languages and cultures in Canada, they were outraged. Several individuals could not comprehend how the French and the English languages were recognized under the Constitution[68] but Aboriginal languages were not. Some people commented on the fact that Aboriginal languages are the first languages of this country and argued that this should be recognized in Canadian law. Others mentioned that Aboriginal languages are sacred rights that were recognized when the Crown agreed to enter into treaties with Aboriginal peoples. The pipe ceremonies that were conducted affirmed this sacred aspect of the treaties. Elders have also articulated that Aboriginal languages were provided to Aboriginal peoples from the Creator.[69] Despite repeated public outcries across the country, there was very little acknowledgement from the government regarding Aboriginal language rights.[70] Many of the court cases ultimately included loss of language and cultures, but the focus was on compensation for sexual and physical abuse.

Class-Action Lawsuits

One of the ways in which some law firms approached the thousands of residential school claims was to launch a class-action suit. This type of lawsuit brings together a large group of people who have been similarly harmed under one case. It also provides equal treatment to the claimants and a more efficient way to deal with the cases. The class-action suits regarding residential schools include the following:

1. The Cloud Class Action, which represented students seeking compensation for abuse that occurred at the Mohawk Institute Residential School in Brantford, ON, between 1922 and 1969;
2. The Baxter National Class Action, which was launched in the Ontario Superior Court of Canada on behalf of all residential school survivors throughout Canada and their families;
3. The Dieter Class Action, which was filed on behalf of students who attended residential schools in one or more of the western provinces between 1 January 1920 and 31 December 1996;
4. The Pauchay Class Action, which represented students of residential schools in Canada from the 1940s to the 1980s who were seeking compensation for abuse;[71] and
5. The Straightnose Class Action, which was launched on behalf of all Saskatchewan citizens who had attended a residential school in that province between 1920 and 1996.

Most recently, Aboriginal people who had attended residential schools in Newfoundland and Labrador between 1949 and 1979 launched a class-action suit for their mistreatment. A major issue in this case is that the federal government is not claiming any responsibility for these schools because it did not directly fund them.[72]

In addition to the class actions, the federal government established an out-of-court dispute resolution process for residential school survivors. It commenced with a series of community exploratory dialogue processes that took place across Canada from September 1998 to June 1999.[73] During these discussions, Aboriginal people identified a variety of barriers to their coming forward and collaborating with the government, including a lack of trust in the government and the government's own refusal, while acknowledging the physical and sexual abuse, to discuss the cultural, spiritual, and psychological mistreatment that transpired. Aboriginal peoples also indicated that they wanted to be full participants in the development of an out-of-court process. As one participant stated, the process had to be empowering to residential school survivors:

> It is critically important that the Native community understand what is going on. . . . I don't want to further dis-empower people. This is about individuals and getting them empowered to make choices. Residential schools took control for so long; getting control back is important. This is a task we take to the community.[74]

Another former student indicated that 'Residential schools happened because the government made decisions for Aboriginal peoples—government took away control at residential schools—I don't want to let that happen as we move to resolutions and to decisions around healing.'[75] In the final report of the exploratory dialogues, the federal government indicated that Aboriginal peoples' concerns would be addressed and that they would be empowered to make choices.

It was therefore surprising when Indian Residential Schools Resolution Canada (IRSRC) emerged as a new federal department in 2001, after very little consultation with Aboriginal peoples. By the time a public announcement was made, IRSRC had established three offices (in Regina, Vancouver, and Ottawa) with full administrative support and approximately 100 lawyers on staff. Two years later, IRSRC launched its dispute resolution process, again without adequate consultation. Immediate criticism came from survivors, lawyers, legal experts, and Aboriginal organizations across the country. One criticism was that the recommendations Aboriginal peoples made during the exploratory dialogues were ignored. Furthermore, the dispute resolution process did not reflect the needs of survivors or their families and seemed likely to cause further harm. Other issues came from the cumbersome application process, which included a 30-page application form and a 50-page guideline booklet. There was also an offensive grid system that allocated points for varying degrees of sexual assault and physical harm. It was generally agreed that the process was similar to court.[76] Aboriginal organizations and lawyers from across Canada, including the Canadian Bar Association, tried to convince the government to change the dispute resolution process. However, the government proceeded full steam ahead.

A radical shift in the government's attitude finally occurred in March 2004 after the AFN (under the leadership of former national chief Phil Fontaine) and the University of Calgary co-hosted a conference entitled 'The Tragic Legacy of the Residential Schools: Is Reconciliation Possible?' The purpose of the conference was to draw national and international attention to the Canadian government's dispute resolution process and expose its flaws. The presenters unanimously concluded that the dispute resolution model in its present form would not meet survivors' needs and would not result in a fair settlement.

A few months after the conference, the AFN organized a team of national and international experts to determine what practical and reasonable changes could be made to the government's dispute resolution process in order to make it more acceptable and accessible to survivors. The team's final report, *Assembly of First Nations Report on Canada's Dispute Resolution Plan to Compensate for Abuses in Residential Schools*, was released in November 2004 and was initially met with a great deal of resistance by the federal government. Three years later, the **Indian Residential School Settlement Agreement** was successfully negotiated.

Lawyers, the churches, the federal government, the AFN, and other Aboriginal organizations negotiated the agreement under the guidance of former Supreme Court justice Frank Iacobucci, with the objective of merging all the residential school lawsuits into one agreement. As a result of the legal nature of the process, the approval of nine courts in Alberta, British Columbia, Manitoba, Ontario, Quebec, Saskatchewan, the Yukon, the Northwest Territories, and Nunavut had to be obtained. The approval process also included a national public communications strategy. Aboriginal peoples were informed that they had until 20 August 2007 to formally opt out of the settlement agreement. According to its terms, if 5,000 or more individuals chose this option, the agreement would be nullified. In other words, a majority of the Aboriginal population had to support the agreement for it to be accepted. Fewer than 200 individuals chose to opt out, and the agreement was approved on 18 September 2007.

This agreement stands as the largest court-ordered settlement agreement in Canadian history. Some of its major components consist of a compensation fund for survivors and the establishment of a 'truth and reconciliation' process. As for compensation, the federal government agreed to pay $1.9 billion to former students as a 'common experience payment'. Every eligible student is entitled to $10,000 for their first school year and $3,000 for each additional year. There is also an independent assessment process for former students who want to seek further compensation for severe incidents of physical or sexual abuse. Money has also been allocated for programs and commemoration for former students and their families. These funds are distributed in a few areas: $125 million for healing, $60 million for research and documentation, and $20 million for national and community commemorative projects. Compensation is distributed under the remit of the TRC.

Truth and Reconciliation

The TRC commenced its five-year mandate on 1 June 2008 with Justice Harry LaForme as chair. Claudette Dumont-Smith, an Aboriginal health expert, and Jane Brewin Morley, a lawyer and public policy advisor, were also appointed as commissioners. After four months, LaForme resigned due to irreconcilable differences with the commissioners and staff. A few months later, the commissioners publically announced their resignation. In June 2010, Justice Murray Sinclair was appointed as the new chair and Marie Wilson and Wilton Littlechild as commissioners. Over the course of its five-year mandate, this group must complete four main tasks:

- prepare a comprehensive historical record on the policies and operations of the schools;
- complete a publically accessible report to the Government of Canada concerning the residential school system, its legacy, and how best to commemorate it;
- establish a research centre that will be a permanent resource for all Canadians; and
- host seven national events in different regions across Canada to promote awareness and public education about the residential school system and its impact.[77]

Regarding the final objective, the first national event was held in Winnipeg from 16 to 19 June 2010. Thousands of people attended the momentous four-day event. My family and I were fortunate to attend some of the sessions. The first day was extremely hot and sunny. During the opening ceremony of the first sharing circle, my sister, brother, mother, and I sat under a tent that sheltered us from the sweltering heat. As an Elder from the Coast Salish territory began to sing and play his hand drum, I heard a louder banging that was impacting my ability to focus on the song. At first I thought the noise was coming from the construction of the Human Rights Museum that was being built relatively close to where we were sitting. When the banging got louder, I asked my sister if she could hear it. She leaned over to me and whispered, 'Yes, I hear it. It's thunder.' I listened more closely and also recognized the sound of thunder. I soon felt overwhelmed when I looked up into the sky and saw only crystal hues of blue. There were no clouds in sight. As soon as the Elder's song was completed, the thunder also stopped. I was thankful for the powerful presence of the Thunderbirds,[78] which gave me comfort. I offered tobacco for the blessings they brought to the opening ceremony.

The event offered a variety of activities, including statement gathering, academic paper presentations, films, musical performances, plays, literary events, powwows, traditional ceremonies, cultural teachings, storytelling, and a sacred fire that burned for the four days to acknowledge the ancestors who have passed away. For me, the most compelling aspect was the sharing circles. The smell of sage filled the room as survivors courageously bared their souls. Some of them closed their eyes tightly as they revealed the darkest memories of their childhood. Others openly wept because the memories were too painful for them to bear. The audience witnessing the sharing circles formed a protective supportive barrier around those survivors sharing their experiences. Many tears were shed as the audience listened. When I took a break from listening, I located a place where I could quietly reflect on what I had heard. I realized that it was strange to be at an Aboriginal gathering where there were no children running around. There must have been an unspoken rule that the sharing circles were not a place for young children and infants because there was nothing mentioned publicly that children could not attend. I also reflected on the presence of the big-screen TV that was placed in the hallway of the building so that individuals who could not fit into the room could be a part of the sharing circle. Some sat and quietly listened while doing their beadwork; others watched the screen attentively. I was struck by the stark silence against the backdrop of the voice of the survivor who was speaking. As I left the area, I recognized that I was part of a very important historic event. All the hard work that Aboriginal peoples had expended for many years in trying to gain government recognition of the crimes committed in the residential schools was paying off. Finally, there was some movement forward from the residential school experiences. Finally, people were openly talking about what had happened.

Concluding Remarks

There were two other events that indicated to me that the silence had been broken. The first occurred on 11 June 2008, when Prime Minister Stephen Harper offered a full apology on behalf of Canadians for the residential school system. He expressed remorse for what had happened and declared that the racism that instigated the creation of the residential schools had no place in Canada. The following is an excerpt of the apology:

> For more than a century, Indian Residential Schools separated over 150,000 Aboriginal children from their families and communities. In the 1870s, the federal government, partly in order to meet its obligation to educate Aboriginal children, began to play a role in the development and administration of these schools. Two primary objectives of the Residential Schools system were to remove and isolate children from the influence of their homes, families, traditions and cultures, and to assimilate them into the dominant culture. These objectives were based on the assumption Aboriginal cultures and spiritual beliefs were inferior and unequal. Indeed, some sought, as it was infamously said, 'to kill the Indian in the child'. Today, we recognize that this policy of assimilation was wrong, has caused great harm, and has no place in our country.[79]

The second event occurred exactly one year later. The Legacy of Hope Foundation, in partnership with the Aboriginal Healing Foundation, coordinated a roundtable conversation on the topic of how to move towards healing and reconciliation. Panelists included then governor general Michaëlle Jean, Phil Fontaine, Chief Robert Joseph of the Kwagiulth Nation, and philosopher and former viceregal consort of Canada John Ralston Saul. Fontaine provided reflective yet hopeful thoughts on reconciliation:

> We haven't been accepted for who we are. We have been denied our place . . . our rightful place in Canada, our history books are absent of stories, sadly most Canadians do not know about us . . . they don't know our stories and they ought to because we are a large part of the history of this country. When you make the point of the length of time it took to be on the floor of the House of Commons to receive the Apology from the Prime Minister . . . the reason is because Canadians did not know that we have been here for a long time. They didn't know the saddest, darkest chapter of their history. June 11, 2008 was a special day because we are no longer going to talk about the apologies we are now embarking on a different part of this long journey together . . . this is about us . . . all Canadians including our people. We are now going to focus on healing and reconciliation. Reconciliation means different things to different people but there are certain inescapable facts about reconciliation and one of them of course has to do with our history and what it's taught Canadians

about themselves and that must include . . . all the ugly manifestations of what was done to us in the good name of Canadians. We have before us an incredible opportunity to fix the many things that are wrong with Canada and there's no better way to start what will be at moments a very difficult journey but we will achieve success because things are different now. Because we [Aboriginal peoples] have come into our own and in the process Canada has come of age and so I am very hopeful and optimistic that we are about to transform Canada in a very positive way.[80]

Although Fontaine's message inspires hope about the reconciliation process, the idea remains controversial for many Aboriginal peoples. There are survivors who are not ready to reconcile. Others are not at a point in their healing journey to recognize that they have been affected. And the 20,000 or more Aboriginal children who are trapped in the child welfare system because of the legacy of the residential schools do not have a voice in this process.

As for me, I have not come to any grand conclusions on my feelings towards reconciliation. There are days when I see my daughter happily thriving in life and I feel very hopeful. Then there are days when I become consumed with grief over the loss of my childhood because of the violence I experienced. I also feel a great deal of anger when I hear about so many youth feeling displaced because they do not have a positive sense of their identity. I do, however, recognize that change is occurring as more people become aware of the legacy of the residential schools.

Despite my conflicting feelings, two good examples come to mind when I think about healing and reconciliation. When I think of my family's healing journey, I perceive enormous courage therein. In spite of what we endured as children, most of us have been able to raise our children in a safe environment. We have greater knowledge of our ceremonies and our beautiful Creation Story that has been passed down by my ancestors for so many years. Many of us have gone through counselling. We are now able to express affection and love towards one another. It is true that we still have a long way to go with language revitalization. None of my cousins know how to speak our language fluently, and the situation has become even more desperate because there are no immersion schools for our children to attend in our region. But I remain hopeful that this will soon change with greater awareness.

This past spring, I also witnessed reconciliation occurring in my classroom. Eleven of my students made presentations on the legacy of residential schools to two other classes. The two groups presenting provided an accurate and compelling account of the impact of the schools. They also offered insightful comments on reconciliation. Although the students did not come to any grand conclusions, their views indicated to me that change is possible with education. These students taught me how important the journey of unveiling the truth about the residential schools is for Canada's future with Aboriginal peoples.

Primary Document

4. Excerpt from the Indian Residential Schools Settlement Agreement, May 2006

Schedule 'N'

Mandate for the Truth and Reconciliation Commission

Terms of Reference

1. Goals
   The goals of the Commission shall be to:

(a) Acknowledge Residential School experiences, impact and consequences;
(b) Provide a holistic, culturally appropriate and safe setting for former students, their families and communities as they come forward to the Commission;
(c) Witness,[81] support, promote and facilitate truth and reconciliation events at both the national and community levels;
(d) Promote awareness and public education of Canadians about the IRS system and its impacts;
(e) Identify sources and create as complete an historical record as possible for the IRS system and legacy. The record shall be preserved and made accessible to the public for future study and use;
(f) Produce and submit to the Parties of the Agreement[82] a report including recommendations[83] to the Government of Canada concerning the IRS system and experience including: the history, purpose, operation and supervision of the IRS system, the effect and consequences of IRS (including systemic harms, intergenerational consequences and the impact on human dignity) and the ongoing legacy of the residential schools;
(g) Support commemoration of former Indian Residential School students and their families in accordance with the Commemoration Policy Directive (Schedule 'X' of the Agreement).

Primary Document

5. Telling Truths and Seeking Reconciliation: Exploring the Challenges

Rupert Ross

The Abuse of Aboriginal Students by Other Aboriginal Students

It should not be surprising that students had abused other students because residential schools were themselves institutions centred on power, position, and force. The children who came into them were suddenly without defences, living completely at the mercy of their surroundings. Many Aboriginal people have confided that they were never abused by nuns, priests, or teachers but were abused regularly by older students. They told me that gangs flourished, bullying was common, and the only protection was membership in parallel gangs. There was no one to complain to, so you just shut up and took it or plotted revenge of your own.

This category of abuse presents unique challenges. In the first place, it is one thing to accuse foreign priests, nuns, or teachers but quite another to accuse one of your own. Many have kept this secret for 30 years or more, even from their own families, because they knew no one wanted to hear about it. Secondly, while most of the abusive priests, nuns, or teachers have died or moved away, those students who abused are likely to be close in age, very much alive, and in many instances, living in exactly the same community, just down the road. If truth-telling happens, it will have immediate consequences. Thirdly, such accusations may well be denounced as personal attacks aimed to further *existing* animosities within the inter-family politics of dysfunctional communities and not be seen for what they really are: major *contributors* to those animosities. Fourthly, such accusations may bring a host of related accusations into the open, for if gangs were operating, they had involved many people, few of whom have elected to speak of it over the decades. The person who opens up this Pandora's box runs the risk of losing their welcome in their community and of compromising their extended family's welcome as well.

Keeping silent, however, may only *perpetuate* the inter-family antagonisms that plague community politics, hiring, education, welfare, housing, and healing. Many Aboriginal communities complain that it is the adversariality of the Western system of government that lies behind the instability, rancour, and occasional violence seen in reserve politics. While that may contribute, it is also likely that the unresolved history of abuse provides the personal, vendetta-like ferocity often seen within that institutional adversariality.

At the very least, it must be difficult to see the sons or daughters of someone who abused you 30 years ago entering into relationships with your own sons or daughters—and difficult as well to pretend cordiality and warmth when there is hurt and anger that has never been acknowledged.

Additionally, much of that abuse was likely witnessed by other students. They know what happened and are likely to translate things they see in today's community dynamics in terms of those secrets from long ago. Many may feel guilt for not having tried to stop it or not having brought it out into the open when it began to poison community relationships. The complex lines of fear, resentment, guilt, and even regret form subterranean spiderwebs that likely ensnare many community and inter-family relationships in ways that defy clear articulation, by anyone.

I do not know what kinds of processes might bring some of those secrets safely into the open. This category of abuse is different from family violence or intergenerational sexual abuse, for there are no family ties or parent/Elder responsibilities to draw on in an effort to have all parties honour their relational responsibilities and come together in healing processes. To the contrary, there may the opposite reaction of 'I owe you nothing because you and your family have always had it in for me.' It is hard to know what might motivate people to acknowledge their misbehaviour and seek reconciliation, unless it is seen by all as a *community* healing process aimed at expunging *all* of the hurt that afflicts today's community relationships.

And I suggest that might be an important role for the Truth and Reconciliation Commission: making a detailed analysis of how children placed in intrinsically violent situations like residential schools begin adopting violence in their relations with each other. If that dynamic can be explained in such a way that whole communities, abused and abusers alike, come to recognize that it was the *situation* that prompted the violence between them, capturing so many children, often turning one year's victim into the next year's perpetrator, then perhaps individual truths could safely be told and true reconciliation could begin.

Questions for Consideration

1. When was the residential school system established? When was it dismantled? What were its goals?
2. What methods did residential schools employ in pursuit of their goals? How did Aboriginal children react to and/or resist these methods?
3. Why does Haig-Brown believe it is essential for all Canadians to remember the residential schools? Do you agree? Why or why not?
4. What were the goals of the Department of Indian Affairs' program of studies for residential schools?
5. What are the long-term consequences of the residential school system?
6. Is reconciliation between the Aboriginal people harmed, either directly or indirectly, by the residential schools and the 'white' Canadian majority possible? If so, how?
7. Did the Truth and Reconciliation Commission provide an appropriate forum for dealing with the legacies of student-on-student abuse? If so, why? If not, what would be the best way to deal with these legacies?

Further Resources

Books and Articles

Knockwood, Isabelle. *Out of the Depths: The Experiences of Mi'kmaw Children at the Indian Residential School at Shubenacadie, Nova Scotia*. Lockeport, NS: Roseway Publishing, 1992.

Miller, J.R. *Shingawauk's Vision: A History of Native Residential Schools*. Toronto: University of Toronto Press, 1996.

Milloy, John S. *A National Crime: The Canadian Government and the Residential School System, 1879 to 1986*. Winnipeg: University of Manitoba Press, 1999.

Wall, Sharon. "'To Train a Wild Bird'": E.F. Wilson, Hegemony and Native Industrial Education at the Shingwauk and Wawanosh Residential Schools, 1873–1893', *Left History* 9, 1 (Fall/Winter 2003): 7–42.

Younging, Greg, Jonathan Dewar, and Mike DeGagné, eds. *Response, Responsibility, and Renewal: Canada's Truth and Reconciliation Journey*. Ottawa: Aboriginal Healing Foundation, 2009.

Printed Documents and Reports

Jack, Agnes, ed. *Behind Closed Doors: Stories from the Kamloops Indian Residential School* rev. edn. Kamloops: Secwepemc Cultural Education Society, 2006.

Films

The Fallen Feather: Indian Industrial Residential Schools. DVD. Directed by Randy N. Bezeau. Fallen Feather Productions, 2007.
Muffins for Granny: and the Restlessness of an Ancient Sadness. DVD. Directed by Nadia McLaren. Feather Productions, 2007.
Older than America. DVD (drama). Directed by Georgina Lightning. Tribal Alliance, 2008.
Where the Spirit Lives. Film (drama). Directed by Bruce Pittman. CBC, 1989.

Websites

Assembly of First Nations
www.afn.ca/index.php/en/policy-areas/indian-residential-schools-unit

Hidden from History
www.hiddenfromhistory.org/

Prime Minister Stephen Harper's apology for the residential school system
www.cbc.ca/news/canada/story/2008/06/11/pm-statement.html

Truth and Reconciliation Commission
www.trc.ca/websites/trcinstitution/index.php?p=3

Where are the Children? Healing the Legacy of the Residential Schools
www.wherearethechildren.ca

TEN

Religion, Culture, and the Peoples of the North

Introduction

This chapter turns its attention to the Inuit and Aboriginal people living in present-day northern Canada. The North, as a region, is often characterized as geographically isolated and forbidding. In part, this myth is a product of the fact that non-Aboriginal people initially expressed little interest in the North aside from furs, mission work, and resource extraction. Until the early twentieth century, few outsiders resided in the North except for fur traders and trappers, missionaries, and the North West Mounted Police (after 1919, the RCMP). As a result, historical interest in the North and its people typically relies on one of the following organizing topics: European exploration, the missionary encounter, or the exploitation of natural resources. At the heart of each of these topics lies a fascination with Inuit and Aboriginal societies in transition. The entry of missionaries into the North and the establishment of permanent missions has been of particular interest. However, most of this literature tends to be one-sided, written from the missionaries' perspective. These conventional narratives focus on the heroic nature of the men and women who travelled north in order to convert Aboriginal people. More recent histories are much more critical of the missionary endeavour, locating it as part of the colonial project; however, the focus of such works continues to be somewhat one-sided and Eurocentric. In these narratives, Aboriginal communities are most often described as previously unchanged societies whose interactions with Christianity and European society and technology set into motion a cultural decline.

Recent examinations of the missionary encounter offer a more sophisticated analysis of the reactions of Aboriginal people to these meetings.[1] Cornelius H.W. Remie and Jarich Oosten offer a new perspective regarding missionaries and contact in the North. By examining the formative years of the Catholic mission at Pelly Bay (in present-day Nunavut), the authors suggest a different and more complex interpretation of the role played by missionaries and missions in Inuit society. They propose that the mission served more than a religious function, fitting into the social, cultural, and economic contours of the community in complex ways. Inuit incorporated Catholicism into their own world views and used the mission itself as a means of accessing goods and services otherwise unavailable to the community during certain periods of the year. Aboriginal people did not indiscriminately adopt Christianity; they 'selectively adapted to or rejected features' of it in accordance with their own needs, desires, and interests.[2]

The article by Naomi Adelson looks at how the northern Cree (*Iiyiyu'ch*) First Nation, Whapmagoostui, negotiated change. Adelson rejects the notion of referring to Whapmagoostui as remote or isolated. While outsiders may perceive the North in this way, the community sees itself as part of a larger and well-established network of families across the region that used to hunt, trap, and trade. Adelson's argument evokes those offered by Susan Sleeper-Smith and others in this volume regarding the centrality of kinship networks to many Aboriginal societies. Even though the Whapmagoostui community is currently more sedentary, its established network of family relations remains. New technologies in telecommunications and the Internet have, in fact, facilitated these connections and reaffirmed feelings of community and family. Both articles in this chapter deal with how Inuit and Aboriginal people came into contact with, understood, and incorporated new ideas and technologies and, in so doing, how they negotiated their own encounters with the outside world.

Chapter Objectives

At the end of this chapter, you should be able to

- understand how and why Aboriginal peoples of the North adopted and used Western religion, customs, culture, and technologies;
- identify ways in which the Inuit modified Christianity to suit their own spiritual and religious needs; and
- understand how the Cree of Whapmagoostui First Nation applied and continue to apply technology to the practice of pre-existing Cree customs.

Secondary Source

1. The Birth of a Catholic Inuit Community: The Transition to Christianity in Pelly Bay, NU, 1935–50

Cornelius H.W. Remie and Jarich Oosten

In this article, we will examine the formative years of the Catholic mission post in Pelly Bay. The paper is based on literary and archival sources and on interviews with one of the Oblate missionaries who spent 27 years in Pelly Bay, Father Franz Van de Velde. With the exception of some brief autobiographical notes, there are no written sources in Inuktitut for the period under scrutiny. The Inuit views of Christianization we discuss are therefore largely inferred from *qallunaat* (non-Inuit) data and research carried out elsewhere in Nunavut. In the next few years, we hope to supplement these data with interviews with older informants from Pelly Bay. Such interviews are indispensable to obtain a more balanced understanding of the transition to Christianity in Pelly Bay.

The *Codex Historicus* of the Pelly Bay mission[3] is an important source for this paper. It was written by the resident missionaries and gives an account of the daily events at the mission post. But the *Codex* is by no means a private diary. We hear little about the private thoughts and the feelings of the missionaries or their views of the Inuit. Neither is it an ethnographic account. We find hardly any references to conversations with Inuit or descriptions of events in the Inuit camps themselves.

Another important source for our paper is the oral comments on the *Codex* by Father Van de Velde, recorded in 1982 by the first author. These comments provide a wealth of detailed explanations of the entries in the *Codex* of Pelly Bay and of the culture of the Nattilingmiut[4] in general.

Oblate Plans and Inuit Strategies

The foundations of [Catholic] missionary expansion [in the far north] were laid by Father Arsène Turquetil, who established the first Oblate mission in Chesterfield Inlet in 1912. The northern move by the Oblate Fathers was a reaction to the expansion of Anglican missionary activities to the Keewatin district.[5]

The first Inuit were converted and baptized in 1917. The Oblates first consolidated their position at Chesterfield Inlet and only expanded their missionary activities in the late 1920s, when Anglican pressure on the Keewatin increased. Their strategy aimed at ensuring control of the land before the Anglicans arrived.[6] In a relatively short span of time, a little over 10 years, 6 new mission posts were established, [including,] in 1933 and 1935, the posts of Repulse Bay and Pelly Bay.

The Repulse Bay mission soon developed into an important logistic centre for the northern missions of the Hudson Bay vicariate. In the first two years of its existence, the Pelly Bay mission was a dependency of Repulse Bay. On 23 August 1937, on the occasion of the vicarial synod held in Chesterfield Inlet, it was recognized as an independent mission. On that same occasion, Father Franz Van de Velde, a newly arrived Flemish Oblate, was appointed socius of [the resident missionary,] Father Henry.[7] He joined the latter in 1938.

The decision to open a mission post at Pelly Bay was taken after a request by converted Pelly Bay people who resided temporarily in the Aivilik [Repulse Bay] area. They belonged to a substantial group of Nattilingmiut that had migrated south at the end of the nineteenth or the beginning of the twentieth century.[8] This migration of about 40 per cent of the total Nattilik population had far-reaching effects. It boosted the female infanticide ratio and made latent factionalism manifest.[9] Such factionalism was quite marked among immigrants from the eastern branch of the Nattilingmiut who had their traditional hunting grounds around Arviligjuaq (Pelly Bay). Within this community existed two groups, the so-called Kukigarmiut and the Irmalingmiut, named after the protagonists of a feud that probably dates back as far as the end of the eighteenth century.[10]

Among the 36 persons baptized prior to the founding of the Pelly Bay mission, only 6 were Irmalingmiut, whereas 26 were of Kukigaq extraction.[11] Apparently, Kukigaq leaders realized the potential benefit of being Catholic earlier than their Irmalik counterparts and made the tactical move to side with the missionaries. This interpretation of the differential rates of baptisms prior to 1935 is further substantiated by the behaviour of the leader of the Kukigarmiut, Qaqsuvik. Not only did he request a missionary to come and live with them, but he also attempted to influence where the missionary would reside. Father Henry noted in the *Codex*:

> Sudden departure of K'arsuvik for Igluriarjuk. Despite their beseeching, I do not want to follow them. I have found an ideal spot to settle in front of the little hill between the river and the sea. I have decided to build a winter house of stone and clay here. Against the approval of my Eskimos who encourage me to settle down farther North.[12]

The reasons for his decision are clear: Father Henry wanted to be independent whereas his Inuit guides preferred him to go with them. We do not know how Qaqsuvik and the other members of the Kukigaq faction took his decision. A comment by Father Van de Velde suggests that it took them quite a while to accept the independent position of the mission:

> Father Henry wanted to be independent in order to be the priest of all and not just the priest of one group. The Father had to be handy, tactful and sometimes firm to express his independence [. . .]. It is only after my arrival in 1938 that the Father was able to make them finally understand that the Mission was there for all.[13]

Thus the Oblate missionaries were not the only ones planning their moves; Inuit also had their own strategies. Although these plans and strategies might sometimes conflict, they often reinforced each other: when the request for a resident missionary in Pelly Bay was made, it was quickly granted because it fitted in the general Oblate strategy of occupying what they considered to be a religious *terra nullius*.

The Founding of the Pelly Bay Mission

In 1934, Father Henry expressed the wish to found a mission at Pelly Bay. Father Clabaut [at Repulse Bay] was only prepared to let him go if a family invited him for instruction, a family that would supply him with the seal blubber for the lamp needed to survive. Once these conditions were met, Father Henry set out on his journey on 26 April 1935. He travelled with the family of Qaqsuvik, the oldest Christian family at Pelly Bay.[14] [Jean Philippe, OMI,] records a brief dialogue between the old Qaqsuvik and the missionary. One evening Qaqsuvik asked him, 'Why are you going to Arviligjuaq (Pelly Bay)?' The missionary answered, 'To tell you about the good God, whom you do not know . . .'. The old man answered, 'You will often be hungry at Ar-vi-lee-goo-ar.'[15]

This brief dialogue reflects the encounter of two worlds: the ambitions of the missionary and the concerns of the Inuit. Both were concerned with each other's welfare: the missionary with the spiritual welfare of the Inuit, the old Inuk with the well-being of the foreign missionary who did not know the land.

After a difficult journey by dog sled, Father Henry arrived at the mouth of the Kuugaarjuk River on 1 June. Almost immediately Father Henry started building a stone house annex chapel, a project that would take several months to complete. In the meantime he had to hunt and fish for his own subsistence. Food was a continuous problem.[16]

By the end of November, Inuit [had] built an igloo for him, as living in the stone house was impossible because of the cold. Qaqsuvik supplied him with oil for the lamp during the winter.[17] Weeks of preparations followed for baptisms that would take place at Christmas when most inhabitants of the area would gather at the mission. At the first Christmas celebration in Pelly Bay, 40 Nattilingmiut attended the festivities.[18] A few days later they departed for their seal hunting camps on the sea ice of Pelly Bay.

In January, February, and March 1936, Father Henry occasionally visited the Inuit in these camps and instructed his catechumens, heard confessions, celebrated Mass, and distributed Communion. In March, preparations for Easter started. At Easter, Inuit from all over Pelly Bay would gather at Kuugaarjuk, as at Christmas. After that, some Inuit would travel to the Hudson's Bay Company (HBC) store in Repulse Bay to trade; others would trade at Gjoa Haven on King William Island, whereas those who stayed behind would engage in various hunting activities. In June and July 1936 Father Henry was engaged in further building activities and, after break-up, in netting seals and fish in the Kuugaarjuk River.

The presence of a resident missionary in Pelly Bay did have considerable demographic effects. Whereas the total population of Pelly Bay consisted of only 54 individuals in November 1935, a year later their number had risen to 83[19] and in February 1937 there were 89 people.[20] In subsequent years this number would further expand until it reached an average of about 125 in the early 1950s.[21]

The Growth of the Mission

In the summer of 1937, the Hudson's Bay Company had established a post at Fort Ross on the south end of Somerset Island.[22] To counter possible Anglican influence, Father Henry visited the Inuit at Iktuaqturvik and Ikpik (Thom Bay) and quickly instructed and baptized a sick Inuk whom he had met earlier in Pelly Bay.[23]

He was barely back in Kuugaarjuk when his socius Father Van de Velde arrived. Father Henry expressed his joy at having a fellow missionary after almost four years of solitude.[24] Father Van de Velde was a young Flemish missionary. His energy and skills proved a great help to Father Henry at the mission. Together they started new building activities and took turns visiting Inuit camps to baptize older catechumens and newborn children. In the next 12 years, Father Henry and Father Van de Velde worked together to develop the mission.

Social and Economic Role of the Mission

Economic Functions

From its very beginning the Pelly Bay mission played an important part in local economics. Since Pelly Bay was landlocked and not accessible by boat, the Roman Catholic mission depended upon bulk freighting by dog sled for its own logistics.

Freighting was done on a voluntary basis by Inuit who often combined the trip with some trading of their own. The compensation for such freighting trips varied over the years and was regularly adapted to price standards. In 1950, Pelly Bay Inuit received $60 for a round trip to Repulse Bay to bring in 800 pounds of freight.[25] At that time, this was sufficient to buy 24 average-sized seals for dog food, 400 pounds of caribou meat, or 4 male dogs.[26] In the early years of the mission, Inuit were also compensated for supplying the mission with country food (seals and fish), for assisting in construction work, and for acting as guides during the missionaries' visits to Inuit camps in the area.

Since its foundation, the Pelly Bay mission operated a small mission store. Through that store, Inuit could obtain scarce commodities when the HBC stores at Repulse Bay and Gjoa Haven were inaccessible as a result of limited mobility, from June till the end of October. Tea, tobacco, flour, sugar, sewing materials, and ammunition were sold at the mission store. Another important product was caribou skins for winter clothing. At the time the Roman Catholic mission was established, caribou were scarce at Pelly Bay. They had disappeared from Simpson Peninsula and could only be hunted far to the south and southwest. To alleviate the problem of deficient winter clothing, the mission bought caribou skins by the hundreds and sold them locally.[27]

The mission also bought products from the Inuit such as seals for dog food, fish, and pelts of arctic foxes. Trapping was a marginal activity in Pelly Bay, and the number of fox pelts bought by the Pelly Bay mission never exceeded 200 in any of the years under review in this paper. The pelts were transported south and sold to the HBC at Repulse Bay or sent to Churchill, from where the economic affairs of the vicariate were handled.[28]

The mission store had considerable advantages for the Pelly Bay Inuit. Pricing was fair and in tune with the Repulse Bay prices, and basic commodities were accessible during periods of the year when otherwise they would have been out of reach. But the mission store had some disadvantages too. These did not stem from the store itself, but from the way its fiercest competitor, the Hudson's Bay Company, perceived it. When the HBC trading post at Fort Ross was closed and moved to Spence Bay in 1949, the new post manager did everything to discourage the Nattilingmiut from trading at the mission. According to Van de Velde, when Catholics from Pelly Bay came to trade at Spence Bay, they were treated with condescension and their furs were systematically depreciated. Counter slips of their purchases were withheld so that they had no means to complain when items they had ordered and paid for were missing when they collected their goods at the post.[29] The manager even called in the RCMP to get the Pelly Bay mission store closed. Father Van de Velde protested vigorously against what he considered to be an injustice. The final result of his protests was that the Pelly Bay mission store received a formal outpost licence in 1952.

Taking Care of the Sick

Until the early 1950s the Oblate mission at Pelly Bay was the only *Qallunaaq* organization that did take care of the sick on a daily basis. The missionaries had received some elementary training in dealing with illnesses; they were equipped with a medical handbook and had some basic medicines at their disposal.[30] When the Oblate mission started using a radio in December 1944,[31] the [missionaries] could contact the doctor at the mission hospital at Chesterfield Inlet for further advice. If necessary, the missionaries were entitled to send patients to the mission hospital or, at the end of the 1940s when planes made their appearance on the northern scene, to call upon the RCMP or the Hudson's Bay Company to arrange for a medical evacuation.

Freighting to Repulse Bay, Gjoa Haven, and Spence Bay increasingly led to outbreaks of small epidemics of flu, as did contact with outside parties that visited the Pelly Bay mission by plane in the 1940s. As communication with the outside world intensified, more epidemics spread. Some were of an increasingly aggressive nature such as the 1949 polio epidemic in the Central Arctic that claimed the lives of many Inuit. In Pelly Bay, only one case occurred, but that same year an influenza epidemic claimed the lives of five victims.[32] In 1953 and 1954 eight patients were evacuated because of tuberculosis and two because of tuberculosis of the dorsal spine.[33]

Religious Life

Religious Feasts and the Celebration of Sunday

The mission post in Pelly Bay immediately became a religious centre in the area as Inuit began to convene at the mission to celebrate the Christian holy days, notably Christmas and Easter. At the Christmas celebrations in 1935, 40 people were present and in 1936, Christmas was celebrated in grand style.[34] A big igloo was built. Sixty people were present. At eight o'clock the vigil started. Every hour, songs were chanted and exhortations made. Games were played. At eleven o'clock the *Veni Creator* was sung, and at midnight six adults were baptized. A mass was celebrated followed by grace and a meal. At eleven in the morning, another mass was celebrated, followed by a copious meal of fish, caribou, and biscuits. After four o'clock various competitions were organized.[35]

The combination of Christian rituals, competitive games, and great meals was characteristic of Inuit Christmas celebrations in northeast Canada and proved very successful in Pelly Bay. In the 1940s, the number of participants gradually increased and at the end of the decade more than 100 people might be present. In 1949 the Christmas meal required 60 fish, 25 gallons of caribou meat and boiled rice, tea, and five biscuits for each participant. Games such as *nugluktaq* (thrusting a stick through a small hoop) and archery were practised. In many respects Christmas seems to have replaced the traditional Inuit winter feasts, of which drum dances were an essential element.[36]

The celebrations of Easter were less well attended [and] we do not find many references to other feasts. All Saints did not appear to be an important holiday. [On] 1 November 1950, the *Codex* states: 'Poor Sunday of All Saints. It is as if it were an ordinary day.' For Epiphany it seems to have been the same: 6 January 1941, 'Epiphany. Seven people present at Holy Mass.' Efforts by the missionaries to turn Assumption (15 August) and Immaculate Conception (8 December) into feast days also do not seem to have been successful.[37]

Like anywhere else in the Catholic world, Inuit were expected not to work on Sunday.[38] However, hunting often occurred.[39] In practice, the Roman Catholics were less strict with respect to hunting and travelling on Sundays than the Anglicans. Thus Father Henry arrived at the mission on Sunday, 25 November 1939.

Sacraments

Baptism had a central place in the program of the Oblates in the Hudson Bay vicariate. Through baptism a person was saved. He or she became a new being, and this was expressed in the adoption of a new name. The name already had a central place in pre-Christian Inuit cosmology as it was assumed that a deceased namesake lived on in persons named after him or her. The Inuit continued this practice and retained their Inuit names beside their Christian names, combining shared identities with their deceased namesakes with the new Christian identity.

According to Catholic usage newborn children were preferably baptized immediately after birth. Fathers Henry and Van de Velde took great pains to baptize infants once they learned about their birth. Concern about the possibility that infants might be killed made them act quickly.[40] A child whose life was in danger could be baptized without instruction. It had to be baptized, even if the parents were opposed.[41]

According to Catholic belief, baptized children who died became little angels watching and protecting people. We find at least five references in the *Codex* where this idea is expressed.[42] It may have been picked up easily by the Inuit who strongly believed in the efficacy of protective spirits.

To assure that newborn children could become little guardian angels, the missionaries taught Inuit how to baptize. Sometimes an invalid baptism occurred:

> The wife of Paul has delivered a premature boy of seven months, alive, at nine in the evening. Paul has baptized him. The child died this morning at ten. Was the baptism performed well? He has said: 'Kobverivagit Ernernerub Anernealub atingni.' It is a pity.[43]

The fact that Paul baptized the child in the name of the Son and the Holy Spirit but not of the Father, is decisive: the child is lost.

This strict adherence to the ritual formulas probably appealed to the Inuit who were well aware of the power of magic words. Missionaries and Inuit shared a strong belief in the miraculous power of prayer. In a number of [*Codex*] entries this power is emphasized as a means to heal.[44] Inuit used prayer in much the same way, as can be inferred from the following entry in the *Codex*: 'Little Jacques was born in the autumn on the river. Konwaksiut almost lost her life in bringing him into the world. Only the incessant prayers of the Inuit miraculously saved her.'[45]

Individual confession, another important aspect of the Catholic dogma, did not present a major problem for Inuit in the transition to Christianity. Father Van de Velde argued that Inuit were accustomed to making public confessions during shamanic séances:

> During the general sorcery séances, the sorcerer usually demanded a general confession from all those present. The Eskimos accused themselves of their most hidden failures and omissions as well as of the most intimate faults of

which they were guilty. These self-accusations were public, made in the presence of the entire community young and old alike. . . .[46]

Confession in the Catholic Church is not a public affair. This confidential nature of the confession must have implied a great change in religious life. On one side shamanism became a tradition that was practised in secrecy; on the other side confession itself became a confidential matter. The traditions of sharing knowledge were changed.

In contrast to confession, Communion was a public affair. It is general practice in the Catholic Church that young children receive their first Communion when they reach the age of reason (i.e., when they are about seven years of age). Pelly Bay was no exception. In the *Codex* we find seven entries referring to First Communion and in all cases it concerned the First Communion of young children.[47] Adults received their first Communion at the time of their baptism.

As a rule a bishop administered confirmation. In the case of Pelly Bay, problems of communication with the outside world sometimes called for another solution. Thus, in 1937, Mgr Turquetil sent Father Clabaut by dog sled to Pelly Bay to confirm 42 Christians. On later occasions, in March 1944, in April 1949, and in May 1950, Bishop Turquetil's successor, Mgr Lacroix, came by plane to Pelly Bay to administer confirmation. The *Codex* mentions only one case in which the missionary confirmed a dying child. This case may have contributed to the perception that confirmation was a *tuqunaqsiuti*, a 'means that makes one die'. [Cornelius] Remie refers to two other cases in which confirmation was seen this way.[48] Van de Velde confirmed that this Inuit view of the sacrament existed.[49]

[When] people died in the vicinity of the mission, they were buried at the nearby cemetery. This gave sometimes rise to avoidance behaviour since Inuit believed that the spirits of the dead would stay around and could cause harm and spread sickness. The frequent occurrence of small or greater epidemics at the mission post was attributed to the spirits of the dead.[50]

Control of Moral Attitudes and Conduct

As religious leaders, missionaries had to see that their parishioners persevered in their conviction and observed the moral standards set by the Catholic faith. The missionary strategy was to never ridicule Native customs. Instead, missionaries should try to point out to Inuit in a benign and kind-hearted way what their shortcomings were and how these could be mended.[51]

The purpose of control of moral attitudes and conduct was to keep the flock religiously on track and prevent them from abandoning the Church. But such control, and in particular reprimand, was not always appreciated by the Inuit, as is clear in the case of Iksivalitaq, the son of the famous shaman Alakkannuaq. Iksivalitaq, a shaman who wore the *kigluraq*, a little tattoo between the eyebrows that signified that he had slain a *tupilaq* (evil spirit), constantly challenged the religious authority of Father Henry. Finally, he renounced the Catholic faith by saying that he did not want to be reprimanded by [the missionaries].[52]

Missionary attempts to control the moral attitudes and conduct of their parishioners did not mean that the Inuit easily gave up their customs and beliefs. Although we find very few references to religious continuity in the first volume of the *Codex*, we do learn that some Inuit still practised *sakkajuq*[53] and *tuumgijuq*,[54] used amulets,[55] [and] believed in evil spirits as the cause of illness.[56] Testimonies by Elders such as Aupilaarjuk from Rankin Inlet and Victor Tungilik from Naujaat, both of Nattilik origin, reflect Inuit perspectives on the religious changes that occurred. Aupilaarjuk remembers the void created by the rejection of traditional beliefs and customs by the missionaries:

> . . . The Catholic priest said that our Inuit ways were evil, and only the ways of God, Jesus and Mary were good. If he had told us that we had to follow the *maligait* [dicta] of Jesus, then I would have understood. We were only told to abandon our Inuit *maligait*, but they did not give us anything to replace them. For example, I would no longer *anijaaq*, go out early in the morning. I felt like I was in a void. I no longer wanted to follow what my parents had taught me. If I did something wrong or something shameful, I did not need to tell anyone about it. I did whatever I wanted. I did not tell anyone if I did something wrong. Before that, we had *angakkuit* [plural of shaman] who could see if we had done something wrong. . . .[57]

The conversion to Christianity often implied a deprivation of cultural traditions that is still resented by Elders. Aupilaarjuk observed:

> I had a lot of *aarnguat* [amulets]. They were taken away by the Catholic missionaries when we were baptized. Now we see a lot of *Qallunaat* in important positions wearing necklaces. The *Qallunaat* took them away because they thought they were evil, but they were not evil. Through the help of the *aarnguat* and through the protection provided by my mother, I have been able to live a long life.[58]

Conflicts between Inuit traditions and the new religions were hard to solve for individual Inuit. Victor Tungilik from Naujaat practised several years as a shaman. In his youth his parents instructed him not to become an *angakkuq*:

> When my parents started following the Anglican faith, they told me that I was going to be following the Catholic religion. I was told that when they accepted religion. They told me to let go of the ways of the *angakkuq*, because the ways of the *angakkuq* were not compatible with religion. . . .[59]

During his youth Tungilik heard a sermon about Judgment Day in Igluligaarjuk that influenced his decision to let go of shamanism:

> If I continued to be an *angakkuq*, I would end up in hell in the great fire. Because I didn't want this to happen I let my *tuurngait* [helping spirits] go [. . .]. When my two in-laws died I regretted having let my *tuurngait* go. Although I knew that I might not have been able to heal them, I still thought that maybe I should have hung on to my *tuurngait* a little longer and not sent them away right away. . . .[60]

Such testimonies are not preserved in the *Codex Historicus*. However, a striking example of cultural continuity, related in the *Codex* entries of 8–14 September 1944, is the death of old Alakkannuaq, a famous shaman. Alakkannuaq was baptized on 2 February 1937 and learned syllabics in order to read the Catholic prayer books. Yet, he committed suicide with the help of two of his sons in accordance with traditional Inuit customs and beliefs. Father Henry wrote a brief account:

> . . . Ovide Allakatnuar, aged 70, suffered a stroke, thus losing the power of speech and part of the use of his limbs. However, his mental capacities stayed intact. . . . Because the camp had to break up and move inland for the caribou hunt, and because the old Allakatnuar had become invalid and an obstacle to break up, Niptayok and Kayaitok decided to make an end to the life of their father, believing that by doing so they would respond to the wishes of their old father. The two sons, aged 50 and 40, prepared a gallows equipped with a rope with a noose outside the tent. Then they brought the sick man there. In a sitting position, he put his head through the noose and let himself fall to strangle himself. . . .[61]

When Father Henry learned about Alakkannuaq's death, he exclaimed: 'But what kind of Christians are we raising?' In a conversation with the first author in the summer of 2001, [Father Van de Velde] emphasized that from an Inuit point of view, Alakkannuaq had sacrificed himself. He wanted to end his days so that the younger generation could move inland to hunt caribou and survive: 'His deed was in fact an altruistic one. Therefore, we should not judge too harshly.' And pointing his finger to heaven, he added, 'You will be surprised whom you will see up there!'

Conclusions

The Oblate fathers attempted to secure the Central Arctic for the Catholic Church and to block the westward expansion of Anglicanism. In doing so they appear to have been much more concerned with the containment of the westward expansion of Anglicanism than with the survival of paganism. Whereas preventing the former was seen as an urgent necessity, the replacement of the latter by Catholicism was perceived as a long-term process.

The way the transition to Christianity in Pelly Bay has usually been described fails to appreciate the role of Inuit in this process. A number of Nattilingmiut had already been baptized before the opening of the mission post at Pelly Bay in 1935. These converted Inuit asked for a missionary to come and live with them. The request fitted well into the Hudson Bay vicariate's policies and was granted. The Oblates were not aware that the vast majority of early converts belonged to one of the two major factions of the Pelly Bay community, the Kukigarmiut. The latter apparently had their own agenda and tried to use the missionaries' presence to strengthen their own position. But [Father Henry] took an independent stance, chose his own location for the mission post, and thereby laid the foundation for what was to become the permanent settlement of Pelly Bay in the late 1960s.

Once the Pelly Bay mission was established, the Oblate missionaries quickly assumed tasks that transcended the boundaries of their religious occupations. In the economic field they incorporated Inuit in the mission post's logistics, introducing paid labour and initiating the production of carvings to be sold on foreign markets. The small mission store facilitated access to *Qallunaaq* products.

The missionaries also assumed responsibility for the treatment of the sick. In the absence of good and quick means of communication with the outside world, health care had to remain elementary. Outside assistance only arrived around 1950.

The missionaries gave the religious guidance the Inuit had requested. They served the religious community, expanded it in concerted effort, and wherever possible established religious routines. As in most Inuit communities, Christmas became the most important religious feast, in many respects replacing the old traditions of the Inuit winter feasts. In the delivery of sacraments, the Oblate fathers adhered to strict norms of ritual correctness, a regime that may well have appealed to the Inuit who were accustomed to the importance of strictly observing ritual rules.

Like shamans, missionaries assumed leadership roles in many fields. Yet, they were often not aware to what extent Inuit continued their traditional practices. Neither were they aware of the extent to which Inuit integrated these practices into Catholicism, thus developing a form of religiosity that responded to their own existential and cultural needs. The missionary perspectives still have to be complemented by the recollections of Inuit Elders participating in the process of transition to Catholicism. Only the Pelly Bay Elders can tell us why and how they decided to make the transition to Christianity.

Primary Document

2.   Excerpt from *Codex Historicus*, 25 December 1940[62]

The missionaries at Pelly Bay kept a journal detailing the activities at the mission. The following is an excerpt describing the Christmas celebrations in 1940.

94
1940

21 – Arrival of Niptayok with his entire family for Christmas. Yesterday evening, return of Julien, Zacharie, Bernard and Dominique with a large catch of fish. Quiet time. Construction of 2 naves at the main igloo of K'agorangoar: Julien and Zacharie.

22 – Sunday, low mass at 8 o'clock and high mass at 10 in the house.

23 – 38 C below (A; very cold, very little wind; construction of porches on the 3 naves, magnificent view. Dimensions of 'naterk': 6 m 2 (about 18 feet) from the entrance i.e. from the 'kattar' to the bed of K'agortangoar, and 7 m (21 feet) wide i.e. from Julien's bed to Zacharie's. The tower's peak is definitely 15 feet from the ground (4 m). Today, arrival of Anemilik, Adgonerk, Paul, K'avik, Papik: 5 initiates.

24 – Mass with the Esk. under the new dome; 6 new initiates present: Padlak, K'épigayok, Taleriktok, Charley, Joani, Kokowak. In total, 16 initiates participating in Christmas celebrations; 48 in attendance, 10 absences due to lack of warm clothes.

The evening, presided over by R. Father VdV [Father Van de Velde]. Opening at 81-.. [*sic*]; the evening took place in the following order: speech; surprises; distribution of the party prizes; some entertainment . . . the chair game, rifle shooting; the candy rain, etc. etc. At 6 o`clock, there was singing, the rosary and a sermon by Father Henri. At midnight, Father Henri sang high mass followed by 2 other masses; finally, Christmas Eve dinner of oatmeal and brioches, cacao.

25 – mass at 11 o'clock by Father VdV who had already celebrated two masses at the house; at about 2 o'clock, lunch: fish and a bouillabaisse of caribou, rice and peas; self-serve brioches and tea. Various games followed: rifle-shooting, archery. Dancing to drums.

26 – Big gun shooting after the St. Etienne high mass; sack race; candy rain. Tug of war: 5 on each side; imitation games, etc.

27 – During the Christmas celebrations, it was extremely cold dropping to 39.1 C below zero.

Secondary Source

3.   Reflecting on the Future: New Technologies, New Frontiers

Naomi Adelson

As I write this article, I am sitting in the home of a long-time friend, watching a thick curtain of clouds descend upon this remote northern community, cloaking it yet again in an impenetrable grey miasma. The dense fog is a standard occurrence here in Whapmagoostui, where the relative warmth of the land along the shore of Hudson Bay draws the chilled ocean air ashore in a confluence of arctic vapours, wind, and land. The density, movement, and altitude of the clouds are significant because they determine whether people, fresh food, and mail will arrive today. Situated 1,400 kilometres north of Montreal and with no access roads, the community is dependent on the daily flights of two regional airlines, the arrivals and departures of which are, in turn, wholly contingent upon seemingly fickle winds. Without an adequate ceiling, planes cannot land—today's low, rolling clouds hint at another flyover.

Movement and communication are the interconnected themes of this article and are the basis of my reflections upon how people, ideas, and things move into and out of northern places. Whereas the planes physically move people and things (weather permitting) to and from communities with no land access, new communications technologies are transforming communication possibilities in the remote reaches of Canada as much as airplanes changed transportation when they first arrived. More specifically, I consider these communication technologies in a remotely situated community in northern Canada through the lens of the shaking tent, a much older form of communication used in Whapmagoostui. This article emerges out of work that I have done with the **Cree** people (*Eeyouch*) of this community and reflects upon a single word—*kusaapihchikin*—that is so vivid and alive with metaphor that I felt compelled to write about it. I will describe and expand upon this metaphor but, first, let me begin with the village and the *Iiyiyu'ch* of Whapmagoostui, QC.[63]

Whapmagoostui and the *Iiyiyu'ch*

Whapmagoostui is one of the smallest and the most northerly of the Eastern James Bay Cree communities in Quebec.[64] Located on the eastern shore of Hudson Bay, this site has been home to the northern Cree since the arrival of a permanent trading post in 1820, which was followed by a missionary station, schools, and other government services. Sitting on a spit of land where the Great Whale River pours into Hudson Bay, the village is bordered by the river to the south, Hudson Bay to the west, and conifer forests to the immediate north and east. The waterways and lands that extend many miles beyond the village are the historic and territorial space of the northern and eastern *Iiyiyu'ch*. Prior to settlement at this site less than 100 years ago, the Indigenous peoples of the region spent most of the year moving across these lands in small familial groups, typically meeting each summer on the south shore of the Great Whale River (where the village currently rests). During this earlier period, the village, as one Elder explained to me, remained but one constituent of the larger place of home.

In the early 1700s, mineral extraction and fur harvesting brought outside economic activity and the first non-Native travellers (i.e., surveyors and traders) to the region. Neither of these ventures was particularly successful, but the start and ultimate success of the beluga whaling industry just a few decades later meant a more permanent presence of non-Native peoples at the mouth of the Great Whale River. The Hudson's Bay Company established one of their posts at Great Whale in 1820 and encouraged fur harvesters from the wider region to travel here to trade their furs for provisions. Soon, more and more Cree and Inuit individuals and families began to make the post a permanent home. With the unanticipated cyclical decline in fur-bearing and larger hunted animals in the first decades of the twentieth century, many of the Cree and Inuit of the surrounding region became reliant on the post and the few amenities, facilities, and services it offered.

In addition to the whaling and fur trade industries, Anglican missionaries made their way into this region in the mid-1800s, bringing with them a Victorian Christian sensibility. Native men and women were lectured on what constituted appropriate dress, actions, habits, and beliefs; were treated as heathens; and were chastened for practising their own ways. These missionaries, acting with a sort of benevolent despotism, had a profound and enduring influence on the people.[65]

In the late 1950s, during the height of the Cold War, the post and mission site was transformed seemingly overnight as the Canadian Armed Forces arrived and built a base to support the Mid-Canada Line, an early warning radar line. The continued presence of the barracks, airplane hangar, and discarded oil drums recall a period of substantive growth.[66] The village was formally recognized in 1958 and was maintained by the provincial and federal governments after the Armed Forces departed in the early 1960s. With both Inuit and Cree people living there, however, it was segregated by the Department of Indian and Northern Affairs into two villages (Kuujjuarapik for the former and Whapmagoostui for the latter) and separately administered, despite the relatively small size of the overall village site and population.[67]

The Whapmagoostui First Nation has grown substantially since the signing of the James Bay and Northern Quebec Agreement in 1975, which provided them with compensation in exchange for the Quebec government's appropriation of Cree land and waterways for its hydroelectric projects.[68] Although the community still had wholly inadequate housing in the early 1980s, it currently boasts modern homes and new buildings and institutions. The population continues to grow; the village has just over 800 residents, with 46 per cent of that total under 19 years of age.[69] Whapmagoostui is, in other words, a small, circumscribed, but growing northern community. Cree remains the first language in the home, workplace, and primary school, while English and French are the principal languages of instruction at the secondary level.[70]

Information and Communications Technologies, Past and Present

While Whapmagoostui is located a distance from any urban centre and is considered a remote community, I hesitate to label it as isolated. The people of this community define themselves in terms of their long-established networks of family, travel, hunting, and trade throughout the region. Indeed, past generations would not have considered the village site as 'home' but as one place of residence within their much larger territorial homeland. With the availability of air transit and the recent addition of an array of technological links (telephone, Internet, satellite television), the site's physically remote status is mitigated significantly. The ways in which current community members define their sense of place also defies characterizing Whapmagoostui as isolated. As past chief Losty Mamianskum comments on the Whapmagoostui First Nation website, 'Although Whapmagoostui is geographically isolated with no access road to the South, the Internet and other telecommunications technology are our link to the outside world.'[71] Communications technologies, in other words, transform the physical and virtual boundaries of home.

It is important to remember that, in this small community, the radio and the landline telephone remain the most immediate means of intracommunity contact and the sources of much local information. Until just a few years ago, one had to dial only the last four digits of a telephone number within this small network, making the phone system seem that much more intimate. Rather than beginning with 'Hello', a caller will dispense with unnecessary formality and ask '*Awaan chi?*', or 'Who are you/ Who am I speaking to?' A similar informality exists with the radio as everyone knows the local announcers. Catching up on local news means turning to the radio first, especially when awaiting updates on someone who has left for emergency medical care in the south. The radio provides regular public service messages; local, regional, and national news feeds; and political announcements broadcast entirely in Cree. It also serves as a major link for the community through such programs as the highly popular live bingo games and, in the recent past, live and recorded transmissions of Elders' stories.

In 2009, the first cellphone tower was constructed in the region, making cellphones available to those who could afford them. Sold through the local band office, the phones can be used only within range of the tower's transmission coverage, which includes the area in and around the village. However, they will soon be integrated with larger communications carriers, making them more available, more affordable, and as commonplace here as they are everywhere else. The real value of this technology will come when the cellphone can replace satellite phones, the mainstay of both emergency and bush communications.

The community's virtual access began with the arrival of the Internet approximately 20 years ago. Since then, advancements in Internet availability and speed have vastly improved this form of communication. Today, for example, my communication with friends, colleagues, and local government officials in the north is conducted almost exclusively by e-mail. That said, there is no simple public access to computers or the Internet in Whapmagoostui. With no access points such as a friendship centre, Internet café, or library, people have very few alternatives to home use.[72] Those who work in the band office, police station, or school have Internet access for work-related communications but not, typically, for personal use.

As a result, household computer use is expanding in Whapmagoostui and the Internet is becoming more accessible. There was only extremely limited Internet connectivity in 1986; however, by 2006, households could purchase two-way (upload/download) satellite relay access technology. Spurred on by a community member's entrepreneurial initiative to bring higher bandwidth and Internet speed to the community, residents can currently purchase their own Internet satellite dish and, for a monthly fee, access the Internet at ever greater speeds (although, at approximately 24 times the speed of dial-up, this is still relatively slow access). The only other option is to purchase slower Internet access, either through existing phone lines or a shared satellite access service. Of the 188 household units in the village, approximately 140 (75 per cent) have Internet access.[73] Almost half have purchased Internet satellite dishes, which are perched on the sides of houses, alongside the ubiquitous television satellite dishes.

In 1994, Arturo Escobar wrote about the potential scope of communications and biotechnologies, referring to a 'technobiocultural' world at the nexus of our communications technologies and our physical and social worlds. 'How', he asked, 'will notions of community, fieldwork, the body, nature, vision, the subject, identity and writing be transformed by these technologies? . . . What continuities do the new technologies exhibit in relation to the modern order? . . . What happens to non-Western perspectives when technologies extend their reach?'[74] In a response to Escobar's thesis, Anastasia N. Panagakos and Heather Horst note that, given the swell of information and communications technologies (ICTs), these questions remain relevant.[75] For example, we currently do not simply contemplate how new communications media will change notions of community or fieldwork. We also consider how these methods will reinvent and reorient, in some fundamental ways, the places and parameters of that research. This is not to say that technologies determine change but that their use, value, and modes of integration are significant areas of study.[76] Panagakos and Horst, in their discussion of 'transnational migrants' uses of ICTs, remind us that, while we must 're-main skeptical of technological determinism and the over-optimistic prophesies about the transformative powers of ICTs', we must also recognize the impact of these technologies on how individuals 'imagine, negotiate and create their social worlds'. They further note that there is an ongoing need for the study of how 'different populations [use] ICTs based on historical circumstances, cultural values, daily needs, access to technology and living conditions'.[77]

Within a First Nations context, and despite persistent issues of limited connectivity, many have written about the inherent value of ICTs in such areas as the continuity and transfer of language and cultural practices and the innovation of new and unanticipated communities of knowledge and activity.[78] The Internet is also increasingly becoming a primary communications medium as a growing number of websites and other online initiatives directly engage First Nations individuals and communities around larger issues of Indigenous action; cultural, political, and social engagement; and entertainment. Similarly, political, social, and educational organizations of all levels now represent themselves primarily via websites, Facebook, and/or other social networking sites. These are all examples of the integrated 'technoscapes' of our connected worlds that Escobar imagined. My own current research project on health information and communications technologies, which includes examining how young adult Cree women use the Internet for health matters, requires me to pay particular attention to these expanding communications networks. While conducting the community-based component of this research, I learned of a wonderfully descriptive linguistic link between these newer technologies and a much older Cree form of communication that reminded me of exactly the kind of engagement described above. In studying the intersections of Cree peoples' virtual and physical worlds, I happened upon an expression that reflected a dense yet delightfully playful and powerfully engaging link between past and present 'technoscapes'.

The Shaking Tent Ceremony as Communication

As new words emerge in any language, so too have Cree words been created to reflect our changing world. The common neologism for the computer in the northern Cree dialect, for example, is *kaamsinaastaahthich*, which roughly translates as 'that which shadow writes by itself'. The term is similar to that for movies, *aahtikaashtaahtihch*,[79] which translates as 'that which shadow plays by itself'.[80] Like so many other Cree words, these are richly descriptive and reflect the actions and functions of the respective machines. An alternate term, however, is also used in Whapmagoostui and links the computer (more specifically, the Internet) and its ability to communicate seemingly by magic to a much older form of communication. Some older Cree people jokingly refer to the Internet as a modern-day *kusaapihchikin*, or 'shaking tent ceremony'. The reference is significant for a number of reasons. The shaking tent is an ancient ceremony with roots as far back, as Elders would say, to the time when humans and animals could speak to one another. It is an intensely powerful and potentially dangerous ceremony and, in more recent history, a highly contentious one. I therefore recognize it as a joking—but not a facile—figure of speech when used to describe the Internet. It is only its capacity as a ceremony of communication, not its spiritual or religious dimensions, that is being referenced by those Elders who make the connection.

Indeed, it is not the first time that the shaking tent has been used in reference to new forms of communication. Fifteen years ago, anthropologist Ronald Niezen interviewed Cree Elders about the transformation of Cree traditional medical practices. One Elder told him, '[the shaking tent] acted like the phone system, but no wires were needed . . . the spirits were the lifelines of the shaking tent.'[81] The shaking tent remains a dense and, for some, controversial symbol of Cree culture and spirituality in both the past and present, making the joking reference to it as being comparable to the Internet even more remarkable.

Early ethnographers spent long hours observing and recounting the details of ceremonies such as the shaking tent, albeit with a different perspective than scholars today. For example, Regina Flannery describes in considerable detail the construction of the tent used, the person who acted as the intermediary for the major spirit that entered the tent, and the events that took place the evening she conducted her observations. Interestingly, she noted that the ceremony would not conclude—in other words, the *mishtaapaau*, or major spirit, would not leave the tent—until she departed (it ended within 15 minutes of her leaving). It seems that the spirit's skepticism about Flannery was reciprocated, as she in turn queried the authenticity of the practice: '[t]he general reaction of the old people, so far as I could judge it, is one of belief.'[82] More recently, Richard Preston, Adrian Tanner, Harvey Feit, and Peter Armitage have all written about the shaking tent not simply as a catalogued practice but, more appropriately, in the broader context of Cree religious ideology and the transformation of the lives of Cree people in the latter half of the twentieth century.[83] Drawing from their example, the discussion that follows should not be read as a decontextualized or idealized re-collection of an irretrievable past but should be understood within the context of the contemporary reality of Cree peoples' everyday lives, including how a reference to a spiritual practice can be appropriated as an apt (if joking) twenty-first-century turn of phrase. This is also by no means a comprehensive review of Cree religious beliefs and practices. I refer readers to other studies to learn more about Cree cultural and spiritual beliefs.[84]

The *kusaapihchikin* is one of many spiritual practices that are part of a system of beliefs integral to Cree peoples' relationship to the land, animals, ancestors, and spirit guides. It is part of what Armitage, in discussing Innu traditional practices, refers to as a larger 'practical' religion where 'knowledge is acquired through years of practice, hunting, and handling animals, showing respect for them, dreaming about them, analyzing dreams, observing and performing ritual actions, . . . learning and reciting myths and being with the Elders in a context which encourages them to share their knowledge.'[85] Ceremonies such as the *kusaapihchikin* exist within the context of a profoundly respectful relationship between humans and animals. That relationship is, in turn, part of a larger cosmological framework that takes for granted the inherent presence of an essence, or spirit, in all living things. Indeed, bush animals are not hunted as much as they 'give themselves' to those who have shown proper and appropriate respect to animals and their respective spirits.[86]

The *kusaapihchikin* was, previously, a very specific kind of communications ceremony. The shaking tent would be used to consult spirits to cure disease or to find medicines, to learn about loved ones who had passed on, to communicate with others still living but at a distance, and to find bush animals and hence food sources. From the mundane task of finding lost objects to the powerful act of confronting enemies, the shaking tent ceremony was an integral part of the lives of not just the Cree but also the Algonquian peoples of the subarctic boreal forest region stretching from present-day Labrador to the eastern foothills of the Rockies.[87]

A shaking tent ceremony was conducted only at someone's request. After the request was made and acknowledged, a tent would be constructed for that particular ceremony. The tent was quite small compared to those used as dwellings, usually only big enough to hold one adult. Fundamental to the shaking tent is the *mishtaapaau*, a spirit intermediary between the shaman (the one with the powers to communicate with the spirit intermediary and who is conducting the shaking tent ceremony) and the animal spirits.[88] It is understood that, while everyone might have a *mishtaapaau*, not everyone would have been aware of theirs. Only those who had the ability to communicate with their spirit intermediaries were called upon to perform these duties. The *mishtaapaau* had to be beckoned in by the shaman in order for the ceremony to begin, and it was only when people outside the tent saw it begin to shake seemingly of its own volition that they knew that the *mishtaapaau* had been successfully called in. As Armitage notes, 'when the shaman entered into the conically shaped tent, it would start to shake, sometimes violently. The commencement of the shaking signified that animal masters and other spirits had joined the shaman in the tent.'[89] The *mishtaapaau* would relay messages between the human and spirit worlds, including the realm of animal spirit beings. Indeed, as one of the functions of the shaking tent ceremony was to locate bush animals, the *mishtaapaau* would act as intermediary between the shaman and a particular animal's spirit or the spirit of an entire class of animals.[90] Shaking tent ceremonies could last for many hours and would conclude only when the final spirits had left the tent (or, as Flannery learned, when certain observers left the grounds).

From Communication to Silence

The arrival of the Christian missionaries in the north profoundly transformed the meaning of ceremonies such as the *kusaapihchikin*. To this day, the *kusaapihchikin* ceremony is recognized as inherently Cree, yet it is also burdened with a history of proscription. The missionaries, facing considerable social and spiritual impediments to the Cree embracing Christian rituals and beliefs, summarily banned practices they deemed heathen, including all that involved the summoning of spiritual beings. As Niezen explains '"Conjuring," or *mitaauwin* (shamanism), was the most significant rival to Christianity, and all activities even remotely associated with it were deemed suspect.'[91] The first missionary in the James Bay region was Reverend Edwin Arthur Watkins, who was stationed on the east coast of James Bay at the Fort George trading post. His diaries offer tremendous perspective on this period and, in particular, some insight into the missionaries' thinking. The missionaries, for example, offered medicines, as well as some food and clothing, to the Cree out of benevolence but also as part of their attempt to simultaneously 'remedy' bodies and souls.[92] In the following excerpt from his diary, we can see Watkins's piety, his conviction of the supremacy of Christianity, his extensive effort in trying to convert the Cree (especially his attempts to learn the Cree language), and his seemingly complete failure to comprehend the Cree world view:

October 26, 1852

This morning I spent in learning Cree. This Afternoon I had a class of Indians for instruction. As one of my scholars was a noted conjurer I requested the interpreter to ask him to remain behind when the others left the school room. His brother who is but little better than himself remained with him, and when they were alone I availed myself of the opportunity of speaking to them plainly and I trust faithfully, as to the evils of their past conduct exhorting them to repentance and endeavoring to set before them the freeness of the Gospel Scheme of Salvation. The brother of the conjurer spoke several times expressing his wishfulness [sic] to obtain instruction in Christianity, but the conjurer himself remained silent till he was pointedly asked if he would promise not to practise conjuring again, when he expressed his willingness to give up his evil ways, but said that the other Indians made a conjuring house for him and then he was obliged to conjur [sic] for them. This afforded me an opportunity to speak of his duty to obey God rather than men, and of the necessity of his taking heed to his own soul's salvation at the risk of gaining a bad name from his fellow Indians.[93]

Another missionary who had an immediate and enduring effect on the Cree of Whapmagoostui was Reverend Walton, synonymous to this day with the movement of Christianity into the Cree north. When Walton arrived at the trading post along the shore of the Great Whale River in 1892, he systematically worked to eliminate all practices that involved 'conjuring'.[94] In her conversations with members of the Whapmagoostui community Elders in the early 1970s, ethnohistorian Toby Morantz found that people recalled the singling out of this particular practice by the resolute Reverend Walton:

Sam Masty, speaking in 1974 in Great Whale River, said Walton was the 'first man to tell people to put away the things they believed; the first to change many people.' Masty explained that the people lost the supernatural powers 'when they heard about Jesus Christ from the missionaries . . . The people wilfully lost these powers because Reverend Walton said to do so. They listened to him and now today no one has any powers like that . . . Reverend Walton didn't think it was all bad to have power like that but he still didn't want people to practice this, also he didn't want people to practice the 'shaking tent'. . .[95]

In my own interviews conducted in the early 1990s, I also found many references to Reverend Walton and his lasting impact with regard to specific practices such as the *kusaapihchikin* and conversion to Christianity more generally.[96] While some were less inclined to accept the missionary's teachings as wholly as Sam Masty seems to suggest, there is no doubt that Walton was a tremendous force in the attempt to eliminate the spiritual ceremonies of the Cree. In one instance, my interlocutor, an Elder of the community, was talking about how people had hunted in the past. He then abruptly changed the direction of the conversation:

Elder: There was this priest who came from far from here, his name was Mr Walton. He was the one who stopped the people from what they were doing—like with the shaking tents.

Q: He was the one who told them?

Elder: Yes, he was the one who told them to stop. So, they stopped using the shaking tent. He must have done the same with the people south of here, at all the places he went to.

Q: But did he say why he stopped the people from using the shaking tents?

Elder: The reason why he stopped them is because he told them there is only one thing we should think about as a Saviour, who we are living for each day and everything that he made, and that is how it is written in the Bible. We should never think: What shall I live for? What shall I eat? How am I going to stay alive? We should never think that way. If someone thinks that way, it seems as if he has lost faith in Him.[97]

Retired archbishop Caleb Lawrence, who was a priest when he ministered to the people of Whapmagoostui from 1965 to 1979, is fondly remembered as much for his active engagement with the community as for his fluency in Cree and Inuktitut. In an interview in 1995, Lawrence told me that he felt he understood why older missionaries were 'deaf to the drum'. He interpreted their actions as a response to what they felt would bring about an altered state of consciousness and, as such, a heathen activity that needed to be abolished. More specifically, he felt that, while other forms of drumming should be incorporated into church service, this sort (and related ceremonies) need not be revived.[98]

Seen by the missionaries as the iconic expression of animistic belief and thus dangerously heathen, the shaking tent was singled out and explicitly forbidden. The practice quickly went underground and only cautiously resurfaced in the middle of the last century. Despite its deep roots in Cree history, the shaking tent remains a controversial practice because of its characterization as emblematic of non-Christian belief.[99]

Discussion: Reclaiming Voice and Power

What I have presented here is a brief overview of Cree cosmology and its articulation in one particular ceremony in the context of the history of the *Iiyiyu'ch* of Whapmagoostui. I have particularly focused on how the shaking tent ceremony was used as a form of communication. Today, the term *kusaapihchikin* is used by some as a light-hearted metaphor when discussing the computer and, more specifically, the Internet. To those unversed in the latest communication technologies, the Internet is as mysterious as the shaking tent ceremony would be to those unfamiliar with Cree cosmology. Each has its own internal expressive logic and technology of communication; therefore, the joking metaphor resonates well.

The reference, joking or otherwise, to such a profoundly Cree practice lends not only a sense of proprietorship to the technology but also a place from which to engage its relevance. It is perhaps even a way to reclaim the value and meaning of previously condemned practices while simultaneously taking ownership of contemporary technologies. As much as the shaking tent might be used for other and specifically spiritual forms of communication, the virtual shaking tent offers a similarly powerful (albeit explicitly non-spiritual) tool for expanding Cree networks of communication and information. Of course, we must not take the analogy too far—the religious ideology inherent in the shaking tent remains powerful and, for some, contentious.[100] This is, after all, a good-natured pun that should neither be overinterpreted nor entirely ignored.

Now back in the city, as I email back and forth to my friends and colleagues in Whapmagoostui and catch up on their Facebook posts, I recall the morning that I began writing this article. I heard the low hum of the turboprop engines as the plane circled three times while looking for a clearing in the dense fog. Suddenly, the engine sound swelled, the high-pitched roar indicating that it was picking up speed and power in order to gain altitude. Visual landing was impossible and the plane bypassed the village. No one returned to or left the community that day and no fresh food or mail arrived, but the poor weather did not, this time, interfere with people's access to the Internet.[101]

Primary Document

4.

Engaging and integrating technologies. (Courtesy of Naomi Adelson.)

Questions for Consideration

1. Why did Inuit convert to Catholicism in Pelly Bay between 1935 and 1950?
2. Discuss the ways that some Inuit preserved their previous beliefs and traditions after converting to Catholicism.
3. What does the excerpt from the *Codex Historicus* tell us about life at the Pelly Bay mission? What light does it shed on the reasons for Inuit converting to Catholicism?
4. Why does Adelson suggest that it is a mistake to describe Whapmagoostui as isolated? Why do most outsiders usually conceive of it in this way?
5. How do pre-existing Cree customs and practices inform the usage of twenty-first-century communications technologies in Whapmagoostui?
6. How does the image on page 273 challenge conventional assumptions about Indigenous people and culture?
7. How have the communities of Pelly Bay and Whapmagoostui evolved and adapted in the face of change? How are the two situations similar?

Further Resources

Books and Articles

Adelson, Naomi. *Being Alive Well: Health and the Politics of Cree Well-Being*. Toronto: University of Toronto Press, 2000.

———. 'Discourses of Stress, Social Inequities, and the Everyday Worlds of First Nations Women in a Remote Northern Canadian Community', *Ethos* 36, 3 (2008): 316–31.

Blaisel, Xavier, Frédéric Laugrand, and Jarich Oosten. 'Shamans, Leaders and Prophets: Parousial Movements among the Inuit of Canada', *Numen* 46 (1999): 370–411.

Buijs, Cunera, ed. *Continuity and Discontinuity in Arctic Cultures. Essays in Honour of Gerti Nooter, Curator at the National Museum of Ethnology, 1970–1990* (Leiden, The Netherlands: Centre of Non-Western Studies, 1993).

Gray, Susan. *I Will Fear No Evil: Ojibwa-Missionary Encounters Along the Berens River, 1875–1940* (East Lansing: Michigan State University Press, 2007).

Morantz, Toby. *The Whiteman's Gonna Getcha: The Colonial Challenge to the Crees in Quebec* (Montreal: McGill-Queen's University Press, 2002).

Printed Documents and Reports

Oosten, Jarich, and Frédéric Laugrand, eds., *Inuit Perspectives on the 20th Century*, 4 vols (Iqaluit: Nunavut Arctic College, 1999–2002).

Van de Velde, Franz, O.M.I. 'Religion and Morals among the Pelly Bay Eskimos', *Eskimo* 39 (1956): 6–16.

Films

Atanarjuat: The Fast Runner. DVD (drama). Directed by Zacharias Kunuk. Isuma Igloolik Productions, 2001.

CBQM. DVD. Directed by Dennis Allen. NFB, 2009.

The Challenge in Old Crow. DVD. Directed by George Payrastre. NFB, 2006.

Christmas at Moose Factory. Film. Directed by Alanis Obomsawin. NFB, 1967.

The Experimental Eskimos. DVD. Directed by Barry Greenwald. Whitepine Pictures, 2009.

Nanook of the North: A Story of Life and Love in the Actual Arctic. DVD. Directed by Robert J. Flaherty. Les Frères Revillon/Pathé Exchange, 1922.

Websites

Grand Council of the Crees
www.gcc.ca/cra/cranav.php

A Guide to Inuit Culture **by the Inuit Women of Canada**
www.pauktuutit.ca/pdf/publications/pauktuutit/InuitWay_e.pdf

Inuit Circumpolar Council
http://inuitcircumpolar.com/index.php?Lang=En&ID=1

Inuit Tapiriit Kanatami heritage
www.itk.ca/publications/5000-years-inuit-history-and-heritage

Whapmagoostui First Nation
www.whapmagoostuifn.ca

ELEVEN

The Economy and Labour

Introduction

Conventional economic and labour histories of Canada overlook the roles of Aboriginal people in the economy and workforce. This oversight is not because Aboriginal people did not participate in the capitalist economy, trade unions, or the labour force; it is a function of persistent misconceptions about Aboriginal people themselves. Stereotypes of them being lazy, dependent, marginalized, or remnants of the past capable only of Euro-Canadian conceptions of 'traditional' Indigenous work make Aboriginal people appear out of place in the 'modern' capitalist economy. This misconception is perpetuated by historians who tend to emphasize the importance of Aboriginal people's labour within the fur and robe trade and imply that the decline of that trade marked the growing irrelevance of Aboriginal people to the Canadian economy, particularly the industrial economy.[1] Acknowledging the contribution of Aboriginal people to the industrialization and modernization of the Canadian economy makes it harder for Euro-Canadians to rationalize the exclusion of Aboriginal people from the benefits of the prosperity that accompanied that process, particularly in the post-World War II period. Recognizing that Aboriginal workers of both sexes played vital roles in Canada's emerging industrial economy is not to suggest that they did not experience racism or that they were not subject to exclusionary formal and informal policies that barred them from many workplaces. It is meant to acknowledge that, as Aboriginal historian Mary Jane McCallum argues, 'marginalization and displacement could and did exist simultaneously with other experiences, and . . . a history of decline or persistence, coercion or autonomy, difference or accommodation cannot adequately represent our past.'[2]

The articles in this chapter look at the wage-for-pay of Aboriginal people at two historical moments in the twentieth century: the turn of the century and the 1950s. In examining the former, John Lutz attempts to understand the processes by which Aboriginal people in British Columbia went from being central actors in the province's economy to being invisible. According to Lutz, 'ignoring Aboriginal participation in the workforce misses the role that wage labour played in the "peaceful subordination" of Canadian Aboriginal peoples and the establishment of modern Canada.'[3] Overlooking these processes, which also made Aboriginal people one of the most impoverished segments of BC society, disregards the actions of the state that regulated (and reduced) the place of Aboriginal labourers in crucial (and lucrative) segments of the economy, such as resource extraction.

In the post-World War II period, the federal government sought to 'save' Aboriginal women from 'failing reserves' through labour placement programs, which were designed to allow Aboriginal women to enjoy the benefits of the modern economy and urban living. These programs also facilitated the assimilationist project outlined by Hugh Shewell and others in this volume. Joan Sangster explores these labour placement programs and the reasons they failed to achieve the goals of the Indian Affairs Branch. While the federal government responded in part to Aboriginal leaders' and communities' calls for economic development, it failed to address the economic and ideological legacies of colonialism. As a result, the government ensured the failure of its half-hearted attempts at stimulating economic development for Aboriginal people.

Chapter Objectives

At the end of this chapter, you should be able to

- recognize the roles that Aboriginal workers have played in Canada's modern economy;
- understand the goals of the labour placement programs for Aboriginal workers in the post-war period and how they fit with the broader goals of federal Indian policy;
- understand how economic policies contributed to the poverty experienced by Canada's Aboriginal peoples; and
- understand how gender shaped Aboriginal peoples' experiences of the labour market and Canadian labour policy.

Secondary Source

1.   Vanishing the Indians: Aboriginal Labourers in Twentieth-Century British Columbia

John Lutz

Visitors to British Columbia in the late nineteenth century were surprised by what they saw. In 1886, famous anthropologist Franz Boas recorded his observations about Indigenous people in Victoria: 'We meet them everywhere. They dress mostly in European fashion. . . . Certain Indian tribes have already become indispensable on the labour market and without them the province would suffer great economic damage.'[4] At the turn of the century, settlers and visitors were astonished not only at the number of Aboriginal people in the province's workforce but also at how wealthy they were.

Ts'msyen Chief A.S. Dudoward's house, 1905. (Residence of A.S. Dudoward, Indian Chief, Port Simpson, BC. Library and Archives Canada.)

This wealth was sometimes reflected in large Victorian homes, such as Tsym'sen Chief Dudoward's in Port Simpson, but it was more often noted at potlatches.[5]

Historians have not generally noticed that Indigenous people were wealthy in the nineteenth century, but consider the evidence from around Victoria, BC. *The British Colonist* estimated that, at a potlatch in April 1869, the Lekwungen people gave away an astounding $20,000 in goods and cash to 700 assembled guests. In April 1874, 'the grandest affair of that kind that has been held upon Vancouver Island for many years, came off . . . at Victoria', hosted by Chief Sqwameyuks (Scomiach) of the Lekwungen. Sqwameyuk personally distributed over $1,000 worth of blankets to the 2,000 assembled, and the total value of goods given away by all the families during that week amounted to between $8,000 and $10,000. The next year, a week-long potlatch saw a similar distribution among a crowd of the same size. Two years later, at a potlatch given by the neighbouring Wsanec people, the Indian superintendent saw 'three members of one family (brothers) give away 3,500 blankets, no doubt the savings of many years . . . Goods to the value of $15,400 were distributed ere the affair ended.'[6] Such amounts would be considered large even today. In the mid- to late nineteenth century, when Aboriginal workers made 50 cents to 1 dollar per day and white labourers made 2 dollars, these sums represent an incredible accumulation of wealth. A sum of $15,000 in 1870 would be the equivalent of more than $315,000 today.[7]

In 1884, a delegation of Nuu-chah-nulth chiefs from Vancouver Island's west coast expressed their views: 'We work for our money and like to spend it as we please, in gathering our friends together; now whenever we travel we find friends; the "potlatch" does that.'[8] Like the Aboriginal people in many parts of the region, they made wage labour work for them, not the other way around. This concept is born out by Helen Codere's study of the Kwakwaka'wakw on northeastern Vancouver Island, which shows that work for wages and the production of goods for sale increased the frequency of potlatches, the number of guests, and

Potlach Gifts at Albert Bay, 1910–12, photographed by A.M. Wastrell. (City of Vancouver Archives, In P1192.)

the wealth distributed. She calls the period between the founding of Fort Rupert in 1849 and 1921 'the potlatch period'.[9]

Historian Robin Fisher has argued that 'the effect of frontier settlement was to diminish Indian wealth,' but Superintendent of Indian Affairs I.W. Powell finished his 1881 overview with the observation that 'there was never a time in the history of the Province when the Indians have been so prosperous as during the present year.'[10] Apparently, Aboriginal people eagerly participated in the foreign economy because they had well-developed potlatch economies of their own. However, instead of hoarding wealth, status in Northwest Coast cultures was achieved by hosting a potlatch and giving away all of one's wealth.

When historians write about British Columbia's Aboriginal peoples, they generally use one of three broad storylines. While each metanarrative has contributed to erasing the history of Aboriginal workers, the earliest and most enduring casts 'Indians' as obstacles to economic development, or 'progress'. This perspective, although found in early-twentieth-century Canadian texts,[11] is best exemplified in the work of an American, Frederick Jackson Turner. His *The Significance of the Frontier in American History* argues that the destruction of Indigenous peoples is part of the trial by fire from which a new nation and people were born.[12] Another 'progressive' variant of this argument states that Aboriginal peoples should exchange their 'primitive existence' for 'civilization' under the guiding hand of the missionary, teacher, or government agent. Although now out of fashion in the scholarly world, these ideas still have wide currency. As recently as 1991, they formed the basis for a major legal decision that rejected Aboriginal land claims.[13]

A second metanarrative can be summed up by the term *fatal impact*. In other words, trade and contact between an avaricious European world and an (often romanticized) Aboriginal culture resulted in the destruction of the latter. The reasons usually given for this outcome are superior European technology, Aboriginal passivity, and the inherently static nature of 'primitive societies'. Such an explanation is often a thinly veiled critique of a capitalist society that has flattened Indigenous cultures that stood in its path. This metanarrative frequently devalues contemporary Aboriginal society as being only the 'debris' of an idyllic Aboriginal past. Both versions portray Aboriginal peoples as victims of superior force and deny them a role in the making of their own history.[14]

The third metanarrative is more subtle. Best known in British Columbia from Fisher's work, it considers the period following first contact as one of cultural florescence. Sometimes called the 'enrichment thesis', this storyline argues that Aboriginal people had a great deal of control over the fur trade and were able to choose the aspects of the immigrant culture they wished to adopt, thereby enriching their own culture. This narrative temporarily restores agency to Aboriginal peoples. The fatal impact of European settlement, it seems, was not averted but only delayed:

> The fur trade had stimulated Indian culture by adding to Indian wealth and therefore to the scope of Indian creativity. Settlement on the other hand, often had the effect of subtracting from Indian wealth and this tended to stultify Indians . . . The Indians had been able to mould the fur trade to their benefit, but settlement was not malleable; it was unyielding and aggressive. It imposed its demands on Indians without compromise.[15]

Thus, settlement, not contact, marked the demise of Aboriginal culture and history.

If Aboriginal people were labouring 'in the sawmill, the logging camp, the field, the store in fact in every department where labour is required . . .'[16] in the 1870s and 1880s, what became of them? Did they continue to work in these enterprises into the twentieth century? If they vanished from the workforce, when did this happen? For the answers to these questions, we can look to the autobiographies written by Aboriginal people during this period. These stories are supplemented by more routine sources generated by an increasingly bureaucratic government. From the mid-1880s to the 1940s, the Department of Indian Affairs (DIA) expanded the types of information it gathered about Registered Indians, including estimated annual incomes.[17] Beginning in the late 1870s, the federal Department of Fisheries (DOF) expanded its collection of data on matters relating to fur sealing, fishing, and canning, with a view to regulating and allocating access to marine resources. Different agencies of the provincial government also became involved in gathering information on Aboriginal people. In 1926, the province established the Game Laws Enforcement Branch, with wardens stationed around the province enforcing hunting and trapping regulations. Due to a general labour shortage during World War II, the provincial labour department began an annual count of Aboriginal people. In fact, we have quite a bit of data on the 'invisible Indian'.

The Industrious Indian

Both the autobiographies and government records allow us to see what was happening in many of the sectors that were major employers of Aboriginal people, including trapping, commercial fishing, and agriculture. The autobiographies show that trapping was the first activity that brought most Aboriginal people into contact with the non-Aboriginal economy.[18] Like sealing, fishing, and other industries employing

Daniel Wigaix (Big Wings), Gistskan, with winter's catch of furs, 1923. (Canadian Museum of Civilization, Marius Barbeau, 1923, 59501.)

concentrations of Aboriginal people, trapping was a seasonal industry. By the 1920s, it remained the main source of income only in the northern part of the province. However, the fur industry was not an entirely reliable source of income because prices and supply fluctuated widely from year to year (see Figure 11.1). Nor were prices the only problem. In his annual report for 1892, the superintendent of Indian Affairs wrote that, for the first time, Aboriginal people were facing significant competition from non-Aboriginal trappers. This situation was exacerbated in 1926, when the provincial government required registration of traplines. Many Aboriginal people found that the traplines that their ancestors had worked for generations had been registered by non-Aboriginal people.

While the decline of the trapping industry was felt primarily in the north, changes in the commercial fishing industry affected much larger numbers. Commercial fishing was concentrated in coastal regions, but people from as far inland as Lillooet (on the Fraser River), Kispiox (on the Skeena River), Telegraph Creek (on the Stikine River), and the Chilcotin Plateau as far east as Kluskus Lake migrated seasonally to participate.[19] Coupled with the existing concentration of Aboriginal people on the coast, these migrations meant that the fishing industry was the largest employer of Aboriginal labour from the 1880s through to the 1960s. The canneries employed 1,400 fishermen in 1882; by 1929, that number had grown to 12,675. Between 1925 and 1940, the fishing fleet was 30 to 40 per cent Aboriginal. The cannery labour force grew as

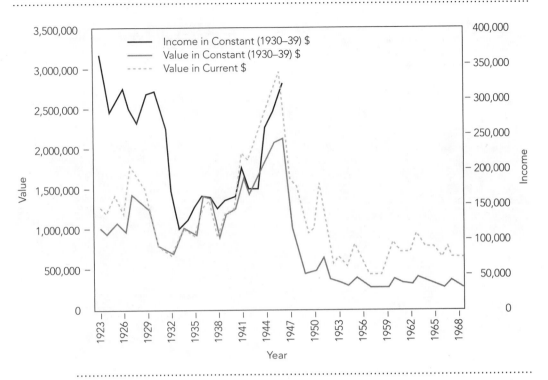

Figure 11.1   Value of Fur Trapped in British Columbia, 1923–70, and Registered Indian Income from Trapping, 1923–46.
Source: Department of Indian Affairs Annual Reports.

well and, by 1929, the DIA estimated that 11,488 Aboriginal people (or 41 per cent of the Aboriginal population in British Columbia) 'engage in the several branches of the commercial fishing operations'.[20]

The importance of the fisheries is also reflected in the autobiographies of Aboriginal people. All but one of the coastal men who wrote their stories fished commercially. Several owned their own fishing boats.[21] The Aboriginal cannery workforce was heavily dominated by women. Children also contributed to the family income by finding employment there: Florence Davidson recalls starting work in the canneries at age 11 and James Sewid and Ed Sparrow started at age 8.[22]

The fishing industry and the canneries that employed such a large percentage of Aboriginal people were, however, in decline over the latter part of the period under study. Several factors, including technological change and financial consolidation, contributed to this decline. The introduction of gas-powered boats in the 1920s meant that greater distances could be travelled faster. In the 1930s and 1940s, refrigeration allowed for the transportation of fish over longer distances. Previously, fish had to be processed within a day of being caught, requiring many small canneries close to the prime fishing sites—sites that Aboriginal people had identified centuries before and established as village locations. Keeping fish fresh for longer periods meant

James Sewid and crew of his fish boat, Twin Sisters, 1963. (Canadian Indians Today, 1963.)

that canneries could be consolidated into large operations located in two main centres: Vancouver and Prince Rupert. Figure 11.2 shows the rise and fall of the cannery industry.[23]

Cannery closures affected both the cannery labour force and the fishermen. Many canneries provided boats to Aboriginal fishermen on a share basis, boats that were no longer available when the canneries closed. At Klemtu, George Brown noted:

> We have about sixty families in the village; only nine or ten people own a fishing boat. When the cannery was still open, our men fished on company boats. The ones that didn't go fishing worked in cold storage. All the women worked during canning season. But the plant closed in 1968. For forty years we had got used to working all the time. Then they closed her down, quit operating. That's when things went from bad to worse. . . . Prices here are about double Vancouver's. Many people are on welfare; that's why it hits us so much.[24]

A different comparison illustrates the same trend. In 1892, 16 Fraser River canneries employed between 640 and 800 Aboriginal women. By 1953, that number was down to 10 canneries and a total of 91 Aboriginal women and men.[25]

Other changes also affected Aboriginal people's involvement in the fishing industry. A long-term decline in the number of fishing licences held by Aboriginal men, discernable from 1925, was temporarily reversed by the internment of

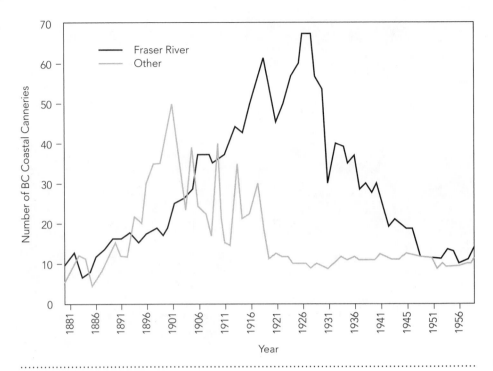

Figure 11.2 Number of BC Coastal Canneries, 1881–1959.
Source: Cecely Lyons, 1969.

Japanese-Canadians during World War II, allowing Aboriginal fisherman to benefit from high prices and reduced competition. After the war, the decline continued. Between 1948 and 1953, the number of Aboriginal fishermen fell even though the total number of fishermen increased. In his autobiography, Harry Assu observed that 'the number of our native people fishing in their own waters here on the coast has fallen off with poor harvests and the restrictions on fishing. While our people lost out in many places, the number of non-Indian "fishermen" buying seiners on these waters built up' (see Figure 11.3).

Although fishing's contribution to Aboriginal income rose during the war years, by 1954 it was in decline. In the northern fishing district, Aboriginal fishermen held their relative position a decade longer, but after 1964 the share of licences going to Aboriginal people in this district also fell off.[26] The year-to-year decline was often small, but the long-term effect was striking. In 1883, the canneries of the Fraser River area alone employed 1,000 to 1,200 Aboriginal fishermen. Seventy years later, less than 100 were employed in fishing in the whole lower coast area.[27]

Another main employer of Aboriginal people was agriculture. Some raised crops and stock as farmers and ranchers, for both the commercial and domestic economies. A larger number worked as wage or piece-rate labour for other farmers. Despite the

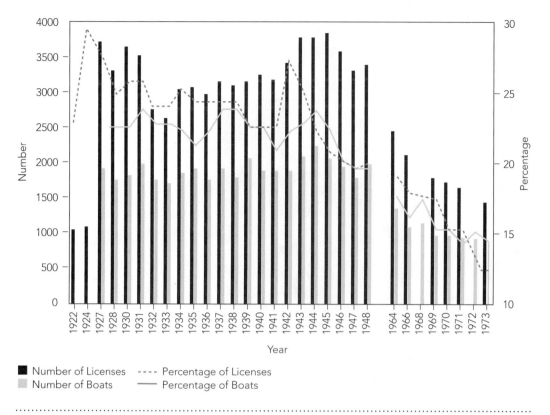

■ Number of Licenses   ---- Percentage of Licenses
  Number of Boats   —— Percentage of Boats

Figure 11.3 Number and Percentage of Fishing Licences and Boats Held by Aboriginal People, Selected Years, 1922–73. Sources: Fisheries and Oceans Canada.

characterization of British Columbia's Aboriginal people as non-agricultural, this sector at the beginning of the century and between 1910 and 1926 supplied more income to British Columbia Indigenous people than any other. In the latter part of the period studied, farming declined in importance as a source of income for Aboriginal people, though it remained, even in 1961, the third largest employer after fishing and forestry.[28]

Although agriculture was concentrated in the southern interior and the coastal river valleys of British Columbia, many Aboriginal people from other parts of the province expanded their seasonal migrations to participate in seasonal paid labour in the Fraser Valley and Puget Sound. Over half of the existing work histories of Aboriginal people describe this practice. A seasonal migration to the hop fields of the area was part of Charley Nowell's and John Fornsby's experiences in the 1880s.[29] John Wallace was born at the Hulbert's Hop Yard in the Fraser Valley on 25 September 1905 while his family was working there. Around the same time, Henry Pennier worked nearby at a single hop farm employing 700 'Indians from all over the

Salmon cannery worker. (BC Archives, I-28895.)

[province]. . . . They'd bawl me out in their own languages and I'll bet my last bale of hay that there were seven or eight different Indian languages there.'[30]

Some calculations suggest that the peak years for the migrations may have been the late nineteenth century.[31] In the summer of 1912, however, a Vancouver newspaper estimated that 1,500 Aboriginal hop pickers were employed in the Fraser Valley alone. This figure shows the continued importance of seasonal agricultural labour for many Aboriginal people. Indian agents' reports reveal that, while seasonal agricultural labour remained a source of Aboriginal income, its importance was dwindling by the early 1950s. The Canadian Regional Employment Offices placed the average number of Aboriginal people migrating to the United States during this time at 1,800 men and 1,555 women. Most of this group were agricultural labourers from British Columbia. The offices also estimated that a similar number migrated within the province to engage in seasonal agricultural labour. But, by 1957, only 300 Aboriginal people from British Columbia participated in the hop harvest in the province and in the United States.[32]

The third main employer of Aboriginal people was the forest industry. However, an overall picture of Aboriginal labour in forestry is hard to come by. We do know that all of the 12 Aboriginal men who left work histories (and who were from all parts of the province) worked at some time as loggers, wood cutters, boom men, sawmill labourers, or pole cutters. Charles Jones turned to logging at the turn of the nineteenth century (when the sealing industry shut down) and was a logger for the rest of his life, though 'when the jobs in the logging industry were scarce, I often went fishing.'[33] Although logging activity was widely distributed throughout the province, it was most intensively pursued in the coastal regions. Helen Codere's study of the Kwakwaka'wakw and James Pritchard's of the Haisla found widespread involvement in hand-logging during the early twentieth century. This is probably true for many of the other coastal Aboriginal communities.[34]

When legislative changes and increasing regulation forced an end to hand-logging in 1910, Aboriginal people, in several cases, formed their own logging companies or found employment as wage labourers for larger logging firms. Pritchard found that the peak of Haisla logging took place between 1917 and 1924, although the Haisla people continued as loggers during World War II and the immediate post-war period. There

Aboriginal hop pickers, Chilliwack, BC. (Courtesy of Chilliwack Museum and Archives, P1622.)

are two indicators of the relative significance of the forestry sector to Aboriginal people. First, the decennial census (1931–61) suggests an increase in the importance of the forest industry and a decline in agriculture. Second, a survey of Aboriginal occupations conducted by Harry Hawthorn in 1954 confirms an increase in the importance of the forest industry as an employer.[35]

Based on the autobiographies and the Indian agents' reports, it is possible to say that the forest industry continued to be a major employer of Aboriginal people in the province. However, it is difficult to chart changing patterns of Aboriginal employment. Interviews with Aboriginal men in the coastal towns of Queen's Cove, Kingcome, and Owikeno show that, while logging employed a part of the male labour force formerly engaged in fishing, the employment was tenuous, especially once the local area was logged out.[36]

The only local study of an Aboriginal economy centred on logging is Douglas Hudson's survey of the Carrier people in north central British Columbia. Based on interviews with a forestry employer, Hudson argues that the period from 1946 to 1964 marked the boom years for logging operations in that area and the peak years of Aboriginal employment in the sector. In the following years, the small, local logging operations and local sawmills that employed most of the Aboriginal forest workers were displaced by multinational firms, who brought in workers from 'outside'.[37] While Aboriginal people were engaged in a wide variety of non-forestry occupations, these comprised a relatively small part of the workforce.

Hank Pennier, Stó:lō logger. (Courtesy of Chilliwack Museum and Archives, Photo 2003.39.7.).

Boom and Bust Cycles

While they do not often appear in our histories of the two world wars and the Great Depression, Aboriginal people were dramatically affected by these major events. World War I created a massive demand for workers to supply the war industry and replace the enlisted men. Like other Canadians, Aboriginal people benefited from the increase in war-time employment. In 1918, the annual report of the DIA recorded:

> The past year has been one of great prosperity for the Indians of south-western British Columbia, . . . [due to] the extraordinarily high price paid for all kinds of fish, and the great scarcity of unskilled labour. Never in the history of the Pacific Coast have such high prices been paid for fish as during the past year. . . . On the West Coast some Indians are known to have earned as much as $1,000 in a single week.[38]

The following year, the DIA's annual report stated: 'The prevailing wage paid for farm labourers and for work in the saw mills and logging camps was higher than at any time previous . . . In the lumbering industry wages were exceptionally high and Indians engaged in that work earned from five to eight dollars per day.'[39] Yet, despite the rising wages, wartime inflation caused a decline in real income. Following the war, real income rose, returning to pre-war levels in 1929–30 before plummeting during the Depression.[40]

Carrier-Dene Mary John described the effect of the Depression on her community: 'Our hard life became harder. . . . Employment for our men became scarce and finally non-existent. By the end of the Depression the only work available for the men was relief work. . . . Many times relief money was the only cash which was circulating on the reserve.' Other evidence indicates that her experience was widely shared among Registered Indians in British Columbia. They rode the roller coaster of the national and international economy along with other Canadians, experiencing the sharp dips in 1914, 1924, and 1927 and the full impact of the Great Depression.[41]

Similarly, recollections of increases in wages and employment levels during World War II are dramatically reflected in the income statistics and other information gathered by the provincial Department of Labour. This data indicate that Aboriginal people were hired in industries and occupational categories outside the range of where they had previously been concentrated. Hundreds of British Columbia's Aboriginal men also joined the military and fought in the war. Employment in these enumerated industries doubled between 1940 and 1941 and almost doubled again to a peak in 1942, when it started to decline.

The plentiful supply of wartime work was used as an excuse by the DOF to further reduce Aboriginal access to food resources. The Chief Inspector of Fisheries wrote the following to one of the Indian agents: 'It is felt that Indians engaged in the commercial fishing during the height of the season do not require food permits.'[42] But when growing numbers of Aboriginal people returned to the relief–subsistence combination after the war, the DOF still withheld fishing permits. In 1955, Andy Paull, editor of *Indian Voice* magazine, told a conference that conditions were better earlier in the century: 'At least then a hungry Indian could go down to the creek and hook a salmon—now they have to watch the salmon swimming by.'[43] Hunting regulations also limited Aboriginal people's ability to hunt food. By the 1950s, the state had game wardens enforcing the law in much of the province. Clam digging remained one of the few means by which the coastal people could still harvest food without restriction for food and sale. However, this freedom

Okanagan men in uniform. (Courtes yof the Historic O'Keefe Ranch and Okanagan Indian Band.).

lasted only until 1960, when the DOF instituted an annual closed season for commercial harvesting of clams between June and November. Lekwungen Chief Albany considered it another step in the federal government's appropriation of Aboriginal resources:

> Now through regulations, it [the season for digging clams] is only seven months. They tell us the clams are no good from June to November, but Indians feel the clam is really at its prime then. Those are the months Indians used to put up their food for the winter. For many hundreds of years Indians were eating clams in those months.

Albany noted that, because Aboriginal people could not sell the clams in order to buy other food, the shellfish was about all they would have to eat. In Victoria, the newspaper headlines on 18 October 1960 read 'Indians Face Starvation.'[44]

The gradual erosion of Aboriginal access to subsistence resources increased their dependency on the wage economy. However, several factors limited Aboriginal success in the capitalist economy: the province and municipalities refused to hire them for public works; the Forest Service refused to give them timber leases; the DOF limited the kind of fishing licences they could have; the Lands Branch gave whites preferential access to irrigation water and range land; the Indian Act criminalized the sale and possession of alcohol by Aboriginal people, which cut them out of the restaurant and hotel business altogether and made running a store less profitable; and the reserve system made it difficult for Aboriginal people to acquire capital for a business because they could not use their homes or land as security to get a loan. More personal kinds of racism, including white customers' refusal to be served by Aboriginal people, meant that they were not hired in restaurants or retail stores, and low educational levels kept them out of white-collar professions. When the wage economy contracted, as it did after World War II, the government's alternative to the subsistence economy was the expansion of the welfare system.

At the turn of the nineteenth century, Indian agents estimated that less than 1 per cent of Aboriginal income came from the government. This figure rose to 4 per cent during the Depression and to 17 per cent by 1954. In 1966, 25.4 per cent of the on-reserve Aboriginal population in British Columbia received financial assistance, more than eight times the provincial average. By 1972–3, the percentage of British Columbia's Aboriginal people dependent on social assistance had increased to 47 per cent.[45]

Indigenous girls trained to be servants at All Hallows Residential School, Yale, BC. (Annual report of the Department of Indian Affairs for the year ended June 30 1902. COP.CA.CI.1 1902 Copy 1, AMICUS 90778)

Conclusion

In the twentieth century, several simultaneous processes affected Aboriginal people's ability to earn a living. First, industry and seasonal work, the main employers of Aboriginal people, were in decline. Second, while educational levels for Canadians and the percentage of jobs requiring high-school and post-secondary education were rising rapidly, this was not the case for Aboriginal people. In residential schools, Aboriginal people were educated for menial, low-paying jobs, many of which were also in decline due to mechanization. Third, the land and sea that Aboriginal people had turned to in the past could no longer provide as good a living as a result of competing economic activities such as logging and commercial fisheries, as well as state regulations that limited hunting and fishing. Fourth, an influx of settlers from eastern Canada and Europe reduced Aboriginal people to a minority in the province. These immigrants produced and supported racist ideologies that characterized Aboriginal people as lazy and worthless, preventing employment in many service industries. Finally, at the beginning of the twentieth century, laws against the potlatch began to be enforced. Because earning wealth to potlatch had been one of the key motivations for Aboriginal people to join the capitalist economy, the government discouraged them from working for their own reasons.

In the latter half of the twentieth century, Aboriginal people vanished from the work force and became one of the most impoverished segments of British Columbia society through a process of increasing state regulation and anti-conquest narrative. This latter approach had different fronts: residential schools, missionaries, literary and media constructions, and derogatory stereotypes. The anti-conquest narrative also existed in workplaces, where Aboriginal people were inundated with capitalist values, and in the regulations that denied Aboriginal people access to their subsistence and capitalist economies. Lekwungen Elder Joyce Albany recognized the challenge. 'Believe me,' she told the *Colonist* in 1973, 'we very often sit down and talk about the White Problem.'[46]

Primary Document

2.   Excerpts from the Diary of Arthur Wellington Clah

Introduction by John Lutz

Arthur Wellington Clah (1831–1916) was a Ts'msyen man who led a varied and rich life as a trader, an Aboriginal healer, a Christian teacher, and a labourer. He mixed his traditional spiritual, family subsistence, and economic practices with those of the immigrant society.[47] In 1857, Clah met William Duncan, a missionary, in Fort Simpson (now Port Simpson) on the BC coast. The two men taught each other their native languages, although (as you will see) Clah's English is very much his own version. As a result of this encounter, Clah kept a daily diary from 1858 to 1916. Because few Aboriginal people could write in English in this period and journal writing was not one of their practices, Clah's diaries are an extremely rare kind of primary source—a view of the nineteenth-century world through the eyes of an Aboriginal man.

What follows are excerpts from Clah's diary from the spring and summer of 1860. We have kept his spelling but have indicated places where we are unsure of his intentions with [?] and placed suggested words in square brackets. The original diaries are housed at the Wellcome Institute in London, England (MS American 140).

Arthur Wellington Clah. (BC Archives, AA-00678.)

5th Months May had 31 Days 1860
Morning and I begin work [?] at New Westminster and of Fraser River 14 of May 1860
I had 15 Days of working at New Westminster an of Fraser River for in May 1860

24th May 1860
Queen is Born[48]

Steamer Wilson G. Hunt started for New Westminster about 7 o'clock on Thursday night the 15 of May 1860. Capt. Wellice Commante [in command?] and Clah going the same steamer Wilson G. Hunt go all night. 9 hours gone an he in New Westminster and Clah Shew [?] in Fraser River on Wednesday morning

6th Months June had 30 Days 1860
I begin work.

Victoria V.I. friday june 29th 1860. I bought a revolver from soldiers and I pay 2 of silver him standing by Sawchuck [?] Indian.
I left New Westminster on Saturday morning on Steamer Wilson G. Hunt.

Steamer Wilson G. Hunt arrived at New Westminster at Fraser River on the 20th June 1860. And I heard some bad news. I hear my brother has been shoot. Blessed are those who die in the Lord and I am very Sorry for my Brother Die. My Brother also was name Wallice Brother of Clah: this man who shooting brother of Clah also name Cayqun [of layqun?] he is Bad Man killing my Brother.
Cayqun [?] him over
Bad Man be his
Place Name
Yellow Jaw [?]
Cay Qun Killing
3 men in one day an in one hour.
On man killing another
day 4 men all together
Wallice Shu claks [?] weth [with] my [me].

7th Months July has 31 days 1860
I had in that month good working do Some things and every Day.

7 of July 1860 and I went Down Victoria on Saturday evening and on steamer hunt and steamer hunt arrived on Sunday morning 8 inst. [inst. meaning of this month] with 9 hours from at Fraser River an at New Westminster.
And 13 at inst. and the same steamer started for New Westminster.
And he arrived at place on Saturday morning carry good lot men.
8th Month August had 31 days 1860

Westminster Fraser River August 6th 1860
Monday morning I have been working for week and when I am done working and

I going back in my house and I shew [saw] one large deer swim an in the River. To when I shew [show] deer them I called Charry [Charley?] he had a little boat uset [used] for carry loaves Bread at Bank and of Soldiers Camp. Clah an them I called Charrly 2 of men siting in little boat and after that one indian came coming to 2 indian sitting an 2 indian first killing Deer and was [?] catching Deer from indian Charrly Tuked [took] Deer in is boat an he going to Shore and all whit [whites?] coming together and some men has knive in them hand to cuting Deer is meat an all the men cuted [cutted]

an Deer is fresh cuted there in pieces an Tooked [taken] away and Charrly angry with them all men and Charrly fighting with one man. fighting for deer

Secondary Source

3.   Colonialism at Work: Labour Placement Programs for Aboriginal Women in Post-War Canada

Joan Sangster

During the 1950s, the Department of Indian Affairs' newsletter *The Indian News* featured optimistic stories of Aboriginal[49] women's successful integration into the world of steady wage labour. 'Indian Girls Achieve Successful Careers—Pave the Way for Others', reprinted on pages 302–4, was typical of these expositions. Another article highlighted 'Treaty Indian' women who had migrated to the city from reserves and had conquered many obstacles to became stenographers, hairdressers, and office workers. Their personal stories projected a positive message: persistent women could overcome time in a sanatorium, rural isolation, or lack of education and triumph in the world of work.[50] In contrast, popular exposées of Indigenous women's downward spiral into poverty and criminality also emerged in the mainstream press, not unlike some of the recent 'sensational' stories of Indigenous women adrift in the city.[51] These women were often portrayed as refugees from dying reserves. In one well-publicized story, two young girls from God's Lake, MB, were sent to Vancouver on a trip funded by MacMillan Bloedel, in the hopes that they would imbibe the benefits of further education and pursue careers as typists. Instead of joining the modern life of 'airplanes, appliances, and bathtubs' that they experienced in the city, the girls returned to the 'futility, despair, unemployment' of the reserve. The article suggested that it was the responsibility of Canadian society to aid and uplift Aboriginal people like these, who were attempting to move from traditional to modern lives by escaping failing reserves.[52]

Aboriginal women's experiences of life and labour were far more complex than these stark morality tales would suggest. While there is no doubt that some faced increasing material and social marginality in the post-war period, their actual labour was misrepresented in this dualistic narrative of moving either up or down the ladder of modernity. At the same time, these narratives do reflect some of the popular prejudices and state perspectives of the post-war period. The Indian Affairs Branch

(IAB), under the purview of the Department of Citizenship and Immigration during the 1950s, believed that Aboriginal women would increasingly migrate to urban areas, that they should be integrated into permanent wage labour in service and clerical jobs (at least until marriage), and that expert guidance from the state was necessary as Aboriginal women made the transition from 'traditional' modes of living to modern employment. This article explores the genesis in the 1950s of federal labour placement programs for Aboriginal women, how these programs were actually implemented on the Prairies, and why they failed to achieve the stated goals of the IAB.[53] Although these programs had some limited successes, they were unable to effectively reverse women's economic marginalization. Indeed, they might simply have modernized or reinvented colonial relationships. This is not to say that Aboriginal peoples had no interest in such initiatives; on the contrary, in testimony before Senate and House of Commons committees, Aboriginal organizations often called for more training, better education, and greater wage labour opportunities, especially for their youth. However, the calls of Aboriginal organizations for employment justice were wider ranging and encompassed a much broader program of economic development, while state-initiated programs were narrowly designed and ultimately unable to address the more pervasive economic and ideological legacies of colonialism.

Labour historians often designate the post-World War II period as that of the 'Fordist accommodation', a tacit pact between organized labour, capital, and the state that offered labour new legal protections in exchange for increased production and regulation of the workplace. While this agreement may have increased economic security for unionized workers, it did not apply to a 'second tier' of the labour force, including many women, immigrants, and non-white workers who faced a gendered and racialized division of labour, less job security, and more limited (if any) unemployment benefits. Not only was Fordism a term that had little resonance for Indigenous peoples, but many Aboriginal communities actually experienced intensified economic marginalization in the post-war period; the Royal Commission on Aboriginal Peoples (RCAP) refers to this as a 'dark era of increased dependency'.[54] The legacies of this economic marginalization remain visible today. The high levels of urban poverty, racism, criminalization, and violence that Aboriginal women face must be seen in the context of the post-war era of deepening 'dependency', a process that labour placement programs were unable to address effectively.

In order to understand the context and rationale for labour placement programs, the questions posed by feminist labour history and political economy are useful starting points. How did men and women sustain themselves as the material conditions around them changed? How did they negotiate, accommodate, and resist economic and social changes, drawing on the cultural resources at hand and, in turn, reshaping their cultures? How did women's role in social reproduction shape daily life and wage labour? What was the role of the state in shaping gender and racial divisions of labour? In this story, life and labour, colonialism and class, gender and race become inseparable categories; the denigration of Indigenous cultures and the racialization of Aboriginal women cannot be separated from their economic exploitation. However, even if hard economic times defined Aboriginal women's lives in the post-war decades, they did not determine them. Women's own accounts indicate how they negotiated the changing economic situation with their own courageous strategies for individual and family survival. Some embraced the possibility that labour placement programs seemed to offer, even if the overall impact of these programs was far less than Aboriginal peoples had hoped.

Context for Labour Placement Programs

Historically, it is difficult to disentangle Aboriginal women's work from family and community or to separate their paid and unpaid labour, especially for those peoples combining different kinds of work, including seasonal and casual wage labour, permanent wage labour, bush production for use, and bush production for market exchange. As one study of Manitoba First Nations concluded, most families on re- serves and in rural areas were enmeshed in a family economy that involved multiple earners and multiple occupations, what Jean Legassé labelled a 'cycle economy'.[55] Aboriginal economies also varied considerably in strength and affluence (or poverty) across the Prairies, but there are still good reasons for the RCAP's negative charac- terization of this period, even though for some communities a downward slide had started in the 1930s. In northern Manitoba, for instance, Aboriginal peoples had adjusted their labour to new markets and resource extraction for decades. However, changes in the fur trade, a decline in fur prices, the dispossession of Aboriginal land title, the incursion of new resource industries, and the loss of casual work that had been essential for Aboriginal families combining multiple forms of labour for survival all made this adaptation more difficult. As Frank Tough concludes, there was 'an in- tensified integration of Indigenous communities into the capitalist market on terms very unfavourable to them'.[56]

There are six brief points to make about the intensification of hard times on the Prairies after the war and the context in which labour placement programs emerged.[57] First, economic changes always interacted dynamically and often negatively with other social and cultural assaults on Indigenous life, such as the legacy of violence and cul- tural denigration associated with residential schooling. Second, economic problems were particularly difficult for those involved in the production of commodities such as fish and fur and for those engaged in multiple occupations or a seasonal cycle of jobs. As many waged jobs were decasualized in northern areas and given to white people, Indigenous families were forced to rely more heavily on trapping at a time of declining fur prices.[58] In northern Saskatchewan, for instance, some families combined trapping with what little wage labour or welfare could be secured, eking out an existence on $300 to $400 a year, an income that was undoubtedly 'Third World' in nature.[59]

Third, in many expert studies by social scientists and in the eyes of IAB, women in these economies were secondary workers, who, for example, might help to bring in extra money as handicraft producers but were not the primary earners. Even re- searchers who recognized that they were dealing with a 'colonial' economy in northern Saskatchewan still referred to Aboriginal 'male breadwinners' as being responsible for all the trapping 'income', while women were responsible for 'domestic affairs'.[60] The interdependent nature of the family economy was thus misread, and women's unpaid labour, essential to family survival, was rendered invisible. Yet, in their autobiograph- ical accounts, Métis and Indian women recall how they produced food for survival, cared for the family, collaborated in the fishing industry, and were part of a chain of production in fur, skinning and creating a pelt for sale in a process that was itself highly skilled and 'artisanal'. Increasingly, Aboriginal women also had to find more wage work to aid the family economy.

Fourth, the state's response to these economic difficulties was often stop-gap and based on decidedly colonial views of Indigenous labour. One example was the sugar beet program in southern Alberta, which employed Indigenous families from across the Prairies who were denied welfare payments in their home reserve if they refused to migrate to the beet fields for summer work. IAB pushed Aboriginal people into seasonal fieldwork during the 1950s because it saw them as well suited for migrant, temporary, physical, low-paid work; moreover, it knew that practices of family-based labour were easily incorporated into the regime of agricultural work.

Fifth, Aboriginal people tried to offer their input on economic development and labour policies. To note only one example, many bands and Indian organizations provided briefs or gave testimony on these issues to federal parliamentary committees in 1947–8 and again in 1959–60. Although the 1947–8 hearings on the Indian Act focused more on issues such as education, treaty rights, and health, these were not completely distinct from economic development. In its submission, the Le Pas Indian Band argued that 'economic conditions are at the heart of the whole problem [of Indian life] . . . without a decent income, the average Canadian, Indian or otherwise, will not be healthy. Only by raising living standards through cooperative industrial development, will there be the basis for a healthy and virile people.'[61] During the 1959–60 joint Senate and House of Commons hearings into Indian Affairs, more calls were made by Aboriginal groups for expanded wage employment in concert with demands such as the protection of trapping rights, the establishment of make-work projects on reserves, and job training off the reserves. In the groups' view, respecting the treaties and protecting the right to subsistence were quite compatible with more education and paid work, but many politicians tended to see an either/or choice for Indigenous peoples: either 'traditional' trapping or 'modern' work roles. Finally, these calls for economic development and justice, while challenging a racial division of labour, did not question the existing gendered division of labour. Chiefs, bands, and advocacy groups generally assumed that women needed access to home aide, clerical, and nursing aide jobs. This is hardly surprising, given the tenacious persistence of a sex-segregated labour market for all Canadian women and the glaring lack of any jobs for Indigenous women in many communities.

Labour Placement Programs

It was precisely these difficult conditions that led to Aboriginal women's increased mobility and search for new economic options in the post-war period. Moreover, leaving reserves allowed Aboriginal people to escape the often invasive and moralistic surveillance of the Indian agent.[62] The high number of women moving to urban areas was also a result of the Indian Act's infamous 'marrying out' clause (section 12(1) (b)), which stated that 'Indian' women lost their status and right to live on the reserve when they married a non-Indian.[63] Like their Métis counterparts, these women were then disadvantaged because they were officially disqualified from participating in the IAB's education and labour placement programs. Whether status or non-status, many

Aboriginal women who were new to urban areas had difficulties finding jobs and housing, coping with low wages, and handling the isolation from their communities. The 1957 Labour Placement and Relocation Program (shortened to Labour Placement Program) was supposed to address at least some of these problems: the solution to Aboriginal economic development, the state reasoned, was 'full time jobs, steady incomes . . . and integration into the industrial economy of Canada'.[64] Initiated with placement officers located in four large cities (three in the Prairie West), the program sought to provide employment counselling, liaison with unions and businesses, on-the-job training, help finding jobs, and loans and aid with relocation. IAB identified the need for 'general' placements in casual jobs and 'permanent' placements for which the candidate might need more training, though it clearly saw more hope in the latter. Although there were some rural dimensions (resource work) to the program, it was generally assumed that relocation to towns and cities would be necessary, especially for female-typed jobs. The program was not unlike the American relocation program begun by the Bureau of Indian Affairs a few years earlier, which encouraged (indeed, pushed) American Indians to leave reservations and relocate in urban centres, where blue- and white-collar jobs were more plentiful.[65]

In developing the program, the IAB could point not only to Aboriginal demands for more employment opportunities but also to contemporary social science experts, many of whom urged greater wage employment as a key solution to the poverty on reserves. The implicit assumption was that Native poverty was the product of their failure to embrace wage labour rather than the result of colonialism and capitalist underdevelopment.[66] Moreover, the IAB chose selectively from the experts. Anthropologist Harry Hawthorn's extensive investigation of contemporary Indian life opened by rejecting the 'assimilation and integration' of Indians as a state objective, yet he also tended to fall back on a model that posited a linear progression from failing subsistence economies to jobs within industrial capitalism; progress was equated with higher paying wage labour, enhanced skills and training, acceptance of new forms of work discipline, and, importantly, the male breadwinner family. Hawthorn believed that this strategy would aid, not destroy, Aboriginal cultures, stemming the tide of 'personal and social disorganization' plaguing Indigenous communities.[67] Hawthorn's anthropological accent on cultural preservation was not necessarily embraced by IAB, which was more inclined to favour integration as a means of replacing what it saw as problematic Aboriginal cultural practices with new ones better suited to the 'modern' workplace.

Labour placement programs had two gender tracks: men were moved into resource work or into (generally) blue-collar jobs in urban areas, while women were trained for white-collar and service occupations.[68] These parallel streams were linked ideologically through the ideal of the 'family wage';[69] women's job options were often predicated on the belief that they would eventually become part of a male breadwinner household. While our historical focus has understandably been on forms of political discrimination against Aboriginal women encoded in the Indian Act, it is important to remember that the state's active promotion of this male breadwinner model was also instrumental in both encouraging patriarchal ideologies in Indigenous families and communities and offering lessons in racialized and gendered labour.

Unfortunately, one of IAB's longer-standing work solutions for Aboriginal women, long before 1957, was domestic service, which was integrated into new placement programs even though some Indian agents admitted that it was not always popular or permanent work for women. Girls coming out of residential schools were presumed to be especially well suited for such work because domestic training was an important part of the curriculum, because girls were forced to perform domestic labour within the schools, and because some girls had worked in domestic placements during their summers.[70] Domestic service was supposed to provide young women with a preliminary introduction into the world of wage labour and serve as the first step towards employment in service or factory jobs. Indeed, in its list of public achievements, the IAB pointed to the domestic courses it offered Aboriginal girls as signs of its success.

The IAB also promoted domestic jobs as a means to prevent female juvenile delinquency, claiming that they kept young women, susceptible to immoral influences, off the streets. Like earlier generations of working-class women, these domestic workers were viewed as morally fragile and susceptible to the 'wrong kind of influence'.[71] However, race and the racialization of urban space were also at issue. Aboriginal women's presence in the city was viewed as alien to the natural Indian character; they were literally out of place in urban spaces or, worse, viewed as 'trespassers' in white space, a colonialist view that exposed women to the threat of racism and violence.[72] As one well-intentioned Winnipeg reformer put it, Aboriginal women are 'displaced persons in their own land, trying to bridge the gap between generations when their proud race *was left behind*'.[73] This image of a 'race left behind' may have inspired the pity of some, but it also encouraged contempt from others, an invitation for discrimination and violence.

Theoretically at least, there was supposed to be more emphasis on training women for jobs in the white- and pink-collar sectors: clerical, hospital, and hairdressing work were three hopeful areas for female employment. IAB also assumed that many Indigenous people needed cultural makeovers if they were to move into jobs requiring 'white' standards of work discipline, as if Aboriginals had had no previous experience with wage labour. Cultural explanations were often used to explain the dissonance between 'Indian' and 'modern' work and as a rationale for special 'catch up' economic aid for Aboriginals. Bush production may have imposed a different timetable and culture of work, but to see it only as intermittent or as a choice that allowed one to escape working year round missed the structured imperatives of the cycle economy in which many Aboriginal communities were enmeshed. IAB attempts to educate the public in this regard are revealing. Its widely circulated pamphlets on Indian life argued that Aboriginal peoples needed sympathy and aid in securing new employment since white incursions onto their land had 'knocked [Aboriginal] cultures off balance . . . leading Indians feeling lost, bewildered and hopeless' and since they now faced 'social and cultural intolerance'.[74] Yet this modicum of sympathy and responsibility was negated by descriptions that made Indigenous peoples sound like 'primitives' needing paternal aid: they were people whose idea of making a living was to 'live only for today'; 'they lived by the sun, moon and tides rather than by the clock or calendar'; and 'nothing in their experience has taught them to deal with crises they now faced.'[75]

The implication that Aboriginal cultures were, by their very definition, incompatible with the rhythms of modern wage labour was also potentially dangerous. Taken in one extreme direction, this determinist view of culture became a rationale for simplistic prejudices. In Winnipeg, a local committee with state, labour, and business

participants was set up to help to integrate Indians into urban jobs. A garment manufacturer told the first meeting that there were many jobs available but that Aboriginal
women had problematic work habits. The union representative agreed: 'Indian women
could be absorbed into the needle trades, dry cleaning, and other service jobs' if only
their work habits and 'social adjustment' improved.[76]

Given IAB's notion that there was an 'Indian' employment personality, placement officers were required to assess not only candidates' formal education and language skills
but also their character traits before enrolling them in the program. Since life in the city
was assumed to involve stressful cultural adaptation, only those with 'stable' personal-
ities who were able to 'mix with non-Indians' and withstand pressure without 'losing
control or resorting to alcoholism' were to be selected. Particular hope was placed on
the young, who were seen to be more malleable. 'With considerable guidance,' it was
believed that 'this younger element could eventually integrate into the non-Indian
communities.' Integration, however, was just another word for assimilation.

For some Aboriginal women, hairdressing was a step up from domestic work; however, it was not necessarily work that could sustain a household. In her autobiography, *Halfbreed*, Maria Campbell recalls getting a job in a beauty salon after taking
a hairdressing course. Within two weeks, it was clear that the 'wages were so poor'
that she could not support herself and her children. She had no choice but to head to
the welfare office.[77] The number of women trained to be hairdressers, however, paled
beside those who ended up in service jobs and domestic work. When Jean Lagassé did
his survey of Aboriginal employment in Winnipeg, he found that the largest groups of
women who came to the city found their first job in 'restaurant kitchen work' (38 per
cent) and their second in housework (38 per cent), with a much smaller group (4 per
cent) in nurse's aide positions. Aboriginal women's wages put them at the bottom of
the economic scale, followed closely by Métis women—statistics that remain similar
today.[78]

Lagassé, like many other well-meaning liberals, called for an end to racial discrimination and special supports for Métis and Aboriginal families, but he too saw
permanent and skilled work for men as *the* solution. Women's economic fate was
largely determined by their ties to men. While recognizing that Aboriginal women had
their own employment dreams, such as nursing jobs, he pointed out that they—unlike
Aboriginal men—could always marry a white man and therefore 'move up' the social
ladder. Some urban Aboriginal women, he said, already 'pass', importing a term usually applied to African Americans. These women did not need special programs since
they 'already fit into urban Canada as contributing members'.[79] Who, then, were the
non-contributing members: Indigenous women who valued their heritage but were
still employed washing dishes? Lagassé implied that these 'passing' women were the
successful ones, but the response of one such woman who was interviewed was a horrific comment on the pervasiveness of racism: 'My husband would kill me [if he knew
I was an Indian],' she said.[80]

One of Lagassé's recommendations, supported by not only the IAB but also groups
such as Indian and Métis friendship centres, was that girls should be taught typing and
other commercial skills because these jobs were seen as better opportunities for young,
urban women. IAB developed an in-house placement experiment for such women,
costing the department a mere $10,000 a year. It had to lobby strenuously to increase

funding and expand the program to 22 placements. Status Indians with high-school or commercial college education but still unable to find employment were given jobs in IAB offices in order to provide them with experience, letters of reference, and extra training. Workers received a weekly allowance but not actual wages, so they were ineligible for unemployment insurance, leaving them vulnerable after the program ended. Moreover, there was no question that the government saw this as a program for single women rather than female 'breadwinners'.

Given the focus on clerical jobs, there was a certain bias towards women, and there were some small but noticeable increases in the number of Aboriginal women in white-collar work by the end of the 1960s. Again, however, a cultural makeover was part of women's training, for the women were often seen as too insecure, shy, re-clusive, and quiet for the work world and not the kind, one IAB pamphlet informed the public, 'likely to sparkle in an interview'.[81] The IAB solution was to require the women to take the federal civil service exam after a period of training, so that they could move beyond the supposed 'safety' of the IAB offices to other jobs. Perhaps a more pressing problem than 'personality' was the limited nature of these in-house programs: 22 jobs do not solve an unemployment problem, let alone address lar-ger issues of economic justice. Even the larger placement program dealt with only about 300 to 600 people a year.[82] One Saskatchewan assessment of labour place-ment programs in 1969 provided a dismal picture: 79 per cent of the women could only obtain jobs as domestics or waitresses, and the majority of women placed were in 'temporary' positions. Placement officers, according to the assessment's radical author, helped employers fulfill hiring targets, while, in private interviews, employ-ers admitted they did not think that 'the vast majority of Indians employed would remain on the job'.[83]

As these labour placement programs were developed, an anxious discourse about the 'problem' of 'Indian in the City' was emerging, a fearful response on the part of whites to the increased urban migration of Indigenous peoples and a clear instance of how space was racialized according to colonial ideologies. While the debate at the time about 'the urban Indian' is a topic onto itself, one aspect of it is important to a discussion of Aboriginal women workers: the preoccupation of experts and reformers alike with Aboriginal women's morals. In the Lagassé report, to cite only one example, an interview section that presented various 'typical' experiences of women coming to Winnipeg to work was excessively preoccupied with their morality. The interview sec-tion discussed the discrimination that Aboriginal women faced in the labour market, their naïveté, and their (often) tragic downward spiral into crime. In one story, a young woman wishing to make good after getting into trouble as a teenager came to the city to find work in the needle trades. Despite her training in this area, she faced discrimin-ation in her job searches. The result: because she was easily led astray by companions, she was soon in conflict with the law.[84] Stories of naive Aboriginal women tricked, led, or forced into prostitution shared parallels with white slave narratives concerning working-class women that circulated at the turn of the nineteenth century; however, the 'promiscuity' of Indian women was sometimes taken as a given and equated with the behaviour of 'lower-class' white women.[85] This image of an available, promiscu-ous Indian woman was a staple of racist ideology, and it became a licence for violence perpetrated against Aboriginal women.[86] While decrying discrimination on the one hand, racist stereotypes were thus perpetuated on the other hand in this report; any critique of Aboriginal women's imprisonment in low-wage job ghettos was comprom- ised by recasting the issue as one of morality. These anxieties and stereotypes were replicated in the popular media in more lurid, sensational, and deterministic terms, intensifying the antipathy to Indigenous women's presence in the city. The material exploitation and sexual condemnation of Aboriginal women were thus closely inter- twined; therefore, the appropriation of women's labour cannot be separated from the appropriation of their sexual dignity.

Conclusion

In the 1950s and 1960s, Aboriginal women increasingly migrated to urban centres in search of work or to escape conditions on reserves, sometimes making use of the few labour placement programs that existed to re-train, find work, or start new lives. Like many working-class women, they were in search of economic survival and new opportunities; however, many Aboriginal women were often already burdened with an inadequate education geared towards cultural assimilation, and they encountered profoundly racist views of their culture, ability, and morality.

The increasingly interventionist role of the state in managing and reorienting Aboriginal labour is an important theme in this period, one that was fundamentally gendered, both in the conceptualization of the problem and in the creation of policy solutions. Informed in part by social science studies of the time—but also by prevail- ing idealized images of the white, middle-class, family—politicians and policy-makers often assumed a male breadwinner family as the ideal. Women were seen as *ancillary* earners who only worked when they were young and single, even though that had never been the case in most Aboriginal communities based on a family economy of pooled resources.

Labour placement solutions to the economic problems faced by Aboriginal peoples took two gender paths: relocation programs to place male breadwinners in blue- col- lar jobs or job training geared towards a small range of gender-specific jobs for sin- gle women. The latter avenue involved both a continuation of earlier efforts to place Aboriginal women in domestic jobs and some new programs intended to foster skills necessary for pink- and white-collar jobs, and it was probably in the second category that some small successes were attained. A similar gendered division of labour was taken for granted by Aboriginal groups lobbying Parliament for more and better labour placement programs; however, their presentations differed from the views of polit- icians, experts, and bureaucrats in other ways. They did not see an irrevocable choice between bush production and 'modern' wage work but promoted a more comprehen- sive, holistic vision of economic justice for Indigenous peoples.

The programs developed, however, were very limited and often reproduced les- sons in gendered and racialized labour that left Indigenous women at the bottom of the employment ladder. Non-Aboriginal women were similarly channelled into a very restricted range of sex-typed jobs by the state, and working-class and poor white women experienced similar efforts to patrol their sexual morality. However, the moral and cultural explanations offered for Aboriginal women's supposed in- ability to adapt to wage labour, their poverty, or their criminalization were also racialized arguments, even if they were dressed up as cultural difference and paternalist protection. As a consequence, Aboriginal women were especially vulnerable to both material disadvantage and racist denigration as supposedly more 'primitive' women. This designation also left them vulnerable to the hostility and violence that we have seen repeatedly directed against Aboriginal women in the most vicious way, from the case of Betty Osborne, murdered in northern Manitoba, to the hundreds of Aboriginal women who have disappeared from Canadian city streets over the past two decades.[87]

While scholarship has understandably focused on the Indian Act's discriminatory 'marrying out' clause, this legislation, as Bonita Lawrence argues, was part of a much larger 'regulatory regime . . . a way of seeing life . . . that ultimately forms an entire conceptual territory on which knowledge is produced and shaped'. The state's image of women as ancillary workers in need of moral protection and its active promotion of a patriarchal male breadwinner model were also ingredients of this regulatory regime. Moreover, Lawrence adds that these ways of thinking often come to 'permeate how Indigenous peoples think of themselves. . . . [and] even [their] attempts to change the system itself'.[88] To focus on this regulatory regime is, admittedly, only one part of the story of Aboriginal women and paid work in this period, obscuring themes of agency and resistance. As Heather Howard-Bobiwash indicates in her study of the Toronto Indian and Métis Friendship Centre, some women who migrated to urban areas to seek out new employment developed strategies for survival, drawing on kin and community and building organizations to aid other women who came after them.[89] By concentrating on state-initiated programs, however, I have tried to emphasize that political choices were made by IAB that rested not only on cultural and racial assumptions about the Aboriginal character but also on suppositions about how the capitalist market should work. More specifically, it relied on the theory that it did work—and for the better—allowing all working people, regardless of race and class, to move up the employment ladder. The story of labour placement programs for Indigenous women suggests the opposite: economic justice was not to be found in piecemeal programs or cultural makeovers but through a more comprehensive challenge to the legacies of colonialism on Aboriginal life.

Primary Document

4.   Indian Girls Achieve Successful Careers— Pave Way for Others

Indian News, June 1958

Indian News *was a newsletter published by the Department of Indian Affairs.*

In recent years numbers of Indian workers have been finding their way to Winnipeg. Many who have settled there have found work to suit their abilities and are happy in their new life. Among those who have become successfully employed are young women working in homes and offices.

Miss Rose Bear came to Winnipeg five years ago from the Pequis Indian reserve near Dallas, Manitoba. At first she worked as a ward aid in a city hospital, later obtained employment with a wholesale firm doing general office work. With financial assistance obtained from the Indian Affairs Branch she studied comptometry at night school for 10 months and now utilizes her skill, coupled with switchboard operating, at the wholesale house.

The loneliness felt by a stranger in an unfamiliar city she allayed by joining a church choir, by going bowling with friends, by visits to relatives and occasional trips back to her home.

Another Treaty Indian girl to take advantage of assistance offered by the Indian Affairs Branch is Mrs. Gordon MacKay who left her home at Cross Lake two years ago to take a course in hair dressing at the Manitoba Technical Institute. She is now employed in a Sargent Avenue beauty salon, and is married to another Treaty Indian employed by a city department store. Between them they are saving to establish a home in the city.

Two teenagers, Ruth Le Tandre of Fairford and Frances McCorrister of Hodgson, attended high school together and came to Winnipeg to complete their education. They have been studying stenography at the Manitoba Technical Institute and learning to like the life of the city where they hope to earn their living.

Another successful migrant from the reserve to the city is young Lorna Kirkness of Koostatak, north of Fisher River. Though she was forced to spend several months in a sanatorium, she afterwards came to Winnipeg to temporary employment with the Manitoba Sanatorium Board. She took a course in shorthand at the Manitoba Technical Institute, with government assistance, and now is a stenotypist in the Board's new office.

Each day more Indian girls from reservations and rural points make their way into Canadian cities, seeking further education and jobs. Many succeed in their quest, thus bridging the gap successfully between an old and a newer life. And, in doing so, they pave the way for others of their race to take their place in Canadian society.

Frontier Nurse

A Treaty Indian, the first in Saskatchewan to be placed in charge of an outpost nursing station, is at work at La Range in the northern section of the province.

She is Jean Cuthland, 29 years of age, and a Registered Nurse. The new head nurse was born on the Little Pine Indian Reserve, just west of North Battleford, attended school at the Reserve, later in Saskatoon, and took her nurse's training at Holy Family Hospital in Prince Albert.

Before taking charge of the La Ronge nursing station, Miss Cuthland served in the Indian Hospital in Fort Qu'Appelle, and is anxious to continue as a "frontier nurse". Her example gives further evidence of the growing responsibility which Indian young people are taking in the country's social life.

Winnipeg Attracts Indian Workers

More Indians now live in Winnipeg than on any single reserve in Manitoba—and the movement is growing.

This surprising fact was revealed by Jean Lagassé, chairman of the housing committee of the fourth annual conference on Indians and Métis, held in Winnipeg in January. A survey had shown that more than 2,000 Indians lived in Winnipeg while the largest reserve in Manitoba—Island Lake—was inhabited by 1,620.

Resolutions presented at the conference stressed the need for increased education, recreation, housing, counselling and improved employment. It was also suggested that a referral service for Indian and part-Indian newcomers to Winnipeg should be established to counsel strangers on matters of employment, housing, education, health, and other community services, that Indians who had adjusted successfully to urban life should be enlisted to aid other Indians.

Questions for Consideration

1. How does Lutz's view of Aboriginal people and labourers in the late nineteenth and early twentieth centuries challenge the usual historical view?
2. What, in Lutz's view, explains the marginalization of Aboriginal peoples in British Columbia and their corresponding impoverishment?
3. What can the excerpts from Arthur Wellington Clah's diary teach us about the following: a) the labour market for Aboriginal workers; b) Clah's lifestyle and the lifestyles of other Aboriginal peoples and workers; and c) settler–Aboriginal relations on the west coast in 1860?
4. What were the goals of the labour placement programs for Aboriginal workers in the post-war period? How did they fit with the goals of federal Indian policy more broadly, as outlined by Shewell and Meijer Drees in Chapter Seven, and with the objectives of the residential schools, as discussed by Haig-Brown and Sekwan Fontaine in Chapter Nine?
5. In what ways were the federal government's attempts to integrate Aboriginal workers into the 'modern' industrial economy gendered and/or racialized?
6. What lessons does the author of the article from *The Indian News* want readers to learn from the examples of 'successful Indian girls' that he or she provides?
7. How integral have Aboriginal workers been to the modern economy? How would you explain the poverty of Canada's Aboriginal peoples?

Further Resources

Books and articles

Fisher, Robin. *Contact and Conflict: Indian-European Relations in British Columbia*, 2nd edn. Vancouver: UBC Press, 1992.

Howard-Bobiwash, Heather. 'Women's Class Strategies as Activism in Indigenous Community Building in Toronto, 1950–75', *American Indian Quarterly* 27, 3&4 (Summer–Fall, 2001): 566–82.

Janovicek, Nancy. 'Assisting Our Own: Urban Migration, Self-Governance, and Indigenous Women's Organizing in Thunder Bay, Ontario, 1972–1989', *American Indian Quarterly* 27, 3&4 (Summer–Fall, 2001): 548–65.

Lutz, John. *Makuk: A New History of Aboriginal-White Relations*. Vancouver: UBC Press, 2008.

Pickles, Katie, and Myra Rutherdale, eds. *Contact Zones: Aboriginal and Settler Women in Canada's Colonial Past*. Vancouver: UBC Press, 2006.

Printed Documents and Reports

Indian and Northern Affairs Canada. *A Survey of the Contemproary Indians of Canada: Economic, Political, Educational Needs and Policies: Part 2* (The Hawthorn Report). Ottawa: Queen's Printer, 1967. Available at http://www.ainc-inac.gc.ca/eng/1291832488245.

Films

Broke. DVD. Directed by Rosie Dransfeld. ID Productions, 2009.
César's Bark Canoe. DVD. Directed by Bernard Gosselin. NFB, 1991.
High Steel. DVD. Directed by Don Owen. NFB, 1965.
Mohawk Girls. DVD. Directed by Tracey Deer. NFB, 2005.

Websites

BC Stats' statistics on Aboriginal peoples in the province
www.bcstats.gov.bc.ca/data/cen01/abor/ap_main.asp

First Nations Employment Society
www.fnes.ca

Human Resources and Skills Development Canada, 'Indicators of Well-Being'
www4.hrsdc.gc.ca/.3ndic.1t.4r@-eng.jsp?iid=16

Statistics Canada, 'Aboriginal Peoples in Canada's Urban Area'
www.statcan.gc.ca/pub/81-004-x/2005003/8612-eng.htm

TWELVE

Aboriginal Women

Introduction

Published in 1978, Kathleen Jamieson's *Indian Women and the Law in Canada: Citizens Minus* was part of a broader political movement to address the discrimination that Aboriginal women faced. This study, commissioned by the Native Women's Association of Canada (NWAC), revealed that this discrimination was not only a function of patriarchy but that it also stemmed from the intersection of colonialism, racism, and sexism in Canadian society. Recent scholarship seeking to make visible the experiences of Aboriginal women has exposed the disproportionate surveillance, restraint, and violence that Aboriginal women were and are subject to under the auspices of the Canadian nation-state. Andrea Smith argues that violence, especially sexual violence, towards Aboriginal women is part of a colonial strategy that seeks to 'not only destroy people, but to destroy their sense of being a people'.[1] As such, this violence is part and parcel of the policies of cultural genocide pursued by the state, including the residential schools system detailed by Celia Haig-Brown and Lorena Sekwan Fontaine in Chapter Nine.

This process of erasure is given form through the disappearance and murder of Aboriginal women, which has become epidemic in Canadian society. In 2004, Amnesty International published *Stolen Sisters: Discrimination and Violence against Indigenous Women in Canada*. This report revealed that young Aboriginal women are five times more likely to die as a result of violence than any other women of the same age.[2] Although this is a horrifying statistic, the depressing reality is that the evidence of this phenomenon is all around us. For example, the Highway of Tears (Highway 16) in northern British Columbia, Vancouver's Downtown Eastside, and the 'Killing Fields' outside Edmonton are all spaces of murderous sexual violence that targets Aboriginal women either disproportionately or exclusively. The violence that Aboriginal women experience today cannot be disassociated from the colonial past.

In this chapter, Sarah Carter's article outlines how Aboriginal women were marginalized in western Canada's nascent white settler society during the late nineteenth and early twentieth centuries. During the late nineteenth century, bylaws that prohibited

Aboriginal women from traversing urban areas without passes and stereotypes that portrayed them as lascivious and sexually available made them appear threatening to the white body politic. Such stereotypes remain shockingly persistent. The dehumanization and objectification of Aboriginal women makes the violence and murder perpetrated on their bodies appear normal and acceptable. According to Carter, the marginalization of Aboriginal women, the sexualization of their bodies, and the violence done to their persons were essential to Canadian nation-building and to assuring 'Euro-Canadian newcomers [of] their belief that their cultural and moral superiority entitled them to the land that had become their home'. In other words, it was Aboriginal people who were out of place.

Cora Voyageur's article seeks to complicate the picture that some historians paint of Aboriginal women's experience of Canadian colonialism. As Sylvia Maracle and others emphasize, Aboriginal women were clearly the victims of oppression, but they were also strong and resilient and, in countless instances, led and continue to lead their communities' attempts to overcome the colonial legacy.[3] Voyageur examines one such woman: Elsie Knott, the first female to become a chief under the revised Indian Act of 1951. According to Voyageur, Knott's life is a testament to the strength, courage, and intelligence of Aboriginal women in the face of overwhelming obstacles. Dedicated to improving the lives of the people in her community, Knott appears to stand in the tradition of the strong Aboriginal women who have played central roles in their families and societies.

Chapter Objectives

At the end of this chapter, you should be able to

- identify some of the most common stereotypes associated with Aboriginal women and explain how these labels helped further the colonial project;
- explain some of the ways that Aboriginal women have resisted these stereotypes;
- identify some strong Aboriginal women; and
- discuss the career of Curve Lake First Nation Chief Elsie Knott.

Secondary Source

1. Categories and Terrains of Exclusion: Constructing the 'Indian Woman' in the Early Settlement Era in Western Canada

Sarah Carter

In 1884 Mary E. Inderwick wrote to her Ontario family from the ranch near Pincher Creek, AB, where she had lived with her new husband for six months.[4] The letter provides a perspective on the stratifications of race, gender, and class that were forming as the Euro-Canadian enclave grew in the district of Alberta. Mary Inderwick lamented that it was a lonely life, as she was 22 miles from any other women, and she even offered to help some of the men near them to 'get their shacks done up if only they will go east and marry some really nice girls'. She did not consider the companionship of women such as 'the squaw who is the nominal wife of a white man near us', and she had dismissed her maid, who had become discontented with her position as a servant. Inderwick had disapproved of a ball at the North-West Mounted Police (NWMP) barracks at Fort Macleod, despite the fact that it was 'the first Ball to which the squaws were not allowed to go, but there were several half breeds'. Commenting on the Aboriginal population that still greatly outnumbered the new arrivals, Inderwick wrote that they should have been 'isolated in the mountains', rather than settled on nearby reserves, and that the sooner they became extinct the better for themselves and the country.

At the time of Mary Inderwick's arrival in the West the consolidation of Canada's rule was not yet secure. The Métis resistance of 1885 fed fears of a larger uprising, and an uncertain economic climate threatened the promise of a prosperous West. There was a sharpening of racial boundaries and categories in the 1880s and an intensification of discrimination in the Canadian West. The arrival of women immigrants like Mary Inderwick after the Canadian Pacific Railway was completed through Alberta in 1883 coincided with other developments such as the railway itself, the treaties, and the development of ranching and farming that were to stabilize the new order and allow the re-creation of Euro-Canadian institutions and society. The women did not introduce notions of spatial and social segregation, but their presence helped to justify policies already in motion that segregated the new community from Indigenous contacts.[5] The Canadian state adopted increasingly segregationist policies toward the Aboriginal people of the West, and central to these policies were images of Aboriginal women as dissolute, dangerous, and sinister.

From the earliest years that people were settled on reserves in western Canada, Canadian government administrators and statesmen, as well as the national press, promoted a cluster of negative images of Aboriginal women. Those in power used these images to explain conditions of poverty and ill-health on reserves. The failure of agriculture on reserves was attributed to the incapacity of Aboriginal men to become other than hunters, warriors, and nomads.[6] Responsibility for a host of other problems, including the deplorable state of housing on reserves, the lack of clothing and footwear, and the high mortality rate, was placed upon the supposed cultural traits and temperament of Aboriginal women. The depiction of these women as lewd and licentious, particularly after 1885, was used to deflect criticism from the behaviour of government officials and the NWMP and to legitimize the constraints placed on the activities and movements of Aboriginal women in the world off the reserve. These negative images became deeply embedded in the consciousness of the most powerful socio-economic groups on the Prairies and have resisted revision.

The images were neither new nor unique to the Canadian West. In 'The Pocahontas Perplex' Rayna Green explored the complex, many-faceted dimensions of the image of the Indian woman in American folklore and literature. The beautiful 'Indian Princess' who saved or aided white men while remaining aloof and virtuous in a woodland paradise was the positive side of the image. Her opposite, the squalid and immoral 'Squaw', lived in a shack at the edge of town, and her 'physical removal or destruction can be understood as necessary to the progress of civilization'.[7] The 'Squaw' was pressed into service and her image predominated in the Canadian West in the late nineteenth century, as boundaries were clarified and social and geographic space marked out. The either/or binary left newcomers little room to consider the diversity of the Aboriginal people of the West or the complex identities and roles of Aboriginal women.

Euro-Canadian Settlement of the West

Following the transfer of the Hudson's Bay Company territories to the Dominion of Canada in 1870, the policy of the federal government was to clear the land of the Aboriginal inhabitants and open the West to Euro-Canadian agricultural settlement. To regulate settlement the North-West Mounted Police was created and 300 of them were dispatched west in 1874. A 'free' homestead system was modelled on the American example, and a transcontinental railway was completed in 1885. To open up the West to 'actual settlers', seven treaties with the Aboriginal people were negotiated from 1871 to 1877, and through these the government of Canada acquired legal control of most of the land of the West. In exchange the people received land reserves, annuities, and, as a result of hard bargaining by Aboriginal spokesmen, commitments to assist them to take up agriculture as their buffalo-based economy collapsed. A Department of Indian Affairs with headquarters in Ottawa was established in 1880, and in the field an ever-expanding team of Indian agents, farm instructors, and inspectors were assigned to implement the reserve system and to enforce the Indian Act of 1876. The people who had entered into treaties were wards of the government who did not have the privileges of full citizenship and were subject to a wide variety of controls and regulations that governed many aspects of life.

Much to the disappointment of the federal government, the West did not begin rapid development until the later 1890s. There were small pockets of Euro-Canadian settlement, but in 1885 in the district of Alberta, for example, the Aboriginal and Métis population was more than 9,500 while the recent arrivals numbered only 4,900.[8] All seemed hopeless, especially by the mid-1880s when immigration was at a near standstill. Years of drought and frost and problems finding suitable techniques for farming the northern Plains account in part for the reluctance of settlers, and the 1885 resistance of the Métis in present-day Saskatchewan did little to enhance the image the government wished to project of the West as a suitable and safe home.

Development of Stereotypes

Particularly irksome to many of the recently arrived 'actual settlers' was Aboriginal competition they faced in the hay, grain, and vegetable markets. Despite obstacles, many Aboriginal farmers had produced a surplus for sale. Settlers' particularly vocal and strident complaints led the government to curtail farming on reserves. To explain why underused reserves had become pockets of rural poverty, Indian Affairs officials claimed that Aboriginal culture and temperament rendered the men unwilling and unable to farm.

Plains women were also responsible: according to government pronouncements they were idle and gossipy, preferring tents to proper housing because tents required less work to maintain and could be clustered in groups that allowed visiting and gossip. Reports of the superintendent general of Indian Affairs claimed that Indians raised dust with their dancing and the women's failure to clean it up spread diseases such as tuberculosis. Administrators blamed the high infant mortality rate upon the indifferent care of the mothers. The neglected children of these mothers grew up 'rebellious, sullen, disobedient and unthankful'.[9] While men were blamed for the failure of agriculture, women were portrayed as resisting, resenting, and preventing any progress toward modernization. As an inspector of Indian agencies lamented in 1908, 'The women, here, as on nearly every reserve, are a hindrance to the advancement of the men. No sooner do the men earn some money than the women want to go and visit their relations on some other reserve, or else give a feast or dance to their friends. . . . The majority of [the women] are discontented, dirty, lazy and slovenly.'[10]

The unofficial and unpublished reports of reserve life show that officials recognized that problems with reserve housing and health had little to do with the preferences, temperament, or poor housekeeping abilities of women. Because of their poverty the people were confined in large numbers in winter to what were little better than one-room and one-storey huts or shacks that were poorly ventilated and impossible to keep clean, as they had dirt floors and were plastered with mud and hay. Tents and tipis might well have been more sanitary and more comfortable. One inspector of agencies noted in 1891 that women had neither soap, towels, wash basins, nor wash pails, and no means with which to acquire these.[11] Officials frequently noted that women were short of basic clothing but had no textiles or yarn to work with. Yet in official public statements, the tendency was to ascribe blame to the women rather than to draw attention to conditions that would injure the reputation of government administrators.

'Licentiousness' and Government Officials

Officials propagated an image of Aboriginal women as dissolute, as the bearers of sinister influences, to deflect criticism from government agents and policies. This image was evoked with particular strength in the wake of an 1886 controversy that focused upon the alleged 'brutal, heartless and ostentatious licentiousness' of government officials resident in Western Canada.[12] The remarks of Samuel Trivett, a Church of England missionary on the Blood Reserve in present-day southern Alberta, became the focus of the controversy. To a special correspondent for *The Mail* of Toronto, Trivett said that Indian women were being bought and sold by white men who lived with them without legally marrying them and abandoned the offspring to life on the reserve.[13]

Trivett strongly hinted that some government agents were involved in licentious behaviour, an accusation seized upon by critics of the administration of Indian affairs in western Canada. In the House of Commons in April of 1886, Malcolm Cameron, Liberal member of Parliament, delivered a lengthy indictment of Indian affairs in the West, focusing upon the unprincipled and unscrupulous behaviour of officials of the

Indian department. Cameron quoted Trivett and further charged that agents of the government, sent to elevate and educate, had instead acted to 'humiliate, to lower, to degrade and debase the virgin daughters of the wards of the nation'. He knew of one young Indian agent from England, unfit to do anything there, who was living on a reserve in 'open adultery with two young squaws . . . reveling in the sensual enjoyments of a western harem, plentifully supplied with select cullings from the western prairie flowers'.[14]

Cameron implicated members of the NWMP in this behaviour, wondering why it was that over 45 per cent of them were reported to have been under medical treatment for venereal disease. Cameron was not the first to raise the matter of police propriety in the House. Concern about possible improper relations between the police and Aboriginal women long predated the Trivett scandal and was one aspect of a larger debate in the press and in the House in the late 1870s over charges of inefficiency, lack of discipline, high desertion rates, and low morale in the force. Lieutenant-Governor of the North-West Territories David Laird alerted NWMP Commissioner James Macleod in 1878 that reports about immoral conduct were in circulation:

> I fear from what reports are brought me, that some of your officers at Fort Walsh are making rather free with the women around there. It is to be hoped that the good name of the Force will not be hurt through too open indulgence of that kind. And I sincerely hope that Indian women will not be treated in a way that hereafter may give trouble.[15]

Although Macleod and Assistant Commissioner A.G. Irvine denied that there was 'anything like "a regular brothel"' about the police posts, such reports persisted. In the House of Commons in 1880 Joseph Royal, a Manitoba member of Parliament, claimed that the NWMP was accused of 'disgraceful immorality' all over the West. Royal had been informed that 'many members of the force were living in concubinage with Indian women, whom they had purchased from their parents and friends.'[16] In 1886 public attention was once again drawn to police behaviour. *The Mail* informed its readers that between 1874 and 1881 the police had 'lived openly with Indian girls purchased from their parents' and only the arrival of settlers had compelled them to abandon or at least be 'more discreet in the pursuit of their profligacy'.[17]

There is little doubt that Trivett and other critics based their accusations of both the police and government officials on some foundation, but remaining evidence is scanty and scattered. Missionaries depended to a large extent on the goodwill of government and were rarely as outspoken as Trivett or John McLean, a Methodist missionary on the Blood Reserve near Fort Macleod, who in 1885 characterized many reserve employees as utterly incompetent and urged the government to employ only married men, 'of sterling Christian character'.[18] But missionaries were instructed in 1886 by Edgar Dewdney, lieutenant-governor of the North-West Territories, not to voice their accusations to the newspapers 'even if allegations against public officials were true', as this would do more harm than good, would affect mission work, and could be used to stir up political strife.[19] Government officials generally investigated reports of government misconduct themselves and this functioned to cover up or to mitigate such allegations. Similarly members of the NWMP themselves looked into any complaints about the force's behaviour.

Tahnoncoach, believed to be a niece of Sitting Bull, was the Lakota wife of George Pembridge, NWMP, Fort Walsh, c. 1878. (Glenbow Archives, NA-935-1.)

Marriages of Aboriginal Women and NWMP Members

There were members of the NWMP, especially among the earliest recruits of the 1870s and early 1880s, who formed relationships with Aboriginal and Métis women, as did a great many other male immigrants of these years. Some of these were marriages of long-standing, sanctioned by Christian ceremony or customary law.

Other relationships were of a more temporary nature. Cecil Denny for example, while a sub-inspector at Fort Macleod, had a daughter with Victoria Mckay, a part-Peigan woman who was the wife of another policeman, Constable Percy Robinson.[20] Denny was forced to resign from the force in 1881 as a result of his involvement in a series of court cases that Robinson brought against him for 'having induced his wife to desert him and also having criminal connections with her'.[21]

D.J. Grier, who served three years with the NWMP beginning in 1877 at Fort Macleod, married Molly Tailfeathers, a Peigan woman, and together they had three children.[22] By 1887, however, Grier had remarried a white woman. For a short time the children from his first marriage lived with their mother on the Peigan Reserve, but the two eldest were taken from her and placed in the care of Grier's parents. Grier was one of the most prominent men of the West. Renowned as the first commercial wheat grower in Alberta, he also served as mayor of Macleod for 12 years, from 1901 to 1913.

Abuse of Aboriginal Women

John O'Kute-sica wrote at length about one unsuccessful Wood Mountain customary marriage, that of his aunt Iteskawin and Superintendent William D. Jarvis. According to O'Kute-sica his aunt consented to marry Jarvis because he promised that her brothers and sisters would have something to eat twice a day, and all of her people were in want and suffering. After only a few weeks of marriage Jarvis, in a jealous rage, publicly assaulted Iteskawin at a Lakota 'Night Dance', an incident that strained relations between the two communities, and she immediately left him.[23] On most of the few occasions that Aboriginal women laid charges against policemen for assault or rape, their claims were hastily dismissed.[24]

Some government employees resident on reserves clearly abused their positions of authority. In 1882, Blackfoot Chief Crowfoot and his wife complained that the farm instructor on their reserve demanded sexual favours from a young girl in return for rations, and when an investigation proved this to be the case the man was dismissed.[25] Both the documentary and oral records suggest that several of the government employees that the Crees killed at **Frog Lake** and Battleford in the spring of 1885 were resented intensely because of their callous and at times brutal treatment of Aboriginal women. The farm instructor on the Mosquito Reserve near Battleford, James Payne, was known for his violent temper—he once beat a young woman and threw her out of his house when he found her visiting his young Aboriginal wife. The terrified and shaken woman, who was found by her father, died soon after, and her grieving father blamed Payne, whom he killed in 1885.[26] As a Touchwood Hills farm instructor told a visiting newspaper correspondent in 1885, the charges of immorality among farm instructors on reserves were in many instances too true, as 'the greatest facilities are afforded the Indian instructor for the seduction of Indian girls. The instructor holds the grub. The agent gives him the supplies and he issues them to the Indians. Now you have a good idea of what semi-starvation is . . .'.[27]

Blaming Aboriginal Women

The most vocal response to the accusations of Trivett and other critics was not to deny that there had been 'immorality' in the West but to exonerate the men and blame the Aboriginal women, who were claimed to have behaved in an abandoned and wanton manner and were supposedly accustomed to being treated with contempt, to being bought and sold as commodities, within their own society. In defending the NWMP in 1880, the Toronto *Globe* emphasized that Aboriginal women had 'loose morals' that were 'notorious the world over' and that 'no men in the world are so good as to teach them better, or to try to reform them in this respect.' The editor of the Fort *Macleod Gazette*, a former NWMP, argued that whatever immorality there might have been came from the women themselves and from the customs of their society. They were prostitutes before they went to live with white men, who did not encourage this behaviour but were simply 'taking advantage of an Indian's offer'. *The Mail* told readers that Aboriginal males had sold their wives and children in the thousands to soldiers and settlers since the time of the French fur trade in exchange for alcohol, and that with the arrival of the police a great deal had been done to end this situation.[28]

The *Gazette* stressed, incorrectly, that there was no marriage in Plains societies, simply a little lively bartering with the father and a woman could be purchased for a horse or two. The argument that Aboriginal women were virtual slaves, first to their fathers, and then to their husbands, was called upon by all who wished to deflect criticism from government officials and the NWMP. In the House of Commons in April 1886 Sir Hector Langevin claimed that to Indians marriage was simply a bargain and a sale and that immorality among them long predated the arrival of government agents in the North-West.[29]

The government published its official response to the criticisms of Indian affairs in the North-West in an 1886 pamphlet entitled 'The Facts Respecting Indian Administration in the North-West'. A government official had again inquired into accusations about the misconduct of employees of the Indian department and, predictably, had found no evidence. The investigator, Hayter Reed, assistant commissioner of Indian affairs, was one of those unmarried officials who had been accused of having Aboriginal 'mistresses' as well as a child from one of these relationships.[30] The pamphlet boldly asserted that Trivett was unable to come up with a shred of actual evidence, although the missionary vehemently denied this.[31] The pamphlet writer admitted that some men had acquired their wives by purchase, but claimed that this was the Indian custom, and that 'no father ever dreams of letting his daughter leave his wigwam till he has received a valuable consideration for her.' If the government stopped this custom, there would be loud protests, over and above the Indians' 'chronic habit of grumbling'. 'The Facts' insisted that it was not fair to criticize the behaviour of the dead, such as Delaney and Payne, who had 'passed from the bar of human judgment'.[32]

Constraints on Aboriginal Women

It was the image of Aboriginal women as immoral and corrupting influences that predominated in the non-Aboriginal society that was taking shape. Authorities used this characterization to define and treat Aboriginal women, increasingly narrowing their options and opportunities. Both informal and formal constraints served to keep Aboriginal people from the towns and settled areas of the Prairies and their presence there became more and more marginal.[33] Their presence was seen as incongruous, corrupting, and demoralizing. Classified as prostitutes, Aboriginal women were seen as particular threats to morality and health. An 1886 pamphlet of advice for emigrants entitled 'What Women Say of the Canadian Northwest' was quick to reassure newcomers that Aboriginal people were seldom seen. The 320 women who responded to the question 'Do you experience any dread of the Indians?' overwhelmingly replied that they rarely saw any. Mrs S. Lumsden, for example, thought they were 'hundreds of miles away with sufficient force to keep them quiet'.[34]

Following the events of 1885, government officials as well as the NWMP made strenuous efforts to keep people on their reserves. A pass system required all who wished to leave to acquire a pass from the farm instructor or agent declaring the length of and reason for absence. A central rationale for the pass system was to keep away from the towns and villages Aboriginal women 'of abandoned character who were there for the worst purposes'.[35] Classified as prostitutes, Aboriginal women could be restricted by a new disciplinary regime. Separate legislation under the Indian Act, and, after 1892, under the Criminal Code governed Aboriginal prostitution, making it easier to convict Aboriginal women than other women. As legal historian Constance Backhouse has observed, this separate criminal legislation, 'with its attendant emphasis on the activities of Indians rather than whites, revealed that racial discrimination ran deep through the veins of nineteenth century Canadian society'.[36]

The pass system was also used to bar Aboriginal women from the towns for what were invariably seen as 'immoral purposes'. Women who were found by the NWMP to be without passes and without means of support were arrested and ordered back to their reserves.[37] In March of 1886 the Battleford police dealt with one woman who refused to leave the town by taking her to the barracks and cutting off locks of her hair. Two years later the Battleford paper reported that 'during the early part of the week the Mounted Police ordered out of town a number of squaws who had come in from time to time and settled here. The promise to take them to the barracks and cut off their hair had a wonderful effect in hastening their movements.'[38]

Accustomed to a high degree of mobility about the landscape, Aboriginal women found that the pass system not only restricted their traditional subsistence strategies but also hampered their pursuit of new jobs and resources. Government officials further limited the women's employment and marketing opportunities by advice such as that given by one Indian agent, who urged the citizens of Calgary in 1885 not to purchase anything from or hire Aboriginal people, so as to keep them out of the town.[39] The periodic sale of produce, art, and craftwork in urban or tourist areas could have provided income to women and their families, as did such sales for Aboriginal [and European-Canadian] women in eastern Canada.

Murders of Aboriginal Women

Community reactions to the poisoning of one Aboriginal woman and the brutal murder of another in the late 1880s in southern Alberta reflect the racial prejudices of many of the recent immigrants. In 1888 Constable Alfred Symonds of the NWMP detachment of Stand Off was accused of feloniously killing and slaying a Blood woman by the name of Mrs Only Kill by giving her a fatal dose of iodine. The woman had swallowed the contents of a bottle given to her by Symonds that apparently held iodine and had died the next morning.[40] In his report on the case, Superintendent P.R. Neale of the NWMP wrote to his superior, 'I do not think any Western jury will convict him.' Symonds appeared before Judge James F. Macleod, former commissioner of the NWMP, in August of 1888 but the Crown prosecutor made application for '*Nolle Prosequi*', which was granted, and the prisoner was released.[41]

During the 1889 trials of the murderer of a Cree woman identified only as 'Rosalie', who had been working as a prostitute, it became clear that there were many in Calgary who felt 'Rosalie was only a squaw and that her death did not matter much.'[42] Instead the murderer gained the sympathy and support of much of the town. The murder was a particularly brutal one, and the accused, William 'Jumbo' Fisk, had confessed and given himself up to authorities, yet there were problems finding any citizens willing to serve on a jury that might convict a white man for such a crime. The Crown prosecutor stated that he regretted having to conduct the case, as he had known the accused for several years as a 'genial accommodating and upright young man'.[43] Fisk was a popular veteran of 1885, and he was from a well-established eastern Canadian family. At the end of the first of the Rosalie trials the jury astoundingly found the accused 'Not Guilty'. Judge Charles Rouleau refused to accept this verdict and he ordered a re-trial at the end of which Rouleau told the jury to 'forget the woman's race and to consider only the evidence at hand', that 'it made no difference whether Rosalie was white or black, an Indian or a negro. In the eyes of the law, every British subject is equal.'[44] It was only after the second trial that Fisk was convicted of manslaughter and sent to prison for 14 years at hard labour. The judge intended to sentence him for life, but letters written by members of Parliament and other influential persons who had made representations to the court as to his good character, combined with a petition from the most respectable people of Calgary, persuaded him to impose the lesser sentence.

The people of Calgary tried to show that they were not callous and indifferent toward Rosalie by giving her 'as respectable a burial as if she had been a white woman', although several months later the town council squabbled with the Indian Department over the costs incurred, as the department did not think it necessary to go beyond the costs of a pauper's funeral. As a final indignity Rosalie was not allowed burial by the priests in the mission graveyard, although she had been baptized into the Roman Catholic Church, because they regarded her as a prostitute who had died in sin. The lesson to be learned from the tragedy, according to a Calgary newspaper, was 'keep the Indians out of town.'[45]

Haunted by an Image

Negative images of Aboriginal women proved extraordinarily persistent. Their morality was questioned in a number of sections of the Indian Act. As late as 1921 the

House of Commons debated a Criminal Code amendment that would have made it an offence for any white man to have 'illicit connection' with an Indian woman. Part of the rationale advanced was that 'the Indian women are, perhaps, not as alive as women of other races in the country to the importance of maintaining their chastity.' The amendment was not passed, as it was argued that this could make unsuspecting white men the 'victims' of Indian women who would blackmail them.[46] By contrast, any critical reflections upon the behaviour of early government officials and the police in western Canada did not survive beyond the controversy of the 1880s. Ideological constraints, combined with more formal mechanisms of control such as the pass system, succeeded in marginalizing Aboriginal women and in limiting the alternatives and opportunities available to them.

Local histories of the Prairies suggest that by the turn of the century many of the settlements of the West had their 'local Indian' who was tolerated on the margins or fringes of society and whose behaviour and appearance was the subject of local anecdotes. A solitary Indian woman known only as Liza camped on the outskirts of Virden, MB, for many years until her disappearance sometime in the 1940s. She lived winter and summer in an unheated tent by the railroad tracks although she spent the long winter days huddled in the livery stable and also at times crept into the Nu-Art Beauty Parlour, where she sat on the floor in front of the window, warming herself in the sun. Liza smoked a corncob pipe as she shuffled about the streets and lanes of Virden, rummaging in garbage tins. She bathed under the overflow pipe at the water tower, sometimes clothed and sometimes not, and dried off by standing over the huge heat register in Scales and Rothnie's General Store. To an extent she was tolerated and even assisted; town employees shovelled out a path for her when she was buried under snow, and it was thought that the town fathers supplied her with food from time to time.

The presence of Liza, and the stories told about her, served to sharpen the boundaries of community membership and to articulate what was and what was not considered acceptable and respectable.[47] Liza was the object of both fascination and repugnance as she violated norms of conventional behaviour, dress, and cleanliness, representing the antithesis of 'civilized' Prairie society. Although economically and socially marginal, Liza was symbolically important. Her role attests to the recurrent pattern through which the new society of the West gained in strength and identity and sought to legitimate its own authority by defining itself against the people who were there before them. Liza was a real person, but what she represented was a Euro-Canadian artifact, created by the settlement. The narratives circulated about Liza were not those she might have told herself—of the disasters that had stripped her of family and community, or perhaps of her strategies in adopting the character role—and this folklore reflected less about Liza than about the community itself. Her solitary life was unique and in contrast to the lives of Aboriginal women; Liza was not representative of a Lakota woman within Lakota society. Yet her presence on the margins of the settlement was tolerated and encouraged in the way these women were not, as she appeared to fit into the well-established category of the 'squaw' that still served to confirm the Euro-Canadian newcomers in their belief that their cultural and moral superiority entitled them to the land that had become their home.

Primary Document

2.   Letter from Mrs Mary McNaughton Concerning the Chattels of Indian Women Married to White Men and Living on the Reserve, dated 15 December 1879

To Sir John A. Macdonald
Superintendant General of Indian Affairs

Honourable Sir

I take the liberty of writing you for the purpose of asking you a few questions which I hope you will be kind and condescending enough to answer, relative to my position as an Indian of the Six Nations on the Grand River. In the first place, I will state as briefly as possible, what I am and in what position I am placed. I am an Indian woman of the Cayuga tribe (Sister to the late Dr. G.E. Bomberry one of the chiefs) married previous to the passing of the act of 1869 to a whiteman (a Scotchman) residing with me with my permission, and working on the farm I occupy, and other lands I have rented, for me, and for the support of my family. I have a family of seven children myself and children are all on the paylist of the Six Nation Indians, and have always and all received our annuities since childhood.

I carry on farming in my own name, and harvesting, leased or bargained for any land that I work because the Superintendant said that my husband could not hold or lease any Indian land at all. The Supt. Allowed Indians to hire whitemen to work their farms, therefore I hired my husband to work for me. I shall now with your permission put a few queries.

1ˢᵗ Is my husband a trespasser on Indian land and liable to be turned off upon the complaint of any Indian, and in the event of my dying has my husband any claim on the land for the support of the children who are minors.

2ⁿᵈ What is my husband, a whiteman, an Indian, alien or what is he. For reference See [undecipherable] Indian Act 1876 c98.s40.

3ʳᵈ Can any bailiff seize and sell on judgement and supposition upon goods and chattels belonging to me jointly with my husband for and on which part of my annuity money has been paid. I had a horse seized and sold by the Bailiff of Onondaga Division Court A took the horse from the plough and sold him for a seven dollars and fifty cent judgement, an unjust debt and for which I nor my husband never received any notice.

4ᵗʰ Is a chattel mortgage made jointly by men and my husband legally binding.

5ᵗʰ Is a chattel mortgage made by my husband without my consent on stock goods and chattels, which have been purchased and acquired, with and by means of myself and families annuities, legally binding. And if I pay the sum mentioned in the said mortgage (which I intend to do legal or not) can any other party take the same goods mentioned in the said mortgage and sell them on a judgement and execution against my husband.

6ᵗʰ Is the crop in the ground belonging to me, on Indian land, the land I have leased from an Indian, liable to be seized and sold for myself or my husbands debts. I do not ask these questions for the purpose of evading paying any of my or his just debts.

7th Can I collection damages for the destruction of any crop by unruly horses, cattle, and sheep belonging to whitemen who do not live on the reserve, and who turn them on the reserve, and will not take care of them, and if I can collect, how can I do it, and is whitemens cattle, horses, and sheep who do not live on the reserve, trespasses when found on the reserve (the chiefs have made no regulations as to pounds) and would the Supt. General be so good as urge the Chief and Supt. to act in the matter, as I lose a large portion of my crop every year, by doing so and answering the above questions you will confer a honour on me and other Indian women placed in the same position as I am and really do not know whether our husbands will have to leave the reserve or not. It is called Indian Reserve, but it should be called Whiteman Reserve. Whitemans cattle and horses roam over it in hundreds destroying the poor Indians crop and if he or she remonstrates, all they get is abuse, and if an Indians animal goes over the line they are at once put in pound.

Honourable Sir I Remain
Your Obedient Servant
Mary McNaughton

Secondary Source

3.   Making History: Elsie Marie Knott, Canada's First Female Indian Act Chief

Cora Voyageur

When Elsie Marie Knott threw her hat into the political ring for her band's election in 1952, little did she know that, if elected, she would be making history. Prior to the 1951 amendments to the patriarchal Indian Act[48], women were banned from voting in or running for office in band elections. By choosing Knott as their chief, the 500 members of the Mississaugas of Mud Lake Indian Band (now called the Curve Lake First Nation)[49] were the first to break the gender barrier. Knott would go on to win an additional seven campaigns, serving as chief for 16 years, from 1952 to 1962 and from 1970 to 1976. In the 1976 election, she was defeated by only 12 votes.[50]

In this paper, I explore Knott's personal and professional experiences in her history-making role as chief. I draw on newspaper and magazine articles, diaries and personal papers, family interviews, and other published works.[51] I found that this energetic woman was not only Canada's first female Indian Act chief but also a person committed to improving the lives of band members and an entrepreneur who was determined to overcome her own financial uncertainty. Through her concerns and experiences, we are given a glimpse into the historical, social, economic, and political conditions of Canada's First Nations population.

Knott was born on 20 September 1922 to Esther Mae and George Henry Taylor. The Taylors were a large and well-established family in the Mud Lake Reserve community, and Knott enjoyed the benefits of a large, traditional, and extended family. As a child, she developed an appetite for band politics, community issues, and social matters. She often accompanied her father, who was the caretaker of the band office, to band meetings and community events.

As an Indian, Knott sensed that she was different from other Canadians. She knew that Indians were wards of the government and, as such, were isolated from the outside world and treated differently. At this time in Canadian history, Indians were warehoused on reserves and thought by mainstream society to be a 'vanishing race' that would simply disappear over time. Their mobility was strictly curtailed by an Indian Affairs policy that prohibited them from leaving the reserve without a pass from the Indian agent. This rule meant that there was little interaction between Indians and non-Indians. As a result of this isolation, the young Elsie was afraid of 'white' people. It did not help matters that her parents would scare her into going to bed by telling her to go to sleep because the 'white man' was coming.[52]

Like most students on the Mud Lake Reserve, Knott's formal education ended at grade eight because transportation to the nearest high school (16 miles away in Lakefield) was not provided. At this time, the government's assimilation policy[53] dominated the curriculum and practices at Indian schools. Proponents of the policy thought that allowing traditional languages in schools would slow the assimilation of Indian children. Therefore, students were expected to cast off all notions of their identity and culture and to speak only English while at school. Knott recalled that, when she started school, speaking an Indian language was strictly prohibited. The names of those students 'caught talking Indian' were listed on the blackboard with big Xs beside them.[54]

Married Life

Elsie Knott grew up at a time when most people believed that women should marry and stay at home with their children.[55] When she was 15 years old, her parents arranged her marriage to Cecil Knott, a fellow band member who was 12 years her senior. Cecil suffered from tuberculosis for their entire marriage and was often unable to work because of his illness. At the age of 20, Elsie had three children and was living on social assistance. Although Cecil found seasonal guiding employment, mainly for American hunters in the summer and fall, the family relied on the $12 they received from the government every month. Their financial circumstances forced Elsie to look for work. Kathleen Taylor, her relative, remembered, 'Elsie's late husband was never really healthy. So I suppose, someone had to be the breadwinner and so Elsie took it upon herself.'[56] Knott was not above doing menial work to support her family. Early in her marriage, she dug worms and caught minnows to sell to fisherman for bait. Her first paying job was berry picking in a town outside Toronto. The job paid poorly, and after five weeks she barely made enough to get back home. She also did a variety of other jobs, including being a chambermaid at the Lakefield Hotel, sewing pajamas for children in federal Indian hospitals for 35 cents a pair, and making quilts to sell to tourists. Importantly, she was creative, had an entrepreneurial spirit, and a keen sense of what services were in demand—traits that manifested themselves throughout her life.

Knott's first opportunity to make a steady income on the reserve came by chance. Five children wanted to attend high school, and the Indian agent hired a local man (at $3 per day) to drive them to and from the main highway, where they were picked up by the county school bus. Before long, the man forgot to pick the children up after school and they had to walk the five miles home. The Indian agent approached Knott about driving them until he could find someone else. Seeing an opportunity, she established the Knott Bus Service and drove the children in the family car. When the number of students attending high school increased, she needed a bigger vehicle.[57] Denied a bank loan, she convinced the Indian agent to co-sign a loan for $200 and bought an old hearse, converting it into a school bus by placing bench seats on the floor.[58] The Knott Bus Service, which remains in operation today, eventually grew to include two 78-passenger school buses. Knott drove a school bus for 31 years (including when she was chief). In 1978, she received an award from Minister of Indian Affairs Hugh Faulkner for her 25 years of accident-free driving.[59] She retired from driving in 1993 and died two years later, at the age of 73.[60]

Political Life

Knott ran for office because there were many things about reserve life that she wanted to change. For example, she did not agree that the government should have total control over Indian people but thought that communities needed autonomy and control over their own affairs. She believed that education was important and that reserve children should be successful in school.[61] She was unhappy that the Indian children attending Lakeview High School were not accepted by the white students, who taunted the reserve children by calling them names and throwing rocks at the school bus.[62] Despite these challenges, some of the children she drove to school became successful professionals.

In newspaper interviews, Knott described herself as shy and slightly afraid when she entered the political world. Being unsure of herself, she thought it was 'the biggest joke ever when community members asked her to run for chief'.[63] In her first election, she ran against two other candidates, including the incumbent, Dan Whetung. Her eldest son, Edward (then a teenager), was so afraid that his mother would lose that he crossed the lake in a boat to avoid hearing the election results.[64] Even Knott was unsure that she could beat the two men running against her, but she liked a challenge: 'When I went in by a real big landslide it never dawned on me that I was making history.'[65] But people were ready for a change in leadership. 'I think women can be good at politics. They are more demanding. Everyone helps a woman.'[66]

After winning the election, Knott faced significant challenges. At 31, she was the elected leader of a 500-member band and worked with five band councillors. The community wanted a leader who would produce results, a daunting task considering that band elections were held every two years. Those in leadership usually need the first year to familiarize themselves with the job and the community, assess the issues, and become fully informed. Producing tangible results in such a short time was difficult; however, one of Knott's biggest obstacles was public speaking. Besides the fear of being in front of a crowd, she did not believe that she had a good command of English because Ojibway was her first language:

> I could explain myself better in Indian than in the white language. I would think in Indian and it was hard to translate that in my head. I was afraid to make a mistake in English. I used to start off my talks with a joke. When you have

them laughing you know they have accepted you and it used to give me a good feeling and then I'd lose my shyness right off.[67]

With time, she became more comfortable with public speaking and ultimately became an effective orator.

As the excitement of winning the election waned, Chief Knott knew that she had much work ahead of her. The reserve was mired in poverty and remedies had to be found. Band Secretary Hannah Johnson recalled, 'Elsie always seemed to know what she wanted and she seemed to know how to get it. And she wasn't afraid of saying what she wanted. She was a real worker too.'[68] Knott lived her entire life in the community and knew what needed to be changed. Her daughter Rita Rose said, 'I think her main goal seemed to be helping the Indian people have a better life. She did not like it when a lot of them were poor and abusing alcohol.'[69] Elsie focused a great deal of effort on these social issues and, through a referendum, later prohibited the sale and consumption of alcohol on the reserve.

As Knott became more active in politics and community activities, life in her household changed. Her husband did not cope well with her success and was envious that she was young and full of energy. Rita was 11 when her mother became chief: 'I guess we were expected to do more housework. I cooked a lot when I was young.'[70] All the children were expected to support their mother by helping out at home. Her husband also helped with the running of the household and with taking care of the children, which allowed her to concentrate on band issues. Rita said that her mother either worked around the children's schedules or took them along with her.[71] In 1962, Cecil Knott died from a stroke. After 24 years of marriage, Elsie found herself a widow at the age of 39. She never remarried but kept herself busy with family, community issues, and political advocacy.

The Years in Office

During her tenure as chief, Knott dealt with many barriers and hardships, but she never viewed being a woman as a disadvantage. During an interview with a British newspaper in September 1973, she said, 'I think I can honestly say I never encountered discrimination because I was a woman. I didn't think about it really. I wanted to play my part.'[72] Although some people thought that a woman should not be chief, she persevered and proved that a woman could carry out all the required duties. Her nephew, artist Norman Knott, commented, 'she had enough spunk to get out there and she was right for the job. That's the way they thought in those days. She made a lot of people realize that women can do a lot of things that men can do . . . she opened our eyes.'[73]

Chief Knott was politically astute and was able to identify the power brokers. She developed a good rapport with the Indian agent, A.E. Adams, who worked out of the Peterborough Indian Affairs office. It was important for her to cultivate this relationship because the Indian agent wielded a tremendous amount of power. His stamp of approval was required for every decision made about reserve life. She earned the agent's respect and was able to claim him as an ally.

Newspaper accounts of her early years in office portray Knott as a housewife who took on community duties but had not lost sight of her responsibilities to home and family. She was shown heading a variety of social activities such as fish fries or corn roasts. A 1955 photograph shows her canning preserves while another undated photo captures her reading to children and wearing a headdress.[74] She was depicted as a benevolent, affable individual who was not in any way threatening to mainstream society. Over time, however, her meek and mild demeanour changed. In later years, she became more outspoken and radical in her opinions and did not shy away from controversy. Her daughter remembers her publicly burning the 1969 White Paper on Indian policy and dancing on the ashes at the opening of the annual Curve Lake powwow. Local Member of Parliament Hugh Faulkner was present at the event and later remarked that 'the incident was done in good fun.'[75]

Introduced by the Trudeau government, the White Paper said,

> The Government believes that its policies must lead to the full, free and non-discriminatory participation of the Indian people in Canadian Society. Such a goal requires a break from the past. It requires that the Indian people's role of dependence be replaced by a role of equal status, opportunity and responsibility, a role they can share with all other Canadians.[76]

To fulfill the plan, the government proposed to eliminate the unique status of Indian people and integrate services provided to Indian people with those of mainstream society.[77] These proposed actions touched off a firestorm of Indian protests across the country. Indian people responded to the White Paper with *Citizens Plus* (also known as the **Red Paper**), which was created under the guidance of the Indian Association of Alberta in 1970. The Red Paper suggested that the government abandon all plans to renege on treaty promises and eliminate Indian status and focus instead on improving living conditions in the communities and promoting economic development.[78] The White Paper was eventually withdrawn in 1971.

In 1975, Knott led a protest against provincial legislation that encroached on Treaty Indians' rights to hunt and fish. Three band members had been charged by provincial wildlife authorities for fishing out of season. More than 200 people representing 10 First Nations in Ontario and the Union of Ontario Indians participated in the protest, using civil disobedience to defend their treaty rights. A newspaper account described the incident:

> They fished through half a dozen holes in the ice in open defiance of provincial wildlife authorities who witnessed the four-hour demonstration from shore . . . The 200 year old Indian Act, and revisions in 1923 [under the terms of the Williams Treaty] give native people rights to self-determination including control over the wildlife and band members' use of it. Fisheries legislation of 1951 gives the provinces power to control, among other things, fishing seasons. Ontario has recently started enforcing the fishing laws, claiming they supersede the Indian Act.[79]

Being the first female Indian chief in Canada also brought Knott into some exclusive circles. She met every prime minister from John Diefenbaker to Jean Chrétien. While on vacation in England in June 1973, she was invited to a luncheon with Queen Elizabeth II and Prince Philip. The event was covered by the *West Sussex County Times*

in an article that described Chief Knott as 'an energetic, exuberant, and most exceptional woman'.[80] Although delighted to meet the royals, she was less impressed with
the spartan meal she was served: a little piece of filet mignon, three tiny potatoes, and
two slices of fried cucumber. On the way home, she stopped for a Denver sandwich
because she was still hungry.[81]

Knott remembered England as a beautiful place. She loved the country's history,
the flowers and gardens, and the hospitality that she received from the British people.
While there, however, she felt out of sorts because she was homesick and unaccus-
tomed to leisure time. She was happy to get back to work, family, and community.

Contributions to Community Life

Committed to improving the lives of Curve Lake community members, Chief Knott
took steps throughout her political career to heighten cultural awareness, both on the
reserve and in the surrounding area, by getting people involved in the community. Rita
said that her mother wanted to change situations that she believed were wrong: 'She
was right against the Indian Act and how it put us on little pieces of land—she made a
lot of changes. And she liked to get other people involved . . . to be leaders. She didn't
do it just to help herself. If she had ... she could have been rich but she wasn't.'[82]

In her first year in office, Knott revived events such as the community powwow,
which she viewed as a means of improving the reserve and preserving its culture. The
proceeds from the powwow helped to fund Christmas hampers for needy families.[83]
Because the powwow was open to people from outside the community, it also served
as an opportunity for non-Aboriginal people to experience First Nation culture in a
welcoming and non-threatening way. Chief Knott used such events to promote awareness and appreciation of First Nations people.

Knott was also involved in a variety of local, regional, provincial, and national
organizations. On the reserve, she was a dedicated community worker, organizer, and
fundraiser. She used the funds raised through dances, regattas, and other activities to
buy groceries for the entire village. She wanted to get everybody involved in some form
of community activity, and she organized everything from Boy Scouts and Girl Guides
for the children to men's baseball tournaments. An avid baseball fan, she pitched for
the married women's team for many years.[84] Later, she served as the sports representative for the southeastern region of the Union of Ontario Indians and participated in
hosting a Native hockey tournament with participants from 60 Ontario reserves.[85] She
also organized the Curve Lake Homemakers' Association. Such clubs were created in
the 1930s by the Indian Affairs Branch to promote home economics. Under Knott's
guidance, the Curve Lake club became a breeding ground for political activism and a
place for Indian women to discuss women's issues and community politics.[86]

At the provincial level, she was involved in the Union of Ontario Indians while she
was chief and later as its southeastern region Elder. The Union was formed in 1890, on
the New Credit Reserve near Brantford, to address matters within the Indian Act and to
obtain Indian representation in the House of Commons. It was reorganized in 1969 with
an extended mandate that included the protection of culture and heritage of Ontario's
First Nations people.[87] This organization mirrored Knott's concerns about the loss of
culture and language among members of her community. On the national level, she

served on the board of directors of the National Indian Brotherhood, the forerunner to the Assembly of First Nations. She also pushed for universal franchise for Indians, claiming that 'Indians felt left out of things as long as they could not vote.'[88] She was referring to Governor General Georges Vanier's Throne Speech on 14 January 1960, in which he said, 'Legislation will be introduced to give Indians the franchise in Federal elections.'[89]

Knott also wanted better living conditions for reserve residents. However, negotiating with the government and obtaining funding for reserve programs or for even the most basic needs were difficult tasks. When she took office, there were no wells, the roads were poor, and the houses were mostly run down. Housing was a major concern for her and, in five years, she was able to obtain the resources to have 45 new houses built on the reserve.[90] She worked to bring better roads, streetlights, new wells, and better social services to the community. 'I took advantage of money available. The government wanted to improve the reserves so there were lots of grants out there. We took everything they handed out.'[91] 'I had a new daycare centre built when I was chief.'[92] She noted that, with the daycare centre, the women of the community were able to go out to work or go to school to improve their education and get better employment.[93]

Chief Knott also started a number of community initiatives that drew on volunteers and not money. One example was Decoration Day, which was started in 1952, the year that she was elected. It was a day of beautification that gathered community members together to clean up the cemetery, plant flowers, and paint, followed by a picnic and fish fry. The Salvation Army band from Peterborough performed for the community. It was a great community-building effort that brought the people closer together.

As mentioned earlier, Chief Knott was concerned about the loss of Ojibway culture due to the assimilation efforts of church, school, and Indian Affairs. She brought traditional teachers to the reserve to help the people re-learn drumming, dancing, and singing and to make their own regalia. She and Gladys Taylor taught weekly Ojibway language classes on the reserve. These classes were included in the schools as part of the educational curriculum for children. She also translated 14 Christmas carols for children to sing at a concert.[94] Adult Ojibway language classes had about a dozen participants at any given time and continued for approximately two years.[95]

Knott also believed in education. She wanted reserve children to succeed in school, and she helped them in a variety of ways. Artist Randy Knott said, 'I was so scared to leave the reserve and go to the other school. But through her we all got brave.'[96] Former student Winston Taylor recalled, 'Her example inspired me when I went back to school. She was that kind of lady who made up her mind to do something and she just did it.'[97] Judge Tim Whetung often stopped to visit her and thank her for having driven him to school when he was a boy.[98]

Political Defeat

While Elsie Knott's political career was lengthy, it was not easy. She was also not without her critics. Hannah Johnson said that people had strong feelings against her.[99] Doug Williams, who defeated Knott in the 1976 election, was critical of her and her council, saying that 'the council she was heading then was a "yes" council. It was practicing nepotism at this time. A lot of grants were forthcoming and many on the council were getting jobs. I was just clearly dissatisfied with the way things were going.

I ran because I wanted to let Elsie know there were ill feelings on the reserve.'[100] Chief Williams also claimed that Knott had taken the election loss hard and was vengeful.[101]

Knott took Williams's criticism personally. She said, 'I worked hard for the little I got. Some say I got ahead too fast.'[102] She was disappointed at losing the election and her role as chief:

> I should have given it up instead of losing it. I think that was a shock. Afterwards, I didn't know who my friends were. I didn't trust anyone. My nerves bother me sometimes. I took things personally. If someone criticized me just a little bit of what I did or didn't do it would bother me for a night. I would toss and turn just thinking about that one subject. But I think I did my best anyway.[103]

Knott believed that she had lost the election because 'the old people did not come out to vote. My supporters thought I would win by a landslide and thought that their votes would not be needed. The young people were pushing for the other guy.'[104] She added, 'the first thing that Williams guy did was change the law that you could not work for the band and run for public office. I could not run as long as I have [sic] the bus contract for the band.'[105] When asked if she would run again, she said that she would have to think twice about it. Given her long term in public office, the electorate believed they wanted a change in leadership.

Later in life, Knott received accolades and recognition from across the country and was the subject of many newspaper and magazine articles. In 1975, International Women's Year, she was named one of Ontario's 25 outstanding women, along with geneticist Irene Ayako Uchinda, women's advocate Grace Hartman, and academic librarian Margaret Beckman. In 1980, Lois Franks of Boston University wrote a play about her called *Elsie, Indian Chief, Bus Driver, Shopkeeper, Grannie*.[106] Elsie Marie Knott died on 3 December 1995, with 3 children, 10 grandchildren, and 13 great-grandchildren to mourn her loss. Honouring her passing in the Ontario legislature, Member of Provincial Parliament R. Gary Stewart described her as a friend, mother, and leader of a community that benefited from her hard work and love of life.[107]

Elsie Knott was an unlikely political leader. She started out as a shy woman married to an unhealthy older man. Over the years, she transformed into a dedicated and effective leader who worked hard to improve the lifestyles and living conditions of members of her community. Financial circumstances caused her to move beyond her comfort zone and take chances that she might not ordinarily have taken. Dalton Jacobs said, 'She was someone with tenacity and a strong work ethic. She would have done well in any community but I am just happy that she was part of my community.'[108] Community members remembered her fondly and commented on her community work. 'She was a pioneer and she made real accomplishments,' according to band member Margaret Spencely.[109]

In the early years of her leadership, Knott was singled out continually as the 'woman chief'. This description was a blessing and a curse. The recognition that came with the position of chief could work to one's benefit. She mentioned that people were more likely to help a woman and less likely to refuse her requests for assistance. She was portrayed in the media as a community worker but also as a woman who maintained the traditional caregiving role of wife and mother. She appeared to have simply increased her family size to include the entire band when she became chief. She was non-threatening as an Indian leader, a characteristic that would have been comforting to local non-First Nations people who had limited contact with and knowledge of First Nations people.

However, being the sole woman in a man's environment brought isolation and loneliness. Her fame and her deep sense of duty invaded her privacy. Her work impinged on family time and occasionally caused resentment among family members. It also left her little personal time for rejuvenation and reflection. Knott dedicated her adult life to the community. She also held various jobs during her political career, working as a domestic, postmistress, bus driver, store owner, and church superintendent. For her, these jobs represented financial security. In a community with high unemployment, however, some people saw her as an elected person seizing opportunities for herself and her family instead of allowing others to compete for them. She was accused of conflict of interest, nepotism, and benefiting from confidential information. In short, her multiple jobs caused resentment in the community, and this resentment was the basis of her political defeat.

Unfortunately, Elsie Knott did not have the opportunity to leave community politics on her own terms. She was forced out. Her final campaign was bitter and she was hurt by allegations that her financial assets had been gained by other than honourable means. The defeat took a huge personal toll on her. For Elsie Knott, being chief was more than just a job. It had served as a means to become a respected and confident person. She used her skills and innovative ways to bring improved living conditions and upgraded services to her community. The job kept her busy and helped her cope after the death of her husband. As chief, she moved from anonymity to fame. In his eulogy, Father Paul Heffernan intimated that sometimes one person can make a difference in a community. Summing up Knott's character, he said, 'With Elsie, the difficult was easy, the impossible took a little longer.'[110]

Primary Document

4.   Excerpt from the Indian Act, 1951

Election of Chiefs and Band Councils

73. (1)   Whenever he deems it advisable for the good government of a band, the Governor in Council may declare by order that after a day to be named therein the council of the band, consisting of a chief and councillors, shall be selected by elections to be held in accordance with this Act.

   (2)   The Council of a band in respect of which an order has been made under subsection (1) shall consist of one chief, and one councillor for every one hundred members of the band, but the number of councillors shall not be less than two nor more than twelve and no band shall have more than one chief.

   (3)   The Governor in Council may, for the purposes of giving effect to subsection (1), make orders or regulations to provide

   (a)   that the chief of a band shall be elected by
      (i) a majority of votes of the electors of the band

or

    (ii) a majority of the votes of the elected councillors of the band from among themselves, but the chief so elected shall remain a councillor,

(b) that the councillors of a band shall be elected by

    (i) a majority of the votes of the electors of the band

or

    (ii) a majority of the votes of the electors of the band in the electoral section in which the candidate resides and that he proposes to represent on the council of the band,

(c) that a reserve shall for voting purposes be divided into not more than six electoral sections containing as nearly as may be an equal number of Indians eligible to vote, and

(d) for the manner in which electoral sections established under paragraph (c) shall be distinguished or identified.

74. (1) No persons other than an elector who resides in a section may be nominated for the office of councillor to represent that section on the council of the band.

   (2) No person may be a candidate for election as chief or councillor unless his nomination is moved and seconded by persons who are themselves eligible to be nominated.

75. (1) The Governor in Council may make orders and regulations with respect to band elections, and without restricting the generality of the foregoing, may make regulations with respect to

(a) meetings to nominate candidates,

(b) the appointment and duties of electoral officers,

(c) the manner in which voting shall be carried out,

(d) election appeals, and

(e) the definition of residence for the purpose of determining eligibility of voters.

   (2) The regulations made under paragraph (c) of the subsection (1) shall make provision for secrecy of voting.

76. (1) A member of a band who is of the full age of twenty-one years and is ordinarily resident on the reserve is qualified to vote for a person nominated to be chief of the band, and where the reserve for voting purposes consists of one section, to vote for persons nominated as councillors.

    (2) A member of a band who is of the full age of twenty-one years and is ordinarily resident in a section that has been established for voting purposes is qualified to vote for a person nominated to be councillor to repreent that section.

77. (1) Subject to this section, chiefs and councillors hold office for two years.

   (2) The office of chief or councillor becomes vacant when

(a) the person who holds that office

    (i) is convicted of an indictable offence

    (ii) dies or resigns his office, or

    (iii) is or becomes ineligible to hold office by virtue of this Act; or

    (b) the Minister declares that in his opinion the person who holds that office

        (i)   is unfit to continue in office by reason of his having been convicted of an offence,

        (ii) has been absent from meetings of the council for three consecutive meetings without being authorized to do so, or

        (iii) was guilty, in connection with an election, of corrupt practice, accepting a bribe, dishonesty or malfeasance.

    (3) The Minister may declare a person who ceases to hold office by virtue of sub paragraph (iii) of paragraph (b) of subsection (2) to be ineligible to be a candidate for chief or councillor for a period not exceeding six years.

78. The Governor in Council may set aside the election of a chief or councillor on the report of the Minister that he is satisfied that

    (a) there was corrupt practice in connection with the election

    (b) there was a violation of this Act that might have affected the result of the election, or

    (c) a person nominated to be a candidate in the election was ineligible to be a candidate.

79. The Governor in Council may make regulations with respect to band meetings and council meetings and without restricting the generality of the foregoing, may make regulations with respect to

    (a) presiding officers at such meetings,

    (b) notice of such meetings,

    (c) the duties of any representative of the Minister at such meetings, and

    (d) the number of person required at the meeting to constitute a quorum.

Questions for Consideration

1. What negative images of Aboriginal women did the Canadian government and Euro-Canadian newcomers promote? Why did they portray Aboriginal women this way?

2. Why did Samuel Trivett's accusations regarding the improprieties of government officials and members of the NWMP cause such a scandal in 1886? Who was blamed for the alleged misbehaviour and why?

3. How does Mary McNaughton's letter to Sir John A. Macdonald contradict the standard image of Aboriginal women during this time?

4. Discuss the historical significance of Elsie Knott's life.

5. How did Elsie Knott's leadership benefit the people of Curve Lake First Nation?

6. According to the excerpt from the 1951 Indian Act, who could become chief of an 'Indian' band? Under what circumstances could a chief be removed by the Governor in Council? Was the retention of this power to intervene in bands' affairs justified? Why or why not?

7. What roles has the Canadian state attempted to consign to Aboriginal women? In what ways have Aboriginal women adopted and resisted these roles?

Further Resources

Books and Articles

Anderson, Kim. *A Recognition of Being: Reconstructing Native Womanhood*. Toronto: Sumach Press, 2001.

Anderson, Kim, and Bonita Lawrence, eds. *Strong Women Stories: Native Vision and Community Survival*. Toronto: Sumach Press, 2003.

Miller, Christine, and Patricia Chuchryk, eds. *Women of the First Nations: Power, Wisdom and Strength*. Winnipeg: University of Manitoba Press, 1996.

Smith, Andrea. *Conquest: Sexual Violence and American Indian Genocide*. Cambridge, MA: South End Press, 2005.

Printed Documents and Reports

Jamieson, Kathleen. *Indian Women and the Law in Canada: Citizens Minus*. Ottawa: Canadian Advisory Council on the Status of Women and Indian Rights for Indian Women, 1978.

Native Women's Association of Canada. *Aboriginal Women and the Implementation of Bill C-31*. Ottawa: Native Women's Association of Canada, 1991.

Films

Finding Dawn. DVD. Directed by Christine Welsh. NFB, 2006.

Nose and Tina. DVD. Directed by Linda Bailey. NFB, 1980.

Places not Our Own (part of the *Daughters of the Country* series). DVD. Directed by Derek Mazur. NFB, 1986.

Senorita Extraviada, Missing Young Woman. DVD. Directed by Lourdes Portillo. Independent Television Services, 2001.

The True Story of Linda M. DVD. Directed by Norma Bailey. NFB, 1995.

Websites

Amnesty International's Stolen Sisters Campaign
www.amnesty.ca/campaigns/sisters_overview.php

Assembly of First Nations' Women's Council
www.afn.ca/index.php/en/policy-areas/afn-womens-council

Curve Lake First Nation
www.curvelakefirstnation.ca

Native Women's Association of Canada
www.nwac.ca

THIRTEEN

Negotiating Health and Well-Being

Introduction

Very little attention has been paid to the importance of the aquatic environment in the lives of Aboriginal people. This oversight was partly caused by Europeans' and Euro-Canadians' long-standing disdain for cultures and diets based on fish and other aquatic foodstuffs. For example, British fur traders working on the West Coast often described Aboriginal people who relied heavily on a diet of fish as 'lazy, feckless, physically weak, and prone to starvation'.[1] Such characterizations say more about the fur traders' cultural ideologies, beliefs about food, and perception of hunting as a manly endeavour than it does about the reality of Aboriginal peoples' lives, cultures, and relationships with the environment.[2] The neglect of the aquatic environment in the history of North America has been perpetuated by the prominence of the fur trade, which continues to be the subject of a great deal of fascination and mythmaking. Consequently, the significance of fish and water to Aboriginal peoples who do not occupy a coastal region remains relatively unrecognized. While the majority of Aboriginal peoples combined a range of economic activities, including fishing, hunting, gathering, and farming, the historical focus has remained on fur. A similar historical myopia exists around the practice of agriculture among Aboriginal groups.[3]

As Betty Bastien makes clear in Chapter One, the Blackfoot (and Aboriginal cultures generally) place a great deal of value on their interconnectedness with their environment. This relationship sustains the people, and, accordingly, environmental degradation represents profound cultural distress. Thus, it is all the more puzzling that historians have looked to the decline of fur-bearing resources as the cause of ill-health and starvation among Aboriginal peoples but have largely ignored the devastating impact of declining access to water resources as a result of commercial fishing and pollution. Liza Piper suggests that both Aboriginal and environmental historians have overlooked the central role that fish played in the freshwater ecosystems in the Canadian Northwest and in the health and well-being of Aboriginal communities. She emphasizes the consequences that severing the connection between the aquatic environment and Aboriginal people had on the latter's health. Piper argues that the rise of industrial fisheries and the interest of Euro-Canadians in this enterprise fundamentally transformed the relationship between fish, people, and freshwater ecosystems. Direct and indirect connections can be drawn between the pollution of the Dauphin River, the depletion of fish stocks, and the well-being of the Aboriginal people who made use of these resources. Contaminated water caused outbreaks of illnesses such as typhoid, and the depletion of fish stocks eroded people's abilities to sustain their families and communities.

Gabrielle Parent's article similarly emphasizes the 'intimate and complex relationship with their aquatic environment' of the Ojibwa and Oji-Cree living in northwestern Ontario. In addition to providing them with food, 'the lakes and rivers shaped the Northern Ojibwa and Oji-Cree's culture and traditions, their stories, their technologies, their population movements, and their economy.' According to Parent, we must acknowledge the importance of this connection in order to understand how the changes wrought by settlement, environmental degradation, the depletion of fish, and the imposition of environmental regulations affected the Ojibwa and Oji-Cree. Trying to understand the health and well-being of people separate from the environment in which they live reduces health and well-being to a biological function and causes historians to misidentify the source of ill-health. As anthropologist Naomi Adelson eloquently writes, 'health and identity are linked as part and parcel of the ongoing struggle for voice and endurance in a world that has, over the years, muted and disenfranchised Native people's existence.'[4]

Chapter Objectives

At the end of this chapter, you should be able to

- understand the important role that the aquatic environment and fisheries played in the economic and personal lives of many Aboriginal communities;
- recognize the interconnectedness of environmental health and personal well-being;
- identify the differences between Western and Aboriginal perspectives on health and well-being; and
- understand the connections between economic activities, personal health, and a community's world views.

Secondary Source

1.   Industrial Fisheries and the Health of Local Communities in the Twentieth-Century Canadian Northwest

Liza Piper

Fish are neglected creatures in Canadian, Aboriginal, and environmental histories. Although Harold Innis's *The Cod Fisheries* (1940) is a much more effective and comprehensive statement on the role of staples in Canadian history, his earlier *The Fur Trade of Canada* (1930) is far better known. In *Traders' Tales* (1997), Elizabeth Vibert explores European cultural preferences for animal flesh, noting explorer and cartographer David Thompson's explicit contrast that fish 'can never compensate the want of Deer,

Sheep, and Goats'.[5] That animals occupied the pre-eminent position in Western food hierarchies meant that European observers often discounted the value and importance of fish to Aboriginal populations and livelihoods—a bias reproduced by historians who have foregrounded fur over fin. The lower status of fish in history is not only a product of culture but also of environment. As mammals, we share our environment most immediately with other warm-blooded terrestrial creatures. Because aquatic environments, whether freshwater, marine, or in-between (such as estuaries, marshes, and mangroves), are much less familiar to us, we have, throughout history, remained much more ignorant of aquatic character and complexity.[6]

The integral role of fish in western Canadian Aboriginal history lies at the heart of this essay. Fish were an essential part of healthy freshwater ecosystems across Canada's Northwest, a region extending from Lake Winnipeg to the Mackenzie Delta. The area encompasses four of Canada's largest lakes—Lake Winnipeg, Lake Athabasca, Great Slave Lake, and Great Bear Lake—among countless mid-sized and small lakes, rivers, marshlands, bogs, creeks, sloughs, and ponds. A saturated place with extreme temperature variations, the Northwest historically offered an immense, rich habitat for a range of fish species. Prior to the late-nineteenth-century rise of industrial fisheries, these fish were central to Northwest Aboriginal and non-Aboriginal peoples' subsistence practices, and, by extension, human health. Fish were ultimately transformed into a commercial export product by the early twentieth century. Part of this transformation involved severing fish from their freshwater habitats while conceptually making these creatures separate from, rather than integral to, human livelihoods across the Northwest. This essay uses the example of the Dauphin River hatchery in Manitoba to explore the health consequences of this transformation and, in particular, of the separation of fish, water, and people. Before we can discuss the specific case of Dauphin River, we need to briefly examine the longer history of freshwater fisheries in the Northwest and the relationship between fish, Aboriginal and non-Aboriginal peoples, and the health of freshwater ecosystems.

Pre-Contact and Colonial Fisheries

In the pre-contact era, freshwater fish flourished in the waters that run across the Precambrian Shield and in the Assiniboine, Red, and Saskatchewan rivers, which cross the western interior. In summer, fish could be easily taken from parkland waters, and the autumn spawning runs provided opportunities to harvest concentrated fish populations on the boundaries between the parkland and the shield.[7] In certain places, as in the radial arms of Great Bear Lake, year-round fishing sites provided a greater, more reliable source of nutrition than could be harvested from the land. Aboriginal technologies and cultures demonstrate the importance of freshwater fishing to pre- and early contact Aboriginal populations west of Lake Superior. The **Dene** of the Northwest and the Ojibwe and Saulteaux of Lake Winnipeg employed the widest range of fishing tools, including traps, spears, hooks, nets, and weirs. Gillnets, nets used to catch fish of a certain size by the gills, predated the arrival of European technology. Aboriginal nets, woven using willow bast, had to be kept moist and required more maintenance than those made of Italian twine, which were introduced later. For Cree and Ojibwe living near Lake Winnipeg, the lake sturgeon figured as a prominent spirit in their cosmology.

With the arrival of Europeans, sturgeon shifted from the spiritual to the earthly realm, marking the onset of the colonial era (contact to *c.* 1880) fishery.[8] Freshwater fish of all kinds, particularly inconnu (*Stenodus leucichthys*), whitefish (*Coregonus clupeaformis*), and sturgeon (*Acipenser fulvescens*) became essential energy sources for the missions and the fur trade. Freshwater fish suited Catholic and Anglican endeavours because it was a reliable source of nutrition and it met with Christian dietary restrictions for Lent. The persistent regularity of fishing in fur-trade records signals its importance to the dominant commerce of the eighteenth- and nineteenth-century Northwest. For example, the Hudson's Bay Company (HBC) hired Orkneymen as expert fishermen. The HBC and its competitors also situated their posts at productive fish sites and kept stores of fish through the winter months. During the winter of 1820, George Simpson (who was then HBC governor-in-chief and was overwintering in the Northwest) described regular work at the Old Fort Fishery on Lake Athabasca.[9] Late-nineteenth-century journals from Norway House describe an annual cycle of harvesting pike (*Esox lucius*, also known as jackfish) in spring, sturgeon in the summer, and whitefish in the fall and winter.[10] Yet the HBC was only ever interested in the fisheries as a support to its fur business, never as a resource opportunity in and of itself. In 1841, Simpson ordered a halt to an export fishery established at Fort William (Thunder Bay) by retired company servants. He expressed concern that local Aboriginal peoples 'expected to be supplied with agricultural implements, seed, [and] permanent occupation as fishermen and otherwise'.[11] Not wanting to divert effort from the fur trade or to become responsible for the maintenance of settlements oriented around other resource pursuits, Simpson and the HBC encouraged fishing only insofar as it fuelled hunters, traders, their families, and their dogs.

The advent of the colonial period of freshwater fish exploitation changed how many and which species of fish were harvested across the Northwest. Nevertheless, there is little evidence to suggest widespread unsustainable relationships with freshwater ecosystems prior to 1880. As Shepard Krech has argued, the sustainability of freshwater ecosystems had less to do with the place of fish in Aboriginal cosmologies than with their material relationships with the rest of nature.[12] In the colonial era, as before, freshwater fish consumption remained within the region. Increased exploitation reflected demographic changes and shifts in the consumption of fish products across the Northwest. For example, fisheries facilitated more permanent settlements during the colonial era. Where previously a large Indigenous population might have met seasonally to harvest a rich fishery, many of these same sites sustained year-round harvesting by the eighteenth and nineteenth centuries. To understand this shift, we can visualize fur trade and mission posts as places of intensified fishing activity. Local depletion at these sites meant that residents increasingly relied on fish from nearby areas and that the harvesting pressures created by colonial era fisheries increasingly radiated outwards from the posts. After 1850, the adoption of dogs—fed and therefore fuelled with fish—as a principal means of winter transportation also significantly increased demand. Collectively, these circumstances meant that freshwater fish populations were more widely and more regularly harvested and that a greater variety of fish species were heavily exploited compared to the pre-contact period, when greater harvests occurred locally and varied over the course of the year and across a given region.

Industrial Fisheries after 1880

The rise of industrial export fisheries in the late nineteenth century significantly changed relationships between fish, people, and freshwater ecosystems across the Northwest. The new industrial fisheries had a much more immediate and negative impact upon freshwater ecosystems than their predecessors. Signs of depletion and ecological damage appeared within a few years of the new fisheries opening, while more serious problems manifested within decades. Lake Winnipeg was the first Northwest lake from which freshwater fish were caught for export markets in the 1880s. Harvesting from Lake Winnipeg reached a historic peak in 1904–05. The harvests crashed shortly after, recovered during the 1910s and 1920s, and collapsed again during the 1930s, never to wholly revive. Lake Winnipeg's neighbour, Lake Winnipegosis, also showed signs of overfishing in the opening decades of the twentieth century. By 1930, the Dominion Fisheries inspector, J.B. Skaptason, observed that there 'can be no doubt' that Lake Manitoba, the third of Manitoba's largest lakes, was 'being fished beyond its capacity'.[13] From the intensification of local harvesting that characterized the colonial era, the industrial export era vastly increased the scale of production across the region. Industrial fishers would identify lakes that had yet to be commercially exploited, harvest the 'virgin' waters until depletion led to decreasing returns, and then move on.

Industrial fisheries affected the health of freshwater ecosystems in a number of ways. Commercial harvesting changed fish populations in lakes and rivers. Gillnet fisheries, which prevailed across the Northwest, preferentially harvested large, heavy, fast-growing fish. As a result, slow-growing, smaller fish were able to thrive. In some places, an alteration in lake demographics led to the extirpation of commercial species (most notably lake sturgeon) and the loss of genetic diversity in freshwater environments. In addition to direct impacts on fish species, industrial harvesting generated enormous quantities of waste, including fish guts (offal), spoiled fish, and 'rough' fish (non-commercial species), that further affected freshwater ecosystems. The majority of this waste was simply dumped back into the lakes or rivers from which the fish were taken. In the 1950s, one federal scientist argued that the waste acted as a fertilizer to help younger generations of fish. Experienced fishermen thought otherwise. According to Fred Fraser, a local government official from the Northwest Territories, 'Old experienced fishermen, who have worked Lake Winnipeg, Winnipegosis, Lesser Slave and Athabasca, are unanimous, and vociferous in condemning the dumping of dead fish or offal in lake water. They blame that practice for the deterioration of fishing in all lakes . . . the rotten offal spreads disease and death.'[14] Rotten fish offal had direct health consequences; not only did it leave the water oily and tasting like fish, but it could also cause gastroenteritis (an inflammation of the gastrointestinal tract leading to acute diarrhea). Fish offal dumped directly offshore at fish-packing sites across the Northwest also led to local eutrophication, with the additional organic nutrients infused into the lake waters.[15] This change in trophic conditions drove whitefish away from the shallow waters.

Across the Northwest, Aboriginal people were repeatedly the first to notice and protest the degradation of freshwater environments. For example, Great Slave Lake was closely monitored by scientists and bureaucrats from the Fisheries Research Board (FRB) since it had been opened to commercial fishing in 1945. However, it was local, predominantly Aboriginal, populations that first identified signs of depletion. It took six years of calling for the restriction of industrial operations before the FRB finally confirmed their findings and responded.[16] In Great Slave Lake and other areas, local Aboriginal people were directly involved in industrial harvesting but lacked sufficient control over resource exploitation to effectively adjust harvesting practices to minimize depletion. Instead, they had to press provincial and federal authorities to make the necessary changes.

Early responses to overfishing focused on using fish hatcheries as the best means to restore populations or to introduce commercial or sport fish into new waters. George Colpitts noted that the Department of Marine and Fisheries began working with fisheries scientists and local protective associations to advance a larger program of fisheries conservation.[17] The department also opened a large whitefish hatchery in Selkirk, just south of Lake Winnipeg, in 1893. Initial hatchery work in the Northwest was focused in Manitoba, with several more hatcheries for whitefish and pickerel opened on lakes Winnipeg, Manitoba, and Winnipegosis after 1907. The federal government built hatcheries further west: in Banff in 1913 and Fort Qu'Appelle in 1915. As one hatchery superintendent, George Butler, reported in 1930, 'The principal work of the Prairie hatcheries has been to replenish the supply of whitefish and pickerel on the large commercial fishing lakes, although of late years increasing attention has been paid to sport fishing lakes and the propagation of sport fish.'[18]

The Manitoba freshwater fish hatcheries reveal the industrial fisheries' significant effect on environmental health in the Northwest. The need for hatcheries to 'restock' commercial populations on the largest lakes in Manitoba exposed the ill-health of freshwater ecosystems caused by rapidly intensified harvesting. Fish populations—particularly the most sought-after commercial species, such as lake whitefish, goldeye (*Hiodon alosoides*), sturgeon, pickerel (or walleye, *Stizostedion vitreum*), and lake trout (*Salvelinus namaycush*)—suffered directly from the new character of the fisheries. People who depended on these fish populations as part of their regular diet, especially people who lived along the lake shores and fished either for their home or as part of the commercial industry, faced seasonal malnutrition or had to adjust their diets in light of the scarcity of once-common fish.

Hatcheries and Health on the Dauphin River

There was more to the role of hatcheries in Aboriginal health than matters of nutrition. One of the richest fishing sites in Manitoba was located where the Dauphin River flowed into Lake Winnipeg, connecting Lake Manitoba to its larger neighbour. Important whitefish and pickerel spawning grounds in this area ensured plentiful harvests. Lake whitefish usually spawned in shallower, inshore waters with hard or stony bottoms. Spawning occurred in the fall, when the eggs were 'deposited more or less randomly over the spawning grounds by the parents'.[19] The eggs remained on the spawning ground until hatching in April or May. Pickerel spawned in the spring or early summer, on coarse-gravelled lake bottoms or in river pools. Unlike whitefish, they moved into tributary rivers (such as the Dauphin River) as soon as the river was ice-free, which preceded the break-up of ice on the lake. They spawned at night in large numbers; eggs would hatch within a few weeks, but the young stayed in deep crevices until late summer.[20] Spawning grounds across the Northwest acted as important harvesting sites: fish congregated there to spawn, and predators (including adults of the same species that cannibalized their young) gathered to feast on the large numbers of juvenile fish. That pickerel and whitefish typically sought shallower, near-shore waters for spawning also facilitated harvesting from shore or in smaller boats than those required to sail the often stormy and turbulent waters of the largest lakes.

Aboriginal people returned to the mouth of the Dauphin River annually as part of their seasonal harvesting patterns. The richness of the site also attracted commercial operators. The first export-oriented commercial fishing company on Lake Winnipeg, Reid and Clarke, set up their first commercial operation at this site in 1881.[21] With the construction of the Gull Harbour hatchery (close to Hecla) in 1914, the government maintained a spawn camp at the Dauphin River to supply the new hatchery. Eggs were transported on a government steamer, the *SS Bradbury*. Unfortunately, many eggs did not survive the journey, and the Gull Harbour hatchery was replaced with a new operation at the Dauphin River itself in 1936. Fisheries officials relied on Aboriginal knowledge of the Dauphin River area to help assess where and when to harvest spawn. As Skaptason wrote to his superior, A.G. Cunningham, 'We were informed at Dauphin River by Indians that there is a considerable run of fish up the River the latter part of August, but that is entirely too early for our purpose.'[22] By the 1940s, Aboriginal people from the St Martin, Fairford, and Dauphin River reserves, as well as nearby communities, such as Gypsumville and Sandy Bay, acquired fishing licences (another twentieth-century regulatory measure introduced to control fishing and address problems of overharvesting) to fish at this site. Some Aboriginal people came to be characterized not as fishers but as 'poachers' because they continued their long-standing harvesting activities in waters now re-defined as restricted to fishing.[23]

Locating a hatchery at Dauphin River, a rich fishing site and seasonal gathering place, was not, of course, a coincidence. Both hatchery work and subsistence harvesting depended on the same environmental opportunities. There is no evidence to suggest that provincial fisheries officials saw any conflict between the hatchery and harvesting at the same site. Indeed, the hatchery superintendent was also responsible for distributing fishing licences. Local Aboriginal men and women were hired to work at the hatchery, in fisheries-related tasks (e.g., collecting spawn), or as cooks, maids, and casual labourers. The hatchery thus became integrated into the social life of the region. Likewise, the buildings and equipment were connected to the physical environment. The hatchery and a neighbouring residence were constructed from nearby timbers. Local wood resources supplied the fuel for the *SS Bradbury* and the hatchery buildings. Local men submitted tenders to cut jackpine, tamarack, and poplar for cord wood.[24] Hatchery work also relied on the provision of water, which closely bound the hatchery to the immediate physical environment. An intake pipe continuously drew 'a large volume of water' from the Dauphin River. This water was essential for the hatchery operations, where eggs, fry, and fingerlings had to be kept submerged in moving water. It was 'also used as a supply for the plumbing systems in both buildings [the residence and the hatchery], and, in addition to being used for ordinary domestic purposes, may also be used for drinking.'[25] Thus, the hatchery became intricately caught up in the hydrological system connecting the Dauphin River with Lake Winnipeg.

In November 1943, word reached the Game & Fisheries administration in Winnipeg of a serious epidemic at Dauphin River. George Butler, now supervisor of Fisheries, was consulted about the history of epidemics at this site. Butler, who had worked at Dauphin River 'spawn-taking' since 1923, remarked that, over the years, he had experienced repeated 'periods of distress and slight dysentery that I attributed to something in the water'.[26] During construction of the new hatchery in 1936, many of the men working on the building had also contracted dysentery, a general term for a range of gastrointestinal disorders that involve the inflammation of the intestine, leading to bloody diarrhea and, possibly, death. Where dysentery is caused by bacteria, it can spread easily through contaminated water. Butler observed that 'after freeze-up it usually passed away' and attributed the ailment to decomposing algae or 'liberating toxins or poisons in the water'.[27] Indeed, he considered it to be a 'seasonal sickness' and hence was unsurprised by the prospect of serious illness in November. Ultimately, the reports of an epidemic in 1943 seemed exaggerated as there was no further news of sickness. The deaths of three small children were confirmed but were ascribed to 'under-nourishment and lack of medical attention, rather than from any epidemic'.[28] While the absence of further evidence prevents conclusive analysis, it is noteworthy from an environmental health perspective that, during a period when the region's fish populations suffered from overharvesting, malnutrition and limited access to health care may have played a role in the deaths. Moreover, malnutrition at Dauphin River would have made the people in this community more vulnerable to other kinds of infections. That said, the characterization of Aboriginal people as unwilling to use Western medicine and unable to feed their children properly reflected widely held attitudes among the dominant society in this period. By 20 November 1943, with no one else apparently ill, the medical director of Health deemed the matter closed.[29]

During the following winter, families from the nearby reserves of St Martin, Fairford, and Dauphin River made their usual journey to fish on Lake Winnipeg. By March, over 300 people had been living at Dauphin River for several months and about 100 fishing licences were issued. The families lived in 20 or more log cabins along the riverbanks and in the bush. They carried water from the river to the cabins for food and washing. Food was harvested from the bush and the lake, although at least one cow and one goat were also kept in the community for milk, and some staple foods could be purchased from a small store situated on the hatchery property. Frequent dances and box socials were held. People fished both for themselves and commercially, with a large fish shed serving as the packing plant for the commercial fishery.

Although the fishing was good that winter, there were tragic consequences. One hatchery worker, a non-Treaty Aboriginal man who lived just outside the northern limit of the Dauphin River Reserve, died from tuberculosis in early April. His death was followed by that of two small girls. In short order, an epidemic broke out—another 26 people fell ill either at Dauphin River or after their return to their own reserves.[30] Among those affected, sixteen were under the age of 20 (and half of those were under the age of 10), nine were adults between the ages of 20 and 50, and only one was over 50.

The epidemic was confirmed as typhoid, an acute, highly infectious disease caused by the bacillus *Salmonella typhi*. Transmitted primarily through contaminated food and water, the disease manifests in a high fever, headache, diarrhea or constipation, coughing, and rose-coloured spots on the skin. Intestinal hemorrhaging can also occur, although it is relatively rare. Prior to the availability of effective antibiotics, approximately 10 per cent of those infected with the bacillus died. These antibiotics were available in North America by 1942; however, more remote communities in the Northwest had limited access to them.

Investigations into the outbreak focused on two key features of the local environment: living conditions at Dauphin River and the character of the hatchery and settlement water supplies. In their reports, Chief Sanitary Inspector John Foggie, L.J. Hunter (one of Foggie's employees), and Director of Health C.R. Donovan concentrated first on the living conditions. This focus reflected in part the character of the outbreak. Because women and children were most significantly affected, it was thought that the typhoid was food-borne rather than water-borne. However, widely held racist attitudes towards Aboriginal people also significantly influenced what the inspectors saw and reported. Donovan and Hunter each drew attention to the 'extremely over-crowded' conditions at Dauphin River. Hunter specified that 'during the fishing and trapping seasons, many families move in [sic] the Dauphin River mouth district. As this migration or trek is annual, the over-crowded living conditions are present every year during certain seasons. It, therefore, follows that each family should provide their own shelter in this area.'[31] This attitude spoke to commonly held attitudes among government officials who, since the nineteenth century, had endeavoured to force Aboriginal people to change how they lived to meet the expectations of the settler society. In this instance, communal housing was seen as a menace to public health—even if it was only for the few months when people came to Dauphin River to fish. Hunter and Foggie characterized general sanitary conditions as 'filthy', 'ill-kept', and 'careless'. As the inspectors' reports made their way through the bureaucracy, greater attention was paid to the issue of living conditions. A.G. Cunningham, the director of Game and Fisheries, wrote to Deputy Minister D.M. Stephens, foregrounding how 'Living conditions among Indians on the Dauphin River reservation are extremely unsanitary and conducive to the breeding of infectious and contagious diseases.'[32] Cunningham wanted this matter brought to the attention of the federal Department of Indian Affairs. He also implied that the presence of the Aboriginal fishing camp posed a potential hazard to the health of hatchery employees (those for whom Cunningham himself was directly responsible).[33]

Only after addressing the living conditions at Dauphin River was close attention given to the water supply itself. It became evident that there were serious issues with sanitation at both the hatchery and in the settlement. At the latter, there was no well; water for drinking and washing was taken from the Dauphin River in galvanized pails without subsequent treatment or boiling. Nine earth pit privies were located along the river banks. By contrast, the hatchery itself and the adjacent manager's residence each had a bath, wash basin, and toilet. The residence also had an additional sink. Water for the residence was taken from a wood-cribbed well with a wooden cover, located about 70 feet from the river. In the hatchery, water was used both in the building's operations and plumbing. This water was drawn directly from the river, 30 feet out from the bank. A log pile crib, filled with stones and gravel, acted as a filter before the water entered the hatchery. While the waste from the privies remained in the soil, waste water from the hatchery and residence septic systems was dumped straight into the river. Thus, as Hunter observed in his report, 'the water used by the Indians living between the fish hatchery and the river mouth could be polluted.'[34] Also problematic was the fact that the water intake pipe for the hatchery, which supplied the building's toilet, bath, and basin, was situated downstream from where waste from the residence was discharged. The currents in the river contributed to a situation where 'effluent from the septic tanks, even in small quantities, may quite readily be passed into the hatchery.'[35]

The design of the hatchery's sanitation system points to some serious human error. However, it also illuminates attitudes towards the hatchery and its purpose and towards Aboriginal people and their use of the lake. Those who designed and constructed the hatchery (including George Butler) viewed it as a space for fish, fish management, and fish science. It was a work space, not a living space. This perspective did not take into account that Aboriginal people living in the area and working in the hatchery would be using the water, an oversight that is apparent in the separation of the hatchery buildings and residence and even more so in the sequence of the pipes. If the hatchery intake was intended only for fish, it would not have mattered (at least to government and hatchery workers) if it took in polluted river water.

Aboriginal uses of the lake appeared to be even further from the minds of those who designed the hatchery. As twenty-first-century observers, we might initially be struck most by the disparity between the availability of treated water at the reserve settlement and the hatchery. In effect, the fish got plumbing, but the reserve did not. However, we should also be mindful that this inequity is not exclusive to the past, as seen in the ongoing issues regarding the availability of clean water on First Nations reserves, particularly in the North.[36] What we can see with the benefit of hindsight is the compartmentalization of the different lake functions. The reports from the typhoid outbreak consistently separated the issue of the settlement (and sanitary conditions there) from the hatchery. As previously mentioned, many of those who lived in the settlement also worked in the hatchery; the families purchased goods at the hatchery store; and those who fished in the lake used the hatchery as headquarters. The hatchery was integrated socially and physically into the life of the Dauphin River community because both the community and the hatchery took advantage of the same environmental opportunities. For those from outside the community (the sanitary inspectors and Winnipeg bureaucrats), there was no such integration. The community was separate; the harvesting of the lake waters (even though providing fish to harvest was the very reason for the hatchery) was separate; and the people who lived in the community and harvested the lake were also separate—clearly othered in the reports on the typhoid outbreak, with responsibility for their well-being passed off onto the federal government. As Foggie noted, 'The Dauphin River . . . may be a hasard [sic] by virtue of the somewhat insanitary conditions that exist at habitations along the banks, and their methods of waste disposal, apart, altogether, from direct discharge of sewage from buildings.'[37] The hatchery and the habitations were two separate things, even though they had been intimately bound together by the rise and intensification of industrial and commercial activity across the Northwest.

These disparities speak to the environmental injustice at work in the Northwest at mid-century. Particularly given that regulations under the provincial Public Health Act required that '<u>all surface waters</u> be regarded with suspicion, and that they be treated or sterilized before being used for drinking or domestic purposes', it is not coincidental that the Aboriginal settlement did not have access to treated water. It is, however, indicative of the segregation of Aboriginal and non-Aboriginal spaces and the different wealth, opportunity, and services available in these spaces.[38] Ultimately, the distance between the imagined separation and the actual integration created fertile ground for the typhoid bacillus.

Conclusion

The twentieth-century rise of industrial fisheries across the Canadian Northwest undermined the health of freshwater ecosystems and Aboriginal people across this region. Industrial harvesting depleted fish stocks, altered freshwater fish demographics, and led to the dumping of wastes that affected nutrient levels and degraded freshwater habitats. Some of these changes to freshwater ecosystems also affected human health. The depletion of the ecosystems contributed to the marginalization of commercial fishing, and it was primarily Aboriginal people who suffered the economic consequences. To the extent that health is linked to economic well-being through, for instance, access to appropriate health care, Aboriginal health can also be seen as indirectly related to the deterioration of freshwater environments. For those people who relied on freshwater fish in their diet, the depletion of fish stocks also contributed to malnutrition well into the mid-twentieth century. In the construction of the Dauphin River hatchery, government officials failed to recognize the ways in which commercial fishing, hatchery operations, freshwater environments, and daily sustenance were all intimately linked. These associations led directly to a typhoid epidemic in the early 1940s, just one instance of how ill-health is sometimes a direct consequence of our interconnection with and impacts on the wider, natural world.

Primary Document

2.   Letter from Chief Pierre Freezie to S.J. Bailey, 9 October 1950

Rocher River, N.W.T.
9th October, 1950.
S.J. Bailey, Esq.,
Room 204,
Norlite Building,
Ottawa, Ont.

Dear Sir,
We, the undersigned, being residents and trappers of the settlement of Rooher River in the Northwest Territories do hereby tender this petition to stop further commercial fishing on Great Slave Lake.

Due to extensive commercial fishing it is becoming more difficult to catch sufficient fish for ourselves and our dogs. Fish is the staple food of dogs and when we do not get enough to feed them it is very difficult for us to travel about the country to visit our trap-lines. Trapping is our only means of livelihood.

Since commercial fishing started a few years ago on Great Slave Lake, we have noticed the fish getting more scarce each year, the quality is also poorer.

During the last two years we have had difficulty in obtaining sufficient fish for ourselves and dogs when we set our nets in the Taltson River which flows in to the Lake. For this reason we have tried setting our nets out in the Lake under the ice during the winter months but this idea has not been successful. It is becoming increasingly difficult for us to live off the country and when we get a year the caribou pass us up, it seems to all of us that certain steps should be taken to safeguard the little that is left.

We beg that the Government should put a stop soon to this extensive commercial fishing on this Lake, because the people living here are going to be in need and may become a Government liability.

Yours truly,
his
mark
Pierre Freezie
(Chief)

Secondary Source

3.   'The Indians Would Be Better Off if They Tended to Their Farms Instead of Dabbling in Fisheries'[39]

Gabrielle Parent

I

On 22 September 1849, Captain T.G. Anderson and Alexander Vidal, representatives of the Canadian government, arrived at Spar Island (just south of Thunder Bay) to negotiate the cession of Ojibwa lands to the British Crown. Anderson held a series of meetings at Fort William with the local Ojibwa population, led by Chief Joseph Peau de Chat and the Illinois, concerning the conditions for the surrender of the territories. These talks were the blueprints for the Robinson Superior Treaty signed the following year. Father Nicolas Frémiot, a Jesuit missionary observing the negotiations, worried about the slight compensation the Ojibwa were to receive for their lands, stating 'Here are our people on the eve of receiving, not a ready-made fortune that will dispense them from work . . . but some weak assistance which, at least, will help them to clothe themselves.' Frémiot was confident, however, that 'fishing will provide sufficient food.'[40]

The Ojibwa and the Oji-Cree residing in the region north and west of Lake Superior relied on fish for nourishment because plant and big-game food resources in the area were less plentiful. However, the Northern Ojibwa and Oji-Cree's connection with water ran far deeper than their need to harvest food. They maintained an intimate and complex relationship with their aquatic environment, which included over 100,000 bodies of water. Besides providing them with sustenance, the lakes and rivers shaped the Northern Ojibwa and Oji-Cree's culture and traditions, their stories, their technologies, their population movements, and their economy.

In this article, I emphasize the significance of the aquatic environment to the Northern Ojibwa and Oji-Cree's culture, belief system, and economy in order to illustrate how settlement and industrial development affected not just their subsistence but also their entire way of life. Although water and fish have typically been overlooked in histories of the Northern Ojibwa and Oji-Cree, there have been some recent exceptions. Charles E. Cleland was among the first to argue that fish was the main staple of the Indigenous populations in the region before contact with Europeans and that Indigenous settlement patterns and cultural development were shaped by access to this resource.[41] Historians such as Victor P. Lytwyn, Leo Waisberg, and Tim Holzkamm have since demonstrated the centrality of fish to the Northern Ojibwa's subsistence and commercial trade, while Laura Peers, Douglas Harris, and Christopher Hannibal-Paci have examined the Northern Ojibwa's fishing practices, commercial economies, and relationships with traders and other Europeans.[42] However, even these groundbreaking studies understate the extent to which bodies of water shaped Ojibwa and Oji-Cree culture and way of life in northwestern Ontario. Only by understanding the centrality of water to the Northern Ojibwa and Oji-Cree can we fully appreciate the impact of non-Aboriginal encroachment on their watery world.

During the last half of the nineteenth century, Indigenous populations faced an influx of immigrants looking to profit from the resources and opportunities in the North. Historians still need to ask how Aboriginal communities responded to both the opportunities and the setbacks that this arrival presented. Research on the impact of resource industries and settlement campaigns on the Ojibwa and Oji-Cree remains limited, as do studies on the effects of the depletion of fish stocks, environmental degradation, and the restriction of movements and fishing rights. Historians Ken Coates, William Morrison, and Kerry Abel have recently begun to examine the role that the Ojibwa played in the development of the northern industries and how these projects affected their livelihood and sovereignty, but their role in the fishing industry remains underrepresented in these works.[43]

II

At the time of contact, the aquatic culture of the Northern Ojibwa and Oji-Cree was highly advanced. Archaeological evidence suggests that Shield Archaic people resided and fished in northwestern Ontario as early as 6500 BCE, using fishhooks, nets, traps, and barbed harpoons.[44] In the Rainy River region, Indigenous people were consistently exploiting sturgeon fisheries from at least 500 BCE, with heavy exploitation taking place around Long Sault Rapids.[45] For over 2,000 years, the McCluskey site (located approximately 60 kilometres southwest of Thunder Bay) was occupied between the spring and fall, the primary fishing seasons.[46]

During the Woodland period (1000 BCE to 1000 CE), Indigenous communities developed a 'multi-fisheries subsistence theme', meaning that Indigenous groups and family units moved seasonally to maximize the fisheries' productivity. Different communities occupied these fishery sites temporarily but repeatedly from the late Woodland period to modern day.[47] Due to the cold climate, major fish harvests were confined to seasonal spawning periods, with the oil-rich whitefish, lake trout, and ciscos taken in the late fall and lake sturgeon, sucker, pike, pickerel, northern catfish, and bullheads in the spring.[48] Excess catches were smoked, dried, or made into pemmican. Sturgeon were sometimes tethered in small ponds for a few weeks for later use.[49] Oji-Cree Elder Mary Fox of Bearskin Lake recalled another way fish was preserved: 'A long time ago, the Natives set nets out to fish. From their catch, they would make fish powder. They were able to store this powder. The elders would make this stuff. They were able to survive by eating fish powder.'[50]

The Northern Ojibwa and Oji-Cree traded a variety of fish products with other Indigenous groups. The Nipissing, for example, maintained a trade relationship with the Huron, procuring corn, wampum, and fish nets for their fresh and dried fish products.[51] Northern Ojibwa groups exchanged sturgeon by-products with the Cree. Groups living in the Rainy River area also conducted a lucrative trade in sturgeon by-products, namely sturgeon oil and pemmican.[52] Sturgeon oil was rendered for use as medicine, lamp oil, hide softening, and, later, machine oil. Isinglass, made from pounding the sturgeon's air bladder, made strong glue. John Bighead, an Oji-Cree Elder from Wunnumin Lake, remembered another use of fish when he recalled how his father kept him alive after his mother's death: 'My father used the stomach of a fish to feed me. That was my bottle.'[53]

From this aquatic environment evolved a dynamic and adaptable culture. The Ojibwa's technological and engineering innovations, notably the birchbark canoe, are further testament to their interconnectedness to their watery world. The Ojibwa canoe is a dexterous watercraft, able to navigate the rough waters of present-day northwestern Ontario's inland lakes and rivers, as well as the sea-like conditions of the Great Lakes, while carrying up to 3,000 pounds.[54] The Ojibwa also fashioned sails, presumably made of animal skins, which they used prior to contact with Europeans.[55]

In northwestern Ontario, waterways were the principal means of transportation in both the summer and winter. As Jesuit Joseph-Urbain Hanipaux described in 1851, 'No matter how far you might want to go from the lake, as far as to the lofty mountains lost in space and in the clouds, it will always be rivers and lakes that will take you to your destination.'[56] During the long winter months, fish were needed to feed the Ojibwa's sled dogs, which were essential for travel over the frozen lakes and rivers. Oji-Cree Elder Ellen Sainnawap of Wunnumin Lake explains, 'They would ice fish and set nets to catch fish to feed the dogs. . . . That is how the people survived by using dogs to carry their things. Many dogs starved too, if the person was unable to kill or catch fish to feed them. Also, people used dogs to go trapping far away.'[57]

The Ojibwa and Oji-Cree used a diverse set of technologies and techniques to catch fish. Gillnets made of willow bark brought in the bulk of the catch.[58] Spears, harpoons, bows and arrows, dip nets, and fishing weirs were also used, as were baited hooks, predominantly for deepwater or ice fishing.[59] The Northern Ojibwa also fished at night by torchlight from their canoes. This practice of *wasswewin*, fishing with a spear in the light, was an extremely effective method for catching fish in the summers or between spawning seasons and allowed the Ojibwa to get fresh fish and replenish stocks in otherwise lean times.[60]

The annual fall and spring fish harvests were also important socio-cultural events for the Ojibwa and Oji-Cree. Between several hundred and a few thousand people would congregate at the spawning fisheries. These semi-annual gatherings allowed families and communities to trade information and news, make political decisions, renew military alliances, and arrange marriages.[61] Religious ceremonies and thanksgiving also took place on these occasions.

The aquatic environment also played a key role in all aspects of the Northern Ojibwa and Oji-Cree identity. The totems of the five great Ojibwa clans in the region are indicative of the formative role of the aquatic environment. For example, the A-waus-e clan claim Me-She-num-aig-way (immense fish) as their totem.[62] During the 1850s, William Warren gathered information regarding this being from Esh-ke-bug-e-coshe, chief of the Pillager and Northern Ojibwa and head of the A-waus-e family:

> Me-she-num-aig-way . . . is equivalent or analogical, to the Leviathan mentioned in the Bible. This being is also one of the spirits recognized in their grand Me-da-we rite. This clan comprises the several branches who claim the Catfish, Merman, Sturgeon, Pike, Whitefish, and Sucker Totems, and in fact, all the totems of the fish species may be classed under this general head.[63]

The Ojibwa in northern Ontario developed a region-specific belief system, based largely on their close relationship with water and fish. The Northern Ojibwa have many *manido* (referring to spirits, patrons, the divine, or animate objects).[64] In the northern Great Lakes region, it is the great manido Micipijiu, the male underwater lynx, that holds the most power.[65] According to the mythology, Micipijiu was sometimes benevolent, providing the Northern Ojibwa with fish and game as well as medicines and power, but maintained strict and sometimes vengeful control over all levels of the world: water, land, and sky.[66] Selwyn Dewdney noted in his study of Ojibwa birchbark scrolls that Micipijiu 'incorporated the fears of a people whose travel was almost exclusively by water'.[67]

There are many other *manido* residing in the lakes and rivers in northwestern Ontario. For instance, Ojibwa storyteller Basil Johnston recounts many tales of *Nebaunaubaewuk* and *Nebaunaubaequaewuk* (mermaids and mermen) in his writing.[68] The *Nebaunaubaewuk* and *Nebaunaubaequaewuk* are known to kidnap human men and women and make them their spouses. Johnston also recounts that the merpeople helped the Anishnaabeg[69]: 'It got to be impossible for the Anishnaubaek to go anywhere without the mermaids following.'[70]

III

By the late 1830s, Lake Superior's fisheries were more lucrative than the fur trade.[71] Fish was in abundance, a fact frequently noted by the French missionaries, traders, and explorers in the region. Only recently have historians realized the extent to which fish were part of the trade economy in northwestern Ontario during the eighteenth and nineteenth centuries, when the Ojibwa traded their surplus catch[72] and generated considerable wealth.[73]

Given the profitability of the Aboriginal fisheries, it is not surprising that a complex web of conservation and fishing regulations existed pre- and post-contact. Evidence that laws and customs related to fisheries management held sway among the Northern Ojibwa exists in stories from the area, which repeatedly underline one basic guideline: the need to preserve species by avoiding waste and overconsumption. Victoria Brehm surveyed multiple versions of the Ojibwa flood myth, illustrating the role that Micipijiu played in preventing overfishing and overhunting. She explains, 'Since Micipijiu raises the flood waters, in his role as guardian of resources he is immortal, reappearing to punish anyone who attempts to upset the balance of ecosocial relations.'[74]

Cleland underlines the Ojibwa's emphasis on sharing between family members and communities, which allowed them to preserve the North's precious, and limited, re-sources.[75] During the fall and spring spawning runs on the Nipigon River, each family fished in a specific location, inherited from their ancestors. Moreover, custom dictated that each family let some fish through to ensure that everyone received their share and that enough fish reached the spawning grounds. For this reason, nets were prohibited in rivers during spawning seasons.[76]

When greater numbers of fur traders began arriving in the region in the late eight-eenth century, the Northern Ojibwa supplied the Hudson's Bay Company (HBC) and North West Company (NWC) trade posts with fish and fish products in exchange for commercial goods.[77] Indeed, traders initially depended on the Northern Ojibwa for their food. However, Europeans did not often appreciate the local fish diet. Most records from the HBC fur posts concerning fish consist of complaints about its domi-nance. The 1792–3 record of staple food consumed by the HBC post at New Brunswick House complained of receiving *only* 18 pounds of deer traded with the Ojibwa, as op-posed to 1,858 pounds of fish.[78] In 1851, Frémiot voiced a common sentiment among newcomers: 'the fishing, however abundant and however excellent it may be, still leaves—even for the native—a desire for some concomitant nourishment.'[79]

When the traders complained about the fish, they were upset about more than their diet: they found it offensive to have to eat fish provided by Native people.[80] The prevalence of fish in the northwestern Ontario diet was, in the eyes of Europeans, correlated to dependence and poverty and consequently perpetuated an image of the Northern Ojibwa as 'needy' and 'lazy'. Jesuit August Kohler's description of Ojibwa fishing economy around Sault Ste Marie in 1850 was typical:

> Too lazy to go hunting, too lazy even to cultivate the soil, they live like parasites, depending on one another, or else they come to trade, for whiskey or for worth-less objects, a few fish they speared by night in the summer in the light of bark torches. During the winter, they open a hole in the ice and lie on their stomachs close to it all day long watching for their prey.[81]

Through the early 1800s, the HBC and other trading companies had little choice but to accept the fish and the Ojibwa's traditional fishing practices. By the 1830s, all the HBC outposts in the Lake Huron district, 24 in total, were provisioned through the winter with salted lake trout and whitefish, the majority of which was procured from local Ojibwa and Odawa.[82] It was also common practice to send fish, salted and packed into barrels, from Fort William's Aboriginal-run fisheries to the more remote trade posts in the area northwest of Lake Superior.[83] The missions in the area were similarly dependent on Aboriginal fisheries.

Despite their initial reservations, the Europeans became more receptive to the local diet, favouring sturgeon, whitefish, and lake trout. This new-found openness was also related to the depletion of game. Fisheries took on greater importance to both the Europeans and the Indigenous populations when the big and small game that had sustained the fur trade and supplemented their diets in the seventeenth and eighteenth centuries began to disappear. Frémiot attributed this phenomenon to the newcomers' failure to pursue, unlike the Ojibwa, a conservationist strategy of moderation: 'The reason for [the disappearance of game] is, in this universal and incessant conspiracy against the denizens of the forests, people do not respect any season whatever.'[84]

In the early 1800s, the shortage of fur-bearing animals affected the Assiniboine-Plains Cree and the Blackfoot more harshly than it did the Ojibwa and other Algonquin-speaking communities living in northwestern Ontario. This difference was because the sturgeon fisheries remained highly productive and allowed these communities a certain freedom of manoeuvre.[85] Many explorers in the region observed the Ojibwa's independence from the fur traders. In the Boundary Waters region, one commented that the Ojibwa could 'feed themselves without having recourse to the supplies of ammunition and clothing with which the Hudson's Bay Company supply their Indians'.[86] In some places, such as Rainy River, the Ojibwa, well fed on fish, were not particularly interested in trade with the Europeans. Traders found them to be 'difficult and expensive trading partners'.[87]

Between 1820 and 1880, fishing in northwestern Ontario increased by 20 per cent every year, thanks to the influx of settlers, missionaries, and others.[88] It was not only Euro-Canadians newly fishing in the waters: Americans, both commercial and sports fishers, were poaching, fishing off-season, and operating commercial fishing boats in Canadian waters, further stressing the fish population.[89]

Non-Aboriginal people believed that they could fish in the Great Lakes region, and they asserted this right vociferously. Before the Fisheries Act was introduced in 1857, common law and the **Magna Carta** governed Euro-Canadian fishing practices.[90] Both recognized the public's right to fish in tidal waters. The Great Lakes and adjacent bodies of water, despite their lack of tide, were treated as communal fisheries, and the public's right to fish superseded any Aboriginal title. Fisheries officials enforced the public right to fish because they believed that the Aboriginal fisheries had not been granted by the Crown and therefore were not protected.[91] This was inconsistent with English legal and historical precedents.[92] The colonial government viewed the fisheries in northwestern Ontario as a largely untapped resource ripe for commercial enterprise: they were not about to let the Ojibwa and Oji-Cree stand in the way.

It took some time for the effects of this attitude to be felt as the immigrant population in the region remained relatively small until the mid-nineteenth century. The American Fur Company (AFC) established the first large-scale non-Aboriginal commercial fisheries in Lake Superior. Its operations began in the early 1820s, with the company purchasing whitefish from the Ojibwa in exchange for commodities from Ohio.[93] After reaching an understanding with the HBC, the AFC moved to the more fruitful Canadian waters and opened major fisheries at Grand Portage (1836), Isle Royale (1837), and La Pointe (1839) and small posts in and around the area. The AFC's profitable ventures inspired both large and small competitors. Aboriginal people remained the primary employees at the fisheries during these formative years. For example, while visiting Siskiwit Bay on Isle Royale in September 1850, Frémiot noted that the local commercial fishing operation 'had to depend only on Natives'.[94]

Interest in the area increased with the discovery of gold and silver in the 1840s. At this time, the federal government began restricting the Northern Ojibwa's fisheries with the imposition of treaty agreements. During negotiations with Captain Anderson at Fort William in 1849, Chief Peau de Chat confessed to Frémiot that he believed 'the Englishman . . . wanted to reduce him to poverty.'[95] Peau de Chat's concerns materialized with the signing of the Robinson Superior Treaty on 7 September 1850. This agreement allowed the Northern Ojibwa 'to fish in the waters thereof as they have heretofore been in the habit of doing, saving and excepting only such portions of the said territory as may from time to time be sold or leased to individuals, or companies of individuals, and occupied by them with the consent of the Provincial Government'.[96] The treaty made no provisions for commercial fishing rights, movement to seasonal fishing sites, or preservation of fish stocks. Similarly, the government intended Treaty 3, which was signed in 1873, to open up the Northwest for settlement and resource extraction. It granted the Ojibwa the right to hunt and fish with a crucial proviso: should there be developments in forestry, mining, or other industries, the treaty was subject to change.[97] This betrayed promises made in 1873 by Simon Dawson and the treaty commissioners, who had convinced the reluctant Rainy River Ojibwa that, 'along with the land reserves and money payments, they would forever have the use of their fisheries.'[98]

The treaties paved the way for settlement of the region and provided for unrestricted access to minerals and lumber. The goal of the government and settlers alike was to extract resources for capitalist exploitation; little heed was paid to sustainable resource management.[99] In December 1850, Kohler wrote about the increasing loss of the Robinson Treaty lands to development and population expansion, stating, 'Only recently the lot of our people was settled by the sale of a large part of their lands, and by the guarantee of their perpetual possession. . . . Every winter a part of what once constituted their riches and their sole means of survival is taken away from the native people.'[100]

The growing population along the shores of Lake Superior adversely affected the fish and aquatic environment in many ways. Kohler spoke of the effects of pollution produced by the HBC forts:

> They wash and throw their garbage in the water at the shore. . . . Moreover, even when the fish would be abundant in those regions, the fish flee from the spot because the filth remaining in backwaters prevents the water from being purified quickly enough. In this way the very finest fishing ground can be lost. This is what brings on famine.[101]

Water-borne diseases, such as cholera, imported by new immigrants to the region and perpetuated by increasingly contaminated waters hit the Indigenous communities fiercely. As Frémiot observed, 'another unfortunate factor that worked against our Natives' fishing season this year was the number of people who had died, or were dying, or were sick. We have just buried the eleventh person within only a few months and most of the deaths took place during the fishing season.'[102]

Throughout the 1840s and 1850s, new fisheries continued to be established on both the American and Canadian shores of Lake Superior despite the noticeable decline in fish stocks. Thereafter, the region's fisheries supplied salted fish to markets in eastern Canada and the mid-western United States. During the 1870s, the total commercial catch from Lake Superior was over 1.8 million kilograms. Unsurprisingly, the impact on fish stocks was profound.[103]

Non-Aboriginal commercial fisheries developed much later in the interior lakes and tributaries. Rainy River and Lake of the Woods did not see settlers or commercial fishermen until the mid-1880s. Thereafter, the inland Ojibwa's fisheries were soon suffering on the same scale as those on Lake Superior. Americans also played a role in overfishing in the interior. As historian J.J. West relates, 'Minnesota's fishermen exercised little discretion in harvesting sturgeon. The commercial catch had risen dramatically between 1888 and 1890, from 40,000 to 200,000 pounds.'[104]

By 1875, logging was also extensive on the Canadian shore of Lake Superior, attracting more non-Aboriginal labourers to the region and putting greater pressure on its natural resources, including fish populations.[105] Logging eroded the shores of lakes and rivers, and the logs were boomed down river systems, devastating fish habitats and destroying fish eggs and fry in spawning grounds. Moreover, allochthonous materials from the lumbering and pulp and paper industries in the area damaged the marine environment.[106] By 1880, entire species were at risk. Fisheries that the Ojibwa had depended on for centuries were wiped out and, for the first time in memory, the ability of the fisheries to sustain the Indigenous population was uncertain.

The federal government, the provincial government, commercial fisheries, and sports anglers also limited, if not destroyed, the Ojibwa and Oji-Cree's subsistence and commercial fishing economies. As early as 1844, the **Bagot Commission** recommended that fishing equipment no longer be given to the Northern Ojibwa.[107] Frémiot commented on the effects that this interdiction had on the Ojibwa in 1850: 'Our people in general had an unsuccessful fishing season because they do not have many nets and even fewer barrels and less salt.'[108]

The British followed the Bagot Commission's recommendation and began to restrict the Ojibwa's fish harvest.[109] The 1857 Fishing Act introduced fishing licences to the Province of Canada in a bid to establish governmental control and end the common fishery. Aboriginal commercial fisheries were given only 12 band leases, whereas the HBC received 14 and Euro-Canadian fishermen 71. By 1869, the Act for Better Protection of Game restricted night fishing and hunting in Ontario, and torchlight fishing became a criminal offence by the end of the century.[110]

Adding to the Northern Ojibwa and Oji-Cree's troubles were the 'Gentlemen Anglers', sports fishermen from North America and Europe. The Northwest was considered one of the best fishing grounds in the world. While Northern Ojibwa were sought-after fishing guides,[111] non-Aboriginal sports fishermen petitioned the government to limit Aboriginal fishing and restrict their methods. Non-Native anglers complained that torches, spears, and other traditional technologies were uncivilized and argued that fly-fishing should be the only method permitted.[112] The success of the sports fishers' unions and clubs (made up of wealthy politicians, businessmen, and professionals) in making this argument is evident by the fact that many lakes and rivers in northwestern Ontario are still governed by 'fly-fishing only' laws.[113] Northern Ojibwa Elder James Masakeyash from Osnaburgh described these nineteenth-century restrictions in this way: 'The Ministry of Natural Resources would not allow them to kill ducks or fish. The Ministry of Natural Resources does not allow them to set a net.'[114]

The Northern Ojibwa fought the restrictions against their fishing practices. Menitoshens, a Northern Ojibwa who ran as a candidate for chief in the Nipigon region in 1856, sought to maintain Ojibwa control over the best whitefish fishing grounds when his band was negotiating the location of their reserve with the government.[115] The Treaty 3 Ojibwa from Rainy River also petitioned against increased encroachment on their fisheries with a letter to the Canadian Government dated 15 July 1892. The Lake of the Woods Ojibwa fought back as well, with the support of the sympathetic Simon Dawson.[116] Unfortunately, the efforts of the Ojibwa and their allies proved fruitless.

By the end of the century, the Ontario government was building hydropower stations in northwestern Ontario, which proved wildly destructive to the aquatic environment.[117] Dams built along the Nipigon and Kaministiqua rivers and elsewhere in Lake Superior's watershed caused soil erosion, disrupted water levels, and disturbed or destroyed spawning grounds. Ojibwa and Oji-Cree fisheries were thus further compromised. By the 1890s, the depletion of the fish in the Great Lakes was so dire that a joint commission was formed between Canada and the United States to preserve and increase stocks. Pollution had also reached crisis levels: many fish became inedible due to contamination from mercury, PCBs, dioxins, chlordane, and other toxic chemicals. By the early 1900s, it had become dangerous, even deadly, to consume large quantities of fish from the Lake Superior watershed. In 1907, Canada and the United States signed the Boundary Waters Treaty, promising to limit pollution in Lake Superior. For the Northern Ojibwa and Oji-Cree, however, this attempt at environmental regulation came too late: fishing no longer provided sufficient food for their survival.

IV

It is clear that the Indigenous population's significantly diminished position in the fisheries was the result of Canadian colonial policy and of campaigns by other non-Aboriginal parties invested in northwestern Ontario. The restrictions placed on the Ojibwa and Oji-Cree's fishing practices limited Aboriginal competition and eroded their independence. The Ojibwa and Oji-Cree's right to participate freely as independent fishermen and as employees in the commercial fisheries and their auxiliary trades was further compromised by discrimination and competition with European settlers in the area.

While fishing rights were promised in both Treaty 3 and the Robinson Superior treaties, there was no recognition that the northern ecosystem needed to be preserved in order for fish to thrive. These treaties neglected to protect the Aboriginal fisheries despite the fact that fish had served as the main food source for the Ojibwa and Oji-Cree for centuries and were central to their culture and lifestyle. The assault on the northwestern ecosystem that accompanied colonization not only undermined the region's fish stocks, but it also devastated the Ojibwa and Oji-Cree's traditional way of life, their culture, and their independence by defiling their lifeblood, the aquatic environment.

Primary Document

4.

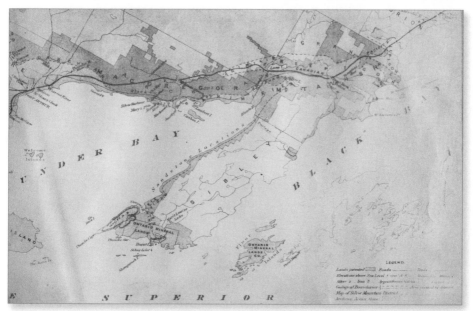

Maps 13.1–13.2 Maps of the Thunder Bay Mining Region of Lake Superior. Geological and National History Survey of Canada, 1887 (Lakehead University Library Archives.).

Primary Document

5.

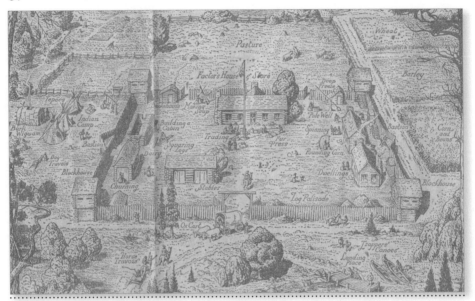

Early Pioneer Fur Trading Settlement, Newspaper Advertisement from Canadian Bank of Commerce, 1954. (Lakehead University Library Archives.)

Primary Document

6.

On the Nipigon River, Whitchers(?) camp at Hamilton Pool, W.F. Langworthy, July 1884. (Lakehead University Library Archives.)

Primary Document

7.

On the Nipigon River, one hour's catch at big Canoe Portage, W.F. Langworthy, *c.* 1884. (Lakehead University Library Archives.)

Primary Document

8.

'This is a real Indian canoe in the picture, White water rapids from below', White Charles, W.F. Langworthy, c.1884. (Lakehead University Library Archives.)

Primary Document

9.

On the Nipigon River, 'Guzz(?) Brother's camp at Pizer(?) Portage. Trout bearing camp, July 1884', W.F. Langworthy. (Lakehead University Library Archives.)

Questions for Consideration

1. What effects did the opening of the Dauphin River hatchery have on the Aboriginal people of the area and the aquatic environment?
2. In Piper's analysis, what were the failings in the design of the Dauphin River hatchery? To what does Piper attribute these problems?
3. Discuss the similarities between the complaints in Chief Freezie's letter and the situation at Dauphin River.
4. How did the Ojibwa and Oji-Cree peoples of northwestern Ontario go from relative affluence in the eighteenth century to a state of government dependence by the end of the nineteenth century?
5. Is Parent's analysis of the importance of the aquatic environment in the lives of Aboriginal people consistent with Piper's? Do the articles in this chapter present a similar picture of Aboriginal world views as the one painted by the articles in Chapter One? Give reasons to support your answers.
6. In what ways do the images on pages 352–54 provide evidence of the importance of the aquatic environment to the Ojibwa and Oji-Cree of northwestern Ontario and of increasing commercial activity in the region?
7. What are the differences between Western and Aboriginal perspectives on health and well-being?

Further Resources

Books and Articles

Krech, Shepard. *The Ecological Indian: Myth and History*. New York: W.W. Norton & Company, 1999.

Lytwyn, Victor P. 'Ojibwa and Ottawa Fisheries Around Manitoulin Island: Historical and Geographical Perspectives on Aboriginal and Treaty Fishing Rights', *Native Studies Review* 6, 1 (1990): 1–30.

Piper, Liza. *The Industrial Transformation of Subarctic Canada*. Vancouver: UBC Press, 2009.

Tough, Frank. *'As their Natural Resources Fail': Native Peoples and the Economic History of Northern Manitoba 1870–1930* (Vancouver: UBC Press, 1996).

Printed Documents and Reports

Rich, E.E. ed. *Journal of Occurrences in the Athabasca Department by George Simpson, 1820 and 1821, and Report*. London: Hudson's Bay Record Society, 1938.

That is what happened. Timmins: Ojibway and Cree Cultural Center, 1999.

Williams, Glyndwr, ed. *London Correspondence inward from Sir George Simpson, 1841–42*. London: Hudson's Bay Record Society, 1973.

Films

Battle for the Trees. DVD. Directed by John Edginton. NFB, 1993.

March Point. DVD. Directed by Tracy Rector and Annie Silverstein. Longhouse Media, 2008.

Uranium. DVD. Directed by Magnus Isacsson. NFB, 1990.

Websites

Aboriginal Affairs and Northern Development Canada, 'Progress on Kashechewan Action Plan'
www.ainc-inac.gc.ca/ai/mr/nr/s-d2005/2-02730-eng.asp

Aboriginal Affairs and Northern Development Canada, *The Robinson Treaty made in the year 1850 with the Ojibewa Indians of Lake Superior Conveying Certain Lands to the Crown*
www.ainc-inac.gc.ca/al/hts/tgu/pubs/trob/rbt/rbt-eng.asp

CBC News, 'Kashechewan: Water crisis in Northern Ontario', 9 Nov. 2006
www.cbc.ca/news/background/aboriginals/kashechewan.html

CTV News, 'Concerns over water on reserve ignored for years', 27 Oct. 2005
www.ctv.ca/servlet/ArticleNews/story/CTVNews/20051027/aboriginal_water_feature_051027/20051027

FOURTEEN

Political Activism

Introduction

The contemporary political activism of Aboriginal people is long-standing and well documented. Some of the most celebrated examples include the 1970 Red Paper, the 1990 Oka Crisis, the 1995 Ipperwash Crisis, the 1995 Gustafsen Lake Standoff, the assertion of Mi'kmaq fishing and lobster-trapping rights following the **Marshall decision** of 1999, the Kitchenuhmaykoosib Inninuwug's more than decade-long battle to prevent drilling for platinum on its traditional lands, and the ongoing Grand River land dispute. These examples illustrate a clear pattern of Aboriginal people's defence of their rights, lands, and traditions.

Historians examining the political activism of Aboriginal people in Canada have tended to draw links between the participation of Aboriginal people in World War II and the development of a 'new political consciousness'.[1] As a result, groups such as the Assembly of First Nations, the League of Indians of Canada, and the Indian Association of Alberta and the men that organized and ran these groups have received a disproportionate amount of attention. This temporal focus has overshadowed centuries of defiance by Aboriginal people. Furthermore, these very public forms of resistance have eclipsed more private acts, including hiding one's children when the Indian agent came to take them away to school or continuing to hunt and trap on ancestors' land despite the fact that it had become the Minai-nipi bombing range.[2] Unfortunately, much of this resistance went unreported and has accordingly remained unacknowledged, especially when listening to or searching for these stories threatens the interests of capital.

Robin Jarvis Brownlie's article shows that Aboriginal people protested the government's actions long before World War II. Brownlie found that the rights articulated in recent court challenges echo concerns expressed to government officials half a century earlier. While Aboriginal people in the early part of the twentieth century had 'little success in their efforts to carve out a space for their people within the Canadian polity . . . their descendants took up their ideas and succeeded in having Aboriginal rights entrenched in Canadian law.' Brownlie's research provides an invaluable service in rescuing early-twentieth-century resistors such as Joseph Traunch from the 'condescension of posterity'[3] and reminds students of history to look beyond the post-World War II era when searching for Aboriginal activism.

David Bentley and Brenda Murphy's article focuses on an often neglected segment of the Aboriginal population—the Non-Status Métis people of Kelly Lake, BC. Prior to the passing of the Constitution Act in 1982, the Métis were not formally recognized by the federal government as Aboriginal people. As a result of their lack of 'status', they could not negotiate treaties or gain access to the same educational and medical services 'guaranteed' to other Aboriginal people by the federal government. However, the Act did not resolve the thorny question of status and access to resources but made questions of who was 'Métis, what rights and resources ought to follow from that definition, and who gets to decide such questions' even more contentious, especially in an era of government cutbacks on and public apathy about Aboriginal affairs. Nonetheless, the Métis of Kelly Lake are asserting their own agency and redefining what being Métis means to their community through grassroots activities such as the hearing aid campaign, which 'challenged the normal practices' of health care delivery and 'reject[ed] the power relationships of the past and creat[ed] new ones in the present'. Together, these articles illustrate that Aboriginal activism assumes many forms in diverse historical contexts.

Chapter Objectives

At the end of this chapter, you should be able to

- identify forms of Aboriginal resistance in the pre- and post-World War II eras;
- identify some of the major watershed moments in Aboriginal activism since 1950;
- discuss how open resistance can affect policy;
- identify the rhetorical strategies that Aboriginal activists have pursued in dealing with provincial and federal governments; and
- debate what constitutes resistance.

Secondary Source

1.   'Nothing Left for Me or Any Other Indian': The Georgian Bay Anishinabek and Interwar Articulations of Aboriginal Rights

Robin Jarvis Brownlie

In 1926, an Anishinabe[4] man living on the northeastern shore of Georgian Bay sent a protest letter to the Department of Indian Affairs (DIA). Joseph Traunch raised a series of issues that illustrate the commonly expressed objections of First Nations people to their treatment by the federal government. Traunch wrote,

. . . your not trying to help and Indian a tall for you not alode to let and Indian
to do eny tingatall on is one reserve [without] lincencs now I want you to
know this the Department he dident give this pice of land to the Indian. . . .
the Department try to take the reserve from [us] the same [as] he don with the
Island . . . and the same with the fishing and a poor Indian can't fish without
license on [h]is [own] reserve . . . We do not like to see a White pepel kill our
fish. . . .

How would the Indian department respond, he wondered, if it had a pond full of fish
and a yard full of cattle, and Aboriginal people came and took the fish and killed the
cattle? He suggested that the department would not like this, 'and us Indian we are
the same. . . .'[5]

Although Traunch's letter was dismissed by DIA officials, it contains most of the
essential ingredients of the protests raised by First Nations people around Georgian
Bay during the 1920s and 1930s. They were engaged in a struggle with the DIA and
the provincial government to correct what they saw as a series of continuing violations of their treaties and rights. While efforts to establish effective political organizations were largely unsuccessful at that time,[6] the prevalence of organizing efforts and
of individually articulated protests reveals strong continuity with a lengthy protest
tradition stretching from the early nineteenth century to the present. At the same
time, it appears that in this period the existing set of grievances crystallized into a
fairly well-codified set of rights arguments that laid the basis for post-war Aboriginal
rights struggles. There is a striking degree of consistency among interwar Anishinabe
spokespersons that suggests an internal conversation in which the Anishinabek,
probably in dialogue with other Aboriginal groups, had mapped out their Indigenous
rights position. In fact, through Aboriginal communications in DIA records, one can
trace the articulation of an Aboriginal rights position that differs little from the kinds
of positions presented today, focusing on the right to self-government, to hunt and
fish without government restriction, and to be governed by the terms of treaties
signed with Britain and Canada. Their paradigm was based not on European or Euro-
Canadian ideologies, but on Indigenous understandings of their inherent right to the
land and its resources.[7]

The exchange of land for goods was profoundly unequal in value and the post-
treaty condition of the Anishinabek dearly exposed that material reality. Moreover,
dispossession was followed by the imposition of a series of new Euro-Canadian
regulatory systems, each of which functioned to divest the people of further elements of their cultures and economies. These impositions included the Indian
agent system, revamped in the 1830s to extend direct government domination over
Aboriginal communities; a state licensing system for fishing, introduced in 1859;
and the provincial game conservation enforcement regime established in the 1890s.
First Nations people had not consented to any of these changes, nor were they
mentioned in the treaties. These impositions stripped the people of their sovereignty, their right to self-determination, and much of the economic activity on which
they had based their livelihoods up to the mid-nineteenth century. The Anishinabek
and other groups never accepted these developments willingly—at times, indeed,
they waged militant resistance.[8] After the report of the Ontario Game and Fisheries

Men at the French River, Georgian Bay, c.1930, enjoying the fruits of a fishing trip. This image is part of a series of photos by the Ontario Ministry of Health documenting tourist camps in the French River/Parry Sound area. The man in the middle is probably an Aboriginal guide, one of many hired in this period for the region's thriving tourist industry, based in part on harvesting and indigenous animals. (Archives of Ontario.)

Commission in 1911, Ontario game policy and legislation shifted toward a more direct criminalization of Aboriginal harvesting activities. Although the province justified its more aggressive approach in the name of conservation, the new regime also served to appropriate game and fish resources for non-Aboriginal commercial interests such as fish companies and tourist outfitters.[9] The result was an intensification of harassment by game wardens and increased protest and resistance by First Nations people.

The period following World War I witnessed a fresh wave of Aboriginal lobbying nationwide on issues such as hunting and fishing rights, economic encroachment, and the authoritarian administration of the DIA. Various circumstances combined to produce this ferment. For one thing, more and more First Nations people could articulate their concerns in English. At the same time, governments were moving steadily towards minimizing and repudiating Aboriginal rights, as well as increasing pressure on First Nations to assimilate and to surrender more lands to non-Aboriginal people. The DIA, under the administration of Deputy Superintendent General Duncan Campbell Scott, increasingly used coercive measures, and in Ontario, the provincial government was intensifying its efforts to prevent Aboriginal hunting and fishing. Having contributed to the war in substantial numbers, the Anishinabek and other First Nations groups felt that they deserved improved treatment rather than legal and political assault. Once back from Europe, veterans were determined to fight for recognition and equality, and many of them involved themselves in efforts to refashion their communities' relations with government and with the broader Canadian society.[10]

In spite of these precedents, in today's public discourse, First Nations people's assertions of Aboriginal rights, land claims, and the right of self-government are often treated as a phenomenon without a history. Linked as they are with current debates over the Constitution and Aboriginal people's place in Canadian society, Native people's assertions appear to be a recent development made possible only by the Charter of Rights and Freedoms and the rights-focused political climate of the late twentieth century. But there is nothing new about these arguments. In the interwar period, individual spokespersons were elaborating and articulating concepts of Aboriginal rights many years before mainstream Canadian society was ready to accept them.

Government Disregard of Treaties

By the late twentieth century, Canadians had become accustomed to the idea that treaties were binding agreements meant to exist in perpetuity, and the courts affirmed this principle. But earlier in the century, governments paid little attention to treaties. In the 1920s and 1930s, First Nations people lived under the authoritarian regime of the Indian department, overseen, administered, and controlled by its Indian agents. DIA officials considered their duties and obligations to be determined by the Indian Act, a creation of the federal government. By contrast, treaties such as those signed with Georgian Bay First Nations people in the mid-nineteenth century were seen as obsolete documents with little or no relevance to the present. '[T]hese treaties are past and done with,' opined John Daly, Indian agent at Parry Sound.[11] DIA officials did not want to hear about treaty violations or faulty implementation, nor did they accept Aboriginal interpretations of the treaties. Spokespersons who raised these issues were regarded as troublemakers and ingrates who repaid the department's benevolence with unwarranted complaints. While some officials attempted to ensure limited access to fish and game in order to reduce the need for departmental aid, they refused to acknowledge First Nations' hunting and fishing rights.

The government's apparent rejection of treaties alarmed and outraged First Nations people. The crucial difference between the Indian Act and treaties was authorship and control. While most treaties were bipartite agreements, the Indian Act was designed and controlled by federal government officials, without the consent of First Nations people. Since they had no vote, they had no power to modify its contents.[12] Not only did it replace and supersede treaties, but the Act was also misrepresented at times as the sole source of Aboriginal benefits. Agent Daly, for instance, once noted that he had explained to the people 'that they are subject to the Indian Act, and that the Indian Act is good for them', adding that 'they believe this around pay day, and believe this when they come for relief. They believe this so long as they can get something for nothing.'[13]

Within the context of a general disregard of treaty rights, certain provisions were particularly subject to violation, and none more so than those relating to harvesting rights. For example, in the Robinson Huron Treaty of 1850, the Crown promised 'to allow the said Chiefs and their Tribes the full and free privilege to hunt over the Territory now ceded by them, and to fish in the waters thereof, as they have heretofore been in the habit of doing' except on surrendered lands actually occupied by newcomers.[14] This provision, however, was routinely breached. Less than a decade after the treaty was signed, the Province of Canada introduced a regulatory system for commercial fishing that shut First Nations people out of the industry by imposing licences and designated fishing grounds. In short order, the Anishinabek's most productive fishing grounds in Georgian Bay were appropriated and transferred to white-owned fishing companies.[15] In 1892, the Ontario government revised and extended its game conservation laws, creating, among other provisions, game wardens to enforce the system and licences for big game hunting, thereby severely restricting Aboriginal access to animals they had always depended on for food and trade.[16] This regime became more restrictive after the final report of the Ontario Game and Fisheries Commission in 1911, a document that assigned priority to the interests of commercial fishing and tourist operations in wildlife policy. Issues relating to fishing and hunting were a major source of grievance, not only because they were of vital economic importance to First Nations people, but also for cultural reasons. A sense of Aboriginal identity was often closely linked to resource harvesting activities that connected the people with their ancestors and with their society's oldest, most cherished roles and traditions. 'Hunting

Trappers at Pikangikum, an Ojibwe community in northwestern Ontario, consult with Wildlife Management Officer Earl Stone at a 1953 trapping meeting. The image is part of a series of photos by John McFie, an employee of the Department of Lands and Forests, documenting aspects of the work of wildlife management officers in northern Ontario. The men are apparently discussing a map, perhaps of their registered traplines. (Archives of Ontario.)

and fishing is part of the Indian identity,' an Anishinabe Elder recently noted. 'You take the hunting and fishing away and you've taken away part of who we are.'[17]

Since the federal government paid little attention to treaty terms, it was awkward for DIA officials when the people learned the precise provisions of these agreements. Thus DIA officials usually preferred that they not have access to copies of written treaties. For example, Daly informed the Indian department that he did not wish Frank Judge, newly elected chief of the Parry Island Reserve, to obtain a copy of the Robinson Huron Treaty, since former chief Francis Pegahmagabow had 'tried to make trouble with his knowledge of these Treaties', and the new chief was 'of the same ilk'.[18]

The failure of both levels of government to respect and uphold the treaties, and the imposition of the Indian Act in their stead, provide the context for understanding the list of Aboriginal grievances expressed in this period. The DIA experienced ongoing criticism from First Nations people concerning administrative practices and alienated lands and resources, as well as officials who failed to defend First Nations people against economic discrimination and the many other unfavourable changes introduced by non-Native settlers.

At least three strong common themes can be discerned in this criticism: the encroachment by non-Aboriginal people, who exploited local resources; government facilitation of that steady encroachment and expropriation; and the injustice of the Indian agent system, which robbed First Nations people of their right of self-determination. Chiefs and band councillors repeatedly objected to their subjugation to the

Non-Aboriginal exploitation of local resources: a successful fisherman at French River holds up his prize muskellunge, 1930. This is another photograph from the Ontario Ministry of Health's series documenting tourist camps in the French River/Parry Sound area. (Archives of Ontario.)

Indian department and fought to regain the ability to govern their own affairs. They persistently sought to transform the elected band councils from powerless mock-democracies into instruments for self-government.

Hunting and Fishing Rights

The sense of an inherent, prior entitlement to the land's resources was nowhere more powerful than in the battle to restore the hunting and fishing rights that the Ontario government had abrogated. Joseph Traunch's letter of 1926 dealt with most of the central issues. A major concern was fishing rights. The regulatory regime, he argued, violated his rights. He protested the expropriation of fish in general and the imposition of licences on First Nations people: 'the Department try to take the reserve from [us] . . . and the same with the fishing and a poor Indian can't fish without license on [h] is [own] reserve.'

Traunch also voiced the belief, widely held among First Nations people and per-petuated in oral tradition,[19] that the treaties had reserved exclusive rights to game and fish. This belief may have rested in part on the conviction that the original treaty signatories would not have agreed to give up fishing and hunting, given the central role of these activities in their economies and cultures. Indeed, the Robinson Huron Treaty guaranteed that harvesting activities would continue unchanged. In part, how-ever, this conviction also rested on the view that First Nations people had an exclusive entitlement to the animals indigenous to North America. In Traunch's view, the killing of white-owned domestic animals was analogous to Euro-Canadians taking wild fish and game because the fish in lakes and rivers really belonged to First Nations people. Thus the massive exploitation of indigenous fish by local whites and the commercial fishing industry was, in Traunch's opinion, nothing but theft on a prodigious scale.

The game laws were another source of anger and vexation. 'I want to ask you ques-tions now. It's my turn,' interjected John Bigwin of the Rama Reserve during a hearing held by Treaty Commissioner Uriah McFadden in 1923. 'It is about my hunting. Why do they make these game laws and say you can't do this and you can't do that and take my game away from me. I want to have that back again. Now they have made laws all over my hunting grounds and I want them to stop it.'[20] Bigwin's profound sense of ownership of his traditional hunting territory is tangible. Like many others, he could not fathom what entitled the government to impose laws on his hunting grounds.

Not all First Nations hunters gave up their ancient occupation. Especially in less densely settled areas, they continued to hunt in defiance of game laws, as the repeated confrontations with game wardens attest. But they paid a considerable price when caught, including fines, confiscation of their game and equipment, and even jail.[21] Even where some treaty rights were honoured, Aboriginal harvesters could still face punishment. For example, on Manitoulin Island treaty fishing rights seem to have been honoured to a limited degree by Game and Fisheries officials, despite Ontario's restrictive Fisheries Act. Yet in 1917, some island fishermen had their boat, net, and equipment seized by an overseer when they were fishing for their own use.[22] Until then, fishing for 'domestic' or 'subsistence' consumption was precisely what overseers had tolerated. In 1923 a new officer was appointed for the area and threatened to abrogate the practice altogether. As Indian Agent Robert Lewis explained to the DIA,

[d]uring past years the Indians at Sucker Creek have been allowed to set short pieces of nets in the waters fronting their reserve . . . but now there is a new Game and Fisheries Overseer . . . and it appears that he has given the Indians to understand that in future any nets that are set without the Indians first obtaining licenses, the nets will be seized . . . Other Game and Fisheries Overseer's [sic] in this district did not interfere with the Indians catching a few fish for food as they considered it was witin the Indian treaty rights.[23]

The phrase 'catching a few fish for food' makes it clear that the people were permitted only small-scale, non-commercial fishing without paying for a provincial fishing licence. In response to the new overseer's threat, the DIA arranged with the Ontario Department of Game and Fisheries that its officials would continue to tolerate very restricted fishing, provided that the First Nations fishers did not use seine nets.[24] In this case, then, the First Nations on Manitoulin Island managed to retain access to a key resource, though it was strictly limited. Treaty or Aboriginal rights, moreover, were not cited—rather, both governments viewed Aboriginal access to fish as an act of grace on the part of government.[25]

Beyond treaty rights, some groups maintained oral traditions that told of unwritten arrangements reached with government officials of earlier generations. These were even more impossible to uphold, since Euro-Canadian society did not recognize the legitimacy of Aboriginal people's oral record-keeping. Once the officials in question were out of the picture, these agreements were likely to lapse rapidly. Nonetheless,

Newcomer exploitation of game: 'Men shooting wild geese' at Sarnia, 1907. Photograph by amateur photographer John Boyd. (Archives of Ontario.)

there were sporadic endeavours to reinstate them. The Shawanaga band, for example, had an oral tradition dating back to 1853 that told of two officials, surveyor John Stoughton Dennis and Indian Superintendent Captain T.G. Anderson. While surveying the reserve, Dennis had set aside a large off-shore fishing ground for Shawanaga's exclusive use, while Anderson had advised the leading men to ensure that no one encroached on the territory without their permission.[26] As Dennis and Anderson knew, these Anishinabek had chosen their reserve for its proximity to rich fishing grounds in Georgian Bay, to serve as a primary basis of their economy. In the second half of the nineteenth century, Shawanaga people conducted commercial fishing on a considerable scale.[27] For part of this time, the band explained, Shawanaga Chief Solomon James had been fishery officer for all of Georgian Bay and had observed the band's right to the designated fishery. In further support of their claim, the Shawanaga people reported that French fishermen from Penetanguishene used to pay them a fee to use their fishing grounds.

The band made two attempts to reinstate its right to these grounds, the first in 1917–18 when it encountered only denial from agent Alexander Logan, the DIA, and Ontario's Department of Game and Fisheries. By the early twentieth century, the Shawanaga people were completely excluded from the fishing industry, and Logan dismissed their assertions in part because, he argued, few of them fished any more.[28]

The band made a second attempt in 1923. Agent John Daly, newly appointed, was initially sympathetic. He wrote the DIA to find out if there was any written record to bolster Shawanaga's case for fishing rights. But his superiors quickly gave him the usual response to such grievances, namely to dismiss Aboriginal spokespersons, to discount their oral traditions, and to hush matters up as speedily as possible. Once Daly was apprised of the claim's previous rejection, he too dismissed it. The band has never regained its lost fishing rights.

Another Anishinabe man, Edward Paibomsai, wrote an eloquent letter to the DIA in 1930 on trapping, the trapper licensing regime, and white appropriation of game and fur-bearing animals. A member of the Whitefish River band, Paibomsai was a trapper working in the bush near Timmins, ON. He was experiencing devastating competition from white trappers who killed every marketable animal in a given area and then moved on. When Paibomsai left some breeding animals behind to replenish their numbers, 'the whiteman has come along and cleaned them out, so that there is nothing left whatever.' He went on to critique the regulatory regime applied to trapping as an injustice to First Nations people *and* an ineffective conservation mechanism:

> There is no more fur of any kind to get in this part of the country now as there has been too many white men trapping around here in the last few years and has cleaned us up on everything, so that there is nothing left for me or any other Indian to make an existence on. There is the odd Moose yet but we are not allowed to sell moose meat and we cannot live on moose meat alone. Sometimes I often wonder how it is or why it is that the Government is trying so hard to protect the fur bearing animals and yet anyone who has the price to buy or pay for a trappers licence can get one....[29]

In other words, First Nations people were twice penalized, first by competition from local whites, then by criminalization of their ancient economy under the guise of conservation. Yet despite the government's claims that game conservation was of special benefit to the First Nations people (a favourite DIA declaration to justify its failure to uphold treaty rights), the admission of outsiders to the trapping industry resulted in wholesale slaughter of animals with no provision for preservation of the species.[30] The conservation regime was unjust to Native people *and* it was resulting in overtrapping.

Government Complicity in Newcomer Encroachment

Thus First Nations people held the DIA responsible, if not for instituting these injustices, at least for failing to correct them. The people were well aware of the division of government powers that assigned them to federal jurisdiction as wards. They were also frequently exposed to the DIA's rhetoric of protection, by which the department's employees justified their exercise of power. In 1930, John Daly authored one of the most arresting instances of this protection rhetoric. In a passage that explicitly linked the DIA's colonial authority with the larger British imperial project, the agent requested that the DIA write a letter that he could read to John Manitowaba, one of Daly's most persistent adversaries, to 'comfort him in the knowledge that the Department, like the flag of the empire, floats over the Indians with a protecting assurance that they will see to it that no one will take advantage of them'.[31]

Despite, or perhaps because of, the DIA's protectionist claims, First Nations people considered department officials remiss in the performance of their duties. As Joseph Traunch put it in his characteristically succinct and unique way, 'your not trying to help and Indian at all.' The failure went well beyond the department's unwillingness to enforce treaty rights such as hunting and fishing. The DIA flatly refused to entertain any claims relating to the misappropriation or misuse of land in the treaty implementation process, or to listen to concerns about issues such as the overexploitation of timber on reserves.[32] It also did nothing to counter the harmful competition of newcomers for local resources or the systematic marginalization of Aboriginal people in the Euro-Canadian economy.

Joseph Traunch's letter of 1926 discussed several points relating to land, including the fairly widespread conviction that the DIA sought to take more land away from the small patches remaining to First Nations people. After all, he wrote, 'the Department try to take the reserve from [us] the same [as] he don[e] with the Island. . . .' By this he meant the islands of Georgian Bay and Lake Huron, which had been bones of contention since the 1850s, shortly after the Robinson Huron Treaty was signed. The Anishinabe signatories believed they had surrendered only the mainland. They soon learned, however, that government officials were leasing and selling islands to newcomers, in the belief that the islands were included in the surrender.[33]

The injustice of the economic and social system imposed by Euro-Canadians was another prominent feature of Aboriginal people's experience. In his letter of 1930, trapper Edward Paibomsai went on to point out the problem of employment discrimination against First Nations people:

> In a great many places of employment they will not employ an Indian to do their work, so I say and have often said before that no one should be allowed a trappers license only a treaty Indian. . . . I have had a pretty hard winter of it

Sioux Lookout, March 1956: Game management by Ontario's Department of Lands and Forests: an American aerial wolf hunter watches as Conservation Officer Mike Semetok of Sioux Lookout counts the wolves he has shot. A small group of such bounty hunters flew planes over the lake shores around Sioux Lookout each March, shooting animals for the bounty paid by the Ontario government. (Archives of Ontario.)

this year sometimes we eat and sometimes we just went through the motions, it is no good for an Indian around here any more . . .[34]

Paibomsai offered a prescription to mitigate the harm caused by racial discrimination. Trapping could be limited to Treaty Indians as a way to ensure their livelihood and compensate for other economic wrongs. In essence, his argument was that non-Aboriginal employers' refusal to hire Aboriginal workers could be offset by granting First Nations people sole access to trapping, their traditional economy, while excluding non-Aboriginal people from this occupation. In addition to balancing the equation somewhat, this solution would have the additional merit of eliminating the non-Native trappers who were recklessly destroying animal stocks and ruining the business for trappers like himself. It is difficult not to read into the last sentence an Anishinabe's powerful sense of a world turned upside down, in which the Anishinabe homeland had become a place of exclusion, alienation, and hunger for its original owners, while newcomers despoiled the land and wiped out the game.

This was one area in which the Anishinabek received some support from Daly, who had sympathy for a limited form of clearly specified Aboriginal rights. Daly agreed that the guiding licence was an unfair imposition, since the people had fished and hunted in their lands from time immemorial. In opposing the fee, Daly argued that it violated Aboriginal people's rights. In 1924, Daly wrote to the deputy minister of Game and Fisheries advocating an Aboriginal exemption from guiding licences. 'They, the Indians,' he explained, 'maintain that they, being natives, should be exempt from paying any fee.'[35] In a second attempt in 1929, the agent used stronger language to make his case against 'the injustice of the Indians having to pay a fee of $2.00 for the privelege [sic] of guiding in the waters that their forefathers knew and paddled in a thousand years before the white men saw them.'[36] Unfortunately, Daly had no power to change the guiding licence system, which had now been established as a legitimated form of government regulation and taxation. The system would subsume Aboriginal guides and appropriate for the provincial government a small percentage of their limited incomes.

Self-Government

Finally, the DIA records reveal a broad-based campaign for self-government during the interwar period. The primary form of this campaign was a diffuse, widespread, and persistent opposition to the Indian agent system, conducted by individuals inside and outside the elected band councils. Jane Manitowaba of the Parry Island band expressed many of the typical sentiments in a letter she wrote in 1917 to Duncan Campbell Scott, deputy superintendent general of the DIA. Manitowaba was trying to get her son discharged from the army. She declared that the Indian agent, Alexander Logan, had 'barred the way', telling her it was no use writing the DIA directly. Manitowaba now sought to circumvent the agent, asking that Scott write to her directly. 'I feel quite capable of handling my own individual matters,' she informed him. She did not want her correspondence 'touched or managed' by the agent, 'as I, or, we have experienced many disappointments . . . through and by the hands of our Indian Agent's management of our affairs, personal or otherwise.'[37]

In response to these frustrations, countless individuals attempted to sidestep the local agent and communicate directly with DIA officials in Ottawa, or with other parts of government that they hoped would be more sympathetic. The most common approach was that taken by Mrs Manitowaba, either attempting to contact high-ranking DIA officials by letter or actually visiting the DIA office in Ottawa. Some also wrote to the King or made appeals to his representatives, reflecting the long-standing relationship many First Nations maintained with the British Crown. Manitowaba contacted the Governor General before writing to Scott, and her husband John wrote to the King about rights violations.[38] Veterans sought the help of the Canadian Legion, which interceded on behalf of Native returned soldiers in matters such as pensions, relief, and potentially harmful actions by the DIA.[39] In addition, federal and provincial members of Parliament were approached, and they often agreed to take action even though

First Nations people could not reward them with votes. Finally, it was not unusual for the people to try to instigate investigations of unpopular agents in order to limit their power or have them replaced.

Another aspect of the DIA administration that came under attack was the elective band council system and the control exercised over it by DIA officials. Section 93 of the Indian Act outlined the features of this system, which was expected to be voluntarily accepted as bands became Europeanized, but could also be imposed by the superintendent general when he deemed it 'advisable . . .'[40] The band councils provided an appearance of Western-style representative democracy, but only for men, since women were not allowed to vote or stand for office until 1951. Besides this patriarchal restriction, the system had another important set of drawbacks: it was intended to eliminate Indigenous governing systems and ensure federal control. This was accomplished primarily by assigning the councils extremely limited powers and subjecting their decisions to an Indian department veto. Aboriginal people, especially those elected to council, were incredulous at the notion that they should have no right to govern themselves.

First Nations people made repeated efforts to return to self-governing status, but were consistently blocked during these years. The dependence and subordinate status imposed on band officials led to a general disregard for the council among First Nations people, thus further undermining their communities' ability to govern themselves. For example, in 1931 Parry Island Chief Frank Judge wrote to Daly that his 'Indians think that I am a dependent, so I told them that I get my instructions from the Indian agent.'[41]

One of the common threads in First Nations protests was the perception that the government had imposed on them a whole new set of conditions and restraints to which they had never consented. They had arguably not even consented to be subject to the Canadian government. None of the nineteenth-century treaties covering southern Ontario contains any mention of the Aboriginal signatories giving up their sovereignty or submitting to Euro-Canadian government or laws. As non-citizens deprived of the franchise, they quite accurately perceived government decisions as the impositions of outsiders who were not responsible to Aboriginal people. They could not help but notice that the government's rhetoric of help and protection cloaked a reality of control and subjugation.

Conclusion

In Ontario and elsewhere during the interwar years, First Nations people nurtured a strong sense of their right to self-determination, to hunt indigenous animals, and to harvest their land's resources. Parallel developments occurred in much of the country: First Nations of British Columbia organized to defend their lands and Aboriginal title, the Six Nations took their sovereignty claim to the League of Nations, and thousands of Aboriginal individuals from Ontario to Alberta joined Mohawk war veteran Fred Loft's League of Indians of Canada.[42] These actions clearly demonstrate the deeply rooted outrage of Aboriginal people in this era and their pressing demands for change.

In trying to obtain recognition of rights, First Nations people faced enormous disadvantages. For mainstream Canadians, the concept of Aboriginal rights did not exist;

nor would Canadian courts deal with the issue. Even treaty rights were largely unen-
forceable in court.[43] But individuals persisted, nonetheless, spurred on by their strong
sense of the injustice of the existing order, and perhaps even encouraged by the federal
government's own rhetoric of protection, which stood in stark contrast to the reality of
subjugation under the DIA's administration.

The men and women who protested had little success in their efforts to carve out
a space for their people within the Canadian polity. But their descendants took up
their ideas and succeeded in having Aboriginal rights entrenched in Canadian law.
National institutions have now been reshaped to sustain Aboriginal rights, which are
affirmed in the Charter of Rights and Freedoms and bolstered by a series of court decisions. It is important to acknowledge that these concepts of rights were first envisioned
and articulated by First Nations people. They are based on Indigenous ideas that the
people have successfully compelled Canada to embrace. In effect, they have inserted
their own Indigenous rights concept into this country's European-style human rights
framework, asserting rights that were theirs not by virtue of any treaty, declaration of
a British king, or Canadian law, but by virtue of their Aboriginal occupation, use, and
ownership of the land.

Primary Document

2. Letter from Elijah Tabobondung to Jon Daly, Indian Agent, 12 August 1923, Copperhead, Perry Sound, ON

*In August 1923, Anishinabe fisherman Elijah Tabobondung wrote a lawyer to inquire about
the legality of his having to pay for a fishing licence even though he had no representation in
either the House of Commons or the Ontario Legislative Assembly.*

Aug. 12th 1923
Copperhead
Mr. Jon Daly Esq.
Perry Sound
Dear Sir,

I am write few words. I was looking for you Saturday night. Reason I want to see you
about that game warden come to see us Saturday ask us to pay guide license. So I refuse.
I was thinking I have no right to pay guide license that I am noncitizen have no vote for
Dominion election also provincial vote an [sic] have no voice in Government. I don't mind
pay guide license, if I am entitle as you are Indian Superintendent to take all that see. Mr.
Walter Willet game warden lives in Perry Sound. Hope you will understand my writing.

From
Elijah Tabobondung
Give me advise
Care Mr. E. Light

Secondary Source

3.   Power, Praxis, and the Métis of Kelly Lake, Canada

David Bentley and Brenda Murphy

Introduction

Agency and power in Aboriginal communities have often not been recognized. Canada's first peoples have typically been positioned as victims who do little either to resist or redefine the hegemonic relations within which they are embedded.[44] Yet, as many authors such as Winona LaDuke have pointed out, the landscape of Native struggles is replete with examples of their dynamic engagement in the issues that affect their lives.[45] Within Canada, Annette Chrétien argues that the Métis have long been actively involved in political struggles, but that the nature of those struggles has evolved over time. She asserts that subsequent to the Canadian Constitution of 1982 and the official recognition of the Métis, Métis politics has shifted away from the 'politics of recognition' towards the 'politics of definition'. By this she means that although the Métis are now officially recognized as one of Canada's first peoples (the other two groups being First Nations and the Inuit), the politics has now shifted towards such questions as who *is* Métis, what rights and resources ought to follow from that definition, and who gets to decide such questions.[46] As compared to Canada's First Nations and Inuit groups, these are particularly thorny issues since the Métis have less clearly defined access to land rights, the government funding of social programs, language rights, and so on.

The [1996] Royal Commission on Aboriginal Peoples (RCAP) addressed some of the complexities involved in the 'politics of definition'. RCAP recognized the existence of Métis peoples throughout Canada yet made the distinction between the Métis Nation and 'other' Métis peoples.[47] In the context of RCAP, the Métis Nation refers to the historical community tied to Red River, MB, and the military conflicts of the nineteenth century involving Louis Riel.[48] The Métis Nation is linked to the Métis National Council (MNC) and has official recognition by the federal government. Regarding the 'other' Métis, RCAP states:

> Several Métis communities came into existence, independently of the Métis Nation, in the eastern part of what we now call Canada, some of them predating the establishment of the Métis Nation. The history of Métis people who are not part of the Métis Nation is not easy to relate. For one thing, their past has not been much studied by historians. If the Métis Nation's story is unfamiliar to most Canadians, the story of the 'other' Métis is almost untold.[49]

Thus, the 'other' Métis is an ambiguous, amorphous category whose boundaries and characteristics remain to be defined. For those potentially encompassed by this category, this is problematic since the 'other' Métis often do not receive the recognition and support that is offered to the Métis Nation or other Aboriginal groups.

Recent steps towards redefinition are captured by the small Métis settlement of Kelly Lake in British Columbia. Through activities associated with addressing a host

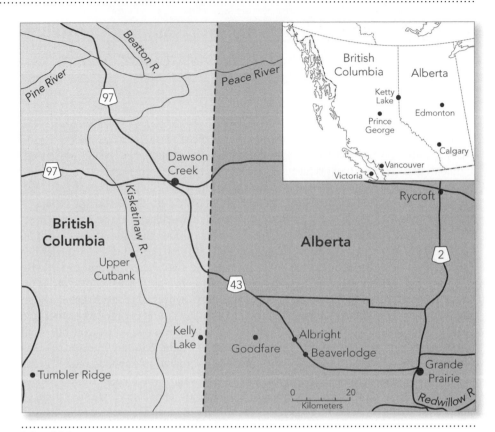

Map 14.1 Kelly Lake, BC. (Bentley, Murphy, 2006.)

of social and environmental issues, this community is altering the hegemonic power relations within which they are embedded. Kelly Lake (population 150), located 60 miles west of Grand Prairie, AB, just inside the British Columbia boundary, was established by a group of Métis with ties to Red River, who were pushed to the foothills of the Rocky Mountains by the rushing influx of European immigrants. For several generations Kelly Lake's relative isolation afforded it some protection from further encroachment and the region had (and to a great extent, still has) abundant sources of country food to sustain a traditional subsistence economy. The Kelly Lake area is also endowed with resources of recent interest to capitalist economies, namely timber, coal, gas, and wind power.

As a Métis settlement, Kelly Lake exhibits both similarities and differences to other Aboriginal communities in Canada. On the one hand, unlike First Nations' territories, the Kelly Lake settlement is not an 'Indian reservation', and so has not suffered the negative consequences nor enjoyed the protection that this designation provides. On the other hand, as a Métis community associated with a distinct settlement location, the situation in Kelly Lake shares several similarities with other Aboriginal communities. For instance, the village has struggled with high unemployment, lack of services, environmental contamination, and resource extraction from their traditional territories. And, like many other Aboriginal communities, Kelly Lake has recently begun to take small steps to challenge the status quo and deal with these ongoing problems, for instance, by facilitating a hearing aid campaign in the community and undertaking negotiations for energy resources in the form of wind energy.

This paper assesses the historic development of Kelly Lake, the problems it faces, and examples of active agency in dealing with those problems. We argue that they are contributing to the redefinition of the place and identity of the Métis within Canadian society, among constitutionally recognized Aboriginal groups, and within the Métis themselves. To structure this assessment a three-dimensional framework of power relations, first articulated by Steven Lukes in the 1970s, is utilized. He argues that there are three dimensions of power: those demonstrated by direct interaction between actors in pluralistic decision-making, by the effects of non-decision-making,[50] and those related to dominant ideologies that obscure the real values and interests of actors.[51] We argue that utilizing this multi-dimensional concept allows for a more nuanced understanding of the predominant multiple and interactive power relations that can affect small communities such as Kelly Lake, as well as the practices through which those relationships are negotiated, reinforced, and/or altered. In other words, the model provides a framework through which we can assess both the oppression and the active agency of the Kelly Lake community.

We maintain that the Métis of Kelly Lake are simultaneously imbricated within a set of evolving multi-dimensional power relationships and practices, involving the various levels of government, private industry, and Aboriginal groups. Even as these power relationships constrain their capacity to achieve their goals, Kelly Lake residents are actively involved in contesting and redefining them, in some cases, by circumventing the touted fiduciary relationship between the federal government and the Métis people.

Lukes and Theories of Power

Simplistic or unidimensional conceptions of the power relationships and practices facing Aboriginal communities do not acknowledge the multiple pathways through which power is mediated and exercised. As outlined below, [Lukes] asserts that there are three levels of power relationships.[52] [Peter] Digeser further observes that, methodologically, each understanding of power is associated with a different empirical question.

- One-dimensional: Focus is on behaviour and decision-making, observable (overt) conflict. Policy preferences and interests are revealed by political participation.[53] Key empirical question: 'Who if anyone, is exercising power?'[54]
- Two-dimensional: Focus is on decision-making and non-decision-making and observable (overt or covert) conflict. Policy preferences or grievances reveal participant interests.[55] Key empirical question: 'What issues have been mobilized off the agenda and by whom?'[56]
- Three-dimensional: Focus in on decision-making and control over the political agenda (not necessarily through decisions), observable (overt or covert) and latent

conflict. The real interests of participants may be obscured by dominant discourses.[57] Key empirical question: 'Whose objective interests are being harmed?'[58]

Hence, the three dimensional power model stresses that power can also be ideological and systemic;[59] power is 'able to influence the thoughts and desires of its victims without their being aware of its effects'.[60]

We contend that the community of Kelly Lake is simultaneously involved with the three dimensions of power through their multiple relationships with the federal and provincial governments, other Aboriginal organizations (both Métis and First Nations), and various private industries such as resource extraction companies and private health care providers. It is also clear that, simultaneously, these other players are involved in their own complex sets of relationships that sometimes impinge on the power positioning and possibilities for residents of Kelly Lake. For instance, in the case of industry–government–Aboriginal relations, resource extraction companies (including timber, gas, and coal) have typically negotiated directly with government authorities and nearby First Nations communities, while ignoring any protests or claims from Kelly Lake residents. Thus, while the other players have benefited from the extraction activity, the residents of Kelly Lake have been excluded from any of the pursuant benefits.

Methodology

This orientation towards highlighting theories of power is directly related to the methodological approach adopted which is concerned with 'activist scholarship' and 'participation research'. Audrey Kobayashi defines activist scholarship concerned with social justice issues as research combining a 'critical perspective on the world' with the personalization of the research undertaking. The former is 'an attempt to understand the systemic ways in which human relations result in oppression, and especially in racialized oppression'. The latter implies that activist research involves emotional experiences, commitment to personal stands on political issues, personal confrontation of oppressive conditions, and personal commitment 'to make a difference'.[61]

In recognition of these issues 'participatory research', as [Frank] Fischer calls it, seeks to develop research practices grounded in social justice and democracy, in which citizens and their local knowledges are brought directly into the research process. At the heart of this type of methodological orientation is the fundamental conviction 'that people can help choose how they live their lives'.[62] One strand of participatory research is called participatory action research (PAR). According to [William] Carroll 'in PAR, research is only one of three elements, with inclusive participation and action to create change being of equal import. PAR is in effect a form of radical pedagogy.'[63] More specifically, Fischer outlines that this form of research involves 1) collaborative learning between the researcher and the subjects; 2) a phenomenological perspective that values experiential knowledge and takes place in the subjects' 'natural' setting in order to understand the sociocultural context of the situation; and 3) [interpreting] the problems faced by subjects as related to social domination and oppression. As such, participatory action research is differentiated by its ideological commitment to empowerment.[64]

The research for this project was conducted within this approach of activist scholarship and participatory action research. The first author is Métis and a university student. This project both fulfilled the requirements for a directed reading course (with the second author) and allowed him to further the social justice work in the Aboriginal communities with which he is involved. The research was conducted over an eight-month period, between September 2004 and April 2005, through an initial four-day visit to the community of Kelly Lake [and] subsequent follow-up visits during which formal and informal discussions were held with a wide range of community members. Further, extensive telephone and email conversations were held with Kelly Lake community members, and interaction, dialogue, and conversations occurred with government authorities, private industry, and other Aboriginal groups to both understand Kelly Lake's problems and help facilitate some amelioration of the situation. Finally, the project also collected archival material, books, articles, and access to information data.

The Historical and Socio-Economic Context of Kelly Lake

The Canadian Constitutional Act of 1982, section 35, defines Aboriginals in Canada as being Indians, Inuit, and Métis. Prior to being included in the Constitution, the Métis in Canada chose to align themselves with Non-Status Indians through the Native Council of Canada since both groups faced similar challenges in obtaining recognition and resources from the federal government.[65] After being included in the Constitution, the Métis National Council (MNC) was formed claiming to be the voice of the Métis Nation.

As Gerry Andrews, schoolmaster at Kelly Lake from 1923 to 1925, offered in *The Métis Outpost*, the community has historic ties to the Red River Settlement in Manitoba during the golden age of the Métis under the leadership of Louis Riel, *circa* 1885.[66] Given this context, one could assume that the people of Kelly Lake would, automatically, be included as part of the Métis Nation. However, particularly prior to 2004, the community of Kelly Lake maintained their autonomy from the Métis National Council. Interestingly, since that time this situation has changed greatly. In 2006, the provincial government in British Columbia signed the Métis Nation Relationship Accord with the Métis Nation British Columbia (MNBC). In February 2007 MNBC signed a Métis Nation Territorial Affiliation Agreement with the Kelly Lake Métis Settlement Society (KLMSS).[67] These agreements are significant as they demonstrate that the residents of KLMSS have been successful in re-positioning themselves politically. A dialogue which had been previously unavailable is now possible. These very recent changes also demonstrate the fluidity of boundary definitions regarding who has official membership in the Métis Nation. This is clearly a social power issue; it is about the definition of who and what is 'Métis'.

In *The Kelly Lake Métis Settlement*, Dorthea Calverly writes about events in 1945 when the people of Kelly Lake tried to exert their legal claim to the land. In an example of one dimensional power (involving overt decision-making) and of the traditional capitalist relationship between governments and industry, the response from the government of British Columbia was to make the land at Kelly Lake a 'reserve'. This was not a reserve in the traditional Indian sense, but rather a 'timber reserve' with lumber companies controlling the wood and all uses. According to Calverly, at that time, the timber company holding title to the land had no intention of cutting the trees. The people had to obtain permission to cut logs to expand their houses for their ever-growing families and were denied work on their traditional lands. Calverly states that this contributed to the dependence on welfare in the community.[68] Today, the capitalist-driven relationships continue to be visible when visiting Kelly Lake; industry trucks constantly speed through the community, loaded with coal and lumber. These are not just trucks; this is money and resources leaving the traditional territory.

Unfortunately, the presence of the lumber, coal, and oil industries has not resulted in job opportunities for members of Kelly Lake. By leveraging their position in the Canadian Constitution as Status Indians (e.g., a third dimension power structure), nearby First Nations are able to demand employment, but the Métis of Kelly Lake rarely benefit. This forces many residents to leave in search of employment and has tended to de-populate the community.

Encana Oil is one of the most recent examples of capitalist exploitation of the Kelly Lake area; it recently invested $369 million for the right to drill and to acquire land in the Kelly Lake area.[69] The Métis of Kelly Lake are fighting Encana Oil and the government of British Columbia in court. In an article titled 'Battling the Ghosts and Death', author Derek Reiber quotes [KLMSS President Lyle] Campbell-Letendre as follows:

> They've drilled quite a bit around our area. We're never consulted. Nothing. I don't know how much harder I can stress that there's a problem. We're not here to stop progress. We're just here to say we want to be able to manage it. I want to be able to eat a moose in 10 years. And I want my grandson to be able to eat one in 40 years.[70]

Currently, due to the excessive drilling and clear-cutting, there are local fears that the wells are being drained and the availability of drinking water is now being questioned.[71] Campbell-Letendre realizes that progress and technology cannot be stopped; however, he maintains it can be controlled in a manner that does not affect the environment in a detrimental manner. Campbell-Letendre has had initial discussions with wind power companies since Kelly Lake is located on prime real estate for such a venture. To date, Campbell-Letendre has been successful in acquiring four meteorological towers for testing the wind capabilities of the area. In a rare agreement with Indian and Northern Affairs Canada (INAC), INAC assisted in acquiring the towers as well as supplying $50,000 in start-up funds.[72] Moreover, in contrast to the way in which they have traditionally been ignored by the resource extraction companies, currently the community has also been invited to undertake consultations with other energy resource companies interested in working in the Kelly Lake area.

Their questioning of status quo attitudes towards progress and the quest for more sustainable energy development initiatives (third dimensional power issues) along with the simultaneous demand for consultation (a first dimensional power concern) are emblematic of the complex power relationships within which Kelly Lake is embedded. Note also that these relationships move beyond the typical theorization of the Aboriginal–government fiduciary relationship, in which it is assumed that the government will negotiate and protect Aboriginal interests. Instead, the Métis of Kelly Lake are challenging both the government and resource extraction companies while simultaneously engaging in potentially positive sum negotiations with other capitalist firms. Through these processes and practices, the Métis of Kelly Lake are attempting to gain the 'power to' manage some of their local resources and striving to alter the power dynamic currently being faced by the community. As [Michel] Foucault would suggest, power here is productive rather than repressive;[73] it is being sought to improve the daily lives and conditions of Kelly Lake residents.

Within Kelly Lake: Infrastructure Issues

Other examples of the power relationships existent within the community are revealed through the community struggles to obtain adequate infrastructure, including telephones and sewage treatment. Until approximately 1998, the community had one telephone; a payphone that only accepted calling cards or allowed them to make collect calls. In a mini-documentary for CBC Television in 1993, Karen Tankard approached BCTel to inquire about the lack of phone service to the community. BCTel claimed that they were willing to invest $270,000 towards running phone lines to Kelly Lake and that the people would be required to pay $27,000.[74] This would have been impossible for the people of Kelly Lake and they remained without phones. Only when a private communications company, Telus, offered to set up the service did they receive phones. The service was installed from Alberta and the community has an Alberta area code, despite being located in British Columbia. However, unlike the second example provided below, the decision to provide the service in Kelly Lake was far less related to the needs of the community than to provide the corporations working in the vicinity with adequate telecommunications. In contrast to the resource extraction industry, in this case practices and decisions made in the interest of private sector players have led to a positive result within Kelly Lake despite the marginalized position of the community.

In another example of infrastructure problems, in the late 1970s and early 1980s housing was constructed in Kelly Lake. According to Campbell-Letendre, the goal was to have suitable houses constructed to replace the cabins of old.[75] The Canada Mortgage and Housing Corporation (CMHC) acted as the government agent for this initiative. Campbell-Letendre maintains that in order for the housing to be constructed, CMHC required that landowners sign off on five-acre parcels of land. Once the construction was completed, CMHC then sold the land back to the landowners at a cost of $1,000 per acre. In some cases, CMHC held the mortgage on the property or used it as a rental property. The $1,000 per acre did not include the mortgage for the actual house. As outlined below, formal ownership to property eventually proved problematic in solving sewage treatment problems.

Part of the housing construction process required CMHC to arrange for, and approve, the construction of a sewage system. A lagoon system was arranged whereby waste would drain into the lagoons and the natural elements would break down the waste. Campbell-Letendre contends that the Métis had no input into development or installation of the lagoons. The lagoons ultimately proved to be faulty resulting in overflowing sewage and raw sewage backing up into the basements of the homes that had been constructed by CMHC. In her documentary, Tankard presented graphic footage of houses that had to be evacuated due to sewage backup and the proximity of children to the overflowing lagoons. With widespread sewage overflow, Campbell-Letendre fears that the wild game has become contaminated, that the poorly constructed lagoons put both the health of the community and the health of the trapper/hunter economy at risk.[76]

As revealed by internal documents, CMHC eventually acknowledged the problems with the lagoons and agreed to undertake the needed repairs. Arrangements were made to assess sewage lines from the houses to the lagoons and to examine the lagoons themselves. However, only houses with which CMHC still had some kind of financial interest were examined. Anyone who had paid off their mortgage was not entitled to testing by CMHC.[77]

Contractors were hired to assess lagoon damage and make recommendations regarding repairs. The inadequacy of the CMHC's sewage management approach is exposed in a letter obtained through Access to Information. Dated 29 July 1993, the letter, from contractor L & M Engineering to CMHC states, 'many of the lagoons are less than 60 metres from the house and closer than 15 metres to the property line, both in contravention of the Peace River Health Unit "Sewage Lagoon Guidelines".' The letter further states, 'Lagoon systems for individual houses have proven to work well in many areas of northern B.C. The systems which have failed typically [sic] have been small, deep lagoons such as most of those in Kelly Lake.' The letter also states, in reference to the Kelly Lake lagoons, 'it is our experience that these systems seldom work.' L & M Engineering went on to recommend 'above ground' lagoons as opposed to the 'in ground' lagoons that had initially been installed.[78]

There were further complications and concerns brought about by CMHC's handling of the initial lagoon installations. Environmental consultants HBT Agra Limited were brought in due to water concerns with the lagoons. They expanded on the above analysis. In a letter dated 27 July 1993, HBT Agra states, 'It is understood that a number of properties use domestic wells as their water supply. An assessment of the ground water quality and the completion details of the wells was not part of the present study, however, it is recommended that an assessment of the potential for cross contamination between the septic disposal facilities and the water wells be carried out.'[79]

L & M Engineering's proposal for the 'above ground' lagoons was presented both to CMHC and the BC Ministry of Health. A letter from then chief environmental health officer Ann Thomas to CMHC stated, 'As the report suggests, it appears the only option for onsite sewage disposal is "above ground" lagoons to replace the present below grade lagoons. However, both myself and Mr. Miller [public health engineer] concur that this is an unacceptable option.'[80] A letter from Geoff Butchart, program manager with CMHC, to Jim Morris, operations manager, expresses some surprise that this option was turned down since 'the proposed corrections were in keeping with their own current guidelines and were prepared by a professional engineer.'[81] Eventually, a sewage system was agreed upon; however, the Métis of Kelly Lake again did not have a say in its design or management. It also does not appear that the problems with the old sewage system have been resolved. On a recent visit to Kelly Lake [by the first author], Campbell-Letendre pointed out pockets of raw sewage still visible on the surface and the stench of raw sewage was acute. From a theoretical perspective, both of these two infrastructure situations—sewage treatment and telephone service—are examples of the powerlessness of the community to meet even some of their most basic needs;

these are examples of both the first and second dimensional power relations facing the community since both direct decision-making and non-decision-making were involved.

Power Shift

History has shown that the Métis of Kelly Lake cannot rely on government to deliver the services and protection that most Canadians enjoy. As Canadians, the Métis of Kelly Lake are landowners and taxpayers, yet they are denied the benefits that mainstream taxpayers enjoy. Whether through active decision-making (e.g., the granting of resource extraction permits), non-decisions (e.g., failure to provide adequate housing and health care), or by recourse to status quo structures (place of the Métis in the Canadian Constitution), Kelly Lake residents have been marginalized. In recent times, however, the Métis of Kelly Lake have been striking out on their own in an effort to improve the various situations in the community. In so doing they are challenging hegemonic patterns and attempting to redefine the social power relations within which they are embedded.

Beyond the alternative energy agreements outlined above, another example of these efforts is a campaign in Kelly Lake that was undertaken to meet a need for hearing care services in the community. The campaign was structured to allow for participation in the campaign by a wide variety of government and industry actors. The intent was to give parties, such as the Peace River School Board, the opportunity to assist. All relevant parties were initially invited to participate in the campaign.

Through contacts in his network, the first author, David Bentley, approached Campbell-Letendre about bringing a hearing aid initiative to Kelly Lake. Bentley sits on the board of CanHear, a charitable organization that does hearing aid campaigns in Third World countries such as Mexico and Haiti. The goal of the campaign was to test the hearing abilities of the people and provide free hearing aids and ongoing care to those who could not afford them. When Campbell-Letendre assured Bentley no health care had been delivered to Kelly Lake in quite some time, [Bentley] approached CanHear founder Martin Heinrich about doing a campaign for Kelly Lake. Approval to proceed came immediately. This campaign challenged second dimensional power relationships since it addresses issues of non-decision-making and neglect. Heinrich and Bentley were determined that CanHear would make this campaign work, with or without government assistance. This challenged the traditional power relationship between the government and the community and challenged the notion that a private sector–Aboriginal relationship will necessarily lead to the marginalization of the latter actors.

The first order of business was to have the hearing abilities of the community tested. Charles Horn, then a consultant for Kelly Lake, was able to contact Fran Thornton, the audiologist responsible for northeastern British Columbia. Despite having never heard of Kelly Lake, [Thornton] did commit to visiting the community for two days of testing.

The Hearing Aid Act of British Columbia is overseen by the Board of Hearing Aid Dealers and Consultants and makes no allowances for giving away hearing aids in the province.[82] Before agreeing to go to Kelly Lake, Thornton requested that Bentley receive permission from the board to do this campaign. The board was willing to give verbal permission but not written. Part of challenging the existing power relationship in the health care sector is to be willing to attempt to influence taken-for-granted preferences and approaches—third dimensional power issues. The bottom line was that the campaign was going to happen with or without permission. The goal in the hearing aid campaign, apart from offering the service to the Métis, was to get other private sector health providers to see the benefits of such campaigns, as well as to encourage the government to provide future services for the community.

Horn had put a request to the school board for access to the school in order to test and have a waiting room for clients. The school is a modern facility that had been closed two years earlier due to budget cuts. It is also the only building suitable for such testing. Repeated requests were denied by the Peace River School Board who cited liability issues, even though the people of Kelly Lake had offered to insure the building for the testing periods. Interestingly, the school has been made available to multinationals when they wished to hold meetings there.[83] Testing was ultimately done in a resident's kitchen. With 10 people at a time crammed into the kitchen, testing was not of the quality it could have been. However, Campbell-Letendre made the best arrangements possible given the lack of co-operation by the school board.

Test results were shipped to Provincial Hearing Consultants and the aids assembled. Chris Auty, national sales manager for GN ReSound ([a] Danish hearing aid manufacturer), offered to supply, free of charge, any hearing aids that may be required. Not only were they free, they would be the best quality aids available. In the end, 72 people were tested with 17 requiring aids.

The objective of the campaign was, first and foremost, to provide necessary health care. Secondly, this was an opportunity to empower the community and its leadership. The provincial government, although officially required to provide health care services for all British Columbia communities, offered only minimal assistance and, at the local level, authorities with the school board refused to allow the use of the school. The minimization of government involvement essentially altered the prescribed health care model of service delivery, shifted power towards the community, and fast-tracked the campaign. The campaign went from concept to delivery in three months. In the end, lack of governmental assistance allowed for more interesting media coverage by CBC Radio and *The Raven's Eye News*. For instance, the front page of *Raven's Eye* featured the headline, 'Rare Health Services Come to Métis of Kelly Lake'.[84] While it was not a huge campaign when compared to government programs, it did draw services into the community that the government would not deliver.

A second campaign for Kelly Lake took place in September 2005. As with the first, Thornton went to the community and tested [residents'] hearing capabilities with the results being sent to Provincial Hearing Consultants in Hamilton, ON. GN ReSound provided any aids that were required. However, since access to the school in Kelly Lake had been denied on the first campaign, people went to Grande Prairie, AB, for the fitting of the aids. Hearing aid practitioner Joanne Lafond and office manager Kristina Wold, of Soundwave Hearing Care in Grande Prairie, offered to donate their time, opening on a Saturday, as well as the facilities at Soundwave in order to fit the required aids. While this required the residents of Kelly Lake to travel to Grande Prairie, it also meant that a proper setting for the campaign was secured.

By bypassing the traditional model of health care delivery, a non-zero sum outcome was achieved wherein all partners benefited. Audiologist Fran Thornton was the only government employee willing to join in this campaign. Thornton gained credibility in the eyes of the people of Kelly Lake. The residents of Kelly Lake benefited as they received testing and the aids. CanHear, Provincial Hearing, and GN ReSound profited from the invaluable publicity they received. Bentley also benefited as he was given the opportunity to coordinate the event and then write about it. This was a win/win/win campaign with the residents of the community given the power to make it happen. In a national context these shifts in power relationships may sound trivial. To the people of Kelly Lake the shift is monumental.

Discussion and Conclusion

The Kelly Lake case study has demonstrated the complex ways in which the three dimensions of power play out in ongoing relationships among the Kelly Lake settlement, various government agencies, other Aboriginal groups, and private industry. It has demonstrated that the power relationships among this group of players are nuanced, multi-layered, and never fully stable. It also provided examples of practices used to bolster, contest, or alter those relationships. In the case of Métis people of Kelly Lake, the fiduciary relationship touted to exist between the Métis and government agencies (in the housing, health care, education, and natural resources sectors) was found to be lacking, leading to examples of first, second, and third dimensions of power, and to the marginalization of Kelly Lake. In terms of the relationship with industry, while an exploitive approach was demonstrated by the resource extraction companies, the more recent agreement regarding alternative energy resources suggests that even this relationship is subject to power shifts. This shift was further demonstrated by companies involved with the hearing aid campaign; by envisioning a non-zero sum approach, all involved benefited and the residents of Kelly Lake gained a modicum of independence and power.

Given the way in which the Métis of Kelly Lake have begun to resist their marginal position within Canadian society as well as the rules and laws that reinforce that positioning (e.g., interpretations of Métis nationhood and the Canadian Constitution), we argue that the people of Kelly Lake are attempting to redefine who they are as active agents. This move towards redefining agency relocates understandings of power beyond the previously outlined three dimensions into a posited fourth dimension. According to Digeser while the first three faces of power are predicated on the idea that the agency and subjectivity of actors (e.g., the nature and needs of As and Bs) are given, the fourth dimension of power postulates that subjects are social constructions and, therefore, agency is contingent. In other words, the fourth dimension of power is linked to the formation of agency and its operation. Under this conceptualization, agency is not based on essential interests or 'true' desires; instead it is created and normalized within society. As such the methodological question becomes 'What kind of subject is being produced?' This dimension of power is, therefore, 'a tool for describing the identities and norms that sustain' the other dimensions of power;[85] it can also be seen as an opportunity to question how we know what we think we know about power, identity, and agency.

In the case of the Métis of Kelly Lake, attention to this fourth dimension of power provides an opportunity to unravel how their subject positions have been shaped and to identify the ways in which this has affected their agency. Drawing heavily from Foucault, Digeser outlines that fourth dimensional power is most clearly visible when the resistance against it is great since the formation of subjects is always resisted by human beings who never completely fit the mould of 'normal'. Thus, this fourth dimension is evidenced by the way in which the residents of Kelly Lake have chosen to resist their 'normal' marginalized identity and are redefining themselves as active agents. It is also evidenced by their own nuanced definition of what it means to be Métis; the community is, in effect, producing their own subject identity and agency. This in turn contributes to the ongoing, evolving political debates regarding who are Canada's Métis, what rights ought to flow from that definition, and who gets to decide.

For the people of Kelly Lake, activities such as the hearing aid campaign have challenged the normal practices for delivering health care to Aboriginal peoples; through this activity they are also redefining their agency. By rejecting the power relationships of the past and creating new ones in the present, it is possible that the seed has been planted for more balanced power relationships in the future. Auty states that GN ReSound is now looking at bringing the Kelly Lake model of hearing aid campaign to remote communities in Russia and Bulgaria.[86] A community of 150 Métis people is having a global impact because they dared to question what is accepted as 'normal' in our society.

Primary Document

4.   Rare Health Services Come to Métis at Kelly Lake

Joan Taillon, Raven's Eye, 2004

Not much has changed in Kelly Lake since the CBC did a 1993 documentary exposing hard living conditions in their community and the lack of essential services, says Lyle Letendre, president of the Kelly Lake Métis Settlement Society. Except more Elders have passed and the people who remain are more disheartened.

Until 1 September, that is. For two days, the Kelly Lake Métis experienced a near miracle brought by some people from Ontario and the only audiologist in northern British Columbia. For a few days the Métis had some hope something can go right. A few with impaired hearing now have hope they'll even hear again.

'That was such a success,' said Letendre. 'Wow. That was so good. I was really happy. All the Elders were there.'

Letendre sounded happy on the phone.

Frances Thornton, the BC doctor who travelled from Fort St John to Kelly Lake tested 72 residents of mixed ages; the youngest was 19. Seventeen will soon receive hearing aids at absolutely no cost to them.

Thornton said, 'I hope to return in the new year when the weather improves and hopefully we'll be able to assess the rest of the community who wish to be tested.'

Letendre said some people who need aids in both ears will receive them. He added only one woman who is totally deaf could not be helped. 'But she knows how to read lips,' Letendre said, wanting to remain upbeat.

Provincial Hearing Consultants, owned by Martin Heinrich and based in Hamilton, ON, is arranging for hearing aids donated by one of their suppliers and is coordinating all services to Kelly Lake. Although the lab work will be done in Ontario, it was a legal requirement to have a licensed BC practitioner oversee the hearing tests. Thornton brought an assistant with her to help with the tests, which had to be done in a private home because there was no clinic or community building.

Impressions were taken of the ears of people with hearing loss. Back in Hamilton the lab will make a mould, which will be matched up with the type of aid that suits an individual's hearing loss. Erin Milward of Provincial Hearing Consultants said their staff would return to Kelly Lake to fit the hearing aids, which will be as 'low-tech' as possible to do the job so that maintenance will be minimal.

The ball got rolling because a 42-year-old Métis man studying emergency preparedness in First Nation and Métis communities at Wilfrid Laurier University in Ontario happens to know Letendre. Dave Bentley also works part-time in a restaurant next to one of Heinrich's clinics, where he got to know Provincial Hearing Consultants' staff. When they learned about the desperate situation in Kelly Lake, they offered to help. Provincial Hearing Consultants are old hands at organizing hearing aid campaigns, only usually they take their services to poor countries such as Mexico and Haiti.

Peterson, general manager of Provincial Hearing Consultants, is incredulous that a community in Canada is without basic services. She said she believed Heinrich, who owns several clinics, would visit Kelly Lake to see conditions for himself when they return to do the fittings.

'We'd be the first country to rush out and fix somebody else's problems if we saw the same thing somewhere else. Or try to. Give aid or something. . . . We do our little bit that we can by reaching out to help the hearing impaired people who can't afford it.'

Peterson said hearing aids cost a minimum of $400 and range up past $2,000.

'The thing is, we had to do it in a house,' said Letendre. 'And it was just pouring, it was just raining.' He said more would have come for tests but they had no transportation, 'and the roads—I won't even go there.'

Letendre is on a high, just the same. He said Thornton told them that when the snow is gone, she'll return to Kelly Lake. 'And Dave Bentley said the same thing,' he said with obvious appreciation. 'And they're coming with a (ear, nose, and throat specialist) and a dentist! The people are . . . I see a smile on their face. That's all I see on them.'

'The community is remote and access difficult,' Thornton said. 'I've only been working in the North for a year and I was unaware that this community existed. I'm looking into how we can deliver better services to remote communities, but as I'm the only audiologist in the northeast of BC, it's a case of using existing resources effectively. I certainly think the two days spent at Kelly Lake was a worthwhile use of resources and I hope the community found this as well.'

Government's excuse for not helping Kelly Lake is a simple declaration that no

Métis community exists in British Columbia, Letendre told *Raven's Eye*. Even though they have a documented history going back 100 years.

Even though some can trace their genealogy back 200 years or more to French and Indian unions.

And even though the Cree-speaking descendents of Iroquois were still living self-sufficient lives in the bush into the 1980s.

Over the past few years, however, life as the Kelly Lake people knew it has changed, because of gas exploration, primarily.

That activity has brought roads and pipelines that cut through the community's hunting and fishing areas. The Kelly Lake people complain that the ground water is contaminated along with the animals, fish, and plants that they still depend upon for food.

The Métis live with the results, even in the face of government denials.

Their only decent building, a school, has been closed and they have been denied access to it. Letendre said the school board refused to let them open up the school to conduct the hearing tests, which is why they had to do it in one of the houses.

The houses are falling down from lack of repair. Many of the people, including Letendre, have to live away from home in order to work.

Curtis De Silva, president of the Métis Nation of British Columbia and a resident of Mission, is familiar with conditions in Kelly Lake. 'The moose are sick; we don't know why yet.' But he added that roads have been built over the natural salt licks moose need.

De Silva echoed Letendre's complaints about the lack of education and health services in Kelly Lake. Dawson Creek is more than 50 kilometres away. The nearest township is Grande Prairie, AB, an hour's drive. He said because they are not affiliated with the Métis National Council, neither recognition nor money comes their way. They can't pay lawyers to defend their rights while large corporations take over the land.

Questions for Consideration

1. What discourse did Aboriginal peoples use to press their claims with the Canadian and provincial governments? When and from where do most people assume this discourse originated? When, according to Brownlie, did it originate?

2. What was the Department of Indian Affairs' attitude towards Canada's treaty obligations? Why did DIA take this position? How did it react to Aboriginal peoples' attempts to assert their treaty rights?

3. In his letter of 12 August 1923, is Elijah Tabobondung asserting Aboriginal rights? Should this letter be seen as evidence of a widespread and conscious strategy of such assertions? Why or why not?

4. In what sense are the Métis of Kelly Lake engaged in 'resistance'? Do you think that Bentley and Murphy are correct to assert that this group has been successful in redefining 'the power relationships of the past'? Give reasons to support your answers.

5. Discuss how PAR and the four dimensions of power can help people to understand the situation at Kelly Lake.

6. Bentley and Murphy claim that the Métis of Kelly Lake seek to 'redefine who they are as active agents'. How does Taillon's article support this statement? How does the article show that the 'politics of definition' have contributed to their marginalization?
7. What forms has Aboriginal resistance to British, French, and Canadian colonialism taken?

Further Resources

Books and Articles

Brownlie, Robin Jarvis. *A Fatherly Eye: Indian Agents, Government Power, and Aboriginal Resistance in Ontario, 1918–1939*. Toronto and New York: Oxford University Press, 2003.

Harris, Cole. *Making Native Space: Colonialism, Resistance, and Reserves in British Columbia*. Vancouver: UBC Press, 2002.

Kulchyski, Peter. 'A Considerable Unrest: F.O. Loft and the League of Indians', *Native Studies Review* 4, 1&2 (1988): 95–117.

LaDuke, Winona. *All Our Relations: Native Struggles for Land and Ute*. Cambridge, MA: South End Press, 1999.

Richardson, Boyce, ed., *Drumbeat: Anger and Renewal in Indian Country*. Toronto: Summerhill Press, 1989.

Printed Documents and Reports

Venne, Sharon Helen, and Gail Hinge, eds. *Indian Acts and Amendments 1868–1975, An Indexed Collection*. Saskatoon: University of Saskatchewan Native Law Centre, 1981.

Films

Incident at Restigouche. DVD. Directed by Alanis Obomsawin. NFB, 1984.
Kanehsatake: 270 Years of Resistance. DVD. Directed by Alanis Obomsawin. NFB, 1993.
Rocks at Whiskey Trench. DVD. Directed by Alanis Obomsawin. NFB, 2000.
Starblanket. DVD. Directed by Donald Brittain. NFB, 1973.

Websites

Indian and Northern Affairs Canada, Royal Commission on Aboriginal Peoples (1996)
www.collectionscanada.gc.ca/webarchives/20071115053257/http://www.ainc-inac.gc.ca/ch/rcap/sg/sgmm_e.html

Ben Parfitt, 'Demanding a Say In the Boom', *The Tyee*, 31 May 2004
http://thetyee.ca/News/2004/05/31/Demanding_a_Say_in_the_Boom

Peace River Region of British Columbia and Alberta
www.calverley.ca

FIFTEEN

Treaties and Self-Governance

Introduction

In order to settle the geographic area that came to be known as Canada with newcomers, and obliged to do so by the Royal Proclamation of 1763, the federal government negotiated a series of treaties (known as the numbered treaties) with Aboriginal people during the late nineteenth and early twentieth centuries. The negotiation of the numbered treaties took place between 1871 and 1921 and involved making enormous tracts of land in the Prairie West, northwestern Ontario, and the Canadian North available for white settlement and industrial development. Widely different interpretations of these treaties exist. In 1952, historians such as George Stanley described the treaties as agreements in which non-negotiable terms were set by the state and accepted by an uncomprehending Aboriginal populace.[1] Such an interpretation tends to characterize Aboriginal people as naive children who possessed no concept of land ownership and misunderstood what the government was doing. This analysis, with slight variations, has remained shockingly resilient in the popular imagination. In part, its persistence rests upon the assumption that the Canadian government would not bargain in bad faith—that it would, in other words, follow through on its treaty obligations—and therefore the disastrous outcomes of the treaties must lie with the misunderstandings of Aboriginal people, not the failure of the government to hold up its end of the deal.

Court challenges from the 1970s to the present have sought to correct this misinterpretation and show that what was negotiated at the time was often not reflected in the written documents or in the verbal promises made by government officials. More importantly, the Aboriginal people who negotiated the treaties were fully cognizant of what they were doing and, in order to address the changing social, political, and economic landscape that faced them, sought to arrive at the best possible terms with the state under difficult circumstances. Aboriginal people consistently called for clothing, housing, farm equipment, animals, agricultural training, education for their children, and medical services as well as for aid during periods of scarcity and famine.[2] Moreover, they perceived the treaties differently than the colonial and Canadian authorities. For example, Treaty 7 was understood to be a peace agreement and not a land surrender.

Map 15.1 Historical Treaties of Canada. (Indian and Northern Affairs Canada.)

In this chapter's first article, Paul Rynard looks at one of the first 'modern' treaties, the James Bay and Northern Quebec Agreement signed by Quebec, the federal government, and the Cree and Inuit of northern Quebec in 1975. Initially, most commentators heralded this agreement as a breakthrough for Aboriginal peoples because it included significant provisions for Aboriginal self-government and participation in the development of the region. However, practice and discourse differed significantly. The implementation of the agreement proved less friendly to Aboriginal interests, particularly when they appeared to conflict with the development of Quebec's capitalist economy. Furthermore, the federal government did not intervene to ensure that the agreement was enforced. As Rynard eloquently writes, public policy 'needs to be analyzed in light of the Canadian state's chronic subservience to the needs of powerful social interests and the exigencies of the market economy'. He suggests (much like sociologist Martha Stiegman and activist Sherry Pictou) that, when it comes to choosing between upholding Aboriginal treaty rights and the advancement of capitalist development, the state will favour the latter every time.

The second article, by Stiegman and Pictou, critiques the use of the legal system by Aboriginal activists in their attempts to reclaim self-government and federal

PUBLIC NOTICE.

NOTICE is hereby given that a Commission representing Her Majesty's Government of the Dominion of Canada will hold Sessions at the places and on the dates hereinafter stated, for the purpose of treating with the Indians and Half-breeds of the Provisional District of Athabasca and of such territory immediately adjacent thereto as may be deemed advisable to include within the said Treaty for the extinguishment of their title to the lands within the said Provisional District and territory, viz :—

Lesser Slave Lake	-	-	-	8th	June,	1899.
Peace River Landing	-	-		13th	do	do
Fort Dunvegan	-	-	-	16th	do	do
Fort St. John	-	-	-	21st	do	do
Fort Vermillion	-	-	-	29th	do	do
Red River Post	-	-	-	3rd	July,	do
Fort Chipeweyan	-	-	-	8th	do	do
Fort Smith	-	-	-	14th	do	do
Fond du Lac (Lake Athabasca)	-	24th	do	do
Fort McMurray	-	-	-	4th August,	do
Wapiscaw Lake	-	-	-	16th	do	do
Athabasca Landing	-	-	23rd	do	do

All Indians and Half-breeds resident within the said Provisional District and territory, except those Half-breeds whose claim to land have already been extinguished in Manitoba or the Territories and who are now resident within the territory proposed to be treated for, are therefore invited to attend the Sessions of the Commission at such of the above mentioned points as may be nearest to their respective places of residence.

CLIFFORD SIFTON,

Minister of the Interior and Supt. Gen'l. of Indian Affairs.

OTTAWA, June, 1898.

Notice for treaty making, 1898. (Library and Archives Canada, C-140890.)

government recognition of their land rights. The authors argue that such methods support the status quo, which underpins a system that facilitates the appropriation of Aboriginal land. By using this system, First Nations are forced to adopt and internalize those understandings and identities of Aboriginality that the state has defined for them. As a result, the current legal system in Canada remains geared towards the extinguishment of Aboriginal cultures and assimilation of Aboriginal peoples, and continuing to work within this framework will ensure that inequities will never be addressed. In the words of Bonny Ibhawoh, 'Discussion about rights within [the] context of colonial law [is] merely part of the many discourses employed to legitimize the colonial state.'[3] Ergo, Stiegman and Pictou believe that Aboriginal activists should disdain the mechanisms for redress provided by the state and thereby deny them legitimacy because the system is the problem.

Chapter Objectives

At the end of this chapter, you should be able to

- understand and explain the motivations of both Aboriginal people and the Canadian government in the process of treaty-making;
- understand why the idea that Aboriginal communities did not understand or negotiate the terms of their treaties remains so pervasive;
- identify ways that Aboriginal communities have resisted colonial power in the late twentieth and twenty-first centuries;
- identify how and why Aboriginal people continue to struggle for self-governance; and
- identify alternative methods employed by Aboriginal people to advocate for change.

Secondary Source

1. Ally or Colonizer?: The Federal State, the Cree Nation, and the James Bay Agreement

Paul Rynard

I. Introduction

This paper argues that current public policies on Aboriginal rights may be insufficient to help ensure that First Nations can thrive as distinct peoples. There are widespread fears that many distinct First Nations cultures will soon disappear, and the evidence suggests that the manner in which governments have interpreted and implemented the James Bay Agreement poses a very real threat to the viability and distinctiveness of the eastern Cree Nation. In turn, this situation is rooted in a deeply entrenched historical pattern of federal evasion of the constitutional and moral obligations owed to First Nations. Finally, it is argued that to best understand this situation public policy needs to be analyzed in light of the Canadian state's chronic subservience to the needs of powerful social interests and the exigencies of the market economy.

Two qualifications are in order: first, the Inuit of northern Quebec (Nunavik) are, of course, partners in the James Bay Agreement, but I do not comment on their unique experience with the treaty here;[4] and second, the focus is primarily on the record of the federal government partly for reasons of manageability, partly because its actions are of general significance for First Nations and for all Canadians across the country, and also because I make extensive use of Alan Penn's important analysis,[5] which emphasizes the province–Cree relationship. Finally, Aboriginal lands and treaties are federal matters under the Constitution.

II. The Historical Setting for the James Bay Agreement

Background

The Crees to the east of James Bay have been trading furs with the Hudson's Bay Company since the early seventeenth century, and missionaries have been active in the region since the mid-nineteenth century. The charter granted by King Charles II of England to the Hudson's Bay Company in 1670 covered a vast territory, including the Cree portion of what is now northern Quebec or **Eeyou Istchee** (the Cree traditional lands). In 1871 the company sold its chartered territories to Canada, but an 1870 Imperial order-in-council stipulated that 'the Indian title' still had to be obtained by the Government of Canada. In 1898 Canada transferred much of the present Cree territory to Quebec, with the rest of present-day northern Quebec being transferred in 1912.

The 1912 transfer—the Quebec Boundaries Extension Act—explicitly reiterated the requirement to negotiate treaties: '. . . the Province of Quebec will recognize the rights of the Indian inhabitants . . . and will obtain surrenders of such rights. . . .'[6] In a sense, then, Canada transferred lands that were not its own, since they had never been ceded by the Crees. The stipulation to negotiate treaties provided an eventual legal basis for clear and 'unburdened' provincial ownership (west of James Bay Treaty 9 had been 'negotiated' in 1905 and 1929). The transfer also involved an attempt to avoid, perhaps unconstitutionally, the federal government's obligations, given that section 91(24) of the Constitution Act of 1867 declares 'Indians, and Lands reserved for the Indians' to be federal jurisdiction.[7] In contrast, in the numbered treaties covering northern Ontario and most of Manitoba, Saskatchewan, and Alberta, federally appointed treaty commissioners representing the Crown conducted the negotiations. So the transfer of the requirement to negotiate treaties in northern Quebec (which was absent Native consent) was an early federal off-loading of responsibilities, not unlike more recent betrayals of the Crees. This understanding of the transfer is also in keeping with a view of the Canadian state that sees both its policies and the evolving shape of its federalism as results of its chronic need to rank the priorities of capitalist accumulation ahead of other concerns and interests, such as the rights and well-being of First Nations: after 1912 in Quebec it was the province that was responsible for rights relating to Indian title.

It was not until the 1930s that either the province or the federal government established a limited presence in Eeyou Istchee. The provincial presence was confined to the regulation of some hunting and trapping in the extreme south of the territory. In the late 1930s the federal department of Indian Affairs began to draw up band lists amongst the Crees and to create, or in most cases to recognize, band councils headed by chiefs.[8] There was no consultation or negotiation about the political implications of the government's new presence and the modified Cree institutions. Indian Affairs came to control the political affairs of the Crees under the Indian Act, and minimal social services such as pensions became available to many. Residential schools were also established as church and state co-operated in a misguided attempt to educate and socialize, sometimes with horrifying consequences.

After 1945, as part of the pan-Canadian use of northern resources to fuel the post-war economy, mining enterprises and some forestry spread into the southern extreme of Eeyou Istchee. Yet although these are provincially regulated industries, it was only in the 1960s that the provincial government began to be a significant presence in most of the Cree territories and in the communities. Prior to the hydro projects, then, the Quebec state lacked a physical presence, in terms of institutions and personnel, in most of Eeyou Istchee, thus underscoring the importance of the federal role and what could have been the basis for a more vigorous defence of Cree rights in the face of sudden massive hydro undertakings.

At the beginning of the 1970s, the Crees continued to live as a distinct people in their traditional homeland. The Crees were also increasing their contacts with the mainstream Canadian economy through wage labour, especially in seasonal jobs with mining and forestry companies but also in guiding and with the Hudson's Bay Company. But the wage work of many Crees did not alter the fact that in 1971 the Cree 'economy' consisted mostly of traditional trapping, hunting, and fishing. The Cree language, culture, and identity were being constantly renewed through traditional practices in ancient patterns—supplemented rather than replaced or threatened by wage work and some federal transfers. For most Crees such income was used to outfit a family for hunting and not to provide an alternative source of subsistence.[9] The strength and relative autonomy of the traditional way of life were reflected in the stability of the Cree system of regulating hunting by dividing the land into traplines and hunting territories overseen by tallymen or stewards. Each tallyman controlled the use of and access to the wildlife in 'his' territory, but under cultural and community pressures to be socially generous and ecologically responsible.[10]

Resistance and Negotiation

Quebec Premier Robert Bourassa announced the James Bay project in April of 1971 without bothering to consult the Crees and without considering their rights and title. A handful of young Cree leaders, fluent in English, enlisted community support and began to fight the project. With construction moving quickly ahead without Native consent, Cree and Inuit leaders went to court and won an injunction that stopped the entire project after a remarkable trial with 71 days of testimony from Cree and Inuit hunters. Justice Albert Malouf ruled that some sort of Aboriginal title and other rights were unextinguished and relevant, and that the hydro project posed a serious threat to the Indigenous peoples and their cultures. However, within only 10 days the project was back on track as the injunction was lifted.[11] The resulting legal uncertainty prompted the province to favour a negotiated solution. The [James Bay and Northern Quebec Agreement] (JBNQA) was signed in November 1975.

The Cree decision to negotiate has been analyzed by others in some detail, but it amounted to a recognition that they had very little choice.[12] Two important rulings made further court support for the Cree position seem extremely unlikely: in December 1973 the Supreme Court refused to overturn the suspension of the injunction against construction, and in November 1974 the Quebec Court of Appeal permanently overturned the suspended injunction (Malouf's sympathetic ruling). The Cree side saw their bargaining power undermined as the negotiations proceeded and as the project became unstoppable. There are other reasons, too, for concluding that the Crees were ultimately under duress during the negotiations. Before 1982 Parliament could unilaterally use legislation to extinguish Aboriginal rights, including title, and the Cree leaders were aware of this possibility.[13] Many basic provisions and the wording of the final agreement must be read in light of the lack of options and bargaining power on the Cree side.

III. Selected Provisions of the James Bay Agreement

The Land Regime

The JBNQA is more than 450 pages and now includes 10 supplementary agreements. Determining the amount of Cree land surrendered is especially complicated given that the agreement confirms varying degrees of Cree rights in the whole region.

Most of the region became category III lands—public lands available for use and development by all Quebecers (although regulated by other sections of the agreement). All the land and resources in category III belong to Quebec. But even on these lands the Crees retained exclusive rights to some species of fish and animals and significant rights to continue all of their wildlife harvesting activities under a regime set up by the agreement. Moreover, the provisions for environmental protection were designed to give the Crees a say in the development of these lands, and the Crees are also supposed to enjoy preferential treatment in the development of outfitting enterprises in category III lands.

Category II lands are defined by the exclusive rights of Native harvesters to hunt, trap, and fish—there is no legal non-Native competition here. However, beyond wildlife the Crees do not own any of the natural resources in these lands, which also became Quebec lands, nor do they control the development that takes place therein.

Finally, category I lands are more under Native control, although even here Aboriginal title is not recognized, and Quebec has subsurface (mineral) rights and other specific development rights. But Cree band councils can pass a wide range of bylaws enforceable on these lands, and all the Cree communities are in category I lands. However, Cree category I lands total only 5,600 square kilometres, or about 1.5 per cent of the land the Crees use (s.5.1). It must also be emphasized that the Crees faced substantial restrictions concerning which lands could be claimed as category I and II lands. Quebec and its Crown corporations effectively asserted priorities of

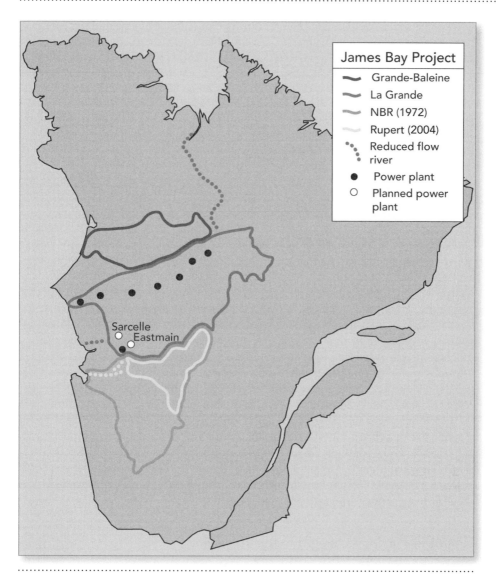

Map 15.2 Map of James Bay Hydro Project.

hydroelectric and natural resource development as pre-existing plans were insisted upon.[14]

Extinguishing Aboriginal Rights

A central component of the treaty is its infamous extinguishment clause, which was presented by Canada and Quebec as absolutely non-negotiable. JBNQA section 2.1 reads:

> In consideration of the rights and benefits herein set forth in favour of the James Bay Crees and the Inuit of Quebec, the James Bay Crees and the Inuit of Quebec hereby cede, release, surrender and convey all their Native claims, rights, titles and interests, whatever they may be, in and to land in the territory.

The surrender is said to be in exchange for all the rights and benefits that are spelled out in the rest of the agreement, in the belief that the agreement then becomes a final and exhaustive list of rights—rights that *were* Aboriginal but have become treaty rights. This clause revived a nineteenth-century policy of using treaties to ensure that business interests and the state would never again have to deal with the issue of Aboriginal 'rights, titles and interests . . . in and to land'. The JBNQA's land regime is therefore effectively frozen even though it reflects, primarily, the interests of the Crown corporations and the province and even though it was negotiated under duress.

The JBNQA also contains a section devoted to 'technical aspects' where the details of the La Grande complex and a variety of other remedial and possible future projects are spelled out. One clause is particularly disturbing in that it explicitly prevents the Native communities from referring to 'sociological factors or impacts' in opposing any future developments (JBNQA 8.1.3). In other words, the clause suggests that the Crown corporations and governments involved are not interested in the human and cultural effects of their resource projects. The intent of this clause has become even more disturbing since we know that Hydro's development of the La Grande complex did in fact have unanticipated and extremely serious impacts of a sociological nature. Chisasibi is the Cree community most directly affected by the hydro projects because of its location on the La Grande River. Due to an alteration in the river's natural flow, the community was relocated. Then it was discovered that many of the residents of Chisasibi were suffering from mercury exposure. The mercury was accumulating in fish, a staple of the traditional Cree diet, as a direct but unanticipated consequence of the flooding required by the hydro developments. The sudden concentration of people in a new village, which had new road access to the south, was also a problem, as was the loss of a great deal of hunting territory.

What the Parties Achieved in the JBNQA

As noted, the mix of circumstances, threats, policies, and court rulings did not give the Cree side many real options, and the agreement finally ratified had some surprisingly promising provisions. The Cree Nation received some compensation and protection from a project they would not have been able to stop in any event, and they bargained for, amongst other things, a whole range of commitments for new services and programs and for increased Cree participation in administration. But most important the Crees also achieved wildlife-harvesting provisions, to help maintain and renew their traditional economy and way of life. Taken together, these sections of the agreement overshadowed money and other considerations in importance during the negotiations in the eyes of the majority of Crees. For those Crees who would or could no longer make a living in the traditional manner, the agreement also contained promises to help them better integrate into the wider Canadian economy.

The agreement held considerable benefits for the provincial government, although it still met with significant resistance in Cabinet from those who seemed to deny the existence of any Aboriginal rights at all.[15] Quebec's negotiator and cabinet minister, John Ciaccia, sold the agreement largely by playing up its nation-building implications.

Quebec gained a legal and constitutional basis—however tainted by coercion—for its claims to the region, just as the hydro project itself and the array of services and programs promised in the agreement meant that the provincial presence in the region would be drastically expanded. All this was achieved at a cost that was a mere fraction of what would be invested in the construction of the project and eventually returned in electricity and other resource revenues.

Ottawa's role in the formation of the agreement is intriguing. Federal officials knew that the treaty-making conditions of the territory transfer agreements had not been met, yet when the hydro project was announced the federal government did not oppose Quebec's unqualified assumption of jurisdiction and ownership. However, the Department of Indian Affairs had little choice but to fund some of the Crees' legal battles and the costs of negotiating, given the prevailing understandings of its constitutional obligations. In fact, in January 1974, Indian Affairs Minister Jean Chrétien threatened to cut off such funding in order to force the Crees to accept Bourassa's original offer of a settlement. According to Roy MacGregor, editorial and public opinion forced Chrétien to back down on the threat when it was made public.[16]

The wider context of federal–Indian relations was also relevant. The government had been forced to abandon—in public statements, at least—its 1969 policy paper, which had proposed an acceleration of the assimilation of Indians and denied the legitimacy of the concept of distinct and ongoing Aboriginal rights. In the summer of 1973 the federal government announced that it would consider negotiating Aboriginal title claims—a response to the Supreme Court's decision in the **Calder case**, in which three of the six judges who addressed the question argued that Nisga'a Nation's title to their homelands remained valid and unextinguished.

In sum, as the federal government apparently saw things, its role was to foster, not to undermine, economic development and capitalist investment, and this in turn required the elimination of the legal uncertainty created by Aboriginal land rights. In the case of James Bay, this broad goal did not conflict with that of trying to manage Quebec nationalism by co-operating with the Quebec Liberals.

IV. Implementation of the JBNQA

Delay, Negligence, and Review in the Initial Phase of Implementation

Neither level of government was ready to live up to the obligations agreed to in the treaty once it was signed. The main piece of federal enacting legislation was delayed for two years and only passed, just before the deadline, after the Crees pressed for action. Neither the financial nor the organizational resources necessary for implementation were made available in the years immediately following the signing, although work with Quebec on the harvesting regime in particular seems to have proceeded reasonably well.

It seems that the federal government was trying to proceed with a business-as-usual approach even though the JBNQA had codified and clarified many of its obligations to the Crees. Perhaps the most important event highlighting government negligence happened about five years after the treaty was signed. A gastroenteritis epidemic in several Cree communities killed several children and made others extremely ill. The deaths were the direct result of poorly planned and half-finished sewers built by the Department of Indian Affairs. Provision 28.11.1(b) of the agreement states that funding and technical assistance are to be provided for 'essential sanitation services in each Cree community', subject to government funding capabilities. Yet initial Cree complaints about the situation were not acted upon until international pressure was applied. After such pressure, and after Cree and Inuit representatives testified before the House Standing Committee on Indian Affairs, the government ordered an internal review of its implementation of the treaty.[17]

The review, which looked at a variety of issues, unconvincingly argued that the government had not broken legal obligations—exaggerating the ambiguity of clauses like the sanitation clause while downplaying the government's fiduciary obligations on the advice of Department of Justice lawyers—but it still made clear that the government had violated the 'spirit and intent' of the JBNQA. In general the report emphasizes what it sees as the ambiguity of most of the obligations in the agreement, and says the federal government was not prepared to implement the spirit and intent of the agreement whenever that required special or additional programs and structures.[18]

Warren Allmand, who was minister of Indian Affairs when the agreement was confirmed into law by legislation, told the Standing Committee on Indian Affairs that he had the same understanding of this issue as did the Crees:

> [it] was crystal clear in the minds of the Crees at the time of the signing that all federal programs, services and benefits would continue, and would be in addition to, and without prejudice to, all the rights, benefits and privileges which the Crees would receive under the . . . Agreement.[19]

Inuit testimony has independently expressed precisely the same understandings of the text of the agreement and of its intent as stated by the negotiators.[20] Therefore, although many specific clauses are somewhat ambiguous and sometimes lack binding language, the principle that the treaty committed both Canada and Quebec to recognize, fund, and provide both normal programs and additional treaty rights and programs was firmly established—a reasonable enough principle if treaties are to be aimed at reconciliation and renewal.

Allmand's testimony came to light in the wake of the gastroenteritis epidemics, as did the implementation review. This public attention to the treaty resulted in the establishment of an implementation office to oversee the JBNQA.

Self-Government for the Crees?

The JBNQA, in section 9, had set out guidelines for negotiations on Cree control of local affairs and service delivery, although such powers were to be delegated by legislation. Yet it was not until 1984, and after considerable lobbying efforts by the Cree leaders, that the Cree–Naskapi Act was passed. This piece of federal legislation replaced the Indian Act for the Crees and Naskapis, and recognized significant powers of local governance, although limited to matters typically given to cities and municipalities. But another major limitation is that the Cree–Naskapi Act only applies on the small parcels of category I lands, so that the decisions made by the band councils are made in the context of the relative isolation from the Quebec economy. This means that there is a lack of an adequate tax base as well as a significant absence of Cree authority over 98.5 per cent of their traditional territories.[21] The Cree–Naskapi Act also involved the creation of the Cree Naskapi Commission. The commission is a panel with equal Cree and federal representation and has usually been chaired by a judge from Quebec.

V. The Canadian State and Cree Nationhood

Explaining the Poor Record of JBNQA Implementation

One explanation for the poor record of federal implementation is fiscal priorities and constraints.[22] The Department of Finance and Treasury Board have repeatedly put pressure on federal officials to contain spending with respect to the JBNQA. But it is not at all clear to what extent such policies and decisions reflect actual fiscal capacities.

From the position of a middle-level bureaucrat with a fixed amount of money to dispense, there may well be a logic and fairness about treating all recipients equally and without reference to special rights, such as James Bay agreement entitlements. For example, when the Cree–Naskapi Commission reviewed the capital-funding disagreements, the federal representatives told the commission that they felt obligated to give the Crees only their fair share of normal Indian Affairs program funding so they could avoid treating other Indians unequally. The commission correctly concludes, 'this implies that government funding is decided upon by policy and not in legal accordance with an agreement.'[23]

There is some ambiguity about the precise nature of the resistance to meeting treaty obligations within Indian Affairs, but it is also true that this merely mirrors the ambiguity about political will closer to the centres of power. Fiscal concerns, whatever their origins, have consistently militated against a fair implementation of a legally binding treaty. The Ambassador of the Crees [notes] that there is such a poor record of treaty implementation simply 'because it is cheaper to pay civil servants to fight Indians than it is to meet treaty obligations.'[24]

Another explanation for poor implementation might be organizational. The government in general is not prepared to restructure operations to meet the new obligations taken on in the treaty,[25] and it also has failed to coordinate properly the various departments and agencies relevant to specific programs or treaty provisions.

Another distinct yet central factor in federal non-implementation is a concern to avoid conflicts with governments of Quebec, as much as possible, in order to check the separatist movement. Several commentators have shown how the Crees have seen the priority attached to their federal relationship subordinated to the general concerns of national unity.[26]

A number of factors are relevant in causing the history of poor treaty implementation. Taken together they reveal an entrenched resistance to acting on the full range of obligations in the JBNQA, a resistance that has spanned nearly 25 years and run through numerous governments and Cabinets. The treaty-breaking can be seen as a contemporary version of the long-standing historical pattern of minimizing or deny-ing Aboriginal rights.

Federalism, Capitalism, and Cree Land Rights

The JBNQA commits the federal government to confront certain powerful interests, most obviously the government of Quebec and Hydro-Quebec, but also various cor-porate interests, like the forestry and mining companies, who directly benefit from the denial of Aboriginal rights by gaining easier and cheaper access to natural resources. The unwillingness to fundamentally restructure the relationship between the state and First Nations is very likely rooted in the limited capacity of, and the lack of incentive for, the federal state to compel all the interests who benefit from the status quo to behave differently.

The evaluation of public policies affecting the Crees is bound up with the com-plexities of Canadian federalism. The James Bay hydro developments and the other ongoing resource industries may be the most immediate and profound threats to the well-being of Cree communities, but they are provincial undertakings. It is in fact ac-curate to speak of a provincial colonization of the Eeyou Istchee, especially since there was such a notable absence of the provincial state from the region before expansion of the hydro projects.

Yet the federal jurisdiction over 'Indians and lands reserved for Indians' means that provincial exploitation of the resources of James Bay could take place only with the co-operation of federal policies, even if the policies amounted to little more than an abrogation of responsibilities and the relatively passive negotiating stance of alert neutrality. The federal policy most obviously implicated here is the JBNQA's extinguish-ment clause, which immediately and decisively 'cleared' the provincial ownership of lands and resources—excepting the limited and defined treaty rights of the JBNQA—from the 'burden' of Aboriginal rights and title. Moreover, the Supreme Court has re-cently clarified that only the federal government can extinguish Aboriginal title,[27] thus reinforcing the dependence of provincial resource based industries on federal policies that minimize Aboriginal land rights.

The specifics of Canadian federalism are only a partial explanation of the tendency for governments to minimize Aboriginal rights. At a deeper level the state–economy relationship of capitalism is structured so that governments face overwhelming pres-sure to allow for the continued plundering of lands and resources by capitalist inter-ests. In Canada these pressures can take on the form of provincial 'rights'. In Quebec this compounds the unity crisis. The essential result of such intergovernmental con-flict is a weakening of the capacity of the state to regulate resource economies in ways that oppose the interests of capital. This means that First Nations must sign treaties with state representatives, but in doing so they sign with only one component of the power structure with which they are dealing. Private capitalist interests—including Crown corporations like Hydro-Quebec which may be arms of the state yet are de-signed and managed to act like corporations—pressure the state to ignore treaty and Aboriginal rights.

It is useful to consider some general estimates that can partly quantify and illus-trate the situation in Eeyou Istchee. Cree reports estimate that electricity revenues from Eeyou Istchee are about $5 billion per year, and about $1 billion worth of lumber is cut annually from Cree traditional territories. In 1996–7 the federal government reports having spent $216 million on the Crees, Inuit, *and* Naskapis ($145 million from Indian Affairs and the rest from 12 other departments). These numbers exclude personal transfer payments—but it must be noted that the Cree band councils do not receive normal municipal transfers and are trying to cope with the legacy of colonial neglect, the social dislocation of the resource projects, and all the problems of youth unemployment and disaffection on the margins of the Quebec economy. The Cree portion of the annual federal expenditures is probably a little over half of the $216 million, while provincially owned corporations and the so-called private sector reap revenues of $6 billion from water and forestry resources on Cree lands. Of course considerable tax revenues then flow back to the governments; about $250 million goes to the federal government from the GST collected on hydro sales alone.[28]

The government's inability and unwillingness to implement fully the James Bay Agreement sheds light on a central fact of the Canadian political economy: the much-discussed financial dependency of the First Nations on the Canadian state is the direct result of the often overlooked dependency of capital on the resources of First Nations' land. This is the contradictory context within which the state–First Nations relationship ought to be understood. However much the minister and the Department of Indian Affairs try to meet the needs of the dispossessed First Nations, they are part of a state that is structured to serve first the needs of those who benefit from the dispossession.

Implications of Rights Denied

It is important not to appropriate or misrepresent Cree experiences in confronting Canadian society, but we are obligated to listen, and Cree leaders have made public statements about Canada's inability to honour its treaties while being quite able to plunder the land's resources. Robbie Dick, former chief of Whapmagoostui, described what the Crees had encountered as 'the bulldozer way of being'.[29] Grand Chief Matthew Coon Come, referring to the plans to dam the Great Whale River, said that examining the reasons for the lack of a proper comprehensive and unbiased environmental review 'questions the whole way that the dominant society does things'.[30] Recent Cree testimony before the Senate Subcommittee on the Boreal Forests pointed out that 'it is our opinion that the [forestry] companies are making decisions for Quebec.'[31]

For the Crees east of James Bay the agreement has meant that the development of the territory has proceeded in a manner not approved of by its residents. Nor has it given them a rightful share in economic benefits. Unemployment and poverty rates remain above the national average, as is the case in most other First Nations communities. The need for federal transfers is maintained and exaggerated by the JBNQA and public policies that deny Cree communities revenues and employment from the resources on their traditional lands. Hydro-Quebec, for example, has fewer than 20 Crees on its payroll while it continuously transfers hundreds of employees from southern Quebec and back.[32] Southern Cree communities like Waswanipi and Ouje-Bougoumou (a village relocated seven times in the twentieth century for the convenience of mining interests)[33] are surrounded by clear-cuts.

There are widespread fears about the strength and distinctiveness of Cree culture. For example, anthropologist Harvey Feit has emphasized the centrality of hunting to Cree culture and the seriousness of the threat to hunting posed by logging. He concludes that 'rapid forestry development, as well as significant increases in non-Cree harvests of wildlife, directly threatens the Cree use of lands and the fabric of Cree society and economy.'[34] The former deputy grand chief of the Crees, Kenny Blacksmith, put it this way:

> the arrogant assumption of all of the jurisdiction by the governments of Canada and Quebec, and their exclusion of the Cree people from both the determination of the regimes concerned and the implementation of the measures required, is a major threat to our society. I would say that, in tandem with megaprojects and forestry development, failure of the regulation of the management of wildlife resources is the major threat to our society, driving our culture towards extinction.[35]

The roots of these problems are deep and complex, but cannot be explained sufficiently by reference to factors such as fiscal constraints, national unity concerns, or administrative organization. I think the evidence suggests it is hardly a coincidence that the public policies threatening Cree culture are policies so well tailored to the needs of corporations.[36]

Primary Document

2. Excerpt from *Cree Regional Authority et al. v. Attorney-General of Quebec*, 1991

Cree Regional Authority and Bill Namagoose
(Applicant)
v.
Raymond Robinson (Respondent)
Indesec as Cree Regional Authority v. Canada (Federal Administrator)
Trial Division, Rouleau J. – Montreal, March 11 and 13, 1991

. . .

In recent months, the government of Quebec along with the James Bay Corporation and Hydro-Quebec have made public their intention to proceed with Phase II of the development called the Great Whale River Hydroelectric Project. It was recently disclosed that the corporation responsible for the development of the project called for the tenders for the clearing of an access road as well as its construction. The **Grand Council of the Crees** became aware of this initiative and were pressing federal authorities to initiate environmental review procedures in the area before the construction was to begin. Conscious of the imminent commencement of site preparation for the road, the Grand Council of the Crees instructed their lawyers to bring proceedings before this Court seeking *mandamus* or an injunction against the appointed federal administrator, Mr. Raymond Robinson. Ultimately the relief requests that he conduct environmental and social impact assessment and review procedures pursuant to sections 22 and 23 of the Agreement.

In a letter dated October 3rd, 1989 and directed to the Minister of the Environment of the Province of Quebec, the federal minister, Lucien Bouchard, indicated that since the federal authorities had become aware of the development of the Great Whale River Hydroelectric Project, it was its view that an environmental assessment should be undertaken since the project involved matters of federal jurisdiction. He contended that sections 22 and 23 of the Agreement applied and he suggested a cooperative approach between both levels of government. The letter went on to indicate that federal officials would look forward to hearing from Hydro-Quebec and hoped to receive from them an outline of the proposed project. He further suggested that taking into account the considerable magnitude of the project, it was extremely important that an environmental assessment be conducted as objectively and independently as possible.

On November 28, 1989, the federal Minister of the Environment once again wrote to the newly appointed Minister of the Environment of the Province of Quebec bringing to his attention that urgency of the environmental review and enclosed a copy of the letter previously forwarded to his predecessor. By a letter dated the 23rd of November 1989, Mr. Raymond Robinson, the federal administrator, corresponded with the vice-president of the environment of Hydro-Quebec and reiterated that this project was subject to a federal environmental review pursuant to sections 22 and 23 of the Agreement. He further requested a summary or outline of the project and confirmed that pursuant to his mandate, he had appointed a tribunal to initiate a study. He also confirmed that he considered that the federal government had an obligation to undertake these studies in light of recent decisions of the Federal Court of Canada, and more particularly, in light of the EARP Guidelines [*Environmental Assessment and Review Process Guidelines Order*, SOR/84-467] which came into effect in June of 1984. He also suggests a cooperative study.

An extensive period of silence then prevails. On the 19th of November 1990, Mr. Robinson wrote to Michel Chevalier of Environment Canada, president of the evaluation committee responsible for the James Bay and Northern Quebec Development. He outlines the federal responsibility with respect to the Great Whale Project and the impact it may have in areas of federal jurisdiction, such as fisheries, migratory birds and the ecology of Hudson's Bay. He advises that the federal appointees are prepared to work in collaboration with their provincial counterparts and he is anxious that a joint agreement be ratified. Should Quebec fail to act, the federal government would be obliged to act unilaterally, he wrote. On November 23, 1990, Mr. Robinson again advises the vice-president of the environment for Hydro-Quebec that this project is subject to federal evaluation pursuant to sections 22 and 23 of the Agreement and he seeks a cooperative effort.

At a meeting in November of 1990, Mr. Robinson changes his position and informs the Cree that he has no mandate to apply federal impact assessment review procedure under the Agreement. As a result of this turn of events, this motion was launched against Mr. Robinson, the federal administrator responsible for environmental evaluation pursuant to section 22 and 23 of the Agreement. Shortly thereafter, having been made aware of the motion, Hydro-Quebec, the federal Department of Justice, and the Attorney General of Quebec sought leave to be added as intervenors. This was granted by the Court without objection by the applicant. The respondent as well as the intervenors challenge the jurisdiction of this Court to grant the relief sought.

It is the applicant's position that the Agreement, which was ratified by the Parliament of Canada, is the law of Canada, that Mr. Robinson, appointed pursuant to the enabling Act of Parliament, has a statutory obligation to appoint Review Panels which he has failed to do; that, pursuant to subsection 3(5) of the ratifying Act, Mr. Robinson, appointed by Order in Council, was a "federal board, commission, or other tribunal" pursuant to paragraph 2(g) of the Federal Court Act . . . and that this Court has jurisdiction to entertain the motion and grant the relief claimed.

The respondent, as well as all intervenors, submit that the Parliament of Canada, has not incorporated the Agreement *per se* into its confirming legislation. They submit that as a result, the appointment of Mr. Robinson was not pursuant to federal legislation and that his powers are derived from a joint provincial and federal authority; and finally, that this Agreement was not an Act of Parliament and therefore this Court does not have jurisdiction.

As mentioned earlier, this rather extensive and complex Agreement involved not only the federal and provincial authorities, but included as signatories Hydro-Quebec, the James Bay Development Corporation, and more importantly, the Grand Council of Cree and Inuit of Northern Quebec. In the document, the aboriginal peoples relinquished their traditional rights over some 3/5 of the territory of the province of Quebec in return for certain assurances and guarantees included in the Agreement. It specifically recognizes the Crees' rights to trapping, fishing, and hunting grounds; considers the social and economic impact that any future development may have, and enshrines, in sections 22 and 23, a procedure to be followed with respect to environmental impact studies which are to be conducted in the event of further projects.

Section 22 refers to the Environment and Future Development Below the 55th parallel, and section 23 refers to the Environment and Future Development North of the 55th parallel. There is no doubt that some of the initial infrastructure development may be undertaken south of the 55th parallel, but nevertheless the major hydroelectric development will occur north of the 55th parallel.

Pursuant to the terms of this Agreement, all parties are to derive certain benefits, and there is no doubt that the Cree and Inuit of the territory were given some guarantees for having surrendered certain rights. The ultimate aim was to provide future safeguards for the occupying aboriginal peoples.

According to sections 22 and 23 of the Agreement, a federal administrator is to be appointed for the purposes of supervising the environmental impact of any future development and to see to the protection of areas of federal jurisdiction which includes, of course, the Indian people of the region. The Agreement specifically indicates that the Administrator is to set up evaluating committees to determine if the development is to have any significant impact on the native people or the wildlife resources of the territory. He is under no obligation to proceed with an assessment in the event that the development contemplates no significant impact. I doubt that anyone can suggest that Phase II of the James Bay Hydroelectric Development Project will not affect both the social and economic future of the native peoples and will certainly interfere with wildlife and its habitat, resulting in drastic changes to the traditional way of life.

As a schedule to the Agreement, it was indicated that future amendments were to be approved by all parties and ratified by the Quebec National Assembly as well as the Parliament of Canada when changes concerned their respective jurisdictions. This would appear to me to indicate that all parties presumed legislative authority or ratification.

The initial submission put forth by the respondents, as well as the intervenors, was to the effect that the statute passed by the Parliament of Canada ratifying the Agreement did not of itself incorporate all terms of the Agreement; was not an enactment and therefore created no federal jurisdiction; it was not a statute, therefore the appointment of Mr. Robinson, by an Order in Council, was not by enactment, and could not clothe this Court with jurisdiction to grant the relief sought.

. . .

The preamble [of the Agreement] goes on to state, that in consideration of the surrender of the native claims to this portion of the territory of Quebec, the government of Canada recognizes and affirms a special responsibility to protect the rights, privileges, and benefits given to the native peoples under the Agreement . . . The Agreement was tabled by the Minister of Indian Affairs and Northern Development and approved and declared valid by Parliament.

. . .

In reaching this conclusion, I cannot help but be directed by the words of Dickson C.J. in *R. v. Sparrow*, [1990] 1 S.C.R. 1075, in which courts are directed that 'the Sovereign's intention must be clear and plain if it is to extinguish an aboriginal right.'

I feel a profound sense of duty to respond favourably. Any contrary determination would once again provoke, within native groups, a sense of victimization by white society and its institutions. This Agreement was signed in good faith for the protection of the Cree and Inuit peoples, not to deprive them of their rights and territories without due consideration. Should I decline jurisdiction, I see no other court of competent jurisdiction able to resolve this issue.

Secondary Source

3.   Recognition by Assimilation: Mi'kmaq Treaty Rights, Fisheries Privatization, and Community Resistance in Nova Scotia

Martha Stiegman and Sherry Pictou

In *R. v. Marshall* (1999), the Supreme Court of Canada recognized the treaty rights of the Mi'kmaq and Maliseet to earn a 'moderate livelihood' through commercial fishing. The case is part of generations of Maritime First Nations' struggle to gain recognition of the eighteenth-century Peace and Friendship treaties and the inherent rights they were meant to protect. Following this decision, many initial Mi'kmaq forays onto the water were met with violent backlash from non-Native fishers, who were struggling after the collapse of northern cod stocks and were battle-worn from a decade of mobilization against neo-liberal Fisheries and Oceans Canada (popularly known as DFO) policy. While the media focused on clashes in Burnt Church, NB, discussions in other places, such as Bear River First Nation (BRFN) in Nova Scotia, focused on potential collaboration between small-scale fishers and First Nations. For those advocating community-based management, the Marshall decision represented hope that such a political alliance might reverse the neo-liberal privatization and rationalization of the fisheries. That window of opportunity quickly slammed shut, however, as DFO negotiated interim agreements on a band-by-band basis, integrating First Nation harvesters into the fishing industry under DFO jurisdiction rather than negotiating with provincial and First Nation governments to establish a treaty-based fishery. This process has undermined Aboriginal and treaty rights, consolidated neo-liberal transformations, and left no room for BRFN's vision of sustainable practices and Mi'kmaq ecological knowledge. A Mi'kmaq fishery grounded in self-governance and Indigenous principles has yet to appear. However, in Nova Scotia, the parameters of such a treaty-based fishery are currently being negotiated within the Mi'kmaq Rights Initiative (MRI), which conducts tripartite discussions to implement the Peace and Friendship treaties.

The treaty rights affirmed through *R. v. Marshall* and debated within the MRI are by no means limited to the fisheries; separating fishing from other traditional practices based on an entire way of life is problematic for many Indigenous peoples. However, in this article we present BRFN's experiences of fisheries negotiations in the post-Marshall environment to highlight concerns about the larger MRI process and Crown–First Nation negotiations in general. Neo-liberal ideology now permeates government policy, as demonstrated by the vicious paces of privatization, commodification, and deregulation in the Atlantic fisheries. In BRFN's traditional territory of Kesputwick, industrial overexploitation and species collapse are advancing to such a degree that survival for subsistence harvesters and independent commercial fishers outside neo-liberal market relations (such as capital-intensive harvesting and aquaculture) has become near impossible. The post-Marshall process has essentially been integrated into this agenda of fisheries rationalization. This enclosure movement, matched with a negotiation policy framework determined to feed into these neo-liberal transformations, presents Aboriginal leaders with a very limited set of options at the negotiation table. It is a political and economic context that places unacceptable limits on the exercise of Indigenous sovereignty.

For Dene political philosopher Glen Coulthard, Canada's once unapologetically assimilationist policy framework has evolved into a deceptively innocuous 'politics of recognition'. Over the last 30 years, recognition—of Canada's treaty obligations and of Indigenous peoples' inherent rights to self-government—has become the main goal of the Aboriginal rights movement. With economic development initiatives, comprehensive land claims and self-government negotiations are resulting in land, money, and political power being delegated from Ottawa to First Nations. Like Taiaiake Alfred, Coulthard sees such legalist strategies as short-sighted. They ease the pain of colonialism but do nothing to challenge its roots, namely a liberal capitalist economy and colonial state, or the Eurocentric world view underpinning them. Instead, the current arrangement creates Aboriginal citizens who define their identities and rights in relation to the Canadian state, a process Alfred calls 'Aboriginalism'. This consequence does nothing to challenge the subjective, internalized oppression of Indigenous people—an equally significant dynamic in colonial power relations.[37]

Anthropologist Paul Nadasdy argues that the co-management regimes emerging from such negotiations reinforce state domination over the Aboriginal communities they seek to empower because colonial power dynamics are unacknowledged and therefore unaddressed. The task of improving science-based 'resource management' by partnering with First Nations and including their 'traditional ecological knowledge' is generally viewed as a technical exercise; its political dimensions are obscured. Nadasdy reminds us that all knowledge systems—including Western science—derive from and depend on an epistemologically distinct social and political context for meaning. In other words, 'resource management' regimes express a world view and belong to a political-economic system that is neither universal nor neutral; the name itself implies a commodification of and domination over nature that makes no sense from an Indigenous perspective. Aboriginal people internalize this world view as they are 'empowered' to participate in management.[38]

This cognitive dimension of colonialism is pivotal for Indigenous scholars such as Linda Tuhiwai Smith, Marie Battiste, and Taiaiake Alfred, who argue that self-determination struggles must target the Enlightenment ideology driving European imperialism.[39] This ideology includes the 'imperial imagination'[40] that conceives of the world as *terra nullius*, an empty wilderness waiting to be claimed by Europe; the ideal of progress that relegates authentic Indigenous people to history; the cult of science that alienates nature from culture and aspires to control the environment; and the fetishization of the individual as rational, free, and compelled to pursue his or her self-interest in a capitalist economy founded on the myth of private property. Alfred argues that, at the heart of Indigenous nations, there is 'a set of values that challenge the homogenizing force of Western liberalism and free-market capitalism; that honor the . . . deep interconnection between human beings and other elements of creation'.[41]

There is debate within the Mi'kmaq community about how to negotiate a balance between 'traditional' values and integration into the modern global economy. The Marshall case, with its emphasis on commercial fishing, is certainly part of that discussion. With Cliff Atleo, Jr, we are cautious about the seeping of 'neoliberal dogma' into discussions of Aboriginal self-determination and are frustrated by the extent to which the current politics of recognition has steered discussions away from peaceful coexistence for First Nations grounded in Indigenous world views.[42] If we take the Aboriginal commercial fishery opened by *R. v. Marshall* as a litmus test, it seems Mi'kmaq treaty rights are in danger of being equated with assimilation into the globalized economy.

Of fundamental concern to BRFN is the world view that this model of development imposes and the respectful relationship with the land—known in Mi'kmaq as *Netukulimuk*—that it severs. In the decade since the Marshall decision, BRFN's struggle to assert *Netukulimuk* has a new battlefront, a process we term treaty right recognition by assimilation. This article tells the story of BRFN's decade of struggle, of grassroots renewal and engagement with traditional values to ground the community's vision, and of the alliances built in order to defend that vision. It is a cautionary story that reveals the vulnerability of Indigenous self-determination struggles in the context of neo-liberal transformations and questions the limited potential of negotiations within the current policy framework. It is also a story of hope that points to the potential of alliances between Indigenous self-determination struggles and broader resistance to neo-liberalism.

We begin with an analysis of DFO's management regime and its success in extending and deepening state control and capitalist relations in non-Native fishing communities— developments that foreshadow the 'Aboriginalism' agenda that Alfred sees crafting Aboriginal-Canadian citizens of the globalized economy. We then ground our discussion of these dynamics as they are illustrated in the BRFN and the Mi'kmaq people's struggle for self-determination. Taking the Marshall decision as a watershed moment in that movement, we explore the ways in which the federal government's response has undermined the rights that *R. v. Marshall* affirmed. Finally, we present BRFN's strategy of resistance to this recognition by assimilation and explore the potential of the alliances that this First Nation is building with non-Indigenous communities and social movements resisting neo-liberal globalization.[43]

Fisheries Privatization and Resistance in Non-Mi'kmaq Communities

Fishing has long defined the culture, economy, and social fabric of coastal communities in Atlantic Canada. Viewed as a barrier to capitalist development, these attributes have been dismantled over the last 30 years by DFO policy aimed at integrating small-scale independent producers into an ever-expanding market and on developing a centralized, corporate-owned fleet capable of large-scale harvesting and processing for international trade.[44] The current policy thrust is consistent with a wider neo-liberal agenda: privatize Crown-owned resources, downsize government services, and de-regulate management. These objectives have been achieved primarily through the imposition of individual transferable quotas (ITQs), intended to create market competition for control of quota and resulting in the survival of only the most 'efficient' and 'competitive' fishers. As a result, Atlantic Canada has experienced a dramatic consolidation of corporate ownership in the fisheries and the near extinction of the family-owned businesses that characterized the industry for generations.[45]

The Atlantic fisheries have always been integrated into an international capitalist market: this association defined the opening phase of the colonial project in eastern Canada. But Anthony Davis describes how the intensification of capitalist relations in the fisheries during the 1980s systematically dehumanized coastal communities, changing fishers' identities and their relationships to the water and to each other. Fishing used to be anchored in a deep attachment to place, to provide a sense of collective destiny, and to be central to the subsistence economy. Fishing rules and access were things harvesters negotiated with their neighbours. With DFO's drive for professionalization, fishers became businesspeople and clients of the state, accountable to the government and their creditors. Competition was embedded in a management regime that both presupposes and creates the atomized, self-interested, rational individual at the heart of liberal capitalist theory. The system also fractures fishers along lines of geography, technology, and fish species, making large-scale collective action difficult.[46]

Davis depicts this shift as one from 'livelihood harvesting', made up of small-scale fishers with control over their means of production, to capital-intensive 'accumulation harvesting', where workers on the water engage in resource extraction for profit.[47] It is a tragic irony that the Marshall decision affirmed the treaty right to a 'livelihood' fishery, the same sector being actively dismantled by the very resource management regime that DFO would impose on First Nations.

David Harvey calls the process driving the expansion and deepening of capitalist relations 'accumulation by dispossession', a movement that dispossess people of the means of production as it coerces them into labour market relations.[48] Resistance in non-Indigenous communities to this enclosure of the ocean commons has been well documented.[49] It has also created painful divisions between fishers who have accepted the ITQ system and those who resist privatization and prefer community-based management. The outrage and sense of betrayal among this former group is so raw that some fishers identify with the displacement and loss of sovereignty experienced by their Mi'kmaq neighbours as a result of Canadian colonialism. But if the management regime enacting this accumulation by dispossession is offensive to non-Native fishers, it is more threatening to the Mi'kmaq for whom assimilation into this development model continues the colonial project that they have confronted for over 400 years.

L'setkuk and Mi'kmaq Struggles for Self-Determination

L'setkuk, or Bear River First Nation, is a tiny community of 150 people[50] located at the headwaters of Bear River, which flows into the Bay of Fundy. In the Mi'kmaq language, L'setkuk means 'water that cuts through' or 'flowing along high rocks'. The name describes the trajectory of the river well, which cuts a swathe through the steep hills. The area was a fishing camp where families gathered over the warm months after spending the winter dispersed, hunting across Kesputwick. The community was largely cut off from its fishing grounds and confined to a reservation in 1801. The reserve is now a postage stamp of green in a sea of clear-cut logging, and most of the fish and animals that the community once relied on for subsistence are now either severely depleted or extinct.

L'setkuk is also a stone's throw from Port Royal, where the French (the first colonial powers in Mi'kmaki) established a settlement in 1604. Colonialism is long-standing in this part of North America: the **Covenant Chain** of treaties that the Mi'kmaq and their Wabenaki allies negotiated with the British Crown stretches back to the 1600s, with the last of the Peace and Friendship treaties negotiated in 1761.[51] Unlike the post-Confederation treaties, these agreements contained no land surrender provisions. They enshrined a vision of sharing the land as 'two states under one crown',[52] with the Mi'kmaq adding an eighth point to the star symbolizing the seven traditional districts of the Mi'kmaq nation.[53] As long as the sun shines and rivers flow, the Mi'kmaq could maintain their way of life; in exchange, they accepted the newcomers to Mi'kmaki. These promises were forgotten by the British as soon as the ink had dried on the page. And so began the Mi'kmaq peoples' long-standing struggle to decipher the double-speak of the British and Canadian governments, to maintain Mi'kmaq values while adapting to non-Mi'kmaq economies, and to negotiate a balance between resisting assimilation and integrating into non-Indigenous society in a self-determined way. Incredibly, the Mi'kmaq have survived over 400 years of relentless colonization despite several obstacles, including the outlawing of traditional government under the Indian

Act, the criminalization of Mi'kmaq language and ceremonies until the early 1950s, the residential school at Shubencadie, and Nova Scotia's attempts in the 1940s to centralize the Mi'kmaq on two reserves at Indian Brook and Eskasoni.

Court cases and police case files provide a public record of Mi'kmaq resistance, from the trial of Grand Chief Syliboy, who was charged in 1928 with illegal hunting and who referred to the 1752 Treaty to defend the Mi'kmaq's right to hunt and trap, to the 1973 and 1981 armed raids by Quebec Provincial Police and DFO wardens on the people of Listiguj, who were defending their traditional fishery.[54] But historical records fail to capture the spirit driving these events: the intention of Mi'kmaq people to live—as Kerry Prosper, an Elder from Paq'tnkek First Nation would say—according to the laws that are rooted in the land and waters of Mi'kmaki.

The Marshall Case

This tradition of resistance is the context for the late Donald Marshall Jr's act of community-supported civil disobedience in 1993 when he fished for *K'at* (eel), a creature and food of tremendous medicinal and spiritual significance.[55] Marshall was arrested for fishing out of season, for not having a licence, and for selling his catch. Marshall held that he was asserting his inherent right to fish, a right protected by the treaties his ancestors had negotiated with the Crown.

Under the 1982 Constitution Act, this right is protected by section 35(1), which recognizes and affirms Aboriginal and treaty rights—a constitutional addition that First Nations across Canada fought hard to have included. The purpose of this section is to reconcile pre-existing Aboriginal and treaty rights that derive from Indigenous peoples' occupation of and responsibility for the land with the underlying sovereignty and title claims of the Crown established through the doctrine of discovery based upon the legal fiction of *terra nullius*. Section 35(1) has provided a powerful, though controversial legal tool for First Nations. Critics point out that Canada acts as defendant, judge, and jury within a framework of colonial state institutions that undermine Indigenous sovereignty and are grounded in a liberal ideology hostile to Indigenous cultures. Nevertheless, appealing to the courts has proven an important strategy for First Nations in dealing with a federal government reluctant to acknowledge, let alone negotiate, their claims.[56]

In the Maritimes, the focus of First Nations' legal activism has been on establishing access to natural resources, based on the contemporary relevance of the historic Peace and Friendship treaties. Until Marshall went fishing, the Mi'kmaq treaty rights recognized by the Crown included the right to hunt, established through *R. v. Simon* (1985), and the right to fish for food and ceremonial purposes, established by *R. v. Sparrow* (1990).[57] Though Mi'kmaq access to resources was increasing, the Union of Nova Scotia Indians and the Confederacy of Mainland Mi'kmaq were frustrated with the limited management authority granted by DFO and the department's unwillingness to discuss Mi'kmaq commercial fishing access. For these organizations, the Marshall case was a chance to expand access to the commercial fisheries.[58] Marshall's defence, referring to clauses in the 1760–1 treaties, asked the court to affirm the Mi'kmaq's constitutionally protected right to earn a living from the land and waters of Mi'kmaki.[59] The Supreme Court affirmed the currency of the Peace and Friendship treaties and the collective rights recognized therein for the Mi'kmaq and Maliseet to obtain a 'moderate livelihood' through participation in the commercial fisheries. The ruling recognized the Crown's prerogative to regulate such rights for the purposes of conservation, though the current regulations were considered an infringement of those rights because they failed to explicitly acknowledge them.[60]

The traditional leadership in Esgenoopotitj, or Burnt Church First Nation, rejected the subjection of inherent Mi'kmaq rights within Canadian domestic law, citing the spirit and intent of the treaties as nation-to-nation alliances of peace and friendship, not surrenders of land or sovereignty. Given DFO's poor conservation record, the leaders judged the department incompetent and its move to place Mi'kmaq fishers under federal jurisdiction illegitimate.[61] It was a stand that resonated with Mi'kmaq across the region and Indigenous people across the country, as reflected by the hundreds of supporters who came to stand with Esgenoopititj during the fishing seasons of 2000 and 2001.[62] In 2000, the Esgenoopotitj Fisheries Act was drafted through community consultation and blended science, harvester knowledge, and Mi'kmaq traditional teachings.[63] It articulated a vision for broad community involvement and resource sharing, one that was radically different than the model of economic development dictated by the DFO management regime. It won the support of conservation groups but was met with violent backlash. Shocking images of RCMP officers beating Esgenoopititj fishers and DFO boats ramming Mi'kmaq dories made headlines for two consecutive summers.

While the media focused on these clashes, fishers around BRFN were quietly negotiating the entry of Mi'kmaq harvesters.[64] This relationship-building approach was motivated by the simple fact that, as one community member put it, 'We have to live here year round. Our children go to school in the neighboring community, and if we can't share the resource there's no point in our even having access.'[65] We have written elsewhere about the remarkable conflict mediation process in southwest Nova Scotia that defused the near-violent crisis triggered by the Marshall ruling.[66] After dialogue was initiated, BRFN discovered that neighbouring fishers shared a similar vision for ecologically sustainable, community-based fishery management grounded in local self-governance and that they had developed a rich critique of the neo-liberal fisheries management regime through years of resistance to the regulations dismantling their local fisheries. Their analysis would provide BRFN with crucial insight in navigating the post-Marshall environment.

Government Response

The government response to *R. v. Marshall* was twofold. Over the long term, the parameters of a treaty-based commercial fishery are to be established as part of formal negotiations between First Nations and provincial and federal governments to implement the historic Peace and Friendship treaties in a present-day context. As previously mentioned, this process is being carried out in Nova Scotia through the MRI. This part of the response comes after three decades of activism on the part of the Nova Scotia Mi'kmaq to have governments address outstanding title and rights questions in Mi'kmaki.[67] A framework agreement was signed in 2007 to guide the MRI negotiations; a final agreement is anticipated in 2011.

In the short term, DFO negotiated interim fishery access agreements, both as an immediate means of responding to First Nations demands and to restore calm on the waters. These agreements, negotiated on a band-by-band basis, offered money for communal commercial licences, vessels, gear, and training. Signing bands agreed to 'shelve' their right to manage their fisheries for the duration of the agreements and to fish by DFO regulations.[68] This paternalistic response triggered resentment within Mi'kmaq communities: the federal government was not so much recognizing treaty rights as pressuring bands to put them aside. There was also dissatisfaction with the funds and the quota put on the negotiating table, as well as with the rushed pace of negotiations and DFO's inflexibility, which gave the department effective control of the negotiation agenda.[69]

BRFN's negotiations with the department are a revealing case in point. For the people of L'setkuk, the Marshall decision represented a deep affirmation of Mi'kmaq identity. It also triggered a renewed exploration of *Netukulimuk* and a grassroots effort to envision a treaty-based livelihood fishery anchored in a renewal of this traditional concept. BRFN's fisheries management plan was drafted with support from neighbouring fishing groups through a community-organizing process that strengthened self-governance, built relationships with neighbouring communities, coordinated BRFN's fishing activities with those of surrounding fishers, and went much farther than DFO regulations in terms of conservation. However, it was completely rejected by DFO, which insisted on assimilating BRFN's fishing activities into the privatized fisheries management regime. Negotiations around scallop harvesting are a poignant example. BRFN proposed to share the scallop dragging licence offered by DFO between several harvesters using traditional, ecologically sensitive methods. Instead, DFO insisted that the band lease the licence and hire a corporate boat using ecologically destructive dragging methods to fish the quota in the band's name.

Given the sharp contrast between BRFN's vision for a livelihood fishery rooted in *Netukulimuk* and the social and ecological relationships imposed through DFO's regulations, BRFN refused to sign an agreement. However, 32 of the 34 eligible bands in the Maritimes did sign interim agreements with DFO. Some have been able to develop innovative community-based fisheries, but, for the most part, First Nations in Nova Scotia have been given little more than local control over the implementation of DFO policy and a token advisory role at the local fisheries management level.[70]

It bears repeating that these interim agreements were not meant to recognize the rights affirmed through *R. v. Marshall* but were supposedly without prejudice to the exercise of treaty rights while MRI negotiations are ongoing. However, BRFN's concern is that, in the future, these agreements will be considered as consultation regarding and compensation for the infringement of treaty rights. We can only hope that the frustrations expressed by the 13 Nova Scotia chiefs at the federal government's reluctance to negotiate a treaty-based fishery within the MRI do not signal that those fears will be confirmed.[71]

A comprehensive evaluation of the Aboriginal commercial fishery that the MRI process put in place has yet to be undertaken. Many chiefs are reluctant to take public positions while MRI negotiations are ongoing. However, it appears that, if the process was successful in easing tensions and helping bands enter the commercial fisheries, it was equally successful at establishing DFO control over the orientation and management of this Aboriginal fishery. While the department uses conservation as justification for this infringement of Aboriginal rights, many suggest that its primary motivation is retaining control over management to further privatization and rationalization of the fishing industry.[72] In the words of one leader in BRFN, 'We don't see any evidence of DFO supporting conservation; we see them supporting big business.'[73]

Resisting Privatization: Towards an Anti-Colonial Commons

Though Mi'kmaq and non-Mi'kmaq communities are affected very differently by this neo-liberal enclosure movement, it is important to frame these experiences of dispossession as moments in the same story—the history of the expansion and intensification of capitalism driven forward by a system of colonial political control. This helps us better understand the forces that BRFN and allied non-Indigenous groups in Kesputwick are resisting as they struggle to assert the treaty relationship between their peoples. It also forms a deepening basis of unity between the various groups.

For BRFN, resistance to this neo-liberal intensification of colonialism begins with what Coulthard would describe as 'on-the-ground practices of freedom', trading the politics of recognition for a process of self-recognition and building a radical alternative to the current neo-colonial arrangement through a critical engagement with traditional culture. Coulthard notes that such a 'transformational praxis' would not only address the internalized oppression of Indigenous people, but it would contribute to the wider society as well. He writes: 'our cultures have much to teach the Western world about the establishment of relationships within and between peoples and the natural world that are profoundly non-imperialist.'[74]

A key element of BRFN's transformational praxis is working with neighbouring communities to learn how the colonial–capitalist project has pitted the interests of Mi'kmaq and non-Mi'kmaq communities against one another and to overcome the de facto segregation that characterizes much of rural Nova Scotia.[75] In Bear River's traditional territory, the conflict mediation sparked by the Marshall ruling opened a dialogue that has matured over the past decade into cross-cultural alliances resisting the successive waves of privatization affecting local communities. The most successful example of this joint action is the opposition that BRFN and non-Mi'kmaq groups mounted against the White Point Quarry project, which forced an environmental assessment process that has delayed, if not thwarted, the mining project.[76] While that political victory is significant, the deepening relationships and political analysis that have resulted from these joint actions are of equal importance.

Battiste sees a liberating potential in dialogue between Western and Indigenous traditions.[77] Together, we can more accurately diagnose colonialism as we imagine and invoke a new society. Creating spaces for such cross-cultural pedagogy is an integral part of BRFN's political action, be it through cultural production, learning circles, or other forums for reflection and cultural sharing. Broadening this discussion to include harvesters, activists, and researchers from across the country is helping BRFN to recognize its position within a broader struggle against the neo-colonial agenda of accumulation by dispossession. Together we are imagining a response to neo-liberal enclosures that resists retrenching the colonial relations embodied in Crown 'public' resources.

Meanwhile, privatization of the resource base that the treaty relationship is meant to protect continues. The most recent example is the de facto privatization of 14 beaches in Kesputwick through 10-year leases signed between the provincial government and Innovative Fisheries Products Inc., a move that gives the latter monopoly control over the clamming sector as it expropriates ancestral clam beds used by BRFN.[78] Though there is a legal duty to consult First Nations on issues that might infringe upon their rights, these consultations happen in a top-down manner through the centralized MRI process, sidestepping and undermining the local alliances so crucial to BRFN's strategy to protect Kesputwick.

Conclusion

The Marshall decision was a moment of hope in the Mi'kmaq's struggle for self-determination that could have led to many things. It could have led—as early declarations from the Atlantic Policy Congress of First Nations Chiefs demanded[79]—to strengthened self-governance and cultural renewal, increased access to hunting and fishing for traditional harvesters, and a meaningful voice for the Mi'kmaq nation in shaping the regulations that govern the fisheries. It could have been, as BRFN hoped, the grounds for alliance, as well as a fundamental challenge to the privatization of marine resources and the intensification of capitalist relations in the fishing industry. Instead, the window of opportunity opened by the Marshall decision slammed shut. In theory, the ongoing MRI negotiations have the power to pry that window open, but the prevailing neo-liberal climate and limited negotiation policy framework leave little room for optimism.

So where do communities who are unwilling to choose between the limited set of options available through such compromised political negotiations find a voice? For BRFN, action at the international level, through participation in social movements such as the World Forum of Fisher People (WFFP; an international alliance of small-scale and Indigenous fishers) has proven crucial. Within Canada, there is a collective denial of the colonial origins of this settler-state. This 'Canadian psychosis'[80] is buttressed by a constitution that supposedly enshrines Aboriginal and treaty rights, despite a modern treaty negotiation framework in which the Canadian state recognizes such title and rights only after First Nations agree to extinguish them. This situation creates a veneer of democracy that makes Canadian colonialism hard to diagnose, let alone confront. But WFFP colleagues in the global south have no problem identifying their resistance to neo-colonialism and globalization with BRFN's experience.

'We were happy—for five minutes.' That is how a South African WFFP comrade describes the euphoria in his country at the fall of apartheid. John Pilger tells the story of the economic conditions that the once-socialist African National Congress (ANC) leadership was pressured to accept in negotiating the end of that system. In exchange for political control of the country, the ANC leadership quickly implemented savage neo-liberal reforms that have seen income for blacks decrease by 19 per cent and for whites increase by 15 per cent in the 15 years since. 'Economic apartheid replaced legal apartheid with the same consequences,' notes Pilger, 'yet is greeted as one of the greatest achievements in world history.'[81] It is an ominous tale for those struggling for Indigenous self-determination in Canada.

Across the global south, overt colonial rule has been replaced by neo-colonial arrangements characterized by the now familiar neo-liberal prescription of privatization, trade liberalization, and deregulation imposed through International Monetary Fund's structural adjustment programs and World Trade Organization-enforced trade agreements. These are the tools of what Harvey calls 'the "new" imperialism', designed to extend the borders of global capital's reach.[82] While trade agreements drive this agenda of accumulation by dispossession forward in the south, the displacement and dispossession of Indigenous peoples in Canada represents a major frontier of capitalist expansion.

BRFN's challenges in asserting *Netukulimuk* demonstrate how Crown negotiations with First Nations continue Canada's long-standing project of assimilating Indigenous nations and extinguishing their rights and title in the interests of capitalist development. We do not mean to understate the tremendous victory that the Marshall decision represents or to underemphasize how hard the Mi'kmaq have fought to force the Crown to acknowledge and then honour the Peace and Friendship treaties and to negotiate a modern interpretation of these nation-to-nation agreements. Our intention is to clarify how the dynamics of accumulation by dispossession, matched with a policy framework determined to feed into these neo-liberal transformations, limit negotiations to such an extent that the notion of self-determination in the current context is highly problematic. This limitation presents a tremendous challenge for First Nation leaders working within established legal channels to find an acceptable compromise. It also points to a need for non-Indigenous social movements challenging neo-liberal globalization to learn from and ally with Indigenous anti-colonial struggles.

Primary Document

4.

The Guides, 1899. Left to right, top row: Louis Peters, John Peters, John McEwan, John Louis; left to right, bottom row: John Labrador, Malti Pictou, Eli Pictou. These men guided a group of sports fishermen into the interior of Digby County, presumably in early May, as the leaves are not yet showing on the trees and bushes, yet there is no snow on the ground. Late April and early May are the best times for going after trout in this area. This picture, one of a series documenting the expedition, was taken at the beginning of the trip, which most likely took place in 1899. (Courtesy of the Nova Scotia Museum Ethnology Collection.)

Primary Document

5.

The Guides, 2009. Harvesters from Bear River First Nation, Bear River First Nation Descendents. (Martha Steigman and Sherry Pictou.)

Questions for Consideration

1. Why was the James Bay Agreement hailed as a landmark agreement for Aboriginal rights?
2. Has the James Bay Agreement served the interests of the Cree in northern Quebec? Does the Quebec government and Hydro-Quebec's behaviour seem consistent with the analysis of treaties, rights, and the politics of recognition offered by Stiegman and Pictou? Give reasons to support your answers.
3. Why did Judge Rouleau rule in favour of the applicants in the Cree Regional Authority case? What, if any, evidence of duplicity on the part of the federal and/or provincial governments exists in the trial record?
4. What criticisms do Stiegman and Pictou offer of the oft-pursued Aboriginal strategy of fighting for Canadian government recognition of treaty rights?
5. What, in Stiegman and Pictou's view, motivates the Canadian government's attempts to dispossess Aboriginal peoples of their rights, lands, and resources? Do you agree with their assessment? Why or why not?
6. What similarities and differences can you see between the two images on pages 414–15? How do these characteristics reflect broader continuity or discontinuity in Mi'kmaq history and the history of Mi'kmaq relations with the Canadian government?

7. Discuss whether treaty-making with the Canadian government has been a positive or negative experience for Aboriginal peoples and whether treaty-making can be a strategy for the advancement of their rights and positions.

Further Resources

Books and Articles

Boldt, Menno, and J. Anthony Long, eds. *The Quest for Justice: Aboriginal Peoples and Aboriginal Rights*. Toronto: University of Toronto Press, 1985.

Issac, Thomas. *Aboriginal and Treaty Rights in the Maritimes: The Marshall Decision and Beyond*. Saskatoon: Purich Publishers, 2001.

Morse, Brad W., ed. *Aboriginal Peoples and the Law: Indian, Metis and Inuit Rights in Canada*. Ottawa: Carleton University Press, 1989.

Nadasdy, Paul. *Hunters and Bureaucrats: Power, Knowledge, and Aboriginal-State Relations in the Southwest Yukon*. Vancouver: UBC Press, 2003.

Peters, Evelyn J. 'Native People and the Environmental Regime in the James Bay and Northern Quebec Agreement', *Arctic* 52, 4 (Dec. 1999): 395–410.

Printed Documents and Reports

Alfred, Taiaiake. *Peace Power Righteousness: An Indigenous Manifesto*. Toronto: Oxford University Press, 1999.

Grand Council of Micmacs, Union of Nova Scotia Indians, and Native Council of Nova Scotia. *The Mi'kmaq Treaty Handbook*. Sydney & Truro: Native Communications Society of Nova Scotia, 1987.

Grand Council of the Crees. *Never Without Consent: James Bay Crees' Stand Against Forcible Inclusion Into An Independent Quebec*. Toronto: ECW Press, 1998.

Films

Dancing Around the Table. DVD. Directed by Maurice Bulbulian. NFB, 1987.

Encounter with Saul Ralinsky, Part II: Rama Indian Reserve. DVD. Directed by Peter Pearson. NFB, 1967.

In the Same Boat? Film. Directed by Martha Stiegman and Sherry Pictou. Bear River First Nation, 2007.

Is the Crown at War with Us? DVD. Directed by Alanis Obomsawin. NFB, 2002.

Websites

Cliff Atleo, Jr, 'From Indigenous Nationhood to Neoliberal Aboriginal Economic Development: Charting the Evolution of Indigenous-Settler Relations', Canada Canadian Social Economy Hub (October 2008)

www.socialeconomyhub.ca/?q=content/indigenous-nationhood-neoliberal-aboriginal-economic-development-charting-evolution-indigeno

Bear River First Nation
www.bearriverculturalcenter.com/aboutbearriverfirstnation.aspx

Cape Breton University, 'The Mi'kmaq'
www.cbu.ca/mrc/the-mikmaq

Anthony Davis, 'Insidious Rationalities: The Institutionalisation of Small Boat Fishing and the Rise of the Rapacious Fisher'. (1991)
www.stfx.ca/research/gbayesp/insidious_report.htm

'Fishing for Answers: An Interview with Video Activist Martha Stiegman'
http://citizenshift.org/node/7047&dossier_nid=1140

Mi'kmaq Association for Cultural Studies
www.mikmaq-assoc.ca/index.htm

Further Resources

Multimedia

Aboriginal Multi-Media Society
Aboriginal Peoples Television Network
Ab-Originals Pod Cast
CBC clip, 'Happy Birthday Hudson's Bay—From Canada's Indians', 12 Dec. 1970
CBC clip, 'Hudson's Bay Company Ends Its Fur Trade', 30 Jan. 1991
CBC clip, 'TB Plagues Northern Natives', 4 Nov. 1991
CBC clips, 'Davis Inlet: Innu Community in Crisis', 1992–2005
CBC clips, 'Tuberculosis: Old Disease, Continuing Threat', 1943–2001

CBC News: Aboriginal Canadians
Cooking with the Wolfman
Dead Dog Café
First Voices imagineNative: Film + Media Arts Festival
Inuit Throat Singing (YouTube clips)
Learn Michif.com
Native Drums
Native Spirit Festival: The Film and Video Festival of Indigenous People
Tusaalanga: Learn the Inuit Language
The Virtual Museum of Métis History and Culture: Indigenous Voices

Radio Stations

Aboriginal Multi-Media Society
Aboriginal Voices Radio
CBC North
CFWE-FM—The Native Perspective
Michif-Cree Online Radio
Muskwachees Radio
Nation Talk

Native Hockey News
NCI: The Spirit of Manitoba
Petaapin Enou Emoo Yaabi
Waskaganish Radio
Wawatay Radio
Wemindji FM

Cultural and Resource Centres

Aboriginal Affairs and Northern Development Canada Departmental Library
Akwesasne Cultural Center
Assembly of First Nations Resource Centre
Bear River First Nation Heritage and Cultural Centre
Canada Aviation and Space Museum
Canada Science and Technology Museum
Canadian Museum of Civilization
Canadian Museum of Contemporary Photography
Canadian Museum of Human Rights
Canadian War Museum
Centre for Indigenous Environmental Resources
Gabriel Dumont Institute Library
Head-Smashed-In Buffalo Jump Interpretative Centre, Alberta
Inuit Tapirisat of Canada Library
Inuvik Centennial Library
Kanhiote—Tyendinaga Territory Public Library
Kanien'kehaka Raotitiohwa Cultural Centre
Kettle and Stony Point First Nation Library
Kwanlin Dun Cultural Centre

Lesser Slave Lake Indian Regional Council
Library and Archives Canada
Lillooet Public Library, First Nations Interest Collection
Mi'kmaq Resources Centre
National Gallery of Canada
Native Law Centre Library
Nisga'a Language & Culture Centre Archives
Ojibway and Cree Cultural Centre
Quw'utsun Cultural and Conference Centre
Saskatchewan Indian Cultural Centre
Squamish Lil'wat Cultural Centre
U'Mista Library and Archives
Union of BC Indian Chiefs Resource Centre
University of Calgary Library, Arctic Institute of North America Collection
University of Toronto, First Nations House Library
Walpole Island Heritage Centre
Woodland Cultural Centre
Xwi7xwa Library
Yukon College Library
Yukon Native Language Centre

Films and Documentaries

Across Arctic Ungava. DVD. Directed by Douglas Wilkinson. NFB, 1949.

As I Am. DVD. Directed by Nadia Myre. NFB, 2010.

The Ballad of Crowfoot. DVD. Directed by Willie Dunn. NFB, 1968.

Battle for the Trees. DVD. Directed by John Edginton. NFB, 1993.

Between: Living in the Hyphen. DVD. Directed by Anne Marie Nakagawa. NFB, 2005.

Broke. DVD. Directed by Rosie Dransfeld. ID Productions, 2009.

Canada: A People's History, series 1–12. DVD. Directed by Claude Lortie, Michelle Métivier, and Serge Turbide. Morningstar Entertainment, 2004.

The Canary Effect. DVD. Directed by Robin Davey and Yellow Thunder. 2006.

CBQM. DVD. Directed by Dennis Allen. NFB, 2009.

César's Bark Canoe. DVD. Directed by Bernard Gosselin. NFB, 1991.

The Challenge in Old Crow. DVD. Directed by George Payrastre. NFB, 2006.

Christmas at Moose Factory. Film. Directed by Alanis Obomsawin. NFB, 1967.

Circle of the Sun. DVD. Directed by Colin Low. NFB, 1960.

Club Native. DVD. Directed by Tracey Deer. NFB, 2006.

Columbus on Trial. DVD. Directed by Lourdes Portillo. 1993.

Dancing Around the Table. DVD. Directed by Maurice Bulbulian. NFB, 1987.

The Desert Is No Lady. VHS. Directed by Shelley Williams in collaboration with Susan Palmer. 1995.

Duncan Campbell Scott: The Poet and the Indians. VHS. Directed by James Cullingham. NFB, 1995.

Encounter with Saul Ralinsky, Part II: Rama Indian Reserve. DVD. Directed by Peter Pearson. NFB, 1967

The Experimental Eskimos. DVD. Directed by Barry Greenwald. Whitepine Pictures, 2009.

The Fallen Feather: Indian Residential Schools. DVD. Directed by Randy N. Bezeau. Fallen Feather Productions, 2007.

Finding Dawn. DVD. Directed by Christine Welsh. NFB, 2006.

First Nations: The Circle Unbroken. DVD. Directed by Geraldine Bob, Gary Marcuse, Deanna Nyce, and Lorna Williams. NFB, 1993.

Foster Child. DVD. Directed by Gil Cardinal. NFB, 1987.

The Gift of Diabetes. DVD. Directed by John Paskievich and O. Brion Whitford. NFB, 2005.

High Steel. DVD. Directed by Don Owen. NFB, 1965.

Hope. DVD. Directed by Thomas Buchan and Stuart Reaugh. NFB, 2008.

Ikwe (part of the *Daughters of the Country* series). DVD. Directed by Norma Bailey. NFB, 1986.

Imagining Indians. DVD. Directed by Victor Masayesva Jr. 1992.

Incident at Restigouche. DVD. Directed by Alanis Obomsawin. NFB, 1984.

In the Same Boat? Film. Directed by Martha Stiegman and Sherry Pictou. Bear River First Nation, 2007.

The Invisible Nation. DVD. Directed by Richard Desjardins and Robert Monderie. NFB, 2007.

Is the Crown at War with Us? DVD. Directed by Alanis Obomsawin. NFB, 2002.

Kanehsatake: 270 Years of Resistance. DVD. Directed by Alanis Obomsawin. NFB, 1993.

March Point. DVD. Directed by Tracy Rector and Annie Silverstein. Longhouse Media, 2008.

The Medicine People: First Nations' Ceremonies. DVD. First Nations Films, 2000.

Mistress Madeleine (part of the *Daughters of the Country* series). DVD. Directed by Aaron Kim Johnston. NFB, 1986.

Mohawk Girls. DVD. Directed by Tracey Deer. NFB, 2005.

Muffins for Granny: Exposing the Restlessness of an Ancient Sadness. DVD. Directed by Nadia McLaran. Mongrel Media, 2008.

Nanook of the North: A Story of Life and Love in the Actual Arctic. DVD. Directed by Robert J. Flaherty. Les Frères Revillon and Pathé Exchange, 1922.

Nose and Tina. DVD. Directed by Linda Bailey. NFB, 1980.

The Other Side of the Ledger: An Indian View of the Hudson's Bay Company. DVD. Directed by Martin DeFalco and Willie Dunn. NFB, 1972.

Places not Our Own (part of the *Daughters of the Country* series). DVD. Directed by Derek Mazur. NFB, 1986.

Qatuwas: People Gathering Together. DVD (available as Part 5 of *First Nations: The Circle Unbroken*). Directed by Barb Cranmer. Qatuwas Productions and NFB, 1997.

Redskins, Tricksters, and Puppy Stew: Native Humour and Its Healing Powers. VHS. Directed by Drew Hayden Taylor. NFB, 2000.

Reel Injun: On the Trail of the Hollywood Indian. DVD. Directed by Neil Diamond. Rezolution Pictures and NFB, 2009.

Richard Cardinal: Cry from the Diary of a Métis Child. DVD. Directed by Alanis Obomsawin. NFB, 1986.

Riel Country. DVD. Directed by Richard Duckworth. NFB, 1996.

Rocks at Whiskey Trench. DVD. Directed by Alanis Obomsawin. NFB, 2000.

Senorita Extraviada, Missing Young Woman. DVD. Directed by Lourdes Portillo. Independent Television Services, 2001.

Six Miles Deep. DVD. Directed by Sara Roque. NFB, 2010.

Spudwrench: Kahnawake Man. DVD. Directed by Alanis Obomsawin. NFB, 1997.

Starblanket. DVD. Directed by Donald Brittain. NFB, 1973.

Third World Canada. DVD. Directed by Andrée Cazabon. The Law Foundation of Canada, 2010.

Totem: The Return of the G'psgolox Pole. DVD. Directed by Gil Cardinal. NFB, 2003.

The True Story of Linda M. DVD. Directed by Norma Bailey. NFB, 1995.

Two Spirits. DVD. Directed by Lydia Nibley. Say Yes Quickly Productions, 2009.

Uranium. DVD. Directed by Magnus Isacsson. NFB, 1990.

Vistas. Various clips available at www.nfb.ca. Directed by Zoe L. Hopkins et al. NFB, 2009.

Waban-aki: People from Where the Sun Rises. Directed by Alanis Obomsawin. NFB, 2006.

A Windigo Tale. DVD. Directed by Armand Ruffo. 2009.

You are on Indian Land. DVD. Directed by Mort Ransen. NFB, 1969.

Websites

Aboriginal Affairs and Northern Development Canada. www.ainc-inac.gc.ca

Aboriginal Healing Foundation. www.ahf.ca/

The Aboriginal Justice Implementation Commission. www.ajic.mb.ca/index.html

Aboriginal Law and Legislation. www.bloorstreet.com/300block/ablawleg.htm

Assembly of First Nations. www.afn.ca

Bear River First Nation. www.bearriverculturalcenter.com/aboutbearriverfirstnation.aspx

BC Stats: Statistical Profiles of Aboriginal Peoples. www.bcstats.gov.bc.ca/data/cen01/abor/ap_main.asp

Canada in the Making: Numbered Treaty Overview. www.canadiana.ca/citm/specifique/numtreatyoverview_e.html

Canadian Human Rights' Commission: National Aboriginal Initiative. www.chrc-ccdp.ca/nai_ina/default-eng.aspx

Canadian Museum of Civilization: Gateway to Aboriginal Heritage. www.civilization.ca/cmc/exhibitions/tresors/ethno/index_e.shtml

Cape Breton University, 'The Mi'kmaq'. www.cbu.ca/mrc/the-mikmaq

CBC News: Aboriginals and the Canadian Military. www.cbc.ca/news/background/aboriginals/aboriginals-military.html

Congress of Aboriginal Peoples. www.abo-peoples.org

Curve Lake First Nation. www.curvelakefirstnation.ca/

Final Trial Statement and Subsequent Renunciation of Louis Riel. www.law.umkc.edu/faculty/projects/ftrials/riel/rieltrialstatement.html

First Nations Employment Society. www.fnes.ca/

First Nations Pedagogy Online. http://firstnations pedagogy.ca/index.html

Grand Council of the Crees. www.gcc.ca/cra/cranav.php

Great Unsolved Mysteries in Canadian History. www.canadianmysteries.ca/sites/klatsassin/home/indexen.html

Health Canada: First Nations and Inuit Health Branch. www.hc-sc.gc.ca/ahc-asc/branch-dirgen/fnihb-dgspni/index-eng.php

Health Canada: First Nations, Inuit, and Aboriginal Health. www.hc-sc.gc.ca/fnih-spni/index_e.html

Hidden from History: The Canadian Holocaust. www.hiddenfromhistory.org/

History of the Peace River Region. www.calverley.ca/

Hudson's Bay Company Heritage Website. www2.hbc.com/hbcheritage/

Human Resources and Skills Development Canada: Indicators of Well-Being. www4.hrsdc.gc.ca/.3ndic.1t.4r@-eng.jsp?iid=16

Indian Act (1985). http://laws-lois.justice.gc.ca/eng/acts/I-5/

Indigenous Bar Association. www.indigenousbar.ca/

Indigenous Peoples Issues and Resources. http://indigenouspeoplesissues.com/

Inuit Circumpolar Council. http://inuitcircumpolar.com/index.php?Lang=En&ID=1

The Inuit Tapiriit Kanatami. www.itk.ca

James Bay Project and the Cree. http://archives.cbc.ca/search?q=JAMES+BAY&RTy=0&RC=1&RP=1&RD=1&RA=0&th=1

The Jesuit Relations and Allied Documents, 1610–1791. http://puffin.creighton.edu/jesuit/relations/

Library and Archives Canada: Index to Federal Royal Commissions. www.collectionscanada.gc.ca/databases/indexcommissions/index-e.html

Manitoba Métis Federation. www.mmf.mb.ca

Métis National Council. www.metisnation.ca

Métis National Council of Women. www.metiswomen.ca/

Métis Nation of Alberta. www.albertametis.com

Métis Nation of British Columbia. www.mnbc.ca/

Métis Nation of Ontario. www.metisnation.org

Métis Nation of Saskatchewan. www.mn-s.ca

Mi'kmaq Association for Cultural Studies. www.mikmaq-assoc.ca/index.htm

MiningWatch Canada. www.miningwatch.ca/

National Aboriginal Document Database. http://epe.lac-bac.gc.ca/100/205/301/ic/cdc/aboriginaldocs/m-stat.htm

National Aboriginal Health Organization. www.naho.ca

Native American Documents Project. http://www2.csusm.edu/nadp/index.html

Native Law Centre of Canada. www.usask.ca/nativelaw/

Native Women's Association of Canada. www.nwac.ca

Nunavut Arctic College: Interviewing Inuit Elders Project. www.nac.nu.ca/OnlineBookSite/index.html

Our Legacy. http://scaa.sk.ca/ourlegacy/

People's Experiences of Colonization: Indian Hospitals. http://web2.uvcs.uvic.ca/courses/csafety/mod1/notes4.htm

Six Nations of the Grand River. www.sixnations.ca/

Statistics Canada: Aboriginal Peoples in Canada's Urban Area. www.statcan.gc.ca/pub/81-004-x/2005003/8612-eng.htm

Truth and Reconciliation Commission. www.trc.ca/websites/trcinstitution/index.php?p=3

Tshinanu. www.tshinanu.tv/accueil_en.html

Turtle Island Native Network. www.turtleisland.org/news/news-courts.htm

The Virtual Museum of Métis Culture and History. www.metismuseum.ca/main.php

Whapmagoostui First Nation. www.whapmagoostuifn.ca/

Where are the Children? Healing the Legacy of the Residential Schools. www.wherearethechildren.ca/

Magazines and Newspapers

Aboriginal Voices
Alberta Sweetgrass
Anishinaabe News
Eeyou Eenou
First Nations Drum
First Nations Voice
First Perspective News
Grassroots News
Indian Country News
Intertribal Times
Inuit Art Quarterly
Inukitut Magazine

Métis National Youth Advisory Gazette
Nunatsiaq News
Raven's Eye
Saskatchewan Sage
Say Magazine
Tekawennake
Turtle Island News
Wawatay News
Weetamah
Windspeaker
Wolf Howls

Journals

AlterNative: An International Journal of Indigenous Scholarship
American Indian Culture and Research Journal
American Indian Quarterly
Canadian Journal of Native Education
Canadian Journal of Native Studies
Ethnic and Racial Studies
Ethnohistory
First Peoples Child & Family Review
Indigenous Law Journal

Indigenous Policy Journal
International Journal of Critical Indigenous Studies
Journal of Aboriginal Economic Development
Journal of Aboriginal Health
Journal of Colonialism and Colonial History
Journal of Indigenous Research
Native Studies Review
Pimatisiwin: A Journal of Aboriginal and Indigenous Community Health

Theses and Dissertations

Brundige, Lorraine. 'Continuity of Native Values: Cree and Ojibwa'. MA thesis, Lakehead University, 1997.

Chrétien, Annette. '"Fresh Tracks in Dead Air": Mediating Contemporary Métis Identities Through Music and Storytelling'. PhD dissertation, York University, 2005.

Fitzgerald, William R. 'Lest the Beaver Run Loose: The Early Seventeenth Century Christianson Site and Trends in Historic Neutral Archaeology'. MA thesis, McMaster University, 1982.

Franks, C.A. 'Elsie, Indian Chief, Bus Driver, Shopkeeper, Grannie'. MA thesis, Boston University, 1980.

Greenberg, Adolph. 'Adaptive Responses by an Ojibwa Band to Northern Development'. PhD dissertation, Wayne State University, 1978.

Hudson, Douglas. 'Traplines and Timber: Social and Economic Change among the Carrier'. PhD dissertation, University of Alberta, 1983.

Huitema, Marijike E. '"Land of Which the Savages Stood in No Particular Need": Dispossessing the Algonquins of South-Eastern Ontario of Their Lands, 1760–1930'. MA thesis, Queen's University, 2000.

Koennecke, Franz. 'Wasoksing. The History of Parry Island an Anishnabwe Community in the Georgian Bay. 1850 to 1920'. MA thesis, University of Waterloo, 1984.

Leslie, John F. 'Assimilation, Integration or Termination? The Development of Canadian Indian Policy, 1943–1963'. PhD dissertation, Carleton University, 1999.

McCallum, Mary Jane Logan. 'Labour, Modernity, and the Canadian State: A History of Aboriginal Women and Work in the Mid-Twentieth Century'. PhD dissertation, University of Manitoba, 2008.

MacKay, Kathryn. 'Warriors into Welders: A History of Federal Employment Programs for American Indians, 1898–1972'. PhD dissertation, University of Utah, 1987.

Nawagesic, Leslie. 'Yuma State: A Philosophical Study of the Indian Residential School Experience'. MA thesis, Lakehead University, 2001.

Newbigging, William James. 'The History of the French-Ottawa Alliance: 1613–1763'. PhD dissertation, University of Toronto, 1995.

Pannekoek, Frits. 'Protestant Agricultural Missions in the Canadian West in 1870'. MA thesis, University of Alberta, 1970.

Simpson, Audra. 'To the Reserve and Back Again: Kahnawake Mohawk Narratives of Self, Home and Nation'. PhD dissertation, McGill University, 2003.

Sparrow, Leona Marie. 'Work Histories of a Coast Salish Couple'. MA thesis, University of British Columbia, 1976.

Spaulding, Philip T. 'The Metis of Ile-a-la-Crosse'. PhD dissertation, University of Washington, 1970.

Weaver, Sally. 'Medicine and Politics among the Grand River Iroquois'. PhD dissertation, University of Toronto, 1967.

White, Pamela Margaret. 'Restructuring the Domestic Sphere — Prairie Indian Women on Reserves: Image, Ideology, and State Policy, 1880–1930'. PhD dissertation, McGill University, 1987.

Williams, Paul. 'The Chain'. LLM thesis, York University, 1981.

Printed Documents and Reports

Amnesty International. *Stolen Sisters: Discrimination and Violence Against Indigenous Women in Canada*. Oct. 2004. Available at http://www.amnesty.ca/campaigns/resources/amr2000304.pdf (accessed 7 Jan. 2010).

Carter, Clarence E., ed. *The Correspondence of General Thomas Gage with the Secretaries of State and with the War Office and the Treasury, 1763–1775*, 2 vols. New Haven: Yale University Press, 1931–3.

Clatworthy, Stewart. *First Nations Membership and Registered Indian Status: Southern Chiefs Organization, Manitoba*. Ottawa: Indian and Northern Affairs Canada, Research and Analysis Directorate, 2001.

———. *Indian Registration, Membership and Population Change in First Nations Communities*. Ottawa: Indian and Northern Affairs, 2005.

Cornet, Wendy. *Executive Summary: First Nation Identities and Individual Equality Rights: A Discussion of Citizenship, Band Membership, and Indian Status*. Prepared for the National Aboriginal Women's Organization, 26 Jan. 2003.

Daugherty, Wayne E. 'Treaty Research Report – Treaty Three (1973)'. Ottawa: Indian and Northern Affairs Canada, 1986. Available at http://www.ainc-inac.gc.ca/al/hts/tgu/pubs/t3/tre3-eng.asp.

Douad, Patrick C. *Ethnolinguistic Profile of the Canadian Métis: Mercury Series – Canadian Ethnology Service Paper 99*. Ottawa: National Museum of Man, 1985.

Duckworth, Harry W. *The English River Book: A North West Company Journal and Account Book of 1786*. Montreal: McGill-Queen's University Press, 1990.

Feit, Harvey. 'The Power to "See" and the Power to Hunt: The Shaking Tent Ceremony in Relation to Experience, Explanation, Action and Interpretation in the Waswanipi Hunter's World'. *Canadian Museum of Civilization, Harvey Feit Papers*, B359, file 6, 1983.

Gilbert, Larry. *Entitlement to Indian Status and Membership Codes in Canada*. Scarborough: Thompson Canada, 1996.

Gough, Meagan. 'The Changing Relationship between First Nations Peoples and Museums'. Available at http://scaa.sk.ca/ourlegacy/exhibit_museums.

Holmes, Joan. *Background Paper - Bill C-31, Equality or Disparity? The Effects of the New Indian Act on Native Women*. Ottawa: Canadian Advisory Council on the Status of Women, 1987.

Indian and Northern Affairs Canada, Royal Commission on Aboriginal Peoples (1996). Available at http://www.ainc-inac.gc.ca/eng/1307458586498.

Jamieson, Kathleen. *Indian Women and the Law in Canada: Citizens Minus*. Ottawa: Canadian Advisory Council on the Status of Women and Indian Rights for Indian Women, 1978.

Kapashesit, R. 'Misiwa Chiwaacheyemitinwaa', in *MoCreebec Council of the Cree Nation 25th Anniversary Commemorative Report*. Moose Factory: MoCreebec Council of the Cree Nation, 2004.

Knox, John. *An Historical Journal of the Campaigns in North America for the Years 1757, 1758, 1759, and 1760*, 3 vols, ed. Arthur G. Doughty. Toronto: Champlain Society, 1914–16.

Native Women's Association of Canada. *Aboriginal Women and the Implementation of Bill C-31*. Ottawa: Native Women's Association of Canada, 1991.

Nourse, J.E., ed. *Narrative of the Second Arctic Expedition Made by Charles F. Hall: His Voyage to Repulse Bay, Sledge Journeys to the Straits of Fury and Hecla and to King William's Land, and Residence Among the Eskimos during the Years 1864–69*. Washington: US Naval Observatory, 1879.

Parry, W.E. *Journal of a Second Voyage for the Discovery of a North-West Passage . . . in the Years 1821–22–23*. London: John Murray, 1824.

Rich, E.E. *The History of Hudson's Bay Company 1670–1870*, 2 vols. London: Hudson's Bay Record Society, 1958–9.

———. *The Fur Trade and the Northwest to 1857*. Toronto: McClelland and Stewart, 1967.

Siggner, Andrew, and Chantal Locatelli. *An Overview of the Demographic, Social and Economic Conditions Among British Columbia's Registered Indian Population*. Ottawa: Research Branch, Corporate Policy, Department of Indian Affairs and Northern Development, 1981.

Surtees, Robert J. *Treaty Research Report: Manitoulin Island Treaty*. Ottawa: Treaties and Historical Research Centre, Indian and Northern Affairs Canada, 1986.

Wallace, W. Stewart, ed. *Documents Relating to the Northwest Company or North-West Company*. Toronto: Champlain Society, 1934.

Williams, Glyndwyr, ed. *Hudson's Bay Miscellany, 1670–1870*. Winnipeg: Hudson's Bay Record Society, 1975.

Wrong, George M., ed. *The Long Journey to the Country of the Hurons*. Toronto: Champlain Society, 1939.

Reference Works

Dickason, Olive Patricia. *Canada's First Nations: A History of Founding Peoples from Earliest Times*, 4th edn. Toronto: Oxford University Press, 2008.

Dictionary of Canadian Biography. Toronto: University of Toronto Press, 1991.

Frideres, James S., and René R. Gadacz. *Aboriginal Peoples in Canada*, 8th edn. Toronto: Pearson/Prentice Hall, 2008.

Grand Council of Micmacs, Union of Nova Scotia Indians, and Native Council of Nova Scotia. *The Mi'kmaq Treaty Handbook*. Sydney & Truro: Native Communications Society of Nova Scotia, 1987.

Helm, June, ed. *Handbook of North American Indians: Subarctic*, vol. 6. Washington: Smithsonian Institution, 1982.

Indian and Northern Affairs Canada, Communications Branch. 'Words First: An Evolving Terminology Relating to Aboriginal Peoples in Canada'. Oct. 2002. Available at http://www.collectionscanada.gc.ca/webarchives/20071124233110/http://www.ainc-inac.gc.ca/pr/pub/wf/wofi_e.pdf.

Jenness, Diamond. *Indians of Canada*, 6th edn. Ottawa: National Museum of Canada, 1963.

Troester, Rosalie Riegle, ed. *Historical Women of Michigan: A Sesquicentennial Celebration*. Lansing: Michigan Women's Studies Association, 1987.

Books and Articles

Abel, Kerry. 'History and the Provincial Norths: An Ontario Example', in Abel and Ken S. Coates, eds, *Northern Visions: New Perspectives on the North in Canadian History*. Peterborough: Broadview Press, 2001, 127–40.

Aberth, John. *The First Horseman: Disease in Human History*. Upper Saddle River, NJ: Pearson Prentice Hall, 2007.

Acuña-Soto, Rodolfo, D.W. Stahle, M.D. Therrell, Chavez Gomez, and M.K. Cleaveland. 'Drought, Epidemic Disease and the Fall of Classic Period Cultures in Mesoamerica (AD 750–950): Hermorrhagic Fevers as a Cause of Massive Population Loss', *Medical Hypotheses* 65 (2005): 405–09.

——, ——, ——, Richard Griffin, and M.K. Cleaveland. 'When Half of the Population Died: The Epidemic of Hemorrhagic Fevers in 1576 in Mexico', *FEMS Microbiology Letters* 240 (1 Nov. 2004): 1–5.

——, Leticia Calderon Romero, and James Maguire. 'Large Epidemics of Hemorrhagic Fevers in Mexico, 1545–1815', *American Journal of Tropical Medicine and Hygiene* 62 (2000): 733–9.

Adams, Howard. *Prison of Grass: Canada from a Native Point of View*. Toronto: New Press, 1975.

——. *Tortured People: The Politics of Colonization*. Penticton: Theytus Books, 1999.

Adelmand, Jeremy, and Stephen Aron, 'From Borderlands to Borders: Empires, Nation-States, and the Peoples in Between in North American History', *American Historical Review* 104 (June 1999): 814–41.

Adelson, Naomi. *Being Alive Well: Health and the Politics of Cree Well-Being*. Toronto: University of Toronto Press, 2000.

——. 'Discourses of Stress, Social Inequities, and the Everyday Worlds of First Nations Women in a Remote Northern Canadian Community', *Ethos* 36, 3 (2008): 316–31.

——. 'The Shifting Landscape of Cree Well-Being', in Gordon Matthews and Carolina Izquierdo, *Pursuits of Happiness: Well-Being in Anthropological Perspective*. Oxford: Berghahn Books, 2009, 109–23.

Alchon, Suzanne Austen. *Native Society and Disease in Colonial Ecuador*. Cambridge: Cambridge University Press, 1991.

——. *A Pest in the Land: New World Epidemics in a Global Perspective*. Albuquerque: University of New Mexico Press, 2003.

Alfred, Taiaiake. *Peace Power Righteousness: An Indigenous Manifesto*. Toronto: Oxford University Press, 1999.

——. *Wasasé: Indigenous Pathways of Action and Freedom*. Peterborough: Broadview Press, 2005.

Allen, Robert S. *His Majesty's Indian Allies: British Indian Policy in the Defence of Canada, 1774–1815*. Toronto: Dundurn Press, 1992.

Anderson, Emma. 'Between Conversion and Apostasy: The Religious Journey of Pierre-Anthoine Pastedechouan', *Anthropologica* 49, 1 (2007): 17–34.

Anderson, Kim. *Life Stages and Native Women: Memory, Teachings, and Story Medicine*. Winnipeg: University of Manitoba Press, 2011.

Anderson, Kim, and Bonita Lawrence, eds. *Strong Women Stories: Native Vision and Community Survival*. Toronto: Sumach Press, 2003.

Armitage, Peter. 'The Religious Significance of Animals in Innu Culture', *Native Issues* 4, 1 (1984): 50–6.

——. 'Religious Ideology among the Innu of Eastern Quebec and Labrador', *Religiologiques* 6 (1992): 64–110.

Atleo Jr, Cliff. 'From Indigenous Nationhood to Neoliberal Aboriginal Economic Development: Charting the Evolution of Indigenous-Settler Relations'. The Canadian Social Economy Hub, 2008. Available at http://www.socialeconomyhub.ca/?q=fr/content/indigenousnationhood-neoliberal-aboriginal-economic-developmentcharting-evolution-indigeno.

Backhouse, Constance. 'Nineteenth-Century Canadian Prostitution Law: Reflection of a Discriminatory Society', *Histoire sociale/Social History* 18, 36 (Nov. 1985): 387–423.

——. *Colour-Coded: A Legal History of Racism in Canada, 1900–1950*. Toronto: University of Toronto Press, 1999.

Baker, Brenda J., and Lisa Kealhofer, eds. *Bioarchaeology of Native American Adaptation in the Spanish Borderlands*. Gainesville: University Press of Florida, 1997.

Balikci, Asen. 'The Netsilik Inuit Today', *Études/Inuit/Studies* 2, 1 (1978): 111–19.

Barker, Adam. 'The Contemporary Reality of Canadian Imperialism: Settler Colonialism and the Hybrid Colonial State', *American Indian Quarterly* 33, 3 (Summer 2009): 325–51.

Barnett, Homer G. *The Coast Salish of British Columbia*. Eugene, OR: University of Oregon, 1955.

Barron, F. Laurie. 'Indian Agents and the North-West Rebellion', in Barron and James B. Waldram, eds, *1885 and After: Native Society in Transition*. Regina: Canadian Plains Research Centre, 1986, 139–54.

Bastien, Betty. *Blackfoot Ways of Knowing*. Calgary: University of Calgary Press, 2004.

Battiste, Marie. 'Introduction, Unfolding the Lessons of Colonization', in Battiste, ed., *Reclaiming Indigenous Voice and Vision*. Vancouver: UBC Press, 2007, xvi–xxx.

——, and James (Sa'ke'j) Youngblood Henderson. *Protecting Indigenous Knowledge and Heritage: A Global Challenge*. Saskatoon: Purich Publishing, 2000.

Benn, Carl. *The Iroquois in the War of 1812*. Toronto: University of Toronto Press, 1998.

Benton-Benai, Edward. *The Mishomis Book: The Voice of the Ojibway*. Lac Courte Oreilles Ojibwe Reservation, WI: Indian Country Communications, 1988.

Betts, Colin M. 'Pots and Pox: The Identification of Protohistoric Epidemics in the Upper Mississippi Valley', *American Antiquity* 71 (2006): 233–59.

Bhabha, Homi K. *The Location of Culture*. New York: Routledge, 1994.

Binnema, Theodore. *Common and Contested Ground: Human and Environmental History of the Northwestern Plains*. Norman: University of Oklahoma, 2001.

——, and Susan Neylan, eds. *New Histories for Old: New Perspectives on Canada's Native Past*. Vancouver: UBC Press, 2007.

Blackman, Margaret. *During My Time: Florence Edenshaw Davidson, A Haida Woman*. Vancouver: Douglas and McIntyre, 1982.

Blaisel, Xavier, Frederic Laugrand, and Jarich Oosten. 'Shamans, Leaders and Prophets: Parousial Movements among the Inuit of Canada', *Numen* 46 (1999): 370–411.

Bogue, Margeret. 'To Save the Fish: Canada, the United States, the Great Lakes, and the Joint Commission of 1892', *The Journal of American History* 79, 4 (Mar. 1993): 1429–54.

Bollet, Alfred J. *Plagues and Poxes: The Impact of Human History on Epidemic Disease*. New York: Demos Medical Publishing, 2004.

Borrows, John. *Recovering Canada: The Resurgence of Indigenous Law*. Toronto: University of Toronto Press, 2002.

Bouchard, Serge, and José Mailhot. 'Structure du Lexique: Les Animaux Indiens', *Recherches Amérindiennes au Québec* 3, 1–2 (1972): 39–67.

Boyle, Susan C. 'Did She Generally Decide? Women in Ste. Genevieve, 1750–1805', *William and Mary Quarterly, 3rd series* 44 (1987): 775–89.

Brandao, Jose Antonio. *'Your Fyre Shall Burn No More': Iroquois Policy toward New France and Its Native Allies to 1701*. Lincoln: University of Nebraska Press, 1997.

Brehm, Victoria. 'The Metamorphoses of an Ojibwa Manido', *American Literature* 68, 4 (Dec. 1996): 677–706.

Brenner, Elise M. 'Sociopolitical Implications of Mortuary Ritual Remains in 17th-Century Native Southern New England', in Mark P. Leone and Parker B. Potter, Jr, eds, *The Recovery of Meaning: Historical Archaeology in the Eastern United States*. Washington: Smithsonian Institution, 1988, 147–81.

Brown, James A. *Aboriginal Cultural Adaptations in the Midwestern Prairies*. New York: Garland Publishing, 1991.

Brown, Jennifer, and Elizabeth Vibert, eds. *Reading Beyond Words: Contexts for Native History*, 2nd edn. Toronto: University of Toronto Press, 2002.

Brownlie, Robin Jarvis. *A Fatherly Eye: Indian Agents, Government Power, and Aboriginal Resistance in Ontario, 1918–1939*. Toronto: Oxford University Press, 2003.

———. 'Intimate Surveillance: Indian Affairs, Colonization, and the Regulation of Aboriginal Women's Sexuality', in Katie Pickles and Myra Rutherdale, eds, *Contact Zones: Aboriginal and Settler Women in Canada's Colonial Past*. Vancouver: UBC Press, 2006, 169–79.

Brundige, Lorraine. '"Ungrateful Indian": Continuity of Native Values', *Ayaangwaamizin: The International Journal of Indigenous Philosophy* 1, 1 (1997): 31–44.

Burnett, Kristin. 'Aboriginal and White Women in the Publications of John Maclean, Egerton Ryerson Young, and John McDougall', in Sarah Carter, Lesley Erickson, Patricia Roome, and Char Smith, eds, *Unsettled Pasts: Reconceiving the West Through Women's History*. Calgary: University of Calgary Press, 2005, 101–22.

———. 'Building the System: Churches, Missionary Organizations, the Federal State, and Health Care in Southern Alberta Treaty 7 Communities, 1890–1930', *Journal of Canadian Studies* 41, 3 (Fall 2007), 18–41.

———. *Taking Medicine: Women's Healing Work and Colonial Contact in Southern Alberta, 1880–1930*. Vancouver: UBC Press, 2010.

Burrows, James. '"A Much Needed Class of Labour": The Economy and Income of the Southern Interior Plateau Indians, 1897–1910', *BC Studies* 71 (Autumn 1986): 27–46.

Butler, G.E. 'Fish culture in the Prairie Provinces, and some of its results', *Transactions of the American Fisheries Society* 60, 1 (Jan. 1930): 119–20.

Callicott, J. Baird. *In Defense of the Land Ethic: Essays in Environmental Philosophy*. Albany: State University of New York Press, 1989.

———. 'Many Indigenous Worlds or the Indigenous World? A Reply to My "Indigenous Critics"', *Environmental Ethics* 22, 3 (2000): 291–309.

Calloway, Colin G. *Crown and Calumet: British–Indian Relations, 1783–1815*. Norman: University of Oklahoma Press, 1987.

Campbell, Maria. *Halfbreed*. Toronto: Seal Books, 1973.

Cardinal, Harold, and Walter Hildebrandt. *Treaty Elders of Saskatchewan, Our Dream Is That Our Peoples Will One Day Be Clearly Recognized As Nations*. Calgary: University of Calgary Press, 2000.

Carstens, Peter. *The Queen's People: A Study of Hegemony, Coercion and Accommodation among the Okanagan of Canada*. Toronto: University of Toronto Press, 1991.

Carter, Sarah. *Lost Harvests: Prairie Indian Reserve Farmers and Government Policy*. Montreal: McGill-Queen's University Press, 1990.

———. *Capturing Women: The Manipulation of Cultural Imagery in Canada's Prairie West*. Montreal: McGill-Queen's University Press, 1997.

———. *Aboriginal People and Colonizers of Western Canada to 1900*. Toronto: University of Toronto Press, 1999.

Cassidy, Maureen. *From Mountain to Mountain: A History of the Gitksan Village of Anpayaxw*. Kispiox: Anpayaxw School Society, 1984.

Cleland, Charles E. 'The Inland Shore Fishery of the Northern Great Lakes: Its Development and Importance in Prehistory', *American Antiquity* 47, 4 (Oct. 1982): 761–84.

———. *Rites of Conquest: The History and Culture of Michigan's Native Americans*. University of Michigan Press, 1992.

Coates, Ken S. *Best Left as Indians: Native-White Relations in the Yukon Territory, 1840–1973*. Montreal: McGill-Queen's University Press, 1991.

———. *The Marshall Decision and Native Rights*. Montreal: McGill-Queen's University Press, 2000.

———, and William Morrison. *The Forgotten North: A History of Canada's Provincial Norths*. Toronto: James Lorimer & Company, 1992.

———, and ———. 'Wintering and the Shaping of Northern History: Reflections from the Canadian North', in Kerry Abel and Ken S. Coates, eds, *Northern Visions: New Perspectives on the North in Canadian History*. Peterborough: Broadview Press, 2001, 23–35.

Codell, Julie F. 'The Empire Writes Back: Native Informant Discourse in the Victorian Press', in Codell, ed., *Imperial Co-Histories: National Identities and the British and Colonial Press*. Madison: Fairleigh Dickinson University Press, 2003, 188–218.

Codere, Helen. *Fighting with Property: A Study of Kwakiutl Potlatching and Warfare, 1792–1930*. Seattle: University of Washington Press, 1972.

Cook, N.D. *Born to Die: Disease and New World Conquest, 1492–1650*. Cambridge: Cambridge University Press, 1998.

———. 'Une primera epidemia Americana de viruela en 1493?' *Revista de Indias* 63 (2003): 49–64.

Coulthard, Glen. 'Subjects of Empire: Indigenous Peoples and the "Politics of Recognition" in Canada', *Contemporary Political Theory* 6 (2007): 437–60.

———. 'Beyond Recognition: Indigenous Self-Determination as Prefigurative Practice', in Leanne Simpson, ed., *Lighting the Eighth Fire: The Liberation, Resurgence, and Protection of Indigenous Nations*. Winnipeg: Arbeiter Ring Publishing, 2008, 187–203.

Culhane, Dara. *The Pleasure of the Crown: Anthropology, Law, and First Nations*. Vancouver: Talonbooks, 1998.

———. 'Aboriginal Women in Eastside Vancouver: Emerging Into Invisibility', *American Indian Quarterly* 27, 3&4 (2003): 593–606.

Culhane Speck, Dara. *An Error in Judgment*. Vancouver: Talonbooks, 1987.

Darnell, Regna. 'Rethinking the Concepts of Band and Tribe, Community and Nation: An Accordion Model of Nomadic Native American Social Organization', in David Pentland, ed., *Papers of the Twenty-Ninth Algonquian Conference*. Winnipeg: University of Manitoba, 1998, 90–105.

Davis, A., and S. Jentoft. 'The Challenge and the Promise of Indigenous Peoples' Fishing Rights — From Dependency to Agency', *Marine Policy* 25, 3 (2001): 223–37.

Davis, Natalie Zemon. 'Iroquois Women, European Women', in Margo Hendricks and Patricia Parker, eds, *Women, 'Race,' and Writing in the Early Modern Period*. New York: Routledge, 1994, 243–61.

Dawson, K.C.A. *Archaeological Survey of Canada, Paper No.25, The McCluskey Site*. National Museum of Man, Mercury Series. Ottawa: National Museums of Canada, 1974.

deMenocal, Peter B. 'Cultural Responses to Climate Change during the Late Colocene', *Science* 292 (2001): 667–73.

Denevan, William N. 'Carl Sauer and Native American Population Size', *Geographical Review* 86 (1996): 385–97.

———. 'The Native Population of Amazonia in 1492 Reconsidered', *Revista de Indias* 63 (2003): 175–88.

Densmore, Christopher. *Red Jacket: Iroquois Diplomat and Orator*. Syracuse: Syracuse University Press, 1999.

Dessert, Daniel, and Jean-Louis Journet. 'Le lobby Colbert: un royaume, ou une affaire de famille?' *Annales: Economies, Societies, Civilizations* 30, 4 (Nov.–Dec. 1975): 1303–36.

Devine, Heather. *The People Who Own Themselves: Aboriginal Ethnogenesis in a Canadian Family, 1660–1900*. Calgary: University of Calgary Press, 2004.

Dewdney, Selwyn. *The Sacred Scrolls of the Southern Ojibwa*. Toronto: Toronto University Press, 1975.

Diamond, Jared. *Guns Germs and Steel: The Fates of Human Societies*. New York: W.W. Norton, 1997.

Dickason, Olive P. 'Reclaiming Stolen Land', in John Bird, Lorraine Land, and Murray MacAdam, eds, *Nation to Nation. Aboriginal Sovereignty and the Future of Canada*, 2nd edn. Toronto/Vancouver: Irwin, 2002, 34–43.

Dobyns, Henry F. *Their Number Became Thinned*. Knoxville, TN: University of Tennessee Press, 1983.

Dorais, Louis-Jacques. 'Le temps des Fetes a Quaqtaq', *Études/Inuit/Studies* 24, 2 (2000): 139–50.

Dosman, Edgar. *Indians: The Urban Dilemma*. Toronto: McClelland and Stewart, 1972.

Douad, Patrick. 'Michif: An Aspect of Francophone Alberta', *Journal of Indigenous Studies* 1, 2 (1989): 80–90.

Douglas, Thomas. *A Sketch of the British Fur Trade in North America; with Observations Relative to the North-West Company of Montreal*, 2nd edn. London: James Ridgway, 1816.

Dowd, Gregory Evans. 'The French King Wakes up in Detroit: Pontiac's War in Rumor and History', *Ethnohistory* 37 (1990): 254–78.

———. *War under Heaven: Pontiac, the Indian Nations, and the British Empire*. Baltimore: Johns Hopkins University Press, 2002.

Dyck, Noel. *Differing Visions: Administering Indian Residential Schooling in Prince Albert, 1867–1995*. Halifax: Fernwood, 1997.

Egan, Patricia Barrios Marcia. 'Living in a Bicultural World and Finding the Way Home', *Affilia* 17, 2 (2002): 206–28.

Ekberg, Carl J., with Anton J. Pregaldin. 'Marie Rouensa-8cate8a and the Foundations of French Illinois', *Illinois Historical Journal* 84 (Fall 1991): 146–60.

Elkins, Caroline, and Susan Pedersen. *Settler Colonialism in the Twentieth Century*. New York: Routledge, 2005.

Ens, Gerhard J. *Homeland to Hinterland: The Changing Worlds of the Red River Métis in the Nineteenth Century*. Toronto: University of Toronto Press, 1996.

Fagan, Brian. *The Little Ice Age: How Climate Made History*. New York: Basic Books, 2000.

Feit, Harvey A. 'Legitimation and Autonomy in James Bay Cree Responses To Hydro-electric Development', in Noel Dyck, ed., *Indigenous Peoples and the Nation State: Fourth World Politics in Canada, Australia and Norway*. St. John's: Memorial University Institute for Social and Economic Research, 1985, 27–66.

———. 'Hunting and the Quest for Power: The James Bay Cree and Whitemen in the Twentieth Century', in R. Bruce Morrison and C. Roderick Wilson, eds, *Native Peoples: The Canadian Experience*. Toronto: McClelland & Stewart, 1995, 181–223.

Fields D.B., and W.T. Stanbury. *The Economic Impact of The Public Sector Upon the Indians of British Columbia*. Vancouver: UBC Press, 1973.

Fisher, Robin. *Contact and Conflict: Indian–European Relations in British Columbia*, 2nd edn. Vancouver: UBC Press, 1992.

Fiske, Jo-Anne. 'Political Status of Native Indian Women: Contradictory Implications of Canadian State', in Mary-Ellen Kelm and Lorna Townsend, *In the Days of Our Grandmothers: A Reader in Aboriginal Women's History in Canada*. Toronto: University of Toronto Press, 2006, 336–66.

———, Susan Sleeper-Smith, and William Wicken, eds. *New Faces of the Fur Trade: Selected Papers of the Seventh North American Fur Trade Conference, Halifax, Nova Scotia, 1995*. East Lansing: Michigan State University Press, 1998.

Fitting, James E., and Charles E. Cleland. 'Late Prehistoric Settlement Patterns in the Upper Great Lakes', *Ethnohistory* 16, 4 (1969): 289–302.

Flanagan, Tom. *First Nations, Second Thoughts?* 2nd edn. Montreal: McGill-Queen's University Press, 2008.

———, and Gerhard Ens. 'Métis Land Grants in Manitoba: A Statistical Study', *Histoire Sociale/Social History* 27, 53 (May 1994): 65–87.

Flannery, Regina. 'The Shaking-Tent Rite among the Montagnais of James Bay', *Primitive Man* 12, 1 (1939): 11–16.

Ford, Clellan S. *Smoke from Their Fires: The Life of a Kwakiutl Chief*. Hamden, CT: Archon, 1968.

Foster, John. 'Rupert's Land and the Red River Settlement, 1820–1870', in Lewis G. Thomas, ed., *The Prairie West to 1905: A Canadian Source Book*. Toronto: University of Toronto Press, 1975, 19–72.

———. 'The Metis: The People and the Term', *Prairie Forum* 3, 1 (1978): 79–90.

———. 'Some Questions and Perspectives on the Problem of Métis Roots', in Jacqueline Peterson and Jennifer S.H. Brown, eds, *The New Peoples: Being and Becoming Métis in North America*. Winnipeg: University of Manitoba Press, 1985, 73–94.

Foster, Martha Haroun. *We Know Who We Are: Métis Identity in a Montana Community*. Norman: University of Oklahoma Press, 2006.

Frederickson, George M. 'From Exceptionalism to Variability: Recent Developments in Cross-National Comparative History', *Journal of American History* 82 (Sept. 1995): 487–604.

Freire, Paulo. *Pedagogy of the Oppressed*, trans. Maria Bergman Ramos. New York: Continuum, 1997.

Fuller, Frank. 'Gilbert Jo', *Labour History* 2, 3 (1980): 16–19

Gaffen, Fred. *Forgotten Soldiers*. Penticton: Theytus Books, 1985.

Garrad, Charles. 'Iron Trade Knives on Historic Petun Sites', *Ontario Archaeology* 13 (1969): 3–15.

Garroutte, Eva Marie. *Real Indians: Identity and the Survival of Native America*. Berkeley: University of California Press, 2003.

Gerber, Linda. 'Multiple Jeopardy: A Socio-Economic Comparison of Men and Women Among the Indian, Métis and Inuit Peoples of Canada', *Canadian Ethnic Studies* 22, 3 (1990): 69–84.

Giokas, John, and Robert K. Groves. *Who Are Canada's Aboriginal Peoples?: Recognition, Definition and Jurisdiction*, ed. Paul Chartrand. Saskatoon: Purich Publishing, 2002.

Goodman, Ronald. *Lakota Star Knowledge, Studies in Lakota Theology*. Rosebud, SD: Sinte Gleska University, 1992.

Gould, Jeffrey L. *To Die in This Way: Nicaraguan Indians and the Myth of Mestizaje, 1880–1965*. Durham and London: Duke University Press, 1998.

Graham-Cumming, G. 'Health of the Original Canadians, 1867–1967', *Medical Services Journal of Canada* 23, 2 (1967): 115–66.

Grande, Sandy. *Red Pedagogy: Native American Social and Political Thought*. Maryland: Rowman and Littlefield Publishers, 2004.

Grant, Agnes. *No End of Grief: Indian Residential Schools in Canada*. Winnipeg: Pemmican Publications, 1996.

Gray, Susan Elaine. *I Will Fear No Evil: Ojibway Missionary Encounters along the Berens River, 1875–1940*. Calgary: University of Calgary Press, 2006.

Graymont, Barbara. *The Iroquois in the American Revolution*. Syracuse: Syracuse University Press, 1972.

Green, J. 'Towards a Détente with History: Confronting Canada's Colonial Legacy', *International Journal of Canadian Studies* 12 (1995): 85–105.

Green, Rayna. 'The Pocahontas Perplex: The Image of Indian Women in American Culture', *The Massachusetts Review* 16, 4 (Autumn, 1975): 698–714.

Guery, Alain. 'L'historien, la crise et l'Etat', *Annales: Histoire, Sciences Sociales* 52 (1997): 233–56.

Gulig, Anthony. 'Sizing Up the Catch: Native–Newcomer Resource Competition and the Early Years of Saskatchewan's Northern Commercial Fishery', *Saskatchewan History* 47, 2 (Fall 1995): 3–12.

———. 'Yesterday's Promises: The Negotiation of Treaty Ten', *Saskatchewan History* 50, 1 (Spring 1998): 25–39.

Hackett, Paul. *A Very Remarkable Sickness: Epidemics in the Petit Nord, 1670 to 1846*. Winnipeg: University of Manitoba Press, 2002.

Hamell, George R. 'Trading in Metaphors: The Magic of Beads: Another Perspective on Indian-European Contact in Northeastern North America', in Charles F. Hayes III, ed., *Proceedings of the 1982 Glass Trade Bead Conference*. Rochester: Rochester Museum and Science Center, 1983, 5–28.

———. 'Strawberries, Floating Islands, and Rabbit Captains: Mythical Realities and European Contact in the Northeast during the Sixteenth and Seventeenth Centuries', *Journal of Canadian Studies* 21 (Winter 1987): 72–94.

Hamer, David. *New Towns in the New World: Images and Perceptions of the Nineteenth Century Urban Frontier*. New York: Columbia University Press, 1990.

Hannibal-Paci, Christopher. 'Historical Representations of Lake Sturgeon by Native and Non-Native Artists', *Canadian Journal of Native Studies* 18, 2 (1998): 214–24.

———. '"Officers of the HBC, Missionaries and other Intelligent Persons in the District of Keewatin": Lake Winnipeg Sturgeon as an Aboriginal Resource', in David Pentland, ed., *Papers of the Twenty-Ninth Algonquian Conference*. Winnipeg: University of Manitoba, 1998, 128–49.

Hansen, Lise C. 'Treaty Fishing Rights and the Development of Fisheries Legislation in Ontario: A Primer', *Native Studies Review* 7, 1 (1991): 1–21.

Harring, Sidney L. *White Man's Law: Native People in Nineteenth Century Canadian Jurisprudence*. Toronto: Published for Osgoode Society for Canadian Legal History by University of Toronto Press, 1998.

Harris, Cole. *Making Native Space: Colonialism, Resistance, and Reserves in British Columbia*. Vancouver: UBC Press, 2002.

Harris, Douglas. *Fish, Law, and Colonialism: The Legal Capture of Salmon in British Columbia*. Toronto: University of Toronto Press, 2001.

Harvey, D. *The New Imperialism*. New York: Oxford University Press, 2003, 137–82.

Hauptman, Laurence M. *Conspiracy of Interests: Iroquois Dispossession and the Rise of New York State*. Syracuse: Syracuse University Press, 1999.

Hawkes, David C., ed. *Aboriginal Peoples and Government Responsibility: Exploring Federal and Provincial Roles*. Ottawa: Carleton University Press, 1989.

Hawthorn, H.B., C. Belshaw, and S.M. Jamieson. *Indians of British Columbia: A Study of Contemporary Social Adjustment*. Toronto: University of Toronto Press, 1959.

Hays, J.N. *Epidemics and Pandemics*. Santa Barbara: ABC Clio, 2005.

Heidenreich C.E., and A.J. Ray. *The Early Fur Trades: A Study in Cultural Interaction*. Toronto: McClelland and Stewart, 1976.

Henige, David. *Numbers from Nowhere: The American Indian Contact Population Debate*. Norman: University of Oklahoma Press, 1998.

Hester, Lee, Dennis McPherson, and Annie Booth. 'Indigenous Worlds and Callicott's Land Ethic', *Environmental Ethics* 22, 3 (2000): 273–90.

Hinderaker, Eric. *Elusive Empires: Constructing Colonialism in the Ohio Valley, 1673–1800*. New York: Cambridge University Press, 1997.

Holzkamm, Tim, Victor P. Lytwyn, and Leo G. Waisberg. 'Rainy River Sturgeon: An Ojibwa resource in the fur trade economy', *The Canadian Geographer* 32, 3 (1988): 194–205.

Howard-Bobiwash, Heather. 'Women's Class Strategies as Activism in Indigenous Community Building in Toronto, 1950–75', *American Indian Quarterly* 27, 3&4 (Summer–Fall, 2001): 566–82.

Howell, Kenneth W. 'In the Wake of Conquest: A Global Perspective on the Depopulation of Indigenous Peoples of Latin America', *Diálogos Latinamericanos* 5 (2002): 58–72.

Hughes, Thomas. *History of the Society of Jesus in North America*. London: Longmans, Green, & Co., 1917.

Hunt, George T. *The Wars of the Iroquois: A Study in Intertribal Trade Relations*. Madison: University of Wisconsin Press, 1940.

Hurlich, Susan. 'Up Against the Bay: Resource Imperialism and Native Resistance', *This Magazine* 9, 4 (1975): 3–8.

Hutchinson, Dale L. *Tatham Mound and the Bioarchaeology of European Contact: Disease and Depopulation in Central Gulf Coast Florida*. Gainesville: University Press of Florida, 2006.

Innis, Harold. *The Fur Trade in Canada*. Toronto: University of Toronto Press, 1970.

Innes, Robert Alexander. '"I'm On Home Ground Now. I'm Safe": Saskatchewan Aboriginal Veterans in the Immediate Postwar Years, 1945–1946', *American Indian Quarterly* 28, 3&4 (Summer–Fall 2004): 685–718.

Isaac, T. *Aboriginal and Treaty Rights in the Maritimes: The Marshall Decision and Beyond*. Saskatoon: Purich Publishers, 2001.

Jacoby, Karl. *Crimes Against Nature: Squatters, Poachers, Thieves and the Hidden History of American Conservation*. Berkeley: University of California Press, 2003.

Jaenen, C. *Friend and Foe*. Toronto: McClelland and Stewart, 1976.

Janovicek, Nancy. 'Assisting Our Own: Urban Migration, Self-Governance, and Indigenous Women's Organizing in Thunder Bay, Ontario, 1972–1989', *American Indian Quarterly* 27, 3&4 (Summer–Fall, 2001): 548–65.

Jarvenpa, Robert. 'The Hudson's Bay Company, the Roman Catholic Church, and the Chipewyan in the Late Fur Trade Period', in Bruce G. Trigger, Toby Elaine Morantz, and Louise Dechêne, eds, *Le Castor fait tout: Selected Papers of the 5th American Fur Trade*. Montreal: The Society, 1987, 485–517.

———, and Hetty Jo Brumback. 'Occupational Status, Ethnicity and Ecology: Métis Adaptations in a Canadian Trading Frontier', *Human Ecology* 13, 3 (1985): 309–29.

Jenness, Diamond. 'The Indian Background of Canadian History', *Canada, Department of Mines and Resources, National Museum of Canada Bulletin No. 86*. Ottawa, 1937, 1–2.

Jilek, Wolfgang G. *Salish Indian Mental Health and Culture Change*. Toronto: Holt, Rinehart and Winston of Canada, 1974.

Johnston, Basil. *Indian School Day*. Toronto: Key Porter Books, 1988.

———. *The Manitous: The Spiritual World of the Ojibway*. Toronto: Key Porter Books, 1995.

Jones, Charles, with Stephen Bosustow. *Queesto, Pacheenaht Chief by Birthright*. Nanaimo, BC: Theytus, 1981.

Kellogg, Louise Phelps. *The French Regime in Wisconsin and the Northwest*. Madison: State Historical Society of Wisconsin, 1925.

Kelm, Mary-Ellen. *Colonizing Bodies: Aboriginal Health and Healing in British Columbia, 1900–1950*. Vancouver: UBC Press, 1998.

———, and Lorna Townsend, eds. *In the Days of Our Grandmothers: A Reader in Aboriginal Women's History in Canada*. Toronto: University of Toronto Press, 2006.

Kettering, Sharon. *Patrons, Brokers, and Clients in Seventeenth-Century France*. New York: Oxford University Press, 1986.

Kidwell, Clara Sue. 'Indian Women as Cultural Negotiators', *Ethnohistory* 39 (1992): 97–107.

Kinietz, W. Vernon. *The Indians of the Western Great Lakes*. Ann Arbor: University of Michigan Press, 1990.

Knockwood, Isabelle. *Out of the Depths: The Experiences of Mi'kmaw Children at the Indian Residential School at Shubenacadie, Nova Scotia*. Lockeport, NS: Roseway Publishing, 1992.

Krech, Shepard. *The Ecological Indian: Myth and History*. New York: W.W. Norton & Company, 1999.

Kue Young, T. *Health Care and Cultural Change: The Indian Experience in the Central Subarctic*. Toronto: University of Toronto Press, 1988.

Kulchyski, Peter. 'A Considerable Unrest: F.O. Loft and the League of Indians', *Native Studies Review* 4, 1&2 (1988): 95–113.

LaDow, Beth. *The Medicine Line: Life and Death on a North American Borderland*. New York: Routledge, 2001.

LaDuke, Winona. *All Our Relations: Native Struggles for Land and Life*. Cambridge, MA: South End Press, 1999.

Lagassé, Jean. *The People of Indian Ancestry in Manitoba*, Vol. 3. Winnipeg: Dept. of Agriculture and Immigration, 1959.

Lagrand, James. *Indian Metropolis: Indigenous Americans in Chicago*. Urbana: University of Illinois Press, 2002.

LaRocque, Emma. *When the Other Is Me: Native Resistance Discourse, 1885–1990*. Winnipeg: University of Manitoba Press, 2008.

Latta, Martha A. 'Archaeology of the Penetang Peninsula', in William M. Hurley and Conrad E. Heidenreich, eds, *Palaeocology and Ontario Prehistory*. Toronto: Department of Anthropology, University of Toronto, 1971, 116–36.

Laugrand, Frederic. 'Le siqqitiq: renouvellement religieux et premier ritue1 de conversion chez les Inuit du nord de la Terre de Baffin', *Études/Inuit/Studies* 21, 1&2 (1997): 101–40.

Lawrence, Bonita. 'Rewriting Histories of the Land: Colonization and Indigenous Resistance in Eastern Canada', in Sherene Razack, ed., *Race, Space and the Law: Unmapping a White Settler Society*. Toronto: Between the Lines, 2002, 21–46.

———. 'Gender, Race, and the Regulation of Indigenous Identity in Canada and the U.S.: An Overview', *Hypatia* 18, 2 (Spring 2003): 3–31.

———. *'Real' Indians and Others: Mixed-blood Urban Native Peoples and Indigenous Nationhood*. Lincoln: University of Nebraska Press, 2004.

Leighton, Douglas. 'The Manitoulin Incident of 1863: An Indian–White Confrontation in the Province of Canada', *Ontario History* 69, 2 (June 1977): 113–24.

Leslie, John F. 'The Policy Agenda of Native Peoples from World War II to the 1969 White Paper', in Jerry P. White, Paul Maxim and Dan Beavon, eds, *Aboriginal Policy Research: Setting the Agenda for Change*, Vol. 1. Toronto: Thompson Educational Publishing, 2004, 15–28.

Lester, Alan. *Imperial Networks: Creating Identities in Nineteenth-Century South Africa and Britain*. London: Routledge, 2001, 189–92.

Livi-Bacci, Massimo. 'The Depopulation of Hispanic America after the Conquest', *Population and Development Review* 32 (2006): 199–232.

Long, John. 'Rev. Edwin Watkins: Missionary to the Cree: 1852–1857', in William Cowan, ed., *Papers of the Sixteenth Algonquian Conference*. Ottawa: Carleton University, 1985, 91–117.

Lutz, John Sutton. *Makúk: A New History of Aboriginal White Relations*. Vancouver: UBC Press, 2008.

———, ed. *Myth and Memory: Stories of Indigenous–European Contact*. Vancouver: UBC Press, 2007.

Lux, Maureen. *Medicine That Walks: Disease, Medicine and Canadian Plains Native People, 1880–1940*. Toronto: University of Toronto Press, 2001.

Lytwyn, Victor P. 'Ojibwa and Ottawa Fisheries around Manitoulin Island: Historical and Geographical Perspectives on Aboriginal and Treaty Fishing Rights', *Native Studies Review* 6, 1 (1990): 1–30.

———. 'Inland Sea Navigators: Algonquian Mastery of the Great Lakes', in H.C. Wolfart, ed., *Papers of the Thirty-Sixth Algonquian Conference*. Winnipeg: University of Manitoba Press, 2005, 255–69.

McCallum, Mary Jane. *Twice As Good: A History of Aboriginal Nurses*. Ottawa: Aboriginal Nurses Association of Canada, 2007.

———. 'Indigenous Labour and Indigenous History', *American Indian Quarterly* 33, 4 (Fall 2009): 523–44.

McClintock, Walter. *The Old North Trail: Life, Legend and Religion of the Blackfeet Indians*. Nebraska: University of Nebraska Press, 1999.

Macdougall, Brenda. *One of the Family: Métis Culture in Nineteenth-Century Northwestern Saskatchewan*. Vancouver: UBC Press, 2010.

McDowell, John E. 'Madame La Framboise', *Michigan History* 56 (Winter 1972): 271–86.

———. 'Therese Schindler of Mackinac: Upward Mobility in the Great Lakes Fur Trade', *Wisconsin Magazine of History* 61 (Winter 1977–8): 125–43.

McFarlane, Peter. 'Aboriginal Leadership', in D. Long and O.P. Dickason, eds, *Visions of the Heart. Canadian Aboriginal Issues*, 2nd edn. Toronto: Harcourt, 2000, 61–4.

MacGregor, Roy. *Chief, The Fearless Vision of Billy Diamond*. Markham, ON: Viking, 1989.

McNab, David T. 'Who Is on Trial? Teme-Augama Anishnabai Land Rights and George Ironside, Junior: Re-Considering Oral Tradition', *The Canadian Journal of Native Studies* 18, 1 (1998): 117–33.

———. 'Herman Merivale and Colonial Office Indian Policy in the Mid-Nineteenth Century', in Ian L. Getty and Antoine S. Lussier, eds, *As Long As The Sun Shines And Water Flows: A Reader in Canadian Native Studies*. Vancouver, UBC Press, 2000, 85–103.

McPherson, Dennis H. 'A Definition of Culture: Canada and First Nations', in Jace Weaver, ed., *Native American Religious Identity: Unforgotten Gods*. Maryknoll: Orbis Books, 1998, 77–98.

———, and J. Douglas Rabb. *Indian from the Inside: A Study in Ethno-Metaphysics*. Thunder Bay: Lakehead University Centre for Northern Studies, 1993.

———, and ———. 'Walking the Talk: An Application of Anishnabe Philosophy or a Tearful Trail toward Culturally Congruent Education', *Ayaangwaamizin: The International Journal of Indigenous Philosophy* 2, 1 (1999): 89–99.

McPherson, Kathryn. 'Nursing and Colonization: The Work of Indian Health Service Nurses in Manitoba, 1945–1970', in Georgina Feldberg, Molly Ladd-Taylor, Alison Li and Kathryn McPherson, eds, *Women, Health, and Nation: Canada and the United States Since 1945*. Montreal: McGill-Queen's University Press, 2003, 223–46.

Mann, Michael C. *1491: New Revelations of the Americas before Columbus*. New York: Alfred A. Knopf, 2005.

Manuel, George, and Michael Posluns. *The Fourth World: An Indian Reality*. New York: The Free Press, 1974.

Marshall Sr, D., A. Denny, and S. Marshall. 'The Covenant Chain', in B. Richardson, ed., *Drumbeat: Anger and Renewal in Indian Country*. Toronto: Summerhill Press, 1989, 71–104.

Martin, Calvin. *Keepers of the Game: Indian–Animal Relationships and the Fur Trade*. Berkeley: University of California Press, 1978.

Martin, Susan Rapalje. 'A Reconsideration of Aboriginal Fishing Strategies in the Northern Great Lakes Region', *American Antiquity* 54, 3 (Jul. 1989): 594–604.

Mary-Rousseliere, Guy. 'The Grave of Kukigaq', *Eskimo* 57 (1960): 18–22.

Meijer Drees, Laurie. *The Indian Association of Alberta: A History of Political Action*. Vancouver: University of British Columbia Press, 2002.

Miller, B. *Invisible Indigenes: The Politics of Nonrecognition*. Lincoln and London: University of Nebraska, 2003.

Miller, Christine, and Patricia Chuchryk. *Women of the First Nations: Power, Wisdom and Strength*. Winnipeg: University of Manitoba Press, 1996.

Miller, Christopher L., and George R. Hamell. 'A New Perspective on Indian–White Contact: Cultural Symbols and Colonial Trade', *Journal of American History* 73 (Sept. 1986): 311–28.

Miller, J.R. 'From Riel to the Métis', *Canadian Historical Review* 69, 1 (1988): 1–20.

———. *Skyscrapers Hide the Heavens: A History of Indian–White Relations in Canada*. Toronto: University of Toronto Press, 1991.

———. *Shingwauk's Vision: A History of Native Residential Schools*. Toronto: University of Toronto Press, 1996.

———. *Reflections on Native–Newcomer Relations: Selected Essays*. Toronto: University of Toronto Press, 2004.

Milloy, John S. 'The Early Indian Acts: Developmental Strategy and Constitutional Change', in Ian A.L. Getty and Antoine S. Lussier, eds, *As Long As The Sun Shines*

And Water Flows: A Reader in Canadian Native Studies. Vancouver: UBC Press, 1983, 56–65.

———. *'A National Crime': The Canadian Government and the Residential School System 1879–1986.* Winnipeg: University of Manitoba Press, 1999.

Milne, Brad. 'The Historiography of Métis Land Dispersal, 1870–1890', *Manitoba History* 30 (Autumn 1995): 30–41.

Milner, George R. 'Warfare in Prehistoric and Early Historic Eastern North America', *Journal of Archaeological Research* 7 (1999): 105–52.

Moran, Bridget. *Stoney Creek Woman: The Story of Mary John.* Vancouver: Tillacum Library, 1988.

Morantz, Toby. *The Whiteman's Gonna Getcha: The Colonial Challenge to the Crees in Quebec.* Montreal: McGill-Queen's University Press, 2002.

Morgan, E.C. 'The North-West Mounted Police: Internal Problems and Public Criticism, 1874–1883', *Saskatchewan History* 26, 2 (Spring 1973): 56–9.

Morrison, James. 'The Robinson Treaties of 1850: A Case Study'. Prepared for the Royal Commission on Aboriginal Peoples, 1993.

Moss, Wendy. 'The Implementation of the James Bay and Northern Quebec Agreement', in Brad W. Morse, ed., *Aboriginal Peoples and the Law: Indian Métis and Inuit Rights in Canada.* Ottawa: Carleton University Press, 1989, 684–94.

Murphy, Lucy Eldersveld. *A Gathering of Rivers: Indians, Métis, and Mining in the Western Great Lakes, 1737–1832.* Lincoln: University of Nebraska Press, 2000.

Nadasdy, P. *Hunters and Bureaucrats: Power, Knowledge, and Aboriginal–State Relations in the Southwest Yukon.* Vancouver: UBC Press, 2003.

Nash, Ronald J. *Archaeological Investigations in the Transitional Forest Zone: Northern Manitoba and Southern Keewatin, NWT.* Winnipeg: Manitoba Museum of Man and Nature, 1975.

Newell, Dianne. *Tangled Webs of History: Indians and the Law in Canada's Pacific Coast Fisheries.* Toronto: University of Toronto, 1993.

Newson, Linda A. 'Patterns of Indian Depopulation in Early Colonial Ecuador', *Revista de Indias* 63 (2003): 135–56.

Neylan, Susan. *The Heavens are Changing: Nineteenth-Century Protestant Missions and Tsimshiam Christianity.* Montreal: McGill-Queen's University Press, 2002.

Nicks, Trudy, and Kenneth Morgan. 'Grand Cache: The Historic Development of an Indigenous Alberta Métis Population', in Jacqueline Peterson and Jennifer S.H. Brown, eds, *The New Peoples: Being and Becoming Métis in North America.* Winnipeg: University of Manitoba Press, 1985, 163–84.

Niezen, Ronald. 'Healing and Conversion: Medical Evangelism in James Bay Cree Society', *Ethnohistory* 44, 3 (1997): 463–91.

Nock, David. *A Victorian Missionary and Canadian Indian Policy: Cultural Synthesis vs Cultural Replacement.* Waterloo: Wilfrid Laurier Press, 1988.

Nute, Grace Lee. 'The American Fur Company's Fishing Enterprises on Lake Superior', *The Mississippi Valley Historical Review* 12, 4 (Mar. 1926): 483–503.

Palm, Mary Borgias. *The Jesuit Missions of the Illinois Country, 1673–1763.* Cleveland: St Louis University, 1933.

Palmer, Jay W. 'A Basketmaker II Massacre Revisited', *North American Archaeologist* 22 (2001): 117–41.

Pannekoek, Frits. 'The Rev. Griffiths Owen Corbett and the Red River Civil War of 1869–70', *Canadian Historical Review* 57 (1976): 133–49.

Parker, Arthur C. 'The Constitution of the Five Nations', in William N. Fenton, ed., *Parker on the Iroquois.* Syracuse: Syracuse University Press, 1968.

Peabody, Sue. *'There Are No Slaves in France': The Political Culture of Race and Slavery in the Ancien Regime.* New York: Oxford University Press, 1996.

Peat, David. *Lighting the Seventh Fire.* Secaucus, NJ: Carol Publishing Company, 1994.

Peers, Laura. *The Ojibwa of Western Canada: 1780–1870.* Winnipeg: University of Manitoba Press, 1994.

Pennier, Henry, with Herbert L. McDonald. *Chiefly Indian: The Warm and Witty Story of a British Columbia Half Breed Logger.* Vancouver: Graydonald Graphics, 1972.

Perdue, Theda. 'Race and Culture: Writing the Ethnohistory of the South', *Ethnohistory* 51, 4 (Fall 2004): 701–23.

Peters, Evelyn J. '"Urban" and "Aboriginal": An Impossible Contradiction?' in J. Caulfield and L. Peake, eds, *City Lives & City Forms: Critical Research & Canadian Urbanism.* Toronto: University of Toronto Press, 1996, 47–62.

———. 'Native People and the Environmental Regime in the James Bay and Northern Quebec Agreement', *Arctic* 52, 4 (Dec. 1999): 395–410.

———, and David Newhouse. *Not Strangers in These Parts: Urban Aboriginal Peoples.* Ottawa: Policy Research Initiative, 2003.

Peyser, Joseph L. 'The Fate of the Fox Survivors: A Dark Chapter in the History of the French in the Upper Country, 1726–1737', *Wisconsin Magazine of History* 73, 2 (Winter 1989–90): 83–110.

Pictou, S. 'How Deep Are Our Treaties?' *Samudra* 54 (2009): 8–9.

———, and A. Bull. 'Resource Extraction in the Maritimes: Historic Links with Racism', *New Socialist* 1 (2009): 38–39.

Pilger, J. *Freedom Next Time.* Ealing: Bantam Press, 2006.

Piper, L. *The Industrial Transformation of Subarctic Canada.* Vancouver: UBC Press, 2009.

Podruchny, Carolyn, and Laura Peers, eds. *Gathering Places: Aboriginal and Fur Trade Histories.* Vancouver: UBC Press, 2010.

Pomedli, Michael M. *Ethnophilosophical and Ethnolinguistic Perspectives on the Huron Indian Soul*. Lewiston: Edwin Mellen Press, 1991.

Ponting, Rick. 'The Report of the House of Commons Special Committee on Indian Self-Government: Three Comments', *Canadian Public Policy* 10, 2 (June 1984): 211–24.

Potts, G. 'Teme-Augama Anishnabai: Last-Ditch Defence of a Priceless Homeland', in B. Richardson, ed., *Drumbeat: Anger and Renewal in Indian Country*. Toronto: Summerhill Press and the Assembly of First Nations, 1989, 201–28.

Pratt, Mary Louise. *Imperial Eyes: Travel Writing and Transculturation*, 2nd edn. New York: Routledge, 2008.

Preston, Richard. *Cree Narrative: Expressing the Personal Meanings of Events*. Montreal: McGill-Queen's University Press, 2002.

Rabb, J. Douglas. 'Prologues to Native Philosophy', *European Review of Native American Studies* 9, 1 (1995): 23–5.

———. 'The Master of Life and the Person of Evolution: Indigenous Influence on Canadian Philosophy', *Ayaangwaamizin: The International Journal of Indigenous Philosophy* 2, 2 (2000): 125–42.

Racette, Sherry Farrell. 'Sewing for a Living: The Commodification of Métis Women's Artistic Production', in Katie Pickles and Myra Rutherdale, eds, *Contact Zones: Aboriginal and Settler Women in Canada's Colonial Past*. Vancouver: University of British Columbia Press, 2005, 17-42.

Ray, Arthur J. *Indians in the Fur Trade: Their role as trappers, hunters, and middlemen in the lands southwest of Hudson Bay, 1660–1870*. Toronto: University of Toronto Press, 1974.

———. 'The Hudson's Bay Company Account Books As Sources for Comparative Economic Analyses of the Fur Trade: An Examination of Exchange Rate Data', *Western Canadian Journal of Anthropology* 6, 1 (1976): 44–50.

———. 'Periodic shortages, Native welfare, and the Hudson Bay Company', in Shepard Krech III, *The Subarctic Fur Trade: Native Social and Economic Adaptations*. Vancouver: UBC Press, 1984, 1–20.

———. *The Canadian Fur Trade in the Industrial Age*. Toronto: University of Toronto Press, 1990.

———. *I have lived here Since the World Began*. Toronto: Key Porter Books, 1996.

———, and Donald Freeman. *'Give Us Good Measure,' an Economic Analysis of Relations between the Indians and the Hudson's Bay Company before 1763*. Toronto: University of Toronto Press, 1978.

Razack, Sherene, ed. *Race, Space and the Law: Unmapping a White Settler Society*. Toronto: Between the Lines, 2002.

Reid, Jennifer. *Louis Riel and the Creation of Modern Canada: Mythic Discourse and the Postcolonial State*. Albuquerque: University of New Mexico Press, 2008.

Remie, Cornelius H.W. 'Culture Change and Religious Continuity among the Arviligjuarmiut of Pelly Bay, N.W.T. 1935–1963', *Études/Inuit/Studies* 7, 2 (1983): 53–77.

———. 'Towards a New Perspective on Netjilik Inuit Female Infanticide', *Études/Inuit/Studies* 9, 1 (1985): 67–75.

———. 'Ermalik and Kukigak. Continuity and Discontinuity in Pelly Bay, Northwest Territories, Canada', in C. Buijs, ed., *Continuity and Discontinuity in Arctic Cultures. Essays in Honour of Gerti Nooter*. Leiden: The Netherlands: Centre of Non-Western Studies, 1993, 78–90.

Rich, E.E. 'Trade Habits and Economic Motivation among the Indians of North America', *Canadian Journal of Economics and Political Science* 26 (Feb. 1960): 35–53.

Richardson, Boyce. 'Wrestling with the Canadian Legal System: A Decade of Lubicon Frustration', in Richardson, ed., *Drumbeat: Anger and Renewal in Indian Country*. Toronto: Summerhill Press and the Assembly of First Nations, 1989, 229–64.

———. *Strangers Devour the Land*. Post Hills, VT: Chelsea Green Publishing Company, 1991.

Richter, Daniel K. 'War and Culture: The Iroquois Experience', *William and Mary Quarterly* 40, 4 (Oct. 1983): 528–59.

Rogers, Edward S., and Mary B. Black. 'Subsistence Strategy in the Fish and Hare Period, Northern Ontario: The Weagamow Ojibwa, 1880–1920', *Journal of Anthropological Research* 32, 1 (Spring, 1976): 1–43.

Rowley, Susan. 'Population Movements in the Canadian Arctic', *Études/Inuit/Studies* 9, 1 (1985): 3–21.

Roy, Susan. *These Mysterious Peoples: Shaping History and Archaeology in a Northwest Coast Community*. Montreal: McGill-Queen's University Press, 2010.

Rushforth, Brett. '"A Little Flesh We Offer You": The Origins of Indian Slavery in New France', *William and Mary Quarterly* 60, 4 (Oct. 2003): 777–808.

Sahlins, Marshall D. *Historical Metaphors and Mythical Realities: Structure in the Early History of the Sandwich Islands Kingdom*. Ann Arbor: University of Michigan Press, 1981.

———. *Islands of History*. Chicago: University of Chicago Press, 1985.

Said, Edward. *Orientalism*. New York: Vintage Books, 1979.

———. *Culture and Imperialism*. New York: Vintage Books, 1994.

Salisbury, Richard F. *A Homeland for the Cree: Regional Development in James Bay: 1971–1981*. Montreal: McGill-Queen's University Press, 1986.

Sandlos, J. *Hunters at the Margin: Native Peoples and Wildlife Conservation in the Northwest Territories*. Vancouver: UBC Press, 2007.

Sangster, Joan. *Regulating Girls and Women: Sexuality, Family and the Law in Ontario, 1920–1960*. Toronto: Oxford University Press, 2000.

———. *Transforming Labour: Women and Work in Postwar Canada*. Toronto: University of Toronto Press, 2010.

Sarazin, Chief Greg. 'Algonquins South of the Ottawa: 220 Years of Broken Promises', in Boyce Richardson, ed., *Drumbeat: Anger and Renewal in Indian Country*. Toronto: Summerhill Press, 1989.

Saum, Lewis O. *The Fur Trader and the Indian*. Seattle: University of Washington Press, 1965.

Sessa, R., C. Palagiano, M.G. Scifoni, M. di Pietro, and M. Del Piano, 'The Major Epidemic Infections: A Gift from the Old World to the New?' *Panminerva Medica* 41 (Mar. 1999): 78–84.

Shewell, Hugh. 'Jules Sioui and Indian Political Radicalism in Canada, 1943–1944', *Journal of Canadian Studies* 34, 3 (1999): 211–42.

———. '"Bitterness behind Every Smiling Face": Community Development and Canada's First Nations, 1954–1968', *The Canadian Historical Review* 83, 1 (Mar. 2002): 58–84.

———. *'Enough to Keep Them Alive': Indian Welfare in Canada, 1873–1965*. Toronto: University of Toronto Press, 2004.

———. 'An Examination of Aboriginal–State Relations in Canada and Their Possible Implications for Aboriginal Participation in the Canadian Armed Forces'. Paper commissioned by the Royal Military College, Kingston, ON, and presented to the Inter-University Seminar on Armed Forces and Society, Ottawa, October, 2006.

———. 'Rassembler nos forces, ou recourir encore à l'aide sociale? La situation socio-économique des premières nations avant et après la Commission royale', *Recherches amérindiennes au québec* XXXVII, 1 (2007): 44–6.

Shoemaker, Nancy. *Negotiators of Change: Historical Perspectives on Native American Women*. New York: Routledge, 1995.

Silver, A.I. 'Ontario's Alleged Fanaticism in the Riel Affair', *Canadian Historical Review* 69, 1 (1988): 21–50.

Silwa, Stephen. 'Treaty Day for the Willow Cree', *Saskatchewan History* 47, 1 (Spring 1995): 3–12.

Sinclair, Donna. 'Living Out the Apology', *The United Church Observer* 64, 4 (2000): 32–4.

Skogan, Joan. *Skeena: A River Remembered*. Vancouver: British Columbia Packers, 1983.

Sleeper-Smith, Susan. *Indian Women and French Men: Rethinking Cultural Encounter in the Western Great Lakes*. Amherst: University of Massachusetts Press, 2001.

Sluman, Norma, and Jean Goodwill. *John Tootoosis: A Biography of a Cree Leader*. Ottawa: Golden Dog Press, 1982.

Smith, Andrea. *Conquest: Sexual Violence and American Indian Genocide*. Boston: South End Press, 2005.

Smith, Linda Tuhiwai. *Decolonizing Methodologies: Research and Indigenous Peoples*. New York: St Martin's Press, 1999.

Smith, Marian L. 'The INS and the Singular Status of North American Indians', *American Indian Culture and Research Journal* 24 (1997): 131–54.

Snow, Dean R. *The Iroquois*. Cambridge, MA: Blackwell, 1994.

Spivak, Gayatri Chakravorty. 'Can the Subaltern Speak?' in C. Nelson and L. Grossberg, eds, *Marxism and the Interpretation of Culture*. Basingstoke: MacMillan Education, 1988, 271–313.

Sprague, D.N. *Canada and the Métis, 1869–1885*. Waterloo: Wilfrid Laurier University Press, 1988.

Stanley, George F. 'The Indian Background of Canadian History', *Report of the Annual Meeting held at Quebec, June 4–6, 1952*. Ottawa: Canadian Historical Association, 1952, 14–21.

———. *The Birth of Western Canada: A History of the Riel Rebellions*. Toronto: University of Toronto Press, 1960.

Steltzer, Ulli, and Catherine Kerr. *Coast of Many Faces*. Vancouver: Douglas and McIntyre, 1979.

Stevenson, J.T. 'Aboriginal Land Rights in Northern Canada', in Wesley Cragg, ed., *Contemporary Moral Issues*. Toronto: McGraw-Hill Ryerson, 1992.

Stiegman, Martha. 'Fisheries Privatization Versus Community-Based Management in Nova Scotia: Emerging Alliances between First Nations and Non-Native Fishers', in Laurie Adkin, ed., *Environmental Conflict and Democracy in Canada*. Vancouver: UBC Press, 2009, 69–83.

———, and Sherry Pictou. 'How do you say Netuklimuk in English? Using Documentary Video to capture Bear River First Nation's Learning through Action', in A. Choudry and D. Kapoor, eds, *Learning from the Ground up: Global Perspectives on Social Movements and Knowledge Production*. New York: Palgrave Macmillan, 2010.

Stoler, Ann Laura. 'Carnal Knowledge and Imperial Power: Gender, Race, and Morality in Colonial Asia', in Micaela di Leonardo, ed., *Gender at the Crossroads of Knowledge: Feminist Anthropology in the Postmodern Era*. Berkeley: University of California Press, 1991, 51–101.

———. 'Rethinking Colonial Categories: European Communities and the Boundaries of Rule', in Nicholas B. Kirks, ed., *Colonialism and Culture*. Ann Arbor: University of Michigan Press, 1992, 319–52.

Summerby, Janice. *Native Soldiers, Foreign Battlefields*. Ottawa: Veterans Affairs, 1993.

Suttles, Wayne. *Coast Salish Essays*. Vancouver: Talonbooks, 1987.

Tanner, Adrian. *Bringing Home Animals: Religious Ideology and Mode of Production of the Mistassini Cree Hunters*. St. John's: ISER, 1979.

———. 'The Origins of Social Pathologies and the Quebec Cree Healing Movement', in Laurence Kirmayer and Gail G. Valaskakis, eds, *Healing Traditions: The Mental Health of Aboriginal Peoples in Canada*. Vancouver: UBC Press, 2009, 249–71.

Tennant, Paul. *Aboriginal Peoples and Politics. The Indian Land Question in British Columbia, 1849–1989*. Vancouver: University of British Columbia Press, 1990.

Thorne, Tanis C. *The Many Hands of My Relations: French and Indian on the Lower Missouri*. Columbia: University of Missouri Press, 1996.

Tilly, Louise. 'Gender, Women's History, and Social History', *Social Science History* 13, 4 (1989): 439–62.

Timpson, Annis May, ed. *First Nations, First Thoughts*. Vancouver: UBC Press, 2010.

Titley, E. Brian. *A Narrow Vision: Duncan Campbell Scott and the Administration of Indian Affairs*. Vancouver: UBC Press, 1986.

———. *The Indian Commissioners: Agents of the State and Indian Policy in Canada's Prairie West, 1873–1932*. Edmonton: University of Alberta Press, 2009.

Tobias, John L. 'Protection, Civilization, and Assimilation: An Outline History of Canada's Indian Policy', In Ian A.L. Getty and Antoine S. Lussier, eds, *As Long As The Sun Shines And Water Flows: A Reader in Canadian Native Studies*. Vancouver: University of British Columbia Press, 1983, 39–55.

Todorov, Tzvetan. *The Conquest of America: The Question of the Other*. New York: Harper & Row, 1984.

Toms, J. Michael. 'An Ojibwa Community, American Sportsmen and the Ontario Government in the Early Management of the Nipigon River Fishery', in Diane Newell and Rosemary Ommer, eds, *Fishing Places, Fishing People: Traditions and Issues in Canadian Small-Scale Fisheries*. Toronto: University of Toronto Press, 1999, 170–92.

Tooker, Elisabeth. 'The Iroquois Defeat of the Huron: A Review of Causes', *Pennsylvania Archaeologist* 33 (July 1963): 115–23.

———. 'The League of the Iroquois: Its History, Politics, and Ritual', in Bruce G. Trigger, ed., *Handbook of North American Indians: Northeast*, 12 vols. Washington, DC: Smithsonian, 1978–2001, 418–41.

Tough, Frank. 'Ontario's Appropriation of Indian Hunting: Provincial Conservation Policies vs. Aboriginal and Treaty Rights, ca. 1892–1930'. Ontario: Ontario Native Affairs Secretariat, 1991.

———. 'Conservation and the Indian: Clifford Sifton's Commission of Conservation, 1910–1919', *Native Studies Review* 8, 1 (1992): 61–73.

———. 'As Their Natural Resources Fail': Native Peoples and the Economic History of Northern Manitoba, 1870–1930. Vancouver: UBC Press, 1996.

Trigger, Bruce G. 'The Historic Location of the Hurons', *Ontario History* 54 (June 1962): 137–48.

———. 'Indians and Ontario's History', *Ontario History* 74 (Dec. 1982): 246–57.

———. *Natives and Newcomers: Canada's 'Heroic Age' Reconsidered*. Kingston: McGill-Queen's University Press, 1985.

———. *The Children of Aataentsic: A History of the Huron People to 1660*. Montreal: McGill-Queen's University Press, 1987.

Van Den Brink, J.H. *The Haida Indians: Cultural Change Mainly between 1876–1970*. Leiden, The Netherlands: E.J. Brill, 1974.

Van de Velde, Franz, Trinette S. Constandse-Westermann, Cornelius H.W. Remie, and Raymond R. Newell. 'One hundred and fifteen years of Arviligjuarmiut Demography, Central Canadian Arctic', *Arctic Anthropology* 30, 2 (1993): 1–45.

Van Kirk, Sylvia. *Many Tender Ties: Women in Fur-trade Society, 1670–1870*. Norman: University of Oklahoma Press, 1983.

———. 'Toward a Feminist Perspective in Native History', in Jose Mailhot, ed., *Papers of the Eighteenth Algonquian Conference*. Ottawa: National Museum of Canada, 1987, 377–89.

Vescey, Christopher. 'Grassy Narrows Reserve: Mercury Pollution, Social Disruption, and Natural Resources: A Question of Autonomy', *American Indian Quarterly* 11, 4 (Autumn, 1987): 287–314.

Vibert, Elizabeth. *Traders' Tales: Narratives of Cultural Encounters in the Columbia Plateau, 1807–1846*. Norman: University of Oklahoma Press, 1997.

Victor, Wenona. *Indigenous Justice: Clearing Space and Place for Indigenous Epistemologies*. Vancouver: National Centre for First Nations Governance, 2007.

Villamarin, Juan, and Judith Villamarin. 'Native Colombia: Contact, Conquest, and Colonial Populations', *Revista de Indias* 63 (2003): 157–74.

Voyageur, Cora, and Brian Calliou. 'Various Shades of Red: Diversity Within Canada's Indigenous Community', *London Journal of Canadian Studies* 16 (2000–01): 103–19.

Waisberg, Leo G., and Tim E. Holzkamm. '"A Tendency to Discourage Them from Cultivating": Ojibwa Agriculture and Indian Affairs Administration in Northwestern Ontario', *Ethnohistory* 40, 2 (Spring, 1993): 175-211.

———, and ———. '"Their Country is Tolerably Rich in Furs": The Ojibwa Fur Trade in the Boundary Waters Region, 1821–71', in William Cowan, ed., *Actes du Vingt-Cinquième Congrès des Algonquinites*. Ottawa: Carleton University Press, 1994, 494–513.

Waite, P.B. *Canada, 1874–1896: Arduous Destiny*. Toronto: McClelland and Stewart, 1971.

Waldram, James. 'The "Other Side": Ethnostatus Distinctions in Western Subarctic Native Communities', in Laurie Barron and James B. Waldram, eds, *1885 and After: Native Society in Transition*. Regina: University of Regina, 1986.

———, D. Ann Herring, and T. Kue Young. *Aboriginal Health in Canada: Historical, Cultural and Epidemiological Perspectives*. Toronto: University of Toronto Press, 1995.

Wall, Sharon. '"To Train a Wild Bird": E.F. Wilson, Hegemony, and Native Industrial Education at the Shingwauk and Wawanosh Residential Schools, 1873–1893', *Left History* 9, 2 (Fall–Winter 2003): 7–42.

Wallace, Anthony F.C. *The Death and Rebirth of the Seneca*. New York: Knopf, 1978.

Walters, Mark. 'The Dimensions of Reconciliation: *Gladstone* and the Great Lakes'. Presented at Reconsidering *R. v. Gladstone*: Aboriginal Rights to Fish Since 1996. 12–14 Oct. 2005. Vancouver, BC.

Walworth, Clarence Alvord. *The Illinois Country, 1673–1818*. Chicago: The Illinois Centennial Commission, 1920.

Warkentin, Germaine, and Carolyn Podruchny, eds. *Decentring the Renaissance: Canada and Europe in Multidisciplinary Perspective, 1500–1700*. Toronto: University of Toronto Press, 2001.

Warriner, Keith. 'Regionalism, Dependence, and the B.C. Fisheries: Historical Development and Recent Trends', in Patricia Marchak, Neil Guppy, and John McMullan, eds, *UnCommon Property: The Fishing and Fish-Processing Industries in British Columbia*. Toronto: Methuen, 1987, 326–50.

Watts, Sheldon. *Epidemics and History: Disease, Power, and Imperialism*. New Haven: Yale University Press, 1997.

Weaver, Jace. *That the People Might Live: Native American Literature and Native Community*. New York: Oxford University Press, 1997.

Weaver, Sally M. *Making Canadian Indian Policy: The Hidden Agenda 1968–1970*. Toronto: University of Toronto Press, 1981.

———. 'A Commentary on the Penner Report', *Canadian Public Policy* 10, 2 (1984): 215–22.

Weber, David J. 'Turner, the Boltonians, and the Borderlands', *American Historical Review* 91 (Feb. 1986): 66–81.

Webster, David. 'The not so Peaceful Civilization: A Review of Maya Warfare', *Journal of World Prehistory* 14 (2000): 65–119.

Wells, Oliver. *The Chilliwacks and Their Neighbours*. Vancouver: Talonbooks, 1987.

West, J.J. 'Ojibwa Fisheries, Commercial Fisheries Development, and Fisheries Administration, 1873–1915: An Examination of the Conflicting Interest and Collapse of the Sturgeon Fisheries of the Lake of the Woods', *Native Studies Review* 6, 1 (1990): 31–66.

Wheeler, Winona. 'Cree Intellectual Traditions in History', in Alvin Finkel, Sarah Carter, and Peter Fortna, eds. *The West and Beyond: New Perspectives on an Imagined Region*. Edmonton: University of Athabasca Press, 2010, 47–61.

White, Leonard D. *The Jeffersonians: A Study in Administrative History, 1801–1829*. New York: Free Press, 1956.

White, Richard. *The Middle Ground: Indians, Empires and Republics in the Great Lakes Region, 1650–1815*. Cambridge: Cambridge University Press, 1991.

———. 'The Nationalization of Nature', *Journal of American History* 86 (Dec. 1999): 976–86.

Wiber, M., and J. Kennedy. 'Impossible Dreams: Reforming Fisheries Management in the Canadian Maritimes after the Marshall Decision', *Law & Anthropology* 11 (2001): 282–97.

Wicken, W.C. *Mi'kmaq Treaties on Trial: History, Land, and Donald Marshall Junior*. Toronto: University of Toronto Press, 2002.

Wightman, Nancy M., and Robert Wightman. 'The Mica Bay Affair: Conflict on the Upper Great Lakes Mining Frontier; 1840–1850', *Ontario History* 83, 3 (1991): 193–208.

Williams Jr, Robert A. *Linking Arms Together: American Indian Treaty Visions of Law and Peace, 1600–1800*. New York: Oxford University Press, 1997.

Wilson, David. 'Residential Schools: History on Trial', *The United Church Observer* 64, 4 (2000): 28–32.

Worsely, P.M., Helen.L. Buckley, and A.K. Davis. *Economic and Social Survey of Northern Saskatchewan*. Saskatoon: Centre for Community Studies, University of Saskatchewan, 1961.

Wray, Charles F., and Harry L. Schoff. 'A Preliminary Report on the Seneca Sequence in Western New York, 1550–1687', *Pennsylvania Archaeologist* 23 (July 1953): 53–63.

Wunder, J.R. *Native Americans: Interdisciplinary Perspectives*. New York: Garland Publishing, 2003.

Yochim, Michael J. 'Aboriginal Overkill Overstated: Errors in Charles Kay's HypoThesis', *Human Nature* 12 (2001): 141–67.

Younging, Greg. 'Talking Terminology: What's in a Word and What's Not', *Prairie Fire* 22, 3 (2001): 130–40.

Glossary

1885 Rebellion Also known as the 1885 Resistance, North-West Rebellion, or North-West Resistance, an armed resistance to Canadian expansion in the North-West territory (particularly present-day Saskatchewan) among some of the Aboriginal peoples of the region. The rebellion involved, in particular, some of the Métis centred around the village of Batoche and led by Louis Riel and Gabriel Dumont, as well as many Cree peoples led by Big Bear and Poundmaker, although some historians see the First Nations uprising as separate from that of the Métis. Beginning in March and defeated in May and June 1885, the rebellion is often considered an extension of the earlier Red River Resistance.

Aboriginal The original inhabitants of a particular territory and their descendants. In Canada, the word refers to First Nations, Inuit, and Métis peoples.

Algonquian One of the largest and most widespread Aboriginal linguistic groups, located from the East Coast all the way to the western Plains.

American Fur Company Founded by John Jacob Astor in 1808, the company monopolized the fur trade in the United States and, by 1830, was one of the largest businesses in the country.

American Revolution (1775–83) Also known as the Revolutionary War or the War of American Independence, a violent rebellion against the authority of the British Empire among the 13 colonies of the present-day eastern United States. The war became global in scale as the Dutch Republic, the Spanish Empire, and the French Empire also declared war on the British and allied with the American rebels. Following several decisive victories by the rebels and their allies, the British conceded American independence in the Treaty of Paris (1783). Notably, neither side's Aboriginal allies were included in the peacemaking process and, accordingly, their concerns went unconsidered.

Anishnabe (also Anishinaabe, Anishinabe, or Anishinaabeg; the plural is Anishinabek) Meaning the 'first' or 'original peoples', the name used by the Ojibwa, Odawa, and Algonquin peoples to refer to themselves.

Assembly of First Nations (AFN) A national organization, formerly known as the National Indian Brotherhood (NIB), representing First Nations in Canada. The AFN advocates in areas such as Aboriginal and treaty rights, economic development, education, languages and literacy, health, housing, social development, justice, taxation, land claims, and the environment.

Bagot Commission (1842–4) Established by Governor General Sir Charles Bagot after the union of the Canadas, the commission's mandate was to review the operations of the Indian Department in Canada and suggest reforms that would facilitate the assimilation of Aboriginal people while simultaneously reducing expenditures. The commission's report led to the centralization of all Indian affairs, especially record-keeping, and laid the foundation for those provisions in the Indian Act pertaining to Indian status, band membership, and enfranchisement.

Band A collection of interrelated nuclear families combined to form a larger unit. According to the Government of Canada, a band is a body of '"Indians" for whose collective use and benefit lands have been set apart, money is held by the Crown, or declared to be a band for the purposes of the Indian Act'. Each band has its own governing council.

Band council The governing body of a band, which usually consists of a chief and councillors selected through either custom or (under the Indian Act) elections. Elected officials hold office for two to three years. Under the Indian Act, the band council is responsible for providing services such as education, water, sewer and fire services, community buildings, schools, roads, and other community businesses and services, without the same funding and infrastructure as non-Native municipalities.

Battle of Seven Oaks Also known as *la Victoire de la Grenouillière*, or the Victory of Frog Plain, a battle that was part of a long-term dispute between the North West Company (NWC) and the Hudson's Bay Company (HBC). In January 1814, Miles Macdonell, governor of Selkirk Colony, issued the Pemmican Proclamation, prohibiting the export of food from the colony. The NWC refused to abide by Macdonell's proclamation and accused the HBC of unfair business practices. On 19 June 1816, a group of Métis led by Cuthbert Grant was transporting a shipment of pemmican from the upper Assinboine River to Lake Winnipeg in order to sell it to the NWC. They were met by Robert Semple (the new governor) and a group of HBC men and local settlers at Seven Oaks. When Semple tried to arrest the Métis, a fight broke out. The Métis defeated Semple, killing him and 20 of his men while sustaining only one casualty of their own. The battle is often referred to as a foundational moment in the development of Métis nationalism.

Bill C-31: An Act to Amend the Indian Act Passed by the Canadian Parliament in 1985, an Act that addressed certain discriminatory membership provisions of the Indian Act that disproportionately affected women.

Most significantly, Aboriginal women who married non-Aboriginal men would no longer lose their status; Aboriginal women who married a member of another band would no longer automatically became a member of that band and lose membership to their natal band; and bands could establish their own membership rules.

Calder case (*Calder v. British Columbia* [1973]) A Supreme Court decision that acknowledged the existence of Aboriginal title to the land prior to the arrival of Europeans. In 1967, Frank Arthur Calder and the Nisga'a Nation Tribal Council brought an action against the BC government for the state's failure to extinguish Aboriginal title to most of the province lawfully.

Charter of Rights and Freedoms Legislation that guarantees Canadian citizens certain rights and extends civil rights to everyone in Canada, regardless of their citizenship. The Charter was enshrined in the Canadian Constitution and signed into law in April 1982. Controversially, Quebec did not endorse the Charter.

Comprehensive land claims Agreements negotiated in regions of the country where Aboriginal rights and title have not been extinguished through treaties with Canada or the British Crown. These agreements are considered to be modern-day treaties between Aboriginal groups, the federal government, and the relevant province or territory.

Constitution Act (1982) Part of the process by which Canada 'patriated' its Constitution, reforming and renaming the British North America Act (1867) as the Constitution Act. The Charter of Rights and Freedoms is usually seen as the most significant reform within the Act. Section 35 of the Act states that 'existing Aboriginal and treaty rights of the Aboriginal peoples of Canada are hereby recognized and affirmed' and that '"Aboriginal Peoples of Canada" includes the Indian, Inuit and Métis peoples of Canada.'

Covenant Chain An alliance between the Iroquois Confederacy (Haudenosaunee) and the British Colonies.

Cree (*Eeyouch*) One of the largest groups of Aboriginal people in North America. The Cree live in areas from Alberta to Quebec, a geographic distribution larger than that of any other Aboriginal group in Canada.

Cree Regional Authority (CRA) The political body that represents the approximately 14,000 Cree of eastern James Bay and southern Hudson Bay in northern Quebec. The CRA was created by the Act respecting the Cree Regional Authority, which was passed by the Quebec National Assembly in 1978. The CRA and the Grand Council of the Crees are two distinct legal entities; however, they have identical membership, board of directors, and governing structures and are de facto managed and operated as one organization by the Cree Nation.

Dene (Dené) Aboriginal people who live in the northern boreal and Arctic regions of Canada.

Department of Indian Affairs (DIA) Formally created in 1880, one of the departments within the federal government that is responsible for meeting the Canadian government's obligations and commitments to First Nations, Inuit, and Métis. In 1966, the DIA became the Department of Indian Affairs and Northern Development. Since May 2011, the department has been known as Aboriginal Affairs and Northern Development Canada.

Eeyou Itschee (Cree for 'the People's Land') The territorial equivalent to a regional county municipality located in northern Quebec. It was created on 20 November 2007 and is governed by the Grand Council of the Crees.

Enfranchisement A term that usually refers to giving someone the right to vote. It can also mean, more broadly, to include someone as a full member of the community with all the rights that entails. In relation to Aboriginal people in Canada, the word often meant gaining the ability to vote and the other rights of Canadian citizenship and renouncing Indian status as defined under the Indian Act.

Factory A trading post. Factories served as markets, warehouses, defensive fortifications, centres of government (as understood by Europeans), and sometimes ports.

First Nations The original inhabitants of a particular territory and their descendants. The term came into common usage in the 1970s to replace the word *Indian*, which many people found both historically inaccurate and offensive. Some groups have adopted the term *First Nation* to replace the word *band*.

Frog Lake Massacre A Cree uprising that took place during the 1885 Resistance. It occurred at the village of Frog Lake in present-day Alberta on 2 April 1885.

Grand Council of the Crees The political body that represents the approximately 14,000 Cree of eastern James Bay and southern Hudson Bay in northern Quebec. The Grand Council has 20 members: a grand chief and deputy-grand chief elected at large by the Eeyouch; the chiefs elected by each of the nine Cree communities; and one other representative from each community. The Grand Council of the Crees and the Cree Regional Authority are two distinct legal entities; however, they have identical membership, board of directors, and governing structures and are de facto managed and operated as one organization by the Cree Nation.

Half-breed A derogatory term used to refer to an individual who is of mixed-race descent. Historically, the term was used to describe individuals who were of Aboriginal and European ancestry. *Métis* is the more common and acceptable term.

Hawthorn Report A report commissioned by the federal government to examine the socio-economic, political, and constitutional conditions of Status Indians in order to advise policy-makers on how to improve the lives of Aboriginal people in Canada. Issued in 1966, the report recommended a 'Citizens Plus' approach, which would give Aboriginal people the same rights and benefits as other Canadians while simultaneously acknowledging that they have special rights and privileges as the original inhabitants of North America and as the signatories of treaties with the British and Canadian governments. Prime Minister Pierre Elliott Trudeau rejected the report.

Hispaniola The second-largest island in the Caribbean and the present-day site of the Dominican Republic and Haiti. Christopher Columbus founded a settlement in Hispaniola in 1492. Some historians argue that the island's Indigenous peoples were entirely wiped out by the end of the sixteenth century.

Hochelaga An Iroquoian village located at the site of present-day Montreal. Jacques Cartier visited Hochelaga in October 1535.

Hudson's Bay Company (HBC) The HBC was incorporated by royal charter in 1670 as 'The Governor and Adventurers of England trading into Hudson's Bay'. The HBC played a central role in Canadian history generally and in the fur trade particularly.

Inca (or Inka) A group of Indigenous people originally located in present-day Cuzco, Peru. In 1442, the Incas expanded their geographic territory under the leadership of Pachacutec, who also founded the Inca Empire, or Tahuantinsuyo. The Inca Empire was the largest empire in the Americas prior to a significant European presence.

Indian Act Canadian federal legislation that governs the lives of Registered/Status Indians 'from cradle to grave' and regulates reserve land, money, and other resources. The Act was formally created in 1876, when all legislation pertaining to Indians was consolidated, and has since undergone over 20 major revisions. In particular, the Act defines who is an 'Indian'.

Indian agent The chief administrator of Indian affairs within a particular district, reserve, or treaty area. Indian agents wield a great deal of power over all aspects of Aboriginal people's lives. The term is no longer used.

Indian Residential Schools Settlement Agreement (IRSSA) The largest class-action settlement in Canadian history. Brought into effect on 19 September 2007, the IRSSA is the result of former residential school students, with the support of the Assembly of First Nations (AFN) and Inuit organizations, taking the federal government

and the churches to court. The agreement includes the following individual and collective measures to address the legacy of the residential school system: a 'common experience' payment to be paid to individuals who attended the schools; the establishment of a Truth and Reconciliation Commission; the creation of an Independent Assessment Process (IAP); the commemoration of the history of residential schools; and the establishment of an Aboriginal Healing Foundation.

Indigenous people The original inhabitants of a particular territory and their descendents. Scholars often use the term to refer to Aboriginal people internationally.

Innu One of the Indigenous inhabitants of present-day northeastern Quebec and Labrador. Innu refer to their territory as Nitassinan.

Inuit One of the Indigenous inhabitants of the Arctic and subarctic regions of present-day Northwest Territories, Nunatsiavut (coastal region of Labrador), Nunavik (northern Quebec), Nunavut, Nunatukavut (coastal region of Labrador), Denmark (Greenland), Russia (Siberia), and Alaska.

Inuk A member of the Inuit people.

Iroquois Confederacy An alliance formed in the sixteenth century by the Seneca, Cayuga, Oneida, Onondaga, and Mohawk, the Iroquois tribes that originally inhabited the northeastern part of present-day New York state. The confederacy was also known as the Five Nations until 1722, when the Tuscarora joined. Thereafter, it has been known as the Six Nations.

Jay Treaty Also known as the Treaty of London (1794), a treaty between the United States and the British Empire. The treaty is credited with avoiding war between the two anglophone powers during the upheavals in revolutionary France. Notably, the British agreed to relinquish several forts in what became the American Midwest, including in the Ohio Valley and present-day Michigan. Article 3 guaranteed Aboriginal peoples the right to cross the boundary between British North America and the United States.

Jesuit A member of the Society of Jesus, a Catholic order of priests and brothers founded by Ignatius Loyola in 1534. Following Loyola's initial vision, the Jesuits were organized along military lines and highly disciplined. Jesuits played a central role in missionary and educational activity in what became Canada, particularly during the period of French colonial rule.

The Jesuit Relations A publication compiling Jesuit missionaries' reports from over 200 years, beginning in 1611. Jesuit missionaries reported regularly to their superiors about the progress of their missionary work, and these documents constitute an invaluable source of information for historians about missionary activity and Aboriginal–Jesuit relations as seen from the Jesuits' perspective.

League of Indians of Canada One of Aboriginal people's first attempts to create a national political organization. The league was formed in 1919 in Ontario by Fred Loft (Six Nations), who wanted to create an organization that could collectively advocate for Aboriginal people across Canada.

Magna Carta An English charter, first issued in 1215, that bound the monarch to respect certain liberties among the aristocracy. The Magna Carta is often hailed as the first document in which an English monarch pledged to respect, to some degree, the rule of law, which provided a check on his power.

Manitoba Act (1870) Legislation that created the province of Manitoba. Given Royal Assent on 12 May 1870, the Act was adopted by Parliament in response to the Métis resistance and the provisional government led by Louis Riel. The Act was based, in part, on Riel's list of Métis rights.

Marshall decision (*R. v. Marshall* [1999]) A landmark Supreme Court decision that recognized the constitutionally protected treaty rights of the Mi'kmaq in Nova Scotia. The decision responded to Donald Marshall Jr's assertion of Aboriginal fishing rights after he had been arrested in 1993 for catching and selling eels out of season and without a licence.

Mayan The Indigenous peoples of present-day south-eastern Mexico and parts of Central America. Ancient Mayan civilization was highly advanced and is credited with passing on many architectural, technological, and cultural advances and characteristics to the other peoples of Central America.

Mesoamerica A region and culture area in the Americas inhabited by a thriving group of Indigenous people prior to the arrival of the Spanish in the sixteenth and seventeenth centuries. The area extends from central Mexico to Belize, Guatemala, El Salvador, Honduras, Nicaragua, and Costa Rica.

Métis Aboriginal people who trace their descent to mixed First Nations and European parentage. The Métis developed a national consciousness in the nineteenth century and played a key role in the fur trade.

Michif A combination of Cree and French that is the language of the Métis people of Canada and the United States.

Mi'kmaq (also Mi'kmaw or Micmac) The original peoples/First Nations of Nova Scotia.

Mohawks (Kanien'gehaga) The most easterly tribe of the Six Nations.

National Indian Brotherhood (NIB) An organization created in 1968 to represent treaty/status groups. In 1981, the NIB changed its name to the Assembly of First Nations.

New France The area colonized by France in North America. The territory of New France extended from Newfoundland to the Rocky Mountains and from Hudson Bay to the Gulf of Mexico. France ceded New France to Great Britain and Spain in the Treaty of Paris (without consulting First Nations people) in 1763.

Non-Status Indian A person who self-identifies as 'Indian' or is a member of a First Nation but is not recognized as such under the Indian Act. Non-Status Indians do not enjoy the same rights and benefits as Status Indians.

North West Company (NWC) A fur-trading business headquartered in Montreal and in operation from 1779 to 1821, when it merged with the Hudson's Bay Company. Before the merger, the rivalry between the two companies resulted in several armed clashes, including the Battle of Seven Oaks, between their respective agents.

North-West Mounted Police (NWMP) A paramilitary police force created by the Canadian government in 1873 to maintain order in the newly acquired North-West territories, including present-day Saskatchewan and Alberta. The force played a key role in forcing Aboriginal peoples onto reserves and in suppressing the Métis and Cree resistance of 1885. The force was renamed the Royal North-West Mounted Police in 1904 and merged with the Dominion Police in 1920 to create the Royal Canadian Mounted Police (RCMP).

North-West Territories Territory created when the Hudson's Bay Company transferred Rupert's Land and the North-Western Territory to the Government of Canada in June 1870. The area was comprised of all non-Confederation Canada except for British Columbia, the coast of the Great Lakes, the Saint Lawrence River Valley, and the southern portions of Quebec, the Maritimes, Newfoundland, and the Labrador coast.

Oblate A member of a male Roman Catholic order who has dedicated his life to the service of God.

Ojibwa (also Ojibwe or Ojibway) One of the largest Aboriginal groups north of Mexico. The group's territories include parts of present-day Manitoba, Ontario, Quebec, Ohio, Michigan, Illinois, Wisconsin, Minnesota, and North Dakota.

Peltry Pelts or furs usually in an unfinished state.

Pemmican A concentrated mixture of meat (such as bison, moose, elk, or deer) and fruit (such as cranberries and Saskatoon berries) made by First Nations people.

Pemmican was widely adopted by fur traders as a light and easily transportable high-energy food.

Penner Report The report of a special committee struck by the House of Commons in 1982 to examine Indian self-government. The committee was chaired by Member of Parliament Keith Penner and recommended recognizing First Nations as self-governing.

Potlatch A gift-giving ceremony practised by the Aboriginal people of the Pacific Northwest Coast. The ceremony was banned by the Canadian government in the 1890s.

Pueblo Revolt of 1680 (Popé's Rebellion) An uprising against the Spanish in New Mexico by the Pueblo.

Récollet(s) A member of the French branch of the Franciscans, a Roman Catholic order of brothers. The Franciscans developed in the fifteenth century out of a reform movement in the Catholic Church.

Red Paper (1970) The Aboriginal response to the federal government's 1969 White Paper which, without Aboriginal consultation, recommended the abolition of the Indian Act and any special status for Aboriginal peoples in Canada. A few of the main points of the Red Paper, also known as *Citizens Plus*, are that the legislative and constitutional basis of Indian status and rights remain as is until Aboriginal people are ready to change them; the only way to maintain Indian culture is to remain as Indians; and Aboriginal people should have self-government and control over their own land and resources.

Red River Resistance The resistance, popularly remembered as the Red River Rebellion, that occurred in the Red River Settlement in present-day southern Manitoba in 1869–70. Following its purchase of Rupert's Land, Canada sent an English-speaking governor to the settlement to survey the land. The French-speaking Métis of the region, led eventually by Louis Riel, refused to give the governor access to their settlement. Riel and his co-resistors then negotiated the terms of Red River's entry into the Canadian federation, laying the groundwork for the founding of the province of Manitoba. The resistance came to an end with the passage of the Manitoba Act in May 1870 and the arrival of a British military expedition to enforce Canadian authority in August of the same year.

Red River Settlement Also known as the Selkirk Settlement or the Red River Colony, a colonization project undertaken by Thomas Douglas, the Fifth Earl of Selkirk, in 1811 along the northern branch of the Red River in present-day southern Manitoba. The settlement became the centre of the Red River Resistance in 1869–70.

Reserve Defined by the Indian Act as 'a tract of land, the legal title to which is vested in Her Majesty, that has been set apart by Her Majesty for the use and benefit of a band'. There are over 600 reserves in Canada.

Residential school apology The apology made on behalf of the government of Canada by Prime Minister Stephen Harper to the former students of Indian residential schools. Harper's statement of apology was delivered in the House of Commons on 11 June 2008.

Residential school system A school system established in the nineteenth century by the federal government in partnership with churches of various Christian denominations and designed to assimilate Aboriginal people into Euro-Canadian society. The schools forcibly separated Aboriginal children from their families, communities, and cultures in order to 'kill the Indian in the child'.

Royal Commission on Aboriginal Peoples (RCAP) A Canadian royal commission established in 1991 to examine issues of Aboriginal status that had come to light as a result of recent events such as the Oka Crisis. The final report was released in 1996 and set out a 20-year agenda for implementing changes. To date, the recommendations of the RCAP have not been implemented.

Royal Proclamation of 1763 A decree issued by King George III after Britain acquired the territories of New France. The proclamation was intended to organize Britain's empire in North America and stabilize relations with First Nations through the regulation of trade, settlement, and land purchases. The Royal Proclamation continues to be of legal significance to First Nations in Canada and the United States.

Rupert's Land A vast territory in British North America that consisted of all the land connected to the Hudson Bay drainage basin. Charles I of England granted the territory to the Hudson's Bay Company in a 1670 royal charter. The HBC sold Rupert's Land to Canada in the late 1860s, although Canada did not formally acquire the land until 1870. The Aboriginal peoples who lived in the territory were not consulted and disputed Canadian sovereignty of the area.

Scurvy A disease that results from a deficiency of vitamin C, which is required for the synthesis of collagen in humans. The disease was common among sailors and other individuals who had little or no access to fruits or vegetables for long periods of time.

Self-government A system considered to provide Aboriginal people with the power to design, establish, and administer their own governments under the Canadian Constitution through a process of negotiation with Canada and, where applicable, the provincial governments.

Shaman A member of some Aboriginal groups who acts as a religious medium between the earthly and spirit worlds. Some shamans are considered to have medicinal skills and/or healing powers. Some scholars consider the term to be outdated.

Six Nations An association of six Iroquois (Haudenosaunee) tribes. The original Iroquois League, known as the Five Nations, consisted of the Mohawk, Oneida, Onondaga, Cayuga, and Seneca. The name changed in 1722, when the Tuscarora joined.

St Lawrence Iroquoians A group of Iroquoian people who lived along the shores of the St Lawrence near present-day Quebec City from the fourteenth to the late sixteenth centuries.

Stadacona A sixteenth-century St Lawrence Iroquoian village near present-day Quebec City.

Status Indian An individual who is registered as an Indian under the Indian Act.

Terra nullius A Latin expression derived from Roman law, meaning 'empty land' or 'land belonging to nobody'. Europeans used this concept to justify their claim to the Americas.

Treaty An agreement recognized under international law and entered into by sovereign parties. In regard to Aboriginal people, treaties refer to agreements between the Crown and First Nations. In Canada, treaties are constitutionally recognized.

Treaty of Paris (1783) Treaty that formally ended the American Revolution. Aboriginal allies on both sides were not consulted during the peacemaking process, and the consequences for many Aboriginal peoples were catastrophic.

Treaty rights Refers to Aboriginal rights as set out in a treaty. These rights are protected under section 35 of the Constitution Act, 1982.

Truth and Reconciliation Commission (TRC) A commission whose mandate is to learn the truth about what happened in the residential schools and to disseminate this information to all Canadians. The establishment of the TRC was one of the conditions of the Indian Residential Schools Settlement Agreement.

Voyageurs Persons engaged in the transportation of furs by canoe during the fur trade.

Wampum belt Belts made of small cylindrical beads used by certain eastern tribes to commemorate treaties, record historical events, and act as currency in both social and material transactions.

White Paper (1967) A policy paper put forth by Minister of Indian Affairs Jean Chrétien, without consultation with Aboriginal people, which proposed the abolition of the Indian Act and the rejection of all land claims. Ultimately, these measures attempted to assimilate First Nations people into Euro-Canadian society. First Nations responded to the policy paper with the Red Paper.

Notes ○○○○○○○○○○○○○○○○○○○○○○○○○○○

INTRODUCTION: ABORIGINAL HISTORY IN A COLONIAL CONTEXT

1. Mary Jane McCallum, 'Indigenous Labour and Indigenous History', *American Indian Quarterly* 33, 4 (Fall 2009): 534.

2. William Lyon Mackenzie King, 18 June 1936. As cited in John Robert Colombo, ed., *Colombo's Canadian Quotations* (Edmonton: Hurtig, 1974), 306.

3. Spivak argues that the colonized subject—the 'subaltern' in her words—cannot speak in a colonial context. Gayatri Chakravorty Spivak, 'Can the Subaltern Speak?' in C. Nelson and L. Grossberg, eds, *Marxism and the Interpretation of Culture* (Basingstoke: MacMillan Education, 1988), 271–313. While other scholars agree with Spivak that the suppression of Aboriginal voices is a key part of the colonial project, they insist on the ability of colonized peoples to make themselves heard. See, for example, Julie F. Codell, 'The Empire Writes Back: Native Informant Discourse in the Victorian Press,' in Codell, ed., *Imperial Co-Histories: National Identities and the British and Colonial Press* (Madison: Fairleigh Dickinson University Press, 2003), 188–218; Alan Lester, *Imperial Networks: Creating identities in nineteenth-century South Africa and Britain* (London: Routledge, 2001), 5–8, 189–92, Edward Said, *Orientalism* (New York: Vintage Books, 1979). In *The Location of Culture* (New York: Routledge, 1994), Homi Bhabha argues that as inhabitants of 'liminal' or 'interstitial' space, colonized peoples are uniquely placed to transcend colonial narratives.

4. John S. Milloy, 'Indian Act: A Century of Dishonour, 1869–1967'. Research Paper for the National Centre for First Nations Governance, May 2008. Available at http://www.fngovernance.org/research/milloy.pdf.

5. Winona Wheeler, 'Cree Intellectual Traditions in History', in Alvin Finkel et al., eds, *The West and Beyond: New Perspectives on an Imagined Region* (Edmonton: University of Athabasca Press, 2010), 59.

6. For examples, see Carolyn Podruchny and Laura Peers, eds, *Gathering Places: Aboriginal and Fur Trade Histories* (Vancouver: UBC Press, 2010); Annis May Timpson, *First Nations, First Thoughts* (Vancouver: UBC Press, 2010); Brenda Macdougall, *One of the Family: Métis Culture in Nineteenth-Century Northwestern Saskatchewan* (Vancouver: UBC Press, 2010); Paul Hackett, *A Very Remarkable Sickness: Epidemics in the Petit Nord, 1670 to 1846* (Winnipeg: University of Manitoba Press, 2002); Susan Roy, *These Mysterious Peoples: Shaping History and Archaeology in a Northwest Coast Community* (Montreal: McGill-Queen's University Press, 2010); Susan Neylan, *The Heavens are Changing: Nineteenth-Century Protestant Missions and Tsimshiam Christianity* (Montreal: McGill-Queen's University Press, 2002); Susan Elaine Gray, *I Will Fear No Evil: Ojibway Missionary Encounters along the Berens River, 1875–1940* (Calgary: University of Calgary Press, 2006); Jennifer Brown and Elizabeth Vibert, eds, *Reading Beyond Words: Contexts for Native History*, 2nd edn (Toronto: University of Toronto Press, 2002); Elizabeth Vibert, *Traders' Tales: Narratives of Cultural Encounters in the Columbia Plateau* (Norman: University of Oklahoma Press, 1997); and Ted Binnema and Susan Neylan, *New Histories for Old: New Perspectives on Canada's Native Past* (Vancouver: UBC Press, 2007).

7. McCallum, 'Indigenous Labour and Indigenous History', 534.

8. Susan Hill and Mary Jane McCallum, 'Guest Editors' Remarks', *American Indian Quarterly* 33, 4 (Fall 2009): xii.

9. Indian and Northern Affairs Canada, Communications Branch, 'Words First: An Evolving Terminology Relating to Aboriginal Peoples in Canada' (Oct. 2002). Available at http://www.collectionscanada.gc.ca/webarchives/20071124233110/http://www.ainc-inac.gc.ca/pr/pub/wf/wofi_e.pdf (accessed 15 Dec. 2010).

10. Métis Community Services, 'Definition of Métis'. Available at http://www.metis.ca/index.php/metis-people/The%20definition%20of%20Metis%20Peoples (accessed 16 Jan. 2011).

11. Edward Said, *Culture and Imperialism* (New York: Vintage Books, 1994), 9.

12. Caroline Elkins and Susan Pedersen, 'Settler Colonialism: A Concept and Its Uses', in *Settler Colonialism in the Twentieth Century* (New York: Routledge, 2005), 2.

13. Adam Barker, 'The Contemporary Reality of Canadian Imperialism: Settler Colonialism and the Hybrid Colonial State', *American Indian Quarterly* 33, 3 (Summer 2009): 328.

14. To put the duration of First Nations' presence in the Americas into perspective, imagine if a home video covering the last 70, 000 years ran for one year, 24 hours a day. In this video, Jacques Cartier,

who came to North America in 1534, would not appear in the video until 11 a.m. on 28 December. Or if the video was to run for just one full day Europeans would not arrive until after 11:49 p.m. In this light, recent comments made by academics such as Tom Flanagan, which characterize all Canadians (Aboriginal people included) as 'recent immigrants', are ludicrous. Such comments need to be viewed as part of a broader project to try to make Aboriginal people appear out of place in the North American landscape. Erasing the history of Aboriginal people on this continent allows non-Aboriginal people to escape the discomfort of confronting Canada's own Eurocentric creation mythology. See Tom Flanagan, *First Nations, Second Thoughts?* 2nd edn (Montreal: McGill-Queen's University Press, 2008).

15. Germaine Warkentin and Carolyn Podruchny, 'Introduction: Other Land Existing', in *Decentring the Renaissance: Canada and Europe in Multidisciplinary Perspective, 1500–1700* (Toronto: University of Toronto Press, 2001), 10.

16. John Sutton Lutz, 'Introduction: Myth Understandings; or First Contact, Over and Over Again', in Lutz, ed., *Myth and Memory: Stories of Indigenous-European Contact* (Vancouver: UBC Press, 2007), 2.

17. Ibid., 4. Mary Louise Pratt defines contact zone as 'shift[ing] the centre view. It invokes the space and time where subjects previously separated by geography and history are co-present, the point at which their trajectories now intersect. The term "contact" foregrounds the interactive, improvisational dimensions of imperial encounters so easily ignored or suppressed in accounts of conquest and domination told from the invader's perspective. A contact perspective emphasizes how subjects get constituted in and by their relations to each other. It treats the relations among colonizers and colonized, not in terms of separateness, but in terms of co-presence, interaction, interlocking understandings and practices, and often within radically asymmetrical relations of power.' See Mary Louise Pratt, *Imperial Eyes: Travel Writing and Transculturation*, 2nd edn (New York: Routledge, 2008), 8.

18. Pratt, *Imperial Eyes*, 31.

19. Richard White, *The Middle Ground: Indians, Empires, and Republics in the Great Lakes Region, 1650–1815* (Cambridge: Cambridge University Press, 1991).

20. Cora Voyageur and Brian Calliou, 'Various Shades of Red: Diversity Within Canada's Indigenous Community', *London Journal of Canadian Studies* 16 (2000/2001): 112.

21. As quoted in E. Brian Titley, *A Narrow Vision:*

22. Robert Alexander Innes, 'I'm On Home Ground Now. I'm Safe.: Saskatchewan Aboriginal Veterans in the Immediate Postwar Years, 1945–1946', *American Indian Quarterly* 28, 3–4 (Summer/Fall 2004): 685–718.

23. 'Aboriginal Group Demands IOC Suspend Pound for "Savages" Remark', *National Post*, 17 Oct. 2008, A6.

24. See, for example, Margaret Wente, 'What Dick Pound Said was Really Dumb, but also True', *The Globe and Mail*, 24 Oct. 2008, A18.

25. Jacques Derrida, 'Structure, Sign, and Play in the Discourse of the Human Sciences', in Richard Macksey and Eugenio Donato, eds, *The Structuralist Controversy: The Languages of Criticism and the Sciences of Man* (Baltimore: Johns Hopkins University Press, 1972), 251.

CHAPTER ONE: WORLD VIEWS

1. Patricia Seed, *Ceremonies of Possession in Europe's Conquest of the New World, 1492–1640* (Cambridge: Cambridge University Press, 1995).

2. Edward Benton-Benai, *The Mishomis Book: The Voice of the Ojibway* (Lac Courte Oreilles Ojibwe Reservation, WI: Indian Country Communications, 1988), 98; Frederick E. Hoxie, ed., *Encyclopedia of North American Indians* (Boston: Houghton Mifflin, 1996), 440, 454, 506.

3. J.T. Stevenson, 'Aboriginal Land Rights in Northem Canada,' in Wesley Cragg, ed., *Contemporary Moral Issues* (Toronto: McGraw-Hill Ryerson, 1992), 301.

4. Ibid., 306.

5. See Donna Sinclair, 'Living Out the Apology', *The United Church Observer* 64, 4 (2000): 32–4; and David Wilson, 'Residential Schools: History on Trial', *The United Church Observer* 64, 4 (2000): 28–32.

6. See J. Douglas Rabb, 'Prologues to Native Philosophy', *European Review of Native American Studies* 9, 1 (1995): 23–5.

7. Michael M. Pomedli, *Ethnophilosophical and Ethnolinguistic Perspectives on the Huron Indian Soul* (Lewiston: Edwin Mellen Press, 1991).

8. Lee Hester, Dennis McPherson, Annie Booth, and Jim Cheney, 'Indigenous Worlds and Callicott's Land Ethic', *Environmental Ethics* 22, 3 (2000): 278.

9. Richard Maundrell, 'From Rupert Lodge to Sweat Lodge', *Dialogue* 34 (1995): 753.

10. Ibid. For Maundrell's source, see Francis Parkman, *The Oregon Trail* (Boston: Francis, Little and Brown, 1885), 270.

11. Calvin Luther Martin, *In the Spirit of the Earth:*

Rethinking History and Time (Baltimore: The Johns Hopkins University Press, 1992), 16.

12. Hester et al., 'Indigenous Worlds', 278.

13. J. Baird Callicott, 'Many Indigenous Worlds or the Indigenous World? A Reply to My "Indigenous" Critics', *Environmental Ethics* 22, 3 (2000): 302.

14. Ibid., 294.

15. Ibid., 298.

16. Ibid., 293.

17. J. Baird Callicott, *In Defense of the Land Ethic: Essays in Environmental Philosophy* (Albany: State University of New York Press, 1989), 212.

18. Dennis McPherson, 'A Definition of Culture: Canada and First Nations', in Jace Weaver, ed., *Native American Religious Identity: Unforgotten Gods* (Maryknoll, NY: Orbis Books, 1998), 81.

19. Samuel Eliot Morison, *Admiral of the Sea: A Life of Christopher Columbus* (Boston: Little Brown and Company, 1942), 231.

20. S.R. Mealing, ed., *The Jesuit Relations and Allied Documents: A Selection* (Ottawa: Carleton University Press, 1990), 45.

21. Donald Purich, *Our Land* (Toronto: James Lorimer and Co., 1986), 31.

22. Frank Waters, *Book of the Hopi* (New York: Ballintine Books, 1963), 312.

23. Ibid., 314.

24. Lorraine Brundige, 'Continuity of Native Values: Cree and Ojibwa' (MA thesis, Lakehead University, 1997), 42. See also Brundige, '"Ungrateful Indian": Continuity of Native Values', *Ayaangwaamizin: The International Journal of Indigenous Philosophy* 1, 1 (1997): 31–44.

25. Reuben Gold Thwaites, ed., *The Jesuit Relations and Allied Documents: Travels and Explorations of the Jesuit Missionaries in New France, 1610–1791*, vol. 3 (New York: Pageant Books, 1959), 271.

26. Brundige, 'Continuity of Native Values', 48.

27. D.H. McPherson and J.D. Rabb, *Indian from the Inside: A Study in Ethno-Metaphysics* (Thunder Bay: Lakehead University Centre for Northern Studies, 1993), 98, 106.

28. British Columbia Ministry of Advanced Education, *Native Literacy and Life Skills Curriculum Guidelines* (Victoria: Ministry of Advanced Education and Job Training and Ministry Responsible for Science and Technology, 1989), 14–15.

29. Arthur C. Parker, 'The Constitution of the Five Nations', in William N. Fenton, ed., *Parker on the Iroquois* (Syracuse: Syracuse University Press, 1968), 101.

30. Ibid., 55–6.

31. Ibid., 10.

32. Robert A. Williams Jr., *Linking Arms Together: American Indian Treaty Visions of Law and Peace,* *1600–1800* (New York: Oxford University Press, 1997), 60.

33. McPherson and Rabb, *Indian from the Inside*, 10–11; J. Douglas Rabb, 'The Polycentric Perspective: A Canadian Alternative to Rorty', *Dialogue* 28 (1989): 107–115; J. Douglas Rabb, 'From Triangles to Tripods: Polycentrism in Environmental Ethic', *Environmental Ethics* 14 (1992): 177–183.

34. Michael Anthony Hart, 'Sharing Circles: Utilizing Traditional Practice Methods for Teaching, Helping, and Supporting', in Sylvia O'Meara et al., eds, *From Our Eyes: Learning from Indigenous Peoples* (Toronto: Garamond, 1996), 65.

35. Jace Weaver, *That the People Might Live: Native American Literature and Native Community* (New York: Oxford University Press, 1997), 33.

36. Marie Battiste and James (Sa'ke'j) Youngblood Henderson, *Protecting Indigenous Knowledge and Heritage: A Global Challenge* (Saskatoon: Purich Publishing, 2000), 105.

37. Michael Ignatieff, *The Rights Revolution* (Toronto: Anansi Press, 2000), 104.

38. See J. Douglas Rabb, 'The Master of Life and the Person of Evolution: Indigenous Influence on Canadian Philosophy', *Ayaangwaamizin: The International Journal of Indigenous Philosophy* 2, 2 (2000): 125–42.

39. Maundrell, 'From Rupert Lodge', 149.

40. Battiste and Henderson, *Protecting Indigenous Knowledge and Heritage*, 105–06.

41. Trevor Herriot, *River in a Dry Land: A Prairie Passage* (Toronto: Stoddart, 2000), 89.

42. Ibid., 81.

43. Ibid., 88.

44. Ibid., 90.

45. Ibid, 97.

46. Ibid., 73.

47. Ibid., 77.

48. Ibid., 72–3.

49. Regna Darnell, 'Rethinking the Concepts of Band and Tribe, Community and Nation: An Accordion Model of Nomadic Native American Social Organization', in David H. Pentland, ed., *Papers of the Twenty-ninth Algonquian Conference* (Winnipeg: University of Manitoba Press, 1999), 99.

50. Ibid.

51. Ibid.

52. Howard Adams, *Tortured People: The Politics of Colonization* (Penticton: Theytus Books, 1999), 54.

53. Alexander Morris, *The Treaties of Canada with the Indians of Manitoba and the North-West Territories: Including the negotiations on which they were based, and other information relating thereto* (Toronto: Prospero Books, 2000), 286.

54. Ibid., 207.

55. Ibid., 206.
56. Ibid., 288.
57. Ibid.
58. Ibid.
59. Ibid., 287.
60. See Paulo Freire, *Pedagogy of the Oppressed*, trans. Maria Bergman Ramos (New York: Continuum, 1997), 45, 76; and Leslie Nawagesic, 'Yuma State: A Philosophical Study of the Indian Residential School Experience' (MA thesis, Lakehead University, 2001).
61. Adams, *Tortured People*, ii.
62. Ibid., 54.
63. Dennis H. McPherson and J. Douglas Rabb, 'Walking the Talk: An Application of Anishnabe Philosophy or a Tearful Trail toward Culturally Congruent Education', *Ayaangwaamizin: The International Journal of Indigenous Philosophy* 2, 1 (1999): 89–99.
64. McPherson and Rabb, *Indian from the Inside*, 22.
65. Battiste and Henderson, *Protecting Indigenous Knowledge and Heritage*, 88–9.
66. Ibid., 89.
67. McPherson and Rabb, 'Walking the Talk', 92.
68. See Linda Tuhiwai Smith, *Decolonizing Methodologies: Research and Indigenous Peoples* (New York: St. Martin's Press, 1999).
69. Battiste and Henderson, *Protecting Indigenous Knowledge and Heritage*, 213.
70. Ibid., 142.
71. Adams, *Tortured People*, 26.
72. For an expanded discussion of Blackfoot beliefs, practices, and pedagogy, see Betty Bastien, *Blackfoot Ways of Knowing* (Calgary: University of Calgary Press, 2004). Much of this essay is based on the research for my book. Hereafter, information taken from this book is not referenced, with the exception of quotations.
73. Ibid., 84–5.
74. Marimba Ani, *Yurugu: An African-Centered Critique of European Cultural Thought and Behaviour* (Trenton: Africa World Press, 1994), 10.
75. Bastien, *Blackfoot Ways of Knowing*, 159–60.
76. Ani, *Yuruguru*, 45–7.
77. Ibid., 98.
78. Ibid.
79. Ibid., 37.
80. Bill Ashcroft, Gareth Griffiths, and Helen Tiffins, *The Empire Writes Back: Theory and Practice in Post-Colonial Literatures* (London and New York: Routledge, 1989), 7.
81. Ibid., 167.
82. Ani, *Yuruguru*, 37–9.
83. Bastien, *Blackfoot Ways of Knowing*, 100.
84. Ibid., 100–01.
85. Ibid., 102–03.
86. Ani, *Yuruguru*, 32.
87. Duane Mistaken Chief, Personal Communication to Betty Bastien, Dec. 1998. See also, Bastien, *Blackfoot Ways of Knowing*, 105.
88. Howard L. Harrod, *Renewing the World* (Tucson: University of Arizona Press, 1992), 67.
89. Ibid., 70.
90. Walter McClintock, *The Old North Trail: Life, Legend and Religion of the Blackfeet Indians* (University of Nebraska Press, 1992), 253–4.
91. Bastien, *Blackfoot Ways of Knowing*, 109.
92. Harrod, *Renewing the World*, 23.
93. Ibid., 25.
94. David Peat, *Lighting the Seventh Fire* (Secaucus, NJ: Carol Publishing Company, 1994), 65.
95. Ronald Goodman, *Lakota Star Knowledge, Studies in Lakota Theology* (Rosebud, SD: Sinte Gleska University, 1992).
96. Bastien, *Blackfoot Ways of Knowing*, 143.
97. Gary Zukav, *The Dancing Wu Li Masters: An Overview of the New Physics* (New York: Bantam Books, 1979), 54–79.
98. McClintock, *The Old North Trail*, 253–4.
99. Bastien, *Blackfoot Ways of Knowing*, 141.
100. Ibid., 140–1.
101. Zukav, *Dancing Wu Li Masters*, 257.

CHAPTER TWO: PERSPECTIVES ON CONTACT

1. Jean Barman, *The West Beyond the West: A History of British Columbia*, 3rd edn (Toronto: University of Toronto Press, 2007), 22, 34–6.
2. John Lutz, 'Introduction', in Lutz ed., *Myth and Memory: Stories of Indigenous-European Contact* (Vancouver: UBC Press, 2007), 2.
3. Bruce Trigger, *Natives and Newcomers: Canada's 'Heroic Age' Reconsidered* (Montreal and Kingston: McGill-Queen's University Press, 1986), 121.
4. Ibid., 89.
5. Carl Becker, 'Every Man His Own Historian', *American Historical Review* 37 (1932): 228, 231.
6. Julius E. Olson and Edward Galord Bourne, eds, *The Northmen, Columbus and Cabot, 985–1503* (New York: C. Scribner's Sons, 1906), 423–4; Samuel Eliot Morison, *The European Discovery of America: The Northern Voyages, A.D. 500–1600* (New York: Oxford University Press, 1871), 206–09; Peter E. Pope, *The Many Landfalls of John Cabot* (Toronto: University of Toronto Press, 1997), 11–42; [Richard Hakluyt the Younger], *Divers Voyages Touching the Discoverie of America, and the Ilands Adjacent until the Same, Made first of All our Englishmen, and Afterward by the Frenchmen and Britons* (London: Thomas Woodcooke, 1582), fols. A1–B4 (2nd pagination); Reuben Gold Thwaites, ed., *The Jesuit Relations*

and Allied Documents: Travels and Explorations of the Jesuit Missionaries in New France, 1610–1791, 73 vols. (Cleveland: Burrows Brothers, 1896–1901), 5, 119–21.

7. Olson and Bourne, *Northmen, Columbus and Cabot*, 423.

8. Hakluyt, *Divers Voyages*, fol. A3v.

9. E.B. O'Callaghan and B. Fernow, eds, *Documents Relative to the Colonial History of New York*, 15 vols. (Albany: Weed, Parsons, 1853–87), 47–51.

10. See, for example, Ruth M. Underhill, *Red Man's Religion: Beliefs and Practices of the Indians North of Mexico* (Chicago: University of Chicago Press, 1965), 20–9.

11. Charles T. Gehring and Willliam A. Starna, trans and eds, *A Journey into Mohawk and Oneida Country, 1634–1635* (Syracuse: Syracuse University Press, 1988), 62; Johannes Megapolensis Jr, 'A Short Account of the Mohawk Indians' (1644), in Dean R. Snow, Charles T. Gehring, and William A. Starna, eds, *In Mohawk Country: Early Narratives about a Native People* (Syracuse: Syracuse University Press, 1996), 45.

12. Hakluyt, *Divers Voyages*, fol. A5v.

13. The following is based on documents published in Lawrence A. Clayton, Vernon James Knight Jr, and Edward C. Moore. eds, *The De Soto Chronicles: The Expeditions of Hernando De Soto to North America in 1539–1543*, 2 vols. (Tuscaloosa: University of Alabama Press, 1993), particularly the accounts attributed to 'A Gentleman of Elvas' (I: 19–219) and Rogrigo Rangel as compiled by Gonzalo Fernandez de Oviedo y Vakdes (I: 247–305).

14. Ibid., I: 257.

15. Ibid., I: 62.

16. Ibid.

17. Ibid., I: 288–9.

18. Ibid., I: 83.

19. Carol Ortwin Sauer, *Sixteenth-Century North America: The Land and the People as seen by the Europeans* (Berkeley, University of California Press, 1971), 158.

20. Clayton, Knight, and Moore, *De Soto Chronicles*, I: 279.

21. Bruce G. Trigger, *Natives and Newcomers: Canada's 'Heroic Age' Reconsidered* (Montreal and Kingston: McGill-Queen's University Press, 1985), 129–35.

22. The published first-hand accounts of Cartier's three voyages to North America, on which the following section is based, are reprinted in Henry S. Burrage, *Early English Voyages Chiefly from Hakluyt, 1534–1604* (New York: C. Scribner's Sons, 1906), 1–102.

23. Ibid., 19.

24. Ibid., 21.

25. Ibid., 25.

26. Ibid.

27. Percy J. Robinson, 'The Origin of the Name Hochelega', *Canadian Historical Review* 23 (1942): 295–6; and Robinson, 'Some of Cartier's Place-Names', *Canadian Historical Review* 26 (1945): 401–05.

28. Ibid., 71.

29. Trigger, *Natives and Newcomers*, 131–2.

30. Burrage, *Early English and French Voyages*, 96.

31. Ibid.

32. Ibid., 102.

33. W.J. Eccles, *The Canadian Frontier, 1534–1760*, rev. edn (Albuquerque: University of New Mexico Press, 1983), 12–18.

34. This article draws chiefly on the author's interviews conducted in Igloolik in 1998 with Rosie Iqallijuq and interpreted by Leah Otak. These are augmented by interviews recorded both with Rosie Iqallijuq and other Elders for the Inullariit Elders' Society and held at the Igloolik Research Centre. All quotations from the Inullariit Elders' Society archives are identified in the notes by the archive file numbers in parentheses.

35. W.E. Parry, *Journal of a Second Voyage for the Discovery of a North-West Passage . . . in the Years 1821–22–23* (London: John Murray, 1824), 269.

36. Ibid., 15 and 17 Apr., 425.

37. Mark Ijjangiaq, Inullariit Elders' Society archives (253).

38. In this article, the author has quoted on a number of occasions from interviews with Rosie Iqallijuq in the Inullariit Elders' Society archives held in the Igloolik Research Centre, notably file numbers 26, 204, and 395.

39. W.E. Parry, *Journal of a Voyage for the Discovery of a North-West Passage . . . in the Years 1819–20* (London: John Murray, 1821), 296.

40. Rosie Iqallijuq, Inullariit Elders' Society archives (445).

41. Parry, *Journal of a Second Voyage*, 230.

42. From personal interviews with the author: Pitseolak Ashoona, Cape Dorset, 1970; Louis Kamookak, Gjoa Haven, 1999.

43. Parry, *Journal of a Second Voyage*, 270.

44. Dorothy Harley Eber, 'Eva Talooki: Her Tribute to Seed Beads, Long Time Jewels of the Arctic', *Inuit Art Quarterly* (Spring 2004): 12–17; Parry, *Journal of a Second Voyage*, 270–2.

45. From 'Tattooing, a Discussion of the Practice across Arctic Regions', in Jens Pederhart Hansen, Jorgen Meldgaard, and Jorgen Nordqvist, eds, *The Greenland Mummies* (Montreal and Kingston: McGill-Queen's University Press, 1991), 102–15.

46. John MacDonald, 'Parry's Flagstaff near Igloolik,

Northwest Territories', *Arctic* 48 (Sept. 1992): 308–12.

47. Parry, *Journal of a Second Voyage*, 410–12.

48. J.E. Nourse, ed., *Narrative of the Second Arctic Expedition Made by Charles F. Hall: His Voyage to Repulse Bay, Sledge Journeys to the Straits of Fury and Hecla and to King William's Land, and Residence Among the Eskimos during the Years 1864–69* (Washington: US Naval Observatory, 1879), 112–14.

49. Hervé Paniaq, Inullariit Elders' Society archives (141).

50. Pauli Kunnuk, Inullariit Elders' Society archives (87).

51. Mark Ijjangiaq, Inullariit Elders' Society archives (86).

52. Noah Piugaattuk, Inullariit Elders' Society archives (303).

53. Alfred Tremblay, *Cruise of the Minnie Maud: Arctic Seas and Hudson Bay, 1910–11 and 1912–13*, trans. and ed. A.B. Reader (Quebec: Arctic Exchange, 1921), 153.

54. Noah Piugaattuk, Inullariit Elders' Society archives (303).

55. Captain Robert Abram Bartlett, with his famous vessel *Effie M. Morrissey*, visited western Baffin in 1927, but he sailed through Hudson Strait and across Foxe Basin to the Strait of Fury and Hecla only in 1933.

56. Rosie Iqallijuq, Inullariit Elders' Society archives (395).

CHAPTER THREE: POPULATION DEBATES

1. Alfred W. Crosby Jr., *The Columbian Exchange: Biological and Ecological Consequences of 1492* (Westport: Greenwood Press, 1973); Henry Dobyns, *Their Number Become Thinned: Native American Population Dynamics in Eastern North America* (Knoxville: University of Tennessee Press, 1983). See also Russell Thornton, *American Indian Holocaust and Survival: A Population History since 1492* (Norman: University of Oklahoma Press, 1990).

2. Jody Decker, 'Country Distempers: Deciphering Disease and Illness in Rupert's Land before 1870', in Jennifer Brown and Elizabeth Vibert, eds, *Reading Beyond Words: Documenting Native History* (Calgary: Broadview Press, 1996), 156–81.

3. Bruce Stutz, 'Megadeath in Mexico', *Discover* 27, 2 (Feb. 2006): 44.

4. For Sauer in particular, see William N. Denevan, 'Carl Sauer and Native American Population Size', *Geographical Review* 86 (1996): 385–97.

5. The history and methodologies of the High Counter movement are discussed at length in David Henige, *Numbers from Nowhere: The American Indian Contact Population Debate* (Norman, OK: University of Oklahoma Press, 1998).

6. For a parroted distillation of a worst-case-scenario disease model, see Kenneth W. Howell, 'In the Wake of Conquest: A Global Perspective on the Depopulation of Indigenous Peoples of Latin America', *Diálogos Latinamericanos* 5 (2002): 58–72.

7. Massimo Livi-Bacci, 'The Depopulation of Hispanic America after the Conquest', *Population and Development Review* 32 (2006): 200.

8. Ibid., 215.

9. In contrast, Elsa Malvido, 'Laepidemiología une propuesta para explicar la despoblación american', *Revista de Indias* 63 (2003): 65–78, finds that disease could have accounted for a 90 plus per cent population decrease, no matter what the maximum figure was.

10. William N. Denevan, 'The Native Population of Amazonia in 1492 Reconsidered', *Revista de Indias* 63 (2003): 175–88, with emphasis in original.

11. Linda A. Newson, 'Patterns of Indian Depopulation in Early Colonial Ecuador', *Revista de Indias* 63 (2003): 135–56.

12. N.D. Cook, 'Une primera epidemia Americana de viruela en 1493?' *Revista de Indias* 63 (2003): 49–64.

13. Massimo Livi-Bacci, 'Las múltiples causas de la catástrofe: consideraciones teoréticas y empíricas', *Revista de Indias* 63 (2003): 38–41, 44–6.

14. Juan Villamarín and Judith Villamarín, 'Native Colombia: Contact, Conquest, and Colonial Populations', *Revista de Indias* 63 (2003): 157–74.

15. W. George Lovell and Christopher L. Lutz, 'Perfil etmodemográfico de la Audiencia of Guatemala', *Revista de Indias* 63 (2003): 105–34.

16. N.D. Cook, *Born to Die: Disease and New World Conquest, 1492–1650* (Cambridge: Cambridge University Press, 1998), 72–83. His only number crunching (21–4) deals with Hispaniola.

17. Suzanne Austin Alchon, *A Pest in the Land: New World Epidemics in a Global Perspective* (Albuquerque: University of New Mexico Press, 2003), 147–72.

18. Ibid., 153.

19. A bizarre, yet minatory, thread about North American contact population has developed among environmental historians, probably deriving from a misreading of the High Counters, to the effect that the population of North America *alone* was in the neighborhood of 100 million at contact. See Michael J. Yochim, 'Aboriginal Overkill Overstated: Errors in Charles Kay's Hypothesis', *Human Nature* 12 (2001): 141–67.

20. Rodolfo Acuña-Soto, D.W. Stahle, M.D. Therrell,

R.D. Griffin, and M.K. Cleaveland, 'When Half of the Population Died: The Epidemic of Hemorrhagic Fevers in 1576 in Mexico', *FEMS Microbiology Letters* 240 (1 Nov. 2004): 1–5, citing a population from 1948. See note 3 above.

21. R. Sessa, C. Palagiano, M.G. Scifoni, M. de Pietro, and M. Del Piano, 'The Major Epidemic Infections: A Gift from the Old World to the New?' *Panminerva Medica* 41 (Mar. 1999): 78–84.

22. Rodolfo Acuña-Soto et al., 'Large Epidemics of Hemorrhagic Fevers in Mexico, 1545–1815', *American Journal of Tropical Medicine and Hygiene* 62 (2000): 733.

23. Acuña-Soto et al., 'When Half the Population Died', 1–2.

24. Rodolfo Acuña-Soto, D.W. Stahle, M.D. Therrell, S. Gomez Chavez, and M.K. Cleaveland, 'Drought, Epidemic Disease and the Fall of Classic Period Cultures in Mesoamerica (AD 750–950): Hermorrhagic Fevers as a Cause of Massive Population Loss', *Medical Hypotheses* 65 (2005): 406.

25. William H. McNeill, *Plagues and Peoples* (Garden City, NY: Anchor Press, 1976).

26. Sheldon Watts, *Epidemics and History: Disease, Power, and Imperialism* (New Haven: Yale Univesity Press, 1997), 84, with emphasis in original.

27. Alfred J. Bollet, *Plagues and Poxes: The Impact of Human History on Epidemic Disease* (New York: Demos Medical Publishing, 2004), 78.

28. John Aberth, *The First Horseman: Disease in Human History* (Upper Saddle River, NJ: Pearson Prentice Hall, 2007), 50–7.

29. Ano Karlen, *Plague's Progress* (London: Gollancz, 1995), 105.

30. J.N. Hays, *Epidemics and Pandemics* (Santa Barbara: ABC Clio, 2005), 79–95 passim.

31. Michael C. Mann, *1491: New Revelations of the Americas before Columbus* (New York: Alfred A. Knopf, 2005), 92–5, 374–5.

32. Jared Diamond, *Guns Germs and Steel: The Fates of Human Societies* (New York: W.W. Norton, 1997), 213.

33. Ibid., 210.

34. Ibid.

35. Michael C. Meyer, William L. Sherman, and Susan M. Deeds, *The Course of Mexican History*, 6th edn (New York: Oxford University Press, 1999), 85, 202.

36. Burton Kirkwood, *The History of Mexico* (West Port, CT: Greenwood Press, 2000), 29.

37. Alicia Hernández Chávez, *Mexico: A Brief History* (Berkeley: University of California Press, 2006), 38; Brian R. Hamnett, *A Concise History of Mexico*, 2nd edn (Cambridge: Cambridge University Press, 2006), 62.

38. David Christian, *Maps of Time: An Introduction to Big History* (Berkeley: University of California Press, 2004), 203–3, 382.

39. Ibid., 550, n47.

40. John F. Richards, *Unending Frontier: An Environmental History of the Early Modern World* (Berkeley: University of California Press, 2003), 312.

41. Massimo Livi-Bacci, *A Concise History of the World Population*, 4th edn (Oxford: Blackwell, 2007), 43–9, 230.

42. Fernand Braudel, *Les structures du quotidien: le possible et l'impossible* (Paris: Armand Colin, 1979), 19–21.

43. Angus Maddison, *The World Economy* (London: OECD, 2006), 234–5.

44. Ibid., 235–6, 491–5.

45. Ibid., 232, 449–51.

46. Bartolomé de las Casas, *Historia de la Indias*, ed. Agustia Millares Carlo and Lewis Hanke, 3 vols (Mexico City: Fondo de Cultura Economica, 1951), 1: 419–20.

47. Columbus to the King and Queen of Spain in Christopher Columbus, *Textos y documentos completos*, ed. Consuela Verla and Juan Gil (Madrid: Alianza, 1992), 284.

48. On American Indians' relationship with their environment, see Shepard Krech III, *The Ecological Indian: Myth and History* (New York: W.W. Norton, 1999).

49. For a recapitulation of this see David Webster, 'The not so Peaceful Civilization: A Review of Maya Warfare', *Journal of World Prehistory*, 14 (2000): 65–119.

50. For example, George R. Milner, 'Warfare in Prehistoric and Early Historic Eastern North America', *Journal of Archaeological Research*, 7 (1999): 105–52; Jay W. Palmer, 'A Basketmaker II Massacre Revisited', *North American Archaeologist*, 22 (2001): 117–41.

51. Richard H. Steckel, 'Health and Nutrition in Pre-Columbian America: The Skeletal Evidence', *Journal of Interdisciplinary History*, 36 (2005): 28–9; cf. Brenda J. Baker and Lisa Kealhofer, eds, *Bioarchaeology of Native American Adaptation in the Spanish Borderlands* (Gainesville, FL: University Press of Florida, 1997); Stephen L. Whittington and David M. Reed, eds, *Bones of the Maya: Studies of Ancient Skeletons* (Washington, DC: Smithsonian Institution, 1997).

52. Climate also contributed to the causes of limiting continuous population growth; see, for example, Peter B. deMenocal, 'Cultural Responses to Climate Change during the Late Colocene', *Science* 292 (2001): 667–73; Brian Fagan, *The Little Ice Age:*

How Climate Made History (New York: Basic Books, 2000).

53. Colin M. Betts, 'Pots and Pox: The Identification of Protohistoric Epidemics in the Upper Mississippi Valley', *American Antiquity* 71 (2006): 233–59.

54. Henry F. Dobyns, *Their Number Became Thinned* (Knoxville: University of Tennessee Press, 1983), 118–19, 291–4.

55. Dale L. Hutchinson, *Tatham Mound and the Bioarchaeology of European Contact: Disease and Depopulation in Central Gulf Coast Florida* (Gainesville, FL: University Press of Florida, 2006), 172–3.

56. Susan A. Alchon, *Native Society and Disease in Colonial Ecuador* (Cambridge: Cambridge University Press, 1991), 12, with emphasis added.

57. William N. Denevan, quoted in W. George Lovell, Henry Dobyns, William Denevan, William Woods, and Charles Mann, '1491: In Search of Native America', *Journal of the Southwest* 46 (2004): 447.

58. The justly famous Little Water Medicine of the Iroquois is described here for the first time, although there are hints to its existence and use in earlier *Relations*. See William N. Fenton, 'Contacts between Iroquois Herbalism and Colonial Medicine', *Annual Report of the Smithsonian Institution for 1941* (Washington: US Government Printing Office, 1942), 503–26.

59. Iroquois shamans today spray the wound with Little Water Medicine in the same manner. William N. Fenton personal observation.

60. *Cigue*, water hemlock (*Cicuta maculata* L.), a powerful alkaloid, was used by the Iroquois for poultices applied to sprains and taken internally in suicide. Its identification from Jesuit sources is recent. See William N. Fenton, 'Iroquois Suicide: A Study in the Stability of a Culture Pattern', Smithsonian Institution, *Bureau of American Ethnology Bulletin* 128 (1941): 79–137.

61. The idea that venereal diseases were brought from America to Europe is often mentioned by writers. The statement may be partially true. There is a slight case for the New World origin of syphilis, which became epidemic in Europe after the return of Columbus, but it has a world wide distribution, as do the other venereal diseases and their agents, which have long old-world histories. See *Encyclopaedia Britannica*, 4th edn, XXIII, 41 ff. W.N.F.

62. John L. Tobias, 'Canada's Subjugation of the Plains Cree, 1879–1885', in James R. Miller, ed., *Sweet Promises: A Reader on Indian-White Relations in Canada* (Toronto: University of Toronto Press, 1991), 215–40.

63. R.G. Ferguson, 'A Study of the Epidemiology of Tuberculosis in a Primitive People', *Edinburgh Medical Journal* 36 (1929): 199.

64. George W. Comstock and Richard J. O'Brien, 'Tuberculosis', in Alfred S. Evans and Philip S. Brachman, eds, *Bacterial Infections in Humans: Epidemiology and Control*, 3rd edn (New York: Plenum, 1998), 781, 790.

65. Ibid., 781.

66. William F. Butler, *The Great Lone Land: A Narrative of Travel and Adventure in the Northwest of America* (Edmonton: Hurtig, 1968), 242.

67. Scrofula was a common name used to identify the non-pulmonary form of tuberculosis that attacked the lymphatic system of the victim. It was especially common among the First Nations people of the west.

68. George M. Grant, *Ocean to Ocean: Sandford Fleming's Expedition through Canada in 1872* (Toronto: Coles, 1973), 96.

69. Ibid., 190.

70. National Archives of Canada (hereafter NAC), RG 18, Vol. 7, File 395-75, Report to the Dept of Justice, 25 Aug. 1875.

71. NAC, RG 18, Vol. 2545, File 11, Report of G.A. French, 27 Apr. 1876.

72. Ronald Atkin, *Maintain the Right: The Early History of the North West Mounted Police, 1873–1900* (Toronto: Macmillan, 1973), 90.

73. The group has been identified elsewhere as Yanktonai Sioux. David McCrady, 'Living with Strangers: The Nineteenth-Century Sioux and the Canadian-American Borderlands', PhD dissertation, University of Manitoba, 1998, 113–15.

74. The term refers to the practice in the military of having the men assemble to report to the medical officer, or of inspecting the men who are ill.

75. John Kittson, 'Report, Swan River, Dec. 19, 1875', in S.W. Horral, ed., *A Chronicle of the West: The North-West Mounted Police Reports for 1875* (Calgary: Historical Society of Alberta, 1975), 20–3.

76. NAC, Robert Bell Papers, MG 29 A 6, Hudson's Bay Company Northern Department Journal of a Voyage . . . from 22nd August 1872 to 28th January 1873 by Hon. Joseph Christie, Inspecting Chief Factor of the Hudson's Bay Company, 26 Jan. 1873.

77. NAC, RG 10 Vol. 3609, p. 3, 229, quoted in Aidan D. McQuillan, 'The Creation of Indian Reserves in the Canadian Prairies, 1870–1885', *The Geographical Review* 70 (1980): 383; NAC, MG 27, David Laird Papers, Indian Affairs N.W.T. Letterbook 1874, C.N. Bell to Laird, 23 Mar. 1874, 18.

78. Nan Shipley, 'The Printing Press Oonikup', *The Beaver* 290 (1960): 48–9.

79. NAC, CMS, Reel A-81, Joseph Reader, Report of Touchwood Hills Mission, 20 Jan.1875, 442.

80. Chief Sweet Grass to Alexander Morris, Edmonton, 13 Apr. 1871, in Alexander Morris, *The Treaties of Canada with the Indians of Manitoba and the North-West Territories* (Saskatoon: Fifth House, 1991), 170–1.

81. Douglas Owram, *Promise of Eden: The Canadian Expansionist Movement and the Idea of the West, 1856–1900* (Toronto: University of Toronto Press, 1980).

82. NAC, RG 10, Vol. 3648, File 8138, Reel C-10113, Personnel File of Dr Daniel Hagarty.

83. NAC, RG 10, Vol. 3643, File 7708, Reel C-10113, Report of Surgeon R.B. Nevitt, N.W.M.P., 2 Jan. 1877.

84. A common name of the time for pulmonary tuberculosis.

85. Grant MacEwan, *Sitting Bull: The Years in Canada* (Edmonton: Hurtig, 1973), 90–1.

86. David D. Smits, 'The Frontier Army and the Destruction of the Buffalo: 1865–1883', *The Western Historical Quarterly* 25 (1994): 334–8.

87. Tobias, 'Canada's Subjugation of the Plains Cree, 1879–1885', 215.

88. Gregg C. Smith, 'Foreword', in Treaty 7 Elders and Tribal Council with Walter Hildebrandt, Dorothy First Rider, and Sarah Carter, *The True Spirit and Original Intent of Treaty 7* (Montreal: McGill-Queen's University Press, 1996), viii.

89. Hugh Dempsey, *Crowfoot: Chief of the Blackfeet* (Norman: University of Oklahoma Press, 1972), 296.

90. NAC, RG 10, Vol. 3659, File 9728, Reel C-11063, R.B. Nevitt, Ft Macleod, Report to the Commissioner, 31 Dec. 1877.

91. NAC, RG 10, Vol. 3659, File 9728, Reel C-11063, Report of Surgeon Kittson, Ft Walsh, to Col Macleod, 19 Feb. 1878.

92. The higher prevalence among women in this instance runs counter to the general epidemiology of the disease, as women tend to have lower case and death rates than men. Michael D. Iseman, *A Clinician's Guide to Tuberculosis* (Philadelphia: Lippincott, Williams and Williams, 2000), 108.

93. Noel Dyck, 'The Administration of Federal Indian Aid in the Northwest Territories, 1879–1885', MA thesis, University of Saskatchewan, 1970, 26.

94. SAB, Innes Papers, A-113, Vol. 3. Canadian Northwest Historical Society Papers, Subject File 12, Ruth Matheson Notes, n.d.. On the effect of the drought and warm conditions at Cumberland House, see George Duck, 'Letters from the West', *The Beaver* 282 (1951): 24. On the effect of the weather anomaly on the far north, see George F.G. Stanley, 'The Fur Trade Party. Part 1. Storm Warnings', *The Beaver* 284 (1953): 38.

95. Commissioners of the North West Mounted Police, *Opening the West: Official Reports of the North West Mounted Police* (Toronto: Coles Canadiana Collection, 1973), Report of Commissioner James Walsh, 1877, 20.

96. Canada, *Sessional Papers 1880*, Report of the Deputy Superintendent-General of Indian Affairs, Lawrence Vankoughnet, 31 Dec. 1879, 12.

97. Commissioners of the North West Mounted Police, *Opening the West*, Report of Surgeon George F. Kennedy, 30 Nov. 1879, 34.

98. Canada, *Sessional Papers*, Report of Indian Agent Edwin Allen, 30 Sept. 1880.

99. NAC, RG 10, Vol. 3726, File 24811, Reel C-10126, Dr Kittson to Lt Col N.T. Macleod, Indian Agent, Fort Macleod, 1 July 1880.

100. Gerald Friesen, *The Canadian Prairies: A History* (Toronto: University of Toronto Press, 1987), 150.

101. Laurie Meijer-Drees, 'Reserve Hospitals in Southern Alberta, 1890 to 1930', *Native Studies Review* 9 (1993–4): 93.

102. Sarah Carter, *Lost Harvests: Prairie Indian Reserve Farmers and Government Policy* (Kingston: McGill-Queen's University Press, 1990), 68–9, 71.

103. Tobias, 'Canada's Subjugation of the Plains Cree', 215.

104. Anthony J. Looy, 'Saskatchewan's First Indian Agent: M. G. Dickieson', *Saskatchewan History* 32 (1979): 111.

105. Walter Hildebrandt, *Views from Fort Battleford: Constructed Visions of an Anglo-Canadian West* (Regina: Canadian Plains Research Centre, 1994), 42.

106. SAB, R.A. Mayson Papers, A-M 455, 4, 'Dr. Andrew Everett Porter First Charter Member of Masonry in Saskatchewan', n.d., 3.

107. Canada, *Sessional Papers 1881*, Report of Indian Agent James C. Stewart, Edmonton, 21 Aug. 1880, 102.

108. Looy, 'Saskatchewan's First Indian Agent: M. G. Dickieson', 110

109. Friesen, *Canadian Prairies*, 150.

110. Tobias, 'Canada's Subjugation of the Plains Cree', 212–39.

111. Hugh Dempsey, 'The Starvation Year: Edgar Dewdney's Diary for 1879', Part 1, *Alberta History* 31 (1983): 13.

112. Canada, *Sessional Papers 1880*, Report of Acting Superintendent M.G. Dickieson, July 1879, 105.

113. NAC, John A. Macdonald Papers, Reel C-1590, A. Campbell to Macdonald, 10 Aug. 1879, 81299.

114. NAC, RG 10, Vol. 3678, File 11683, Reel C-10119, Report of Hagarty Vaccinations 1879, 4–5 Aug. 1879.

115. NAC, RG 10, Vol. 3648, File 8138, Reel C-10113.

Personnel File of Dr Daniel Hagarty, Memorandum of J.D. Cote, Privy Council, 14 June 1880.

116. NAC, RG 10, Vol. 3648, File 8138, Reel C-10113, 14 June 1880.

117. Robert Jefferson, *Fifty Years on the Saskatchewan: Being a History of the Cree Indian Domestic Life and the Difficulties which Led to Serious Agitation and Conflict of 1885 in the Battleford Locality* (Battleford: Canadian Northwest Historical Society, 1929), 39.

118. Peter D. Elias, *The Dakota of the Canadian Northwest: Lessons for Survival* (Winnipeg: University of Manitoba Press, 1988), 151.

119. Ibid., 57.

120. Canada, *Sessional Papers 1881*, Annual Report of the Department of Indian Affairs for the Year Ended 31st December 1881, x.

121. Positive deviance is an approach to identifying solutions to health problems that focus on the successful behaviours of healthy individuals in impoverished populations, and has commonly been applied to issues of childhood nutrition. However, we would argue, it can also be applied to understand how some Aboriginal groups such as the Standing Buffalo band were able to maintain their health compared to other neighbouring groups who faced similar negative circumstances. On positive deviance, see D.R. Marsh, D.G. Schroeder, K.A. Dearden, J. Sternin, and M. Sternin, 'The Power of Positive Deviance', *British Medical Journal* 329 (2004): 1177–9.

122. David Meyer, *The Red Earth Crees, 1860–1960* (Ottawa: National Museum of Man, 1985), 89.

123. CMS, microfilm A-112, John Hines, Assissippi Journal, 9 Mar. 1884.

124. CMS, Rupert's Land Mission Letters, Reel A-111, Joseph Reader to C.C. Fenn, 20 Sept. 1882, 131.

125. Comstock and O'Brien, 'Tuberculosis', 782.

126. R.G. Ferguson, *Tuberculosis among the Indians of the Great Canadian Plains: Preliminary Report of an Investigation Being Carried Out by the National Research Council of Canada* (London: Adlard & Son, 1929), 45.

CHAPTER FOUR: WAR, CONFLICT, AND SOCIETY

1. Sarah Carter, *Capturing Women: The Manipulation of Cultural Imagery in Canada's Prairie West* (Montreal: McGill-Queen's University Press, 1997).

2. P. Whitney Lackenbauer, 'Introduction', in Lackenbauer and Craig Leslie Mantle, eds, *Aboriginal Peoples and the Canadian Military: Historical Perspectives* (Kingston: Canadian Defence Academy Press, 2007), xi.

3. J.R. Miller, *Skyscrapers Hide the Heavens: A History of Indian–White Relations in Canada*, 3rd edn (Toronto: University of Toronto Press, 2000), 123.

4. Baptism, 13 Dec. 1723, in Gaetan Morin, ed., *Répertoire des actes de baptême, mariage et sépulture du Québec ancien, 1621–1799*, CD-ROM, record no. 65055. Registres Notre-Dame-de-Québec, 13 Dec.1723, Family History Library, Salt Lake City, Utah; Marcel Trudel, *Dictionnaire des esclaves et de leurs propriétaires au Canada français*, nouvelle édition revue et corrigée (Ville LaSalle, QC: Hurtubise, 1990), 141. Marguerite-Genevieve's 1725 burial record indicates that she was still Vaudreuil's slave two years later (burial, 2 Oct. 1725, in Morin, *Répertoire*, no. 73772).

5. Vaudreuil au ministre, 2 Oct. 1723, in Correspondence générale, Canada, série C11A, vol. 45, fol. 136-41v, Le Centre des archives d'outre-mer, Aix-en-Provence, France; Vaudreuil to French minister, 2 Oct. 1723, in Reuben Gold Thwaites, ed., *Collections of the State Historical Society of Wisconsin* (Madison: State Historical Society of Wisconsin, 1902), 16: 431 (quotation).

6. Only one historian of the Fox Wars has even acknowledged the slave trade: Joseph L. Peyser, 'The Fate of the Fox Survivors: A Dark Chapter in the History of the French in the Upper Country, 1726–1737', *Wisconsin Magazine of History* 73, 2 (Winter 1989–90): 83–110.

7. R. David Edmunds and Joseph L. Peyser, *The Fox Wars: The Mesquakie Challenge to New France* (Norman, OK: Oklahoma University Press, 1993), 14–17; Louis Hennepin, *A New Discovery of a Vast Country in America* (1698, repr., Chicago: A.C. McClurg, 1903), 1: 134; Claude Charles LeRoy, Sieur de Bacqueville de la Potherie, in Emma Helen Blair, ed. and trans., *The Indian Tribes of the Upper Mississippi Valley and Region of the Great Lakes . . .* (Cleveland: A.H. Clark Co., 1911), 1: 356–72.

8. Gilles Havard, *The Great Peace of Montreal of 1701: French-Native Diplomacy in the Seventeenth Century*, trans. Phyllis Aronoff and Howard Scott (Montreal: McGill-Queen's University Press, 2001), esp. chap. 5; appendix to W. Vernon Kinietz, *The Indians of the Western Great Lakes: 1615–1760* (Ann Arbor: University of Michigan Press, 1965), 383 ('devils on earth').

9. Lettre de Lamothe Cadillac au Ministre à propos de l'établissement du Detroit, 18 Oct. 1700, in série C11A, 14: 56-59, Le Centre des archives d'outre-mer.

10. Edmunds and Peyser, *Fox Wars*, 59–61 (quotation, 59). For 1703 and 1708 raids, see Réponse de Vaudreuil aux Indiens, 29 July 1709, in série C11A, 30: 85-92v (quotation, 89), Le Centre des archives d'outre-mer.

11. Vaudreuil à Dubuisson, 13 Sept. 1710, in série C11A, 31: 79v, Le Centre des archives d'outre-mer.

Vaudreuil au ministre, 1710, in série C11A, 31: 81-88v, Le Centre des archives d'outre-mer.

12. Edmunds and Peyser, *Fox Wars*, 64–71.

13. Pierre François Xavier de Charlevoix, *History and General Description of New France*, ed. and trans. John Gilmary Shea (New York: F.P. Harper, 1900), 5: 260.

14. Charlevoix, *History*, 5: 261, 263.

15. Dubuisson to governor, [1712], 'Official Report . . . to the Governor General of Canada . . . 1712 . . .', in Thwaites, ed., *Wis. Hist. Coll.*, 16, 282.

16. Richard White, *The Middle Ground: Indians, Empires, and Republics in the Great Lakes Region, 1650–1815* (Cambridge: Cambridge University Press, 1991), 145.

17. See documents in Thwaites, *Wis. Hist. Coll.*, 16: 345.

18. Vaudreuil au Conseil de Marine, in série C11A, 36: 59-60v, Le Centre des archives d'outre-mer; baptism, 1 Dec. 1716, Sainte-Famille de Boucherville, Archives nationales du Québec, Centre régional de Montréal. For treaty, see Délibération du Conseil de Marine sur des lettres de Vaudreuil et Louvigny, 28 Dec. 1716, in série C11A, 36: 280v, Le Centre des archives d'outre-mer; Vaudreuil to the Council of the Marine, 14 Oct. 1716, ibid., 36: 71-74v; Thwaites, *Wis. Hist. Coll.*, 16: 341–4, 343 (quotation).

19. Vaudreuil au Conseil de Marine, 30 Oct. 1716, in série C11A, 36: 59-59v, Le Centre des archives d'outre-mer.

20. Perrot, in Blair, *Indian Tribes of the Upper Mississippi*, 1:268; Charlevoix, *History*, 5: 306.

21. Vaudreuil to Council, 30 Oct. 1718, in Thwaites, *Wis. Hist. Coll.*, 16: 377–8.

22. Morin, *Répertoire*, records for 'renard', 'renarde', 'renards', 'outagami', and 'outagamis'; supplemented by Trudel, *Dictionnaire*, 7-263.

23. Baptism, 2 Feb. 1714, in Morin, *Repertoire*, no. 44212. For Vincenne at the Fox siege, see [Gaspard-Joseph Chaussegros de Léry], '1712: Another Account of the Siege of Detroit', in Thwaites, *Wis. Hist. Coll.*, 16: 294 (quotations).

24. Baptism, 21 Sept. 1713, in Morin, *Répertoire*, no. 44145; Registres Notre-Dame-de-Montréal, film 111, Archives nationales du Québec, Centre régional de Montréal. For Repentigny's activities, see Paul-André Dubé, 'Legardeur de Repentigny, Pierre', in *Dictionary of Canadian Biography*, vol. 2, s.v. 'Legardeur'. For Rivard-Loranger, see baptism, 17 Feb. 1714, in Morin, *Répertoire*, no. 7941; baptism, 13 Jan. 1715, ibid., no. 7962; Trudel, *Dictionnaire*, 7.

25. Francis Jennings, 'Bisaillon (Bezellon, Bizaillon), Peter', *Dictionary of Canadian Biography*, vol. 3, s.v.

'Bisaillon'; sale dated 28 Nov. 1717, Greffe Barrette (Montreal), Archives nationales du Québec, Centre régional de Montréal.

26. For Gamelin, see baptisms, 21 Sept. 1713, in Registres Notre-Dame-de-Montréal, film 111, Archives nationales du Québéc, Centre régional de Montréal. For Gamelin's slave trading, see Brett Rushforth, 'Savage Bonds: Indian Slavery and Alliance in New France' (PhD dissertation, University of California, Davis, 2003), 141–2. For Gamelin's own slave, see baptism, 11 Feb. 1714, in Morin, *Répertoire*, no. 44219. For Biron, see baptism, 19 May 1714, Notre-Dame-de-Montréal, Family History Library film no. 375842; burial, 14 Feb. 1733, ibid.; trial beginning 17 July 1725, in Les dossiers de la Juridiction royale de Montréal, Cote TL4, S1, file no. 053-3159, Archives nationales du Québec, Centre regional de Montréal.

27. Baptism, 21 Sept. 1713, in Morin, *Répertoire*, no. 44146; baptism, 3 June 1713, ibid., no. 44087; baptism, 26 Nov. 1713, ibid., no. 63501; baptism, 9 July 1719, ibid., no. 64333; Trudel, *Dictionnaire*, 331.

28. See Vaudreuil to French Minister, 2 Oct. 1723, in Thwaites, *Wis. Hist. Coll.*, 16: 428.

29. For Lefebvre, see sale of 7 Oct. 1722, Greffe Barrette (Montreal), Archives nationales du Québec, Centre régional de Montréal.

30. For hemp, see Rushforth, 'Savage Bonds', 71–3. For riverfront, see trial beginning 13 June 1728, in file no. 059-3432, Les dossiers de la Juridiction royale de Montréal. For prices, see, for example, sale of 7 Oct. 1722, Greffe Barrette (Montreal), Archives nationales du Québec, Centre régional de Montréal; 'Vente d'une Sauvagesse nommee Angélique, de la nation des Renards', 5 Oct. 1733, in Greffe Dubreuil, Family History Library; 'Vente d'une Renarde de nation nommee Therese', 14 Sept. 1737, in Greffe Boisseau, ibid.; 'Vente d'une femme âgée de 36 ans, Sauvagesse de nation renarde, esclave', 31 Oct. 1740, in Greffe Pinguet de Vaucour, ibid.

31. Vaudreuil to French Minister, 2 Oct. 1723, in Thwaites, *Wis. Hist. Coll.*, 16: 430. Vaudreuil to Boisbriant, 17 Aug. 1724, in Thwaites, *Wis. Hist. Coll.*, 16: 442–3 (quotation). Baptism, 13 Dec. 1723, Notre-Dame-de-Québec, Family History Library; Trudel, *Dictionnaire*, 407.

32. De Lignery to Boisbriant, 23 Aug. 1724, in Thwaites, *Wis. Hist. Coll.*, 16: 445.

33. Du Tisné to Vaudreuil, 14 Jan. 1725, in Thwaites, *Wis. Hist. Coll.*, 16: 451.

34. For the 1726 meeting, see Lignery à Deliette, 15 June 1726, in série C11A, 48: 415-18v, Le Centre des archives d'outre-mer.

35. Conseil de marine à Perriers, 22 July 1737, in série B, 50: 543, Le Centre des archives d'outre-mer; Beauharnois et Depuy au ministre, 25 Oct. 1727, in série C11A, 49: 48-49v, ibid.; Beauharnois à Liette, 20 Aug. 1737, ibid., 49: 120–1.

36. Beauharnois to French Minister, 1 July 1733, in Thwaites, *Wis. Hist. Coll.*, 17: 182–3. For Beauharnois's Fox slaves, see Trudel, *Dictionnaire*, 276–7.

37. Charlevoix, *History and General Description of New France*, 5: 256–7. For Fox population, see Résumés de lettres concernant les Renards, n.d., 1733, in série C11A, 60: 448-63, Le Centre des archives d'outre-mer.

38. Hocquart au ministre, 14 Nov. 1730, in série C11A, 53: 207-8v, Le Centre des archives d'outre-mer. Belamy never received his gift, however, since the ship wrecked on its first day of sailing from Quebec (see Beauharnois et Hocquart au ministre, 15 Jan. 1731, in série C11A, 54: 3-9v, Le Centre des archives d'outre-mer).

39. Archives départementales de la Charente-Maritime, La Rochelle, série B, vol. 225, fol. 2-3 (quotation, 3). Transcript, film C-9182, National Archives of Canada.

40. White, *Middle Ground*, 143, 145.

41. This baptismal register was transcribed and translated by Geoff Read. Illegible words are indicated by [. . .] and names as signatures by [signature].

42. David J. Weber, 'Turner, the Boltonians, and the Borderlands', *American Historical Review* 91 (Feb. 1986): 66–81; Richard White, *The Middle Ground*.

43. For a borderlands study of Canada and the United States, see Reginald C. Stuart, *United States Expansionism and British North America, 1775–1871* (Chapel Hill: University of North Carolina Press, 1988). Stuart does not examine the role of Indians in the construction of that borderland. A more recent work on a later, more western portion of the border does illuminate the pivotal role of Native people; see Beth LaDow, *The Medicine Line: Life and Death on a North American Borderland* (New York: Routledge, 2001).

44. Red Jacket, speech, 21 Nov. 1790, Timothy Pickering Papers (Massachusetts Historical Society, Boston), Red Jacket, speech, 10 July 1791, ibid.

45. Dean R. Snow, *The Iroquois* (Cambridge, MA: Blackwell, 1994), 141–57.

46. Barbara Graymont, *The Iroquois in the American Revolution* (Syracuse, NY: Syracuse University Press, 1972), 259–91.

47. Ibid., 259–62;

48. Allan MacLean to Haldimand, 13, 18 May 1783, Reel A-681, Add. Mss. 21763, 111, 118,
Manuscript Group 21 (Haldimand Papers), National Archives of Canada; Major John Ross to Haldimand, 14 May 1783, Reel A-688, Add. Mss. 21784, 132, Manuscript Group 21, ibid.; Major A. Campbell to Col Barry St Leger, 6 Aug. 1785, in E. A. Cruikshank, ed., 'Records of Niagara, 1784–7', Niagara Historical Society, *Publications*, no. 39 (1928), 69; Haldimand to Lord North, 30 Aug. 1783, 43: 241, and Haldimand to North, 27 Nov. 1783, 46: 41, both in Reel B-37, Manuscript Group 21, Colonial Office 42 (National Archives of Canada); Haldimand to Sir John Johnson, 14 June 1784, Reel A-664, Add. Mss. 21723, 131, Manuscript Group 21 (Haldimand Papers).

49. Robert S. Allen, *His Majesty's Indian Allies: British Indian Policy in the Defence of Canada, 1774–1815* (Toronto: Dundurn Press, 1992), 56–7; J. Leitch Wright Jr, *Britain and the American Frontier, 1783–1815* (Athens, GA: University of Georgia Press, 1975), 20–6, 36, 42–3; Lord Sydney to Gen. Henry Hope, 6 Apr. 1788, in Cruikshank, ed., 'Records of Niagara, 1784–7', 88.

50. White, *Middle Ground*, 416–17; Richard Butler, 'Fort Stanwix Proceedings', in Neville B. Craig, ed., *The Olden Time*, 2 vols (Pittsburgh: J.W. Cook, 1848), 2: 410 (11 Oct. includes quotation) and 425 (20 Oct. gives the boundary). For the Iroquois refutation of the treaty, see Anthony F.C. Wallace, *The Death and Rebirth of the Seneca* (New York: Knopf, 1978), 173.

51. Henry Knox, report to the President, 15 June 1789, *American State Papers, Indian Affairs*, 1: 13; Alan Taylor, 'Land and Liberty on the Post-Revolutionary Frontier', in David Thomas Konig, *Devising Liberty: Preserving and Creating Freedom in the New American Republic* (Stanford: Stanford University Press, 1995), 81–108; Wallace, *Death and Rebirth of the Seneca*, 172–9; White, *Middle Ground*, 457–8.

52. Chapin to Pickering, 2 June 1792, Pickering Papers; Chapin to Knox, 17 July 1792, *American State Papers, Indian Affairs*, 1: 242; Simcoe to Alured Clarke, 21 Apr. 1793, in Cruikshank, ed., *Correspondence of Simcoe*, 1: 317; Chapin to Knox, 29 Apr. and 30 July 1794, in O'Reilly Collection (New York Historical Society, New York).

53. Samuel Kirkland, 'A Statement of the Number &; Situation of the Six United Nations of Indians in North America', 15 Oct. 1791, Miscellaneous Bound (Massachusetts Historical Society). For the return to the Allegheny, see Richter, 'Onas, the Long Knife', 131–3; Wallace, *Death and Rebirth of the Seneca*, 168–9.

54. Samuel Kirkland, 'A Statement of the Number & Situation of the Six United Nations of Indians in North America'; Bureau of the Census, *Heads of*

Families at the First Census of the United States Taken in the Year 1790: New York (Baltimore, 1966), 9; Israel Chapin Jr to Oliver Phelps, 16 Mar. 1791, Phelps and Gorham Papers (New York State Library, Albany); Captain Bowman, Journal, 28 Apr. 1791, Pickering Papers.

55. Thomas Proctor, Diary, 27 Apr. 1791, *American State Papers, Indian Affairs*, 1: 155.

56. Wright, *Britain and the American Frontier*, 92–8.

57. William N. Fenton, ed., 'The Journal of James Emlen Kept on a Trip to Canandaigua, New York.', *Ethnohistory* 12 (Fall 1965): 279–342; William Savery, 'Journal', *Friends' Library* 1 (Philadelphia, 1837): 353–67.

58. Israel Chapin Jr to James McHenry, 4 Sept. 1796, O'Reilly Collection.

59. Captain James Bruff, speech, 21 Sept. 1796, and Bruff to unknown, 25 Sept. 1796, ibid.

60. Red Jacket, speech, 23 Sept. 1796, ibid.

61. Charles Williamson, 'Description of the Settlement of the Genesee Country', in O'Callaghan, ed., *Documentary History of the State of New York*, 2: 1141.

62. Wallace, *Death and Rebirth of the Seneca*, 179–83.

63. Secretary at War Henry Dearborn to Israel Chapin Jr, 15 June 1802, and Chapin to Dearborn, 6 July 1802 (includes the quotations), O'Reilly Collection; Joseph Brant to Oliver Phelps, 17 Aug. 1802, Phelps and Gorham Papers.

64. Secretary at War Henry Dearborn to Israel Chapin Jr, 15 June 1802, and Chapin to Dearborn, 6 July 1802 (includes the quotations), O'Reilly Collection.

65. Erastus Granger, notes, 11 Oct. 1810, and Red Jacket, speech, 13 Feb. 1810, in Snyder, ed., *Red and White on the New York Frontier* (Harrison, NY: Harbor Hill Books, 1978), 31, 40; Red Jacket, speech, 8 July 1812, in E.A. Cruikshank, ed., *Documentary History of the Campaign on the Niagara Frontier in 1812* (Welland, ON, Lundy's Lane Historical Society, n.d.), 110. For the removal agitation, see Christopher Densmore, *Red Jacket: Iroquois Diplomat and Orator* (Syracuse: Syracuse University Press, 1999), 88–9; Laurence M. Hauptman, *Conspiracy of Interests: Iroquois Dispossession and the Rise of New York State* (Syracuse: Syracuse University Press, 1999), 144–61.

66. Isaac Chapin Jr to Henry Dearborn, 1 Aug. 1802, O'Reilly Collection; Red Jacket, speeches, 18, 20, Aug. 1802, in A1823 Assembly Papers, 40 (Indian Affairs, 1780–1809).

67. Red Jacket, speech at Canandaigua, quoted in William Leete Stone, *Life and Times of Red-Jacket* (New York: Wiley & Putnam, 1841), 175.

68. Leonard D. White, *The Jeffersonians: A Study in Administrative History, 1801–1829* (New York: Free Press, 1956), 496–512.

69. George Clinton to Henry Dearborn, 21 Aug. 1802, *American State Papers, Indian Affairs*, 1: 667; Dearborn to Clinton, 14 Feb. 1803, and Ontario County Grand Jurors to New York State Legislature, 25 Feb. 1803, Assembly Papers, 40 (Indian Affairs, 1780–1809); *People v. George, a Seneca Indian*, 22 Feb. 1803, Ontario County Court of Oyer & Terminer, Record Book for 1797–1847, 20 (Ontario County Archives, Hopewell, NY); Charles Z. Lincoln, ed., *State of New York: Messages From the Governors*, vol. 2: 1777–1822 (Albany, 1909), 531; chap. 31, 'An Act to pardon George, a Seneca Indian', New York State, *Laws of the State of New York passed at the Twenty-Sixth Session of the Legislature* (Albany, 1803), 64.

70. Hauptman, *Conspiracy of Interests*, 133–4.

71. Charles D. Cooper, Oliver Phelps, and Ezra L'Hommedieu to Gov. George Clinton, 12 July 1802, and Red Jacket, speech, 19 Aug. 1802, both in A1823, Assembly Papers, 40 (Indian Affairs, 1780–1809); New York State treaty with the Seneca, 20 Aug. 1802, John Tayler to Henry Dearborn, 19 July, 23 Aug. 1802, and George Clinton to Dearborn, 21 Aug. 1802, all in *American State Papers, Indian Affairs*, 1: 664, 666–7.

72. Erastus Granger, speech, 6 July 1812, in Cruikshank, ed., *Documentary History of the Campaign on the Niagara Frontier in 1812*, 105.

73. Carl Benn, *The Iroquois in the War of 1812* (Toronto: University of Toronto Press, 1998), 29–66; Carl F. Klinck and James J. Talman, eds, *The Journal of Major John Norton, 1816* (Toronto: Champlain Society, 1970), 286–91.

74. Benn, *Iroquois in the War of 1812*, 86–174.

75. Eric Hinderaker, *Elusive Empires: Constructing Colonialism in the Ohio Valley, 1673–1800* (New York: Cambridge University Press, 1997), 267.

76. Marian L. Smith, 'The INS and the Singular Status of North American Indians', *American Indian Culture and Research Journal* 24 (1997): 131–54; Jolene Rickard, 'The Indian Defense League of America', *Akwesasne Notes* 1, 2 (1995): 48–54, (quotation at 53).

77. This speech has been transcribed by the editors. Places where we were unsure of the transcription are indicated by [?]. Words that could not be transcribed are indicated by [. . .].

78. Likely referring to Benjamin Barton, 1766–1815, a botanist and member of the team that surveyed Pennsylvania's western boundary. Barton was associated with Lt-Col John Butler (see below).

79. Referring to Lt-Col John Butler, 1728–96, a loyalist who fought for the British during the American

Revolution, leading Six Nations warriors in an invasion of New York, among other things. Butler was also one of the primary backers of the Niagara Genesee Company, which, like the New York and Genesee Company, was engaged in land speculation.

80. Referring to Buffalo Creek, New York, a Seneca village established by the British during the revolutionary war.
81. Referring to Seneca chief Little Billy.
82. Referring to Seneca chief Heap of Dogs.
83. Referring to Seneca chief Farmer's Brother.
84. Referring to Samuel Street, 1753–1815, an agent of the New York and Genesee Company, who helped the company circumvent state law by leasing, rather than purchasing, land from the Six Nations.
85. Referring to Captain John Obeil, better known as Cornplanter (c. 1750–1836) a Seneca chief. Cornplanter's father was Dutch.
86. Referring to Samuel Kirkland, 1741–1808, a Presbyterian missionary and later the founder of Hamilton College.
87. Referring to US General Arthur St Clair, 1737–1818.
88. Referring to the town of Big Flats, NY.

CHAPTER FIVE: THE FUR TRADE

1. Harold A. Innis, *The Fur Trade in Canada* (New Haven: Yale University Press, 1930).
2. Arthur J. Ray, *Indians in the Fur Trade* (Toronto: University of Toronto Press, 1974).
3. Sylvia Van Kirk, *Many Tender Ties: Women in Fur Trade Society, 1670–1870* (Winnipeg: Watson & Dwyer, 1980); Jennifer S.H. Brown, *Strangers in Blood: Fur Trade Company Families in Indian Country* (Vancouver: UBC Press, 1980).
4. Howard Adams, *Prison of Grass* (Toronto: New Press, 1975), 41.
5. Ibid., 43.
6. The most notable example was probably Harold Innis. See Innis, *The Fur Trade in Canada*, 386–92.
7. See, for example, Innis, *The Fur Trade*; A.S. Morton, *The History of the Canadian West to 1870–71*, 2nd edn (Toronto: University of Toronto Press, 1973); and E.E. Rich, *The Fur Trade and the Northwest to 1857* (Toronto: McClelland and Stewart, 1967).
8. C. Jaenen, *Friend and Foe* (Toronto: McClelland and Stewart, 1976), 1–11.
9. Innis and Rich deal extensively with the fur trade as an aspect of imperial history. See Innis, *The Fur Trade*, 383; and Rich, *Fur Trade and Northwest*, xi and 296. Several corporate histories have been written. See, as examples, L.R. Masson, *Les Bourgeois de la Compagnie du Nord-Ouest*, 2 vols. (1889–90; reprint edn, New York: Antiquarian

Press, 1960); E.E. Rich, *The History of the Hudson's Bay Company 1670–1870*, 2 vols. (London: Hudson's Bay Record Society, 1958–9); and W.S. Wallace, *Documents Relating to the North West Company* (Toronto: Champlain Society, 1934).
10. This point of view was perhaps most strongly expressed by Diamond Jenness. See Diamond Jenness, 'The Indian Background of Canadian History', Canada, Department of Mines and Resources, National Museum of Canada Bulletin No. 86 (Ottawa, 1937), 1–2; and *Indians of Canada*, 6th edn (Ottawa: National Museum of Canada, 1963), 249. See also George F. Stanley, 'The Indian Background of Canadian History', Canadian Historical Association, *Papers* (1952), 14.
11. A notable example of this interest as it pertains to Western Canada is the early work of Frits Pannekoek. See Frits Pannekoek, 'Protestant Agricultural Missions in the Canadian West in 1870' (MA thesis, University of Alberta, 1970). More recently, Pannekoek has begun to consider the divisive role these groups played in terms of race relations in Western Canada. See Frits Pannekoek, 'The Rev. Griffiths Owen Corbett and the Red River Civil War of 1869–70', *Canadian Historical Review* 57 (1976): 133–49.
12. A notable exception to this viewpoint is that expressed by Stanley in 1952. He pointed out that programs oriented towards assimilating the Indians into the dominant white society lead to cultural extinction of the former group. This is offensive to any people having a strong sense of identity. See Stanley, 'The Indian Background of Canadian History', 21.
13. R.G. Thwaites, ed., *The Jesuit Relations and Allied Documents*, vol. 6 (New York: Pagent Book Company, 1959), 297–9.
14. K.G. Davies, ed., *Letters from Hudson Bay, 1703–40* (London: Hudson's Bay Record Society, 1965), 136.
15. E.E. Rich, ed., *Minutes of the Hudson's Bay Company, 1671–74* (Toronto: Champlain Society, 1942), 26–7, 58–9.
16. Ibid., 91.
17. Arthur J. Ray, *Indians in the Fur Trade* (Toronto: University of Toronto Press, 1974), 75.
18. For example, in the eighteenth century Arthur Dobbs charged that the company advanced the prices of its goods above the Standards of Trade to such an extent that it discouraged the Indians from trading. Arthur Dobbs, *An Account of the Countries Adjoining to Hudson's Bay in the Northwest Part of America* (London, 1744), 43. More recently the company has been attacked for its pricing policy by Adams, *Prison of Grass*, 24.
19. C.E. Heidenreich and Arthur J. Ray, *The Early Fur

Trades: A Study in Cultural Interaction (Toronto: McClelland and Stewart, 1976), 82–3.

20. Arthur J. Ray, 'The Hudson's Bay Company Account Books As Sources for Comparative Economic Analyses of the Fur Trade: An Examination of Exchange Rate Data', *Western Canadian Journal of Anthropology* 6, 1(1976): 44–50.

21. The principal exception was at Eastmain where the prevailing rates exceeded the 50 per cent markup level from the late 1690s until about 1720. However, it should be pointed out that French opposition was relatively weak in this area. See Ray, 'Hudson's Bay Company Account Books', 45–50.

22. For example, one of the virtues of Indian leaders was generosity. And, generalized reciprocity or sharing was practised amongst band members. These values and practices served to discourage any individual, regardless of his position, from accumulating wealth in excess of that of his kinsmen.

23. Generally, alcohol was diluted with water by a ratio of one-quarter to one-third at the Hudson's Bay Company posts in the eighteenth century. See Davies, *Letters from Hudson Bay*, 268.

24. Ray, *Indians in the Fur Trade*, 117–24.

25. Adams, *Prison of Grass*, 51; and Susan Hurlich, 'Up Against the Bay: Resource Imperialism and Native Resistance', *This Magazine* 9, 4 (1975): 4.

26. As a dogger, the *Messenger* would have only two masts, a main and a mizzen. As a 'pinke' she would have a foremast, mainmast, and mizzen. In both cases she would have a square blunt stern. See E.E. Rich, 'Introduction', in Rich, ed., *Minutes of the Hudson's Bay Company, 1671-1674* (Toronto: Champlain Society, 1942), xxx and lv.

27. Harold Innis, in *The Fur Trade in Canada*, views the North American fur trade as an extension of a European economic system. The effect of trade as destructive of Indigenous cultures is described by many, including Lewis O. Saum in *The Fur Trader and the Indian* (Seattle: University of Washington Press, 1965).

28. Richard White, *The Middle Ground: Indians, Empires and Republics in the Great Lakes Region, 1650–1815* (Cambridge: Cambridge University Press, 1991), x–xi, 50, 52.

29. Clara Sue Kidwell, 'Indian Women as Cultural Negotiators', *Ethnohistory* 39 (1992): 97–107. The term *negotiators of change* is borrowed from Nancy Shoemaker's *Negotiators of Change: Historical Perspectives on Native American Women* (New York: Routledge, 1995).

30. 'Marriage "after the custom of the country" was an indigenous marriage rite which evolved to meet the needs of fur trade society.' Van Kirk, *Many Tender Ties*, 28.

31. Sylvia Van Kirk, 'Toward a Feminist Perspective in Native History', in Jose Mailhot, ed., *Papers of the Eighteenth Algonquian Conference* (Ottawa: National Museum of Canada, 1987), 386.

32. Nancy Shoemaker, 'Kateri Tekawitha's Torturous Path to Sainthood', in Shoemaker, ed., *Negotiators of Change*, 49–71; Natalie Zemon Davis, 'Iroquois Women, European Women', in Margo Hendricks and Patricia Parker, eds, *Women, 'Race,' and Writing in the Early Modern Period* (New York: Routledge, 1994), 243–61.

33. The number eight appears throughout the St Joseph Baptismal Register and indicates the phonetic equivalent for parts of Native American languages that were not spelled in French. Eight was a digraph or shorthand for *ou*.

34. Clarence Walworth Alvord, *The Illinois Country, 1673–1818* (Chicago, 1920), 41–6.

35. James E. Fitting and Charles E. Cleland, 'Late Prehistoric Settlement Patterns in the Upper Great Lakes', *Ethnohistory* 16 (1969): 295–6; W. Vernon Kinietz, *The Indians of the Western Great Lakes* (Ann Arbor: University of Michigan Press, 1990), 270–4.

36. Carl J. Ekberg with Anton J. Pregaldin, 'Marie Rouensa-8cate8a and the Foundations of French Illinois', *Illinois Historical Journal* 84 (Fall 1991): 146–60; John E. McDowell, 'Therese Schindler of Mackinac: Upward Mobility in the Great Lakes Fur Trade', *Wisconsin Magazine of History* 61 (Winter 1977–8): 126–7; David A. Armour, 'Magdelaine Marcot La Framboise', *Dictionary of Canadian Biography* (hereafter *DCB*) (Toronto: University of Toronto Press, 1991), 7: 582–3; McDowell, 'Madame La Framboise', *Michigan History* 56 (Winter 1972): 271–86; Keith R. Widder, 'Magdelaine La Framboise, Fur Trader and Educator', in Rosalie Riegle Troester, ed., *Historical Women of Michigan: A Sesquicentennial Celebration* (Lansing, MI: Michigan Women's Studies Association, 1987), 1–13.

37. White, *Middle Ground*, 70–5.

38. Louise Tilly, 'Gender, Women's History, and Social History', *Social Science History* 13 (1989): 439–62.

39. Emily J. Blasingham, 'The Depopulation of the Illinois Indians', *Ethnohistory* 3 (1956): 193.

40. Reuben Gold Thwaites, ed., *The Jesuit Relations and Allied Documents, Travels and Explorations of the Jesuit Missions in New France, 1610–1791* (hereafter *JR*) (Cleveland: Burrows, 1896–1901), 64: 195–205.

41. 'Kaskaskia Church Records', *Transactions of the Illinois Historical Society,* vol. 2 (Springfield, IL, 1904), 394; Marthe F. Beauregard, *La population des forts français d'Amérique* (Montreal: Bergeron, 1982), 2: 108.

42. *JR*, 64: 213.

43. Kimball Brown and Laurie C. Dean, *The Village of Chartres in Colonial Illinois, 1720–1765* (New Orleans, LA, 1977), 871; Ekberg, 'Marie Rouensa', 156.

44. Mary Borgias Palm, *The Jesuit Missions of the Illinois Country, 1673–1763* (Cleveland, 1933), 42–3, 80.

45. Susan C. Boyle, 'Did She Generally Decide? Women in Ste. Genevieve, 1750–1805', *William and Mary Quarterly* 44 (1987): 783–4.

46. Thomas Hughes, *History of the Society of Jesus in North America* (London: Longmans, Green, & Co., 1917), 2: 418–19.

47. See Chapter 3, 'Structures, Habitus, Practices', in Pierre Bourdieu, *The Logic of Practice* (Stanford, CA: Stanford University Press, 1990), 52–65.

48. 'St. Joseph Baptismal Register', *Mississippi Valley Historical Review* 13 (June 1926–Mar. 1927): 212.

49. Marcel Mauss, *The Gift: The Form and Reason of Exchange in Archaic Societies* (New York: Routledge, 1990).

50. Certificate, Montreal, signed de Villiers, 18 July 1745; *ANCol*, C11A, 117: 325.

51. 'St. Joseph Baptismal Register', Rev George Paré and M.M. Quaife, eds, *The Mississippi Valley Historical Review* 13 (June 1926–Mar. 1927): 213. 'The Mackinac Register', *Collections of the State Historical Society of Wisconsin* (hereafter *WHC*)19:4.

52. James A. Brown, *Aboriginal Cultural Adaptations in the Midwestern Prairies* (New York: Garland Publishing, 1991), 60; *JR*, 55: 195.

53. 'Petition of Louis Chevallier', reprinted from the Haldimand Papers, Canadian Archives, Ottawa, *Michigan Pioneer and Historical Society: Collections and Researches* (hereafter *MPHC*), 13 (1889): 61.

54. Boyle, 'Did She Generally Decide?' 788–9.

55. 'Mackinac Baptisms', *WHC*, 19: 24–5; 'Mackinac Register', *WHC*, 18: 475; 'Mackinac Register,' *WHC*, 18: 476; *Rapport de l'Archiviste de la Province de Québec, 1929–30* (hereafter *RAPQ*), 244–408; and Webster and Krause, *Fort Saint Joseph*, 115.

56. John M. Gram, 'The Chevalier Family and the Demography of the Upper Great Lakes', (unpublished paper, Mackinac Island State Park Commission, Lansing, MI, 1995).

57. See, for example, Gregory Evans Dowd, 'The French King Wakes up in Detroit: Pontiac's War in Rumor and History', *Ethnohistory* 37 (1990): 254–78.

58. 'To General Gage from Lt. Campbell, 10 April 1766', Gage Papers #308, Ayers Manuscript Collections, Newberry Library, Chicago, Illinois; 'To General Haldimand from A.S. DePeyster, 15 August 1778', *MPHC*, 9: 368.

59. Gérard Malchelosse, 'St. Joseph River Post', *French Canadian and Acadian Genealogical Review 3–4* (1970): 189.

60. 'The St. Joseph Baptismal Register', *MVHR*, XIII: 202–39; 'The Mackinac Register', *WHC*, 19: 1–161; 'The Mackinac Register, 1725–1821: Register of Marriages in the Parish of Michilimackinac', *WHC*, 18: 469–513; 'Kaskaskia Church Records', *Transactions Illinois State Historical Society*, 395–413.

61. Memorial of Louis Joseph Ainsse, 5 Aug. 1780, *MPHC*, 13: 58–9, 10: 415.

62. Thimotée is also called Marie Neskesh by the Jesuits. 'Mackinac Register', *WHC*, 19: 86.

63. 'Census of the Post of St. Joseph', *MPHC*, 10: 406–07.

64. 'Marguerite-Magdelaine Marcot (La Framboise)', *DCB*, 582; Milo M. Quaife, *Lake Michigan* (Indianapolis: Bobbs Merrill Co, 1944), 201–06.

65. *WHC*, 19: 86, 117, 118; 11: 164–5.

66. Quaife, *Lake Michigan*, 115.

67. 'Mackinac Register', 18: 507–08.

68. Claude La Framboise to John Kinzie, 11 June 1807, Solomon Sibley Papers, Burton Historical Collection, Detroit Public Library.

69. Elizabeth Thérèse Baird, 'Reminiscences of Early Days on Mackinac Island', *WHC*, 14: 38–9.

70. Ibid., 22; Elizabeth Thérèse Baird, 'Reminiscences of Life in Territorial Wisconsin', *WHC*, 15: 213.

71. 'Account Book of Mackinac Merchant', Michigan Manuscripts, C, in Archives Division, State Historical Society of Wisconsin; *Michigan Pioneer and Historical Collections*, 37: 143; McDowell, 'Therese Schindler', 135–6.

72. Baird, 'Reminiscences of Mackinac', *WHC*, 14: 22; Baird, 'Reminiscences of Life in Territorial Wisconsin', 213; 'Account Book of a Mackinac Merchant', Michigan Manuscripts, C, in Archives Division, State Historical Society of Wisconsin; *MPHC*, 27: 143; McDowell, 'Therese Schindler', 128, 135–6.

73. John Denis Haeger, *John Jacob Astor: Business and Finance in the Early Republic* (Detroit: Wayne State University Press, 1991), 149–52.

74. Tanis C. Thorne, *The Many Hands of My Relations* (Columbia, MO: University of Missouri Press, 1996).

75. DePeyser to Gen Haldimand, 15 Aug. 1778, *MPHC*, 368; DePeyser to Sinclair, 12 Mar. 1780, *MPHC*, 9: 581; *WHC*, 9: 93, 95; Mr Claus to Secretary Foster, 22 May 1815, *MPHC*, 115.

CHAPTER SIX: LOCATING MÉTIS IDENTITY

1. John Giokas and Paul L.A.H. Chartrand, 'Who are the Métis? A Review of the Law and Policy', in Paul L.A.H. Chartrand and Harry W. Daniels, eds, *Who Are Canada's Aboriginal Peoples? Recognition,*

Definition, and Jurisdiction (Saskatoon: Purich Publishing, 2002), 83–125.

2. Jacqueline Peterson and Jennifer S.H. Brown, 'Introduction', in Peterson and Brown, eds, *The New Peoples: Being and Becoming Métis in North America* (Winnipeg: The University of Manitoba Press, 1985), 6.

3. See, for example, Sarah Quick, 'The Social Poetics of the Red River Jig in Alberta and Beyond: Meaningful Heritage and Emerging Performance', *Ethnologies* 30, 1 (2008): 77–101.

4. Trudy Nicks and Kenneth Morgan, 'Grand Cache: The Historic Development of an Indigenous Alberta Métis Population', in Peterson and Brown, eds, *The New Peoples*, 163–81.

5. Ute Lischke and David T. McNab, eds, *The Long Journey of a Forgotten People: Métis Identities and Family Histories* (Waterloo: Wilfrid Laurier University Press, 2007). See also Heather Devine, *The People Who Own Themselves: Aboriginal Ethnogenesis in a Canadian Family, 1660–1900* (Calgary: University of Calgary Press, 2004); Brenda Macdougall, *One of the Family: Métis Culture in Nineteenth Century Saskatchewan* (Vancouver: UBC Press, 2009); Gwen Reimer and Jean-Philippe Chartrand, 'Documenting Historic Métis in Ontario', *Ethnohistory* 51, 3 (Summer 2004): 567–607; Nicole St-Onge, *Saint-Laurent, Manitoba: Evolving Métis Identities, 1850–1914* (Regina: Canadian Plains Research Centre, 2004).

6. David Bentley and Brenda Murphy, 'Power, Praxis, and the Métis of Kelly Lake, Canada'.

7. John Knox, *An Historical Journal of the Campaigns in North America for the Years 1757, 1758, 1759, and 1760*, 3 vols, Arthur G. Doughty, ed. (Toronto: Champlain Society, 1914–16), 1: 51, 54, 83–4, 179, 182, 309–20; 2: 607–08, 613–15.

8. Captain Charles Lee to Miss Sidney Lee, 30 July 1759, in New York Historical Society, *Collections* 4 (1871): 19–20.

9. Gregory Evans Dowd, *War under Heaven: Pontiac, the Indian Nations, and the British Empire* (Baltimore: Johns Hopkins University Press, 2002), 41–190.

10. Richard White, *The Middle Ground: Indians, Empires, and Republics in the Great Lakes Region, 1650–1815* (Cambridge, MA: Cambridge University Press, 1991), 315–517.

11. The term *Métis* by the early nineteenth century was not synonymous with 'mixed-blood' but referred to those fathered by North West Company members and their Native wives. For an example of this usage by Hudson's Bay Company retainers, see Samuel Gale, *Notices of the Claims of the Hudson's Bay Company and the Conduct of Its Adversaries* (Montreal: William Gray, 1817), 44–5.

12. Alexander V. Campbell, *The Royal American Regiment: An Atlantic Microcosm, 1755-1772* (Norman: University of Oklahoma Press, 2010), 162-9.

13. Major-General Thomas Gage to the Earl of Halifax, 7 Jan. 1764, in Clarence E. Carter, ed., *The Correspondence of General Thomas Gage with the Secretaries of State and with the War Office and the Treasury, 1763–1775*, 2 vols (New Haven: Yale University Press, 1931–3), 1: 8–9.

14. Colonel Henry Bouquet to Brigadier-General John Forbes, 16 June 1758, in Sylvester K. Stevens and Donald Kent, eds, *The Papers of Henry Bouquet* (hereafter *BP*), 6 vols (Harrisburg: Pennsylvania Historical and Museum Commission, 1951–94), 2: 97.

15. Major George Etherington to Lieutenant-General Thomas Gage, 12 May 1772, Thomas Gage Papers American Series (hereafter TGPAS), vol. 110 (unpaginated), William L. Clements Library (hereafter WLCL), Ann Arbor, MI.

16. Pierre Pouchot, *Memoirs on the Late War in North America between France and England*, trans. Michael Cardy and ed. Brian L. Dunnigan (Youngstown, NY: Old Fort Niagara Association, 1994), 449; Sylvia Van Kirk, *Many Tender Ties: Women in Fur-Trade Society, 1670–1870* (Winnipeg: Watson and Dwyer, 1980), 28–33, 75–86.

17. See, for example, James Sterling to Ensign [Francis] Schlosser, 12 June 1762, James Sterling Letterbook (hereafter JSLB), (unpaginated), WLCL.

18. Lieutenant-Colonel Arent DePeyster quoted by Mark F. Odintz in 'The British Officer Corps, 1754–1783', 2 vols (PhD dissertation, University of Michigan, 1988), 1: 84.

19. 'Bouquet: General Orders: Staff Appointments', 5 Aug. 1764, in *BP*, 6, 599.

20. Harry W. Duckworth, *The English River Book: A North West Company Journal and Account Book of 1786* (Montreal: McGill-Queen's University Press, 1990), xvi, xviii; *Sakitawak Bi-Centennial Ile-à-La-Crosse 1776–1976* (Ile-à-la-Crosse, SK: Ile-à-la-Crosse Bi-Centennial Committee, 1977), 4–9. See 'Patrick Small', in W. Stewart Wallace, ed., *Documents Relating to the Northwest Company or North-West Company* (Toronto: Champlain Society, 1934), 498–9.

21. Entry from McDonald family Bible (hereafter MFB), in John McDonald of Garth's hand. A copy of this register is in the author's possession. Archibald de Lery McDonald to Harry Pirie-Gordon, 22 Sept. 1936, Fonds Quesnel, P4/C2, 821, (2), McDonald, (Famille), Le Centre d'historie La Presqu'ile (hereafter ChP), Vaudreuil, QC; Larry Green, 'John McDonald of Garth: The Last Nor'Wester', *Alberta History* 47 (1999): 2–12; C.M. Livermore

and N. Anick, 'John McDonald', in Frances G. Halpenny, Jean Hamelin, and Ramsay Cook, eds, *Dictionary of Canadian Biography* (hereafter *DCB*), vol. 9 (Toronto: University of Toronto Press, 1976), 481–3.

22. 'Deed of Sale', John and Amelia McDonald to Eliza Campbell, 11 Mar. 1824, #1235, Stormont County Land Registry Office, Cornwall, ON; Robert J. Burns, 'Inverarden: Retirement Home of Fur Trader John McDonald of Garth', *History and Archaeology* 25: 154, 164–5, 174.

23. 'Obituary', [Antoine Eustache de Bellefeuille MacDonald], n.d., Fonds Quesnel, P4/C2, 821 (1), McDonald, (Famille), ChP; 'Insolvency of de B. Macdonald and Company', 7 Feb.1870, Fonds Quesnel, P6/D3, 6, (1), McGillis, (Famille), ChP; Burns, 'Inverarden', 166–7; 'Map of Cornwall Township', in H. Belden and Company, *Illustrated Historical Atlas of the Counties of Stormont, Dundas, and Glengarry Ont.* (Toronto: H. Belden and Company, 1879), 6.

24. Quotation: Eustache Antoine Lefebvre de Bellefeuille to Jacob Oldham, 7 Oct. 1823, John MacDonald, Correpondence famille MacDonald, P30/E,1, (ChP); Mary MacDonald to John McDonald of Garth, 9 Apr. 1858, ibid., Correspondence famille MacDonald, P30/E, 1, ChP; *List of Provincial Land Surveyors for Lower-Canada* (n.p, n.d.), Canadian Institute for Historical Microreproductions, Microfiche series, #38502.

25. John G. Harkness, *Stormont, Dundas, and Glengarry: A History, 1784–1945* (Oshawa: Mundy-Goodfellow, 1946), 190; Joseph O. Coté, *Political Appointments and Elections in the Province of Canada from 1841 to 1865*, 2nd edn (Ottawa: Lowe-Martin Company, 1918), 76.

26. Quotation: 'Obituary', [Mrs John Duncan Campbell], n.d., Fonds Quesnel, P4/C2, 821, (1), McDonald, (Famille), ChP; 'Campbell Family of Breadalbane', Manuscript Group 25, G 17, National Archives of Canada, Ottawa, ON. See Susan M. Trofimenkoff, 'Ann Cuthbert (Knight, Fleming) Rae', *DCB*, vol. 8, 1851–60, 734–5.

27. Lieutenant-Colonel William Eyre to Major-General Jeffery Amherst, 20 Apr. 1760, War Office (hereafter WO) 34/21/35, Public Record Office (hereafter PRO), London, England; Walter Rutherfurd to Same, 28 Apr. 1761, ibid., 147, PRO; Walter Rutherfurd to Lieutenant-General Jeffery Amherst, 9 Apr. 1761, WO 34/74/155, PRO; 'A Proclamation', 10 Apr. 1761, ibid., PRO.

28. James Sterling to James Syme, 10 Jan. 1762, JSLB (unpaginated), WLCL; Same to John Sterling, 26 Aug. 1762, ibid., WLCL; Same to John Duncan,

26 Aug. 1762, ibid., WLCL; Major John Wilkins to John Duncan, 29 Sept. 1762, WO 34/22/93–4, PRO; Lieutenant-General Jeffery Amherst to Major John Wilkins, 17 Oct. 1762, ibid., 163, PRO; Captain Francis Legge to [ ], 24 Aug. 1764, Simon Gratz Manuscripts, 'Colonial Wars', Case 4, Box 7, Historical Society of Pennsylvania, Philadelphia.

29. James Sterling to Lieutenant William Leslye, 3 June 1762, JSLB (unpaginated), WLCL; Same to Captain George Etherington, 31 May 1762, ibid., WLCL; Same to James Syme, June 1762, ibid., WLCL; Same to Lieutenant Edward Jenkins, 14 Apr. 1763, ibid., WLCL; Henry Bostwick to James Beekman, 10 Dec. 1764, in Philip L. White, ed., *The Beekman Mercantile Papers, 1746–1799*, 3 vols (New York: New York Historical Society, 1956), 2:952–3; 'Petition of English and French Traders at Detroit', 24 July 1767, TGPAS, vol. 67 (unpaginated), WLCL; Captain George Turnbull to Major-General Thomas Gage, 25 July 1767, ibid., WLCL.

30. Quotation: James Sterling to Ensign [Francis] Schlosser, 12 June 1762, JSLB (unpaginated), WLCL; Royden W. Vosburgh, ed., *Records of the High and Low Dutch Reformed Congregation at Schoharie, Now the Reformed Church in the Town of Schoharie, Schoharie County, New York*, 3 vols (New York: New York Genealogical and Biographical Society, 1917–18), 1:87. See J.K. Johnson, 'Richard Duncan', *DCB*, vol. 5, 1801–20, 281–2.

31. 'Assignment of Abraham Maumis et al., to John Duncan et al.', 8 Apr. 1767, in Edmund B. O'Callaghan, ed., *Calendar of New York Colonial Manuscripts: Indorsed Land Papers in the Office of the Secretary of State of New York, 1643–1803* (Albany, NY: Weed, Parsons and Company, 1864), 442; Journal of John Lees of Quebec, Merchant, 8 (entry of 27 June 1768), Manuscript Group (hereafter MG), 21, Add. MSS. 28605, National Archives of Canada (hereafter NAC), Ottawa; 'Evidence on the Claim of Alexander Campbell, Late of Schohary', 1 Nov. 1787, in Alexander Fraser, ed., *Second Report of the Bureau of Archives for the Province of Ontario* (Toronto: King's Printer, 1905), 359–61.

32. John Van Sice to Sir William Johnson, 6 Mar. 1756, Loudoun Papers, #883, Henry E. Huntington Library, San Marino, CA; Same to Same, 15 Feb. 1772, in Sullivan et al., eds, *SWJP*,12: 940; 'List of Wintering Partners, Clerks, and Interpreters in the Service of the North West Company', 1797, in Gustave Lancot, ed., *Report of the Public Archives of Canada for the Year 1939* (Ottawa: King's Printer, 1940), 53; Jonathan Pearson, *Contributions for the Genealogies of the Descendants of the First Settlers of the Patent and City of Schenectady, from 1662 to 1800* (Albany, NY: J. Munsell, 1873), 32, 238; James E.

Seaver, *DEH-HE-WA-MIS, or A Narrative of the Life of Mary Jemison*, 3rd edn (Batavia, NY: William Seaver and Son, 1844), 73.

33. Quotation: John J. Bigsby, *The Shoe and Canoe or Pictures of Travel in Canada*. 2 vols., (London: Chapman and Hall, 1850), 1:125.

34. 'List of Indictments against the North West Company', n.d., Selkirk Papers, vol. 12, 4009, MG 19, E-l, NAC; [Samuel Gale], *Notices of the Claims of the Hudson's Bay Company*, (Montreal: William Gray, 1817), 90–3; *Report of the Proceedings Connected with the Disputes between the Earl of Selkirk and the North-West Company: At the Assizes, Held at York, in Upper Canada, October, 1818* (Montreal: James Lane and Nahum Mower, 1819), 151, 203–04; [Halkett], *Statement Respecting the Earl of Selkirk's Settlement upon the Red River*, xxxv, xliv–xlv; Wallace, ed., *Documents Relating to the North West Company*, 188–93, 431.

35. Quotation: John Pritchard in *Narratives of John Pritchard, Pierre Chrysologue Pambrun, and Frederick Damien Heurter, Respecting the Aggressions of the North-West Company, Against the Earl of Selkirk's Settlemmt upon Red River* (London: John Murray, 1819), 14.

36. Harold A. Innis, *The Fur Trade in Canada: An Introduction to Canadian Economic History* (Toronto: University of Toronto Press, 1970), 279; Thomas Douglas, *A Sketch of the British Fur Trade in North America; with Observations Relative to the North-West Company of Montreal*, 2nd edn (London: James Ridgway, 1816), 71–6.

37. W.L. Morton, 'Louis Riel', *DCB*, vol. 9, 1861–70, 663; George F.G. Stanley, *Louis Riel* (Toronto: Ryerson Press, 1963), 2–4, 56.

38. Quotations: (those lawless Rascals . . .) Hudson's Bay Company Archives, (hereafter HBCA), B 60/a/15, fo. 50, and ("countrymen") Donald McIntosh to Christy McIntosh, 22 August 1816, North West Company Records, F 431, MU 2198, Box 3, Item 1, Archives of Ontario, (hereafter AO), Toronto, Ontario.

39. Thomas Douglas, *The Memorial of Thomas Earl of Selkirk: to his Grace, Charles, Duke of ichmond*, (Montreal: Nahum Mower, 1819), 5.

40. Quotations: ("Bois Brules" and "metifs") and (children of the partners . . .), [Halkett], *Statement Respecting the Earl of Selkirk's Settlement*, xxxiv, xlix.

41. Manuscript by Lord Selkirk Relating to Red River," n.d., Selkirk Papers, MG 19-E1, 12857, LAC; *Reply to the Letter Lately Addressed to the Right Honorable The Earl of Selkirk, by The Hon. And Rev. John Strachan*, (Montreal: W. Gray, 1816), 44; Frances M. Staton and Marie Tremaine, eds., *A Bibliography of Canadiana*, (Toronto: Toronto Public Library, 1934), 243-58.

42. Entry of 4 October 1815, Colin Robertson's Diary, 1814-1817, Page 228, HBCA E/10/1; Miles Macdonell to the Earl of Selkirk, 14 September 1815, Selkirk Papers, MG 19-E1, Pages 1707-8, LAC; *Papers Relating to the Red River Settlement, viz: Return of an Address from the Honourable House of Commons to His Royal Highness the Prince Regent*, (London: 1819), 172.

43. Entry of 13 September 1815, Colin Robertson's Diary, 1814-1817, Page 210, HBCA E/10/1; Narrative of James Sutherland Respecting Proceedings at Qu'Appelle in Winter of 1815-16, Selkirk Papers, MG 19-E1, Pages 1946-51, LAC; Brandon House Journal, 1815-1816, HBCA B 22/a/19, Folios 36-7; *Papers Relating to the Red River Settlement*, 172-3.

44. [Gale], Notices of the Claims of the Hudson's Bay Company, 90-3; Report of the Proceedings Connected With the Disputes Between the Earl of Selkirk and the North-West Company: at the Assizes, Held at York, in Upper Canada, October, 1818, (Montreal: James Lane and Nahum Mower, 1819), 151, 203-4.

45. Quotation: Glyndwyr Williams, ed., *Hudson's Bay Miscellany, 1670-1870*, (Winnipeg: Hudson's Bay Record Society, 1975), 222; Entry No. 1180, 9 November 1804, Registers of Reverend John Bethune, St. Andrews Presbyterian Church, Williamstown, F 798, Church Record Collection, AO; *Papers Relating to the Red River Settlement, 186; Report of the Proceedings Connected With the Disputes Between the Earl of Selkirk and the North-West Company*, 295.

46. Quotation: Samuel Gale to William Coltman, 11 September 1817, Selkirk Papers, MG 19-E1, Pages 4037-8, LAC; Samuel H. Wilcocke, "Narrative of Circumstances Attending the Death of the Late Benjamin Frobisher, Esq., A Partner of the North-West Company," in Louis. R. Masson, ed., *Les Bourgeois de la Compagnie du Nord-Ouest: Récits de Voyages, Lettres et Rapports Inédits Relatifs au Nord-Ouest Canadien*, 2 vols. (New York: Antiquarian Press, 1960), 2:179-210.

47. MFB. A copy of this register is in the author's possession. Alexander V. Campbell, "The Campbells of Inverardine," in Robert B. Campbell, ed., *The Campbells and Other Glengarry-Stormont and Harrington Pioneers*, (Ottawa: Privately Printed, 1983), 434-8; Burns, "Inverarden," 177-8; "Campbell Family of Breadalbane," MG 25-G17, LAC.

48. Heather Devine, 'Ambition vs. Loyalty', 270.

49. Quotation: 'Obituary' [Mrs John Duncan Campbell], n.d., Fonds Quesnel, P4/C2, 821, (1), McDonald, (Famille), ChP; Minutes of the Court

of General Quarter Sessions Eastern District and United Counties, 12–14 Oct. 1830, RG 22-47-0-5, AO; 'List of the Names of Persons Who Are Recommended to Be Appointed Justices of the Peace for the Eastern District', 18 Nov. 1824, RG 5, A1, vol. 69, 36492, LAC; William Boss, *The Stormont, Dundas, and Glengarry Highlanders, 1783–1951* (Ottawa: Runge Press, 1952), 415.

50. Thomas G. Anderson, in *Appendix to the Sixth Volume of the Journals of the Legislative Assembly of the Province of Canada* (Montreal: G. Desbarats & T. Cary, 1847), T-144.

51. [Dumont was the first Métis to serve as lieutenant governor. See John Weinstein, *Quiet Revolution West: The Rebirth of Métis Nationalism* (Calgary: Fifth House, 2007), 135.]

52. [At the time Dumont spoke, Eastern Europeans had recently toppled communism and rid themselves of Soviet/Russian domination. See Tony Judt, *Postwar: A History of Europe Since 1945* (New York: Penguin, 2005), 559–633.]

53. [Dumont was likely referring to efforts, then ongoing, by the Manitoba Métis Federation to have the courts recognize that the Manitoba Métis had Aboriginal title in the province. These efforts eventually resulted in a decision favourable to the Métis in 2008. See Weinstein, *Quiet Revolution West*, 112, 121–2; Sam Adkins and Thomas Issac, 'Manitoba Métis Federation at al. v. A.G. of Canada et al.', 15 Jan. 2008. Available at http://www.mccarthy.ca/article_detail.aspx?id=3879 (accessed 30 May 2011).]

54. [Dumont was referring to the Oka Crisis of 1990. See Olive Patricia Dickason with David T. McNab, *Canada's First Nations: A History of Founding Peoples from Earliest Times* 4th edn (Don Mills: Oxford University Press, 2009), 319–24.]

55. In this article, the rebellions will be referred to as Métis resistance because the legitimacy of Canada's sovereignty in 1869–70 is questionable and these incidents were part of a larger pattern of anti-colonial resistance.

56. D.N. Sprague, *Canada and the Métis, 1869–1885* (Waterloo: Wilfrid Laurier University Press, 1988).

57. http://www.mmf.mb.ca/ (accessed 25 May 2011).

58. Gerhard J. Ens, *Homeland to Hinterland: The Changing Worlds of the Red River Metis in the Nineteenth Century* (Toronto: University of Toronto Press, 1996); Thomas Flanagan and Ens, 'Métis Land Grants in Manitoba: A Statistical Study', *Histoire Sociale/Social History* 27, 53 (May 1994): 65–87.

59. See, for example, A.I. Silver, 'Ontario's Alleged Fanaticism in the Riel Affair', *Canadian Historical Review* 69, 1 (1988), 21–50; Jennifer Reid, *Louis Riel and the Creation of Modern Canada: Mythic*

Discourse and the Postcolonial State (Albuquerque: University of New Mexico Press, 2008), 72–158.

60. See, for example, Lawrence J. Barkwell, Leah Dorion, and Darren R. Préfontaine, eds, *Métis Legacy* (Winnipeg: Pemmican Publications, 2001); Ute Lischke and David T. McNab, eds, *The Long Journey of a Forgotten People: Métis Identities and Family Histories* (Waterloo: Wilfrid Laurier University Press, 2007).

61. John E. Foster, 'Some questions and perspectives on the problem of métis roots', in Peterson and Brown, eds, *The New Peoples*, 77.

62. Homi K. Bhabha, *The Location of Culture* (New York: Routledge, 1994), 3–9.

63. Gayatri Chakravorty Spivak, 'Can the Subaltern Speak?' in C. Nelson and L. Grossberg, eds, *Marxism and the Interpretation of Culture* (Basingstoke: MacMillan Education, 1988), 271–313. See also pp. 69, 80, and 104.

64. See, for example, Julie F. Codell, 'The Empire Writes Back: Native Informant Discourse in the Victorian Press', in Codell, ed., *Imperial Co-Histories: National Identities and the British and Colonial Press* (Madison: Fairleigh Dickinson University Press, 2003), 188–218; Alan Lester, *Imperial Networks: Creating identities in nineteenth-century South Africa and Britain* (London: Routledge, 2001), 5–8, 189–92.

65. Sarah Carter, *Aboriginal People and Colonizers of Western Canada to 1900* (Toronto: University of Toronto Press, 1999), 62–82; Gerald Friesen, *The Canadian Prairies: A History* (Toronto: University of Toronto Press, 1984), 91–7; Sherry Farrell Racette, 'Sewing for a Living: The Commodification of Métis Women's Artistic Production', in Katie Pickles and Myra Rutherdale, eds, *Contact Zones: Aboriginal and Settler Women in Canada's Colonial Past* (Vancouver: University of British Columbia Press, 2005), 17–42.

66. Louis Riel to Ulysses S. Grant, 10–15 Dec.(?) 1875, in George F.G. Stanley, Raymond J.A. Huel, Gilles Martel, Thomas Flanagan, and Glen Campbell, eds, *The Collected Writings of Louis Riel* (Edmonton: The University of Alberta Press, 1985), 2: 6–7.

67. Michael Barnholden, trans., *Gabriel Dumont Speaks*, rev. edn (Vancouver: Talonbooks, 2009), See also Carter, *Aboriginal People and Colonizers*, 70–3, 105–11, 150–61; George F.G. Stanley, *The Birth of Western Canada: A History of the Riel Rebellions* (Toronto: University of Toronto Press, 1960).

68. Gabriel Dumont, quoted in George Woodcock, *Gabriel Dumont: The Métis Chief and his Lost World* (Edmonton: Hurtig Publishers, 1985), 240.

69. Stanley et al., eds, *Collected Writings of Louis Riel*, 1:77, 1:42–5, 3:521, 3:533, 3:543, 3:549–50.

70. 'Affairs at Red River', *The Globe*, 12 Feb. 1870, 2; '"President" Riel's Latest', 26 Feb. 1870, 2.

71. 'Who is Responsible?' *The Globe*, 4 Apr. 1870, 2; 'The Expedition to Red River', *The Globe*, 4 Apr. 1870, 2; 'The Red River Affair', (London) *Times*, 22 Apr. 1870, 5; *The Anglo-American Times*, 23 Apr. 1870, 10.

72. 'The Nor'-West Trouble', *The Globe*, 28 Apr. 1870, 2.

73. 'The Week', *The Anglo-American Times*, 2 Apr. 1870, 9; (London) *Times*, 6 May 1870, 9; 'Canadian Affairs', *The Anglo-American Times*, 7 May 1870, 15.

74. 'Riel Released', *Manitoba Free Press*, 17 Nov. 1885, 4.

75. 'Riel', *Toronto Daily Mail*, 16 Mar. 1885, 4.

76. *Toronto Daily Mail*, 13 Apr. 1885, quoted in Maggie Siggins, *Riel: A Revolutionary Life* (Toronto: Harper Collins, 1994), 368.

77. 'The Riel Case', *The Globe*, 14 Aug. 1885, 4; 'The Government and the Rebellion', *Manitoba Free Press*, 27 Mar. 1885, 2; 'The Rebellion', *Toronto Daily Mail*, 29 May 1885, 2.

78. 'The Rebellion', *Toronto Daily Mail*, 29 May 1885, 4; 'Riel's Diary', *The Globe*, 15 July 1885, 5; 'Riel and Dewdney', *Manitoba Free Press*, 17 Apr. 1885, 2.

79. 'The Week', *The Anglo-American Times*, 24 Apr. 1885, 13. See also (London) *Times*, 31 Mar. 1885, 9; *Northern Whig*, 22 Apr. 1885, 4; 'The Rebellion in Canada', (London) *Times*, 16 May 1885, 7.

80. *Freeman's Journal*, 14 May 1885, 5; 'The Uprising in Northwest Canada', *The Anglo-American Times*, 17 Apr. 1885, 8–9; 'Canada', *Guardian*, 22 Apr. 1885, 580; 'Riel and the Rebels', *Northern Whig*, 29 May 1885, 8.

81. (London) *Times*, 31 Mar. 1885, 9.

82. 'The Insurrection in Manitoba', *Brisbane Courier*, 16 May 1885, 1.

83. Writing to Macdonald from his jail cell, Riel repeatedly compared the Métis' position in Canada to that of the Irish in the United Kingdom: Louis Riel to John A. Macdonald, 16 July 1885, in H. Bowsfield, ed., *Louis Riel: Rebel of the Western Frontier or Victim of Politics and Prejudice?* (Toronto: The Copp Clark Publishing Co., 1969), 144–5.

84. 'The Canadian Disturbance', *Brisbane Courier*, 23 May 1885, 1; (London) *Times*, 3 Apr. 1885, 7; *Northern Whig*, 8 May 1885, 5.

85. Similar transatlantic networks have been explored in Alan Lester, 'British Settler Discourse and the Circuits of Empire', *History Workshop Journal* 54 (2002), 24–48.

86. 'The Red River Rebellion', *The New York Times*, 16 Jan. 1870, 5. See also *The New York Times*, 28 Dec. 1869, 1; *The New York Times*, 6 Feb. 1870, 1; 'The Red River Council in Session', *New York Tribune*, 8 Feb. 1870, 1.

87. 'A Winnipeg Policy', *New York Tribune*, 23 Apr. 1870, 6.

88. 'Louis Riel', *The New York Times*, 11 May 1874, 2.

89. 'Some Hit and Miss Chat', *The New York Times*, 5 Apr. 1885, 3; 'The Canadian Revolt', *New York Tribune*, 3 Apr. 1885, 4.

90. *The New York Times*, 19 Oct. 1884, 2.

91. 'Some Hit and Miss Chat'.

92. 'Negotiating with Riel', *New York Tribune*, 11 Apr. 1885, 4.

93. 'The Conviction and Sentence of Riel', *New York Tribune*, 4 Aug. 1885, 4; 'The Respite of Riel', *New York Tribune*, 23 Oct. 1885, 4; 'The Hanging of Riel', *New York Tribune*, 17 Nov. 1885, 4.

94. 'Bulletin du jour', *Le Nouveau Monde*, 19 Nov. 1869, 1.

95. 'Editorial', *Le Nouveau Monde*, 15 Nov. 1869, 1.

96. Un Métis, 'Le Piano dans le Nord-Ouest', *Le Courrier de St.-Hyacinthe*, 5 July 1870, 2.

97. 'Lettre de la Rivière-Rouge', *Le Courrier de St. Hyacinthe*, 1 Mar. 1870, 2.

98. 'La question du Nord-Ouest', *Le Nouveau Monde*, 30 Dec. 1869, 1. For the piece detailing the Métis' grievances in France, see 'Lettres des États-Unis', *Le Temps*, 1 Apr. 1870, 2.

99. Joseph Édouard Cauchon, 'Le Nord-Ouest: Détails intéressants', *Le Pionnier de Sherbrooke*, 6 May 1870, 1.

100. 'Lettres des États-Unis'.

101. 'La révolte au Canada', *Le Cri du peuple*, 11 May 1885, 2.

102. 'L'Insurrection du Nord-Ouest', *Le Courrier de St. Hyacinthe*, 9 May 1885, 1. See also Sarah Carter, *Capturing Women: The Manipulation of Cultural Imagery in Canada's Prairie West* (Montreal: McGill-Queen's University Press, 1997), 48–86.

103. 'Trouble au Nord-Ouest', *La Minerve*, 24 Mar. 1885, 3; 'Servilisme', *La Patrie*, 27 Apr. 1885, 1.

104. 'La révolte du Nord-Ouest', *La Patrie*, 9 Apr. 1885, 1; 'L'inhumation de Louis Riel', *Le Pionnier de Sherbrooke*, 24 Dec. 1885, 2; Edmond Johanet, 'Riel: Le condamné à mort', *Le Figaro*, 13 Aug. 1885, 1.

105. Edward Said, *Orientalism* (New York: Vintage Books, 1979).

106. See, for example, 'Les Métis', *La Minerve*, 7 Apr. 1885, 2; L. de L., 'Mort de Riel', *Le Figaro*, 2 Dec. 1885, 3.

107. 'Une révolte au Nord-Ouest', *Paris-Canada*, 1 Apr. 1885, 1–2.

108. 'La fin de l'insurrection', *Paris-Canada*, 27 May 1885, 1.

109. 'Trouble au Nord-Ouest', *La Minerve*, 24 Mar. 1885, 3.

110. 'Bulletin de l'étranger', *Le Figaro*, 21 Apr. 1885, 2; L. de L., 'Mort de Riel'.

111. Mgr Alexandre Taché, 'La Situation', *Le Manitoba*, 10 Dec. 1885, 2.

112. Henri Rochefort, 'Riel et ses assassins', *L'Intransigeant*, 19 Nov. 1885, 1.

113. 'L'Exécution de Louis Riel', *Le Cri du peuple*, 19 Nov. 1885, 2; 'L'exécution de Riel jugée en Europe', *Le Pionnier de Sherbrooke*, 10 Dec. 1885, 2; P.-Ernest Tremblay, 'Chronique: Riel', *La Patrie*, 21 Nov. 1885, 1.

114. Charles Longuet, 'L'exécution de Riel', *La Justice*, 19 Nov. 1885, 1.

115. See, for example, Léon Millot, 'Chronique: Louis Riel', *La Justice*, 25 Oct. 1885, 1.

116. Edmond Johanet, 'Riel: Le condamné à mort', *Le Figaro*, 13 Aug. 1885, 1.

117. 'Débats sur le Nord-Ouest', *Le Pionnier de Sherbrooke*, 13 May 1870, 2; Rochefort, 'Riel et ses assassins'.

118. For a discussion of this continued activity, see John Weinstein, *Quiet Revolution West: The Rebirth of Métis Nationalism* (Calgary: Fifth House, 2007), 24–5.

119. Bowsfield, ed., *Louis Riel*, 146–51.

120. *House of Commons Debates*, 6 July 1885, 3113.

121. Louis Riel, statement to the court, in Bowsfield, ed., *Louis Riel*, 156.

CHAPTER SEVEN: FEDERAL INDIAN POLICY

1. Duncan Campbell Scott in E. Brian Titley, *A Narrow Vision: Duncan Campbell Scott and the Administration of Indian Policy in Canada* (Vancouver: UBC Press, 1986), 50.

2. For further information, see Maureen Lux, *Medicine that Walks: Disease, Medicine, and the Canadian Plains Native People, 1880–1940* (Toronto: University of Toronto Press, 2001) and Mary-Ellen Kelm, *Colonizing Bodies: Aboriginal Health and Healing in British Columbia, 1900–1950* (Vancouver: UBC Press, 1999).

3. J.R. Miller, *Skyscrapers Hide the Heavens: A History of Indian-White Relations in Canada*, 3rd edn (Toronto: University of Toronto Press, 2000), 352.

4. When I was with the Department of Indian Affairs at the time of the Penner Report, a few of my superiors were heard to say, 'Well, it's time to turn out the lights!'

5. John L. Tobias, 'Protection, Civilization, Assimilation: An Outline History of Canada's Indian Policy', in Ian A.L. Getty and Antoine S. Lussier, eds, *As Long As The Sun Shines And Water Flows: A Reader in Canadian Native Studies* (Vancouver: UBC Press, 1983), 40–1.

6. E. Brian Titley, *The Indian Commissioners: Agents of the State and Indian Policy in Canada's Prairie West,* *1873–1932* (Edmonton: University of Alberta Press, 2009), 3.

7. David T. McNab, 'Herman Merivale and Colonial Office Indian Policy in the Mid-Nineteenth Century', in Getty and Lussier, eds, *As Long As The Sun Shines*, 85–7.

8. See, for example, John S. Milloy, 'The Early Indian Acts: Developmental Strategy and Constitutional Change,' in Getty and Lussier, eds, *As Long As The Sun Shines*, 56, 59.

9. McNab, 'Herman Merivale', 87.

10. Milloy, 'The Early Indian Acts', 58. Enfranchisement generally refers to full citizenship together with the right to vote, a right which, at that time, was generally restricted to men of property.

11. C.B. Macpherson, *The Political Theory of Possessive Individualism: Hobbes to Locke* (Oxford: Oxford University Press, 1964), 263–71.

12. Tobias, 'Protection, Civilization, Assimilation', 42.

13. Milloy, 'The Early Indian Acts', 62–3.

14. Titley, *The Indian Commissioners*, xi, 4, 9; Hugh Shewell, *'Enough to Keep Them Alive': Indian Welfare in Canada, 1873–1965* (Toronto: University of Toronto Press, 2004), 13–16.

15. E. Brian Titley, *A Narrow Vision: Duncan Campbell Scott and the Administration of Indian Affairs in Canada* (Vancouver: UBC Press, 1986), 41.

16. Library Archives Canada (LAC), RG-10, Red Series, Vol. 3086, File 279, 222-1A, General Instructions to Indian Agents in Canada, issued by Duncan Campbell Scott, Ottawa, 25 Oct. 1913.

17. Ibid., 97.

18. Duncan Campbell Scott, cited in E. Brian Titley, *A Narrow Vision*, 34.

19. Shewell, *'Enough to Keep Them Alive'*, 94, 109.

20. Thomas Deasy, 'Civilizing Influences', in LAC, RG-10, Black Series, Vol. 4093, File 570,970, c. Dec. 1920.

21. One exception to this was the Home Industry Program initiated in 1926. It promoted the making and selling of Indian handicrafts for tourists, especially in more northern areas. See Shewell, *'Enough to Keep Them Alive'*, 125.

22. See, for example, Robin Jarvis Brownlie, *A Fatherly Eye: Indian Agents, Government Power, and Aboriginal Resistance in Ontario, 1918–1939* (Toronto: Oxford University Press, 2003), 106.

23. Titley, *A Narrow Vision*, 67–73.

24. Ibid., 73.

25. Hugh Shewell, 'An Examination of Aboriginal-State Relations in Canada and Their Possible Implications for Aboriginal Participation in the Canadian Armed Forces'. Paper commissioned by the Royal Military College, Kingston, ON, and presented to the Inter-

University Seminar on Armed Forces and Society, Ottawa, Oct. 2006, 7–9.

26. Shewell, 'Enough to Keep Them Alive', 157.

27. J.R. Miller, Reflections on Native-Newcomer Relations: Selected Essays (Toronto: University of Toronto Press, 2004), 183–4.

28. Titley, A Narrow Vision, 90–1, 93.

29. Shewell, 'Enough to Keep Them Alive', 158.

30. Ibid., 114–15.

31. Hugh Shewell, 'Jules Sioui and Indian Political Radicalism in Canada, 1943–1944', Journal of Canadian Studies 34, 3 (1999): 227.

32. LAC, RG-10, Red Series, Vol. 3212, File 527,787-4, Transcript of Speech Delivered by the Minister, T.A. Crerar, to the Convention of Indians, Ottawa, 7 June 1944.

33. John F. Leslie, 'Assimilation, Integration or Termination? The Development of Canadian Indian Policy, 1943–1963', (PhD dissertation, Carleton University, 1999), 177.

34. Ibid., 102.

35. Ibid., 174, 179, 181.

36. Tobias, 'Protection, Civilization, Assimilation', 52.

37. Shewell, 'Enough To Keep Them Alive', 238, 262–3.

38. Leslie, 'Assimilation, Integration or Termination?', 286–300.

39. Sally M. Weaver, Making Canadian Indian Policy: The Hidden Agenda 1968–1970 (Toronto: University of Toronto Press, 1981), 46. Col. Hubert M. Jones was director of Indian Affairs from 1953 to 1963.

40. Leslie, 'Assimilation, Integration or Termination?', 387–8.

41. John F. Leslie, 'The Policy Agenda of Native Peoples from World War II to the 1969 White Paper', in Jerry P. White, Paul Maxim, and Dan Beavon, eds, Aboriginal Policy Research: Setting the Agenda for Change, Vol. 1 (Toronto: Thompson Educational Publishing, 2004), 18–19.

42. Ibid., 21.

43. Canada, Department of Citizenship and Immigration, Indian Affairs Branch, Annual Report, 1959-1960 (Ottawa: The Queen's Printer, 1960), 46.

44. LAC, RG-10, CR Series, Vol. 8194, File 1/29-6, Part 3, Memorandum to Cabinet, 'Community Development', Indian Affairs Branch, item 5, Feb. 1964.

45. Hugh Shewell, 'Rassembler nos forces, ou recourir encore à l'aide sociale? La situation socio-économique des premières nations avant et après la Commission royale', Recherches amérindiennes au Québec 37, 1 (2007): 44–6.

46. Ibid.

47. Miller, Skyscrapers Hide the Heavens, 329.

48. Canada, Department of Indian Affairs and Northern Development, Statement of the Government of Canada on Indian Policy (Ottawa: Indian Affairs, 1969).

49. Weaver, Making Canadian Indian Policy, 187.

50. James S. Frideres and René R. Gadacz, Aboriginal Peoples in Canada, 8th edn (Toronto: Pearson/ Prentice Hall, 2008), 368–9.

51. Shewell, 'Rassembler nos forces', 46–7.

52. Frideres and Gadacz, Aboriginal Peoples in Canada, 369.

53. Shewell, 'Enough To Keep Them Alive', 310.

54. Miller, Skyscrapers Hide the Heavens, 343.

55. Ibid., 341.

56. Ibid., 350–1.

57. Frideres and Gadacz, Aboriginal Peoples in Canada, 270–1.

58. Ibid., 271.

59. Sally M. Weaver, 'A Commentary on the Penner Report', in Paul Tennant, Sally M. Weaver, Roger Gibbins and J. Rick Ponting, 'The Report of the House of Commons Special Committee on Indian Self-Government: Three Comments', Canadian Public Policy – Analyse de Politiques 10, 2 (1984): 217–18.

60. Frideres and Gadacz, Aboriginal Peoples in Canada, 272–3.

61. Ibid., 280–1.

62. Although used throughout this article in reference to Aboriginal health practices, medicine is a Western biomedical term. The traditional meaning of the word does not capture the range of therapeutic practices and understandings used by Aboriginal peoples.

63. Until 1945, the piecemeal but growing services to Aboriginal peoples operated as a marriage of church and state. Aboriginal populations in the southern provinces were served primarily by federal Indian hospitals. Northern locations, like the Northwest Territories, were served entirely by mission hospitals, which were partially, although inconsistently, funded through the federal department of Indian Affairs. In 1945, Indian Health Services (IHS) consolidated and reorganized health services for Canada's Indigenous communities. Creation of the IHS reflected attempts by the federal government to prioritize public health care services for all Canadians—including Indian people. Under this new bureaucratic regime, Indian Affairs was no longer directly responsible for Indian health care. See James B. Waldram, D. Ann Herring, and T. Kue Young, Aboriginal Health in Canada: Historical, Cultural and Epidemiological Perspectives (Toronto: University of Toronto Press, 1995); T. Kue Young, Health Care and Cultural Change: The Indian Experience in the Central Subarctic (Toronto: University of Toronto Press, 1988);

G. Graham-Cumming, 'Health of the Original Canadians, 1867–1967', *Medical Services Journal of Canada*, 23, 2 (1967): 115–66.

64. Few researchers have taken on the challenge of investigating Aboriginal epistemologies in relation to definitions of 'health' and engagement with formal Western-style health care systems; however, in the field of medical anthropology Naomi Adelson's *'Being Alive Well': Health and the Politics of Cree Well-Being* (Toronto: University of Toronto Press, 2000) is an excellent example, as is Young's *Health Care and Cultural Change*. Other relevant histories include Dara Culhane Speck, *An Error in Judgment* (Vancouver: Talonbooks, 1987), and Lux, *Medicine That Walks*. Doctoral dissertations include Sally M. Weaver, 'Medicine and Politics among the Grand River Iroquois', University of Toronto, 1967; and Kristin Burnett, 'The Healing Work and Nursing Care of Aboriginal Women, Female Medical Missionaries, Nursing Sisters, Public Health Nurses and Female Attendants in Southern Alberta First Nations Communities, 1880–1930', York University, 2006.

65. Kelm, *Colonizing Bodies*, 127–9.

66. Kathryn McPherson, 'Nursing and Colonization: The Work of Indian Health Service Nurses in Manitoba, 1945–1970', in Georgina Feldberg, Molly Ladd-Taylor, Alison Li, and Kathryn McPherson, eds, *Women, Health, and Nation: Canada and the United States Since 1945* (Montreal: McGill-Queen's University Press, 2003), 223–46, 232–4.

67. Kelm, *Colonizing Bodies*, 153; McPherson, 'Nursing and Colonization', 234.

68. McPherson, 'Nursing and Colonization', 235.

69. Kelm, *Colonizing Bodies*, 164.

70. Ibid., 122.

71. Canada, Indian Health Services and Indian Affairs Branch, *Circular Letter to All Superintendents, Indian Agency, Regional Supervisors, and the Indian Commissioner for BC, and to all Medical Officers, Indian Health Services*. File L.3 (Ottawa: Claims and Historical Research Centre, 1953).

72. Canada, House of Commons, Sessional Papers, Department of National Health and Welfare, *Annual Report, Indian Health Services*, 1949–50, 80.

73. Canada, House of Commons, Sessional Papers, Department of National Health and Welfare, *Annual Report, Indian Health Services*, 1947–8, 41.

74. Graham-Cumming, 'Health of the Original Canadians', 123. He points out how governmental services for Indian health grew 'under pressure of growing need and public outcry'.

75. Provincial Archives of Alberta, Accession No. 96.2/7, file 1, 'Indian Health Services', speech, 1949, 4.

76. This discussion of *snuwuyulth* is based on information shared with me by Florence James (Penelekut First Nation), Ray Peter (Cowichan Tribes), Delores Louie (Chemainus First Nation) and Ellen White (Snuneymuxw First Nation) between 1999 and 2009 as part of my work in the First Nations Studies Department, Vancouver Island University. Interestingly, descriptions of such teachings are missing from the standard ethnographies dealing with Coast Salish cultures, including Homer G. Barnett, *The Coast Salish of British Columbia* (Eugene, OR: University of Oregon, 1955); Wayne Suttles, *Coast Salish Essays* (Vancouver: Talonbooks, 1987).

77. Interview with Ellen White, Nanaimo, BC, 25 Oct. 2007.

78. Interview with Delores Louie, Cedar, BC, 28 May 2008.

79. Interview with Violet Charlie, Duncan, BC, 14 May 2008.

80. Information derived from http://www.wellsphere.com/healthy-eating-article/oolichan-grease-and-my-big-fat-diet/548833, accessed 16 May 2009.

81. Information derived from http://www.cbc.ca/thelens/bigfatdiet/grease.html, accessed 16 May 2009, and http://www.livinglandscapes.bc.ca/northwest/oolichan_history/preserving.htm, accessed 16 May 2009.

82. Kelm also mentions the importation of grease into the Indian hospital setting in her work on Indian Health Services before 1950. See Kelm, *Colonizing Bodies*, 163–4.

83. Wolfgang G. Jilek, *Salish Indian Mental Health and Culture Change* (Toronto: Holt, Rinehart and Winston of Canada, 1974), 105.

84. McPherson, 'Nursing and Colonization', 241.

CHAPTER EIGHT: SURVIVANCE AND THE INDIAN ACT

1. William Roseberry as quoted in Jeffrey L. Gould, *To Die in This Way: Nicaraguan Indians and the Myth of Mestizaje, 1880–1965* (Durham and London: Duke University Press, 1998), 12.

2. Wendy Cornet, *Executive Summary: First Nation Identities and Individual Equality Rights: A Discussion of Citizenship, Band Membership, and Indian Status* (Prepared for the National Aboriginal Women's Organization, 26 Jan. 2003).

3. Bonita Lawrence, 'Rewriting Histories of the Land: Colonization and Indigenous Resistance in Eastern Canada', in Sherene Razack, ed., *Race, Space and the Law: Unmapping a White Settler Society* (Toronto: Between the Lines, 2002), 27–9, 36–41.

4. Kathleen Jamieson, *Indian Women and the Law in Canada: Citizens Minus* (Ottawa: Canadian Advisory

Council on the Status of Women and Indian Rights for Indian Women, 1978), 29–30.

5. Ibid., 25.

6. Theda Perdue, 'Race and Culture: Writing the Ethnohistory of the South', *Ethnohistory* 51, 4 (Fall 2004): 701–02; Eva Marie Garroutte, *Real Indians: Identity and the Survival of Native America* (Berkeley: University of California Press, 2003), 118–19.

7. Brad Milne, 'The Historiography of Métis Land Dispersal, 1870–1890', *Manitoba History* No. 30 (Autumn 1995).

8. Wayne E. Daugherty, 'Treaties and Historical Research Centre, Self-Government', Indian and Northern Affairs Canada, 1986. Available at http://www.ainc-inac.gc.ca/al/hts/tgu/pubs/t3/tre3-eng.asp (accessed 27 Mar. 2010).

9. Ibid.

10. As quoted in James Waldram, 'The "Other Side": Ethnostatus Distinctions in Western Subarctic Native Communities', in Laurie Barron and James B. Waldram, eds, *1885 and After: Native Society in Transition* (Regina: University of Regina, 1986), 281.

11. Larry Gilbert, *Entitlement to Indian Status and Membership Codes in Canada* (Scarborough: Thompson Canada, 1996), 15.

12. The Caldwell band in Ontario is an example of the former and the MoCreebec Council of the Cree Nation in Quebec and Ontario the latter. See D. Smoke, 'Caldwell War Underway', *Turtle Island Native Network News* (April 2001). Available at http://www.turtleisland.org/news/news-smokecaldwell.htm (accessed 7 Mar. 2010); R. Kapashesit, 'Misiwa Chiwaacheyemitinwaa', *MoCreebec Council of the Cree Nation 25th Anniversary Commemorative Report* (MoCreebec Council of the Cree Nation: 2004).

13. For example, the Teme-Augama Anishnabai in central Ontario were left out of the Robinson Huron Treaty in 1850, while the Lubicon Cree of northern Alberta were not included in Treaty Eight in 1899. Because of this, both groups were administratively eliminated as recognized groups, despite the fact that both had asserted their rights over their traditional territories for generations and at times had been acknowledged to have those rights by representatives of the federal governments. For the Teme-Augama Anishnabai, see D. McNab, 'Who Is on Trial? Teme-Augama Anishnabai Land Rights and George Ironside, Junior: Re-Considering Oral Tradition', *The Canadian Journal of Native Studies* 18, 1 (1998): 117–33; and G. Potts, 'Teme-Augama Anishnabai: Last-Ditch Defence of a Priceless Homeland', in Boyce Richardson, ed. *Drumbeat: Anger and*

Renewal in Indian Country (Toronto: Summerhill Press and the Assembly of First Nations), 201–28. For the Lubicon Cree, see Richardson, 'Wrestling with the Canadian Legal System: A Decade of Lubicon Frustration', in *Drumbeat: Anger and Renewal in Indian Country*, 229–64; and Bruce Miller, *Invisible Indigenes: The Politics of Nonrecognition* (Lincoln and London: University of Nebraska, 2003), 146–52.

14. B. Lovelace, 'An Algonquin History', Available at http://www.aafna.ca/history.html (accessed 10 Mar. 2010); Marijike E. Huitema, '"Land of Which the Savages Stood in No Particular Need": Dispossessing the Algonquins of South-Eastern Ontario of Their Lands, 1760–1930' (MA thesis, Department of Geography, Queen's University, 2000), 170, 174–8; Rose Cunha, interview with author, Sept. 1998.

15. Art Cota III, interview with author, 4 Nov. 2007.

16. Jamieson, *Indian Women*, 44.

17. Ibid., 30.

18. Ibid., 72. However, as Jamieson's work shows, it is the personal and cultural losses of losing status that Indian women have most frequently spoken about. Some of the costs have included being unable to participate with family and relatives in the life of their former communities, being rejected by their communities, being culturally different and often socially rejected within white society, being unable to access cultural programs for their children, and, finally, not even being able to be buried with other family members on the reserve.

19. Bonita Lawrence, *'Real' Indians and Others: Mixed-Blood Urban Native People and Indigenous Nationhood* (Vancouver: UBC Press, 2004), 143–51.

20. See, for example, Lawrence, *'Real' Indians*.

21. Stewart Clatsworthy, 'Roundtable on Citizenship and Membership Issues', *Summary of the 2nd Institute on Governance Roundtable Series* (Ottawa, Oct. 2004).

22. For example, Maria Campbell, author of the definitive work addressing Métis identity, *Halfbreed*, in many respects focuses on Cree cultural heritage rather than the notion of building a 'national' identity as 'Métis'. Meanwhile, one of the crucial figures in the Métis revival of the 1970s, Duke Redbird (whose Master's thesis, 'We Are Métis', is an impassioned history of the Métis), now focuses primarily on his Saugeen Ojibway heritage. And Lee Maracle, who in the 1970s referred primarily to her mother's Métis heritage, now refers primarily to her Sto'lo heritage.

23. 'Métis Nation of Ontario Harvesting News'. Available at http://www.mno.ca/harvesting/powley_case/news.html (accessed 6 Mar. 2010).

24. Paul Barnsley, 'New National Métis Organization Forming', *Windspeaker* (Feb. 2003), 15.

25. Miller, *Invisible Indigenes*, 20.

26. Ibid., 24.

27. Kirby Whiteduck, 'Pikwakanagan's Presentation to the Assembly of First Nations Renewal Commission', 26 Feb. 2004. Available at http://www.afn.ca/afnrenewal/ottawa.pdf (accessed 10 Mar. 2010).

28. Sharon McIvor regained her Indian status in 1985. McIvor's children also have status even though their father is a 'non-Indian'. Her son Charles married a non-Indian woman. As a result of what has been dubbed the 'second generation cut-off', Charles's children do not have Indian status. Conversely, the children of Charles's sister have status because their father is an Indian. McIvor claims that the denial of status to Charles's children is discriminatory on the basis of gender. The problem arises from the 1985 amendments, which reinstated women who lost their status as a result of marrying non-Indian men (Indian men who married non-Indians kept their status and their wives gained status as well). The second generation cut-off therefore operates differently for those who trace their Indian heritage maternally versus those who trace it through their paternal lineage. See John Rowenski, 'Indian Status: Changing the Status Quo', Media K-Net, 2009. Available at http://media.knet.ca/node/7330 (accessed 29 Mar. 2010).

29. Glen Coulthard, 'Beyond Recognition: Indigenous Self-Determination as Prefigurative Practice', in Leanne Simpson, ed., *Lighting the Eighth Fire: The Liberation, Resurgence, and Protection of Indigenous Nations* (Winnipeg: Arbeiter Ring Publishing, 2008), 199.

30. Ibid., 194.

31. Taiaiake Alfred, *Wasase: Indigenous Pathways of Action and Freedom* (Peterborough: Broadview Press, 2005), 44.

32. Bonita Lawrence, 'Gender, Race, and the Regulation of Native Identity in Canada and the United States', *Hypatia: A Journal of Feminist Philosophy* 18, 2 (2003): 25.

33. E. Brian Titley, *A Narrow Vision: Duncan Campbell Scott and the Administration of Indian Affairs in Canada* (Vancouver: UBC Press, 1988).

34. J.R. Wunder, *Native Americans: Interdisciplinary Perspectives* (New York: Garland Publishing, 2003), 24.

35. Bonita Lawrence, *'Real' Indians*, 51.

36. Ibid., 50.

37. Enfranchisement was a legal process in which Status Indians lost their status under the Indian Act. The term refers to both voluntary and involuntary enfranchisement, which primarily affected women with Indian status who married non-status men. Enfranchisement was considered by the government as an opportunity to assimilate into Canadian society.

38. Native Women's Association of Canada (NWAC), *Aboriginal Women and the Implementation of Bill C-31* (Ottawa: Native Women's Association of Canada, 1991), 8.

39. Ibid., 8.

40. Lawrence, 'Gender, Race, and the Regulation of Native Identity', 13.

41. Joan Holmes, *Background Paper - Bill C-31, Equality or Disparity? - The Effects of the New Indian Act on Native Women* (Ottawa: Canadian Advisory Council on the Status of Women, 1987), 6.

42. Kathleen Jamieson, *Indian Women*, 1.

43. NWAC, *Aboriginal Women and the Implementation of Bill C-31*, 11.

44. Indian and Northern Affairs Canada (INAC), 'Basic Departmental Data', INAC (Mar. 2004). Available at http://www.ainc-inac.gc.ca/ai/rs/pubs/sts/bdd/bdd-eng.asp (accessed 1 Nov. 2010).

45. James Frideres and René R. Gadacz, *Aboriginal Peoples in Canada* (Toronto: Pearson Prentice Hall, 2008), 28.

46. Ibid., 30.

47. Holmes, *Background Paper*, 37.

48. Canadian Human Rights Act, 'Expanding Knowledge National Aboriginal Initiative', Canadian Human Rights Commission, 8 Sept. 2010. Available at http://www.chrc-ccdp.ca/nai_ina/default-eng.aspx.

49. Joanne Fiske and Evelyn George, *Seeking Alternatives to Bill C-31: From Cultural Trauma to Cultural Revitalization through Customary Law* (Ottawa: Status of Women Canada, 2006), v.

50. Stewart Clatworthy, *Factors Contributing to Unstated Paternity* (Ottawa: INAC Strategic Research and Analysis Directorate, 2003), 2.

51. Stewart Clatworthy, *Indian Registration, Membership and Population Change in First Nations Communities* (Ottawa: Indian and Northern Affairs, 2005), 17.

52. Holmes, *Background Paper*, 37.

53. NWAC, *Aboriginal Women and the Implementation of Bill C-31*, 5.

54. Frideres and Gadacz, *Aboriginal Peoples in Canada*, 30.

55. Joanne Fiske, 'Political Status of Native Indian Women: Contradictory Implications of Canadian State Policy', *American Indian Culture and Research Journal* 19, 2 (1995): 2.

56. Wolfgang Jilek, 'Culture and Psychopathology Revisited', *Culture* 3,1 (1983), 51.

57. Patricia Barrios and Marcia Egan, 'Living in a

Bicultural World and Finding the Way Home', *Affilia* 17, 2 (2002): 212.

58. Wenona Victor, *Indigenous Justice: Clearing Space and Place for Indigenous Epistemologies* (Vancouver: National Centre for First Nations Governance, 2007), 13.

59. Ibid., 13.

60. Sandy Grande, *Red Pedagogy: Native American Social and Political Thought* (Maryland: Rowman and Littlefield Publishers, 2004), 92.

61. INAC, *Registered Indian Population Projections for Canada and Regions from 2000–2021* (Ottawa: INAC, 2001), 4.

62. Ibid., 42.

63. Stewart Clatworthy, *First Nations Membership and Registered Indian Status: Southern Chiefs Organization, Manitoba* (Ottawa: Indian and Northern Affairs Canada, Research and Analysis Directorate, 2001), 39.

64. John Giokas and Robert K. Groves, *Who Are Canada's Aboriginal Peoples?: Recognition, Definition and Jurisdiction*, Paul Chartrand, ed. (Saskatoon: Purich Publishing, 2002), 68.

65. Ibid., 73.

66. NWAC. *Bill C-31 Amendment*, 14.

67. Holmes, *Background Paper*, 37.

68. Statistics Canada, *Women in Canada: Gender Based Report* (Ottawa: Statistics Canada, 2006), 185.

69. Garroutte, *Real Indians*.

70. Ibid., 99.

71. Holmes, *Background Paper*, 35.

72. Ibid., 38.

73. Audra Simpson, 'To the Reserve and Back Again: Kahnawake Mohawk Narratives of Self, Home and Nation' (PhD dissertation, McGill University, 2003), 240.

74. Ibid., 249.

75. Evelyn J. Peters and David Newhouse, *Not Strangers in These Parts: Urban Aboriginal Peoples* (Ottawa: Policy Research Initiative, 2003), 9.

76. INAC, 'Changes to the Indian Act Affecting Registration and Band Membership McIvor v Canada', Indian Affairs and Northern Development, 11 Mar. 2010. Available at www.ainc-inac.gc.ca/br/is/mci-eng.pdf.

77. Sharon McIvor, 'Sharon McIvor's Response to the August 2009 Proposal of Indian and Northern Affairs Canada', 6 Oct. 2009. Available at www.afn.ca/misc/SM-Proposal.pdf.

CHAPTER NINE: RESIDENTIAL SCHOOLS

1. Canadian Tuberculosis Association, Annual Reports, 1906, 26–7, LAC, Records of the Canadian Tuberculosis Association, vol. 23.

2. John S. Milloy, *A National Crime: The Canadian Government and the Residential School System, 1879 to 1986* (Winnipeg: University of Manitoba Press, 1999), v.

3. Colleen Seymour, Secwepemc friend and former student of the Native Indian Teacher Education Program, ends all her correspondence with these words.

4. The term *Indian* is used for individuals designated Indian under the Canadian Indian Act. This Act remains in force as this chapter is being written. Reference to Inuit, Métis, and First Nation refer to groups now recognized either by the Constitution of Canada and/or by formal organizations within Canada. Use of the word *Native* indicates this is in original text. In some parts of Canada, the word *Aboriginal* is considered to be inclusive of all individuals with ancestry related to the original peoples of Canada. *Indigenous* is another term for the original peoples of a particular land (i.e. those who can trace ancestry to the time before written records often through oral histories); it is often used in international contexts.

5. George Manuel and Michael Posluns, *The Fourth World: An Indian Reality* (New York: The Free Press, 1974), 63.

6. Basil H. Johnston, *Indian School Days* (Toronto: Key Porter Books, 1988), 6.

7. Isabelle Knockwood, *Out of the Depths: The Experiences of Mi'kmaw Children at the Indian Residential School at Shubenacadie, Nova Scotia* (Lockeport, NS: Roseway Publishing, 1992), 7.

8. John Milloy, *A National Crime*, xviii.

9. Emma Anderson, 'Between Conversion and Apostasy: The Religious Journey of Pierre-Anthoine Pastedechouan', *Anthropologica* 49, 1 (2007): 17–34.

10. See Agnes Grant, *No End of Grief: Indian Residential Schools in Canada* (Winnipeg: Pemmican Publications, 1996), 59.

11. Robin Fisher, *Contact and Conflict* (Vancouver: UBC Press, 1977), 144–5.

12. Alison L. Prentice and Susan E. Houston, *Family, School and Society in Nineteenth-Century Canada* (Toronto: Oxford University Press, 1975), 218.

13. Ibid., 220.

14. Nicholas F. Davin, *Report on Industrial Schools for Indians and Halfbreeds* (Ottawa: 14 Mar. 1879). PABC, RG 10, Vol. 6001, File 1-1-1, Pt.1.

15. Ibid., 2.

16. See also Noel Dyck, *Differing Visions: Administering Indian Residential Schooling in Prince Albert, 1867–1995* (Halifax: Fernwood, 1997), 96. 'Underlying denominational and government educational programs for Indians in Saskatchewan and elsewhere was the firm belief that Aboriginal

cultures and modes of social organization were "primitive" and "inferior" to those of Euro-Canadians. This racist belief had, of course, provided the justification for appropriating Aboriginal lands across Canada.'

17. Rita Flammand recounts her Métis mother's time in residential school, pointing out that she was there to fill the quota 'while they were in the process of rounding up the Treaty Indian children from the north.' Greg Younging, Jonathan Dewar, and Mike DeGagné, eds, *Response, Responsibility, and Renewal: Canada's Truth and Reconciliation Journey* (Ottawa: Aboriginal Healing Foundation, 2009), 74.

18. Miller, in Celia Haig-Brown, *Resistance and Renewal: Surviving the Kamloops Indian Residential School* (Vancouver: Tillicum Library, 1988), 30.

19. See Aboriginal Healing Foundation, *Directory of Residential Schools in Canada* (Ottawa: Aboriginal Healing Foundation, 2003).

20. People from locations as diverse as Nigeria and Wales speak of the resonances of their experiences in colonially-controlled boarding schools with those of students in Canada. See also Randy Fred's reference to the Coorgs, Indigenous people of India. Foreword to Haig-Brown, *Resistance and Renewal*, 15.

21. Text accessed from http://www.shannonthunderbird.com/residential_schools.htm, 9 Aug. 2010.

22. Rosa Bell, 'Journeys', in Linda Jaine, ed., *Residential Schools: The Stolen Years* (Saskatoon: University of Saskatchewan Extension Press, 1993), 8–9.

23. Sophie, in Haig-Brown, *Resistance and Renewal*, 50–1.

24. Jose Amaujaq Kusugak, in Younging et al., *Response, Responsibility and Renewal*, 19–20.

25. Dan Kennedy, in Grant, *Grief*, 19 (n.p.).

26. Anonymous, in Agnes Jack, ed., *Behind Closed Doors: Stories from the Kamloops Indian Residential School* rev. edn (Kamloops: Secwepemc Cultural Education Society, 2006), 47.

27. Elliot Eisner, *The Educational Imagination: On the Design and Evaluation of School Programs* 3rd edn (New York: Macmillan College Publishing, 2001).

28. Johnston, *Indian School Day*, 27–8.

29. Betsey Paul, in Knockwood, *Out of the Depths*, 31.

30. Sophie, in Haig-Brown, *Resistance and Renewal*, 59.

31. Grant, *Grief*, 163–4.

32. Ibid., 164–5.

33. Jack Funk, 'Une Main Criminelle, L'École St. Henri—the Delmas Boarding School', in Jaine, ed., *Residential Schools*, 73.

34. Peter Julian, in Knockwood, *Out of the Depths*, 34.

35. Grant, *Grief*, 189.

36. Knockwood, *Out of the Depths*, 98.

37. Marlene Starr, 'Foreword', in Agnes Grant, *Finding My Talk: How Fourteen Native Women Reclaimed Their Lives after Residential School* (Calgary: Fifth House, 2004), vii.

38. One example of notable exception is Emmanuel College's Principal Mackay, who became a fluent Cree speaker, speaking it with students. See Dyck, *Differing Visions*, 23.

39. Although a number of critics of the existing literature suggest that they over-emphasize the bad stories, when one reads closely, they almost all document positive moments and aspects. However, the weighting most often favours the negative: perhaps because those who enjoyed their experiences feel they have little to contribute or because there simply were more negative than positive ones.

40. Bill Williams, 'Foreword', in Terry Glavin and Former Students of St Mary's, *Amongst God's Own: The Enduring Legacy of St. Mary's Mission* (Mission: Mission Indian Friendship Centre, 2002), 10.

41. Introduction, Ibid., 11.

42. Bev Sellars, 'Opening Address to the First National Conference on Residential Schools, 18 June 1991', in Elizabeth Furniss, *Victims of Benevolence: The Dark Legacy of the Williams Lake Residential School* (Vancouver: Arsenal Pulp Press, 1995), 125. Emphasis in original.

43. Phil Fontaine, 'We Are All Born Innocent', in Jaine, ed., *Residential Schools*, 63.

44. 'Bear', in Dyck, *Differing Visions*, 45.

45. Starr, in Grant, *Finding*, viii.

46. Grant, *Grief*, 225.

47. 'Foreward', in Haig-Brown, *Resistance and Renewal*, 21.

48. Furniss, *Victims*, 115.

49. Grant, *Grief*, 229.

50. For examples, see Dyck, *Differing Visions*, 17; Funk, in Jaine, ed., *Residential Schools*, 84; Furniss, *Victims*, 62; Haig-Brown, *Resistance and Renewal*, 110; Knockwood, *Out of the Depths*, 108.

51. See, for example, Grant, *Grief* ; Haig-Brown, *Resistance and Renewal*; Agnes Jack, ed., *Behind Closed Doors: Stories from the Kamloops Indian Residential School* (Penticton: Theytus Books, 2006).

52. Ibid., 141.

53. David Nock argues convincingly that these are the words of E.F. Wilson, former principal of Shingwauk and Wawanosh schools. In David Nock, *A Victorian Missionary and Canadian Indian Policy: Cultural Synthesis vs Cultural Replacement* (Waterloo: Wilfrid Laurier Press, 1988), 165. Emphasis in original.

54. Cited in Grant, *Grief*, 145.

55. Jaine, ed., *Residential Schools*, 63.

56. Patrick White, 'Together they've turned shame into pride', *The Globe and Mail*, 18 June 2010, A10.

57. Tom Hill, Museum Director, 2005, http://www.statemuseum.arizona.edu/aip/leadershipgrant/natlconf/tom_hill.shtml. 26 July 2010.

58. Grant, *Finding*, 171–2.

59. Ibid., 172.

60. Knockwood, *Out of the Depths*, 132.

61. Funk, in Jaine, ed., *Residential Schools*, 86.

62. Grant, *Finding*, 209.

63. Gregory Younging, 'Inherited History, International Law, and the UN Declaration', in Younging et al., *Response, Responsibility, and Renewal*, 327.

64. Ibid., 85.

65. Truth and Reconciliation Commission of Canada, 'Remarks at Witnessing the Future Ceremony'. Available at http://www.trc.ca/websites/trcinstitution/File/pdfs/TRC_Chair_Murray_Sinclair_speech.pdf (accessed 2 June 2010).

66. Gregory Younging, 'Inherited History', 327.

67. An Act to further amend the Indian Act, 1894, section 137: The Governor in Council may make regulations either general or affecting the Indians of any province or of any named band, to secure the **compulsory attendance of children at school**. 2. Such regulation, in addition to any other provisions deemed expedient, **may provide for the arrest and conveyance to school, and detention there, of truant children and children who are prevented by their parents or guardians from attending: and such regulations may provide for the punishment, upon summary conviction, by fine or imprisonment, or both, of parents and guardians, or persons having the charge of children, who fail, refuse or neglect to cause such children to attend school**. Section 138: The Governor in Council may establish an industrial school or a **boarding school for Indians**, or may declare any existing Indian school to be an industrial school or boarding school . . . 2. The Governor in Council may make regulations, which shall have the force of law, for committal by justices or Indian agents of **children of Indian blood under the age of sixteen years**, to such industrial school or boarding school, there to be kept, cared for and educated for a period not extending beyond the time at which children shall reach the age of eighteen years. (my emphasis) 68. Official Languages of Canada, Canada's Constitution Act 1982, sections 16–22. Section 16 (1): 'English and French are the official languages of Canada and have equality of status and equal rights and privileges as to their use in all institutions of the Parliament and government of Canada.'

69. Harold Cardinal and Walter Hildebrandt, *Treaty Elders of Saskatchewan, Our Dream Is That Our Peoples Will One Day Be Clearly Recognized As Nations* (Calgary: University of Calgary Press, 2000), 5.

70. Task Force on Aboriginal Languages, *Towards A New Beginning, Report to the Minister of Canadian Heritage by The Task Force on Aboriginal Languages and Cultures*, June 2005, 4: 'They attributed language loss to Canada's assimilation policies, particularly the residential school system, as well as to individual, institutional and government complacency.'

71. Assembly of First Nations website: http://www.afn.ca/residentialschools/PDF/Notice_of_Class_Actions.pdf (accessed 11 Aug. 2010).

72. CBC News, 'N.L. Residential School Lawsuit Can Proceed', 9 June 2010. Available at http://www.cbc.ca/canada/newfoundland-labrador/story/2010/06/08/nl-residential-schools-608.html (accessed 12 June 2010).

73. Ministry of Indian and Northern Affairs, *Reconciliation and Healing: Alternative Resolutions for Dealing with Residential School Claims* (Ottawa: Ministry of Indian and Northern Affairs Development, Mar. 2000).

74. Ibid., 5.

75. Ibid., 33.

76. Canadian Bar Association, *The Logical Next Step: Reconciliation Payments for All Indian Residential School Survivors* (Ottawa: Canadian Bar Association, Feb. 2005).

77. CBC News, 'Facts and Questions Truth and Reconciliation Commission'. Available at http://www.cbc.ca/canada/story/2008/05/16/f-faqs-truth-reconciliation.html (accessed 31 July 2010).

78. According to Cree Elder Doris Young, the Thunderbird is a powerful supernatural sacred being. When it beats its enormous wings, it causes thunder and stirs the wind.

79. *Statement of Apology - to former students of Indian Residential Schools*. Available at http://www.ainc-inac.gc.ca/ai/rqpi/apo/index-eng.asp (accessed 1 June 2010).

80. 'A Day of Hope'. Available at http://www.cpac.ca/forms/index.asp?dsp=template&act=view3&pagetype=vod&lang=e&clipID=2913 (accessed 28 July 2009).

81. [This refers to the Aboriginal principle of 'witnessing'.]

82. [The Government of Canada undertakes to provide for wider dissemination of the report pursuant to the recommendations of the Commissioners.]

83. [The Commission may make recommendations for such further measures as it considers necessary

for the fulfillment of the Truth and Reconciliation Mandate and goals.]

CHAPTER TEN: RELIGIONS, CULTURE, AND THE PEOPLES OF THE NORTH

1. Susan Neylan, *The Heavens Are Changing: Nineteenth-Century Protestant Missions and Tsimshian Christianity* (Montreal: McGill-Queen's University Press, 2003).

2. Susan Elaine Gray, *'I Will Fear No Evil': Ojibwa-Missionary Encounters Along the Berens River, 1875–1940* (Calgary: University of Calgary Press, 2006), 1.

3. *Codex Historicus* (hereafter *Codex*), Mission Pelly Bay, vol. I: 26 avril 1935–31 déc. 1950, (manuscript).

4. In this article, we use the term *Nattilingmiut* to refer to the group classified by Knud Rasmussen as the Netsilik Eskimos. See Knud Rasmussen, *The Netsilik Eskimos. Social Life and Spiritual Culture*, Copenhagen, Report of the Fifth Thule Expedition, 1921–24, vol. 8, no. 1 (1931).

5. Esquisse synthétique sur la Baie d'Hudson, Document LCB3.C56Rl, Archives Deschâtelets, Ottawa (typescript), 4–5.

6. Ibid., 9.

7. *Codex*, août 1937. A socius was an associate.

8. See Susan Rowley, 'Population Movements in the Canadian Arctic', *Études/Inuit/Studies* 9, 1 (1985): 3–21.

9. See Cornelius H.W. Remie, 'Culture change and religious continuity among the Arviligjuarmiut of Pelly Bay, N.W.T., 1935–1963', *Études/Inuit/Studies* 7, 2 (1983): 53–77; and Cornelius H.W. Remie, 'Towards a new perspective on Netjilik Inuit female infanticide', *Études/Inuit/Studies* 9, 1 (1985): 67–75.

10. See Guy Mary-Rousselière, 'The grave of Kukigaq', *Eskimo* 57 (1960): 18–22; Cornelius H.W. Remie, 'Ermalik and Kukigak. Continuity and Discontinuity in Pelly Bay, Northwest Territories, Canada', in C. Buijs, ed., *Continuity and Discontinuity in Arctic Cultures: Essays in Honour of Gerti Nooter, Curator at the National Museum of Ethnology, 1970–1990* (Leiden, The Netherlands: Centre of Non-Western Studies, 1993), 78–90; Geert van den Steenhoven, *Leadership and Law among the Eskimos of the Keewatin District, Northwest Territories* (Rijswijk: Excelsior, 1962).

11. Franz Van de Velde, Statistiques objectives sur la population Netjilique, vols. I–IV, Hall Beach, NT, 1979, 1980, 1981, 1984 (typescripts).

12. *Codex*, 6 mars 1935.

13. Van de Velde, Statistiques objectives, 1979, 69.

14. *Codex*, 2 févr 1937.

15. Jean Philippe, OMI, 'Realizing a dream', *Eskimo* (May 1946), 6.

16. See *Codex*, 2 sept. 1935.

17. *Codex*, 27 janv. 1936.

18. *Codex*, 27 déc. 1935.

19. *Codex*, 7 nov. 1936.

20. *Codex*, 4 févr 1937.

21. See Franz Van de Velde, O.M.I. Trinette S. Constandse-Westermann, Cornelius H.W. Remie, and Raymond R. Newell, 'One hundred and fifteen years of Arviligjuarmiut Demography, Central Canadian Arctic', *Arctic Anthropology* 30, 2 (1993): 12.

22. See Ronne Heming, ed., *NWT Data Book 1986–87: A Complete Information Guide to the Northwest Territories and its Communities* (Yellowknife: Outcrop, 1986), 210.

23. *Codex*, 13 févr. 1938.

24. *Codex*, 23 avril 1938.

25. See Simon et Fabien, Cie de transport pour R.B. Document LCB330.C56R4, Archives Deschâtelets, Ottawa (manuscript).

26. See R.C. Mission Pelly Bay, N.W.T., Invoice to R.C.M. Police, G Division, Ottawa, Ont., Document LCB321.C56R7, Archives Deschâtelets, Ottawa (typescript).

27. Van de Velde, Comments on the *Codex Historicus*, Part 2.

28. Ibid.

29. Ibid.

30. Ibid., Part 1.

31. *Codex*, 16 déc. 1944.

32. See Van de Velde et al., 'One hundred and fifteen years of Arviligjuarmiut', 13.

33. Ibid., 5.

34. Franz Van de Velde, OMI, Comment la traite se faisait-elle dans le temps? Miscellaneous notes compiled by Father Franz Van de Velde, Hall Beach, N.W.T., Volume A: 178–80, 1982 (typescript).

35. *Codex*, 25 déc. 1936.

36. In the *Codex*, we found two entries where drum dances are mentioned as part of the Christmas celebrations: 26 déc. 1930, 25 déc. 1940.

37. *Codex*, 15 août 1940, 15 août 1944, 15 août 1950, 8 déc. 1941.

38. The Inuktitut name for Sunday is *sanattaili*, i.e. day on which manual work is forbidden. See Lucien Schneider, O.M.I, *Ulirnaisigutiit: An Inuktitut-English Dictionary of Northern Quebec, Labrador and Eastern Arctic Dialects (with an English-Inuktitut Index)* (Québec: Les Presses de l'Université Laval, 1985), 339.

39. *Codex*, 27 sept. 1941 and 27 juin 1948; Van de Velde, Comments on the *Codex Historicus*, Part 2.

40. Van de Velde, Comments on the *Codex Historicus*, Part 2. It has been suggested that female infanticide

quickly disappeared under the influence of the Pelly Bay mission; Asen Balicki, 'The Netsilik Inuit Today', *Études/Inuit/Studies* 2,1 (1978): 113.

41. In volume 1 of the *Codex* of Pelly Bay we find one entry by Father Henry that refers to such a case: 2 juin 1948.

42. *Codex*, 10 févr 1942; 11 déc. 1946; 25 févr 1947; 1 juil. 1948; 9 déc. 1949.

43. *Codex*, 10 févr 1946.

44. See *Codex*, 4 juin 1935; 30 oct.1936.

45. *Codex*, 18 janv. 1938.

46. Franz Van de Velde, OMI, 'Religion and Morals among the Pelly Bay Eskimos', *Eskimo* 39 (1956): 8.

47. *Codex*, 4 janv. 1937; 12 août 1945; 9 sept. 1945; 8 déc. 1945; 23 mars 1946; 18 août 1946 ; and 12 juil. 1947.

48. Remie, 'Culture Change and Religious Continuity', 68.

49. Van de Velde, Comments on the *Codex Historicus*, Part 2.

50. Remie, 'Culture change and religious continuity', 68.

51. Turquetil, Textes des résolutions, 22–3.

52. Franz Van de Velde, OMI, Statistiques objectives sur la population Netjilique, vol. III, 241; Van de Velde, Comments on the *Codex Historicus*, Part 2.

53. *Sakkajuq* means 'performs witchcraft over a sick person', See Lucien Schneider, OMI, *Dictionnaire esquimau-français du parler de l'Ungava et contrées limitrophes* (Québec : Les Presses de l'Université Laval, 1970), 308.

54. *Tuumgijuq* means 'invokes the (protective) spirits'. See ibid., 370.

55. *Codex*, 9 août 1949.

56. *Codex*, 19 janv. 1940.

57. Jarich Oosten, Frédéric Laugrand, and Wim Rasing, eds, *Perspectives on Traditional Law: Interviewing Inuit Elders*, vol. 2 (Iqaluit, Nunavut Arctic College, 1999), 22–3.

58. Ibid., 29.

59. Jarich Oosten and Frédéric Laugrand, eds, *The Transition to Christianity: Inuit Perspectives on the 20th Century*, vol. 1 (Iqaluit: Nunavut Arctic College), 63.

60. Ibid., 111.

61. Notes sur le suicide d'Allakatnuar, Document HEF3244.F83D.6, Archives Deschâtelets, Ottawa (undated manuscript).

62. This entry was translated by Geoff Read.

63. The Cree people as a whole refer to themselves as *Eeyouch*, while the Cree people who live in Whapmagoostui also call themselves *Iiyiy'ch*.

64. The material detailing the history of the Great Whale region is drawn primarily from Naomi Adelson, *Being Alive Well: Health and the Politics of*

Cree Well-Being (Toronto: University of Toronto Press, 2000); Naomi Adelson, 'The Shifting Landscape of Cree Well-Being', in Gordon Matthews and Carolina Izquierdo, eds, *Pursuits of Happiness: Well-Being in Anthropological Perspective* (Oxford: Berghahn Books, 2009), 109–23.

65. See William K. Barger, 'Great Whale River, Quebec', in June Helm, ed., *Handbook of North American Indians: Subarctic*, vol. 6 (Washington: Smithsonian Institution, 1982), 673–82; Adelson, *Being Alive Well*; Naomi Adelson, 'Discourses of Stress, Social Inequities, and the Everyday Worlds of First Nations Women in a Remote Northern Canadian Community', *Ethos* 36, 3 (2008): 316–31.

66. Concerns remain to this day regarding the toxic waste, including PCBs, which were never cleared from the Mid-Canada Line sites across Canada. See www.merc.ontera.net/reports/pcbws.pdf (accessed 3 Nov. 2009).

67. Adelson, *Being Alive Well*.

68. See Richard F. Salisbury, *A Homeland for the Cree: Regional Development in James Bay: 1971–1981* (Montreal: McGill-Queen's University Press, 1986).

69. http://www12.statcan.ca/census-recensement/2006/dp-pd/prof/92-591/details/Page.cf (accessed 20 Oct. 2009).

70. As noted earlier, the Cree share the land at the mouth of the Great Whale River with the neighbouring Inuit community of Kujuuaraapik. Separately maintained and governed, the two communities have different governing bodies, schools, services, and facilities.

71. Whapmgoostui First Nation Band Council, www.whapmagoostuifn.ca/bandcouncil.html (accessed 20 Oct. 2009)

72. The Aboriginal Portal indicates that the closest Friendship Centre is approximately 300 kilometres to the southwest of Whapmagoostui in Moosonee, ON. There are no transportation links between these two communities. See Government of Canada, 'Aboriginal Connectivity Survey'. Available at http://www.aboriginalcanada.gc.ca/abdt/apps/connectivitysurvey.nsf/ (accessed 19 Oct. 2009).

73. The household census numbers are from Cree First Nation census data (2008) and personal communication (S. Gilpin). The 188 households exclude 3 trailers, 3 social housing units, 11 Cree Health Board units, and the 27 public buildings. The household connectivity data comes from two sources: a personal communication in 2008 with Andrew Eastman, the dealer for the Xplornet system in Whapmagoostui and Government of Canada, 'Aboriginal Canada Connectivity Survey'.

74. Arturo Escobar, 'Welcome to Cyberia: Notes on the Anthropology of Cyberculture', *Current*

Anthropology 35, 3 (1994): 214. See also Bryan Pfaffenberger, 'Social Anthropology of Technology', *Annual Review of Anthropology* 21 (2002): 491–516.

75. Anastasia N. Panagakos and Heather Horst, 'Return to Cyberia: Technology and the Social World of Transnational Migrants', *Global Initiatives* 6 (2006): 109–24.

76. David Hakken, 'Non-Western Studies of Cyberspace Identity Formation', *Antopologi Indonesia* 73 (2004): 32–9.

77. Panagakos and Horst, 'Return to Cyberia', 124.

78. KTA Aboriginal Practice Group, 'Aboriginal Culture in the Digital Age: Aboriginal Voice Cultural Working Group Paper'. 2005. Available at www.kta.on.ca/documents/AboriginalCultureinaDigitalAge.pdf (accessed 27 Oct. 2009).

79. Wherever possible, I have used the transliteration of Cree words (northern dialect) from the online Cree dictionary (www.eastcree.org/creedictionary/index.php), developed by the Interactive Cree Language Project based at Carleton University.

80. E. Masty, personal communication with author, 2009.

81. Ronald Niezen, 'Healing and Conversion: Medical Evangelism in James Bay Cree Society', *Ethnohistory* 44, 3 (1997): 463–91.

82. Regina Flannery, 'The Shaking-Tent Rite among the Montagnais of James Bay', *Primitive Man* 12, 1 (1939): 11–16.

83. Peter Armitage, 'Religious Ideology among the Innu of Eastern Quebec and Labrador', *Religiologiques* 6 (1992): 64–110; Harvey Feit, 'The Power to "See" and the Power to Hunt: The Shaking Tent Ceremony in Relation to Experience, Explanation, Action and Interpretation in the Waswanipi Hunter's World', Canadian Museum of Civilization, Harvey Feit Papers, B359, file 6. 1983; Adrian Tanner, 'The Origins of Social Pathologies and the Quebec Cree Healing Movement', in Laurence Kirmayer and Gail G. Valaskakis, eds, *Healing Traditions: The Mental Health of Aboriginal Peoples in Canada* (Vancouver: UBC Press, 2009), 249–71. The eastern James Bay Cree are related culturally, linguistically, and historically to the Innu (referred to as Montagnais-Naskapi in older literature) as well as to the western Cree.

84. Peter Armitage, 'The Religious Significance of Animals in Innu Culture', *Native Issues* 4, 1 (1984): 50–6; Serge Bouchard and José Mailhot, 'Structure du lexique: les animaux indiens', *Recherches amérindiennes au Québec* 3, 1–2 (1972): 39–67; Richard Preston, *Cree Narrative: Expressing the Personal Meanings of Events* (Montreal: McGill-Queen's University Press, 1977/2002); Adrian Tanner, *Bringing Home Animals: Religious Ideology and Mode of Production of the Mistassini Cree Hunters* (St. John's: ISER, 1979).

85. Armitage, 'Religious Ideology', 66.

86. Feit, 'The Power'; Bouchard and Maillot, 'Structure du lexique'.

87. See, for example, Armitage, 'Religious Ideology'.

88. For a fuller discussion of the role of the *mishtaapaau* see Armitage, 'Religious Ideology'; Preston, *Cree Narrative*.

89. Armitage, 'Religious Ideology', 58.

90. Armitage, 'Religious Ideology'; Feit, 'The Power'.

91. Niezen, 'Healing and Conversion', 472.

92. See, for example, John Long, 'Rev. Edwin Watkins: Missionary to the Cree: 1852–1857', in William Cowan, ed., *Papers of the Sixteenth Algonquian Conference* (Ottawa: Carleton University, 1985), 91–117.

93. Edwin Arthur Watkins, *Journal*, Church Missionary Society, General Synod Archives of the Anglican Church of Canada, Toronto, Reel A97/98, 1852.

94. Niezen, 'Healing and Conversion'.

95. Toby Morantz, *The Whiteman's Gonna Getcha: The Colonial Challenge to the Crees in Quebec* (Montreal: McGill-Queen's University Press, 2002), 84.

96. See Adelson, *Being Alive Well*.

97. Ibid., 42–3. In my interviews, I retain the anonymity of participants.

98. Bishop Caleb Lawrence to Naomi Adelson, personal communication, 1995.

99. Niezen, *Healing and Conversion*; Preston, *Cree Narrative*.

100. Tanner, 'The Origins'.

101. This chapter is dedicated to my friend Emily, who originally pointed out the playful use of language I have described in this chapter. I would also like to thank the entire Cree community, which continues to make me feel so welcome and so at home and, in particular, the Band Council for their support of my research. I would also like to acknowledge the financial support of the Social Science and Humanities Research Council of Canada.

CHAPTER ELEVEN: THE ECONOMY AND LABOUR

1. Mary Jane Logan McCallum, 'Labour, Modernity, and the Canadian State: A History of Aboriginal Women and Work in the Mid-Twentieth Century' (PhD dissertation, University of Manitoba, 2008), 4.

2. Ibid., 16.

3. John Lutz, *Makuk: A New History of Aboriginal-White Relations* (Vancouver: UBC Press, 2008), 8.

4. Franz Boas, *The Ethnography of Franz Boas: Letters and Diaries of Franz Boas Written on the Northwest Coast from 1886–1931*, ed. Ronald Rohner, trans. Hedy Parker (Chicago: University of Chicago,

1969), June 1889. I use the terms *Aboriginal peoples*, *Indigenous people*, and *Native people* to describe the descendants of the pre-European population in the Americas. See, for one suggested usage, Greg Younging, 'Talking Terminology: What's in a Word and What's Not', *Prairie Fire* 22, 3 (2001): 130–40.

5. Potlatch refers to a variety of feasts held by Northwest Coast Indigenous peoples. While the feasts might mark weddings, deaths, or the passing of titles or ownership to rights or resources, the common feature was that the hosts fed visitors—sometimes numbering in the thousands—and provided goods as gifts to all that attended. The higher status a guest, the more valuable the gift.

6. Reverend H.B. Owen in 'Reports of the Rev. H.B. Owen . . . to the United Society for the Propagation of the Gospel', Rhodes House Library, Oxford, as cited in Grant Keddie, *Songhees Pictorial: A History of the Songhees People as Seen by Outsiders, 1790–1912* (Victoria: Royal British Columbia Museum, 2004); *British Colonist*, 23 and 28 Apr. 1874; *Victoria Daily Standard*, 22 Apr. 1874; see also W.W. Walkem, *Stories of Early British Columbia* (Vancouver: News Advertiser, 1914), 114–15; I.W. Powell, Department of Indian Affairs Annual Report (DIAR), 1877, 32–4.

7. From 1870 to 1975, adjusted by F.H. Leacy, *Historical Statistics of Canada* (Ottawa: Statistics Canada, 1983), Index K44–6; and from 1975 to 2008, adjusted by the Consumer Price Index historical summary from Statistics Canada, http//www.40.statcan.ca/cstolecon46.htm (site now discontinued; see new summary tables site at http://www40.statcan.ca/l01/cst01/econ46a.htm?sdi=consumer%20price%20index%20historical%20summary).

8. DIAR, 1882, 160, 170; DIAR, 1885, 101; J.H. Van Den Brink, *The Haida Indians: Cultural Change Mainly between 1876–1970* (Leiden, The Netherlands: E.J. Brill, 1974), 42.

9. Helen Codere, *Fighting with Property: A Study of Kwakiutl Potlatching and Warfare, 1792–1930* (Seattle: University of Washington Press, 1972), 126.

10. I.W. Powell in DIAR, 1882, 130–60; Robin Fisher, *Contact and Conflict: Indian-European Relations in British Columbia*, 2nd edn (Vancouver: UBC Press, 1992), 111. This pattern differs from the experience in the rest of Canada, but wherever you look, Indigenous peoples' poverty worsened as areas were settled by Europeans.

11. F.W. Howay and E.O.S. Scholefield, *British Columbia from the Earliest Times to the Present* (Vancouver: S.J. Clarke, 1913). E.O.S. Scholefield and R.E. Gosnell, *Sixty Years of Progress: A History of British Columbia*, 2 vols (Vancouver, Victoria: British Columbia Historical Association, 1913); see also H.H. Bancroft, *History of British Columbia, 1792–1887* (San Francisco: History, 1887).

12. Frederick Jackson Turner, *The Frontier in American History in 1920* (New York: Holt, Rinehart and Winston, 1962). See also Richard Slotkin, *Regeneration through Violence: The Mythology of the American Frontier, 1600–1860* (Middleton, CT: Wesleyan University Press, 1973).

13. In April 1991, Justice McEachern, in *Delgamuukw v. BC*, took this position in denying the claim. See *BC Studies* 95 (1992) and Dara Culhane, *The Pleasure of the Crown: Anthropology, Law, and First Nations* (Vancouver: Talonbooks, 1998).

14. An example of this perspective is Peter Carstens, *The Queen's People: A Study of Hegemony, Coercion and Accommodation among the Okanagan of Canada* (Toronto: University of Toronto Press, 1991).

15. Fisher, *Contact and Conflict*, 111, 211.

16. James Lenihan, Canada Sessional Papers, (Cda. S.P.) 1876, p. 56; see also Indian Superintendent Powell, Cda. S.P. 1877, 33–4.

17. Library and Archives of Canada, (LAC) RG 10 vol. 1350 file: Cowichan Agency Departmental Circulars, 1892–1910, A.W. Vowell, 9 Mar. 1896.

18. James Spradley, ed., *Guests Never Leave Hungry: The Autobiography of James Sewid, a Kwakiutl Indian* (Kingston: McGill-Queen's University Press, 1989), 27; Bridget Moran, *Stoney Creek Woman: The Story of Mary John* (Vancouver: Tillacum Library, 1988), 29, 78, 81; Beth White in Yukon Archives (YA), Yukon Women's Project Sound Recording (Transcripts) file 13-5; Margaret Blackman, *During My Time: Florence Edenshaw Davidson, A Haida Woman* (Vancouver: Douglas and McIntyre, 1982), 109; Harry Assu, *Assu of Cape Mudge: Recollections of a Coastal Indian Chief* (Vancouver: UBC Press, 1989), 62; Leona Marie Sparrow, 'Work Histories of a Coast Salish Couple' (Master's thesis, University of British Columbia, 1976), 263.

19. Maureen Cassidy, *From Mountain to Mountain: A History of the Gitksan Village of Ans'payaxw* (Kispiox: Ans'payaxw School Society, 1984), 39; DIAR, 1901, 285; Joan Skogan, *Skeena: A River Remembered* (Vancouver: British Columbia Packers, 1983), 77.

20. Department of Fisheries, *Annual Report*, 1929–30, 105; M.C. Urquhart and K.A.H. Buckley, *Historical Statistics of Canada* (Toronto: MacMillan, 1965), 396.

21. Sayachi'apis, John Fornsby, August Khatsahlano, George Swanaset, John Wallace, and James Spradley fished but do not mention owning their own boats.

22. Sparrow, 'Work Histories', 30; Spradley, *Guests*, 58;

Blackman, *During My Time*, 82; Collen Bostwick, 'Oral Histories: Theresa Jeffries', *Labour History*, 2, 3 (1980): 8–15.

23. John McMullan, 'State, Capital, and the B.C. Salmon Fishing Industry', and Keith Warriner, 'Regionalism, Dependence, and the B.C. Fisheries: Historical Development and Recent Trends', in Patricia Marchak, Neil Guppy, and John McMullan, eds, *UnCommon Property: The Fishing and Fish-Processing Industries in British Columbia* (Toronto: Methuen, 1987), 107–52, 326–50; Dianne Newell, *Tangled Webs of History: Indians and the Law in Canada's Pacific Coast Fisheries* (Toronto: University of Toronto, 1993).

24. Ulli Steltzer and Catherine Kerr, *Coast of Many Faces* (Vancouver: Douglas and McIntyre, 1979), 46, 49.

25. British Columbia, *Sessional Papers* (BC S.P.), 1893, 'Report of the British Columbia Fishery Commission' estimated that canneries employed an average of 40–50 Aboriginal women; 1953 figure from H.B. Hawthorn, C. Belshaw, and S.M. Jamieson, *Indians of British Columbia: A Study of Contemporary Social Adjustment* (Toronto: University of Toronto Press, 1959), 113.

26. Hawthorn et al., *Indians of British Columbia*, 115; M.J. Friedlaender, *Economic Status of Native Indians in British Columbia Fisheries* (Vancouver: Environment Canada, Fisheries Operations Branch, Technical Report Series PAC/T-75-25, 1975).

27. *Resources of British Columbia*, 1, 4 (June 1883), 4; Cda, S.P. 1886, vol. 4, 84; Hawthorn et al., *Indians of British Columbia*, 114.

28. Lutz, *Makúk*, Table VII.

29. Clellan S. Ford, *Smoke from Their Fires: The Life of a Kwakiutl Chief* (Hamden, CT: Archon, 1968), 133–4; June Collins, 'John Fornsby: The Personal Document of a Coast Salish Indian', in Marian Smith, ed., *Indians of the Urban Northwest* (New York: Columbia University Press, 1949), 329; Oliver Wells, *The Chilliwacks and Their Neighbours* (Vancouver: Talonbooks, 1987), 197; Harry Robinson, *Write It on Your Heart: The Epic World of an Okanagan Storyteller*, ed. and comp. Wendy Wickwire (Vancouver: Talonbooks/Theytus, 1989), 11.

30. Henry Pennier, with Herbert L. McDonald, *Chiefly Indian: The Warm and Witty Story of a British Columbia Half Breed Logger* (Vancouver: Graydonald Graphics, 1972), 57.

31. James Burrows, '"A Much Needed Class of Labour": The Economy and Income of the Southern Interior Plateau Indians, 1897–1910', *BC Studies* 71 (Autumn 1986): 27–46; DIAR, 1886 vol. 4, 81, 84.

32. LAC, Department of Citizenship and Immigration, RG 26 vol. 106 file: 1/1-15 part 8: 'Indian Migrant Workers', Report for the International Labour Organization, Oct. 1953; LAC, RG 10, vol. 8423 801/21-1, reel C-13835, W.S. Arneil to Indian Affairs Branch, 27 May 1957.

33. Charles Jones with Stephen Bosustow, *Queesto, Pacheenaht Chief by Birthright* (Nanaimo: Theytus, 1981), 91.

34. Frank Fuller, 'Gilbert Joe', *Labour History* 2, 3 (1980): 16–19; Blackman, *During My Time*, 109; Jones with Bosustow, *Queesto*, 90–1; Interviews with Dave Dawson at Kingcome and Charlie Johnson at Owikeno, in Steltzer and Kerr, *Coast of Many Faces*, 68, 82, 135.

35. Hawthorn et al., *Indians of British Columbia*, 113.

36. Helen Codere, *Fighting With Property: A Study of Kwakiutl Potlatching and Warfare, 1792–1930* (Seattle: University of Washington, 1972), 43–8; Blackman, *During My Time*, 109; Assu, *Assu*, 66; Spradley, *Guests Never Leave Hungry*, 75; Pritchard, 'Economic Development and the Disintegration', 122–7; Jones with Bosustow, *Queesto*, 94.

37. Douglas Hudson, 'Traplines and Timber: Social and Economic Change among the Carrier' (PhD dissertation, University of Alberta, 1983), 145.

38. DIAR, 1918, 38.

39. DIAR, 1919, 52–3.

40. Ibid.

41. Moran, *Stoney Creek Woman*, 77–81; see also Pennier, *Chiefly Indian*, 58; Assu, *Assu*, 66; Spradley, *Guests Never Leave Hungry*, 95; Blackman, *During My Time*, 120; Lutz, *Makúk*, Figure VII.

42. LAC, RG 10, vol. 11,147 file: Shannon 'Fishing 1914–41', J.A. Motherwell, Chief Supervisor of Fisheries to M.S. Todd, M.S. Indian Agent, Alert Bay, 20 May 1940; LAC, RG 10, vol. 11,147 file: Shannon 'Fishing 1914–41,' W.M. Halliday to W.E. Ditchburn, 16 June 1919.

43. LAC, RG 10, vol. 8570, file: 901/1-2-2-2, Andy Paull speaking at a conference on the Indian Act, 20–1 July 1955.

44. Albany claimed clam digging and commercial fishing accounted for 80 per cent of their livelihood, *Colonist*, 18 Oct. 1960, 1; LAC, RG 10, vol. 9,170 file: Cowichan Agency General B-45 Lizzie Fisher to H. Graham, Cowichan Indian Agent, Aug., 1932; Charles to H. Graham, 6 Aug. 1932; Robbie Davis to H. Graham, 8 Dec. 1934.

45. D.B. Fields and W.T. Stanbury, *The Economic Impact of The Public Sector Upon the Indians of British Columbia* (Vancouver: University of BC, 1973), 46; Andrew Siggner and Chantal Locatelli, *An Overview of the Demographic, Social and Economic Conditions Among British Columbia's Registered Indian Population* (Ottawa: Research Branch, Corporate

Policy, Department of Indian Affairs and Northern Development, 1981), 39.

46. *Colonist*, 30 Jan. 1973.

47. To learn more about Arthur Wellington Clah, see Robert Galois, 'Colonial Encounters: The Worlds of Arthur Wellington Clah', *BC Studies* 5–6 (Autumn–Winter 1997/98): 105–47.

48. [Clah is noting the celebration of the Queen's birthday, Victoria Day.]

49. I use *Aboriginal* here in the inclusive way that RCAP did, to include Métis, Status, and Non-Status Indians. *Indigenous* is sometimes used as a synonym. Federal programs were generally directed at 'Status Indians'. When referring to documents of the time, I sometimes use their terms: e.g. *Indian*.

50. 'Indian Girls Achieve Successful Careers—pave the way for others,' *Indian News*, June 1958, 6–7.

51. Dara Culhane, 'Aboriginal Women in Eastside Vancouver: Emerging Into Invisibility', *American Indian Quarterly* 27, 3&4 (2003): 593–606.

52. AM, Hudson's Bay Company Records (HBC), RG 7/1/760, Reports from Posts, Newspaper clippings, 12 and 20 July 1966.

53. For a more detailed analysis of women's work in this period, see Mary Jane McCallum, 'Labour, Modernity and the Canadian State'.

54. Canada, *Royal Commission on Aboriginal Peoples*, vol. 2 (Ottawa, 1996), 777.

55. Jean Lagasse, *The People of Indian Ancestry in Manitoba*, vol. 3 (Winnipeg: Dept. of Agriculture and Immigration, 1959), 54.

56. Frank Tough, *As Their Natural Resources Fail: Native Peoples and the Economic History of Northern Manitoba, 1870–1930* (Vancouver: UBC Press, 1996).

57. For more on context, see Joan Sangster, *Transforming Labour: Women and Work in Postwar Canada* (Toronto: Univeristy of Toronto Press, 2010), chap. 6.

58. Arthur Ray, *I Have Lived Here Since the World Began* (Toronto: Key Porter Books, 1996), 291.

59. P.M. Worsely, Helen.L. Buckley, and A.K. Davis, *Economic and Social Survey of Northern Saskatchewan* (Saskatoon: Centre for Community Studies, University of Saskatchewan, 1961).

60. J.M. Kew, *Cumberland House, 1960, Report #2, Economic and Social Survey of Northern Saskatchewan* (Saskatoon: Centre for Community Studies, University of Saskatchewan, 1962), 31, 90.

61. Canada, Senate and House of Commons Joint Committee on the Indian Act (JCI Act), 1947–48, #15, 665.

62. Joan Sangster, *Regulating Girls and Women: Sexuality, Family and the Law in Ontario, 1920–1960* (Toronto: Oxford University Press, 2000), chap.

6; Robin Jarvis Brownlie, 'Intimate Surveillance: Indian Affairs, Colonization, and the Regulation of Aboriginal Women's Sexuality,' in Katie Pickles and Myra Rutherdales, eds, *Contact Zones: Aboriginal and Settler Women in Canada's Colonial Past* (Vancouver: UBC Press, 2006), 169–79.

63. Nancy Janovicek, 'Assisting Our Own: Urban Migration, Self-Governance, and Indigenous Women's Organizing in Thunder Bay, Ontario, 1972–1989', *American Indian Quarterly* 27, 3&4 (Summer–Fall, 2001): 548–65.

64. Canada, Dept. of Citizenship and Immigration, *The Indian in Transition: The Indian Today* (Ottawa, 1962), 10, 15.

65. James Lagrand, *Indian Metropolis: Indigenous Americans in Chicago* (Urbana: University of Illinois Press, 2002); Kathryn MacKay, 'Warriors into Welders: A History of Federal Employment Programs for American Indians, 1898–1972' (PhD dissertation, University of Utah, 1987).

66. See Hugh Shewell, *'Enough To Keep Them Alive' Indian Welfare in Canada, 1873–1965* (Toronto: University of Toronto Press, 2004).

67. Indian and Northern Affairs Canada, *A Survey of the Contemporary Indians of Canada Economic, Political, Educational Needs and Policies: Part 2* (The Hawthorn Report), (Ottawa, Indian Affairs Branch, 1967), 127.

68. There were distinct programs for Aboriginal nurses. See Mary Jane McCallum, *Twice As Good: A History of Aboriginal Nurses* (Ottawa: Aboriginal Nurses Association of Canada, 2007).

69. Michele Barrett and Mary McIntosh, 'The Family Wage: Some Problems for Socialists and Feminists', *Capital and Class* 9, 1/2 (Summer 1980): 51–72.

70. LAC, RG 10, vol. 8415, 1/ 21-1, Summer Placement from Mohawk Residential School, 1961.

71. LAC, RG 10, vol. 8413, 1-21-1, Hilda Holland to Mr Matters, Indian Affairs, 18 Mar. 1948.

72. Evelyn Peters, '"Urban" and "Aboriginal": An Impossible Contradiction?', in J. Caulfield and L. Peake, eds, *City Lives & City Forms: Critical Research & Canadian Urbanism* (Toronto: University of Toronto Press, 1996), 47–62; Sherene Razack, ed., *Race, Space and the Law Unmapping a White Settler Society* (Toronto: Between the Lines, 2002).

73. AM, Beatrice Brigden Papers, P 820, f 2, clipping, *Winnipeg Free Press*, 18 Jan. 1958 (my emphasis).

74. The pamphlet distinguished the latter from 'racial intolerance'. George Mortimer, *The Indian in Industry: Roads to Independence* (Ottawa: Dept. of Citizenship and Immigration, 1965), 9.

75. *The Indian in Transition*, 6, and George Mortimer, *The Indian in Industry*, 7, 4.

76. LAC, RG 10, vol. 8574, 1/1-2-2-17, 14 Feb. 1963.

77. Maria Campbell, *Halfbreed* (Toronto: Seal Books, 1973), 154.

78. Lagasse, *The People of Indian Ancestry*, 65; Linda Gerber, 'Multiple Jeopardy: A Socio-Economic Comparison of Men and Women Among the Indian, Métis and Inuit Peoples of Canada', *Canadian Ethnic Studies* 22, 3 (1990): 69–84.

79. Lagasse, *The People of Indian Ancestry*, 129.

80. Ibid.

81. George Mortimore, *The Indian in Industry*, 7.

82. In 1959, it was reported that 262 Indians were established in urban employment as a result of the efforts of placement officers. The numbers did increase, but not dramatically so. LAC, RG 10, vol. 8414, file 1/21-1, pt 6, introduction, placement manual.

83. Edgar Dosman, *Indians: The Urban Dilemma* (Toronto: McClelland and Stewart, 1972), 133. Only 12 of 216 women in the sample had obtained permanent jobs. He did note that the 'best off' were women with some high-school education who secured white-collar jobs.

84. Lagasse, *The People of Indian Ancestry*, 111–12.

85. Lagasse makes this equation more than once in *The People of Indian Ancestry*.

86. Andrea Smith, *Conquest: Sexual Violence and American Indian Genocide* (Boston: South End Press, 2005).

87. Amnesty International, *Stolen Sisters: Discrimination and Violence Against Indigenous Women in Canada*, Oct. 2004. Available at http://www.amnesty.ca/campaigns/sisters_overview.php.

88. Bonita Lawrence, 'Gender, Race, and the Regulation of Indigenous Identity in Canada and the U.S.: An Overview', *Hypatia* 18, 2 (Spring 2003): 3–31.

89. Heather Howard-Bobiwash, 'Women's Class Strategies as Activism in Indigenous Community Building in Toronto, 1950–75', *American Indian Quarterly* 27, 3&4 (Summer–Fall, 2001): 566–82.

CHAPTER TWELVE: ABORIGINAL WOMEN

1. Andrea Smith, *Conquest: Sexual Violence and American Indian Genocide* (Cambridge, MA: South End Press, 2005), 3.

2. Amnesty International, *Stolen Sisters: A Human Rights Response to Discrimination and Violence Against Indigenous Women in Canada*. Oct. 2004. Available at http://www.amnesty.ca/campaigns/resources/amr2000304.pdf (accessed 12 Jan. 2011).

3. Sylvia Maracle, 'The Eagle Has Landed: Native Women, Leadership and Community Development', in Kim Anderson and Bonita Lawrence, eds, *Strong Women Stories: Native Vision and Community Survival* (Toronto: Sumach Press, 2003), 70–1.

4. Mary E. Inderwick, 'A Lady and Her Ranch', in Hugh Dempsey, ed., *The Best from Alberta History* (Saskatoon: Western Producer Prairie Books, 1981), 65–77.

5. See Margaret Strobel, *European Women and the Second British Empire* (Bloomington: Indiana University Press, 1991). See also Ann Laura Stoler, 'Carnal Knowledge and Imperial Power: Gender, Race, and Morality in Colonial Asia', in Micaela di Leonardo, ed., *Gender at the Crossroads of Knowledge: Feminist Anthropology in the Postmodern Era* (Berkeley: University of California Press, 1991), 51–101, and Stoler, 'Rethinking Colonial Categories: European Communities and the Boundaries of Rule', in Nicholas B. Kirks, ed., *Colonialism and Culture* (Ann Arbor: University of Michigan Press, 1992), 319–52.

6. See Sarah Carter, *Lost Harvests: Prairie Indian Reserve Farmers and Government Policy* (Montreal: McGill-Queen's University Press, 1990).

7. Rayna Green, 'The Pocahontas Perplex: The Image of Indian Women in American Culture', in Ellen Carol DuBois and Vicki Ruiz, eds, *Unequal Sisters: A Multicultural Reader in U.S. Women's History* (New York: Routledge, 1990), 15–21, 5.

8. P.B. Waite, *Canada, 1874–1896: Arduous Destiny* (Toronto: McClelland and Stewart, 1971), 149.

9. Canada, *Sessional Papers*, Annual Report of the Superintendent General of Indian Affairs for the year ending 20 June 1898, xix. For the year ending 31 Dec. 1899, xxiii, xxviii, 166; *The Toronto Mail*, 2 Mar. 1889; Pamela Margaret White, 'Restructuring the Domestic Sphere—Prairie Indian Women on Reserves: Image, Ideology, and State Policy, 1880–1930' (PhD dissertation, McGill University, 1987); W.H. Withrow, *Native Races of North America* (Toronto: Methodist Mission Rooms, 1895), 114 (quoted).

10. Canada, *Sessional Papers*, Annual Report of the Superintendent General of Indian Affairs for the year ending Mar. 1908, 110.

11. Inspector Alex McGibbon's report on Onion Lake, Oct. 1891, Library and Archives of Canada (LAC), Record Group 10 (RG 10), records relating to Indian Affairs, Black Series, vol. 3860, file 82, 319-6.

12. *The Globe* (Toronto), 1 Feb. 1886.

13. *The Toronto Mail*, 23 Jan. 1886.

14. Canada, *House of Commons Debates*, Malcolm Cameron, Session 1886, vol. 1, 72021.

15. E.C. Morgan, 'The North-West Mounted Polic: Internal Problems and Public Criticism, 1874–1883', *Saskatchewan History* 26, 2 (Spring 1973): 56–9, Laird quoted 56.

16. Canada, *House of Commons Debates*, 21 Apr. 1880, Joseph Royal, Fourth Parliament, Second Session, 1638.

17. *The Toronto Mail*, 2 Feb. 1886.

18. John Maclean, 'The Half-breed and Indian Insurrection', *Canadian Methodist Magazine* 22 (1 July 1885): 173–4.

19. Edgar Dewdney to the Bishop of Saskatchewan, 31 May 1886, NA, RG 10, vol. 3753, file 30613.

20. *Blackfeet Heritage: 1907–08* (Browning: Blackfeet Heritage Program, n.d.), 171.

21. A.B. McCullough, 'Papers Relating to the North West Mounted Police and Fort Walsh', Manuscript Report Series no. 213 (Ottawa: Parks Canada, Department of Indian and Northern Affairs, 1977), 132–3.

22. Personal interview with Kirsten Grier, great-granddaughter of D.J. Grier, Calgary, 19 May 1993. See also *Fort Macleod—Our Colourful Past: A History of the Town of Fort Macleod from 1874 to 1924* (Fort Macleod: Fort Macleod History Committee, 1977), 268–9.

23. John O'Kute-sica Correspondence, Collection no. R-834, file 17b, p. 3, Saskatchewan Archives Board (SAB).

24. S.B. Steele to Commissioner, Fort Macleod, 20 July 1895, LAC, RG 18, vol. 2182, file RCMP 1895 pt. 2, and Gilbert E. Sanders' Diaries, 20 Oct. 1885, Edward Sanders Family Papers, M1093, File 38, Glenbow Archives, 26.

25. F. Laurie Barron, 'Indian Agents and the North-West Rebellion', in F. Laurie Barron and James B. Waldram, eds, *1885 and After: Native Society in Transition* (Regina: Canadian Plains Research Centre, 1986), 36.

26. Norma Sluman and Jean Goodwill, *John Tootoosis: A Biography of a Cree Leader* (Ottawa: Golden Dog Press, 1982), 37.

27. Newspaper clipping, 'Through the Saskatchewan', n.p., n.d., William Henry Cotton Collection, SAB.

28. *The Globe* (Toronto), 4 June 1880; [Fort] *Macleod Gazette*, 23 Mar. 1886; *The Toronto Mail* 2 Feb. 1886.

29. Canada, *House of Commons Debates*, Session 1886, vol. 1, 730.

30. William Donovan to L. Vankoughnet, 31 Oct. 1886, LAC, RG 10, vol. 3772, file 34983.

31. *The Globe* (Toronto), 4 June 1886.

32. Department of Indian Affairs, 'The Facts Respecting Indian Administration in the North-West' (Ottawa: Department of Indian Affairs, 1886), quoted 9, 12.

33. David Hamer, *New Towns in the New World: Images and Perceptions of the Nineteenth Century Urban Frontier* (New York: Columbia University Press, 1990), 17, 213.

34. 'What Canadian Women Say of the Canadian North-West', *Montreal Herald*, 1886, 42–5.

35. L. Vankoughnet to John A. Macdonald, 15 Nov. 1883, LAC, RG 10, vol. 1009, file 628, no. 596-635.

36. Constance B. Backhouse, 'Nineteenth-Century Canadian Prostitution Law: Reflection of a Discriminatory Society', *Histoire sociale/Social History* 18, 36 (Nov. 1985): 420–2.

37. Canada, *Sessional Papers*. Annual Report of the Commissioner of the North-West Mounted Police Force for the Year Ended 1889, reprinted in *The New West* (Toronto: Coles Publishing Company, 1973), 101.

38. *Saskatchewan Herald* (Battleford), 15 Mar. 1886, 13 Mar. 1888.

39. *Calgary Herald*, 5 Mar. 1885.

40. *Macleod Gazette*, 18 July 1888.

41. R.C. Macleod, *The North-West Mounted Police and Law Enforcement, 1873–1905* (Toronto: University of Toronto Press, 1976), 145; see also LAC, RG 18, vol. 24, file 667-1888.

42. Donald Smith, 'Bloody Murder Almost Became Miscarriage of Justice', *Herald Sunday Magazine*, 23 July 1989, 13.

43. James Gray, *Talk to My Lawyer: Great Stories of Southern Alberta's Bar and Bench* (Edmonton: Hurtig Publishers, 1987), 7.

44. Rouleau, quoted in Smith, 'Bloody Murder', 15.

45. *Calgary Herald*, 24 July, 10 Sept., 27 Feb., and 8 Mar. 1889.

46. Canada, *House of Commons Debates*, Session 1921, vol. 4, 26 May 1921, 3908.

47. Diane Tye, 'Local Character Anecdotes: A Nova Scotia Case Study', *Western Folklore* 48 (July 1989): 196.

48. The Indian Act was amalgamated in 1876 to consolidate all government legislation pertaining to Indian people in Canada. It governs virtually every aspect of Indian life from cradle to grave.

49. The Mississaugas of Mud Lake/Curve Lake First Nation is an Ojibway band in southeastern Ontario with a land base of about 1,600 acres in the area covered by the Williams Treaty of 1923. It is on a peninsula surrounded by Buckhorn and Chemong lakes and is located about 20 miles from Peterborough, ON.

50. 'Williams Upsets Knott at Curve Lake Election', *Cortaid News* 4, 13 (1976): 28.

51. Other published works include an unpublished Master's thesis by C.A. Franks from Boston University, 1980, newsletters, and obituary notices.

52. C.A. Franks, 'Elsie, Indian Chief, Bus Driver, Shopkeeper, Grannie' (MA thesis, Boston University, 1980).

53. In 1920, Deputy Superintendent General Duncan Campbell Scott, an advocate of assimilation, stated, 'I want to get rid of the Indian Problem. Our object

is to continue until there is not a single Indian in Canada that has not been absorbed in the body politic and there is no Indian question and no Indian Department.' E. Brian Titley, *A Narrow Vision: Duncan Campbell Scott and the Administration of Indian Affairs* (Vancouver: UBC Press, 1986), 50. The intent of the policy was to eliminate the 'Indian Problem' by eliminating the Indian, their culture, and their language. In Duncan Campbell Scott's time, Canada's Indian population numbered a mere 113,724—an all-time low.

54. Linda Post, 'Honouring the Memory of Elsie Knott', *Anishinabek News* (Fall 1998). Available at http://www.tyendinaga.net/amsp/2nd/story8.htm (accessed 28 May 2004)

55. 'Canada's First Woman Chief', *Indian Life* (1996): 12.

56. Franks, 'Elsie, Indian Chief'.

57. 'Canada's First Woman Chief', 1996.

58. 'Elsie Marie Knott, Enterprising Woman First Female Chief', *The Globe and Mail*, 1995, E6.

59. 'She Has Driven Bus for Twenty-Five Years. Curve Lake Honours Elsie Knott', *The Peterborough Examiner*, 9 May 1978, 8.

60. Personal interview, Rita Rose, Curve Lake First Nation, Aug. 2002.

61. Post 'Honouring the Memory of Elsie Knott', 2.

62. Ibid.

63. Ibid., 8.

64. 'Elsie Knott: A Curve Lake Elder and Crusader', *Prime Time: Peterborough County's Newspaper for People Fifty-Plus, May 1995*, 5.

65. Franks, 'Elsie, Indian Chief', 8.

66. Secretary of State, *Speaking together: Canada's Native women* (Ottawa: Secretary of State, 1975), 100.

67. Franks, 'Elsie, Indian Chief', 59.

68. Ibid., 8.

69. Personal interview, Rita Rose, Curve Lake First Nation, Aug. 2002.

70. Telephone interview with Rita Rose, 2005.

71. Ibid.

72. 'For a Start: Grannie is a Real Chief', *West Sussex County Times*, 7 Sept. 1973, 21.

73. Post, 'Honouring the Memory of Elsie Knott', 3.

74. *The Peterborough Examiner*, 1955, n.p.

75. Post, 'Honouring the Memory of Elsie Knott', 3.

76. Canada, House of Commons, *Statement of the Government of Canada on Indian Policy* (White Paper) (Ottawa: Supply and Services, 1969), 2.

77. Ken Coates, *The Marshall Decision and Native Rights* (Montreal: McGill-Queen's University Press, 2000), 76.

78. Laurie Meijer-Drees, *The Indian Association of Alberta: A History of Political Action* (Vancouver: UBC Press, 2002).

79. P. Armstrong, '100 Indians Break the Ice in Fish Fight', *The Peterborough Examiner*, 10 Feb. 1975, n.p.

80. 'For a Start', 21.

81. 'Elsie Knott: A Curve Lake Elder and Crusader'.

82. Telephone interview with Rita Rose, 2005.

83. Franks, 'Elsie, Indian Chief'.

84. Telephone interview with Rita Rose, 2005.

85. D. Clifford, 'Indians 5000 Strong Coming to Peterborough', *The Peterborough Examiner*, 9 Mar. 1977, 9.

86. Canada, *Royal Commission on Aboriginal Peoples* (Ottawa, 1996).

87. Union of Ontario Indians, 'A History of the Anishnabek Nation'. Available at http://www.Anishnabek.ca/uoi/uoiorghish.htm (accessed 5 Jan. 2005).

88. Canada, House of Commons, *Governor General Georges Vanier's Speech from the Throne* (Ottawa: Queen's Printer, 1960).

89. Ibid.

90. Franks, 'Elsie, Indian Chief'.

91. Ibid.

92. Cited in Post, 'Honouring the Memory of Elsie Knott', 3.

93. Secretary of State, *Speaking together*.

94. Interview with Rita Rose, 2005.

95. Ibid.

96. Post, 'Honouring the Memory of Elsie Knott', 2.

97. Ibid.

98. Ibid.

99. Franks, 'Elsie, Indian Chief'.

100. Ibid., 65.

101. Ibid.

102. Ibid., 70.

103. Ibid.

104. Ibid.

105. Ibid., 68.

106. 'Elsie Marie Knott'.

107. Ontario, Legislative Assembly of Ontario, Speech by Mr R. Gary Stewart. *Hansard*, 1995, 4–5.

108. Father Heffernan, 'Elsie Knott's legacy is one of community first and foremost', *The Peterborough Examiner*, 15 Dec. 1995, 15.

109. Franks, 'Elsie, Indian Chief', 67.

110. Heffernan, 'Elsie Knott's legacy', 15.

CHAPTER THIRTEEN: NEGOTIATING HEALTH AND WELL-BEING

1. Elizabeth Vibert, 'The Contours of Everyday Life: Foot and Identity in the Plateau Fur Trade', in Carolyn Podruchny and Laura Peers, eds, *Gathering Places: Aboriginal and Fur Trade Histories* (Vancouver: UBC Press, 2010), 126.

2. Elizabeth Vibert, 'Real Men Hunt Buffalo: Masculinity, Race, and Class in British Fur Traders'

Narratives', *Gender and History* 8, 1 (Apr. 1996): 4–21.

3. Sarah Carter, *Lost Harvests: Prairie Indian Reserve Farmers and Government Policy* (Montreal: McGill-Queen's University Press, 1990).

4. Naomi Adelson, *Being Alive Well: Health and the Politics of Cree Well-Being* (Toronto: University of Toronto Press, 2000), 110.

5. As cited in Elizabeth Vibert, *Traders' Tales: Narratives of Cultural Encounters in the Columbia Plateau, 1807–1846* (Norman: University of Oklahoma Press, 1997), 172.

6. It is only in the twenty-first century that scientists have engaged in a wholesale census-taking of marine life. See Census of Marine Life, http://www.coml.org/ (accessed 1 Sept. 2010).

7. Arthur J. Ray, *Indians in the Fur Trade: Their role as trappers, hunters, and middlemen in the lands southwest of Hudson Bay, 1660–1870* (Toronto: University of Toronto Press, 1974), 27–32 and figure 15, p. 47.

8. Christopher Hannibal-Paci, 'Historical Representations of Lake Sturgeon by Native and Non-Native Artists', *Canadian Journal of Native Studies* 18, 2 (1998), 214–24.

9. E.E. Rich, ed., *Journal of Occurrences in the Athabasca Department by George Simpson, 1820 and 1821, and Report* (London: Hudson's Bay Record Society, 1938), 197, 3 n.5, 110, 139. See also George Colpitts, *Game in the Garden: A Human History of Wildlife in Western Canada* (Vancouver: UBC Press, 2002), 21.

10. Frank Tough, *'As their Natural Resources Fail': Native Peoples and the Economic History of Northern Manitoba 1870–1930* (Vancouver: UBC Press, 1996), 175.

11. George Simpson to the Governor, Deputy Governor, and Committee of the Honourable Hudson's Bay Company, 20 June 1841, in Glyndwr Williams, ed., *London Correspondence inward from Sir George Simpson, 1841–42* (London: Hudson's Bay Record Society, 1973), 25–6.

12. Shepard Krech, *The Ecological Indian: Myth and History* (New York: W.W. Norton & Company, 1999).

13. Manitoba, Department of Mines and Natural Resources, Annual Report, 1930.

14. Fred Fraser to C.H. Herbert, 25 June 1951, file 40-6-4B, part 2, vol. 249, series 1-A-a, RG 22, Library and Archives Canada (hereafter LAC).

15. Eutrophication refers to the process whereby a body of water receives excess nutrients, which in turn can promote the excessive growth of aquatic plant life.

16. For more on this case study, see Chapter 7 in Liza Piper, *The Industrial Transformation of Subarctic Canada* (Vancouver: UBC Press, 2009).

17. George Colpitts, 'Science, Streams and Sport: Trout Conservation in Southern Alberta, 1900–1930' (MA thesis: University of Calgary, 1993).

18. G.E. Butler, 'Fish culture in the Prairie Provinces, and some of its results', *Transactions of the American Fisheries Society* 60, 1 (Jan. 1930): 119–20.

19. W.B. Scott and E.J. Crossman, *Freshwater Fishes of Canada* (Ottawa: Fisheries Research Board of Canada, 1973), 269–77.

20. Scott and Crossman, *Freshwater Fishes*, 767–74.

21. Tough, *As Their Natural Resources Fail*, 177.

22. J.B. Skaptason to A.G. Cunningham, Re Airplane Patrol to Dauphin River, 28 Oct. 1935, GR1600 G4555, Archives of Manitoba (hereafter AM).

23. Skaptason to Cunningham, 28 Oct. 1935. For the historiography of this transition, see Karl Jacoby, *Crimes Against Nature: Squatters, Poachers, Thieves and the Hidden History of American Conservation* (Berkeley: University of California Press, 2003) and J. Sandlos, *Hunters at the Margin: Native Peoples and Wildlife Conservation in the Northwest Territories* (Vancouver: UBC Press, 2007).

24. A.G. Cunningham to Capt P.M. Pearson, 18 Sept. 1935; A.G. Cunningham to C.H. Attwood, 31 Oct. 1936; C.H. Attwood to A.G. Cunningham, 2 Nov. 1936, all in GR1600 G4555, AM.

25. J. Foggie, Chief Sanitary Inspector, Report of Inspection, Water Supply – Fish Hatchery, Dauphin River, Manitoba. 29 July 1944, GR1600 G4555, AM.

26. G.E. Butler to A.G. Cunningham, 3 Nov. 1943, GR1600 G4555, AM.

27. Ibid.

28. A.G. Cunningham to J.G. Cowan, 11 Nov. 1943, GR1600 G4555, AM.

29. C.R. Donovan to J.G. Cowan, 20 Nov. 1943, GR1600 G4555, AM.

30. J.G. Cowan to A.G. Cunningham, 25 Apr. 1944; G.E. Butler to A.G. Cunningham, 26 Apr. 1944; C.R. Donovan, Investigation of Typhoid Fever, 25 May 1944, all in GR1600 G4555, AM.

31. L.J. Hunter, Sanitary Inspector, 'Sanitary survey following Typhoid Fever Investigation', 4 May 1944, GR1600 G4555, AM.

32. A.G. Cunningham to D.M. Stephens, 19 June 1944, GR1600 G4555, AM.

33. For discussion of how non-Aboriginal people perceived Aboriginal people and communities as repositories for disease, see Maureen Lux, *Medicine that Walks: Disease, Medicine and Canadian Plains Native People, 1880–1940* (Toronto: University of Toronto Press, 2001).

34. Hunter, 'Sanitary survey'.

35. Foggie, 'Report of Inspection'.

36. See, for example, CBC News, 'Kashechewan: Water crisis in Northern Ontario', 9 Nov. 2006. Available at http://www.cbc.ca/news/background/aboriginals/ kashechewan.html; CTV News, 'Concerns over water on reserve ignored for years', 27 Oct. 2005. Available at http://www.ctv.ca/servlet/ArticleNews/ story/CTVNews/20051027/aboriginal_water_ feature_051027/20051027/; Indian Affairs and Northern Development, 'Progress on Kashechewan Action Plan', 3 Nov. 2005. Available at http://www. ainc-inac.gc.ca/ai/mr/nr/s-d2005/2-02730-eng.asp.

37. Foggie, 'Report of Inspection'.

38. As cited in Foggie, 'Report of Inspection'.

39. William Gibbard, in Victor P. Lytwyn, 'Torchlight Prey: Night Hunting and Fishing by the Aboriginal People in the Great Lakes Region', in John Nichols, ed., *Actes du Trente-Deuxième Congrès des Algonquinistes* (Winnipeg: University of Manitoba Press, 2001), 311. William Gibbard was the first government-appointed fishery overseer for Lake Huron and Lake Superior after the Fisheries Act was introduced in 1857. He served until his murder in 1863.

40. Nicolas Frémiot, 'Letter #62: Fr. Frémiot to his Superiors in New York. From the Immaculée Conception Mission, October 18, 1849', in William Lonc and George Topp, trans., Lorenzo Cadieux, S.J. ed., *Letters from the New Canada Missions, 1843–1852 Part 2: Letters #45–93* (hereafter *LNCM*) (Halifax: W. Lonc, 2001), 99.

41. Charles E. Cleland, 'The Inland Shore Fishery of the Northern Great Lakes: Its Development and Importance in Prehistory', *American Antiquity* 47, 4 (Oct. 1982): 768–71.

42. Christopher Hannibal-Paci, '"Officers of the HBC, Missionaries and other Intelligent Persons in the District of Keewatin": Lake Winnipeg Sturgeon as an Aboriginal Resource', in David Pentland ed., *Papers of the Twenty-Ninth Algonquian Conference* (Winnipeg: University of Manitoba, 1998), 128–49; Douglas Harris, *Fish, Law, and Colonialism: The Legal Capture of Salmon in British Columbia* (Toronto: University of Toronto Press, 2001); Victor P. Lytwyn, 'Inland Sea Navigators: Algonquian Mastery of the Great Lakes', in H.C. Wolfart, ed., *Papers of the Thirty-Sixth Algonquian Conference* (Winnipeg: University of Manitoba Press, 2005), 255–69; Lytwyn, 'Ojibwa and Ottawa Fisheries Around Manitoulin Island: Historical and Geographical Perspectives on Aboriginal and Treaty Fishing Rights', *Native Studies Review* 6, 1 (1990): 1–30; Laura Peers, *The Ojibwa of Western Canada: 1780–1870* (Winnipeg: University of Manitoba Press, 1994); Leo G. Waisberg and Tim E. Holzkamm, '"A Tendency to Discourage Them from Cultivating": Ojibwa Agriculture and Indian Affairs Administration in Northwestern Ontario', *Ethnohistory* 40, 2 (Spring 1993): 175–211; Waisberg and Holzkamm, '"Their Country is Tolerably Rich in Furs": The Ojibwa Fur Trade in the Boundary Waters Region, 1821–71', in William Cowan, ed., *Actes du Vingt-Cinquième Congrès des Algonquinites* (Ottawa: Carleton University Press, 1994), 494–513.

43. Kerry Abel, 'History and the Provincial Norths: An Ontario Example', in Kerry Abel and Ken S. Coates, eds, *Northern Visions: New Perspectives on the North in Canadian History* (Peterborough: Broadview Press, 2001), 127–140; Ken S. Coates and William Morrison, 'Wintering and the Shaping of Northern History: Reflections from the Canadian North', in *Northern Visions*, 23–35.

44. Norman Risjord, *Shining Big Sea Water: The Story of Lake Superior* (St Paul: Minnesota Historical Society, 2008), 15.

45. Tim Holzkamm, Victor P. Lytwyn, and Leo G. Waisberg, 'Rainy River Sturgeon: An Ojibwa resource in the fur trade economy', *The Canadian Geographer* 32, 3 (1988): 198.

46. K.C.A. Dawson, *Archaeological Survey of Canada, Paper No.25, The McCluskey Site*, National Museum of Man, Mercury Series (Ottawa: National Museums of Canada, 1974), 1, 83.

47. Susan Rapalje Martin, 'A Reconsideration of Aboriginal Fishing Strategies in the Northern Great Lakes Region', *American Antiquity* 54, 3 (July 1989): 596, 602–03.

48. Lytwyn, 'Ojibwa and Ottawa Fisheries', 8; Cleland, 'The inland shore fishery', 766–7.

49. Sir George Simpson on the sturgeon fishery at Rainy River, 1841, in Holzkamm et al., 'Rainy River Sturgeon', 197.

50. Mary Fox, 'This is the way it was, recorded 28 July 1977 Bearskin Lake', in *This is what happened* (Timmins: Ojibway and Cree Cultural Centre, 1999), 109.

51. Heindenreich, in Lytwyn, 'Ojibwa and Ottawa Fisheries', 8; Holzkamm et al., 'Rainy River Sturgeon', 199.

52. Holzkamm et al., 'Rainy River Sturgeon', 199.

53. John Bighead, 'It is not like the way it used to be, 17 July 1975, Wunnumin Lake', in *This is what happened*, 74.

54. Pierre Pouchot, in Lytwyn, 'Inland Sea Navigators', 256.

55. Lytwyn, 'Inland Sea Navigators', 259.

56. Joseph-Urbain Hanipaux, 'Letter #79: Fr. Hanipaux to his Superior, Paris. From Holy Cross Mission,

Manitoulin Island, November 14, 1851', *LNCM*, 246–7.

57. Ellen Sainnawap, 'This is how poor the people were, 27 July 1975, Wunnumin Lake', in *This is what happened*, 10.

58. Great Lakes Fishery Commission, *Fish-Community Objectives for Lake Superior* (Ann Arbor, MI: Great Lakes Fishery Commission, 2003), 12.

59. Edward S. Rogers and Mary B. Black, 'Subsistence Strategy in the Fish and Hare Period, Northern Ontario: The Weagamow Ojibwa, 1880–1920', *Journal of Anthropological Research* 32, 1 (Spring, 1976): 7–8.

60. Lytwyn, 'Torchlight Prey', 304.

61. Peers, *The Ojibwa*, 23.

62. William Warren, *History of the Ojibway People* (St Paul: Minnesota Historical Press, [1885] 1984), 45–6.

63. Ibid., 20.

64. Basil Johnston, *The Manitous: The Spiritual World of the Ojibway* (Toronto: Key Porter Books, 1995), 2.

65. Victoria Brehm, 'The Metamorphoses of an Ojibwa Manido', *American Literature* 68, 4 (Dec. 1996): 681–2.

66. Ibid., 677–706.

67. Selwyn Dewdney, *The Sacred Scrolls of the Southern Ojibwa* (Toronto: Toronto University Press, 1975), 124.

68. Basil Johnston, 'Nebaunaubaewuk and Nebaunaubaequaewuk', in *The Manitous* (Toronto: Key Porter Books, 1995), 136.

69. *Anishnaabeg* is an autonym for members of the Ojibwa, Odawa, and Algonquin nations.

70. Basil Johnston, 'Mermaids', in *The Star Man and Other Tales* (Toronto: Royal Ontario Museum, 1997), 31.

71. A.H. Lawrie and Jerold F. Rahrer, *Lake Superior: A Case History of the Lake and its Fisheries, Technical Report No. 19* (Ann Arbor, MI: Great Lakes Fishery Commission, 1973), 30.

72. Martin, 'A Reconsideration', 594.

73. See, for example, Peers, *The Ojibwa*, 7.

74. Brehm, 'The Metamorphoses', 683–4.

75. Charles E. Cleland, *Rites of Conquest: The History and Culture of Michigan's Native Americans* (Ann Arbor, MI: University of Michigan Press, 1992), 55–7.

76. J. Michael Toms, 'An Ojibwa Community, American Sportsmen and the Ontario Government in the Early Management of the Nipigon River Fishery', in Diane Newell and Rosemary Ommer, eds, *Fishing places, fishing people: Traditions and issues in Canadian small-scale fisheries* (Toronto: University of Toronto Press, 1999), 174, 175.

77. Adolph Greenberg, 'Adaptive responses by an Ojibwa band to northern development' (PhD dissertation, Wayne State University, 1978), 1686.

78. Ibid., 55.

79. Nicolas Frémiot, 'Letter #75: Frémiot to Rev. Micard, Superior of the Seminary of Saint-Dié. From Sault-Sainte Marie, February 2, 1851', in *LNCM*, 202.

80. Vibert, *Traders' Tales*, 180.

81. August Kohler, 'Letter #74: Fr. Kohler to his Superior. From Sault-Sainte-Marie, December 28 1850', *LNCM*, 188.

82. Lytwyn, 'Ojibwa and Ottawa Fisheries', 8–9.

83. Lawrie and Rahrer, *Lake Superior*, 30.

84. Frémiot, 'Letter #75', 204.

85. Authur J. Ray, 'Periodic shortages, Native welfare, and the Hudson Bay Company', in Kenneth Coates and William Morrison, eds, *Interpreting Canada's North: Selected Readings* (Copp Clark Pitman Ltd, 1999), 99–101.

86. Waisberg and Holzkamm, '"Their Country is Tolerably Rich in Furs"', 494.

87. Holzkamm et al., 'Rainy River Sturgeon', 199.

88. Margeret Bogue, 'To Save the Fish: Canada, the United States, the Great Lakes, and the Joint Commission of 1892', *The Journal of American History* 79, 4 (Mar. 1993): 1432.

89. Ibid, 1433–4.

90. Harris, *Fish, Law, and Colonialism*, 27.

91. Ibid., 31.

92. Mark Walters, 'The Dimensions of Reconciliation: *Gladstone* and the Great Lakes'. Presented at Reconsidering *R. v. Gladstone*: Aboriginal Rights to Fish Since 1996. 12–14 Oct. 2005, Vancouver, BC.

93. Grace Lee Nute, 'The American Fur Company's Fishing Enterprises on Lake Superior', *The Mississippi Valley Historical Review* 12, 4 (Mar. 1926): 486.

94. Nicolas Frémiot, 'Letter #69: Fr. Frémiot to Fr. Provincial. From Immaculate Conception near Fort William, Lake Superior, September 27, 1850', *LNCM*, 138–9.

95. Frémiot, 'Letter #62', 97.

96. Indian and Northern Affairs Canada, *The Robinson Treaty made in the year 1850 with the Ojibewa Indians of Lake Superior Conveying Certain Lands to the Crown*. Available at http://www.ainc-inac.gc.ca/al/hts/tgu/pubs/trob/rbt/rbt-eng.asp (accessed 15 Apr. 2008).

97. Christopher Vescey, 'Grassy Narrows Reserve: Mercury Pollution, Social Disruption, and Natural Resources: A Question of Autonomy', *American Indian Quarterly* 11, 4 (Autumn 1987), 289.

98. As cited in Holzmann et al., 'Rainy River Sturgeon', 201.

99. Coates and Morrison, 'Wintering', 30–2.

100. August Kohler, 'Letter #73: Fr. Kohler to his superior. From Sault-Sainte-Marie, December 21, 1850', *LNCM*, 173.

101. Ibid., 178.

102. Nicolas Frémiot, 'Letter #64: Fr. Frémiot to Fr. Provincial in Paris. From the Immaculée Conception Mission, January, 1850', *LNCM*, 103.

103. Coates and Morrison, 'Wintering', 31.

104. J.J. West, 'Ojibwa Fisheries, Commercial Fisheries Development, and Fisheries Administration, 1873–1915: An Examination of the Conflicting Interest and Collapse of the Sturgeon Fisheries of the Lake of the Woods', *Native Studies Review* 6, 1 (1990): 35–6.

105. Abel, 'History and the Provincial Norths', 129–30.

106. Lawrie and Rahrer, *Lake Superior*, 58.

107. Lytwyn, 'Torchlight Prey', 309.

108. Frémiot, 'Letter #64', 103.

109. Lytwyn, 'Torchlight Prey,' 311.

110. Ibid., 312.

111. Patricia Jasen, *Wild Things: Nature, Culture, and Tourism in Ontario, 1790–1914*, (Toronto: University of Toronto Press, 1995), 93, 133–4.

112. Lytwyn, 'Torchlight Prey', 313.

113. Bogue. 'Fishing the Great Lakes', 297–8.

114. James Masakeyash, 'This is what would make us Happy, 9 May 1978', in *This is what happened* (Timmins: Ojibway and Cree Cultural Center, 1999), 42.

115. Dominique du Ranquet, *Journal 1856*, unpublished, trans. Gabrielle Parent, 129.

116. Holzkamm et al., 'Rainy River Sturgeon', 202.

117. Todhunter, Schollen, & Associates, *North Shore Environmental Services, Lake Nipigon Fisheries Direction Report, 1996–2016*, prepared for Land of the Nipigon Waterways Development Association Inc (Mar. 1996), 2–9.

CHAPTER FOURTEEN: POLITICAL ACTIVISM

1. Robert Alexander Innes, '"I'm On Home Ground Now. I'm Safe": Saskatchewan Aboriginal Veterans in the Immediate Postwar Years, 1945–1946', *American Indian Quarterly* 28, 3&4 (2004): 685–718.

2. In the late 1980s and early 1990s, Innu men, women, and children occupied the Minai-nipi bombing range and the runway at CFB Goose Bay to stop the bombing of the territory in which they had hunted and trapped for centuries.

3. E.P. Thompson, *The Making of the English Working Class* (London: Penguin Books, 1991), 12.

4. *Anishinabek* (*Anishinabe* in the singular) means 'the people' in the Algonkian languages. While the term is sometimes used to refer to First Nations people in general, more often it is used to describe members of the Ojibwe, Odawa, and Potawatomi peoples.

5. Wasauksing First Nation, Franz Koennecke Collection, Joseph Traunch, Collins Inlet, to DIA, Jan. 1926. The letter's spelling has been left largely in its original form, with some minimal editorial changes to clarify the meaning.

6. See Robin Jarvis Brownlie, *A Fatherly Eye: Indian Agents, Government Power, and Aboriginal Resistance in Ontario, 1918–1939* (Toronto and New York: Oxford University Press, 2003).

7. Frank Tough, 'Ontario's Appropriation of Indian Hunting: Provincial Conservation Policies vs. Aboriginal and Treaty Rights, ca. 1892–1930' (Toronto: Ontario Native Affairs Secretariat, 1991), 2.

8. See, for example, Nancy M. Wightman and Robert Wightman, 'The Mica Bay Affair: Conflict on the Upper Great Lakes Mining Frontier; 1840–1850', *Ontario History* 83, 3 (1991): 193–208, and Douglas Leighton, 'The Manitoulin Incident of 1863: An Indian-White Confrontation in the Province of Canada', *Ontario History* 69, 2 (June 1977): 3–23.

9. Frank Tough, 'Conservation and the Indian: Clifford Sifton's Commission of Conservation, 1910–1919', *Native Studies Review* 8, 1 (1992): 70.

10. Paul Williams, 'The Chain' (LLM thesis, York University, 1981), 18.

11. Wasauksing First Nation, Franz Koennecke Collection, John M. Daly to DIA, 15 July 1932.

12. See Theodore Binnema, 'Aboriginal Canadians and the Development of Canada's Indian Act, 1868–1876'. Paper presented at the annual meeting of the Canadian Historical Association, Halifax, 2003.

13. Wasauksing First Nation, Franz Koennecke Collection, John M. Daly to DIA, 4 Apr. 1930.

14. National Archives of Canada (NA), RG 10 (Indian Affairs), vol. 1844, Treaty 60.

15. See Victor P. Lytwyn, 'Ojibwa and Ottawa Fisheries around Manitoulin Island: Historical and Geographical Perspectives on Aboriginal and Treaty Fishing Rights', *Native Studies Review* 6, 1 (1990): 1–30.

16. See Tough, 'Ontario's Appropriation of Indian Hunting', esp. 2–3.

17. Dalton Jacobs of Curve Lake First Nation, interviewed in the 1990s, cited in Cynthia C. Wesley-Esquimaux and Dr I.V.B. Johnson, 'United Anishnaabeg Elders: the Treaties Revisited [with particular emphasis on the 1913 Williams Treaty]', (unpublished report, n.d.), 61–2, in possession of Chippewas of Georgina Island First Nation.

18. Wasauksing First Nation, Franz Koennecke Collection, John M. Daly to DIA, 11 July 1932.

19. See Wesley-Esquimaux and Johnson, 'United Anishnaabeg Elders'.

20. NA, RG 10, vol. 2332, f. 67.071-4C, Testimony of John Bigwin of Rama, 1923.

21. See Tough, 'Ontario's Appropriation of Indian Hunting'; Chief Greg Sarazin, 'Algonquins South of the Ottawa: 220 Years of Broken Promises', in Boyce Richardson, ed., *Drumbeat: Anger and Renewal in Indian Country* (Toronto: Summerhill Press, 1989), 190.

22. NA, RG 10, vol. 10599, Lewis to Mr G.W. Parks, District Warden, North Bay, 22 Oct. 1923.

23. NA, RG 10, vol. 10599, Robert J. Lewis to DIA, 24 Apr. 1923.

24. NA, RG I0, vol. 10599, Lewis to Chief Charles Obotossaway, 25 May 1923.

25. NA, RG 10, vol. 6964, f. 488/20-2, pt. 1, Lewis to DIA, 8 Dec. 1930.

26. NA, RG 10, vol.10820, f. 475/20-2, pt.2, Daly to J.D. McLean, 12 Jan. 1923.

27. See Franz Koennecke, 'Wasoksing. The History of Parry Island an Anishnabwe Community in the Georgian Bay. 1850 to 1920' (MA thesis, University of Waterloo, 1984), 106.

28. NA, RG 10, vol. 1082.0, f. 475/20-2, pt.2, Alex Logan to DIA, 23 Mar. 1918.

29. NA, RG 10, Series B-3, vol. 7225, f. 8019-39, 'Manitoulin Island Agency–Enfranchisement–Paibomsai, Edward', Edward Paibomsai to DIA, 15 Mar. 1930.

30. Tough, 'Ontario's Appropriation of Indian Hunting', 10.

31. Wasauksing First Nation, Franz Koennecke Collection, John Daly to Duncan C. Scott, DIA, 18 Mar. 1930.

32. See Brownlie, *A Fatherly Eye*, 70–5.

33. See James Morrison, 'The Robinson Treaties of 1850: A Case Study'. Prepared for the Royal Commission on Aboriginal Peoples (1993), 150–1.

34. RG 10, Series B-3, vol. 7225, f. 8019-39, 'Manitoulin Island Agency–Enfranchisement–Paibomsai, Edward', Edward Paibomsai to DIA, 15 Mar. 1930.

35. Wasauksing First Nation, Franz Koennecke Collection, Daly to Deputy Minister of Game and Fisheries, Toronto, ON, 20 Aug. 1924.

36. Wasauksing First Nation, Franz Koennecke Collection, Daly to DIA, 11 Aug. 1929.

37. NA, RG 10, vol. 6767, f. 452-15, pt. 1, Jane Manitowaba to D.C. Scott, 27 Jan. 1917.

38. NA, RG 10, vol. 6767, f. 452-15, pt. 1, Jane Manitowaba to D.C. Scott, 27 Jan. 1917. John Manitowaba's letter to the King is mentioned in a letter from Agent Daly to the DIA, Wasauksing First Nation, Franz Koennecke Collection, Daly to DIA, 5 Aug. 1931.

39. See Fred Gaffen, *Forgotten Soldiers* (Penticton: Theytus Books, 1985), 37.

40. Indian Act, Revised Statutes of Canada 1906, c. 81, in Sharon Helen Venne, ed., *Indian Acts and Amendments 1868–1975, An Indexed Collection* (Saskatoon: University of Saskatchewan Native Law Centre, 1981), 208.

41. Wasauksing First Nation, Franz Koennecke Document Collection (DIA files), Chief Frank Judge to J.M. Daly, 17 May 1931.

42. See Paul Tennant, *Aboriginal Peoples and Politics. The Indian Land Question in British Columbia, 1849–1989* (Vancouver: UBC Press, 1990), 84–125; Cole Harris, *Making Native Space: Colonialism, Resistance, and Reserves in British Columbia* (Vancouver: UBC Press, 2002), 216–65; Peter Kulchyski, 'A Considerable Unrest: F.O. Loft and the League of Indians', *Native Studies Review* 4, 1&2 (1988): 95–117; Peter McFarlane, 'Aboriginal Leadership', in D. Long and O.P. Dickason, eds., *Visions of the Heart. Canadian Aboriginal Issues*, 2nd edn (Toronto: Harcourt, 2000), 61–4; Constance Backhouse, *Colour-Coded: A Legal History of Racism in Canada, 1900–1950* (Toronto: Published for Osgoode Society for Canadian Legal History by University of Toronto Press, 1999), 103–31.

43. See Tough, 'Ontario's Appropriation of Indian Hunting', and, for an earlier period, Sidney L. Harring, *White Man's Law: Native People in Nineteenth Century Canadian Jurisprudence* (Toronto: Published for Osgoode Society for Canadian Legal History by University of Toronto Press, 1998), 121–3.

44. Paul W. DePasquale, '"Worth the Noting": European Ambivalence and Aboriginal Agency in Meta Incognita, 1576–78', in J.S.H. Brown and E. Vibert, eds, *Reading Beyond Words: Contexts for Native History* (Peterborough: Broadview Press, 2003), 5–38.

45. Winona LaDuke, *All Our Relations: Native Struggles for Land and Ute* (Cambridge, MA: South End Press, 1999).

46. Annette Chrétien, '"Fresh Tracks in Dead Air": Mediating Contemporary Métis Identities Through Music and Storytelling' (PhD dissertation, York University, 2005).

47. Indian and Northern Affairs Canada (INAC), Royal Commission on Aboriginal Peoples (Ottawa: Indian and Northern Affairs Canada, 1996). Available at http://www.collectionscanada.gc.ca/webarchives/20071115053257/http://www.ainc-inac.gc.ca/ch/rcap/sg/sgmm_e.html

48. Chrétien, '"Fresh Tracks in Dead Air"'.

49. INAC, 1996.

50. Non-decision-making is defined as 'an act that suppresses potential issues and ensures that they do not even enter the decision-making process'. John Scott, *Power* (Cambridge: Polity Press, 2001), 58.

51. Steven Lukes, *Power: A Radical View* (London and Basingstoke: The MacMillan Press Ltd, 1974).

52. Steven Lukes, *Power: A Radical View*, 2nd edn (Hampshire and New York: Palgrave MacMillan, 2005), 29.

53. Ibid.

54. Peter Digeser, 'The Fourth Face of Power', *Journal of Politics* 54, 3–4 (1992): 980.

55. Lukes, *Power*, 2nd edn.

56. Digeser, 'The Fourth Face', 980.

57. Lukes, *Power*, 2nd edn.

58. Digeser, 'The Fourth Face', 980.

59. Gerald Jacob, *Site Unseen: The Politics of Siting a Nuclear Waste Repository* (Pittsburgh: University of Pittsburgh Press, 1990).

60. Barry Hindess, *Discourses of Power: From Hobbes to Foucault* (Oxford: Blackwell Publishers, 1996).

61. Audrey Kobayashi, 'Negotiating the Personal and the Political in Critical Qualitative Research', in M. Limb and C. Dwyer, eds, *Qualitative Methodologies for Geographers: Issues and Debates* (London: Arnold, 2001), 66.

62. Frank Fischer, *Citizens, Experts, and the Environment: The Politics of Local Knowledge* (Durham and London: Duke University Press, 2005), 175.

63. William K. Carroll, *Critical Strategies for Social Research* (Toronto: Canadian Scholar's Press Inc, 2004), 276.

64. Fischer, *Citizens, Experts, and the Environment*.

65. Martin F. Dunn, 'Métis 101, Understanding Métis Today in Canada, Part 2—A Look at Métis Organisations'. Available at http://www.othermetis.net/Papers/Dunn/Understanding/Metis%20102/Metis102%20-%20History.htm#History; Chrétien, '"Fresh Tracks in Dead Air"'.

66. Gerry Andrews, *Métis Outpost* (Victoria: Pencrest Publications, 1985).

67. Keith Henry, Government of British Columbia, Hearing Aid Act (2007). Available at http://www.qp.gov.bc.ca/statreg/stat/H/96186_01.htm (accessed 16 Feb. 2005).

68. Dorothea Calverly, 'The Kelly Lake Métis Settlement' (n.d.) Available at http://www.calyerley.ca/Part0l-FirstNations/0l-135.html (accessed 16 Feb. 2005).

69. Ben Parfitt, 'Demanding a Say In the Boom', *The Tyee*, 31 May 2004. Available at http://thetyee.ca/News/2004/05/31/ (accessed 11 Dec. 2004).

70. Derek Reiber, 'Battling the Ghosts of Death', 2004. Available at http://www.tidepool.org/greentide/greent61104.cfm (accessed 16 Feb. 2005).

71. Lyle Campbell-Letendre, president of Kelly Lake Métis Settlement Society, personal communication to David Bentley, 2005.

72. Ibid.

73. Michel Foucault, *Power/Knowledge* (New York: Pantheon Books, 1980).

74. Karen Tankard, *Kelly Lake* (documentary). CBC, 1993.

75. Campbell-Letendre, personal communication.

76. Ibid.

77. Doug Pelly, HBT Agra Ltd, letter to Stu Lawrence–L.M. Engineering, 27 July 1993. Access to Information.

78. S.N. Lawrence, L.M. Engineering, letter to Geoff Butchart of Canada Mortgage and Housing, 29 July 1993. Access to Information.

79. Pelly to Lawrence.

80. Ann V. Thomas, British Columbia Ministry of Health, letter to Geoff Butchart (CHMC), 3 Sept. 1993. Access to Information.

81. Geoff Butchart, CMHC, memorandum to Jim Moms, Operations Manager, 1 Dec. 1993. Access to Information.

82. Henry, 'Hearing Aid Act'.

83. Campbell-Letendre, personal communication.

84. Joan Taillon, 'Rare Health Services Come to Métis of Kelly Lake', *Raven's Eye* 8, 4 (2004), 1.

85. Digeser, 'The Fourth Face of Power', 980, 991.

86. Chris Auty, national sales manager of GN ReSound, personal communication to David Bentley, 2005.

CHAPTER FIFTEEN: TREATIES AND SELF-GOVERNANCE

1. George F.G. Stanley, 'The Indian Background of Canadian History', *Report of the Annual Meeting of the Canadian Historical Association* 31, 1 (1952): 14–21.

2. Jean Friesen, 'Magnificent Gifts: The Treaties of Canada with the Indians of the Northwest, 1869–76', *Transactions of the Royal Society of Canada* 1, 5 (1986): 41–51.

3. Bonny Ibhawoh, 'Stronger than the Maxim Gun: Law, Human Rights and British Colonial Hegemony in Nigeria', *Africa: Journal of the International African Institute* 72, 1 (Jan. 2002): 55.

4. Evelyn J. Peters, 'Native People and the Environmental Regime in the James Bay and Northern Quebec Agreement', *Arctic* 52, 4 (Dec. 1999): 395–410.

5. Alan Penn, 'The James Bay and Northern Quebec Agreement: Natural Resources, Public Lands, and the Implementation of a Native Land Claim Settlement', Oct. 1995. Available in the 'research reports' section of the RCAP (Royal Commision

on Aboriginal People's) CD-ROM, 'For Seven Generations', records 106607-106769.

6. Quoted in Billy Diamond, 'Aboriginal Rights: The James Bay Experience', in Menno Boldt and J. Anthony Long, eds, *The Quest for Justice: Aboriginal Peoples and Aboriginal Rights* (Toronto: University of Toronto Press, 1985), 273–4.

7. Renée Dupuis and Kent McNeil, *Canada's Fiduciary Obligation to Aboriginal Peoples in the Context of Accession to Sovereignty by Quebec*, vol. 2. Domestic Dimensions (Ottawa: Minister of Supply and Services Canada, 1995). (Also available on the RCAP CD-ROM, 'For Seven Generations'), 29–33.

8. Harvey A. Feit, 'Hunting and the Quest for Power: The James Bay Cree and Whitemen in the Twentieth Century', in R. Bruce Morrison and C. Roderick Wilson, eds, *Native Peoples: The Canadian Experience* (Toronto: McClelland & Stewart, 1995), 198.

9. R.F.A. Salisbury, *Homeland for the Cree: Regional Development in James Bay 1971–1981* (Kingston: McGill-Queen's University Press, 1986), 5–6; 20–3.

10. Harvey A. Feit, 'Legitimation and Autonomy in James Bay Cree Responses To Hydro-electric Development', in Noel Dyck, ed., *Indigenous Peoples and the Nation State: Fourth World Politics in Canada, Australia and Norway* (St John's: Memorial University Institute for Social and Economic Research, 1985), 27–66.

11. Boyce Richardson, *Strangers Devour the Land* (Post Hills, VT: Chelsea Green Publishing Company, 1991), 301.

12. Harvey A. Feit, 'Negotiating Recognition of Aboriginal Rights', *Canadian Review of Anthropology* 1, 2 (1980): 255–78; Diamond, 'Aboriginal Rights', esp. 277.

13. See Grand Council of the Crees (GCC), *Never Without Consent: James Bay Crees' Stand Against Forcible Inclusion Into An Independent Quebec* (Toronto: ECW Press, 1998), 120–6; and Diamond, 'Aboriginal Rights', 279.

14. See Penn, 'The James Bay and Northern Quebec Agreement'.

15. Roy MacGregor, *Chief, The Fearless Vision of Billy Diamond* (Markham, ON: Viking, 1989), 129.

16. Ibid., 115–16.

17. Wendy Moss, 'The Implementation of the James Bay and Northern Quebec Agreement', in Brad W. Morse, ed., *Aboriginal Peoples and the Law: Indian, Metis and Inuit Rights in Canada* (Ottawa: Carleton University Press, 1989), 684– 94; Evelyn J. Peters, 'Federal and Provincial Responsibilities for the Cree, Naskapi and Inuit Under the James Bay and Northern Quebec, and Northeastern Quebec Agreements', in David C. Hawkes, ed., *Aboriginal*

Peoples and Government Responsibility: Exploring Federal and Provincial Roles (Ottawa: Carleton University Press, 1989), 173–242.

18. *The Tait Review*, (Department of Indian Affairs and Northern Development), The James Bay and Northern Quebec Agreement Implementation Review, 'Report', 3 Aug. 1981, esp. 32–3; 68–9.

19. House of Commons, Minutes of Proceedings and Evidence of the Standing Committee on Indian Affairs and Northern Development (Respecting: Main Estimates 1980-81, Vote 1 under Indian Affairs and Northern Development, Issue No. 23:45, 1700-1735), Thursday, 26 Mar. 1981.

20. *The Tait Review*, 20–2.

21. J.P. Rostaing, as cited in Peters, 'Federal and Provincial', 181.

22. Moss, 'The Implementation of the James Bay and Northern Quebec Agreement', 688.

23. Cree–Naskapi Commission, 'Report of the Cree-Naskapi Commission' (Ottawa, 1991), 50.

24. Ted Moses, 'Address by Chief Ted Moses', Yellowknife, 13 June 1988, 6.

25. Peters, 'Federal and Provincial'.

26. Penn, 'The James Bay and Northern Quebec Agreement'.

27. *Delgamuukw v. British Columbia*, paragraph 173.

28. The resource revenue and GST estimates are from GCC, '1997–8 Annual Report'. The federal spending figures are from Indian and Northern Affairs Canada, *The 1997 Annual Report: The James Bay and Northern Quebec Agreement*, 14.

29. As quoted in Michael Posluns, *Voices from the Odeyak* (Toronto: NC Press Ltd, 1993), 93.

30. GCC, Presentation to the RCAP, Montreal, 18 Nov. 1993, 978.

31. Jack Blacksmith in GCC, To the Subcommittee on the Boreal Forest. Proceedings of the Subcommittee on the Boreal Forest. Issue 17, Evidence. 2 Dec. 1998; and Issue 9, Evidence, Morning Sitting, Rouyn-Noranda, 28 Oct. 1998.

32. This figure comes from the Cree magazine, *The Nation* 4, 16 (4 July 1997): 11.

33. John Goddard, 'In From the Cold: The Oujé-Bougoumou Crees Build a Model Community After 60 years of Mistreatment and Dislocation', *Canadian Geographic* (July/Aug. 1994): 38–47.

34. Feit, 'Hunting', 218.

35. Kenny Blacksmith, to the House Standing Committee on the Environment and Sustainable Development, Evidence, 25 Apr. 1995.

36. At the time of the final revisions of this essay a major agreement-in-principle between the Grand Council of the Crees and the government of Quebec was announced. It commits Quebec to funding a Cree Development Corporation and

to revised forestry practices with Cree input into forestry management. In exchange the Crees have agreed to a new hydro undertaking and to drop several legal actions. The agreement is not yet ratified, but it appears to be a significant breakthrough in Cree–Quebec relations. However, it is also, in part, a response to the ongoing court proceedings over breaches of JBNQA and to the public campaign in the United States against provincial forestry practices. See Kevin Dougherty, 'Crees get $3.5 billion', *Montreal Gazette*, 24 Oct. 2001.

37. Taiaiake Alfred, *Wasasé: Indigenous Pathways of Action and Freedom* (Peterborough: Broadview Press, 2005); Glen Coulthard, 'Subjects of Empire: Indigenous Peoples and the "Politics of Recognition" in Canada', *Contemporary Political Theory* 6 (2007): 437–60.

38. Paul Nadasdy, *Hunters and Bureaucrats: Power, Knowledge, and Aboriginal-State Relations in the Southwest Yukon* (Vancouver: UBC Press, 2003).

39. Taiaiake Alfred, *Peace Power Righteousness: An Indigenous Manifesto* (Toronto: Oxford University Press, 1999); Marie Battiste, 'Introduction, Unfolding the Lessons of Colonization', in Battiste, ed., *Reclaiming Indigenous Voice and Vision* (Vancouver: UBC Press, 2007), xvi–xxx.

40. Linda Tuhiwai Smith, Decolonizing methodologies: Research and Indigenous peoples (New York: St Martin's Press, 1999), 22.

41. Alfred, *Peace Power*, 60.

42. Cliff Atleo, Jr, 'From Indigenous Nationhood to Neoliberal Aboriginal Economic Development: Charting the Evolution of Indigenous-Settler Relations', Canadian Social Economy Hub (Oct. 2008). Available at http://www.socialeconomyhub. ca/?q=content/indigenous-nationhood-neoliberal-aboriginal-economic-development-charting-evolution-indigeno (accessed 23 Nov. 2009).

43. This article is a product and an embodiment of these alliances, written collaboratively by Martha Stiegman, a non-Indigenous doctoral student at Concordia University, and Sherry Pictou, a grassroots community leader and former chief of Bear River First Nation. The analysis presented here comes out of three decades of Pictou's community-based political work, as well as the last six years of Stiegman's participatory-action doctoral research. For a detailed presentation of the authors' collaborative, video-based research methodology, see Stiegman and Pictou, 'How do you say Netuklimuk in English? Using Documentary Video to capture Bear River First Nation's Learning through Action', in Aziz Choudry and Dip Kappoor, eds, *Learning from the Ground up: Global Perspectives*

on Social Movements and Knowledge Production (New York: Palgrave Macmillan, 2010).

44. Henry Veltmeyer, 'The Restructuring of Capital and the Regional Problem', in Bryant Douglas Fairley, Colin Leys, and R. James Sacouman, eds, *Restructuring and Resistance from Atlantic Canada* (Toronto: Garamond Press, 1990), 79–104.

45. Patrick Kerans and John Kearney, *Turning the World Right Side Up: Science, Community, and Democracy* (Halifax: Fernwood, 2006): 100–02; 180–5.

46. Anthony Davis, 'Insidious Rationalities: The Institutionalisation of Small Boat Fishing and the Rise of the Rapacious Fisher' (1991). Available at http://www.stfx.ca/research/gbayesp/insidious_report.htm (accessed 15 Oct. 2006).

47. Anthony Davis, 'Barbed Wire and Bandwagons: A Comment on ITQ Fisheries Management', *Reviews in Fish Biology and Fisheries* 6 (1996): 97–107.

48. David Harvey, *The New Imperialism* (New York: Oxford University Press, 2003), 137–82.

49. Kerans and Kearney, *Turning the World*; M. Stiegman, *In the Same Boat?* 39 min. Canada: V-Tape.

50. There are roughly 300 registered band members of Bear River First Nation, approximately half of whom live on-reserve.

51. Grand Council of Micmacs, Union of Nova Scotia Indians, and Native Council of Nova Scotia, *The Mi'kmaq Treaty Handbook* (Sydney & Truro: Native Communications Society of Nova Scotia, 1987).

52. Donald Marshall Sr, Alexander Denny, and Simon Marshall, 'The Covenant Chain', in Boyce Richardson, ed., *Drumbeat: Anger and Renewal in Indian Country* (Toronto: Summerhill Press, 1989), 71–104.

53. Grand Council et al., *The Mi'kmaq Treaty Handbook*, i.

54. Alanis Obomsawin, *Incident at Restigouche*, 45 min 57 s. (Canada: National Film Board of Canada, 1984).

55. Kerry Prosper, Mary Jane Paulette, and Anthony Davis, 'Traditional Wisdom can build a Sustainable Future', *Atlantic Fisherman* (Aug. 2004): 2.

56. J. Marshall, 'Kmitkinu aq Maqmikewminu—Our Birthright and our Land', *Mi'kmaq Maliseet Nations News* 13, 3 (2006): 3.

57. Thomas Isaac, *Aboriginal and Treaty Rights in the Maritimes: The Marshall Decision and Beyond* (Saskatoon: Purich Publishers, 2001), 54–60.

58. William C. Wicken, *Mi'kmaq Treaties on Trial: History, Land, and Donald Marshall Junior* (Toronto: University of Toronto Press, 2002), 3–6.

59. Ken Coates, *The Marshall Decision and Native Rights* (Montreal & Kingston: McGill-Queen's University Press, 2000), 3–7.

60. *R v. Marshall*, 1999.
61. Kwegsi, 'Modern Day Treaty (Self-assimilation)' (2001). Available at www.turtleisland.org/news/kwegsi.doc; Kwegsi, 'Injustice? Duress and the Burnt Church First Nation Fisheries Agreement with Canada' (2002). Available at http://www.turtleisland.org/news/news-onemans-kwegsi.htm (accessed 12 Jan. 2003).
62. Alanis Obomsawin, *Is the Crown at War with Us?* 96 min 31 s. (Canada: National Film Board of Canada, 2002).
63. James Ward and Lloyd Augustine, 'Draft for the Esgenoopotitj First Nation (EFN) Fishery Act' (2000). Available at http://www.tc.edu/centers/cifas/socialdisparity/index.html (accessed 12 Jan. 2003.
64. Pauline McIntosh and John Kearney, 'Enhancing Natural Resources and Livelihoods Globally through Community-Based Resource Management', *Proceedings from the Learning and Innovations Institute* (6–9 Nov. 2002).
65. Interview with Martha Stiegman, 2005.
66. Stiegman and Pictou, 'How do you say'.
67. Marshall, 'Kmitkinu'.
68. Chris Milley and Anthony Charles, 'Mi'kmaq Fisheries in Atlantic Canada: Traditions, Legal Decisions and Community Management'. Unpublished paper presented at the 'People and the Sea: Maritime Research in the Social Sciences: An Agenda for the 21st Century, Amsterdam' (2001).
69. Martha Stiegman, 'Fisheries Privatization Versus Community-Based Management in Nova Scotia: Emerging Alliances between First Nations and Non-Native Fishers', in Laurie Adkin, ed., *Environmental Conflict and Democracy in Canada* (Vancouver: UBC Press, 2009), 69–83.
70. Atlantic Policy Congress of First Nations Chiefs, 'The Management of Fisheries on Canada's Atlantic Coast: A Discussion Document on Policy Direction and Principles' (2001). Available at http://www.apcfnc.ca (accessed 14 Apr. 2006).
71. Maureen Googoo, 'NS chiefs want feds to implement Marshall decision' (2009). Available at http://radiogoogoo.ca/2009/09/17/ns-chiefs-want-feds-to-implement-marshall-decision/ (accessed 5 Dec. 2009).
72. Anthony Davis and Svein Jentoft, 'The Challenge and the Promise of Indigenous Peoples' Fishing Rights—From Dependency to Agency', *Marine Policy* 25, 3 (2001): 223–7; Melanie G. Wiber and Julia Kennedy, 'Impossible Dreams: Reforming Fisheries Management in the Canadian Maritimes after the Marshall Decision', *Law & Anthropology* 11 (2001): 282–97.
73. Interview with Martha Stiegman, 2003.
74. Coulthard, 'Subjects of Empire', 457.
75. Sherry Pictou and Arthur Bull, 'Resource Extraction in the Maritimes: Historic Links with Racism', *New Socialist* 1 (2009): 38–9; Stiegman and Pictou, 'How do you say'.
76. Sherry Pictou, 'How Deep Are Our Treaties?' *Samudra* 54 (2009). Available at http://icsf.net.
77. Battiste, 'Introduction'.
78. Wiber and Bull, 'Rescaling Governance'.
79. Atlantic Policy Congress, 'The Management of Fisheries'.
80. Joyce A. Green, 'Towards a Détente with History: Confronting Canada's Colonial Legacy', *International Journal of Canadian Studies* 12 (1995): 85–105.
81. John Pilger, *Freedom Next Time* (Ealing: Bantam Press, 2006), 287.
82. Harvey, *The New Imperialism*.

Credits ○○○○○○○○ ○ ○○○○ ○○ ○○○○ ○○○ ○○○ ○

CHAPTER ONE

1. Dennis H. McPherson and J. Douglas Rabb, 'Indigeneity in Canada: Spirituality, the Sacred and Survival', *International Journal of Canadian Studies* 23 (Spring 2001): 57–79.
2. Bastien, Betty. *Blackfoot Ways of Knowing.* Calgary: University of Calgary Press, 2004.

CHAPTER TWO

1. Imagining a Distant New World,' reprinted by permission of the publisher from *Facing East from Indian Country: A Native History of Early America* by Daniel K. Richter, pp. 11–40, Cambridge, Mass.: Harvard University Press, Copyright 2001 by the President and Fellows of Harvard College.
4. Eber, Dorothy. 'Into the Arctic Archipelago: Edward Parry in Igloolik and the Shaman's Curse,' in *Encounters on the Passage: Inuit Meet Explorers* (Toronto: University of Toronto Press, 2008), 12–36, 145–8 with some deletions from the original material. Reprinted with permission of the publisher.
5. 'Excerpt from an Interview with Rosie Iqallijuq,' Igloolik Research Centre, Inullariit Elders' Society Archives, Tape Number: IE-204, 8 October 1991. Interview and translation by Louis Tapardjuk. Edited by Leah Otak

CHAPTER THREE

1. Henige, David. 'Recent Work and Prospects in American Indian Contact Population', *History Compass* 6, 1 (2008): 183–206.
2. Lafitau, Joseph-François. 'Natural [Herbal] Medicine,' in *Customs of the American Indians Compared with Customs of Primitive Times, 1681-1746*, volume 2, (Toronto: Champlain Society, 1977), pp. 204–6.
3. Daschuk, J.W., Paul Hackett, and Scott MacNeil, 'Treaties and Tuberculosis: First Nations People in Late 19th-Century Western Canada, A Political and Economic Transformation', *Canadian Bulletin of Medical History* 23, 2 (2006): 307–30.
4. 'Report of Acting Superintendent M.G. Dickieson, July 1879'. Canada, *Sessional Papers 1880*, 105.

CHAPTER FOUR

1. Rushforth, Brett. 'Slavery, the Fox Wars, and the Limits of Alliance', *William and Mary Quarterly* 63, 1 (2006): 53–80.

2. 'Baptism, Sept. 21, 1713', in Gaeten Morin, ed., *Repertoire des actes de baptême, mariage et sepulture du Québec ancien, 1621–1799*, CD-ROM, entry # 44145. Archives nationales du Quebec, Centre régional de Montreal, Registres Notre-Dame de Montreal, film 111.
3. Taylor, Alan. 'The Divided Ground: Upper Canada, New York, and the Iroquois Six Nations, 1783–1815,' *Journal of the Early Republic* 22, 1 (Spring 2002): 55–75. Reprinted and abridged with permission of the University of Pennsylvania Press.
4. 'Speech by Red Jacket, 21 November 1790'. Timothy Pickering Papers, Massachusetts Historical Society, Boston.

CHAPTER FIVE

1. Ray, Arthur J. 'Fur Trade History as an Aspect of Native History', Reprinted with permission of the Publisher from One Century Late edited by Ian Getty and Donald Smith © University of British Columbia Press 1978. All rights reserved by the Publisher.
2. 'Minutes from the Excise Committee of the Hudson's Bay Company, 24 March 1673,' from E.E. Rich, ed., *Minutes of the Hudson's Bay Company, 1671–1674* (Toronto: Champlain Society, 1942), 91.
3. Sleeper-Smith, Susan. 'Women, Kin, and Catholicism: New Perspectives on the Fur Trade', in *Ethnohistory*, Vol. 47, no. 2, pp. 423–52. Copyright, 2002, the American Society for Ethnohistory. All rights reserved. Reprinted by permission of the publisher, Duke University Press. www.dukeupress.edu
4. Baird, Elizabeth Thérèse. 'Reminiscences of Early Days on Mackinac Island', in Reuben Gold Thwaites ed., *Collections of the Historical Society of Wisconsin*, vol. 14 (Madison: Democrate Printing Co., 1898), 38–40.

CHAPTER SIX

1. Campbell, Alexander V. '"I Shall Settle, Marry, and Trade Here": British Military Personnel and Their Mixed-Blood Descendants', in Ute Lischke and David McNab, eds, *The Long Journey of a Forgotten People: Métis Identities and Family Histories* (Waterloo: Wilfred Laurier Press, 2007), 81–107.
2. Dumont, Yvon. 'Métis Nationalism: Then and Now'. Address given at a symposium on the

Battle of Seven Oaks, University of Manitoba, October 1991.

4. 'The Insurrection in Manitoba', *Brisbane Courier*, Saturday, 16 May 1885, 1.

CHAPTER SEVEN

2. 'Civilizing Influences,' a proposed pamphlet by Thomas Deasy, Indian Agent. Library and Archives Canada. LAC, RG-10, Black Series, V. 4093, File 570970. 1920.

CHAPTER EIGHT

2. Indian Act, 1876, Sections 3(3)–3(6). Statutes of Canada, 39 Vict., c. 18, 1876.

5. Indian Act, 1985, Section 6. Statutes of Canada, 1985, c. I-5

CHAPTER NINE

2. 'Program of Studies for Indian Schools, 1897,' from Canada, 'Annual Report of the Department of Indian Affairs for the year Ended June 1897', *Sessional Papers*, 1897, 398–9.

4. Excerpt from the Indian Residential Schools Settlement Agreement, May 2006. Available at http://www.residentialschoolsettlement.ca/ SCHEDULE_N.pdf (accessed 5 Jan. 2011).

5. Ross, Rupert. 'Telling Truths and Seeking Reconciliation: Exploring the Challenges', in Marlene Brant Castellan, Linda Archibald, and Mike DeGagne, *From Truth to Reconciliation: Transforming the Legacy of Residential Schools* (2008), 147–9. Available at http://www.ahf. ca/downloads/from-truth-to-reconciliation-transforming-the-legacy-of-residential-schools. pdf (accessed 5 Jan. 2001).

CHAPTER TEN

1. Remie, Cornelius and Jarich Oosten, 'The Birth of a Catholic Inuit Community. The Transition to Christianity in Pelly Bay, Nunavut, 1935–1950', *Etudes/Inuit Studies* 26, 1 (2002): 109–41.

2. Excerpt from Codex Historicus, 25 December 1940. *Codex Historicus* Mission Pelly Bay, Volume I: 25 December 1940 entry, Archives Deschâtelets, Oblats de Marie Immaculée (Ottawa ON).

CHAPTER ELEVEN

2. Excerpts from the Diary of Arthur Wellington Clah. From the diary of Arthur Wellington

Clah (T'amks), 1860–1916. (London: Wellcome Institute, MS American 140).

4. Indian Girls Achieve Successful Careers—Pave Way for Others. *Indian News* (June 1958): 6–7.

CHAPTER TWELVE

1. Carter, Sarah. 'Categories and Terrains of Exclusion: Constructing the Indian Woman in the Early Settlement Era in Western Canada', *Great Plains Quarterly* 13, 3 (Summer 1993): 147–61.

2. Letter from Mrs. Mary McNauhton Concerning the Chattels of Indian Women Married to White Men and Living on the Reserve, dated 15 December 1879. Library and Archives Canada. LAC RG10, vol. 2100, File 17,638

4. Excerpt from the Indian Act, 1951. Statutes of Canada, 1951, c. 149.

CHAPTER THIRTEEN

2. Letter from Chief Pierre Freezie to S.J. Bailey. Library and Archives Canada. LAC, RG 85, Series D-1-A, vol. 1254, file 431-178, part 2.

CHAPTER FOURTEEN

1. Brownlie, Robin Jarvis. 'Nothing Left for Me or Any Other Indian: The Georgian Bay Anishnabek Inter-War Articulation of Aboriginal Rights', *Ontario History* 96, 2 (Autumn 2004): 116–41.

2. Letter from Elijah Tabobondung to Jon Daly, Indian Agent dated 12 August 1923, Copperhead, Perry Sound ON. Franz Koennecke Collection, Wasauksing First Nations

3. Bentley, David and Brenda Murphy, 'Power, Praxis and the Métis of Kelly Lake, Canada', *The Canadian Journal of Native Studies* 26, 2 (2006): 289–312.

4. Taillon, Joan. 'Rare Health Services Come to Métis at Kelly Lake', *Raven's Eye* 8, 4 (2004): 1.

CHAPTER FIFTEEN

1. Rynard, Paul. 'Ally or Colonizer: The Federal State, the Cree Nation and the James Bay Agreement', *Journal of Canadian Studies* 36, 2 (Summer 2001): 8–48.

2. Excerpt from *Cree Regional Authority et al. v. Attorney-General of Quebec* (1991) 42 Federal Trial Records, p. 168.

University of
Lethbridge   Faculty of Health Sciences
4401 University Drive
Lethbridge, AB, Canada
T1K 3M4

FIAT LUX